The Environmental Planning Handbook

for Sustainable Communities and Regions

The Environmental Planning Handbook

for Sustainable Communities and Regions

Tom Daniels
and Katherine Daniels, AICP

PLANNERS PRESS
AMERICAN PLANNING ASSOCIATION
Chicago, Illinois
Washington, D.C.

Copyright 2003 by the American Planning Association
122 S. Michigan Ave., Suite 1600, Chicago, IL 60603

ISBN (hardbound edition): 1-884829-66-X
Library of Congress Control Number: 2003110667
Printed in the United States of America
All rights reserved

Interior composition and copyediting by Joanne Shwed, Backspace Ink
Cover design by Susan Deegan

Cover photos (clockwise from top): Bureau of Land Management/Colorado;
Photodisc; Eyewire Images; and Tim McCabe, U.S. Department of Agriculture

Acknowledgements

We would like to thank many people for sharing their ideas, comments, and encouragement. Harvey Carter supported the initial project proposal and made important suggestions. Bill Page read an entire draft of the manuscript and gave us a valuable assessment. In 2000, Robert Freilich included me (Tom) in three regional workshops on growth management, and gave me many insights about sprawl and the environment. As part of those workshops, architect-planner Kite Singleton shared his knowledge with me of transportation planning and urban design.

David Schuyler, Jay Parrish, and Deborah Bowers gave us both useful information and friendly support.

Several students in our environmental planning classes wrote papers that provided good information and analysis: David Adams, Michelle Carpenter, Elizabeth Citowicz, Ryan Dodd, Jackie Hakes, Jessica Johnson, Jason Kemper, Ken Kovalchik, Linda Mandarano, Leon Scott, Riti Pritam, Robert Witt, Michael Wyatt, and John Zepko. Our son, Ethan, did the graphics for the book along with Matt Van Slyke from SUNY-Albany. Chuck Eaton also supplied graphics expertise. Finally, we wish to thank Jim Hecimovich at APA for his constructive comments, Joanne Shwed of Backspace Ink for her tireless and cheerful copyediting skills, and our editor, Sylvia Lewis, for her enthusiasm and support for the book.

To Ethan and Jason,
our guardians of the future

Contents

List of Tables   xiii
List of Figures   xv
List of Acronyms   xvii
Preface   xix

Introduction: Guarding the Future: Sustainable Environmental Planning and Development   1
Sustainable Development   3
A Community Perspective on Planning for the Environment   4
A Regional Perspective on Planning for the Environment   5
Managing the Environment: Problems and Possibilities   6
A Note on "Good Science"   6

Part I. The Environmental Planning Process   9

1. Taking Stock of the Local Environment and Creating an Environmental Action Plan   11
Adding Environmental Planning to the Traditional Comprehensive Land Use Planning Process   11
The Environmental Planning Process   17
Sidebar 1-1. The Private Sector and Environmental Planning   27
Day-to-Day Planning Decisions: Review of Development Proposals   30
Case Studies   30
    Case Study 1-1. Columbus, Ohio: The City's Environmental Snapshot   32
    Case Study 1-2. The Twin Cities: A State of the Region Report and Growth Scenarios   34

2. The Legal, Economic, Ethical, and Ecological Foundations of Environmental Planning   37
Legal Issues in Environmental Planning   37
Sidebar 2-1. The Occupational Safety and Health Act of 1970   43
Sidebar 2-2. The U.S. Environmental Protection Agency   45
Economic Reasons for Environmental Planning   48
Sidebar 2-3. The Political Economy of Sustainable Environments   52

Ethical Reasons for Environmental Planning   57
Ecology and Environmental Planning   60

Part II. Planning for Sustainable Public Health   65

3. Planning for Sustainable Water Supply   67
Water Supply Challenges   67
Sidebar 3-1. Tampa Bay Looks to the Sea for Drinking Water Supplies   72
The Need for Water Supply Planning   73
Sidebar 3-2. Drought and Water Supply Planning   73
The Federal Approach to Water Supply Planning   75
Sidebar 3-3. The Colorado River Compact and Water Supply   76
The Safe Drinking Water Act   78
State Water Supply Planning   81
Regional and County Water Supply Planning   83
Sidebar 3-4. Wastewater Reuse   85
Local Planning for Water Supply   92
What to Look for in a Development Review   95
Case Study   95
    Case Study 3-1. New York City's Water Supply Protection Program   95

4. Planning for Sustainable Water Quality   99
Land Use Impacts on Water Quality   99
Sidebar 4-1. Potentially Deadly E. Coli Bacteria   104
Sidebar 4-2. Lakes and Ponds and Eutrophication   106
Federal Water Quality Standards and Pollution Control   107
Sidebar 4-3. Water Quality in Cost-Benefit Analysis and Risk Assessment   113
State Water Quality Protection and Clean-up   114
County and Regional Partnerships and Nonprofit Groups   117
Local Planning for Water Quality   119
What to Look for in a Development Review   122
Case Studies   123
    Case Study 4-1. Barton Springs and Austin, Texas   123

Case Study 4-2. The Maryland Stream
ReLeaf Program   124

5. Planning for Sustainable Air Quality   125

Sources of Air Pollution   125
Types of Air Pollution   127
Federal Air Quality Legislation   128
The Clean Air Act and the 1970
and 1977 Amendments   129
The 1990 Clean Air Act Amendments   131
Sidebar 5-1. Atlanta, Air Quality, and the Georgia
Regional Transportation Authority   132
Sidebar 5-2. California's Crackdown
on Motor Vehicle Emissions   133
Sidebar 5-3. The Energy, Air Quality,
and Water Quality Link   134
Sidebar 5-4. Radon Gas: A Persistent Toxic
Substance   135
Progress and Continuing Challenges in
Solving Air Pollution Problems   138
State Air Quality Management Plans   141
Local Planning for Air Quality   144
What to Look for in a Development Review   146
Case Studies   146
Case Study 5-1. Acid Deposition and Federal
and State Air Quality Standards   147
Case Study 5-2. The Land Use, Air Quality, and
Transportation Study in Portland, Oregon   148

6. Planning for Solid Waste and Recycling   151

The Challenge of Solid Waste   151
Solid Waste: The Federal Response   154
State Solid Waste Disposal Programs   156
Sidebar 6-1. Landfill Gas to Energy   156
Local and Regional Solid Waste Disposal
Options   157
Local Planning for Solid Waste Disposal, Reuse,
and Recycling   160
Sidebar 6-2. Eco-Industrial Parks   160

**7. Planning for Toxic
Substances and Toxic Waste**   165

The Challenge of Toxic Substances
and Hazardous Waste   165
Toxic Waste Disposal   166
Sidebar 7-1. Rachel Carson and *Silent Spring*   166

Sidebar 7-2. Toxic Nightmares: Rocky Flats
and Woburn   168
Federal Action on Toxic Substances   169
Sidebar 7-3. Cleaning Up Leaking Underground
Fuel Storage Tanks   172
Sidebar 7-4. Hazardous Waste and the
New Information Economy   174
Sidebar 7-5. A Toxic Clean-up Dilemma   175
Sidebar 7-6. Mining and Toxic Waste   176
Sidebar 7-7. Notice of Intent to Redevelop
a Brownfield Property   178
Local Planning for Hazardous Substances
and Toxic Waste   179
Sidebar 7-8. Chemical Exposure and Local
Governments   180

Part III. Planning for Natural Areas   183

8. Protecting the Nation's Landscape Treasures   185

The Challenge of Landscape Protection   185
Federal Planning for Protecting the Nation's
Landscape Treasures   187
State Programs to Protect Landscape
Treasures   191
Sidebar 8-1. Sierra Club Sues Hawaii Over Tourism
Funding   191
Local and Regional Acquisition of Open Space   193
Local Planning for Landscape Treasures   202

9. Planning for Wildlife Habitat   207

Pressures on Wildlife Habitat   207
Biodiversity, Landscape Ecology, and Wildlife
Habitat   208
Federal Efforts to Protect Wildlife Habitat   212
Sidebar 9-1. Gap Analysis Program   216
Sidebar 9-2. The Wildlands Project   216
Sidebar 9-3. Fisheries and Extinction   217
State Planning for Wildlife Habitat   220
Local Planning for Plant and Wildlife Habitat   223
Sidebar 9-4. Species Conservation in
San Diego County, California   223

10. Planning and Managing Wetlands   229

Pressures on Wetlands   229
Federal Wetlands Protection Efforts   230

Sidebar 10-1. Constructed Wetlands
for Wastewater Treatment 234
State Wetlands Management 236
Sidebar 10-2. Big-Time Wetlands Restoration:
The Florida Everglades 237
Local Planning for Wetlands 238

11. Coastal Zone Management **241**

The Challenge of Coastal Zone Management 242
Federal Planning and Management
of Coastal Resources 243
State and Regional Coastal Protection
Programs 248
Sidebar 11-1. Protecting the Chesapeake Bay 250
Local Planning for Coastal Resources 251
Sidebar 11-2. Local Planning and Coastal
Storms 252
Case Studies 254
Case Study 11-1. The California Coastal
Commission 255
Case Study 11-2. The California Coastal
Conservancy 256

**12. Planning for Natural Hazards
and Natural Disasters** **257**

The Challenge of Planning for Disaster-
Resistant Communities 257
Federal Planning for Natural Disasters
and Hazard Mitigation 262
Sidebar 12-1. California Wildfires 269
State Planning for Natural Disasters
and Hazard Mitigation 271
Sidebar 12-2. A Few Million
Dollars of Prevention . . . 271
Local Planning for Natural Disasters and
Hazard Mitigation 272
Sidebar 12-3. National Model Building Codes 275

Part IV. Planning for Working Landscapes **277**

**13. Planning for Sustainable Working
Landscapes: Farmland and Ranchland** **279**

Challenges to Maintaining Working Agricultural
Landscapes 281
Federal Planning for Farmland Protection 285

Federal Soil and Water Conservation
Programs 285
State Farmland Protection Programs 288
Sidebar 13-1. Land Trusts and Farmland
Preservation 292
Local Planning for Farmland Protection 293
Sidebar 13-2. Agricultural Economic
Development 296
Case Study 303
Case Study 13-1. Confined Animal Feeding
Operations 303

**14. Planning for Sustainable
Working Landscapes: Forestry** **305**

Pressures on Forests 306
Forest Types 308
Federal Forestland Programs 309
State Forestland Programs 311
Sidebar 14-1. Third-Party Certification:
A Voluntary Approach to Sustainable
Private Forest Management 313
Land Trusts and the Protection of Forestland 314
Local Planning for Forestlands 315
Sidebar 14-2. Forests and Carbon Sequestration 315
Case Studies 318
Case Study 14-1. The Northern Forest Initiative 318
Case Study 14-2. The Headwaters Forest 319
Case Study 14-3. The Spotted Owl Controversy 320

15. Planning for Mining **323**

The Challenges of Mineral and Aggregate
Mining 324
Federal Mining Regulations 326
State Mining Regulations 327
Local Planning for Mineral and Aggregate
Resources 328

Part V. Planning for the Built Environment **333**

**16. Transportation Planning
and the Environment** **335**

Transportation Planning Challenges 335
Federal Approaches to Transportation
Planning 340
Regional Approaches to Transportation
Planning 342

Sidebar 16-1. A Tale of Two Rivals   347
Alternative Transportation Modes   348
Sidebar 16-2. Energy, Transportation,
     and the Internet   349
Sidebar 16-3. Airport Planning and
     Development   349
Local Planning for Transportation   352
Case Studies   355
     Case Study 16-1. Kansas City, Missouri   356
     Case Study 16-2. Transportation Planning in
          Mecklenburg County, North Carolina   356

17. Planning for Energy   **359**

America's Energy Challenges: Production,
     Consumption, Efficiency, and
     Conservation   359
America's Energy Sources   361
Sidebar 17-1. Energy Extraction and Water
     Pollution   363
Federal Energy Planning   366
State Energy Planning   367
Local Energy Planning   369
Sidebar 17-2. Promoting "Green" Buildings   369
Sidebar 17-3. The Building Code and Energy
     Conservation   370

**18. Planning for a Sustainable
Built Environment**   **373**

Challenges to Creating a Sustainable Built
     Environment   375
Sidebar 18-1. The Americans with
     Disabilities Act   379
Sidebar 18-2. A Note on Land-Value Taxation   382
Sidebar 18-3. The Ahwahnee Principles
     for Development Design   385
Federal Efforts in Urban Redevelopment   386
State Efforts to Revitalize Cities   389
Local Planning for the Built Environment   391
Case Study   395
     Case Study 18-1. Chattanooga, Tennessee:
          From Worst to First   396

**19. Planning for the Built Environment:
Greenfield Development and Site Design**   **399**

The Challenge of Sprawl   400

Federal Programs to Manage Greenfield
     Development   403
State Programs to Manage Greenfield
     Development   404
Regional and Local Management of Greenfield
     Development   406
Sidebar 19-1. Los Angeles: Can the Environment
     Keep Pace?   406
Sidebar 19-2. Density Choices, Comprehensive
     Planning, and Zoning   414
Sidebar 19-3. A Note on Golf Courses   416
Local Planning for Greenfield Development   420
Case Studies   424
     Case Study 19-1. Newhall Ranch, Los
          Angeles County, California   424
     Case Study 19-2. Prairie Crossing, Illinois   425
     Case Study 19-3. Tracking Greenfield and
          Urban Development in Lancaster County,
          Pennsylvania   425

**Part VI. Environmental Planning
Challenges at Home and Abroad**   **427**

**20. Positive Trends and Urgent Needs
for Sustainable Environmental Planning**   **429**

Positive Environmental Trends   429
Environmental Planning Needs and
     Challenges   435
Sidebar 20-1. The Supplemental Environmental
     Project Policy of the Environmental Protection
     Agency   439
International Environmental Planning Needs   447
A Final Note on Sustainable Environmental
     Planning   449

**Appendix: Sample Environmental Impact
Assessment Report within the Local Subdivision
and Land Development Regulations**   **451**

Glossary   **455**
Contacts   **465**
Bibliography   **475**
Index   **503**

List of Tables

Table 1-1   Eight Steps in Creating an Environmental Action Plan

Table 1-2   Natural Environmental Features to Be Shown on the Natural Resources Inventory Maps

Table 1-3   Innovative Techniques for Implementing an Environmental Action Plan

Table 1-4   Environmental Impact Checklist for Reviewing Proposed Development Projects

Table 1-5   Examples of Columbus, Ohio, *Priorities '95* Project Issues

Table 1-6   Implementation Progress, Columbus, Ohio and Franklin County, Ohio (1996–2000)

Table 1-7   Natural Environment Trends in the Metropolitan Twin Cities (1999)

Table 2-1   Major Federal Environmental Laws (1970–1999)

Table 3-1   Water Use by Selected Manufacturing and Processing Operations

Table 3-2   Stream Ratings

Table 3-3   Community Water Systems by Size and Estimated Infrastructure Needs (1994–2014)

Table 3-4   Sample Public Water Supply Goals and Objectives in the Comprehensive Plan

Table 3-5   A Checklist of Water Supply Issues in a Development Review

Table 4-1   Nonpoint Water Pollution Sources

Table 4-2   Clean Water Act Programs

Table 4-3   Water Quality Ratings

Table 4-4   U.S. Wastewater Treatment Facilities (1996)

Table 4-5   Recommended Best Management Practices for Construction Sites

Table 4-6   Sample Water Quality Goals and Objectives in the Comprehensive Plan

Table 4-7   A Checklist of Water Quality Issues in Development Review

Table 5-1   National Primary and Secondary Ambient Air Quality Standards

Table 5-2   Sample Air Quality Goals and Objectives in the Comprehensive Plan

Table 5-3   A Checklist of Air Quality Issues for a Development Review

Table 6-1   U.S. Municipal Solid Waste and Recycling by Type (2000)

Table 6-2   Sample Solid Waste Goals and Objectives in the Comprehensive Plan

Table 6-3   A Checklist of Solid Waste and Recycling Issues in a Development Review

Table 7-1   Sample Hazardous Waste Goals and Objectives in the Comprehensive Plan

Table 7-2   A Checklist of Hazardous Substance and Toxic Waste Issues in a Development Review

Table 8-1   A Sample of Local Land Preservation Ballot Measures Passed in 2000

Table 8-2   Valuing the Donation of a Conservation Easement

Table 8-3   America's 15 Most Endangered Natural Lands Identified by the Wilderness Society (1999)

Table 8-4   America's 10 Most Endangered Rivers (2001)

Table 8-5   Sample Special Landscapes Goals and Objectives in the Comprehensive Plan

Table 8-6   A Checklist of Natural and Scenic Environment Issues in a Development Review

Table 9-1   Land and Water Bioregions of the United States

Table 9-2   Federal Information Sources Related to Wildlife Habitat

Table 9-3   Listed Threatened and Endangered Species by Top Ten States and Territories (2003)

Table 9-4   Biological Principles for Local Habitat Protection

Table 9-5   Sample Plant and Wildlife Protection Goals and Objectives in the Comprehensive Plan

Table 9-6   Wildlife Habitat Protection Tools

Table 9-7   A Checklist of Plant and Wildlife Habitat Issues in a Development Review

Table 10-1   Section 404 Approval Process for Federal Wetlands Permit

Table 10-2   Sample Wetlands Goals and Objectives in the Comprehensive Plan

Table 10-3   A Checklist of Wetlands Issues in a Development Review

Table 11-1   Sample Coastal Resources Goals and Objectives in the Comprehensive Plan

Table 11-2   Development Controls in Coastal Communities

Table 11-3   A Checklist of Coastal Resource Issues in a Development Review

Table 12-1   Sample Natural Disaster Response and Hazard-Prone Areas Goals and Objectives in the Comprehensive Plan

Table 12-2   A Checklist of Hazard-Prone Areas Issues in a Development Review

Table 13-1   Ownership of Land and Land Uses in the Lower 48 States (1997)

Table 13-2   Revised Universal Soil Loss Equation

Table 13-3   Farmland Capability Ratings

Table 13-4   Conservation Programs of the Natural Resources Conservation Service of the U.S. Department of Agriculture

Table 13-5   Leading State Programs in Farmland Preserved (2002)

Table 13-6   Leading Counties in Farmland Preserved (2002)

Table 13-7   Example of Purchase of Development Rights

Table 13-8   Sample Goals and Objectives for Farmland and the Farming Industry in the Comprehensive Plan

Table 13-9   Determining the Land Evaluation Score Based on Soil Productivity

Table 13-10 Land Evaluation and Site Assessment System for Sample 300-Acre Farm

Table 13-11 A Checklist of Farm-Related and Nonfarm Development Issues in a Development Review

Table 14-1   Forestland in the Lower 48 United States by Region and Ownership (2000)

Table 14-2   Riparian Management Areas for Logging in Oregon

Table 14-3   Sample Goals and Objectives for Forest Resources in the Comprehensive Plan

Table 14-4   A Checklist of Forestry-Related and Nonforestry-Related Issues in a Development Review

Table 15-1   Sample Goals and Objectives for Mineral and Aggregate Mining in the Comprehensive Plan

Table 15-2   A Checklist of Mineral and Aggregate Resource Issues in a Development Review

Table 16-1   Energy Efficiency of Different Transportation Modes

Table 16-2   Advantages of Transit-Oriented Developments

Table 16-3   Metro Areas with Light-Rail Systems (2000)

Table 16-4   Sample Transportation Goals and Objectives in the Comprehensive Plan

Table 16-5   A Checklist of Transportation Issues for a Development Review

Table 17-1   Sample Energy Goals and Objectives in the Comprehensive Plan

Table 17-2   A Checklist of Energy Issues for a Development Review

Table 18-1   Typical and Recommended Residential Design in Suburbs

Table 18-2   Vermont Forum on Sprawl Smart Growth Principles

Table 18-3   Sample Built Environment Goals and Objectives in the Comprehensive Plan

Table 18-4   A Checklist of Built Environment Issues in a Development Review

Table 19-1   The Six Metropolitan Areas Most Likely to Sprawl (2000–2025)

Table 19-2   Savings Through Compact Development vs. Sprawl for 25 Million Dwelling Units (2000–2025)

Table 19-3   Available Acreage vs. Needed Acreage in Delaware (1997–2020)

Table 19-4   A Comparison of Cluster Development Approaches

Table 19-5   Sample Greenfield Development Goals and Objectives in the Comprehensive Plan

Table 19-6   A Checklist of Greenfield Development Issues in a Development Review

Table 20-1   Leading Environmental Planning Challenges in America

Table 20-2   The Predicted Ten Fastest Growing States (1995–2025)

List of Figures

1-1   General zoning map.
1-2   Geographic Information System database layers.
1-3   Map of soil types from a county soil survey.
1-4   Map identifying steep slopes for the Natural Resources Inventory.
1-5   Land use trends in the greater Twin Cities, 2000–2020.
2-1   Optimal pollution clean-up.
3-1   River basins of the central United States.
3-2   Water withdrawals in the United States, 1995.
3-3   Watershed signs alert people to the connection between land use and water supply.
3-4   New York City's water supply system.
4-1   Sources of groundwater contamination.
4-2   Soil erosion and sedimentation along a streambank where trees have been removed.
4-3   Acres of impervious surface in a regional shopping mall parking lot increase stormwater runoff.
4-4   Abandoned gas station.
4-5   Grass filter strip and woodland stream buffer control stormwater runoff from entering stream.
4-6   "No dumping" sign on storm sewer to protect water quality, Seattle, Washington.
5-1   Air pollution measurements, greater Seattle, Washington, 1997.
5-2   Clean Air Act pollution emission reduction budgets.
5-3   Clean Air Act air pollution management planning.
5-4   Layout of Orenco Station, near Hillsboro, Oregon.
6-1   Curbside recycling by households is required in many communities.
6-2   Scrap metal recycling.
9-1   Fish farm, Puget Sound, Washington.
10-1 Fresh-water wetland, Albany County, New York.
12-1 Map of California earthquakes, July 13, 2001.
12-2 Floodplain with 100-year floodway.

12-3 Low-lying coastal areas in the southeastern United States.
13-1 Farmers and ranchers own most of the privately held land in America, about 930 million acres.
13-2 A block of 3,000 acres of preserved farmland—Maytown, Lancaster County, Pennsylvania.
13-3 The Metropolitan Service District growth boundary of greater Portland, Oregon.
13-4 Urban growth boundary separating residential development and farmland.
14-1 Forest cover of the United States.
14-2 National forests of the United States.
14-3 Map of the Pacific Lumber Habitat Conservation Plan, 1999.
15-1 Quarry site, Fishkill, New York.
16-1 Traffic delays result in the use of billions more gallons of gasoline and add to air pollution.
16-2 Transit-oriented development.
16-3 Light-rail train and automobile sharing the street in Portland, Oregon.
17-1 Promoting energy conservation awareness in Portland, Oregon.
18-1 Downtown Portland, Oregon.
18-2 Percentage change in metropolitan population, central city and surroundings, 1990–1999.
18-3 The Church Street pedestrian mall has been a big success in Burlington, Vermont.
18-4 Suburban "snout houses" emphasize housing cars rather than people.
19-1 Houses encroaching on a farm in the competition for space.
19-2 Typical suburban residential "pod" layout.
19-3 Residential strip development and cluster residential development.
19-4 Residential pod reconfigured to retain open space.
19-5 Tracking of new development in Lancaster County, Pennsylvania, 1993–1996.
20-1 Percentage growth of U.S. population by states, 1990–2000.

List of Acronyms

ADA	Americans with Disabilities Act	DRI	development of regional impact
AFT	American Farmland Trust	EIA	environmental impact assessment
APA	American Planning Association	EIS	environmental impact statement
ASCE	American Society of Civil Engineers	EPA	[U.S.] Environmental Protection Agency
AUM	Animal Unit Monthly	EQIP	Environmental Quality Incentives Program
BACT	Best Available Control Technology		
BART	Bay Area Rapid Transit	ESA	Endangered Species Act
BCDC	[San Francisco] Bay Conservation and Development Commission	FAA	Federal Aviation Administration
		Fannie Mae	Federal National Mortgage Association
BLM	Bureau of Land Management	FEMA	Federal Emergency Management Agency
BMP	best management practice		
BOCA	Building Officials and Code Administrators International, Inc.	FERC	Federal Energy Regulatory Commission
BOD	biochemical oxygen demand or biological oxygen demand	FIFRA	Federal Insecticide, Fungicide, and Rodenticide Act
		FTA	Federal Transit Administration
CAFE	Corporate Average Fuel Economy	FWS	[U.S.] Fish and Wildlife Service
CAFO	confined animal feeding operation	GAO	[U.S.] General Accounting Office
CAP	Central Arizona Project	GAP	Gap Analysis Program
CAUSE	Citizens Against Urban Sprawl Everywhere	GIS	Geographic Information System
		GNP	Gross National Product
CBF	Chesapeake Bay Foundation	GPM	gallons per minute
CCC	California Coastal Commission	GRP	Grasslands Reserve Program
CCLT	Colorado Cattleman's Land Trust	GRTA	Georgia Regional Transportation Authority
CDBG	Community Development Block Grant		
CERCLA	Comprehensive Environmental Response, Compensation, and Liability Act	HCP	Habitat Conservation Plan
		HOV	High Occupancy Vehicle
		HUD	[U.S. Department of] Housing and Urban Development
CERCLIS	Comprehensive Environmental Response, Compensation, and Liability Act Information System		
		ICBO	International Conference of Building Officials
CFC	chlorofluorocarbon		
CIP	capital improvements programs	IPM	integrated pest management
CNE	Chattanooga Neighborhood Enterprise	IRS	Internal Revenue Service
CRA	Community Reinvestment Act	ISTEA	Intermodal Surface Transportation Efficiency Act
CRP	Conservation Reserve Program		
CZMA	Coastal Zone Management Act	LAER	Lowest Achievable Emissions Rate
DART	Dallas Area Rapid Transit	LESA	Land Evaluation and Site Assessment
dB	decibels	LRMP	land and resource management plan
DDT	dichlorodiphenyltrichloroethane	LULU	Locally Unwanted Land Use
DENR	Department of Environment and Natural Resources	MARTA	Metropolitan Area Rapid Transit Authority
DEP	Department of Environmental Protection	mpg	miles per gallon
DNA	deoxyribonucleic acid	MPO	Metropolitan Planning Organization
DOE	[U.S.] Department of Energy	MTA	Metropolitan Transportation Authority
DOT	[U.S.] Department of Transportation	MTBE	methyl tertiary butyl ether

MTC	Metropolitan Transportation Commission	SEP	Supplemental Environmental Project
NAAQS	National Ambient Air Quality Standards	SEPA	State Environmental Policy Act
NAHB	National Association of Home Builders	SIP	State Improvement Plan
NEPA	National Environmental Policy Act	SPDES	State Pollutant Discharge Elimination System (or "Speedies")
NFIP	National Flood Insurance Program	SRBC	Susquehanna River Basin Commission
NOAA	National Oceanic and Atmospheric Administration	STPP	Surface Transportation Policy Project
		SUV	sport utility vehicle
NPDES	National Pollutant Discharge Elimination System	SWAP	Source Water Assessment and Protection
		TCE	trichloroethylene
NRCS	[U.S.] Natural Resources Conservation Service	TCSP	Transportation and Community and System Preservation Pilot
NRDC	Natural Resources Defense Council	TDR	transfer of development rights
NWF	National Wildlife Federation	TEA-21	Transportation Equity Act for the 21st Century
ODLCD	Oregon Department of Land Conservation and Development	TIP	Transportation Improvement Plan
OSHA	Occupational Safety and Health Administration	TMDL	Total Maximum Daily Load
		TNC	The Nature Conservancy
PAYT	"pay-as-you-throw" program	TND	traditional neighborhood development
PCB	polychlorinated biphenyl	TOD	transit-oriented development
PDR	purchase of development rights	TPL	Trust for Public Land
PILTS	payments-in-lieu-of-taxes	TPZ	Timber Production Zone
POP	persistent organic pollutant	TVA	Tennessee Valley Authority
PSD	Prevention of Significant Deterioration	UNEP	United Nations Environmental Program
PUD	planned unit development	USDA	U.S. Department of Agriculture
PVC	polyvinyl chloride	USFS	U.S. Forest Service
RCRA	Resource Conservation and Recovery Act	USGS	U.S. Geological Survey
		USOMB	U.S. Office of Management and Budget
RTP	Regional Transportation Plan	VLT	Vermont Land Trust
SBCCI	Southern Building Code Congress International, Inc.	VMT	vehicle miles traveled
		VOC	volatile organic compound
SDWA	Safe Drinking Water Act	WHIP	Wildlife Habitat Incentives Program

Preface

The only thing certain about the future is that it brings change. Planning describes how people anticipate needs, set goals and objectives, and act to shape change for their personal and collective benefit. Planning as a private act involves deciding how to use assets to achieve personal, family, and business goals. Planning as a public act is a political process of translating social values into government policies and programs to protect the public health, safety, and welfare of a community or region. Public planning does not mean total government control, but rather setting guidelines within which the market system of supply, demand, and prices will operate. In fact, public planning works best as a partnership based on cooperation between governments and the private sector.

Environmental planning involves shaping a community or region by protecting and improving air and water quality; conserving farming, forestry, and wildlife resources; reducing exposure to natural hazards; and maintaining the natural features and built environment that make a place livable and desirable. Good, effective planning produces a sustainable quality environment that stands the test of time.

Environmental planning has become a profession with highly trained and dedicated men and women from a variety of educational backgrounds including land use and community planning, geography, geology, hydrology, biology, botany, zoology, chemistry, landscape architecture, climatology, public policy, economics, law, and journalism. Environmental planners represent hunting and fishing groups; wildlife conservation organizations; watershed associations; land trusts; developers; corporations; consulting firms; and local, regional, state, and federal government agencies.

* * *

People think of themselves as belonging to a place. Familiar open spaces, landmarks, and buildings give us a sense of order and identity. Yet, in the 20th century, America underwent enormous changes in population, settlement patterns, technology, and wealth that transformed both the natural and built environments. During the 20th century, the nation's population increased from 76 million to more than 281 million people. Industrial cities and small towns surrounded by farms have given way to sprawling metropolitan areas. The mass-produced automobile has revolutionized the way Americans live and work by affording greater mobility and the ability to commute long distances. The construction of the interstate highway system not only linked the lower 48 states, but also helped create burgeoning suburbs around the major urban centers. Millions of acres of farmland, forestland, and wildlife habitat were transformed in the development of housing subdivisions, shopping centers, and office parks. By 1990, four out of five Americans lived in metropolitan areas, and more people were living in suburbs than in central cities for the first time in the nation's history.

Americans have amassed more wealth than any other country. At the beginning of the 21st century, Americans made up slightly less than 5% of the world's 6.2 billion people but accounted for more than 20% of the natural resources consumed annually. But America's growth and prosperity have come at a price. The combination of population growth, scattered development patterns, and motor vehicle dependence has unleashed a widespread assault on the nation's air, water, landscapes, and wildlife. Moreover, the decline of central cities coupled with the rapid changes in the suburbanizing landscape have produced metropolitan dwellers who are less knowledgeable and less in touch with the natural environment.

xix

The 20th century also marked America's growing recognition of the need to protect the environment and conserve natural resources. For example, the concept of sustained yield of natural resources began with noted forester Gifford Pinchot and led to the creation of the National Forest System early in the century. Improvements in farming practices to reduce soil erosion from wind and water started during the New Deal through the Soil Conservation Service (now the Natural Resources Conservation Service) formed in 1934. However, it was not until the 1960s that serious degradation of the nation's air and water and loss of open space spurred widespread public support for legislation to clean up the environment, to maintain standards of environmental quality, and to conserve valuable landscapes.

Federal laws created standards to maintain air and water quality, established procedures for reviewing federal development projects, protected endangered species habitats, placed millions of acres of public lands off limits to development, and required safeguards in disposing of municipal solid waste and handling toxic materials. Congress authorized billions of dollars to state and local governments for the construction of sewage treatment plants to improve water quality. Businesses were compelled to invest additional billions to reduce air and water pollution from factories and power plants.

The 1960s and 1970s also marked the beginning of state-level, land use planning efforts with an emphasis on land conservation and environmental quality. Hawaii (1961), Vermont (1970), Florida (1972), and Oregon (1973) adopted pioneering programs.

The 1980s and early 1990s were a low point for federal environmental action. In response, citizens across America formed nonprofit land trusts to protect land and water resources in their communities and regions. By 1999, over 1,200 land trusts had protected a total of more than 4 million acres.

The 1990s also saw a shift in environmental responsibility from the federal government to state, regional, and local governments. States gained primary control of air- and water quality programs. Metropolitan regions drafted transportation plans that were required to meet air quality goals. Local governments began to implement growth management and "smart growth" programs. In 1998 through 2002, voters in more than 30 states approved over 500 ballot measures involving more than $20 billion for land conservation and "smart growth" projects.

The U.S. Bureau of the Census has estimated that the nation's population will grow to just over 400 million by 2050, an increase of 40% above the 281 million in 2000 and equivalent to adding the population of nearly *four Californias*. Where will these people live, work, and play? How will new developments affect air and water quality; food, timber, and mineral supplies; plant and animal habitats; and the integrity of cultural resources? Will the environment be sacrificed to accommodate this surge in growth, or will growth have to adapt to the limited carrying capacity of the natural environment?

We recognize the challenge of understanding environmental problems in the face of changing and often inexact scientific information. But we see the need to continue to take action to protect past improvements in environmental quality and to make further gains in order to create truly sustainable communities and regions over the long run. Governments, businesses, and consumers will need to change many practices in order to protect the environment and conserve natural resources. This will require both new spending and a change in priorities. The environment is not a partisan political issue. There are conservatives who respect and defend the environment just as there are liberals who support environmental quality. Forging partnerships and alliances will be necessary not only across party lines but across income classes; between the public and private sectors; and among urbanites, suburban dwellers, and country people. In this way, planning becomes ingrained and accepted as a way to work out community and regional problems and avoid costly mistakes.

* * *

Expanding the capacity of communities and regions to plan for environmentally sustainable development is a fundamental goal of this book. Comprehensive environmental protection and natural resource management are necessary for long-term public health, safety, and economic success. Most people think locally but act regionally: they live in one community yet work and shop in another. It is important for people to think regionally to address a host of environmental planning issues. Watersheds, airsheds, and wildlife habitats are examples of regional environmental systems, and solid waste and transportation are regional infrastructure networks that require a regional planning approach.

Regional thinking also means a concern with social equity, by which we mean both social justice through equal access to a quality environment and a broad distribution of incomes. Environmental planning will not be successful if people perceive it as a way to create elite green enclaves and to impose health costs and dangers on those with low incomes.

We reject the notion that protecting the environment means sacrificing jobs. Technology and human innovation are key to building an economy that is also environmentally sustainable. Communities and regions with good environmental quality are often able to attract well-paying, high-tech industries and skilled workers. Also, many businesses are adopting environmentally friendly production processes, and creating healthy products and services because they are more profitable.

Planning is most effective as a truly participatory process. If people take an active part in shaping a plan for their community or region, they will want it to succeed. Successful planning happens when actions transform a common vision into a reality. We have been surprised at the number and the creativity of recent community and regional actions throughout the United States. We are optimistic that positive changes are happening, but we are aware that much remains to be done. We offer this book as a set of environmental planning tools, techniques, and processes from which others may learn and profit. We believe the future environment of Americans living now and tomorrow should not be squandered. Rather, the environmental quality of this wonderful nation is well worth guarding.

* * *

This book is intended for public sector planners, private planning consultants, developers, politicians, environmentalists, concerned citizens, and students—in short, anyone interested in taking an active role in the future of the environment in their community or region.

The book is divided into six parts:

- **Part I** begins with a chapter on how communities and regions can incorporate environmental planning into their comprehensive planning process. Chapter 2 then provides an overview of the disciplines that influence decision making about the environment: law, economics, ethics, and ecology.

- **Part II** presents the case for environmental planning to protect public health. Chapters 3 through 7 describe the challenges involving water supply; water and air quality; solid and toxic waste; and the federal, state, and local government regulations and spending programs.

- **Part III** discusses challenges to and planning programs for the protection of natural areas, including wilderness (Chapter 8), wildlife habitat (Chapter 9), wetlands (Chapter 10), coastal areas (Chapter 11), and natural hazards (Chapter 12).

- **Part IV** focuses on planning for the working landscape: Chapter 13 on farming and ranching, Chapter 14 on forestry, and Chapter 15 on mining.
- **Part V** begins with Chapter 16 on how transportation shapes the built environment. Chapter 17 discusses the role of energy, renewable energy supplies, and energy conservation. Chapter 18 presents ways to revitalize the built environment in America's cities and older suburbs, and Chapter 19 discusses planning for development on greenfield sites.
- **Part VI** summarizes in a single chapter the encouraging trends in environmental planning that further the concept of sustainability as well as remaining environmental planning challenges and needs at the local, state, federal, and international levels.

We have provided a List of Acronyms and their definitions at the beginning of the book. In each chapter, we define an acronym the first time it is used. We have listed the authors of literature cited in the text (e.g., "(Daniels 1999)"). When we quote a source directly or refer to a particular page as a source of information, we list the page number (e.g., "(Lugar 2002, A15)"). We have included chapter-by-chapter bibliographies so that readers may pursue particular issues in greater depth, an Appendix on local environmental impact assessment, and a list of contacts of public and private information sources.

Introduction

Guarding the Future: Sustainable Environmental Planning and Development

Then I say the Earth belongs to each . . . generation during its course, fully and in its own right. The second generation receives it clear of the debts and encumbrances, the third of the second, and so on. For if the first could charge it with a debt, then the Earth would belong to the dead and not to the living generation. Then, no generation can contract debts greater than may be paid during the course of its own existence.

THOMAS JEFFERSON, SEPT. 6, 1789

America faces several environmental challenges in the 21st century, most of which are related to sprawling development patterns caused by the outward spread of suburban development; scattered, low-density residential development in the countryside; and commercial strip development along arterial roads leading into and out of cities and suburbs.

1. *There has been a decline in the quality of the built environment in many inner cities and older suburbs.* Heavy investment in the development of housing, factories, shopping malls, and office parks on new suburban "greenfield sites" has resulted in disinvestment in housing, businesses, and infrastructure of many inner cities and older suburbs. Ironically, through a host of public tax breaks and spending programs, the cities and inner suburbs are in effect subsidizing the expanding newer suburbs.

2. *Sprawling suburbs are converting farmland, forests, and natural areas to housing subdivisions, shopping malls, and office parks at a fairly rapid pace.* According to the Natural Resources Conservation Service's January 2001 Natural Resources Inventory, the loss of productive lands, habitats, and open space topped 2 million acres a year from 1992 to 1997. Good-quality natural areas, working landscapes of farms and forests, and built environments are all necessary for human survival. Sprawl has upset the balance among these land uses, resulting in the wasteful use of land in low-density residential developments and an exodus from existing cities and villages.

3. *The sprawling land use patterns are fueled by heavy energy consumption in cars and trucks.* Americans are importing more than half of the oil they consume, at a cost of more than $50 billion each year. Meanwhile, Americans are steadily using up their own oil resources (U.S. Department of Energy 2001).

4. *Sprawling development has proceeded faster than new infrastructure (sewer and water facilities, roads, and schools) can keep pace or older infrastructure can be maintained.* A 2001 report by the American Society of Civil Engineers (ASCE) rated the nation's infrastructure a "D+" and said that America needed $1.3 *trillion* in infrastructure improvements over the next five years (ASCE 2001). The infrastructure shortfall typically shows up in overcrowded schools and congested roads. The more roads and schools are built in the growing suburban areas, the more sprawling development occurs as people are initially drawn to the newer, "better" facilities; however, soon the new roads and schools become crowded. Meanwhile, older infrastructure in the cities and inner suburbs is barely maintained or allowed to deteriorate.

5. *Sprawl has led to serious environmental degradation.* Cars and trucks generate most of

1

the air pollution in many metropolitan regions. Runoff from suburban lawns laden with weed killer and fertilizer washes into rivers and streams, and seeps into groundwater. Oil and gasoline runoff from thousands of miles of streets and roads pollutes waterways. Poorly sited and maintained on-site septic systems contaminate groundwater and pose health hazards. In many cases, sewer and water lines must be extended a mile or more to provide sewer and water service to relieve developments with contaminated water supplies. The loss of natural areas and wildlife habitats to human developments is the leading threat to biodiversity and rare and endangered species.

6. *Americans have not yet taken full advantage of opportunities for energy conservation and alternative energy sources.* Energy conservation is often more cost effective than developing new sources of fossil fuels or constructing new power plants. Solar, wind, biomass, and hydrogen energy sources have far less impact on air and water quality than burning fossil fuels. In addition, unlike fossil fuels, the sun and wind are renewable energy sources.

7. *Americans have not found satisfactory ways to recycle, reuse, or dispose of solid and hazardous wastes.* America's "throw-away" culture has caused a growing shortage of landfill capacity. Although recycling efforts are improving, there are often inadequate markets for recyclables, and too little reuse of products and materials. The safe disposal of nuclear waste from power plants and military sites has yet to be solved.

8. *Americans have not reduced the production and use of toxic chemicals when there are ready substitutes or alternatives.* For instance, stormwater runoff laden with pesticides, herbicides, and fertilizers from farm fields

and suburban lawns is a leading source of water pollution. Toxic chemicals used in a variety of manufacturing processes pose a risk of groundwater pollution, and may threaten human health and wildlife from spills in transport.

9. *Adequate supplies of clean water are becoming increasingly important as America's population continues to grow.* In the 1990s, Nevada was the fastest growing state, with a 66% jump in population. Arizona was second, with a 40% increase. These states are mostly desert, and water supplies may not be able to keep pace with continued rapid population growth.

Federal and state environmental laws and programs have established quality standards and provide funding for pollution clean-up and protection. Yet, land use planning, regulation, and spending programs at local and regional levels can do much to shape the built environment and minimize the effects of development on the natural environment. Land use planning is a public process about first identifying land capabilities and constraints, and then deciding where private and public developments and infrastructure should or should not be located. However, plans alone will do nothing unless they are implemented through day-to-day decisions about proposed development projects and coordinated with long-term "green infrastructure" spending programs for parks, natural areas, and working landscapes as well as "hard" infrastructure investment in schools, sewer and water facilities, and transportation networks.

Transportation systems are the single most significant factor in shaping the development patterns of metropolitan areas today. Different modes of transportation produce variations in land use patterns and environmental impacts. Cars and trucks are both necessary and convenient in a low-density settlement pattern. However, in high-density cities and suburbs, cars and trucks are not as effective, especially during the congestion of rush hour. Motor vehicles use huge amounts of energy and generate significant amounts of air pollutants. Mass transit—commuter trains, light rail, and buses—depends on a fairly dense settlement pattern, yet produces less air pollution than cars and trucks.

Land use planning in America has traditionally meant planning for development. This must change because simply continuing to allow sprawling development is neither financially nor ecologically sustainable over time. Land use planning, along with public and private investments, needs to emphasize redevelopment and infill within cities and suburbs, maintaining quality built environments, preserving valuable natural areas and working landscapes, and carefully designing greenfield developments. In short, communities and regions must plan to preserve those sensitive environmental resources—air, water, shorelines, wetlands, and productive farm and forestlands—on which the built environment depends.

SUSTAINABLE DEVELOPMENT

The term "sustainable development" has become very popular in recent years because it implies that the production and consumption of goods and services and the building of houses, offices, factories, and stores can be done without harming the natural environment. The natural environment provides the air, water, and land resources that sustain human life and serves as a "sink" for human wastes. The natural environment, however, does not have a limitless ability to absorb and assimilate waste or to provide "natural capital" for human consumption. Natural environments have a limit or "carrying capacity" for how much waste and human development they can accommodate.

The 1987 Bruntland Report for the United Nations defines sustainable development as "development that meets the needs of the present without compromising the ability of future generations to meet their own needs" (The World Commission 1987, 43).

Economist Herman Daly emphasizes the concept of environmental carrying capacity in stating, "Sustainable development means qualitative improvement without quantitative growth beyond the point where the ecosystem cannot regenerate" (Greider 1998, 454-55).

Planners Philip Berke and Maria Conroy provide a more expansive definition of sustainable development as "a dynamic process in which communities anticipate and accommodate the needs of current and future generations in ways that reproduce and balance social, economic, and ecological systems, and link local actions to global concerns" (Berke and Conroy 2000, 23).

Sustainability implies durability and quality. Sustainable development suggests buildings that last for several generations. It also suggests a continuous yield of renewable resources, such as timber and fish. Air and water quality, soils, and wildlife resources remain healthy. Sustainability also implies a manageable "ecological footprint"; usually, the higher a community's standard of living and material well-being, the greater the area of land (the larger the footprint) needed to support that community. The United States enjoys a high standard of living and has a large ecological footprint, estimated by the American Planning Association (APA) at 25.5 acres per person in 2000, compared to 6 acres per person in India (APA 2000). Americans:

- import huge amounts of food, minerals, and oil from other countries;
- consume enormous amounts of wood, paper, minerals, food, energy, and water; and
- produce millions of tons of solid waste and toxic waste, of which only a small fraction is recycled.

In turning the ideal of sustainability into reality, one must ask whether it is possible to achieve sustainable development when environmental damage is caused by the long-term increase in human population levels and expanding settlement patterns as well as by natural disasters.

Sustainable development is not an end in itself, but rather a means to an end. Sustainable development carries the promise of long-term economic security, social equity, and environmental integrity. Sustainable development suggests the need for individual, community, regional, national, and international responsibility to maintain a healthy, quality environment.

To bring about orderly, environmentally sound development, the choice is not between an unfettered free market and total government control. Rather, selecting the right regulations, spending programs, and incentives will enable markets to function in socially rewarding ways and will compel governments, businesses, and consumers to be good stewards of the natural and built environments.

We contend that, on the one hand, it is wise to avoid blindly embracing technology and economic growth, and, on the other, to avoid adamantly calling for a halt to growth and development. We believe that sustainable development principles must embrace the following goals:

- the creation and maintenance of healthy environments, featuring clean air and water
- the conservation of energy, soils, and water supplies
- the reduction, reuse, and recycling of waste
- the requirement for polluters to pay for cleaning up the pollution they create
- the clean-up of brownfield sites
- an emphasis on the reuse of existing buildings and infill development rather than building on open greenfields in the outer suburbs
- the promotion of mass transit and compact, transit-oriented development
- the construction of mixed-use commercial and residential development that includes public parks and emphasizes walking and biking
- the practice of environmental justice in the siting of controversial land uses

- the designation of compact growth areas that have services available to support development
- the separation of developing areas from sensitive natural areas, to avoid natural hazards and to protect wilderness areas and wildlife habitats
- the creation of greenways—linear paths and corridors—to connect cities and towns to the countryside and to each other
- the protection of productive farming and forestry regions

To achieve these goals, government tax and procurement policies, spending and incentive programs, and land use and environmental regulations will need to be evaluated and in some cases reformed. Educational programs will be needed to increase the awareness of the public about the value of the environment, the pros and cons of development, and public actions that can maintain or improve environmental quality. An educated public can then become active in planning efforts and elect or lobby politicians to make needed changes. The public and private sectors will have to work together to set goals and objectives for environmental improvement. Progress toward achieving these goals and objectives should be monitored on an annual basis.

A COMMUNITY PERSPECTIVE ON PLANNING FOR THE ENVIRONMENT

A community is perhaps best thought of as people who live in close proximity, share public services and private institutions, and interact socially with one another. A community is often thought of as a village or a city neighborhood, but how many of us live in one community and work in another? Or shop in another? Or attend church in another? In fact, when most of us think of a community, we think locally; however, in practice, we often act regionally.

Even so, planning for environmental quality begins at the community level. Planning is a political process of public decision making, and it is therefore important to form a vision of environmental quality—clean air, clean water, and pleasing surroundings. Ultimately, it is essential to take action to protect and sustain a community's environmental assets and quality of life.

Many local governments do not understand how their land use decisions affect the environment. One of the key roles planners can play is to educate local officials about the environmental consequences of development proposals, public infrastructure spending, and land use and design regulations. Planners can be effective in promoting proactive, comprehensive planning that seeks to avoid water and air pollution and land use problems before they happen, and thus protect the community's quality of life and potential for economic growth.

The results of reactive community planning are all too common. Many ad-hoc citizens' groups have sprung up to address single environmental issues in their communities, such as opposing a proposed development. The citizens must raise funds, attend meetings, and generally disrupt their lives. The developers usually defend their proposal as permitted under the land use rules of the local government, and the local government sometimes appears ineffective. Unfortunately, the case is often decided at considerable expense in a court of law.

After the development proposal is denied or approved, the ad-hoc group disbands. When the next threat comes along, the process repeats itself. A new ad-hoc group is patched together, the developers go on the defensive, and the local government is forced to take sides. This reactive approach to environmental protection is inefficient, combative, and costly for citizens, developers, and local governments.

Proactive environmental planning is much more effective in that it recommends appropriate land uses and land-management regulations before development proposals are made. It makes more sense for the concerns of the public to be incorporated into the comprehensive plan, zoning, and capital improvements programs of the local government. This provides predictability for all parties about where certain types of development are and are not allowed. This greater certainty in the planning process saves everyone time, money, and effort while protecting the environment.

A REGIONAL PERSPECTIVE ON PLANNING FOR THE ENVIRONMENT

A region can be identified in many ways. Political boundaries can define a region, such as a county. Population, such as a Metropolitan Statistical Area that usually contains more than one county, is another way to identify a region. Regions can also be defined economically, such as Silicon Valley. Culture and history also give a region identity, such as New England or the Tidewater area of Virginia. Natural features can define a region, such as the Adirondack Mountains of New York, North Carolina's Outer Banks, or Florida's Everglades. Ecological systems can also define regions, such as the New Jersey Pinelands or the West's Great Basin. The size of natural or ecological regions can vary greatly. In the western United States, river basins of the Colorado and Missouri Rivers encompass tens of thousands of square miles in several states. The Rocky Mountains stretch from Mexico to Canada. The larger the size of the region, the more complex the planning because of the greater number of political jurisdictions involved.

A regional perspective on planning for the environment is necessary because few ecological systems are contained solely within a single political jurisdiction. Also, people live, work, shop, and play across a region. Large developments, such as ski resorts, shopping malls, major highways, and paper mills, can have impacts on air and water quality that are felt in more than one town or county. Local governments must recognize their dependence on one another if they are to achieve effective regional environmental planning. For example, in New York State, three towns, Suffolk County, and the state government jointly formed the Long Island Pine Barrens Commission to tightly control development in a 100,000-acre area with a major aquifer drinking water source and a high concentration of rare and endangered plant and animal species.

Regional planning enables a more comprehensive and integrated way to manage the environment and development, but new management institutions may have to be created. Through the 1990s, no metropolitan region in America sprawled as much as Atlanta. Toward the end of the decade, the region's air quality did not meet federal air quality standards, and the federal government temporarily withheld additional highway funds from metropolitan Atlanta. In 1999, the Georgia legislature created the Georgia Regional Transportation Authority, a regional land use and transportation authority for greater Atlanta with the power to promote mass transit and approve or deny major new building projects. The regional perspective on environmental planning is becoming increasingly popular, and it will be successful if it can encourage and meld together local community planning efforts.

MANAGING THE ENVIRONMENT: PROBLEMS AND POSSIBILITIES

Barry Commoner in *The Closing Circle* (1971) lists three Laws of Ecology, which can serve as rules of thumb for environmental decision making and stewardship of natural resources.

The First Law is: *There isn't any such thing as a free lunch;* that is, every action has a cost. For environmental planning, different development choices will impose different costs on the environment. For instance, a regional mall with acres of parking lot will create a higher volume of runoff and more polluted runoff than the forest it replaced.

The Second Law helps explain why there is no free lunch: *Everything is connected to everything else.* For instance, the clear cutting of old-growth forest

may lead to the extinction of a rare animal species by destroying habitat. The clear cutting may also cause soil erosion and flooding, thus decreasing watershed protection. Similarly, in the case of waste disposal, the waste must go somewhere—into the air, the land, or the water. For example, when liquid, carbon-based gasoline is burned, harmful carbon monoxide gas is released into the atmosphere.

The Third Law is: *You can't fool Mother Nature.* Human attempts to manage the environment don't always work. Houses built in a 100-year floodplain may avoid flood damage for 30 years, but then may be swept away in year 31. The houses should not have been built in the floodplain in the first place.

A corollary to the Third Law might be: *Each environmental system has a carrying capacity—a physical limit to the amount of development, pollution, and (human, plant, or animal) population beyond which environmental quality is not sustainable.* This carrying capacity or limit to growth may be stretched by new technologies; however, once a carrying capacity is reached, decline in environmental quality is likely to be sudden rather than gradual. A challenge to planners is that carrying capacity is often difficult to identify with scientific accuracy.

A NOTE ON "GOOD SCIENCE"

In making choices about how to use our environment, we must have accurate information on which to base our decisions. Environmental planning relies on information from a variety of sciences, including biology, botany, chemistry, physics, agronomy, meteorology, geology, epidemiology, hydrology, engineering, and ecology.

"Good science" is objective, technical information based on empirical evidence, past experience, and tested technology. There is much about the environment that is not known with certainty. In some cases, there may be evidence but not conclusive proof. Scientists may disagree about sources of environmental problems and possible solutions. They may also disagree over what is an acceptable level of risk of harm from polluting activities. Moreover, an enormous amount of misinformation has been circulated about the environment. Environmentalists often support the "precautionary principle," which holds that the absence of complete scientific certainty should not be an excuse for refusing to take action (Dernbach 2002). For instance, a ban on the use of a particular chemical with a tendency to produce cancer in laboratory animals could be taken as a precautionary measure.

The use of good science faces three main obstacles:

1. It may be expensive to gather and analyze information in a timely fashion.
2. The results may become highly politicized when debated by political parties with different interests.
3. It may be difficult to anticipate the impacts on the environment of a proposed development that may not become evident for several years.

A proposed development may seem environmentally benign and be granted approval. However, elected officials who make public rulings on development proposals often spend a relatively short time in office. The negative consequences of their decisions may not occur until they are no longer in office and no longer accountable.

Good science evolves over time. It is important to have reputable, objective scientific research. The National Academy of Sciences and its National Research Council are often called upon by Congress to provide objective scientific research, free from the "politics" of science. New studies and discoveries can and will change our thinking about the environment. For example, in the 1970s, the U.S. Environmental Protection Agency (EPA) promoted the concept "The solution to pollution is dilution." This concept resulted in taller smokestacks on coal-fired electrical plants in the Midwest to reduce local air pollution.

Unfortunately, the taller smokestacks emitted pollution higher into the sky where winds could carry the pollution eastward to contribute to acid rain in the Northeast. Now, at the beginning of the 21st century, the emphasis is on reducing air pollution emissions altogether.

Take the case of global warming. In the late 1980s, there was considerable controversy within the scientific community about global warming, but the 1990s were the warmest decade since weather measurements were first regularly recorded in the 1890s. Today, nearly all scientists agree that global warming is real and poses serious long-term threats to humans and ecological systems. (See U.S. EPA *Climate Action Report 2002* in the Bibliography.)

While it is impossible to remove all risks to human health and ecosystems, scientists may be able to identify and reduce the risks of long-term and potentially irreversible effects on human health and ecosystems from air and water pollution, toxic waste, transportation systems, developments amid natural hazards, and certain agricultural practices. Scientists, citizens, businesses, and governments must work together to decide which risks pose intolerable threats and which are acceptable.

Technological inventions can influence good science, but it is difficult to predict what new technologies will occur and when. Environmental management is based on a variety of approaches: regulations, standards, financial incentives, markets, and best management practices—each with its advantages and disadvantages. It is important to understand the costs and benefits of selecting one environmental management approach over another, or how to blend a number of approaches into a strategic environmental management package. Ideally, our individual and collective actions will be beneficial to ourselves, our community, our region, and future generations.

The Environmental Planning Process

1

Taking Stock of the Local Environment and Creating an Environmental Action Plan

---

If we cannot imagine a healthy, bountiful, and sustaining environment today, it will elude us tomorrow.

MARK DOWIE, *LOSING GROUND* (1995, 7)

Planning is about organizing resources and making choices to achieve goals and objectives. The term "environment," as first used by Rachel Carson in *Silent Spring* (1962), refers to both natural places and processes and the condition of human settlements. Environmental planning is deciding how to use natural resources, financial capital, and people to achieve and maintain healthy communities and a high quality of life. Planning also involves avoiding problems before they happen. Environmental planning can help communities avoid or minimize air and water pollution, loss of wildlife, the conversion of farm and forestlands, and degradation of the built environment.

The environment is made up of three main land uses:

1. *Natural areas* that provide environmental services, including wildlife habitats, wetlands, water supplies, most coastal and riparian regions, national and state parks, and wilderness areas; natural areas that also contain lands that pose environmental constraints, such as natural hazards, including floodplains and landslide areas;

2. *Working landscapes,* including farms, rangelands, forests, mines, and recreation areas, that provide jobs and contribute to the health of rural economies; and

3. *Built environments* of cities, suburbs, and towns that involve the design, siting, and type of buildings, transportation systems, sewer and water facilities, and public spaces and parklands.

How these three land uses interact with one another affect a community's appearance, size, functioning, and environmental quality. Deciding how, when, and where these land uses should or should not change is the primary challenge of environmental planning.

ADDING ENVIRONMENTAL PLANNING TO THE TRADITIONAL COMPREHENSIVE LAND USE PLANNING PROCESS

Public environmental planning is put into practice through federal, state, and local government laws, regulations, and taxation and spending programs that discourage, encourage, or require certain actions by companies, individuals, and governments. State governments have environmental agencies that coordinate compliance with federal laws and regulations, and in some cases set their own environmental standards. Private businesses and nonprofit citizens' groups also do environmental planning to guide their actions that influence environmental quality. The focus of this book is mainly on environmental planning by cities, towns, and counties.

Municipal and county governments have primary responsibility for land use planning, though local planning programs may be influenced by federal and state requirements and guidelines. The main purposes of local land use planning are to:

- decide the appropriate uses of land;
- regulate the location, timing, and design of development; and
- invest in infrastructure, such as sewer and water facilities and roads, to address current needs and to influence the siting, design, and intensity of future development.

Most communities have already adopted a traditional comprehensive land use plan that describes the built environment, estimates future population growth, and identifies areas for future development. But many community plans focus on residential, commercial, and industrial land uses and do not adequately address issues of air and water quality, water supply, solid waste disposal, farmland, forestland, wildlife habitat, or physical constraints to development such as steep slopes and wetlands.

The concept of sustainability can become a guiding principle for communities and regions as they undertake environmental planning. Sustainability involves planning for the long-term health of the natural environment, productive working landscapes, efficient public investments, a durable built environment, economic prosperity, and opportunities and access to a quality environment for all income groups. It is especially important for a community or region to recognize its air, water, and land resources as economic assets and "green infrastructure" that can attract responsible new businesses to the area as well as contribute much to residents' well-being.

Environmental planning should strive to be comprehensive and holistic. Planning for one aspect of the environment (such as water quality) without recognizing the impacts of other activities (such as air pollution affecting water quality) will result in less effective plans, regulations, and incentives for environmental improvement. Environmental planning must also be economically and technologically feasible. It makes little sense to advocate tax policies, capital spending programs, or technologies that a community or region cannot afford.

The Comprehensive Plan

The comprehensive plan is the foundation for local and regional planning. The plan sets forth a vision of how a community or region should look, function, and grow over the next 10 to 20 years. The plan provides direction through an inventory of current conditions and the identification of future needs through goals and objectives dealing with topics including housing, the economic base, public facilities and services, transportation, land use, parks and recreation, and the environment.

Fundamental to the comprehensive plan is a projection of population change over the next 20 years. More people mean greater demands for housing, jobs, water, sewage treatment, and land for development. On the other hand, some communities may be losing population or experiencing little population change, but population shifts and new developments within such communities can influence environmental quality. How a community grows or declines will have a significant impact on the built environment, the natural environment, and overall quality of life.

Particularly important is the comprehensive plan's future land use map, which details what land uses are desired where and lays the foundation for the zoning map. The comprehensive plan is meant to be a working document. Private development proposals and public infrastructure programs should be evaluated according to the goals and objectives of the plan, and the future land use map. The comprehensive plan provides a legal basis for the zoning ordinance and subdivision regulations that, along with the capital improvements program (CIP), put the comprehensive plan into action. Consistency among the comprehensive plan, implementing regulations, and spending programs is essential. A lack of consistency creates confusion for developers, planning commissions, and the public about the purpose of the plan, the legality and fairness of the regulations, and the need for infrastructure spending.

A common problem is that the traditional comprehensive land use planning process usually emphasizes growth and development, and does not place a high priority on environmental planning. Economic development, transportation, and housing receive far more attention. It is not uncommon to find comprehensive plans that have little to say about the capabilities and constraints of the natural environment. This is frequently the case with larger cities that have small amounts of open, developable land, and rural communities that are hungry for economic development. Communities on the metropolitan fringe often designate their remaining farmland as "vacant" in the comprehensive plan, as if the land has no legitimate current use and is just waiting to be developed. Many smaller communities in particular try to save time and money by drafting a "policy plan" that does not include an inventory of facts or an analysis of environmental conditions. As a result, policy recommendations are likely to be flawed and often sound like nothing more than a wish list.

Many communities overlook the fact that a quality environment is an economic asset. Two of the largest economic sectors in America are high technology and tourism. High technology includes computer-related businesses, health care, biotech, optics, and aerospace. Many high-tech companies are footloose; they can locate just about anywhere. Moreover, they employ well-paid and highly educated workers who value quality surroundings and quality of life. Attractive cities, towns, and villages with good air and water quality and access to open space will be competitive for high-tech businesses and workers.

Tourists are looking for enjoyable sights and activities. Scenic vistas; wildlife; recreation areas; clean air and water; historic sites and buildings; and places to eat, shop, and spend the night all contribute to positive experiences in places that can be visited again and again. This is not to say that everyone should be writing computer software or employed in hotels. Heavy manufacturing is still important to many communities, as are retail trades, finance, and a variety of service- and government-related jobs. However, there is a close link between sustainable economic growth and a sustainable environment.

Many communities have comprehensive plans that are more than 10 years old and no longer reflect the community's conditions or goals and objectives for growth and development. All too frequently, planning commissions and planning staff find themselves overwhelmed with reviewing development proposals and have little or no time to devote to updating the comprehensive plan, the zoning and subdivision regulations, or the CIP. The suburban Town of Williston, Vermont, addressed this problem by appointing two separate planning boards. One deals with current planning issues; the other handles long-range planning, including drafting or updating the comprehensive plan, zoning, subdivision and land development regulations, and the CIP.

Another common problem is that the plan of a single community or county may not recognize the environmental impacts of their land use and development activities on neighboring jurisdictions or environmental impacts from neighboring jurisdictions. For instance, the destruction of wetlands upstream will create more flooding downstream. Most land use and environmental problems are regional, not local. Yet, many local governments try to address these problems by themselves, rather than cooperatively.

Zoning

Zoning is the most widely used land use control in the United States to guide the future growth and development of a municipality or county. The zoning ordinance consists of two parts: a text describing the rules for each zoning district (Residential, R-1 Single Family, R-2 Multifamily, Commercial C-1, Manufacturing M-1, etc.) and a map showing the location and boundaries of the zoning districts (Figure 1-1).

Zoning has several purposes. First, it serves to implement the goals and objectives of the comprehensive plan—in particular, the plan's future land use map. Thus, the zoning ordinance should be consistent with the comprehensive plan. In some states, a zoning ordinance that is not consistent with the comprehensive plan could be ruled invalid in a court of law.

Another purpose of zoning is to separate potentially conflicting land uses, such as a factory from single-family homes, to protect public health, safety, and welfare. Each zoning district has different rules for permitted uses, special exceptions, and conditional uses. Permitted uses are normally allowed outright after a review by planning commission staff. Special exceptions are usually reviewed by the zoning board after a public hearing, while conditional uses are typically reviewed by the planning commission and the elected governing body after public hearings. Each zoning district also has specific regulations on lot size, height of buildings, building setbacks from property lines, lot coverage (how much of a site can be covered with impervious surfaces), and other requirements.

Zoning must not remove all economic use of a private property. Otherwise, zoning will violate the takings test of the Fifth Amendment to the U.S. Constitution (see Chapter 2). Zoning must also be reasonable. The reasonableness test is largely a matter of common sense, based on land capabilities and constraints. However, there should be a clear link between the goals of the comprehensive plan and what the zoning ordinance requires. Zoning, for example, can be used to protect farmland from intense development, but farmland protection should be described as a goal in the comprehensive plan for environmental, fiscal, aesthetic, and local economic reasons.

A valid criticism of traditional zoning is that it often separates commercial and residential land uses, and forces people to travel by car from where they live to where they work or shop. This situation creates more energy dependence, air pollution, and sprawling development. The zoning ordinances of most cities and suburbs do not allow for the mixing of commercial and residential uses. Many commercial and residential uses can

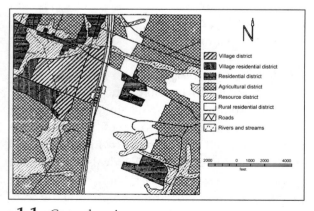

1-1   General zoning map.

Source: Albany County, New York

be safely combined in a mixed-use zone of small shops, houses, offices, and apartments to create a more attractive, compact, and pedestrian-friendly built environment. Zoning tends to be rigid, resulting in "cookie-cutter" housing developments, and may also be poorly administered through the frequent granting of use variances, illegal spot rezonings, and other rezonings that defeat the goals of the comprehensive plan.

Local zoning ordinances and especially rezoning decisions have too often been based on the hunt for new development to expand the property tax base, rather than on topography, hydrology, soils, wildlife habitat, or the availability of adequate infrastructure to support development. Many communities allow commercial, industrial, and large-lot residential development that will increase the property tax base, but openly discourage multifamily housing for fear of a greater property tax burden. This fiscal zoning is discriminatory and tends to promote both large-lot residential sprawl and arterial commercial sprawl, instead of compact, mixed-use developments.

Also, if the planning and zoning process does not examine the cumulative environmental impacts of development projects, a community may jeopardize its environmental quality in the long run. Over time, many small developments can create impacts as great as a few large projects.

Finally, many zoning ordinances are long, dry texts. It is a good idea to place drawings or photos depicting correct zoning practices in the zoning text. These illustrations will help landowners, developers, politicians, and concerned citizens to better understand and implement the zoning concepts.

Subdivision and Land Development Regulations

The subdivision and land development ordinance establishes rules for the proper design and layout of lots, necessary roads, sewage disposal, drinking water supplies, and stormwater drainage as well as the retention of open space and vegetation. In some states or communities, the subdivision ordinance may require an environmental impact assessment for all major subdivisions and land development plans (see Appendix).

The subdivision and land development process typically requires the planning commission to review and approve a development proposal in three stages: the sketch plan, the preliminary plat, and the final plat. In the sketch plan stage, the developer presents a conceptual layout of the proposal. This is a brainstorming and negotiation process between the developer and the planning commission or staff, rather than a rigorous review of requirements. The planning commission or staff recommends ways to improve the proposal, and the developer then prepares a preliminary plat.

The preliminary plat shows a considerable amount of information about the proposal, including planned lot configurations, building locations, streets, utilities, neighboring landowners and land uses, and environmental features such as streams, slopes, and vegetation. The planning commission and staff review the proposed development according to the subdivision and land development regulations, and provide an opportunity for the public to comment. The planning commission may approve the preliminary plat, approve it with conditions, or deny it. Most often, the planning commission imposes conditions to ensure that the proposal meets the standards of the subdivision ordinance. The developer may be required to put up a bond for installing streets and utilities for the development.

Once the planning commission approves the preliminary plat, there is little the public can do to change the project. The developer responds to the conditions attached to the preliminary plat approval and then submits a final plat for approval. In this stage, the municipality or county determines whether the developer has met the conditions attached to the preliminary plat and, if so, signs the final plat and it is recorded with the recorder of deeds at the county courthouse. Then the land may be developed or subdivided.

From the date the final plat is approved, the developer is usually allowed up to three years to commence the project and five years to complete it. If the project is not begun within three years or completed within five years, the final plat is null and void and a new application for a subdivision would be required. Exceptions may be granted for large developments that are phased in over time, such as for some planned-unit developments that can take several years to complete. Time limits for most types of development are a good idea because environmental and other factors can change over time. In the past, many substandard subdivisions were laid out, legally approved, and then never developed. Substandard lots in such subdivisions are often constrained by small size, steep slopes, lack of road access, and lack of water.

In many communities, subdivision regulations, together with rigid zoning ordinances, have produced "cookie-cutter" residential layouts, varied only by the use of road loops and cul-de-sac "lollipops." Curvilinear street patterns that maximize driving and disorientation are all too common. Any open space that is preserved is typically fragmented and often not useful for recreation, wildlife habitat, or other purposes.

The subdivision review process should require developers to present detailed studies of the likely environmental impacts of large proposed projects. Developers may be asked to consider alternative project designs that may be more compatible with the environment. For instance, local subdivision and land development regulations may require developers to mitigate environmental impacts, such as restoring wetlands or creating new wetlands off site, to provide long-term protection of important natural resources.

The Capital Improvements Program

Public roads, schools, parks, and sewer and water facilities have a powerful effect on where development occurs, when it occurs, and the type of development. A CIP describes:

- what public infrastructure a community will build, repair, or replace;
- where these services are or will be located;
- when construction, repair, or replacement will happen; and
- how these infrastructure projects will be funded.

A CIP will look five to 10 years into the future, but this may vary according to a community's estimates of future population growth and service needs.

The purpose of the CIP is to anticipate the location and amount of public service needs and to provide adequate services at a reasonable cost. The CIP can help coordinate projects and avoid mismanagement, such as paving a street one year and tearing it up the next to install a sewer line.

A CIP commonly covers roads and bridges, school buildings, sewer and water treatment plants and lines, municipal buildings, parks, solid waste disposal sites, and police and fire equipment. The program should contain detailed information on the capacity of current facilities, the projected future demand for public services, standards for road construction, and sewer and water treatment plants and lines; and estimated future costs and financing arrangements in relation to expected municipal or county budgets.

The CIP needs to be coordinated with the comprehensive plan and the zoning ordinance and map. Lack of coordination has often resulted in extensions of central water and sewer by municipalities, authorities, and private developers that create leapfrog development and the premature conversion of farmland and open space. Sewer line extensions mean that local water bodies will be receiving more treated effluent. More highways and wider roads generate more traffic, air pollution, and stormwater runoff into waterways. The construction of public buildings (such as the town hall, post office, and schools) outside of downtowns and on arterial strips promotes automobile dependence, energy consumption, air pollution, and sprawl.

Concurrency is a policy that requires infrastructure to be in place before public or private development can begin. This policy can be written into the subdivision and land development regulations to ensure that new development will not exceed infrastructure capacity or impose an unreasonable tax burden on a community. Concurrency is a good way to promote phased growth. Florida requires local governments to practice concurrency as part of its 1985 state land use program, and many local governments in other states have adopted the concurrency policy. Communities may choose to allow privately financed infrastructure to meet concurrency requirements. However, it is important to note that a concurrency policy on public infrastructure may not stop the development of building lots that rely on private wells and individual on-site septic systems.

Finally, the CIP should not just feature "bricks and mortar infrastructure" but also the provision and protection of "green infrastructure." Financial incentives and land purchases can protect sensitive environmental lands and working landscapes, provide recreational opportunities, and keep new development away from steep slopes and other natural hazards.

THE ENVIRONMENTAL PLANNING PROCESS

To emphasize sustainability in the traditional planning process, we recommend that communities and counties adopt an Environmental Action Plan. An Action Plan can be used to influence the goals and objectives of several areas of the comprehensive plan, especially the Natural Resources, Economic Base, Land Use, and Community Facilities sections. It can also identify regulations, spending programs, and other actions to achieve a sustainable environment and sustainable development.

The Environmental Action Plan may be drafted separately from the comprehensive plan or as part of the comprehensive plan. We recommend that it be made part of the comprehensive plan, because the comprehensive plan is a widely circulated public document, the legal basis for local land use regulations, and a guide for community and regional infrastructure investment and development. In short, *comprehensive land use planning is environmental planning.*

Chapters 3 through 19 discuss specific environmental issues that should be addressed in local comprehensive planning. Each chapter presents Action Strategies for innovative zoning, subdivision regulations, and CIPs as well as design guidelines and cooperation from nonprofit groups, to implement environmental quality goals and objectives. It is important to consult your state's planning and zoning enabling legislation to determine which land use regulatory tools are allowed in your state. Finally, each chapter contains a discussion of what a planning staff or planning commission should look for in reviewing a development proposal in order to minimize environmental impacts.

The Environmental Action Plan

The Environmental Action Plan process has eight main steps, most of which contain a mix of technical planning and political "selling" (see Table 1-1).

Recognizing the Need for Environmental Planning

To start the environmental planning process, elected officials must be convinced that certain environmental problems exist or are potential threats to public health, safety, and welfare. It helps if interest groups, business leaders, and the general public recognize the need for environmental planning and voice their concerns to the elected officials. Recognizing the need for environmental planning may result from a study done by the local government, such as a comprehensive plan. Sometimes, as in the case of Columbus and Franklin

Table 1-1
Eight Steps in Creating an Environmental Action Plan

1.	The public and elected officials recognize the need for environmental planning.
2.	Officials then commit people and funding to the environmental planning effort, and appoint an environmental advisory committee to assist the planning commission.
3.	The planning commission, staff, and the environmental advisory committee conduct an Environmental Needs Assessment Survey and solicit public input.
4.	The planning commission, staff, and the environmental advisory committee develop a factual base of environmental conditions and analyze the information.
5.	The planning commission, staff, and the environmental advisory committee draft a vision statement, broad goals, and specific objectives for the Environmental Action Plan.
6.	The planning commission, staff, and the environmental advisory committee draft an Action Strategy to articulate a set of land use controls, infrastructure spending, tax programs, and other regulations that will put the Environmental Action Plan into practice.
7.	Elected officials solicit public input and adopt the Environmental Action Plan.
8.	The planning commission and elected officials implement, monitor, and evaluate the performance of the Environmental Action Plan through an annual review, and make revisions and updates as needed.

County, Ohio, a partnership of citizens and local government will do a study that alerts public officials about environmental needs and compels them to act (see Case Study 1-1, below). Keep in mind that politicians are more likely to adopt an Environmental Action Plan and support specific actions to implement the plan if they receive credit for supporting the planning effort from the beginning.

Committing People and Money to the Environmental Planning Effort

Elected officials either give the planning commission and staff the task of drafting an Environmental Action Plan or hire a professional planning consultant to do the job. It is recommended that the elected officials or planning commission appoint an environmental advisory committee to help with drafting the plan. Many communities in the northeastern states have appointed a standing local conservation commission to assist the planning commission and elected officials in drafting the environmental elements of the comprehensive plan. The conservation commission can also review and comment on the potential environmental impacts of proposed developments. A local conservation commission or environmental advisory committee should ideally have between eight and 12 members, and should include people from a range of backgrounds (e.g., business, the local university, environmental groups, a local planner, a representative of any adjacent municipality that may share a common natural resource, and citizens from different areas of the community). For technical expertise, it is a good idea to include a biologist and an engineer on the committee.

Some communities may want to hire a consultant to help with the Environmental Action Plan. A consultant should be able to show examples of work on Environmental Action Plans. Make sure the consultant is willing and able to tailor the Action Plan to the needs and desires of the community. A pitfall to avoid is allowing a consultant to present a "boilerplate plan" used by several communities—an all-too-common practice among consultants. Spell out in a contract what is expected of the consultant, when the work is due, the amount of the consultant's fee, and payment dates.

The Environmental Action Plan should include an acknowledgment of public and private sources of funding that paid for the plan as well as the major participants, including the planning commission, any advisory committees and volunteers, any consultants, and, of course, the elected officials who will be asked to adopt the plan.

Surveys and Soliciting Public Input

An Environmental Action Plan must involve broad and meaningful participation from the public and various interest groups. A good way for the planning commission and advisory committee to involve the public in the planning process is to conduct an Environmental Needs Assessment Survey. The survey gives people in the community the opportunity to voice their opinions about environmental conditions and needed improvements. The survey can ask specific questions about a range of environmental issues as well as include open-ended questions about what improvements are needed. Other questions might ask for levels of willingness to pay for new environmental services such as parks, water treatment facilities, or recycling programs.

Surveys may be distributed in a variety of ways, but the most meaningful and representative results will be from mailings to each household or a sample of households in the community. Surveys that are clear and short, and include a self-addressed stamped envelope and cut-off date for responses, will have the best return rates. The survey responses will indicate issues of concern in the community or region, and will help the advisory committee and planning commission in drafting a vision statement, evaluating alternative actions, and formulating general goals and specific objectives for the community or region.

Community or neighborhood public meetings, newsletters, and spots in the local media are also helpful in publicizing the needs assessment effort and eliciting public comments. Public participation is essential for building political support for spending, regulatory programs, and incentives that put the plan into action. At least two sets of meetings are recommended. The first set is to solicit input from the public. The advisory committee and planning commission members should ask people to identify important environmental aspects of their communities and the improvements they would like to see. This can be done effectively in small group brainstorming sessions or focus groups to draw people out and hear from everyone.

Later, after the surveys and informational meetings have been completed and incorporated in a draft of the plan, the planning commission and advisory committee should present their findings and recommendations at a second set of public meetings to get feedback from the public. Does the Action Plan reflect a public consensus? Keep in mind that a consensus does not mean 100% support—there will always be opposition. Were important environmental issues left out? Taking the extra time to involve the public and make changes to the Environmental Action Plan will pay off in the long run. The public will appreciate the opportunity to voice concerns and opinions, and will gain a better understanding of what the Environmental Action Plan is trying to do. Public support is crucial in convincing elected officials to adopt the Environmental Action Plan.

Public meetings should be well organized. A professional facilitator can help to keep the meeting focused and give a fair, impartial sense to it. Speakers should be given about five minutes to have their say. Politeness and courtesy should be observed. A public meeting that dissolves into a shouting match or is dominated by one or two speakers will reflect poorly on the overall planning effort. Well-run, informative public meetings with good discussion are good advertising. People want to become part of the planning and implementation process, and they want it to succeed.

Gathering Data About Environmental Conditions and Analyzing the Data

Studies of the natural and built environments, including projected future impacts of population on environmental resources, create a factual base. The factual base should include a Natural Resources Inventory and a Built Environment Inventory. These studies should present accurate, unbiased information on the current condition of the local or regional environment. The factual base will help to answer a variety of questions, such as: What is the quality of the community's air and water? What type of wildlife and wildlife habitats exist? Where are the best farming and forestry soils in the community? What is the suitability of lands and water resources in the community for different types of development? Federal, state, regional, and local governments are good sources of information. Local and state universities and nonprofit environmental organizations may also be helpful. Private consultants may be useful for specific tasks.

Natural Resources Inventory

Natural resources include air, water, soils, geologic formations, farmlands, forests, minerals, wetlands, and plant and animal species. The inventory should identify the location, quantity, and quality of these resources, and their vulnerability to development or overuse. The inventory should also identify natural hazards and development constraints, such as steep slopes and floodplains.

One challenge in putting together a Natural Resources Inventory is that communities have political boundaries that are likely to differ from geologic or ecological boundaries. For example, the community may be part of a river basin or wildlife migration route. A community may need to consult with neighboring communities, counties, and regional planning agencies to gather complete inventory data.

Resource maps are very useful, and a composite map of natural resource layers, generated by a Geographic Information System (GIS), is highly recommended (see Figure 1-2). Several states have GIS clearinghouses with data accessible on line. If available, remote sensing information may be helpful, especially on a regional level. Topographic maps from the U.S. Geological Survey (USGS) display elevations, roads, water bodies, and settlements. Other USGS maps can help to identify historic, current, and projected community land use patterns.

Aerial photos of the community or region can be especially helpful in showing the pattern of development (whether sprawled or compact), the amount of built-up area and undeveloped land, and where future development might best be accommodated (Humstone *et al.* 2001). Orthopho-

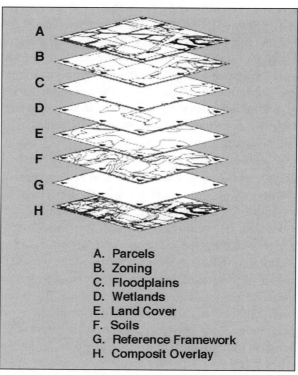

A. Parcels
B. Zoning
C. Floodplains
D. Wetlands
E. Land Cover
F. Soils
G. Reference Framework
H. Composit Overlay

1-2   Geographic Information System database layers.

Source: Lancaster County, Pennsylvania

Table 1-2
Natural Environmental Features to Be Shown on the Natural Resources Inventory Maps

1.	Soils, geology, and topography
2.	Watersheds, streams, water bodies, floodplains, and wetlands
3.	Aquifer recharge areas and delineated wellhead areas
4.	Wildlife habitats
5.	Vegetation (forest cover, croplands, pastures, prairies, etc.)

tos are computerized aerial photographs that are scale-corrected and distortion-free. This information is available from most local offices of the Natural Resources Conservation Service (NRCS). Digitized property tax maps showing property boundaries and land parcel patterns can be overlaid on top of the orthophotos. The resulting GIS maps can then add layers from the Natural Resources Inventory maps (see Table 1-2) and built environment maps. Land parcels can be identified from local tax maps. Areas with many small parcels will not be suitable for development that requires large acreages, such as industrial parks or natural resource uses. Areas with large parcels have better potential for natural resource uses, such as farming, forestry, and mining. Linking parcel patterns with soils, topography, and proximity to sewer, water, and major roads pro-

1-3 Map of soil types from a county soil survey.

Source: Natural Resources Conservation Service

vides a picture of development potential for specific sites. Also, it is important to identify any lands owned by federal, state, or county governments that are generally off limits to development.

The following are discussions of the natural resources that should be included in a Natural Resources Inventory.

Soils. Soils information should include slope, erosion potential, wetness, strength, depth to bedrock, frost action, shrink-swell, prime agricultural soils, forest soils, and suitability for on-site septic systems. County soil surveys produced by the federal NRCS provide all of this information (see Figure 1-3). In many counties, soil surveys have been digitized for GIS applications. Soils information indicates the ability of an area or parcel of land to support buildings, absorb water, and grow plants (see Table 13-2).

Soils with high productive capability for agriculture and forestry are deep, level, and well drained; contain a wealth of microorganisms and organic matter; and can produce crops with a minimum of fertilizers. They also tend to be the same soils that can best support development and are most suitable for the use of on-site septic systems. Slopes of more than 15% should be avoided for building sites. Shallow depth to bedrock, poor drainage, and wet soils can also hamper the construction and stability of buildings. Low weight-bearing soils, which might support development of single-family houses, might not be able to support heavier commercial, industrial, or institutional buildings. Septic systems in porous soils run a high risk of polluting groundwater, while septic systems in heavy clay soils may result in the back-up of effluent to the surface. Soil types inappropriate for buildings, agriculture, or forestry can be designated for uses that are appropriate to the particular conditions, such as parks, wildlife habitats, and other open space uses.

Geology and Topography. The geology of the community or region includes underlying rocks and mineral and aggregate deposits, and the topography of the landscape. Geology can help to identify areas likely to have productive groundwater aquifers and areas vulnerable to groundwater contamination. Geology and underground faults that could lead to subsidence, landslides, or earthquakes should be mapped. There may also be unique geological features such as caves, mesas, and rock outcroppings that should be noted. Topographic maps will show ridges and steep slopes (see Figure 1-4) and reveal stormwater drainage patterns. A study of topography will also be helpful in viewshed analysis with an eye toward protecting outstanding vistas. Data on geology and topography can be obtained from the USGS, state environmental agencies, and state universities.

Water Resources. Important water resources include ground and surface water sources, public water supplies, wetlands, and floodplains. Communities should obtain or draft maps on the location and extent of water resources as well as watershed and aquifer boundaries (see Chapter 3). Topographic quadrant maps from the USGS and maps of wetlands from the National Wetlands Inventory are helpful. Information on the flow or yield of surface and groundwater may be available from state water resources or environmental agencies and the U.S. Environmental Protection Agency (EPA). Current water system use and treatment capacity should be noted. Use of water for wildlife, recreational purposes, and energy use should also be described, along with minimum streamflows to sustain these uses. If

there are known pollution problems that could threaten water supplies, they should be explained and noted on a map (see Chapter 4). For instance, known hazardous waste sites and landfills should be mapped and nearby groundwater tested.

The quality of surface and groundwater resources should also be described (see Table 4-3). Water quality data can be obtained from a variety

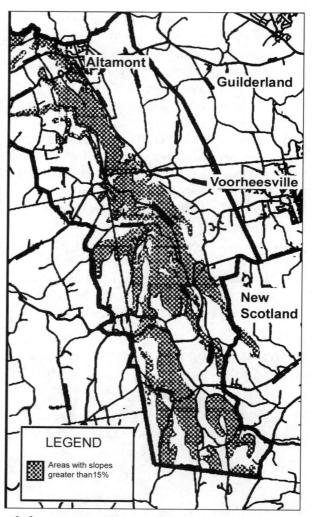

1-4 Map identifying steep slopes for the Natural Resources Inventory.

Source: Albany County, New York

of sources, including public water suppliers, the local municipality, and the state environmental or water resources agency.

It is essential to identify and map wetlands (see Chapter 10). Good sources of information include the National Wetlands Inventory from the U.S. Fish and Wildlife Agency and state-level wetlands maps from the state environmental agency. The county soil survey has maps that identify the location of wet or hydric soils, although not all hydric soils are considered wetlands.

Identifying floodplains is important to avoid building in these dangerous areas (see Chapter 12). The Federal Emergency Management Agency (FEMA) publishes floodplain maps for all communities in the nation with floodplains. While much of the mapping is now dated, FEMA is in the process of updating mapping for many communities. Communities may also refine FEMA mapping by using detailed floodplain studies that may have been commissioned for proposed developments close to the floodplain. Additional information may be available from the state environmental or water resources agency.

Wildlife Habitat. Significant wildlife habitat, migration routes, fish spawning grounds, nesting areas, and feeding spots should be described and mapped. Wildlife habitat can be identified by knowledgeable local volunteers, conservation groups, and personnel from the state university and state fish and wildlife department. Habitats should be rated for importance and vulnerability. Any rare and endangered plant or animal habitats should be generally identified so as to protect species from possible poaching or habitat destruction (see Chapter 9).

Vegetation. Lands in forest cover, farm use, or other type of vegetation should be described and mapped. Sources of information include satellite imagery and aerial photos. This information can be digitized into a GIS database and can be combined with the wildlife habitat map.

Air Quality. An inventory of air quality should include average measurements of carbon monoxide, particulates, nitrogen dioxide, lead, ozone, and sulfur oxides, which are the main air pollutants identified by the federal government under the Clean Air Act Amendments of 1970 (see Chapter 5). Mention should be made of how many days each year the air quality fails to meet one or more of the standards for the above six pollutants. Information on air quality is available from the state environmental agency and from the regional office of the EPA. Air quality is normally described but not mapped.

Built Environment Inventory

A Built Environment Inventory can show the location, number, age, and condition of the housing stock, commercial and industrial buildings, parks, and public buildings. The inventory should also include the location and condition of public infrastructure, including roads, sewer and water lines, schools, landfills, and police and fire stations. The built environment has important connections with the natural environment. The amount of developed land, land with development potential, and the location of different land uses have implications for stormwater management, transportation and energy use, and air and water quality.

The Built Environment Inventory should identify and map buildings and neighborhoods with historic and cultural value, public buildings and spaces, streetscapes, and blighted areas. These are all areas with potential for improving the quality of life for residents in the neighborhood. Historic buildings and streetscapes have been key ingredients in the redevelopment of many cities and towns across America. Public buildings and spaces draw people together and create a sense of community. Open spaces and greenways provide parklands, wildlife habitats, filter runoff, and buffer watercourses. Information on the built environment can be found through the state historic preservation office and city and county planning offices.

*Analysis of the Natural Resources
Inventory and Built Environment Inventory*

The analysis of the Natural Resources Inventory and the Built Environment Inventory consists of three parts:

1. a Land and Water Suitability Analysis;
2. an Environmental Quality Analysis; and
3. a Current Trends Analysis.

Land and Water Suitability Analysis. A key product of the Natural Resources Inventory is a Land and Water Suitability Analysis, which identifies those areas of the community that are appropriate for development, places that have moderate limitations for developments of various types, and areas that should be protected in their natural state because of severe environmental constraints. The suitability analysis for the community can be shown on one or more GIS maps with several layers of environmental information (see Table 1-2). The analysis should also identify land with particular capabilities, such as productive farm and forest soils as well as areas that will maintain critical natural processes such as wetlands and aquifer recharge areas. Overall, the Land and Water Suitability Analysis can provide important information on the carrying capacity of the community; that is, how many people and how much development the community can sustainably support before serious negative impacts on the natural environment occur. For this reason, the Land and Water Suitability Analysis is a primary building block of the comprehensive plan.

Rating Natural Resources and Development Suitability. The Land and Water Suitability Analysis should use a method to rate or classify the development potential of different lands. Development constraints and natural hazards can be identified with a color code on GIS maps (red for severe limitations, orange for moderate limitations, and yellow for few limitations) or a numeri-

cal points system, with developable lands receiving higher points than lands with development limitations.

Natural resources worthy of preserving should be identified using a separate color code, such as shades of green. For instance, high-quality, actively farmed land and land managed for timber production might be identified on the land suitability map by different green colors.

Natural resources should be prioritized for protection according to:

- whether the resource is renewable or irreplaceable (if irreplaceable, the resource is more valuable);
- the rarity of the site (the less common, the more valuable the resource, particularly in the case of habitats of rare and endangered plant and wildlife species);
- the size of the site (generally, the larger the site, the more important it is);
- the diversity of plants, wildlife, scenic views, and other natural features (the greater the diversity, the more important the site is); and
- the fragility of the site, including the quality of the undisturbed site and human threats to the site.

The development potential classification system should be clear and understandable to nonexperts. The system, and especially maps, will help planners and elected officials in creating the future land use and zoning maps as well as in the day-to-day development review process.

Environmental Quality Analysis. This analysis compares state and federal environmental standards with actual conditions in the community. For example, local air and water quality are measured against air and water pollution standards. This analysis provides baseline information that can help a community rank its natural resources for protection, identify environmental quality problems, evaluate alternative solutions, and set priorities for action. The baseline information can be used to set environmental quality targets and can be readily updated to measure progress toward environmental quality benchmarks.

Current Trends Analysis. Recent trends in population growth, acreage developed, acreage in public parks, vehicle miles traveled (VMT), recycling efforts, loss of endangered plant and animal species, air and water quality, and water use give indications of the direction of environmental quality. The Current Trends Analysis asks the questions: Where are we going in terms of population growth, land development, and environmental quality? Are these trends sustainable? What will be the environmental costs if these trends continue? What will be the economic costs? Will new sewer and water facilities have to be built? A Current Trends Analysis should project recent environmental trends to help answer these questions.

The Current Trends Analysis should discuss the environmental strengths, weaknesses, opportunities, and threats to the community or region based on the information provided in the Natural Resources and Built Environment Inventories together with population projections. Strengths for a particular community might include a pleasant setting with scenic views, good quality water, and a collection of solid historic buildings. Weaknesses might feature poor air quality and a lack of public transportation. Opportunities might include creating a greenway along a riverfront and rehabilitating historic buildings for commercial purposes in the downtown. Threats might include flooding, sprawling suburbs, and loss of open space. The Current Trends Analysis will be useful in drafting the environmental vision statement for the community together with broad goals and specific objectives to achieve that vision.

Carefully researched and drafted population projections should be the basis for estimating future environmental impacts and designating future land uses. The amount of remaining buildable land and infrastructure capacity are crucial factors for communities to consider. For instance, how many people can the community or region ultimately accommodate? In some cases, lands with high natural resource values will also get a high rating in terms of development potential. The community will need to decide which lands are appropriate for development and which for natural resource protection. In determining development capability, a planner will need to combine the Land and Water Suitability Analysis with information about access to public infrastructure. This is the concept behind the Land Evaluation and Site Assessment system created by the NRCS to help communities decide which lands are best suited to development and which are highly productive farmland with long-term economic viability for agriculture (see Chapter 13). If a community looks only at land in terms of development potential, large amounts of farm and forestland might be designated for development.

The Vision Statement, Broad Goals, and Specific Objectives

The planning commission and advisory committee combine input from the public Environmental Needs Assessment Survey and the analysis of the factual base data into a vision statement for the community or region. The vision statement describes what the quality of the natural, working, and built environments of the community or region should be in 20 years. The vision statement serves as an overall policy directive for the local government, and as the foundation for a variety of environmental goals and objectives. The vision statement typically advocates four outcomes:

- compliance with state and federal environmental standards;
- a healthy, sustainable environment;
- a sustainable economy; and
- a good quality of life for all citizens.

Next, the planning commission and advisory committee should articulate environmental goals and objectives that reflect community desires and priorities, and provide direction for elected officials on public spending, taxation, and land use regulation. This is the first step in making the environmental vision a reality. The goals and objectives must be based on a solid technical analysis of the natural and built environments, realistic costs, and an understanding of relevant state and federal environmental requirements. A common problem is that a goal or objective may be deemed "politically unfeasible," even though it would significantly improve or protect environmental quality. Goals and objectives should address the full range of environmental issues facing the community or region, and should build on strengths (such as a good water supply) as well as address weaknesses (a lack of parkland), opportunities (wildlife and ecotourism), and threats (groundwater pollution).

Setting Goals and Objectives

Goals

Goals are broad statements reflecting a community's desires. Because they provide direction to local officials in their decision making, they should be clear and decisive, avoiding the use of "should." Sample environmental goals might include the following:

- to ensure compliance with state and federal environmental standards for air and water quality;
- to increase the recycling of trash into useful products;
- to conserve the amount of land used for development by promoting compact, mixed-use development;
- to expand mass transit and thus reduce reliance on the automobile and air pollution;
- to increase the amount of public parkland; and
- to protect farmland from conversion to non-farm uses.

Objectives

Objectives spell out specific ways in which goals can be attained. More than one objective per goal is often needed. The following sample objectives would help meet each of the goals above, though additional objectives would also be needed:

- Adopt a wellhead protection ordinance to limit development near public water supplies.
- Contract with a private recycling firm to increase the amount of trash recycled.
- Revise the zoning ordinance to allow smaller minimum lot sizes and a mix of commercial and residential uses.
- Explore funding for additional buses or the construction of a commuter light-rail system.
- Revise the subdivision ordinance to require mandatory dedication of parkland or fees in lieu thereof.
- Explore the creation of a local purchase or transfer of development rights (TDR) program to preserve farmland.

To help draft realistic goals and objectives, the advisory committee or the planning commission should consider the environmental strengths, weaknesses, opportunities, and threats summarized in the Current Trends Analysis. The general strategy is to protect one's strengths, address weaknesses, take advantage of opportunities, and avoid or minimize threats. It is very important to coordinate the goals and objectives of the Environmental Action Plan. A major problem with many traditional comprehensive plans is that they have several conflicting goals that create confusion and effectively cancel each other out. The goals and objectives should be linked by the common theme of sustainability. Some communities may find it useful to prioritize goals and objectives.

The Action Strategy

The chief reason so many comprehensive plans end up sitting on a shelf is because they do not include a detailed Action Strategy as follow-through to the goals and objectives. An Action

SIDEBAR 1-1

The Private Sector and Environmental Planning

One of the most important trends since 1970 is the growth in private sector environmental planning. To comply with government regulations, businesses have had to form environmental management units. Moreover, in working to reduce the costs of environmental compliance, businesses have been challenged to operate more responsibly and sustainably. New technologies are enabling businesses to reduce waste and toxic substances, save energy and water, and produce more durable products. These trends are encouraging because they show that businesses can be both environmentally friendly and profitable (Hawken *et al.* 1999).

Land developers in several states and many communities have had to address a wide range of questions about the impacts of their proposed developments on the natural and built environments, from air and water quality to transportation and aesthetics. Some developers have abandoned the uniform "cookie-cutter" designs of residential subdivisions in favor of mixed-use residential and commercial projects that emphasize pedestrian access over motor vehicles.

The private nonprofit sector has earned a rapidly expanding role in environmental planning, especially in the protection of natural areas, wildlife habitat, working landscapes, and historic buildings. The number, size, and importance of land trusts, conservancies, watershed associations, and citizens' groups have grown impressively. No longer is environmental planning conducted solely by governments. The result has been an increasing number of public-private partnerships in local and regional planning, land preservation, watershed protection, and redevelopment efforts.

Strategy should articulate a set of land use controls, infrastructure spending, tax and incentive programs, and other regulations that will put the Environmental Action Plan into practice. These recommended actions should be the same as or consistent with the plan's objectives. The Action Strategy may identify who is expected to do the work, funding mechanisms, and time lines for completion, and should be set out in an easy-to-read table format. Short-term, medium-range, long-run, and ongoing proposed activities can be identified and described. A clearly presented Action Strategy will keep the comprehensive plan alive in the minds of the public and local government and help ensure its full implementation.

Adoption of the Environmental Action Plan

The Environmental Action Plan should be presented to the local governing body for review at a public meeting. The elected officials may adopt, amend and adopt, or reject the Environmental Action Plan. In the case of Columbus, Ohio, for example, the city government reviewed the recommendations and decided that about half of them were feasible given financial and regulatory constraints (see Case Study 1-1, below).

If there has been broad participation from the public and various interest groups in drafting the Action Plan's vision statement and goals and objectives, elected officials will be more likely to adopt most, if not all, of the plan's recommendations for action. Also, public support is needed to ensure that the planning commission and elected officials have the political will to adhere to the plan and to implement it in their day-to-day decisions and longer term policy and budgetary decisions.

The goals, objectives, technical background studies, and analysis of the Environmental Action Plan may be incorporated into the community or regional comprehensive plan or may stand alone. The former approach is recommended because the comprehensive plan is the legal basis for zoning and subdivision ordinances and the CIP that govern land development and affect environmental quality.

Plan Implementation, Monitoring, and Evaluation

A plan is only meaningful if it is implemented. As the City of San Francisco said in its Sustainability Plan, "The only goal of producing this plan is to begin implementing it." The successful implementation of an Environmental Action Plan requires the use of effective spending programs, incentives, and environmental and land use regulations. Above all, it requires cooperation among government, businesses, citizens' groups, and private individuals.

Monitoring of the implementation efforts not only points out successes and shortcomings, but can be the basis for recommending changes to existing programs as well as the use of new techniques. To monitor the progress of the Action Plan and to keep the local government accountable, it is a good idea to use benchmarking. Benchmarks are measurable targets, such as acquisition of a certain number of acres of parkland, improvements in water quality from Class C to Class B, and slowing the annual loss of open space. Each year, the planning commission or elected officials could set targets tied to specific goals and objectives in the Environmental Action Plan. The planning commission can then assess the progress toward the benchmarks and publish an annual *Environmental Action Report*. The report can indicate which benchmarks were met and which were not, and suggest needed adjustments in policy priorities, regulations, and spending programs. Above all, benchmarking and the annual *Environmental Action Report* keep the Environmental Action Plan and implementation programs in front of the public, businesses, and elected officials. Finally, the Environmental Action Plan should be reviewed and updated by the planning commission every three to five years to reflect changes in community desires and priorities, to keep the plan responsive to changes in environmental quality, and to keep the community on course toward long-range goals of sustainability.

Innovative Techniques to Put the Environmental Action Plan into Practice

Several proven techniques go beyond the traditional zoning-subdivision-capital improvements method of implementing comprehensive plans (see Table 1-3). Traditional "Euclidean zoning" regulates the location of different uses and controls density and setback requirements. Zoning can be revised to include overlay zones that protect sensitive environmental areas. Overlay zones typically apply to one or more environmental features and their boundaries may not coincide with property lines. An overlay zone creates a double zone; any development proposal must comply with both the requirements of the "base" zone (such as single-family residential) and the overlay zone (such as a floodplain zone). If provisions of the two zones conflict, the overlay zone would take precedence.

Communities can use performance zoning to regulate the likely impacts of land uses rather than limiting land uses to those generally thought to be compatible with the area. If it can be demonstrated that a land use in a certain location will not adversely affect water quality or traffic or other environmental features, then the land use will be allowed. Performance zoning can be used in communities with adequate staff to implement and enforce it. We do not recommend performance zoning in rural areas with little planning staff or local planning expertise.

Subdivision and land development regulations can incorporate an environmental impact review of proposed development. An adequate public facilities ordinance can guide CIPs by requiring concurrency of infrastructure before new development is approved and thus avoid premature development and leapfrog development patterns.

Table 1-3
Innovative Techniques for Implementing an Environmental Action Plan

Zoning	
1.	Special overlay zones protect sensitive resources, such as wildlife areas, steep slopes, wellhead protection areas, floodplains, and wetlands.
2.	Performance zoning regulates impacts rather than uses.
3.	Historic districts can be designated by a community and the federal government to help protect historic areas and make property owners eligible for federal investment tax credits (see Chapter 18).
Subdivision	
1.	To evaluate the potential impacts of development, especially for a large development, a local environmental impact statement can be required of the developer.
2.	Vegetation requirements can include buffers between properties and the replacement of trees and vegetation removed in the development process.
Capital Improvements Programs	
1.	Urban or village growth boundaries link capital improvements with zoning. They also provide a way to resolve annexation disputes, identify urban service areas for public sewer and water service, and separate developed areas from rural areas (see Chapters 13 and 19).
2.	A policy of concurrency can be linked to an adequate public facilities ordinance in order to encourage phased growth.
3.	Impact fees and exactions require developers to pay for the cost of the development of public services, including parkland and traffic improvements (see Chapter 19).
4.	Property tax incentives in the form of reductions in property tax assessments for farm and forestlands or historic properties can provide an incentive not to convert property from these uses (see Chapters 13, 14, and 18).
5.	Fee simple land acquisition, purchase of development rights (PDR), and transfer of development rights (TDR) are techniques to keep land undeveloped. The public purchase of land in fee simple gives the public ownership of the land, as in the case of purchasing land for a park. In a PDR program, a landowner voluntarily sells to the public the right to develop his or her land; the landowner still owns the land but can use it only for farming, forestry, or open space purposes. A TDR program to protect farmland and open space areas or historic structures allows landowners to sell transferable development rights to developers who transfer the development rights to properties they are then allowed to develop more intensively (see Chapters 8, 13, and 14).
Other Regulations	
1.	Building codes are standards for the construction of new buildings and renovations, and can address energy conservation as well as safety (see Chapter 17).
2.	Nuisance ordinances can regulate light and noise pollution (see Chapter 18).

Innovative techniques for CIPs include urban and village growth boundaries (see Chapters 13 and 19), public acquisition of land and development rights (Chapters 8, 13 and 14), TDR (Chapter 13), impact fees, exactions, and property tax incentives (Chapter 18).

Communities should not be afraid to try out new tools and techniques to implement the goals and objectives of the Environmental Action Plan. This book presents a variety of tax incentives, spending programs, regulations, and public-private cooperative efforts that can help maintain and improve environmental quality. Planners may want to seek legal advice about how to implement these tools and techniques and if they are legal in their particular state or community.

DAY-TO-DAY PLANNING DECISIONS: REVIEW OF DEVELOPMENT PROPOSALS

The day-to-day implementation of the Environmental Action Plan and comprehensive plan occurs through the recommendations and decisions made by planning commissions, zoning boards, zoning officers, and elected officials as they review proposed development projects for consistency with the zoning ordinance, subdivision regulations, CIP, and other local standards.

When a development proposal is submitted to the planning commission, the commission should make an assessment of the potential environmental impacts. First, the commission should refer to any state or federal review requirements. If federal funds are involved in a proposed project, the developer must follow the federal environmental impact statement procedures according to the National Environmental Policy Act (see Chapter 2). If there is a State Environmental Policy Act, its rules may affect the proposed development project. Air and water quality, wetlands, and rare and endangered species are examples of environmental issues that might require federal or state review.

The planning commission should next refer to the local zoning and subdivision regulations in reviewing a development proposal. If the Natural Resources Inventory has been properly used in drafting the future land use map, zoning map, and ordinance language, development will tend to be guided toward the most appropriate locations, and inappropriate development proposals will be rare. The subdivision and land development regulations should require developers to provide information about on-site environmental conditions in greater detail than the Natural Resources Inventory. The environmental impact review should evaluate both site-specific impacts and the contribution of the proposed development to the cumulative environmental impact of development in the community or region. The purpose of the environmental impact review is not to delay development needlessly, but to ensure good design and that the development will not have significant negative impacts. This is not to say that all developments should be approved. Development review is very much a case-by-case process, depending on size, location, design, and current environmental conditions. Small developments, often referred to as minor subdivisions of three or fewer lots, should have a more streamlined review than major subdivisions. Though some flexibility in development projects can be allowed, planners and elected officials should not rely on voluntary negotiations to obtain environmentally acceptable developments.

The checklist in Table 1-4 can be used as a guide in reviewing the impacts of proposed developments on the natural environment at a specific location. The answers to the questions in the checklist will help the planning commission in making findings of fact to support its recommendations about a proposed development.

CASE STUDIES

The following three case studies illustrate innovative efforts in conducting inventories of environmental conditions and drafting Environmental

Table 1-4
Environmental Impact Checklist for Reviewing Proposed Development Projects

1.	Is the proposed development consistent with the goals and objectives of the comprehensive plan and the future land use map?
2.	Is the proposed development consistent with the zoning ordinance or is a rezoning requested?
3.	Is the proposed development consistent with the subdivision and land development regulations?
4.	Is the proposed development consistent with a capital improvements program?
5.	What use or uses are proposed in the development?
6.	What is the size of the proposed development, including buildings, acreage, and lot coverage (impervious surface) by buildings, roads, driveways, and sidewalks?
7.	Can the development be considered a "development of regional impact"?
8.	Could the development have an impact on groundwater supplies or quality?
9.	Could the development affect the quality or supply of water to a lake, pond, stream, or wetland?
10.	What will be the source of water? If on-site water is proposed, is there sufficient water to accommodate the development? Could the proposed water source be contaminated from nearby landfills or commercial or industrial uses? Could the on-site use of water reduce water availability to adjoining properties?
11.	Could the development change stormwater drainage patterns or increase runoff off site?
12.	Could the development produce significant soil erosion and sedimentation?
13.	How will sewage be disposed of? If on-site sewage disposal is proposed, are soils appropriate and the lot large enough to provide an adequate absorption field?
14.	How will the development affect air quality?
15.	How will the development affect transportation use and patterns?
16.	How will solid waste, including any toxic substances, from the development be disposed of?
17.	What kind of energy will the development use and where will it come from?
18.	Could the development affect any rare or endangered plant or animal species, sensitive wildlife habitat, or hunting and fishing areas?
19.	Is the development proposed for an area with known natural hazards, especially floodplains and steep slopes?
20.	Would the development affect any scenic views or unique land forms?
21.	Could the development adversely affect nearby agricultural or forestry operations?
22.	How will the development fit in with the existing built environment in terms of scale, use, and aesthetics?
23.	Will the development spur additional development in the vicinity?
24.	Will the development affect any known archaeological or historic sites or historic buildings?
25.	Will the development generate unreasonable noise, odor, glare, or other off-site impacts?
26.	What state and federal reviews and permits are needed for approval of the proposed development and have they been obtained?

Action Plans. In Columbus, Ohio, volunteers worked with the local health department and the city government to forge environmental quality indicators or benchmarks and a list of proposed actions and projects, and to monitor progress toward environmental goals. A citizens' group in Alabama drafted regional environmental goals for a 12-county area. The Metropolitan Council of the Greater Twin Cities in Minnesota has described recent environmental trends and developed alternative growth scenarios to show how much land a sprawled development would consume compared to compact development.

CASE STUDY 1-1
Columbus, Ohio: The City's Environmental Snapshot

Columbus is the capital of Ohio and the state's largest city. Located in the south central part of the state, Columbus had an estimated population of 657,000 in 1996, ranking it 16th in size among American cities. That year, the Columbus Department of Health published its first *Environmental Snapshot* of the city and adjoining Franklin County. The *Snapshot*, which the Department of Health has been updating each year, grew out of *Priorities '95*, a two-year project that brought hundreds of volunteers together to identify, analyze, and rank the city's environmental threats. The volunteers then wove dozens of recommendations into a comprehensive environmental blueprint (see Table 1-5). Columbus City officials reviewed the recommendations and responded that of the 103 suggested actions, 54 could and would be implemented, and 49 were not immediately possible to implement. Each year since 1996, city department heads have been asked to review the actions of their departments in addressing the project recommendations. This process has given a clearer picture of progress, or sometimes lack of progress, in meeting the city's environmental goals (see Table 1-6).

Table 1-5
Examples of Columbus, Ohio, *Priorities '95* Project Issues

Category	Project Issue	Number of Recommendations
Greenspace	Lack of Greenspace/Habitat Destruction	63
	Urban Sprawl/Blight	17
Consumer Issues	Indoor Air Contaminants	12
	Lead Exposure	5
Industrial Issues	Storage Tank Leakage	2
	Hazardous Materials	2
Solid Waste	Industrial Solid Waste Disposal	8
	Municipal Solid Waste Disposal	6
Urban Issues	Noise Pollution	3
	Road Salt	3
Water Issues	Surface Water–Nonpoint Source Pollution	8
	Drinking Water Safety	5

Source: Columbus Health Department, *Environmental Snapshot* (1998)

Table 1-6
Implementation Progress, Columbus, Ohio and Franklin County, Ohio (1996–2000)

Issue	1996	2000
Solid Waste (Columbus) Tonnage Collected	336,000	380,000
Tonnage Recycled	7,900	15,000
Greenspace (Columbus) Trees Planted	2,000	4,798
Greenspace (Franklin County) Farmland Acres	103,000	102,000
Air Pollution (Franklin County) Toxic Releases (millions of pounds per year)	1.6	1.3
Ozone (parts per billion)	114	117
Particulates (PM-10) (in micrograms per cubic meter)	55	67
Vehicle Miles Traveled Each Day (in millions of miles)	25.5	26

Source: Columbus Health Department, *Environmental Snapshot* (2001)

The *Snapshot* measured the progress of the city and county according to several environmental benchmarks and goals. These measurements applied to population, construction permits, farmland loss, air and water quality, and solid waste. This benchmarking process is known as "green accounting," and documents changes in environmental quality and overall quality of life in a community or region.

The *Snapshot* helps to educate the public about the health of their environment and gives elected officials information on the success of their past efforts and continuing problems in need of attention. Positive achievements from 1996 to 2000 included an increase in tree plantings and tons of solid waste recycled, and a decrease in the release of toxic chemicals. Farmland loss was only 1,000 acres from 1996 to 2000. On the negative side, Columbus generated more solid waste and more particulates were detected in the air in Franklin County. One of the reasons for the decline in air quality can be traced to an increase in VMT each day.

Columbus and Franklin County can already point to a number of achievements in redeveloping vacant lots, such as dedication of greenspace, tree planting, and pollution reduction. However, challenges remain, particularly for industrial waste disposal, transportation-related pollution, and the persistent presence of pesticides, herbicides, and fertilizers in water supplies. Still, the *Priorities '95* and *Snapshot* projects have raised community awareness and spurred public action to improve the quality of the environment in greater Columbus. The effort underscores the fact that planning to protect the environment requires broad community participation, annual monitoring of environmental quality, and a long-term commitment from the public and elected officials to make the changes called for in the *Snapshot*.

The Columbus experience demonstrates that public action can fairly quickly result in beneficial changes to the environment, but such progress requires good information, cooperation between the private and public sectors, and political will and action. Without these ingredients, the Columbus environmental planning and implementation process would not have gained measurable results and a self-sustaining momentum. The visibility and success of the planning process have made it politically difficult for city officials to abandon the *Snapshot* and the efforts underway to improve and protect environmental quality.

Columbus is not the only city that is taking stock of its environment. In the 1990s, nearly 150 cities were

Table 1-7
Natural Environment Trends in the Metropolitan Twin Cities (1999)

1.	*Air Quality:* Air quality in the Twin Cities area is basically good and seems to be improving.
2.	*River Water Quality:* The water quality of the region's rivers has been maintained or improved in the last decade, despite increased environmental stress caused by regional growth, including a growing population and economy. The separation of sanitary and storm sewers, a 10-year project carried out in Minneapolis, St. Paul, and South St. Paul, has produced dramatic improvements in fecal coliform levels in the Mississippi River.
3.	*Lake Water Quality:* Most "priority lakes" in the region are suitable for swimming based on algae blooms and water clarity. Fish consumption advisories on tested Twin Cities lakes recommend only minor reductions in consumption. The number of lakes infested with Eurasian milfoil is increasing but at a slower rate.
4.	*Water Supply:* The region is increasing its reliance on groundwater sources. Much of the region's future development, especially in the north and west, will be served by less productive and potentially more contaminated aquifers. Metropolitan area water utilities are becoming more interconnected to provide water to the communities they serve, especially during water system emergencies.
5.	*Municipal Solid Waste Management:* The rate at which municipal solid waste was landfilled steadily increased between 1995 and 1997. Despite a steady increase in the amount of mixed municipal solid waste recycled between 1993 and 1997, the percentage of garbage recycled has stayed relatively flat since then.
6.	*Hazardous Waste Management:* The amount of household hazardous waste collected by the seven counties in the region grew by 15%, from 5.6 million pounds in 1996 to 6.4 million pounds in 1997. The amount of toxic substances released into the air, land, and water was reduced by 51% between 1991 and 1997.

Source: Adapted from the Minneapolis-St. Paul Metropolitan Council, State of the Region (1999)

developing sustainability indicators of environmental, social, and economic well-being (www.cabq.gov/profress/sir/summsry.html). For instance, in 1995, Albuquerque, New Mexico, appointed a Sustainable Community Committee. The following year, the city adopted a set of indicators for energy and environment; land use and transportation; and education, employment, and social services (www.cabq.gov/profress/sir/summsry.htm).

Sustainable Seattle, a nonprofit organization founded in 1991, developed a set of environmental indicators for green accounting in 1993. The watchdog group has published three reports on environmental quality in Seattle and King County, with an emphasis on gauging progress toward goals of sustainable living and development. For example, the group found that between 1994 and 1998, both fuel consumption per capita and VMT per capita increased by 7% in King County. On the other hand, water consumption in King County declined by 12% from 1993 to 1998, thanks to con-

servation programs, higher water prices during peak summer months, and a new state plumbing code (Sustainable Seattle 1998).

CASE STUDY 1-2
The Twin Cities: A State of the Region Report and Growth Scenarios

Entire regions are also starting to plan for a sustainable future. The Metropolitan Council of the seven-county Twin Cities region of Minnesota has produced a *State of the Region* report that tracks trends in the economy and public services as well as the environment. A summary of trends in environmental quality noted in the 1999 report follows (see Table 1-7).

A separate study for the Minnesota legislature projected land use and development trends from 1995 to 2020 for the seven-county Twin Cities region based on trent scenarios: sprawl and "smart growth" with compact development (Center for Energy and Environment 1999). The sprawl scenario would accommodate 330,000 new households at a density of only 2.1 dwelling units per acre and use up 135,500 acres. The compact alternative features a density of 5.5 dwellings per acre and would consume 47,900 acres (see Figure 1-5). The compact scenario would have a mix of 50% single-family detached dwellings, 25% single-family attached dwelling units, and 25% multifamily units. The sprawl scenario would have 70% single-family detached housing units, 16% single-family attached units, and 14% multifamily units. The compact development option would place 34% of the new households in core cities and established suburbs, 55% in developing suburbs, and 11% in unsewered areas. The sprawl scenario would have only 18% of the new households locating in the core cities and established suburbs, 70% in developing suburbs, and 12% in unsewered areas. The sprawl scenario would result in a greater loss of open space and farmland as well as involve greater dependence on the automobile for transportation.

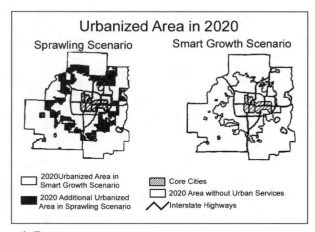

1-5   Land use trends in the greater Twin Cities, 2000–2020, based on a sprawling scenario and a smart growth compact.

Source: Metropolitan Council of the Twin Cities, Minnesota

2

The Legal, Economic, Ethical, and Ecological Foundations of Environmental Planning

It is the continuing policy of the Federal Government, in cooperation with State and Local Governments, and other concerned public and private organizations, to use all practical means and measures . . . to create and maintain conditions under which man and nature can exist in productive harmony, and fulfill the social, economic, and other requirements of present and future generations of Americans.

NATIONAL ENVIRONMENTAL POLICY ACT
(NEPA) OF 1970 [NEPA, 4331, TITLE 1]

An ecosystem is greater than the sum of its parts.
EUGENE P. ODUM

Planning is a technical and political process, but it occurs within a framework of laws and regulations, economic and technical feasibility, personal values, and natural resource systems. This chapter explores each of these contexts as it relates to environmental planning.

LEGAL ISSUES IN ENVIRONMENTAL PLANNING

The law is a set of rules of behavior for individuals, companies, and governments. Environmental laws spell out the ground rules for protecting air and water quality, public health, wildlife, and sensitive lands. Environmental law is embodied among many laws, regulations, and a variety of legal rulings. Local officials, planning staffs, business operators, and interested citizens should understand how the many federal and state environmental laws and regulations influence local and regional environmental planning efforts. Environmental plans and planning decisions must be legally sound or they risk being overturned in the courts. We do not offer legal advice here. For legal opinions and advice, we recommend that you consult an attorney.

Constitutional Law

Constitutional law stems from interpretations of the United States Constitution by the nation's courts. The 5th, 10th, and 14th Amendments to the U.S. Constitution form the basic legal framework for environmental and land use laws. These three Amendments are especially important to consider when communities are setting up new land use and environmental management programs.

The 5th Amendment

The 5th Amendment states ". . . nor shall private property be taken for public use without just compensation." A government regulation goes too far and results in a "taking" of private property if it restricts the use of that property to the point that no reasonable economic use of the property remains. In such a case, the courts will find the regulation unconstitutional and strike it (*Pennsylvania Coal v. Mahon* 260, US 393 (1922)). For example, in *Lucas v. South Carolina Coastal Commission,* 112 S.Ct. 2886 (1992), the U.S. Supreme Court ruled that the commission went too far in restricting all of Lucas's rights to build on his beachfront property without paying him just compensation. The Supreme Court held that the government regulation violated Lucas's 5th Amendment rights and so was invalidated.

Government regulations may legally reduce private property values or dampen their potential increase if they further a public interest and protect the public health, safety, or welfare. For example, limitations on building on wetlands, floodplains, or steep slopes may be justified as protecting public health and safety (*Planning* 1999, 23). Regulations must have a "rational nexus" or connection to the protection goal, and any reduction in property value must be "proportional" to the potential impacts of proposed development.

Governments, however, must be careful in negotiating with developers over exactions of money for infrastructure and dedications of land in the subdivision review process. Exactions and dedications must reflect the impacts of that particular development. *Dolan v. City of Tigard,* 512 U.S. 374 (1994), arose over the city's requirement that the Dolans donate land for a bicycle path in return for permission to expand their hardware business. The Supreme Court ruled in favor of the Dolans, saying there was no link (rational nexus) between what the Dolans were proposing and what the city was asking. Also, the requirement of the bicycle path was not "proportional" to the size of the Dolans's land development proposal, and hence was unreasonable. In short, the donation of land for a bicycle path would have been a "taking" of private property. Nonetheless, the court did affirm the standards of rational nexus and proportionality. Developers may still be required to dedicate land for roads as part of the land development process, but local governments need to have clear standards and not ask for dedications that are unrelated to the development in question (Freilich 1999).

While a government cannot take private property without paying just compensation, a government is also under no obligation to guarantee a private landowner's return on a land investment. Holding property for investment, just like owning stocks and bonds, carries an element of risk. Government investments in infrastructure may increase the value of privately owned land, just as government land use regulations may reduce or limit private property value.

In the 1990s, 18 states passed laws requiring governments to compensate landowners for new regulations that reduce the value of a property by a certain percentage. Ironically, many of the complaints from landowners have come from federal government regulations on wetlands and endangered species, not local zoning regulations. Properties declared wetlands under the Clean Water Act and properties on which federally listed plant or animal species are found may be severely restricted as to their use. In response, since 1990, the federal government has offered compensation to farmers who voluntarily participate in the Wetlands Reserve Program and sell easements banning the development of wetlands over 30 years or in perpetuity. By 2001, the federal government had purchased easements on more than 1 million acres of privately owned wetlands (Natural Resources Conservation Service 2001). The federal government has not, however, offered compensation to owners of lands with endangered plant and animal species.

The 10th Amendment

The 10th Amendment allows state governments to use their "police power" to protect the public health, safety, welfare, and morals. Each state has in turn delegated this authority to local governments. State governments use the police power to impose safety standards, such as speed limits on roads. Local governments exercise police power when they adopt zoning and subdivision regulations over the use of privately held land.

The U.S. Supreme Court upheld the legality of zoning as a valid exercise of government police power under the 10th Amendment in the landmark case *Village of Euclid, Ohio v. Ambler Realty Co.,* 272 U.S. 365 (1926). Zoning separates potentially conflicting land uses, such as houses and factories, which could otherwise put people at risk of injury or ill health. Similarly, subdivision regulations require that new developments meet standards in design, safety, and services, such as water supply, stormwater management, and sewage disposal.

Tension between the 5th and 10th Amendments persists in environmental and land use law, and will continue to be at the center of legal battles involving property owners, governments, and citizens' groups. Landowners typically view their property as a financial asset. The more development the property can support, the higher the value of the property. However, the development of property has implications for community public service costs, environmental quality, and overall quality of life. The government as regulator is placed in a middle position between the property owner and the rest of the community.

The 14th Amendment

The 14th Amendment proclaims that "No State shall . . . deprive any person of life, liberty, or property, without due process of law; nor deny to any person within its jurisdiction the equal protection of the laws." Due process means that a person has a right to a fair and speedy trial or government decision. Governments that seek to delay development by dragging out their deliberations not only cost developers and taxpayers money, they violate the developers' rights to a decision within a reasonable time frame. Governments must also follow correct procedures, including public notice of public hearings and meetings, or else risk legal challenge.

Equal protection means that governments cannot enact laws or regulations that discriminate against anyone, based on race, creed, color, or sex. An important issue that arises under the 14th Amendment is environmental justice. All Americans have the same right to a clean and healthy environment, but in practice this is not always the case. For instance, according to the American Planning Association (APA), ". . . in Los Angeles County, California, minorities are three times as likely as whites to live within one half mile of a large hazardous waste treatment, storage, or disposal facility" (APA 2000).

The equal protection clause seeks to ensure that governments treat all citizens and like-situated properties similarly. For example, the practice of "spot zoning"—such as allowing a large commercial use in the middle of a single-family residential zone—could be interpreted as an illegal act of favoritism toward one property owner. Government officials may not make "arbitrary and capricious" decisions, and must support their decisions with written findings of facts that are available to the public.

The 14th Amendment also guarantees an individual's right to free travel under the equal protection clause. The right of free travel means that an American citizen may live anywhere in the United States. A state, county, town, or township cannot prevent a person from moving into that jurisdiction by banning new residential construction. The exception to this is a temporary moratorium on new construction, usually for no more than one year in order to upgrade sewer or water facilities or to draft a new comprehensive plan or zoning ordinance. The right of free travel is one of the fundamental liberties that Americans enjoy, especially in a society where many people move several times during their lives. But the right of free travel can pose challenges to communities as they seek to provide a sustainable quality environment in the face of increasing populations.

In 1972, voters in rapidly growing Boca Raton, Florida, approved an eventual limit of 40,000 dwelling units and a cap on population of 100,000 (up from 32,000 in 1972). This was the first attempt by a city to impose an ultimate population cap. A local builder filed suit (*Boca Villas Corporation v. City of Boca Raton*, 45 Fla. Supp. 65 (15th Cir., 1976)), and the limit on the number of dwelling units was overturned in court. The judge did not rule the population cap unconstitutional, but rather found that Boca Raton had set an arbitrary cap that was not based on an objective study. The case was settled out of court in the midst of an appeal.

The courts have supported attempts to limit building permits and the extension of sewer and water lines that would induce premature growth and adversely impact the environment. In Petaluma, California, 40 miles north of San Francisco, the city enacted a growth control ordinance in the early 1970s to limit the number of building permits involving projects with five or more units to no more than 500 dwelling units a year, based on sewer and water capacity. Petaluma also established a city growth boundary for at least five years, with a goal of limiting the population to 55,000. Although a federal district court found the Petaluma ordinance a violation of the right of free travel under the 14th Amendment, the U.S. Court of Appeals for the Ninth Circuit overturned the decision. The Court of Appeals ruled that Petaluma had not been unreasonable or arbitrary in setting the cap on building permits and supported the city's ordinance as a valid use of the 10th Amendment police power to promote the public welfare:

> We conclude therefore that under *Belle Terre* and *Los Altos Hills* the concept of the public welfare is sufficiently broad to uphold Petaluma's desire to preserve its small town character, its open spaces and low density of population, and to grow at an orderly and deliberate pace (*Construction Industry Association of Sonoma County v. City of Petaluma*, 375 F. Supp. 574, 6ERC 1453 (N.D. Cal. 1974)).

The goal of orderly and deliberate growth was also at the heart of the *Golden v. Planning Board of the Town of Ramapo*, 30 N.Y.2d 359, 334 N.Y.S.2d 138, 285 N.E.2d 291 (1972), appeal dismissed, 409 U.S. 1003 (1972). In the late 1960s, Ramapo, New York, located about 40 miles northwest of New York City, set up a permit development system that required what is now known as concurrency; that is, a developer had to show that adequate infrastructure to service a proposed development was in place or would be put in place by the developer before development could occur. The town had drafted its capital improvements program for the next 18 years and would allow "phased growth" in "tiers" of land over time. The tier closest to the town center would have infrastructure for development in years one to six, the next tier further out would receive public infrastructure in years seven to 13, and the outermost tier would have infrastructure in years 14 to 18. The premature expansion of sewer, water, police, fire, and schools to the outer tiers would not be allowed, unless private developers were willing to pay for it.

The *Ramapo* case is significant because the courts upheld as legitimate the public goals of concurrency and phased growth, and rejected arguments of takings and restriction of free travel. *Ramapo* did not place a cap or moratorium on growth, nor did it try to be exclusionary. The New York Supreme Court determined that the Town of Ramapo's permit system and capital improvements plan would "provide a balanced cohesive community dedicated to the efficient utilization of land" (*ibid.* at 302). Ironically, the Town of Ramapo scrapped its growth management system in the early 1980s, but the concepts of phased growth, adequate public facilities, and concurrency soon became standard practices in other communities in the battle against sprawl and environmental degradation.

Legislative and Statutory Law

Both Congress and state legislatures may enact legislation that becomes legislative law. Legislative law changes the law, unlike judicial law, which interprets the law. New legislative laws become statutory laws and are compiled in federal and state law books. Legislative law also refers to actions by county legislatures and commissioners, and local councils that create new laws and ordinances. For instance, a city council could pass a local nuisance ordinance banning noise above 80 decibels.

Federal environmental legislative law emerged from a broad public concern about threats to public health and the loss of wilderness areas and wildlife habitat. The Clean Air Act of 1970, the Clean Water Act of 1972, and the Safe Drinking Water Act (SDWA) of 1974 have led to improve-

ments in the nation's air and water quality. The Resources Conservation and Recovery Act of 1976 and the Superfund Law of 1980 have established rules for the manufacture, handling, disposal, and clean-up of toxic substances. The Wilderness Act of 1964 created the nation's wilderness system, currently at 103 million acres, and the Endangered Species Act (ESA) of 1973 was passed to avert the extinction of plant and animal species on public and private land. Except for the Wilderness Act, which covers federal land, the above laws apply to all governments, businesses, and individuals. Some of the laws are reactive in responding to pollution damage, and some are proactive in preventing pollution or degradation (see Table 2-1).

Table 2-1
Major Federal Environmental Laws (1970–1999)

1970	National Environmental Policy Act (Public Law 90-190); Clean Air Act Amendments (PL 91-224) Resources Recovery Act (PL 91-512); Occupational Safety and Health Act (PL 91-596)
1972	Federal Environmental Pesticide Control Act (PL 91-224) Federal Water Pollution Control Act Amendments (Clean Water Act) (PL 92-500) Marine Protection, Research and Sanctuaries Act (PL 92-532) Ocean Dumping Act (PL 92-532); Noise Control Act (PL 92-574) Coastal Zone Management Act (PL 92-583)
1973	Endangered Species Act (PL 93-205); Flood Disaster Protection Act (PL 93-234) Safe Drinking Water Act (SDWA) (PL 93-523)
1976	Toxic Substances Control Act (PL 94-469); Resource Conservation and Recovery Act (PL 94-580)
1977	Surface Mining Control and Reclamation Act (PL 95-87)
1980	Comprehensive Environmental Response Compensation and Liability Act ("The Superfund Law") (PL 96-510)
1984	Hazardous and Solid Waste Amendments (PL 98-616)
1985	Food Security Act (PL 99-198)
1986	Superfund Amendments and Reauthorization Act (PL 99-499)
1990	Oil Pollution Act (PL 101-380; Pollution Prevention Act (PL 101-508); Clean Air Act Amendments (PL 101-549)
1994	National Flood Insurance Reform Act (PL 103-325)
1996	Food Quality Protection Act (PL 104-170); SDWA Amendments (PL 104-182)
1999	Chemical Safety, Site Security and Fuels Regulatory Relief Act (PL 106-40)

National Environmental Policy Act

NEPA, Public Law 91-190 (1969), 42 U.S.C., Section 4331 *et seq.*, established a process to review federal projects and policies that could affect environmental quality and result in the irreversible use of natural resources. NEPA created the Council on Environmental Quality to draft regulations for NEPA, oversee the NEPA process, and publish an annual report on the nation's environmental conditions and progress.

The expressed purposes of NEPA are to:

- fulfill the responsibilities of each generation as trustee of the environment for succeeding generations;
- ensure for all Americans safe, healthful, productive, and aesthetically and culturally pleasing surroundings;
- attain the widest range of beneficial use of the environment without degradation, risk to health or safety, or other undesirable or unintended consequences;
- preserve important historic, cultural, and natural aspects of our national heritage, and maintain, wherever possible, an environment that supports diversity and a variety of individual choice;
- achieve a balance between population and resource use that will permit high standards of living and a wide sharing of life's amenities; and
- enhance the quality of renewable resources and approach maximum attainable recycling of depletable resources.

The heart of NEPA is the environmental impact statement (EIS) process, which screens all proposed federal projects, funding, permits, policies, and actions for potential environmental effects. NEPA also applies to federal agency decisions to approve, fund, or license actions by state and local governments or the private sector.

The EIS must describe and evaluate:

- the current conditions and the environmental impact of the proposed action;

- any adverse environmental effects which cannot be avoided should the proposal be implemented;
- alternatives to the proposed action and the likely impacts of those alternatives;
- the relationship between local, short-term uses of man's environment, and the maintenance and enhancement of long-term productivity;
- any irreversible and irretrievable commitments of resources that would be involved in the proposed action, should it be implemented; and
- ways to minimize the negative impacts of the proposed action (42 U.S.C., Section 4332(2)(c)).

A federal agency must first decide whether NEPA applies. A federal agency decision that NEPA does not apply to a proposed action can be challenged in court. Several court cases have involved the question of whether NEPA applies to a specific action. In *Hanly v. Kleindienst*, F.2d, 2 ELR 20720 (2nd. Cir. 1972), for example, the Second Circuit Court of Appeals defined NEPA qualifying actions by:

1) the extent to which the action will cause adverse environmental effects in excess of those created by existing uses in the area affected by it, and 2) the absolute quantitative adverse environmental effects of the action itself, including the cumulative harm that results from its contribution to existing adverse conditions or uses in the affected area.

If the agency decides that NEPA does apply, the agency must then determine whether an EIS is required before it can implement its project or action. If a proposed project involves more than one federal agency, a lead agency may be named to conduct the NEPA review. The federal agency has two options: it may make a Finding of No Significant Impact or it may decide that an EIS is necessary. If the agency rules that an EIS is necessary, it must publish a notice in the *Federal Register*. The agency then must draft an EIS and circulate it for

---

---

comments to federal, state, and local government agencies with expertise and jurisdiction as well as to the public. The comment period typically lasts 90 days.

Following the comment period, the agency drafts a final version of the EIS, spelling out environmental protection measures that must accompany the proposed agency action. As an alternative to project-by-project review under NEPA, a federal agency may also prepare a "program impact statement" to allow for a single review of several related projects, such as logging in a national forest (Mandelker 1997).

The U.S. Department of Transportation writes the most EIS reports among federal agencies, mainly for road construction projects. The Army Corps of Engineers is another leading agency in preparing EIS reviews, usually for water-related projects. NEPA also requires all federal agencies to review their statutory authority, administrative regulations, and current policies to determine necessary measures to comply with the act. However, the U.S. Environmental Protection Agency (EPA) is exempt from NEPA when taking actions under the Clean Air Act and in issuing pollution discharge permits under the Clean Water Act Amendments of 1972. The Clean Water Act exemption does not apply to new point sources of water pollution.

The EIS process is designed to provide full disclosure of the impacts of federal actions that may affect the environment. State and local governments and the public have the opportunity to participate in the review of proposed federal actions. Public scrutiny is necessary because the quality of EIS reviews can vary from federal agency to agency and because federal actions under NEPA may involve major projects that affect important natural resources and large geographic areas. Consider the following major NEPA cases:

- *Calvert Cliffs' Coordinating Committee v. Atomic Energy Commission*, 449 F.2d 1109, 2ERC 1779 (D.C. Cir. 1971), mandated an EIS for the licensing of a private utility to construct a nuclear power plant.

- *Named Individual Members of the San Antonio Conservation Society v. Texas Highway Department*, 446 F.2d 1013, 2 ERC 1871 (5th Cir. 1971), resulted in a ruling that a major road project could not be reviewed as small, individual segments as a way to try to avoid NEPA review. This ruling has important implications for developing master plans that propose construction over several years.

- *United States v. 247.37 Acres of Land*, F. Supp, 12 ELR 20513 (S.D. Ohio 1971) ruled that an EIS was required for the condemnation of 247 acres of land for a flood-control project.

Environmental groups have filed numerous legal challenges under NEPA in order to delay or thwart proposed development projects. For instance, completion of the Tellico Dam was halted by *Tennessee Valley Authority v. Hill,* 437 U.S. 153 (1978), in which the court ruled that building the dam would endanger the survival of a small fish, the snail darter, under the ESA of 1973.

When local and regional planners review development proposals, the first question they might ask is: Is any federal money or permitting involved? If the answer is yes, the next question should be: Has a federal agency made a determination whether NEPA applies? If no determination has been made, the project should be tabled until the federal agency has rendered a decision. If a Finding of No Significant Impact is made, the local review can continue. If an EIS is required, it should be thoroughly reviewed by local planners and officials, and they should decide whether to submit comments in writing within the allowed comment period.

State Planning and Zoning Enabling Legislation

In the 1920s, the federal government drafted the model Zoning Enabling Act and the model Planning Enabling Act. All states borrowed from these acts in drafting their own planning and zoning enabling legislation that allows local governments to undertake planning and zoning. The planning and zoning enabling legislation varies from state to state. In some states, the legislation has not been updated for decades. Also, the specific land use controls that are allowed may differ from state to state (e.g., Connecticut does not allow local governments to zone land for agriculture while California does).

State constitutions describe the powers of state governments and the authority that the states delegate to cities, counties, villages, and townships. State legislatures may enact specific enabling legislation to grant additional powers to local governments. Some states are known as "home rule" states because they have granted their local governments the authority to adopt comprehensive plans and land use and environmental regulations. In states without home rule, the state legislature must pass enabling legislation for local governments to use certain practices, such as purchasing development rights to protect farmland and open space (see Chapter 13). Most states, however, permit a wide variety of planning and zoning techniques. Some states—notably Oregon, Florida, and Washington—require local governments to adopt comprehensive plans that then must be reviewed and approved by the state according to statewide planning goals.

State Environmental Policy Acts

Twenty-two states have adopted State Environmental Policy Acts (SEPAs), which are similar to NEPA in allowing a review of state projects and actions, and sometimes local government and private projects and actions, that could adversely impact the environment. Fifteen states require state agencies to follow the EIS, and six states extend this requirement to local government actions. Some states (specifically Hawaii, Massachusetts, Minnesota, New York, and Washington) have extended the environmental review process to cover private developments that are subject to land use regulations. Four states apply the EIS only to certain public projects. Three states adopted the EIS approach administratively rather than through legislation. Planners should check whether their state has a SEPA and what it requires in the review of development proposals. (For a list of states requiring review, see Mandelker 1997, 10-11.) As under NEPA, these states, localities, and private parties must either obtain a "negative declaration" (known in shorthand as a "neg dec") of no significant impact or draft an acceptable EIS.

NEPA and SEPA cannot take the place of the community or regional comprehensive planning process involved in developing and implementing

---

SIDEBAR 2-2

The U.S. Environmental Protection Agency

The Environmental Protection Agency (EPA) was created through an Executive Order by President Nixon in December of 1970, partly in response to the first Earth Day on April 22, 1970. The agency has broad regulatory powers that affect nearly every industry and local government in the nation. The EPA has the authority to implement and enforce a wide variety of environmental laws, such as the Clean Water Act; the Safe Drinking Water Act; the Clean Air Act; the Toxic Substances Control Act; the Federal Insecticide, Fungicide and Rodenticide Act; the Resource Conservation and Recovery Act; the Comprehensive Environmental Response, Compensation and Liability Act (the Superfund for toxic waste clean-up); and others. The regulations that the EPA administers to implement these laws are found in Chapter 40 of the Code of Federal Regulations (40 CFR).

As of 2002, the EPA had 18,000 employees (including nearly 2,000 scientific researchers); 10 regional offices in addition to its Washington, D.C., headquarters; 18 research laboratories; and an annual budget of slightly more than $7 billion.

The EPA has the authority to:

- present testimony on Environmental Impact Statements through the National Environmental Policy Act;
- block large development projects that the EPA feels would do irreversible environmental damage or violate federal environmental laws;
- bring enforcement actions against state and local government agencies that are not carrying out environmental laws and regulations;
- levy fines on violators of environmental laws and standards;
- undertake legal actions against polluters;
- initiate the clean-up of hazardous waste sites;
- ban the production of hazardous substances, such as dichlorodiphenyltrichloroethane (DDT) and polychlorinated biphenyls (PCBs);
- require states to link land use planning and the management of air quality;
- withhold federal highway funds from states and metropolitan regions that do not meet National Ambient Air Quality standards; and
- conduct research on toxic substances and set safety standards for air and water quality based on "good science."

The EPA has a difficult job. On the one hand, the agency serves as the primary guardian of America's public health and environment. On the other, it is subject to the whims of whichever political party is in the White House. Finally, the extent of the EPA's administrative authority is often challenged in long and expensive legal battles.

---

a comprehensive plan with an Environmental Action Plan component. The Environmental Action Plan (described in Chapter 1) can help to estimate environmental carrying capacity and help identify the best location for different types of development.

Both NEPA and SEPA processes react to development proposals rather than create proactive planning. They allow for the review of projects at locations that may not be appropriate for the type of development proposed. For instance, the proposed site may not be planned or zoned, or the planning or zoning may be out of date. The site may have severe development constraints, inadequate infrastructure, or important on-site or nearby environmental resources. Yet, the typical NEPA or SEPA applicant has already invested heavily in one particular site. The applicant has often acquired the site and has spent a large amount of money on engineering and other costs in planning the development of the site. Applicants and reviewing bodies may be reluctant to seriously consider alternative locations. Moreover, NEPA and SEPA reviews only occasionally result in the outright denial of a project.

The quality of EIS reviews can vary significantly, especially given the option of government agencies simply to make a "negative declaration" and let development proceed. Another shortcoming is that NEPA and SEPAs involve only a case-by-case review of projects, not a cumulative assessment of the impact of development projects over time on the environment. In implementing NEPA and SEPAs, government administrators and the courts have often emphasized procedural aspects rather than "good science" or comprehensive ecosystem management. Finally, NEPA and SEPAs can result in considerable delay for government agencies and private developers, adding to project costs, frustration, and uncertainty about the environmental review process.

While NEPA and SEPAs can enhance local environmental planning, they should not be relied upon as a substitute for it. Proactive local and regional planning can balance growth with environmental protection while saving developers, governments, and concerned citizens a lot of time and money. The State of Washington has recognized this, and has combined local reviews of development under its 1990 Growth Management Act with its SEPA. The combined review is more thorough, coordinated, and quicker than separate state and local development reviews.

Administrative Law

Whenever statutory law sets up a government program, government agencies need to adopt rules and regulations to implement the statute. These rules and regulations are known as administrative law. When government agencies make decisions based on the rules and regulations, those decisions have the force of law. For example, Chapter 40 of the Code of Federal Regulations describes the regulations that the EPA follows and enforces to implement a host of environmental statutes. When a state air pollution control agency grants an Indirect Air Pollution Control Permit so a regional mall can expand the amount of parking by 2,000 spaces,

that is administrative law in action. Similarly, a state agency's reclassification of a body of water from Class A (drinkable) to Class B (swimmable, but not drinkable) would be an exercise of administrative law (Sargent *et al.* 1991, 215).

There are four federal agencies that set rules and regulations that directly affect the environment: the Department of the Interior, the Department of Agriculture, the Department of Energy, and the EPA. State environmental agencies go by several different names, such as the department of natural resources, the department of environmental conservation, and the department of environmental protection, among others. These state agencies are responsible for administering state environmental laws and regulations, and for coordinating state compliance with federal laws and regulations. Local government agencies that draft environmental regulations may include county planning departments, county health departments, a township planning department, a city planning department, and, in larger cities, a city department of environmental affairs.

Judicial Law (Case Law)

Judicial law (or case law) is created through legal rulings on cases brought before a court. A judge is asked to interpret how the constitution and existing laws and regulations apply to a particular situation. In rendering a decision, the judge in effect "makes law." For example, in *Just v. Marinette County*, 210 N.W.2d 761 (1972), a Wisconsin court upheld a county shoreline zoning ordinance that restricted resource lands (in this case, a wetlands) to natural uses, as a reasonable exercise of the police power.

Judicial law has been important in interpreting the 5th, 10th, and 14th Amendments and in understanding, upholding, and enforcing laws. Nonprofit environmental organizations have been especially active in filing suits against the federal government to compel the government to enforce its own environmental laws. Environmental organizations also have sued corporations to force them to comply with federal statutes. Both the Clean Air Act and Clean Water Act allow private citizens to sue violators, even though private citizens cannot collect damages in those cases; instead, if fines are levied by a court, they go to the federal treasury. Also, a polluter cannot avoid a fine by agreeing to abide by the pollution laws after a suit has been initiated.

State courts have jurisdiction over state and local land use and environmental laws. State courts often differ about how far environmental management techniques may go in restricting land use. For instance, Pennsylvania courts have upheld conservation zoning of one dwelling per 10 acres, and agricultural zoning of one dwelling per 50 acres.

Quasi-judicial Rulings

Judicial actions interpret the law. Quasi-judicial rulings (quasi, meaning "as if") also interpret the law based on facts, but the ruling is made by a publicly appointed board or elected officials, not by a judge. Government boards and elected officials make quasi-judicial rulings on the basis of a record of facts following a hearing. A quasi-judicial ruling usually applies to a single landowner or a single property where the applicant has requested an exemption from or a change to a local land use ordinance, such as a waiver, variance, or rezoning. In these cases, elected officials or appointed boards are called on to render a judgment on an issue that benefits one individual rather than the general public. Therefore, the officials or boards must observe due process by giving proper notice of a public hearing and make written findings of fact to support their decision. For instance, planning commissions often make quasi-judicial rulings when deciding whether to allow the rezoning of a property. The Zoning Board of Adjustment commonly makes quasi-judicial rulings on zoning variances for setback requirements for additions to buildings. A quasi-judicial ruling may be appealed to a court of law.

Common Law and Property Rights

Some judicial decisions are based on common law. Common law comes from the traditions of English law that are hundreds of years old. For example, there are landowners who believe that they should be able to do whatever they want with their land. However, this sentiment runs counter to the common law tradition that a person cannot use land in ways that bring harm to neighbors. Another example of common law is the public trust doctrine, which dates back to Roman law. The public trust doctrine holds that government has an obligation to make certain resources available for the enjoyment of all citizens. Today, the public trust doctrine most often applies to providing public access to navigable waterways. On this basis, many states claim that all lands below the mean high water mark are state property and should be managed for the public benefit.

Common law contributed significantly to the origins of private property rights in America. In early colonial days, the creation of private property in land was not meant to give landowners total control. As William Cronon explains in *Changes in the Land,* "the passage of land from town commons to individual property was intended to create permanent property rights. These rights were never absolute since both town and colony retained sovereignty and could impose restrictions on how land might be used" (Cronon 1983, 73). The use of private property has been an important liberty and a major source of wealth creation in America. However, it is almost inevitable that as the number of Americans increases, the greater are the chances that the actions of one landowner may infringe on the welfare of neighbors or the community at large.

A private landowner owns a bundle of rights to a property. These rights include air rights, water rights, mineral rights, the right to sell all or part of the property or pass the property on to heirs, the right to lease the property, the right to use the property, and the right to develop the property.

Any single right may be separated from the bundle and sold or given away. For instance, it has long been a common practice for landowners to sell mineral rights to mining companies.

Responsibilities also come with rights. A landowner cannot use or develop the property in ways that would harm others. A landowner has the right to defend his or her property through legal means against trespass across the property and against nuisances occurring on neighboring properties. A property owner also has the right to challenge government land use regulations.

The Legal Pecking Order

Which type of environmental law takes precedence over another? Constitutional law cases, especially rulings by the U.S. Supreme Court, have the most clout. The Supreme Court, for instance, can rule that laws passed by Congress or a state legislature are unconstitutional.

Generally, legislative law supersedes administrative law. The issue here often is whether the administrative rules adopted by a government agency are consistent with the letter or intent of legislation passed by Congress or a state legislature that established the program for the agency to administer. That determination is usually made by a court judge.

Federal laws have greater authority than state or local laws. Federal laws can mandate that state and local governments take certain actions. Sometimes the federal government will make money available for state and local governments to carry out these mandates, such as federal funding for water treatment plants. In some instances, however, the federal government enacts "unfunded mandates" that require state and local governments to take certain actions without the help of federal funding.

State laws may be more protective of the environment than federal laws, and local laws more protective than state laws, provided that there is no violation of the constitution. In such cases, a law from a lower level of government may supersede that of a higher level.

Legal Aspects of the Comprehensive Plan and What to Look for in a Development Review

Planners and elected officials should work with an attorney who specializes in land use law to ensure that the management programs have a solid legal foundation and are operated fairly, openly, and with careful attention to proper procedure. The attorney should review the comprehensive plan and especially the purpose and goal statements in the plan that help resist legal challenge. The attorney should also review the zoning ordinance and subdivision regulations for legal correctness and consistency with the comprehensive plan. It is also a good idea to have a book on land use law available as a reference (Callies *et al.* 1999).

As local planners and elected officials review development proposals, they should be aware of the state and federal laws and regulations that may apply, in addition to local ordinances. In some cases, the development review approval process can go beyond the local jurisdiction to involve state environmental agencies and the EPA. The more levels of government review, the more costly and time-consuming the review process is likely to be. In Chapters 3 through 19, we discuss specific state and federal laws and programs that shape local government decisions about proposed developments.

ECONOMIC REASONS FOR ENVIRONMENTAL PLANNING

Economics is the study of how scarce resources of land, labor, and capital are allocated among competing uses. A central principle in economics is scarcity: there are not enough resources to satisfy everyone's needs and desires (Barnett and Morse 1963; Smith 1979). Therefore, individuals, businesses, and governments must make choices about the use of resources. Environmental economics is the study of how scarce natural resources are allocated among competing choices, and how human production and consumption choices affect environmental quality.

Economic Efficiency

An important concept in evaluating choices is efficiency. A choice is efficient if it gives a consumer the most satisfaction or a producer the most profit. The use of natural resources is efficient if it produces the most output per unit of input, with the least amount of waste. Government is efficient if it maximizes the general welfare of its constituents. For instance, government programs that protect air and water quality may be efficient in improving the quality of life in a community or region. Yet, there may be very real differences between decisions that are efficient for private individuals and businesses and those that promote the welfare of the general public. That is why the private use of air, water, and land resources is often tempered by government regulations. Moreover, every decision in the use of natural resources comes at the cost of a foregone opportunity. Economists stress the need to be aware of who gains and who loses from economic decisions as well as the size of the gains and losses.

Renewable and Nonrenewable Resources

There are two general types of natural resources: renewable and nonrenewable. A renewable resource is able to regenerate, either by itself or with human help, over a short to moderate time horizon (e.g., fish, food crops, and trees). A nonrenewable resource cannot create more of itself within a time horizon that is useful to humans (e.g., oil, hard-rock minerals, and water trapped in deep aquifers). Land has elements of both renewable and nonrenewable resources. Land can provide crops on a renewable basis, but the quantity and quality of land on the earth is essentially fixed, like a nonrenewable resource. Land is also fixed in location. Access to land, the uses to which

land can be put, and the proximity of land to amenities are the sources of land value.

We can think of natural resources as a stock of resources, such as oil reserves or fish, or as a renewable flow, such as crops from the land. The stock of renewable resources, such as fish, can increase or decrease over time, but it is possible to turn a renewable resource into a nonrenewable resource through depletion and extinction.

Natural resources can also be described in terms of physical supply and economic supply. The physical supply is the total amount of a resource that exists. The economic supply is the amount that is cost-effective to obtain through mining, harvesting, hunting, and fishing. For example, the economic supply of oil tends to increase in response to a rise in the market price of oil, even though the physical supply does not change.

Valuing Environmental Resources— Prices, Markets, and the Government's Role

America's economic system is based on private property and markets for goods, services, and resources in which buyers and sellers make decisions based on prices. Prices provide information to individuals as they decide what to purchase, and to companies as they decide what to produce, how to produce it, and for whom.

For instance, prices of nonrenewable resources tend to follow a U-shaped path over time. Initially, nonrenewable resources are expensive to develop. Then, thanks to technology, they become abundant and prices fall. Later, as supplies dwindle, they become expensive again. Renewable resources, on the other hand, tend to be initially abundant and cheap to exploit, but become more scarce and expensive over time as the renewable resource is depleted (Fisher 1981, 107). Over time, natural resource prices can fluctuate widely, driven by changes in demand, inflation, deflation, technology, government policies, subsidies, taxes, and substitute products. Economists assume that under perfect competition, no one buyer or seller would be able to influence prices, but Saudi Arabia controls about one-fifth of the world's oil supply and can influence world oil prices by deciding how much oil to sell.

Prices must accurately reflect the costs of production (land, labor, capital, and management), and market prices and "social prices" (costs of production to society) must be the same for the market system to operate efficiently. Flaws in the price system, known as "market failures," have long been recognized, especially when it comes to putting a value on natural resources and environmental services (Bator 1958, 351-379).

- *Market prices typically do not include the external costs created in the processing and manufacturing of products.* Market prices may cause companies to overproduce environmentally undesirable by-products. For example, when a coal-fired electrical plant in the Midwest generates electricity, it does not charge its customers a price that includes the cost of the acid rain damage (reduced human health and degraded water quality) that it imposes on residents of the Northeast. In this case, a government-imposed tax may be needed to raise the price of the electricity so that less electricity will be produced, less coal will be burned, and less air pollution will be generated. This tax, originally proposed in the 1920s by the economist A.C. Pigou, improves efficiency by bringing private costs and public costs in line.

  In economic terms, the Pigouvian tax is a way to compel companies to "internalize their externalities"; that is, the tax forces companies to charge a price for the electricity that includes the health costs of the air pollution. This new price accounts for all of the costs, private and public, in generating coal-fired electricity. As a general rule, it is less costly and hence more efficient to prevent pollution than to clean it up later.

- *Market prices may not accurately reflect the value of goods and the environment over time.* Economic decisions involve trade-offs, such as whether to consume a resource today or at some future date. Prices are a measure of scarcity and should include the opportunity costs of foregone future benefits from consuming a resource now rather than at some future date, or using a resource for one purpose rather than another. For example, if a farm field is developed into a housing subdivision, an economist would say that the price of the house lots should be greater than or equal to the cost of developing the lots, plus the opportunity cost of not having the land available for farming. There tends to be a bias, however, in favor of consuming sooner instead of later. As we shall see, this bias shows up particularly in weighing the costs and benefits of an investment project that has major environmental impacts.

  The branch of economics known as welfare economics embodies the concept of equity or fairness. This is particularly important in the case of intergenerational equity. By consuming nonrenewable resources today, the current generation may well be reducing the ability of future generations to provide a quality standard of living. Recall the definition of sustainability from the Bruntland Report: "development that meets the needs of the present without compromising the ability of future generations to meet their own needs" (The World Commission 1987, 43).

- *Market prices result in the underproduction of public goods.* A public good is something that society values, such as a city park. The park is publicly owned, and no one can be excluded from the park because access is free. The private market has little incentive to provide public goods, hence the market will create fewer public goods—in this case, parks—than society wants. Thus, it is common for local governments to buy land to create parks, or require developers to set aside land or money for parks (known as an exaction) in return for receiving approval for large residential subdivisions.

Some privately held resources may have public good aspects, such as the view of privately owned farmland that people who drive by enjoy, but there may be no means of forcing the public to pay the farmer for their enjoyment of the view. Moreover, if a community pays to keep farmland open, a visitor from outside the community can enjoy the view without paying. This is an example of the free rider problem: how to get everyone who benefits to pay for that benefit.

- *The market is limited in its ability to allocate common property resources, and to account for situations of uncertainty and irreversibility.* No one owns a common property resource, such as the air or the fish in the ocean. Because there are no clearly defined property rights, everyone has an incentive to use as much of the common property resource as they want. Unfortunately, this self-interest can easily lead to the degradation or depletion of the common property resource.

In his famous essay entitled "Tragedy of the Commons" (1968), biologist Garrett Hardin describes the commons of New England towns of the 17th and 18th centuries where any family could freely graze cattle. Because there was no limit on grazing, each family had an incentive to graze as many cattle as possible on the free land. This resulted in overgrazing of the commons and the eventual reduction of cattle production for everyone. The recent drastic decline in many of the fishing stocks in the world's oceans is a startling example of the tragedy of the commons. In the New England fishery, limits on access to fishing grounds have been used at times to enable the fish stocks to recover.

The economic model of perfect competition assumes that producers and consumers have perfect information on which to base their choices. However, prices reflect the private cost of producing goods and services today, not the uncertainty of supplying future goods and services. Moreover, the effects of many decisions are irreversible. As a popular bumper sticker says, "Extinction Is Forever." Some decisions may not be irreversible forever, but are so within our lifetimes. A bumper sticker from a Skagit County, Washington, farmland protection group says, "Pavement Is Forever." While pavement can be torn up and removed at considerable expense, how many of us know of a shopping center parking lot that has been torn up and returned to a farm field?

- *The market is a voting system according to dollar votes, and wealth and income are not evenly distributed throughout society.* Willingness to pay for goods and services is largely predicated upon ability to pay. Economists, however, shy away from making value judgments about wealth or income distribution. Consumers and producers have different levels of buying power and thus vary in their ability to influence the demand for goods and services that have certain environmental consequences.

Because of these flaws in markets and the price system, government intervention may be necessary to establish environmental quality standards and financial incentives to encourage a more efficient and equitable use of natural resources. However, there is no guarantee that a government regulation or spending program will produce a more efficient or equitable allocation of environmental resources than a market-based decision; that is, market flaws are only a necessary condition for government intervention; they are not a sufficient condition.

A common criticism of government programs is that they "throw money at a problem" for polit-

SIDEBAR 2-3

The Political Economy of Sustainable Environments

In its 18th and 19th century origins, economics was better known as "political economy." This term was used to describe how wealth and power are exercised in a community or a society as a whole; that is, some people have political clout that enables them to influence government taxation, regulation, and spending programs. These programs in turn affect the market price, allocation, and use of natural resources.

In America, companies hire lobbyists and make contributions to political campaigns to influence legislation. For instance, certain industries have enjoyed significant subsidies from the federal government: timber companies have had access to timber on federal land at prices below market value; farmers have received direct payments for growing certain crops, and in the Southwest, farmers and ranchers have received publicly subsidized water; oil companies receive a tax "depletion allowance" for each barrel of oil they pump; and car makers have benefited from publicly financed highways.

Perhaps the largest subsidy is the deduction of home mortgage interest for federal income tax purposes. Since World War II, this subsidy has encouraged sprawl and the conversion of millions of acres of farm and forestlands. Recently, Americans have been building and buying "McMansions" on large suburban and exurban lots, in an attempt to own as much house as possible and maximize the interest deduction.

The federal government apparently believes that food, timber, gasoline, and housing are basic necessities and that it is in the nation's best interest to provide these goods at discount prices, but the cost of these subsidies has been great. All of these subsidies encourage the misuse of natural resources by causing the market to respond as though plentiful supplies of resources and working landscapes exist. In reality, these subsidies reward behavior that degrades the environment through air and water pollution; the depletion of soil, water, and energy; and the loss of working landscapes and natural ecological systems.

What if federal subsidies rewarded the recycling and reuse of wood and paper products and the production of organically grown crops? There would be less demand for virgin timber, less destruction of wildlife habitat, and less use of energy and water in producing new lumber and paper. There would be less use of pesticides, herbicides, and chemical fertilizers in growing crops. What if the government taxed the use of oil at levels comparable to the Europeans to encourage conservation? There would be less driving, less air pollution, and a strong incentive to drive smaller, more energy-efficient cars and trucks. What if there were no mortgage interest deduction, as in Canada? There would be less demand for large houses on large lots, and more demand for small houses on small lots. Less space would be needed to accommodate new development, and hence more working landscapes and natural areas would not be converted to housing subdivisions.

ical reasons, rather than pursue a clear, cost-effective, problem-solving strategy. Also, governments may subsidize environmentally harmful activities (such as mining, forestry, oil, and certain farming practices) that waste huge amounts of water, release toxic chemicals, and degrade soil quality (Hawken *et al.* 1999, 13). Yet, sometimes a combination of market-based decisions and government standards can result in the conservation of natural resources and greater efficiency, as producers streamline production and cut waste. For example, the EPA's lighting efficiency standards, which were encouraged by the 1990 Clean Air Act to reduce the demand for electricity, could save industry an estimated $20 billion a year (Easterbrook 1996, 319).

How Much Should We Pay to Clean Up Pollution?

Economics focuses on incremental effects, such as the effect on the price of a good caused by the cost of producing one more unit of a good or the increase in satisfaction to a consumer from obtaining one more unit of a good. These incremental effects are known as marginal costs and marginal benefits. Ideally, marginal costs equal marginal benefits and both equal the market price.

In a perfect world, the extra (marginal) benefit to society from achieving a certain level of clean-up, say in air quality, should equal the extra (marginal) cost to society of cleaning up the air (see Figure 2-1). The optimal price of pollution clean-up would be price P, and the level of clean-up or the cleanliness of the air would be level Q_1, where marginal social costs and benefits are equal (point X). This would provide the most efficient economic solution, even though the maximum benefit of clean-up over cost is at point Z. Cleaning up air beyond the point at which the marginal social cost and marginal social benefits are the same (point X) would be inefficient. The cost of an extra unit of cleaner air would be greater than the benefit.

The shortcoming with this model is that market prices do not account for public health standards or "threshold effects." An economically efficient

solution may still impose unacceptable health risks and premature deaths. A threshold effect is the amount of pollution that an ecosystem can absorb before it "crashes" and can no longer support life. For instance, in the 1960s, Lake Erie was considered biologically dead. The lake had become so polluted that there were virtually no fish left. However, the price of the goods that the polluters of the lake made and the price households paid for sewage disposal (or lack thereof) did not reflect the fact that pollution was killing the lake. If the price of the goods and sewage disposal had included the externality costs of pollution, less pollution would have been generated and Lake Erie would have been better able to assimilate the lower pollution level. In the case of Lake Erie, government intervention in the form of water quality standards and requirements for sewage treatment appear well justified. The lake has since recovered as a fishery and recreation area.

The following data, taken from the Council on Environmental Quality (1996, 249, 250, 255), make it clear that the United States has taken pollution abatement seriously. From 1972 to 1994, Americans spent more than $1.5 *trillion* to control and reduce air and water pollution and solid waste; in 1972, the public and private sectors spent $15.45 billion to clean up and reduce pollution; in 1994, using current dollars, pollution control expenditures reached $117.62 billion, with an additional $4 billion for regulation and research. In 1994, about $37 billion was spent on air pollution abatement, $42 billion on water quality, and $42 billion on solid waste disposal; individuals paid almost $10 billion for pollution control, businesses $76 billion, and governments $31 billion. Employment in environmental industries rose from 462,500 in 1980 to more than 1.3 million workers in 1996; and revenues from these businesses climbed from $52 million in 1980 to more than $184 million in 1996.

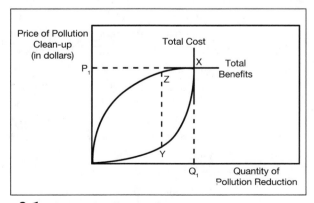

2-1   Optimal pollution clean-up.

Valuing Environmental Services and Analyzing Environmental Improvement Projects

One of the biggest challenges economists face is obtaining information to put a value on the services that the environment performs. Globally, according to the APA, natural systems provide life-supporting services estimated to be worth nearly as much as total annual gross world economic output, or about $33 *trillion* (APA 2000). On a local level, take, for example, the value of a coastal wetland. The private market price for the wetland is likely to be low, especially if it is unlikely that the wetland can be filled in for farming or to support buildings. However, the value of the wetland to society is probably much greater because of the environmental benefits that the wetland generates. Coastal wetlands are breeding grounds for shellfish and a variety of waterfowl. They also serve as a buffer against storm surges and can act as water recharge areas. In addition, wetlands filter pollutants. All of these services have real dollar values, but these values are not reflected in the private market price. Economists have tried to estimate "shadow prices" for environmental services to reflect their value to society. These shadow prices are based on how much the public would be willing to pay for the environmental services.

The divergence between private price as an indicator of value and the public value or "shadow price" of the wetland means that the private sector alone will not maintain enough wetlands. Because the private market understates the environmental value of wetlands, private landowners have little incentive to protect them, and government regulations and subsidy programs may be necessary.

Contingent Valuation

A question that politicians often want answered is: What price is the public willing to pay for environmental amenities? Economists have responded with a technique called contingent valuation. Contingent valuation is usually done through a survey that asks taxpayers how much they would be willing to pay for an environmental benefit, such as buying 100 acres to add to the community park system. Because there is no private market for public parks, economists try to estimate the "public" price (or shadow price) taxpayers would be willing to pay. Another way to estimate willingness to pay is through the travel-cost method; people reveal their preferences for a park by saying how much they are willing to pay to get there.

Contingent valuation may include the concept of option demand; that is, a person may derive satisfaction from knowing that there will be a park that the person or others could use. In other words, the option of being able to go to the park has value to the person.

Contingent valuation studies can be very helpful to politicians, planners, and citizens' groups interested in putting a spending measure on the ballot. If the contingent valuation study shows strong support for increased funding for parks or other environmental projects, a bond measure on the ballot would probably have a good chance of passing.

Cost-Benefit Analysis

Economists traditionally use cost-benefit analysis as a way to estimate the costs and benefits of a proposed large development project, government program, or government regulation. Cost-benefit analysis is a guide to decision making; it does not provide conclusive evidence of all costs or benefits. Monetary costs and benefits can be measured, but it is often difficult to put a dollar value on environmental costs (loss of wildlife or scenic views) and benefits (e.g., less flooding). Similarly, it is rather easy to measure the monetary costs and benefits to a private company but difficult to measure the costs and benefits to society as a whole.

Cost-benefit analysis is a convenient way to organize information to help decide:

- whether a certain project should be built, program undertaken, or regulation adopted; and
- which projects to build, programs to enact, or regulations to adopt among several alternatives.

Cost-benefit analysis is an application of discounted cash flow analysis, commonly applied in the business world. The dollar values of project costs and benefits accrue in different amounts over a number of years, but there is a time value of money; that is, a monetary benefit received a year from now is worth less than the same monetary benefit received today. Hence, the monetary benefit received after one year is "discounted" or reduced according to an interest rate. Say the monetary benefit is $100 and the interest rate is 8%. The monetary benefit today is worth $100 and in year one is worth $92; the $100 monetary benefit would be worth about $85 in year two, and so on. Discounting shows the value today of a project's future stream of net benefits (benefits minus costs), corrected for the value lost in waiting to receive those net benefits.

The formula is:

$$NPV = \sum_{t=0}^{n} \frac{B_t - C_t}{(1 + r)^t}$$

in which

NPV = net present value

t = the time horizon or the life of the project up to the nth year

Bt = the benefits of the project

Ct = the costs of the project

r = the rate of time preference, also known as the discount rate or rate of interest

The goal of cost-benefit analysis is to select projects with the greatest net present value, indicating the highest return on investment. In comparing two projects using the same discount rate, the project with the greater net present value would be the more desirable. If a project shows a negative net present value, the project should be avoided altogether.

The main elements to consider in cost-benefit analysis are:

- the size of the costs and benefits;
- when they will happen;
- the time horizon or life of the project;
- the discount rate used; and
- how the costs and benefits of one proposed project compare with another project.

Let's take the case of a proposed dam. The functional life of the dam may be 75 years. The major costs—the cost of building the dam, the cost of relocating residents who will be flooded out, and the environmental costs of the loss of wildlife habitat, farmland, and timberland—will occur early in the life of the dam. Also, no benefits will accrue until the dam is completed. So for the first three years, say, the costs significantly exceed the benefits, but beginning in year four, the benefits of flood control and recreation are expected to be greater than the cost of operating the dam.

Deciding what discount rate to use is key. A high discount rate, such as 10%, would mean that capital is scarce and the benefits of the dam will have to be quite high to justify construction. On the other hand, a low discount rate, such as 4%, would mean that capital is plentiful and future benefits will not be heavily discounted; hence, the project will be easier to justify. In many cases from the 1950s to the 1970s, the U.S. Army Corps of Engineers was criticized by environmentalists for using low discount rates and inflating anticipated benefits in estimating the net present value of dam projects (Reisner 1986, 208-09, 328). There is considerable debate about whether the discount rate for public projects should be the same interest rate that businesses have to pay to borrow money or a lower "social" discount rate that reflects the desirability of public projects.

The discounting of costs and benefits tends to create a bias in favor of projects with short-term benefits. Projects that would produce net benefits only in the long run will not compare as favorably. Above all, cost-benefit analysis does not address the question of who will bear the costs and who will reap the benefits of a project over time.

Have environmental regulations produced greater benefits than costs? The EPA estimated that the 1970 Clean Air Act and 1977 Clean Air Act Amendments created about $23 trillion worth of health and ecological benefits between 1970 and 1990, compared to $523 billion in costs (U.S. EPA 1997). The EPA projected that the 1990 Clean Air Act Amendments would generate $110 billion in human health and ecological benefits in 2010 compared to $27 billion in costs to governments, businesses, and individuals (*ibid.*, 1999). On the other hand, the Superfund Law for cleaning up hazardous waste sites may have failed the cost-benefit test. Between 1980 and 1999, only 595 sites had been cleaned up at a cost of more than $10 billion, or about $25 million per site (Dowie 1995, 58). It is unclear whether the benefits to human health and the health of the environment equaled or exceeded the high clean-up costs.

Fiscal Impact Studies

Fiscal impact studies attempt to estimate the likely net costs to a community associated with a proposed development project or the ultimate build-out of the community based on alternative development scenarios. While cost-benefit analyses are geared to evaluating the monetary and environmental impacts of large public projects and programs, fiscal impact studies generally address the anticipated public financial impacts of large private development projects (e.g., a shopping mall might bring major highway construction and traffic management needs, or a residential subdivision of 300 homes might create a need for a new elementary school). The public might be expected to pay for the increases in infrastructure through higher property taxes.

A fiscal impact analysis typically looks at the demands for new infrastructure (sewer, water,

roads, schools, parks, police, and fire service) compared to the property taxes and sales taxes that the proposed development or build-out would generate (Burchell 1978). However, a fiscal impact study could also include the estimated environmental costs, such as loss of open space and wetlands, highway congestion, and impacts on air and water quality and supply. The fiscal impact analysis can show whether a project is desirable in the first place, or the analysis can suggest certain steps that a developer or the community can take to minimize the infrastructure and environmental impacts of proposed and anticipated development (Burchell 1978 and Burchell *et al.* 1998).

Economic Development and Economic Growth

Most economists are firm believers in economic growth: increased productivity (defined as output per person per hour, or higher quality and hence higher valued products) and more jobs mean more income, a broader tax base, better public services, and a higher standard of living. Yet economic growth has also come from a greater consumption of natural resources, especially oil, natural gas, minerals, land, and wood. Can the increased consumption of these resources sustain economic growth indefinitely?

In 1972, the book *The Limits to Growth* (Meadows *et al.*) caused an uproar by predicting when the world would run out of certain natural resources. The book suggested that economic growth from exploiting natural resources could not go on forever. Some economists point to the rationing mechanism of markets for an answer. As a certain natural resource becomes scarcer, its price rises. This, in turn, drives consumers and businesses to use less of the resource, to search for new supplies of the resource, and to adopt substitutes. For example, after the price of oil jumped in 1979, the demand for oil decreased, drilling for oil increased, and people began to use more natural gas.

Another factor is technological change. In his 1798 essay on population, Thomas Robert Malthus predicted that because food output increased mathematically but population grew exponentially, population would outstrip the food supply, resulting in mass starvation. Based on this conclusion, Malthus dubbed economics "The Dismal Science," but overlooked the role of technological advances. Since 1945, food output has increased many times over, while the world population has doubled. In America, the main problem that farmers have is chronic overproduction of food, which keeps prices low. Nationwide and worldwide, an even distribution of food, not food production, is the central challenge.

Perhaps the concept of growth needs to be redefined. Economist Herman Daly, in *Toward a Steady-State Economy* (1973), posited that there was a difference between physical growth and economic growth. Physical growth meant more, whereas economic growth meant better. In a steady state, there would be a fixed level of population, and economic growth would occur without depletion of natural resources; that is, there would be no waste, and all materials and natural resources would be recycled. The same amount of natural resources would be available to future generations, thus maintaining intergenerational equity.

From a national standpoint, the traditional method of accounting for economic growth is the Gross National Product (GNP): the annual value of all goods and services produced. However, the GNP does not discriminate between environmentally beneficial and harmful economic activity. The GNP includes such environmentally degrading activities as the production of toxic chemicals, the cutting of old-growth forests, and the consumption of gasoline in vehicles that get less than 20 miles per gallon. In effect, the GNP counts the depletion of nonrenewable resources as a plus, even though this is akin to living off one's capital rather than the interest.

Some economists have offered an alternative "green" accounting that adjusts the GNP for changes in environmental quality. Herman Daly developed the Index of Sustainable Economic Welfare as a measure of national quality of life and the condition of the nation's natural capital, such as air, water, soil, and other natural resources. For example, if water quality showed improvements and water conservation resulted in less consumption, the green GNP would rise. The green GNP is perhaps a more accurate measure of how well off a country is. This concept of green accounting can be used by cities and counties in the environmental benchmarking process discussed in Chapter 1.

What Economic/Environmental Balance to Look for in a Development Review

A starting point in a development review is to ask: What are the economic costs of the project to the public? Will the developer pay for or install streets, traffic signals, and sewer and water lines or hook-ups? Will the development require new schools, parks, and recreation areas? Next, what are the environmental costs? What is the impact on air and water quality? On wildlife habitat? Will wetlands be disturbed or filled in? Will active farm or forestland be lost?

These questions are all aimed at ascertaining a Full Cost Accounting of the fiscal and environmental impacts and the overall potential costs to the community. Too often in the past, communities have rushed through development approvals without thinking of the environmental impacts on the community or how public services would be paid for. Communities need to promote and encourage developments that are fiscally and environmentally sustainable, and thus have net positive financial and environmental benefits.

ETHICAL REASONS FOR ENVIRONMENTAL PLANNING

Ethics are the values, standards, and philosophies that people live by. Ethics help individuals establish codes of personal behavior, and, collectively, ethics become translated into institutional, business, and governmental policies and programs. Ethics form the basis of legal systems, economic systems, political action, and public policy on the environment. Yet, what one person values about the environment may not mesh with someone else's beliefs. Hence, there are almost always competing interests for using natural resources, the working landscape, and the built environment.

From Nature as Servant to Humans to Nature as Sacred and Worthy of Stewardship

The Anthropocentric/Utilitarian View

There are several different ethical ways to look at the environment. The first and most common view is anthropocentric; that is, the environment exists primarily for its utility and benefit to humans. This view dates back to the Biblical edict to "be fruitful and multiply" and to have "dominion over the fish of the sea and over the birds of the air and over every living thing that moves upon the surface of the earth" (Genesis 1:29). In short, the human-centered perspective justifies the conquest, shaping, and management of nature to satisfy human needs and desires.

Yet, within the anthropocentric view of the environment, there is a concern about "environmental justice," the right of all people to enjoy a safe, clean, and healthy environment. Environmental benefits and costs are not evenly distributed. Typically, lower income people have been subjected to living closer to polluting industries, landfills, and natural hazards. A more open debate about the siting and operation of Locally Unwanted Land Uses and improving the quality of the air, water, and built environment in lower income neighborhoods are key elements of environmental justice.

Environmentalist/Preservationist Views

Deep ecologists believe that nature is sacred in itself, above and beyond human needs. To the deep ecologists, the sustainability of the natural environment is paramount. Humans present threats to that sustainability and must learn to make their needs subservient to the needs of nature. A more moderate philosophy sees humans as part of a larger ecosystem in which plants, animals, and humans share equal rights to exist and thrive. One of the most profound statements of this philosophy was made by Christopher Stone in his famous essay "Should Trees Have Standing?" (Stone 1996). Stone argues that nature has a right to be represented in legal proceedings in the same way as humans do.

Aldo Leopold, in *A Sand County Almanac* (1970), emphasized the concept of human stewardship for the land and its resources. He wrote:

> All ethics rest upon a single premise: that the individual is a member of a community of interdependent parts. . . . The *land ethic* enlarges the boundaries of the community to include soils, waters, plants and animals, or collectively: the land. . . . A thing is right when it tends to preserve the integrity and stability and beauty of the biotic community. It is wrong when it tends otherwise. [pp. 238, 239, 262; emphasis added]

The concept of stewardship is fundamental to the principle of sustainability: leaving the earth in at least as good shape for future generations as one found it.

The debate between preservationists and utilitarians has been going on since the early 20th century. Initially, the debate featured two well-known figures: John Muir, founder of the Sierra Club, for the preservationists; and Gifford Pinchot, father of the National Forest System and a favorite of President Theodore Roosevelt, for the utilitarians. However, the arguments have become more heated as the number of Americans increased nearly fourfold, from 76 million in 1900 to 281 million in 2000. There are simply more competing demands on the natural resources. (Note: The utilitarians should not be confused with The Wise Use Movement that sprang up in the 1980s. The Wise Use

Movement advocates private property rights of landowners. The Wise Use Movement essentially believes that landowners should be able to do whatever they want to with their land.)

Both the preservationists and utilitarians have valid points. Wilderness areas are refreshing to visit; exciting to view in photos; important for wildlife, watersheds, and air quality; and valuable for scientific studies. In addition, some people find it satisfying to know that there are wild areas remaining even if they never visit them. On the other hand, working landscapes are necessary to produce food, fiber, minerals, and energy. Working landscapes mean jobs, incomes, and a tax base for rural communities. The preservationist-utilitarian debate often centers on the national forests, which are supposed to be managed according to the principle of multiple use and maximum sustainable yield of natural resources. The multiple uses include timber harvesting, recreation, livestock grazing, watershed protection, and wildlife habitat. Balancing these multiple uses is an ongoing challenge, which is supposed to be addressed in the management plans of individual national forests.

Three More Views About Ethics and the Environment

Beyond the preservation-utilitarian views are three other ethical approaches to environmental planning: the cornucopians, the alarmists, and the cautionaries. The main differences among the three groups are their ethical beliefs, how they interpret data, their faith in technological advances, and the amount and pace of change they feel can be accommodated consistent with a sustainable environment.

Some people believe that there is no environmental crisis that technology and human ingenuity cannot solve. These people are often called cornucopians, derived from the bountiful harvest symbol, the horn of plenty. Cornucopians tend to be anthropocentric and utilitarian, and emphasize the abundance of natural resources. They have

faith in the market system to allocate goods and services efficiently, and feel that the price mechanism will successfully regulate the use of natural resources over time. Cornucopians can point to the inflation-adjusted price of oil to show that oil was cheaper in 2002 than it was during the energy crisis of 1979. Conservation, substitutes for oil, and more fuel-efficient cars were successful responses to the oil price hikes of the 1970s.

Cornucopians, however, tend to overlook the impacts of population growth and some technologies on the environment. For example, according to the National Resources Inventory, which is conducted every five years by the U.S. Department of Agriculture (USDA), between 1982 and 1997, 22 million acres of open spaces, farms, and forests were converted to urban and suburban development (USDA 2001). In an example of the unknown outcomes of technological change, nuclear power was supposed to produce power that was "too cheap to meter." Unfortunately, nuclear power plants were expensive to build and nuclear waste has been difficult to dispose of. No nuclear power plants have been built in America since 1978.

Alarmists tend to be closely allied with preservationists and feel that environmental disasters are imminent unless humans change their lifestyles and consumption patterns. Alarmists seek to shake people out of taking the environment for granted. Often it takes a major crisis or disaster to alert the public, to change household and business behavior, and to get government action. For instance, the discovery of the Love Canal hazardous waste site in Niagara Falls, New York, which caused illness and loss of property values, led to the passage of the federal Superfund Law for cleaning up hazardous waste sites nationwide. On the other hand, alarmists can be wrong. The Malthusian vision of widespread food shortages in the face of rising populations has not yet materialized.

In between the cornucopians and the alarmists are the cautionaries, who are most closely allied with the concept of stewardship. Cautionaries believe in taking preventive measures and responding to existing environmental problems before they get out of hand. Perhaps the first American environmental cautionary was George Perkins Marsh, a Vermont native who served as Ambassador to Italy in the years after the American Civil War. In *Man and Nature*, Marsh (1864) warned about destructive floods that resulted from cutting trees high in the hills and mountains. Virgil Carter and Tom Dale (1955) pointed out that ancient civilizations fell because of severe soil erosion; the Fertile Crescent of yore is now the desert nation of Iraq. Leo Marx (1967) suggested that technology was a cause of environmental destruction rather than a mark of human progress.

Projected increases in population in some parts of the United States are cause for concern, if not alarm. Already the environmental footprint of the major metropolitan areas—the space needed to provide the natural resources, to produce the goods they consume, and to absorb their waste— is enormous. In effect, several major metropolitan areas already exceed their carrying capacity in terms of poor air quality and the need to bring water long distances. Consider the persistent smog of Houston. Think of the 300-mile-long aqueduct, known as the Los Angeles River, that draws water from the Owens Valley of eastern California to greater Los Angeles. Without the Owens Valley water and diversions from the Colorado River, Los Angeles would be pretty much a desert. Can metropolitan Los Angeles, with 12 million people and growing, be sustained dozens or hundreds of years into the future?

Planning is about anticipating change, and population projections and the needs of future populations form the heart of public planning efforts. It is always risky to predict what will happen in the future, but it is prudent to err on the side of caution. Polluted air and water, depleted water supplies, and toxic waste sites are difficult and expensive to remediate, and the loss of unique ecosystems and plant and animal species cannot be undone.

ECOLOGY AND ENVIRONMENTAL PLANNING

Ecology and economics share the same root word from the Greek, *oikos,* which means "household." Ecology is the study of the household or one's surroundings. Economics refers to the management of the household. Ecology is the science of how plants, animals, air, water, soil, and climate interact in a specific environment. For example, there is forest ecology, coastal ecology, and prairie ecology, among others. These ecological relationships occur in ecosystems, a concept created by ecologist Eugene Odum.

Ecosystem Dynamics

An ecosystem consists of individual organisms, a population of each type of species, and a community of several types of species. To many ecologists, the diversity of plant and animal species defines the health of ecosystems. Ecosystems are thought to evolve through stages from immaturity to a more stable "climax" stage. The greatest amount of species diversity is thought to occur at the climax stage at which an ecosystem is likely to be the most resilient to natural or human disruption; and the ecosystem is most able to maintain a closed loop of growth, death, decay, and reuse. The loss of certain species or the disruption of ecological processes can reduce the ability of an ecosystem to recycle waste, to cycle vital chemicals, and to support a variety of life forms. Hence, many ecologists place importance on maintaining "biodiversity" in a community or region. Ultimately, humans depend upon ecosystems for food, water quality and quantity, air quality, and the absorption of waste. Thus, humans have a very real interest in maintaining healthy, functioning ecosystems that are biologically diverse.

Natural disturbances to ecosystems include fire from lightning, hurricanes, volcanoes, floods, earthquakes, meteors, and the invasion of plants and animals from outside the ecosystem. Some ecosystems, such as a prairie or a forest, may benefit from occasional fires. Human disturbances to ecosystems feature clear cutting forests, filling wetlands, damming rivers, introducing nonnative plants and animals, covering land with buildings and pavement, and destroying wildlife habitats.

Natural ecosystems recycle all of their waste. As plants and animals die, their remains are transformed by microorganisms into the soil to become nutrients for new plants, which are then eaten by animals, and the cycle continues. Humans do not recycle all of their waste. Instead, it piles up in landfills or is incinerated, or remains untreated in the environment. The reduction of waste and pollution from human activities is thus an important element of environmental planning.

Ecosystems play a valuable role in several continuous, natural chemical cycles in which essential chemicals are transferred from the air, water, and earth to living beings and back again. These cycles are important to sustaining life on planet earth; how well they function is a reflection of environmental health. The earth can be seen as a single organism, as biologist James Lovelock asserts in his classic book, *Gaia* (1979). Or, as biologist Barry Commoner (1971) defines the first law of ecology: everything is connected to everything else. Ecology underscores the need for individuals and communities to adopt Environmental Action Plans that embody the motto "think globally, act locally."

Natural Cycles

The hydrologic cycle, also known as the water cycle, provides a life-sustaining substance to plants, animals, and humans. The water cycle purifies and removes salts from water so that it can be safely absorbed by living organisms. The water cycle is the system of precipitation that is partly taken up by plants, animals, and humans, and partly recycled back into the air through evaporation, or evapotranspiration as the plants breathe. The effect of aggressive harvesting of forests, particularly rainforests, on the water cycle can result in a reduction in evapotranspiration and a subsequent decline in precipitation, leading to drier soil and slower plant growth. Water pollution makes it more difficult for the water cycle to perform its water-purifying function, and in turn reduces the ability of aquatic life and water-dependent plants and animals to survive. Water pollution from industrial and agricultural waste and stormwater runoff also poses major health threats to humans.

The carbon cycle features the process of photosynthesis, in which energy from the sun converts carbon and water in plants into sugar molecules that plants absorb as food. The sugar molecules break down to release energy, and through plant decay, carbon enters the atmosphere. Trees, for example, can be seen as large stores of carbon. Trees breathe in carbon dioxide and breathe out oxygen. When a tree is harvested, a carbon "sink" is lost. Coal and oil are fossil fuels from carbon-based fossilized plants. Humans can distort the carbon cycle by burning fossil fuels that release carbon, in the form of carbon monoxide and carbon dioxide, into the atmosphere. Carbon monoxide has been listed under the Clean Air Act as one of the six "criteria" air pollutants that pose major health threats (see Chapter 5). The build-up of carbon dioxide in the atmosphere is a leading cause of global warming, which may be causing changes in weather and in the functioning of ecosystems worldwide.

The oxygen cycle starts with trees and plants that take in carbon dioxide and give off oxygen. Humans breathe in oxygen and exhale carbon dioxide, which returns to the atmosphere. Trees and plants also act as filters to clean the air. The loss of vegetation reduces the amount of oxygen in the atmosphere as carbon dioxide increases, contributing to global warming.

Nitrogen is one of the most important nutrients for life. In the nitrogen cycle, bacteria in the soil "fix" nitrogen so it can be taken up by plants. Animal manure is rich in nitrogen and is commonly used to fertilize crops. When plants and animals die, nitrogen is broken down by microorganisms and made available to new plants. Bacteria in the soil also release nitrogen back into the atmosphere, thus completing the nitrogen cycle. Farmers can distort the nitrogen cycle if they apply more manure or fertilizer than the soil or plants can absorb. In such cases, nitrogen often runs off into rivers and streams and causes harmful algae blooms, or seeps into groundwater and raises the nitrate concentration to potentially harmful levels.

Phosphorus is a necessary nutrient for deoxyribonucleic acid (DNA) and cell development. In the phosphorus cycle, inorganic phosphorus rock is broken down by weather and erosion until it can be dissolved in water and absorbed by plants. Some plants are then eaten by animals and humans. When plants and animals die, phosphorus decomposes back into inorganic phosphorus. The excess application of phosphate fertilizer, as in the case of nitrogen, can cause algae blooms in water bodies.

How Humans Fit into Ecosystems

Ecosystems vary in their ability to respond to human activity. Wetlands, for instance, are vulnerable to the dredging and filling that degrade or destroy their natural functions. An ecosystem is not a static phenomenon. It is constantly changing. What is important for the functioning of the ecosystem is the degree of change and the pace of change.

Ecosystems have a carrying capacity: the amount of human consumption of natural resources that an ecosystem can support, or the amount of waste and pollution that an ecosystem can assimilate, before environmental damage occurs. Carrying capacity depends on soil and water quality, water quantity, air quality, and topography. For instance, deep, level, well-drained soils can support development better than thin, clayey soils on steep slopes. However, carrying capacity is not necessarily fixed; it can be either increased or reduced by human intervention. For example, sewage treatment and drinking water facilities can increase the ability of a settlement to absorb waste and thus expand carrying capacity, or the dumping of toxic waste can reduce the ability of an ecosystem to support life.

Yet, to what degree can humans actually manage and control ecosystems and not cause them to exceed their carrying capacities? Or can humans achieve an optimal use of environmental resources without harming ecosystems? In his book *The Control of Nature*, John McPhee gives an example of the constant and expensive struggle to subject nature to the human will. Since 1963, the Army Corps of Engineers has been working to hold the Mississippi River in its channel by diverting part of it through the Atchafalaya River. This diversion provides flood control for New Orleans—a city barely above sea level—and maintains ocean access for the extensive petrochemical industry along the banks of the Mississippi. Said Norris F. Rablais of the Army Corps, "We are fighting Mother Nature. . . . It's a battle we have to fight day by day, year by year" (McPhee 1989, 7). Yet, if Mother Nature were allowed to take its course, New Orleans would be submerged. One could argue that New Orleans grew up in the wrong place.

A comprehensive plan with a Natural Resources Inventory and a well-crafted zoning ordinance can help identify sensitive environmental areas and keep development away from them. Once mistakes are made in a development, it is expensive to maintain that development in the face of repeated assaults by nature.

The planning of human developments must be sensitive to four environmental issues:

1. the compatibility of the development with the surrounding ecological systems

2. the suitability of a site to support different types of development
3. the limitations and constraints of a site, including the vulnerability to natural hazards, such as flooding and landslides
4. the sustainability of the development over time; that is, how well the development fits with the local and regional ecological systems in the long run

The idea of humans living in balance with ecosystems is important for sustainable environmental planning. It is also important for sustainable economic development. Mayors, city councils, and county commissioners may ask why to invest in parks, greenbelts, water quality, and other environmental improvements. If they were to access the web site of any industrial development authority in America, they would find the answer. These web sites tout available industrial sites and a capable workforce as well as the quality of the environment in the community and region. In short, a good environment has become essential for economic development in the new Information Age because companies and workers are able to move easily and are seeking places with a high quality of life. Tourism also is often a major local industry and tourists want to visit quality environments. Thus, investment in green infrastructure may be as important to economic development as investment in sewer and water lines and roads. Nor should this lesson be lost on those communities and regions that are losing population rather than growing. A quality environment can play an important role in stimulating an economic turnaround and can also slow economic decline. For instance, adequate supplies of clean water are especially key to any future economic growth. Renewable natural resources, such as trees, fish, and farmlands, can produce yields well into the future if they are not overharvested.

Decisions on what developments should go where, what we produce and consume, and how we dispose of waste will have powerful implications for the maintenance and health of ecosystems, on which humans ultimately depend. The health of ecosystems should be continually assessed, such as through the benchmarking process described in Chapter 1. Planning for sustainable ecosystems, sustainable economies, and utilities is vital for communities and regions, and will pose a continuing long-term challenge, especially as human populations increase.

Planning for Sustainable Public Health

3

Planning for Sustainable Water Supply

*We've reached a point in water management where if
it's not water reuse, it's water abuse.*

DON BEARD, U.S. BUREAU OF
RECLAMATION COMMISSIONER

The frog does not drink up the pond in which he lives.

AMERICAN PROVERB

Water is a special resource. People, plants, and
animals need water to stay alive. Water provides
essential wildlife habitat, enables crops to grow,
and is important in many manufacturing processes. People use water to drink and bathe and to
clean clothes. Dirty water spreads disease and
poses a variety of health threats. Water is a renewable resource that is replenished through the
water cycle. But some water supplies, especially
groundwater, are essentially nonrenewable because
they recharge themselves very slowly.

Identifying the location, amount, and quality of
water supplies and protecting them over time are
essential actions in planning for the future of a
community, county, or region. Water supply planning is especially important in places experiencing
rapid population growth and development, and
where water supplies are scarce. Pollution from
existing and new development can contaminate
surface water and groundwater, at the same time
that demand for clean, fresh water from these
sources may be increasing. Accommodating more
people and development while protecting water

supplies requires careful land use planning. Lack
of a reliable water supply can be a serious limit to
growth or can hasten a community's decline.

We discuss water planning in two chapters:
water supply planning in this chapter and planning for water pollution clean-up and control in
Chapter 4. Yet, the two types of water planning
are closely linked. A water supply is not useful if
it is polluted, and clean water in short supply will
not meet community demands.

WATER SUPPLY CHALLENGES

America possesses about 8% of the world's supply
of fresh water. According to the U.S. Environmental Protection Agency (EPA) (1996), America has
3.6 million miles of rivers and streams; 41 million
acres of lakes, including much of the five Great
Lakes; 58,000 miles of shoreline; 34,400 square
miles of estuaries (outside of Alaska); 278 million
acres of wetlands; and 33 trillion gallons of
groundwater.

Americans use about 400 billion gallons of
water every day (*ibid.*). Irrigating crops and watering livestock account for about one-third of the
nation's water consumption. Farmers irrigated an
estimated 55 million acres in 1997, accounting for
nearly two-thirds of all groundwater withdrawals.
Manufacturing products (see Table 3-1) and generating electricity account for about 55% of America's water consumption. Residential uses account
for about 10% of America's water consumption,

Table 3-1
Water Use by Selected Manufacturing and Processing Operations

Activity	Gallons of Water Used
Making a board foot of lumber	5
Processing a chicken	12
Making one pound of plastic	24
Refining one barrel of crude oil	1,851
Making a new car, including tires	39,090

Source: U.S. Environmental Protection Agency, *Liquid Assets* (1996)

and more than half of all residential water use goes for watering lawns and gardens and washing cars. Competing uses of water often arise, especially between farming and urban uses and between farming and wildlife habitats. Water rights are an attempt to decide who can use water, but there are few limitations on how much water a landowner, homeowner, or business may use.

Fresh water is necessary both to support life and to enable economic growth. Wildlife and domestic animals rely on water for drinking and habitat needs. Fresh water is needed for virtually every manufacturing process. Even the New Information Economy requires large amounts of fresh water. For instance, the production of a 6-inch silicon wafer uses 2,800 gallons of clean, fresh water (Natural Resources Defense Council 2001, 38).

Most of the nation's easily accessible water supplies have already been harnessed or tapped. Nearly all of the once free-flowing rivers have been dammed, and some waters have been diverted hundreds of miles to their ultimate destinations. Cities attempting to access distant water supplies often face local opposition in the hinterlands. For instance, in the mid-1980s, Boston proposed to increase withdrawals from the Connecticut River, 80 miles away, but eventually dropped the proposal when residents near the Connecticut River complained. Instead, Boston opted for greater water conservation (Lowy 2000, A9).

Landowners and governments with existing water rights are often reluctant to yield them or even sell them to others. Moreover, local citizens may become actively involved in protecting local water supplies. For example, in the late 1990s, residents of Waterbury, Connecticut, successfully sued the city to block a proposed increase in withdrawals from the Shebaug River (*ibid.*). In the foreseeable future, many major cities and even some smaller communities will face difficulties in trying to expand their water supplies. Water shortages and rationing will likely occur.

Residents of the eastern United States often take water supplies for granted because of generally adequate average rainfall and an abundance of rivers and lakes. However, in the West, access to water can mean the difference between valuable real estate and desert. As author Marc Reisner (1987, 12) explained, "To easterners, conservation of water usually means protecting rivers from development; in the West, it means building dams." But several areas of the East have experienced water shortages in recent years. Maryland and Virginia have gone to court over water withdrawals from the Potomac River (Jehl 2003, 1, 21). North and South Carolina are negotiating the use of the Peedee River, which flows through both states. Georgia and Florida have verged on a water war over supplies coveted by both states. The lesson is that for rapidly growing cities and towns anywhere, the lack of adequate long-term water supplies can pose a very real limit to growth.

Hydrology

Only 3% of the earth's water is fresh, and only one-third of that (1%) is surface or groundwater (Owen *et al.* 1998). Water supply depends on the hydrologic cycle of precipitation and evaporation. When precipitation hits the ground, some water infiltrates into the soil and becomes groundwater. A portion of rainfall and snowmelt enters rivers and streams as surface runoff, but most precipitation evaporates or transpires through plants back into the atmosphere. Local differences in impervious surface, slope, soil type, and vegetation can create wide variations in amounts of runoff and infiltration. Significant regional variations in rainfall, sizes of water bodies, streamflows, and aquifers exist among America's humid eastern third, the drier Great Plains, the desert Southwest, and the rainforests of the Pacific Northwest, Hawaii, and Alaska.

A key concept in water availability is the replacement period, or time it takes for water to replenish itself through the hydrologic cycle. Water in the atmosphere is recycled about every nine to 12 days, rivers take 12 to 20 days, soil moisture cycles in about 280 days, fresh water lakes take 10 to 100 years depending on depth, groundwater of up to a depth of half a mile takes 300 years, and groundwater below half a mile—also known as "fossil water"—takes 4,600 years to completely recycle (*ibid.*, 177). Withdrawals of fossil water are very much like mining a nonrenewable resource.

Watersheds and Surface Water

Water supplies may be thought of as belonging to specific watersheds or river basins. A watershed consists of the land area that drains into a particular river system, including its tributaries. Most watersheds consist of several smaller watersheds and eventually drain into the ocean (see Figure 3-1). For example, the Mississippi River watershed—the nation's largest—begins with its headwaters in Minnesota, includes the Missouri and Ohio River systems, and ultimately flows into the Gulf of Mexico. Watersheds vary in size, from the vast Colorado River Basin in the West to the more typical Connecticut River Basin in New England. (An exception to this description of watersheds is the very arid Great Basin in Nevada and Utah, where the watershed does not drain into the ocean.) The location and size of watersheds, along with the average annual precipitation and variations due to microclimates, are important factors to consider in assessing the quantity of water that is available to a community or region.

Watershed boundaries rarely reflect political boundaries. Hills or mountain ridges typically define the boundaries of a watershed. The slope and soil type of watersheds affect how much water infiltrates and how fast water runs off. The steeper the topography and the greater the rock and clay content in the soil, the faster the runoff and the greater the potential for flooding and soil erosion. Water passes fairly easily through sandy soils and loamy soils into groundwater, but less water filters through soils with a high clay con-

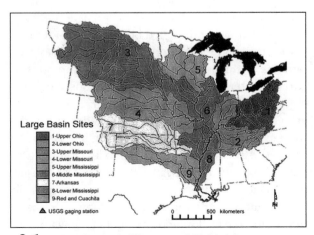

3-1 River basins of the central United States.

Source: U.S. Geological Survey

Table 3-2
Stream Ratings

Stream Category	Streamflow	Normal Depth	Normal Width	Uses
First Order	Intermittent, Seasonal	up to 1.5 ft.	1 to 5 ft.	Natural Area
Second Order	Intermittent or Constant, Storm Runoff	1 to 3 ft.	3 to 12 ft.	Natural Area
Third Order	Low Continuous Flow	2 to 5 ft.	10 to 25 ft.	Linear Parks, Trails
Fourth Order	Moderate Flow with Slight Channel	3 to 6 ft.	20 to 40 ft.	Canoeing, Trails, Fishing
Fifth Order	Continuous Flow with Shifting Channel	1 to 10 or more ft.	50 to 200 ft.	Boating, Fishing

tent. Vegetative cover and impervious surface are also important. Shrubs and grasses soak up water and hold soil in place, and trees with large canopies and extensive root systems absorb large quantities of rainwater and runoff. Watersheds may also be classified by the quality of water within them. Federally designated exceptional value and high-quality watersheds have very clean water, and discharges into the water bodies are tightly controlled (see Chapter 4).

Surface water provides about 75% of the total water used annually in the United States and half of the nation's drinking water supply. Surface water availability is usually measured in millions of gallons per day or in acre-feet. An acre-foot covers 1 acre to a depth of 1 foot and is considered a sufficient amount of water to meet the needs of two families of three people for a year. The amount of surface water available in some locations is considerably greater than the surface runoff to lakes, reservoirs, and streams, because of baseflow recharge from groundwater sources. However, in an average dry year, surface runoff can drop to less than 10% of normal, and in a drought year to far less. Reservoirs, lakes, streams, and rivers are vulnerable to heavy withdrawals and drought. Many states have minimum streamflow requirements to sustain fish, wildlife, and aquatic ecosystems, which means that some surface water is not available for human use.

Rivers, lakes, streams, and wetlands store water during floods and storms, and replenish groundwater aquifers. Wetlands in particular do more to safeguard both water quality and quantity than any other land feature on an acre-for-acre basis. Wetlands—which include swamps, marshes, and bogs—act as natural catchment basins during floods and storms by retaining excess waters and gradually releasing them into the ground or nearby surface waterways. During dry seasons, wetlands also release waters to ground and surface sources, thus helping to maintain relatively stable flows during low-flow periods. In addition, wetlands purify the quality of water by filtering and biodegrading pollutants (see Chapter 10). Streams are classified according to size and appropriate uses (see Table 3-2). Headwater streams in mountains are important drinking water sources and provide essential wildlife habitats. Development and any sewage discharges should be kept well away from these streams, which mainly fall into the first three stream orders. Larger, four-season streams are attractive for recreational boating, canoeing, and fishing.

Aquifers and Groundwater

About half of the nation's drinking water comes from groundwater supplies. In rural America, groundwater is the primary source of water for both community and individual water systems, accounting for about 90% of the overall water supply. Groundwater availability depends on the size and location of aquifers. Aquifers are underground areas that contain usable amounts of groundwater. Aquifers may be large (such the Ogallala Aquifer that lies beneath Nebraska, Kansas, Oklahoma, and west Texas) or they may be as small as a pond. Most aquifers are found within a half-mile of the surface. Water in aquifers moves at various speeds and not in clearly defined channels, unlike surface rivers and streams.

Below the earth's surface lies the aeration or unsaturated zone, an area with small spaces between the rock and soil that contain air and water in varying amounts. When precipitation infiltrates the soil, it passes through the zone of aeration. Any water that is not taken up by plant roots continues downward until it runs into impermeable bedrock. The water then backs up to form what is known as a water table. This water-saturated area below the zone of aeration is called the saturation zone and should be thought of more as a sponge than an underground lake. Water tables often correspond fairly well to topography and are seldom level. They may lie just below the land's surface or hundreds of feet below ground. Wetlands are areas with water tables that lie at the earth's surface.

The infiltration process restores or recharges the groundwater within underground aquifers. Depending on the porosity of soils and rock, the infiltration process usually can take from hours to months. The amount of precipitation and infiltration and rate of recharge of groundwater are important factors in estimating sustainable water supply.

The rate of recharge depends on the texture and composition of the soil, underlying rock strata, depth to the water table, the slope of the land, the amount of vegetative cover, and impervious surface areas. Sandy and loamy soils are more pervious than clay soils, and level ground absorbs more water than steep slopes. Soil with a shallow soil depth to bedrock means that less water will percolate down to the water table. The lower the water table, the longer it will take water to percolate down to the aquifer. Vegetation helps groundwater recharge as do surface wetlands. Impervious surfaces hinder recharge.

Different rock types and structures affect groundwater movement rates and water yield. The chemical composition of rock can also influence the chemical content of groundwater and the vulnerability of groundwater to potential contamination. Groundwater recharge is enhanced in sedimentary geology, particularly in the unconsolidated geology of stream valleys and carbonate "Karst" areas with sinkholes. However, these same pervious characteristics make groundwater in these areas prone to pollution from human activities on the land's surface.

Groundwater may be discharged from aquifers in one of three ways. Most groundwater that is used is pumped up from underground water tables by wells. Springs, which are found at locations where the water table intersects the land surface, are a second source of discharge. Artesian wells—a third discharge type—have their source in underground aquifers that lie between two layers of impermeable bedrock. Because they are under pressure, these wells gush water out of the ground.

In dry years, groundwater availability is reduced, particularly in shallow wells and springs and at higher elevations. Some community water systems and individual wells experience difficulty in meeting water demands during periods of drought. A decrease in rainfall or snowfall can reduce infiltration and lower the water table, resulting in higher pumping costs or even the need to drill new wells.

Threats to Water Supplies

The availability of water supplies to meet future needs will be greatly influenced by existing and future land uses. Open lands such as wetlands, forests, grazing land, and cropland provide large per-

SIDEBAR 3-1

Tampa Bay Looks to the Sea for Drinking Water Supplies

The Tampa-St. Petersburg-Clearwater area on the Gulf coast of south Florida had about 2.3 million residents in 2000 and enjoys abundant rainfall. Public water has long come from wells. But sprawling development has threatened the water quality of those wells, and heavy pumping has depleted some of the aquifers. Moreover, the region's population, which grew by a factor of five from 1950 to 2000, is expected to continue to increase along with the retiring baby boom generation.

The Southwest Florida Water Management District proposed and built a desalinization plant, which in 2003 began providing 25 million gallons of fresh water each day, or 10% of the region's fresh-water needs. The plant cost an estimated $95 million, and water from the plant is expected to add about $90 a year to the typical residential water bill. A second desalinization plant, to open sometime after 2008, is already being discussed (Jehl 2000, 1, 32; *The New York Times* 2003, A21).

Two questions arise: What are the residents and businesses of the Tampa Bay region doing to conserve water supplies, and what is the region doing to control growth to better balance water demands with water supplies?

Over the next few decades, several coastal regions are expected to look to the sea for freshwater supplies. For instance, the Metropolitan Water District of Southern California, which serves 17 million people in greater Los Angeles, is expecting to rely on desalinization plants within the next 20 years (Shigley and Krist 2002, 7). Yet, potential drawbacks of desalinization plants are the high costs of operation because of the need to filter water, generation of saline waste, and the disruption of coastal wildlife habitats as large amounts of seawater are withdrawn.

vious areas capable of absorbing enormous quantities of precipitation into aquifers. Impervious surfaces consisting of buildings, streets, parking lots, and driveways greatly reduce the infiltration of groundwater and raise pollution levels in surface and groundwater supplies. Impervious surfaces raise the volume and speed of stormwater runoff, which increases erosion and sedimentation, and washes oil and other chemicals from roadways and parking lots into surface waters. Development on steep slopes or on lands where vegetation has been removed also reduces groundwater recharge. A general rule of thumb is that when more than 10% of a watershed is covered in impervious surfaces, serious and continued water quality problems will result (Beach 2002).

Groundwater supplies may be depleted by overdrafts for drinking water, irrigating farmland or watering livestock, mining and quarrying, industrial uses, or commercial uses. For instance, according to the American Planning Association (APA), groundwater overdrafts in California average 1.6 billion cubic meters a year, which accounts for 15% of the state's groundwater use (APA 2000). In the San Joaquin Valley of California, overpumping of groundwater for irrigation has increased the salinity of the soil, which reduces productivity for growing crops. In some aquifers, excessive drawdown can lead to aquifer collapse and a permanent loss of the water source. Overdrafts indicate overreliance on a water source that cannot be sustained over time. One of the most prominent examples is the south central Great Plains where rainfall is typically less than 18 inches a year and the recharge rate into the Ogallala Aquifer is very slow. Since World War II, farmers and ranchers have withdrawn huge amounts of water from the aquifer to irrigate wheat fields and water livestock. The pumping has lowered the water table to the point where several experts predict that much of the region above the Ogallala will return to lower yield dry-land farming, which uses no irrigation, within 30 to 50 years.

THE NEED FOR WATER SUPPLY PLANNING

In many parts of America, particularly in the Southwest, water supplies are the most important element in determining carrying capacity and the limits to population and economic growth. Effective water supply planning and implementation will be crucial to sustaining livable communities (see Figure 3-2). For example, the Atlanta Regional Commission estimates that the demand for water in fast-growing greater Atlanta will increase by 50% from 2000 to 2020 (Firestone 2000, A16). A good part of this expanding demand will come from watering lawns and landscaping. In fact, summer water usage in greater Atlanta is about twice winter usage. Water supply planning can help communities and regions anticipate both future growth and droughts by building in reserve supplies and

water conservation programs. Finally, since the attacks of September 11, 2001, protecting water supplies from sabotage by terrorists has become an issue of community and national security.

The two main strategies in water supply planning are ensuring a reliable long-term water sup-

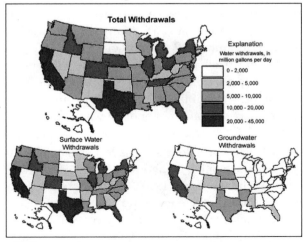

3-2 Water withdrawals in the United States, 1995.

Source: U.S. Geological Survey

ply and managing water demand. Communities can create water budgets to identify existing and future capacity to meet anticipated water needs and ways in which to limit water use. Any major new development or expansion of a water service area should be reviewed against projected future water supplies.

A major portion of the water supplies of several large cities comes from sources many miles away. Phoenix has gone out to the countryside to purchase "water ranches" (properties valued more for their underlying groundwater than the land on the surface). Phoenix also takes a share of the distant Colorado River. Los Angeles not only receives Colorado River water but also pumps water from the Owens Valley in eastern California over 200 miles via the concrete Los Angeles River, and receives water pumped from northern California through the Central Valley Project.

California had the largest population of any state in 2000, with more than 34 million people, and is expected to grow to 49 million in 2025, according to 1997 U.S. Bureau of the Census projections. In the 1990s, the Intermountain West between the Rocky Mountains in the east and the Sierra Nevada Mountains in the west was the fastest growing region in the United States. Most states in the region experienced population increases of more than 20%. Many communities in the Intermountain West and southern California are having trouble finding new water sources to serve their growing populations. Water conservation alone will not be sufficient. There are simply too many people and not enough water.

The good news is that America's average annual water use seems to have peaked in 1980 and has since fallen by about 9% as of 1999 (Belsie 1999, 4). In the early 1990s, Congress mandated national water efficiency standards for new toilets (1.6 gallons per flush), showerheads (2.5 gallons per minute (GPM)), and faucets. In addition, about one-third of water utilities have moved to charge water rates that rise as households use more water. This change to rising block-rate pricing is significant because traditionally utilities have employed a declining rate structure that charges customers less per gallon as they use more water. The declining rate structure in effect encourages water use, while the rising rate structure promotes water conservation. Other demand-side policies include restrictions on water use (e.g., no watering lawns between 8 AM and 6 PM) and programs that subsidize consumers who adopt more water-efficient technologies, such as the purchase of low-flow showerheads. Public education campaigns for water conservation can also help (Renwick and Green 2000, 37-55). Water conservation surveys and home and business retrofit programs can involve recording water use, checking for leaks, and installing water-saving devices.

More stringent demand-side policies feature limiting the number of new water hook-ups to avoid excess demands on the community's water supply. A more extreme action would be to impose a moratorium on new hook-ups where water supplies are in serious danger of falling short of demand. However, usually a moratorium can be legally imposed for not more than about 18 months or until the problem is fixed. Finally, a community could use water offsets to achieve a goal of no net increase in water consumption; that is, a proposal for a new development would have to be combined with reductions in water use from existing customers. Also, gray water use by industry can recycle water from residential and commercial sources.

The mismatch between water supplies and population concentrations, the uncertain replenishing and expansion of water supplies, and threats to water supplies from competing uses all underscore the need for state and national efforts to plan for long-term supplies of high-quality fresh water. States can plan for water supplies within their borders, but many rivers and lakes fall into two or more states. Here, either a federal role or a regional watershed commission is needed to help allocate water among states and competing uses.

THE FEDERAL APPROACH TO WATER SUPPLY PLANNING

The federal government's water supply policy has traditionally emphasized building dams and diverting water for irrigation. The government has relied on state water boards, water companies, landowners, municipally owned water utilities, and quasi-public water authorities to conduct water supply planning. However, planning by these many entities is often not coordinated with local or regional land use planning. Moreover, because water supply planning and land use planning rarely occur using a watershed as the planning unit, there is often a confusion of plans and claims on water supplies. Only since the passage of the 1974 Safe Drinking Water Act (SDWA) and subsequent Amendments has the federal government compelled state and local governments to consider a watershed management approach to protect their drinking water supplies.

Western Water Projects

For more than a century, the federal government has been actively involved in developing water projects, especially in the western states. Two federal agencies in particular—the Bureau of Reclamation and the Army Corps of Engineers—have long competed in building dams for flood control, hydroelectricity, irrigation, recreational reservoirs, and drinking water supplies.

Bureau of Reclamation

The Bureau of Reclamation was created in 1902 to develop water projects in 17 western states and Hawaii. The Bureau gained prominence in the 1930s for building the enormous Hoover Dam on the Colorado River and a series of dams on the Columbia River, including the Grand Coulee Dam. In the 1960s, the Bureau constructed the Central Valley Project in California to dam and pump bil-

lions of gallons from the water-rich north to water-starved southern California. Water from the Bureau irrigates about 9 million acres of farmland, provides water to nearly 20 million people, and generates nearly 10 million kilowatts of electricity.

The Bureau's sale of subsidized water to farmers has been the subject of much criticism. Originally, each farmer was entitled to low-cost water for 160 acres. In 1982, the 160-acre limit was raised to 960 acres and in 1987 to an unlimited number of 960-acre paper farms (large farms that are divided into 960 acre-ownerships by deed but are in effect controlled by one landowner or corporation) (Reisner 1987, 352-53). Especially in California, farms of thousands of acres in size have been

3-3 Watershed signs like this one alert people to the connection between land use and water supply.

Source: Katherine Daniels

SIDEBAR 3-3

The Colorado River Compact and Water Supply

One of the boldest attempts to ration water supplies dates back to the Colorado River Compact of 1922. The Compact was an attempt by the federal government to allocate water among several western states and Mexico. The Compact estimated the available water at 17.5 million acre-feet per year. At the time the Compact was signed, an acre-foot was thought to be enough water for a family of four for a year. Today, because of improved technology, an acre-foot can probably meet the needs of two three-person families for a year. The upper basin states of Colorado, Utah, Wyoming, and New Mexico received rights to withdraw 7.5 million acre-feet per year, as did the lower basin states of Arizona, California, and Nevada. Mexico was entitled to 1.5 million acre-feet per year. Yet, historically, the Colorado makes available only 11.5 million acre-feet per year—not nearly enough to satisfy the agreed-upon allotments.

By 1952, California was already withdrawing 5.3 million acre-feet from the Colorado, which exceeded its annual allotment of 4.4 million acre-feet. In southern California alone, farmers control 3.85 million acre-feet of the state's allotment (Greene 2000, A1, A27). In 2003, the U.S. government cut in half the amount of Colorado River water going to the Metropolitan Water District of Southern California, or about 800,000 acre-feet (Perry 2003). Southern California will need to buy water from farmers, build desalinization plants, store more water, increase conservation efforts, or implement some combination of these measures.

Colorado's growing urban areas also face tight water supplies. Of the 3.1 million acre-feet of the Colorado River allocated to the State of Colorado, only 500,000 acre-feet are reserved for the Front Range cities of Colorado Springs, Denver, and Boulder. Most of the remainder is used to irrigate large agricultural areas on the western slope.

In the early 1980s, the Central Arizona Project (CAP) was built to supply Colorado River water to Phoenix and Tucson. The CAP is an open concrete river that loses huge amounts of water to evaporation in the desert sun and dry heat. Tucson has decided to rely mainly on groundwater. Meanwhile, Phoenix continues to grow and is expected to reach 3.5 million people by 2020. In greater Phoenix, cities have purchased ranchlands just to be able to tap into the underlying water supplies. These so-called "water ranches" appear to be at best a short-term solution in the hot and arid Valley of the Sun.

In the 1990s, greater Las Vegas, Nevada, was the nation's fastest growing metropolitan region. About 85% of the water the region uses comes from Lake Mead behind the Hoover Dam. While Nevada has not yet reached its water allotment of 300,000 acre-feet per year, Las Vegas has been taking advantage of a return flow credits policy in the 1922 Compact. For every gallon of treated wastewater returned back into Lake Mead, Las Vegas can draw another gallon. The city returns all of its treated effluent to Lake Mead and 6.5 miles downstream pumps drinking water out! (Ward 1999, 139). In 1990, the population of metropolitan Las Vegas was 842,646; in 2000, it was 1.4 million. This number does not include the 35 million people who visit Las Vegas each year (Egan 2001, A1). By 2020, there could be more than 2 million people living in greater Las Vegas. Unless the Colorado River Compact is renegotiated, Las Vegas could face water shortages or be forced to pipe in water from hundreds of miles away. As a precaution, Las Vegas has been "banking" millions of gallons of water in underground aquifers.

Renegotiation for any city or state will not be easy because all of the Colorado's water is already allocated, and in many years, the Colorado is only a trickle by the time it reaches the sea in the Gulf of California (Reisner 1987, 125). As of 2000, the Colorado River was the primary source of drinking water for 30 million people. From 2000 to 2025, the cities and regions dependent on Colorado River water in the lower basin alone are expected to grow by 9 million people.

receiving Bureau water for years and at a cost of less than $20 an acre-foot (about 326,000 gallons), compared to the average cost of $431 per acre-foot for nonfarm water uses in the Metropolitan Water District of Southern California in 1999.

The cost of many Bureau of Reclamation dams was to be paid back by farmers who purchased irrigation water from the Bureau; however, with very low water prices, farmers have not come close to paying the cost of the dams.

Army Corps of Engineers

Since the 1930s, the Army Corps of Engineers has built more than 250 dams, mainly for flood control and hydroelectricity. To date, more than 70,000 dams have been built in the United States, nearly all of them before environmental impact statements were required under the National Environmental Policy Act. The environmental impacts of dams have been enormous, including the flooding of thousands of acres of productive farm and forestland, wilderness, geologic and archaeological sites, wetlands, and wildlife habitat as well as the decimation of anadramous fish runs such as the salmon on the Columbia River. Anadramous fish are born in fresh water, migrate to the sea, and then return to the fresh water where they were born to spawn and die. Dams hinder or prevent migration to the sea and the return spawning trip; hydroelectric turbines also kill the fish.

For decades, decisions on dam construction have been subject to cost-benefit analysis, but discount rates (interest rates) used to estimate the net benefits have often been skewed in favor of building dams. For example, in the early 1970s, the Bureau of Reclamation proposed to erect a dam on the Teton River in Idaho, primarily for irrigation. Yet, according to Marc Reisner (*ibid.*, 402), the Teton dam realistically could not provide greater benefits than its cost. The dam made it through the environmental impact process and was mostly completed by 1975. In June 1976, the Teton dam ruptured, killing 11 people and destroying or damaging 4,000 homes. Total damage was estimated at $2 billion.

Congress has long used water projects as a way to deliver jobs and dollars back to the states and congressional districts. But, starting in the late 1990s, it became clear that few new dams and water diversions were likely to happen. In fact, pressure is growing for the Federal Energy Regulatory Commission to deny the renewal of licenses for small hydroelectric dams because of growing public desire to restore fish and wildlife habitat.

Federal water projects for transportation and flood protection have also included stream and river channeling, diversions, dams, locks, dikes, and levees—all of which have destroyed large areas of wildlife habitat and fresh-water ecosystems. In addition, efforts to modify streamflows have often led to increases in the volume and velocity of floodwaters and increased downstream flooding.

River Basin Planning

Perhaps America's greatest example of river basin planning was the creation of the Tennessee Valley Authority (TVA) in 1933. The TVA was the first attempt to bring federal funds and administration to bear in taming a river for a combination of flood control, hydroelectricity, shipping, and recreation. The series of dams on the Tennessee River brought electricity to one of the nation's most impoverished regions, and provided jobs and good housing during the height of the Great Depression. The success of the TVA was based on its regional orientation and multiple purposes it served.

In 1965, Congress authorized the creation of river basin commissions to undertake planning for entire watersheds extending across state boundaries. River basin commissions have been formed for the Delaware, Susquehanna, Ohio, Missouri, and Columbia Rivers, among others. A key feature of river basin planning is bringing together water users to discuss water needs and allocations. River basin commissions have the authority to regulate large water withdrawals. For example, in the Susquehanna River Basin in Pennsylvania, groundwater withdrawals of 100,000 or more gallons per day are regulated by the Susquehanna River Basin Commission (SRBC). In addition, the SRBC's Agricultural Water Use Program requires agricultural water use to be reported. Reported agricultural water use, however, is estimated to be only about 10% of that actually used.

Effective river basin planning is about allocating water among competing uses. Interest in river basin planning has increased since the late 1990s when the EPA was ordered by the courts to plan for water quality on a watershed basis. Such planning gives the EPA and individual states an opportunity to work with river basin commissions to:

- set minimum streamflows and set maximum water withdrawals to support wildlife habitats, maintain adequate water supplies and the integrity of groundwater aquifers, and maintain the ability of rivers and streams to assimilate point and nonpoint pollution;

- establish total daily maximum loads of pollutants allowed in order to help revive polluted rivers and tributaries (see Chapter 4); and

- issue drought declarations and require water-rationing measures.

THE SAFE DRINKING WATER ACT

The primary goal of public water system planning has been to protect the water quality of the systems, rather than maintaining or increasing water supplies. Congress passed the SDWA of 1974 (with Amendments in 1986, 1988, and 1996) to reduce contaminants in public drinking water supplies. The SDWA enabled the EPA to:

- set national drinking water quality standards;

- require water quality monitoring, water treatment, and the public reporting of contaminants in drinking water systems;

- fund source-water protection programs to protect watersheds, aquifers, and wellheads from potential contamination; and

- ban the underground injection of hazardous wastes.

Public Water Systems Defined

The EPA has the authority to regulate some 170,000 public water systems that provide 90% of the nation's drinking water. It is the responsibility of these systems to provide an adequate water supply of potable water to meet present and projected future needs in the communities they serve. In 1999, public water systems included over 53,000 community water systems serving at least 15 connections or 25 year-round residents. Community water systems include municipal and private water systems serving cities, towns, and villages as well as private systems serving larger subdivisions and mobile home parks. Public water systems also include more than 100,000 noncommunity water systems serving at least 25 people daily for six months or more a year primarily at larger business, recreational, and public sites and buildings. Only private water systems serving fewer than 25 people are not regulated by the EPA. Thus, owners of individual wells supplying homes and small businesses need to test their own wells. According to the EPA's Office of Ground Water and Drinking Water, 10,728 of the nation's community water systems use surface water to supply 167.4 million people, and 43,195 draw on groundwater to supply 86.4 million people.

Maximum Contaminant Levels

The SDWA established mandatory maximum contaminant levels for each drinking water contaminant, of which there were 90 in 2000. These contaminant levels include 77 primary standards on volatile organic compounds, synthetic organic chemicals, inorganic chemicals, radiation, and coliform bacteria to protect human health. The EPA also set secondary standards on heavy metals, color, corrosiveness, and turbidity. Under the primary standards, public drinking water must be monitored for those contaminants known or suspected to be present in the water. Where contaminants are found above the maximum contaminant levels, the water must be treated to achieve the applicable standards prior to distribution to customers. For the secondary standards, monitoring and treatment are also required.

Surface Water Treatment Rule

In 1989, the EPA adopted the Surface Water Treatment Rule under the SDWA, requiring all public water systems using surface water to filter the water before distributing it to customers. Prior to this, many smaller public water systems used only chlorination as treatment.

The 1996 SDWA Amendments set new drinking water standards for public systems that rely either on surface water or on groundwater that is under the influence of surface water. For instance, wells that are less than 50 feet deep, are adjacent to streams, or that experience turbidity after a storm may be under the influence of surface water and must be evaluated. In 1996, the EPA adopted the Enhanced Surface Water Treatment Rule to require nearly all communities that rely on surface water or surface-influenced groundwater to filter and disinfect their water before it is distributed. These new standards have resulted in many smaller communities abandoning their surface water or surface water-influenced sources and seeking out new groundwater sources, to avoid the cost of building a filtration plant. Other small communities without good groundwater options face considerable expense in building a filtration plant.

The EPA may allow a waiver from the Enhanced Surface Water Treatment Rule if a public water system has good water quality and the community in which it is located has an active water source protection program and has demonstrated the ability to control potential contamination. For instance, New York City is attempting to avoid building a $6 billion filtration plant by protecting water supplies in the Catskill and Delaware Watersheds (see Case Study 3-1, below).

In 2000, the EPA added new rules under the SDWA to require public water systems that rely on groundwater sources for drinking water to monitor for bacteria and disease-carrying parasites. If bacteria or parasites are found, the water must be disinfected above normal disinfection levels.

Wellhead Protection and Source Water Assessment and Protection

The 1986 SDWA Amendments established the Wellhead Protection Program, which required each state to develop a program to protect wellhead areas for community water supplies. This program was expanded in the 1996 SDWA Reauthorization to require states to develop Source Water Assessment and Protection (SWAP) programs that address not only wellhead areas but entire watersheds. SWAP programs require states to assess both surface and groundwater drinking water sources that serve public water systems for their susceptibility to pollution, and to use this information as a basis for building voluntary, community-based programs to prevent contamination. A SWAP program must map the boundaries of the area providing source drinking water and identify the origins of contaminants in the delineated area. SWAP program findings must be made available to community water systems, municipalities, and the public.

Source Water Assessment Plans must include strategies for source-water protection. This protection may include the purchase of land or conservation easements and the implementation of wellhead protection ordinances and other land use planning techniques to significantly limit new development and other potential sources of contamination near water supplies. In this way, communities and water systems may be able to reduce the variety and quantity of contaminants in the water supply for which treatment would otherwise be needed. The EPA may designate a groundwater supply as a sole-source aquifer if the water supply is the sole or primary source of drinking water for a city or area. If a federally funded project has the potential to pollute a sole-source aquifer, the project must undergo a stringent review. The EPA has set a goal that "by the year 2005, 60% of the population served by community water systems will receive their water from systems with source water protection programs in place" (U.S. EPA 1999, 3).

The SDWA Amendments also include a Public Reporting requirement that calls on water suppliers serving larger populations to inform their customers about where their water comes from, what contaminants are in it, and how their water compares to state Health Department standards, including any violations that occurred in the previous year. Water suppliers must provide this information through an annual *Consumer Confidence Report* that can be either mailed to customers or published in a local newspaper. Finally, public water systems must demonstrate adequate financial, technical, and management capacity.

Future Infrastructure Needs

The reauthorization of the SDWA in 1996 included $9.6 billion for the EPA to make grants to state and local governments and public water systems. States have used the Drinking Water State Revolving Fund to make loans to public water suppliers for constructing and upgrading water treatment plants and transmission systems and to protect water sources. For example, the State of Maine loaned money to public water systems to purchase land needed to protect drinking water sources and thus avoid expensive water treatment (U.S. EPA 2000a). In fiscal 2000, the EPA made $94 million in grants to public water systems through the Public Water Supply Supervisory program on a 75% federal/25% local match basis (U.S. EPA 2000b).

Despite these state efforts and federal funding, a 1997 survey by the EPA estimated that commu-

nity water systems would require investments of $138.4 billion between 1994 and 2014 to meet SDWA requirements for water quality (U.S. EPA 1997a, 4). Most of the money would be needed for water system installation and upgrading (see Table 3-3). Many systems are more than 50 years old, and smaller community systems often do not meet the 1996 SDWA requirements.

State water quality boards or departments of natural resources work with operators of small systems serving fewer than 3,300 people to develop their technical, financial, and management capacity to provide safe drinking water. Small public water systems that lack sufficient capacity may be best assisted through interconnections with other systems, shared-water delivery contracts and procurement, or mergers with stronger systems. Financially strong water systems should be encouraged to assist weaker neighboring systems, and small new systems should be discouraged in areas where strong public systems can meet demand. Federal guidance and funding of water system improvements will continue to be important, but states, counties, localities, and individual public water systems will bear greater responsibility for finding creative and effective ways to implement new and stricter water quality standards.

As of 2000, about 90% of the nation's drinking water from public systems met the federal standards. Still, more rigorous federal water quality standards and enforcement appear likely, given continued violations of federal standards by some—usually smaller—public water systems, and because of outbreaks of potentially deadly microbes.

Enforcement

Most states have primary enforcement authority for the SDWA, but the EPA Office of Enforcement and Compliance Assurance has the power to enforce the act if a state does not have primary enforcement authority or does not do a proper job

Table 3-3
Community Water Systems by Size and Estimated Infrastructure Needs (1994–2014)

Size	Infrastructure Needs
Large Systems, serving more than 50,000 people	$58.5 billion
Medium Systems, serving 3,301–50,000 people	$41.4 billion
Small Systems, serving 3,300 or fewer people	$37.2 billion
Native American Systems	$1.3 billion
	Total $138.4 billion
Type of Water System Infrastructure and Cost	
Water Source Development and Protection	$11 billion
Water Storage	$12.1 billion
Water Treatment	$36.2 billion
Water System Installation, Transmission, Distribution, and Repair	$77.2 billion
Other	$1.9 billion

Source: U.S. Environmental Protection Agency, Office of Water, *Drinking Water Infrastructure Needs Survey: First Report to Congress*, 1997a.

of enforcing the act. States that have assumed responsibility for enforcing the EPA's drinking water standards must:

- maintain an inventory of the public water systems in the state;
- conduct sanitary surveys of public water systems;
- collect annual compliance reports from public water systems;
- certify lab testing of public water quality;
- ensure that new or modified water systems comply with state drinking water regulations;
- require public water systems to keep records and report violations;
- assess fines for violations;
- require emergency response plans for public water systems; and
- certify operators of public water systems.

STATE WATER SUPPLY PLANNING

Planning and regulating surface water and groundwater are often done by different state agencies, counties, local water districts, water authorities, municipal water utilities, and private water companies. Streamflow withdrawals are regulated by state water resources boards or departments of natural resources, while groundwater withdrawals in many states are not regulated at all. States have the power to declare drought emergencies and may call on public water systems to enforce volunteer or mandatory conservation measures.

State planning for public water systems is done in conjunction with the federal government through the SDWA. However, some states have begun to require local governments to plan for water supplies as part of their planning for growth and development. In 1995, California began requiring all cities and counties to include a study of water supplies in drafting their comprehensive plans and in reviewing large development proposals. In 2001, California enacted a more specific water supply law requiring developers who propose to build 500 or more housing units to demonstrate an ample water supply for the next 20 years (Sanchez 2001, A3). Developers will have to work with local water agencies to identify and certify the necessary water supplies. Vermont's Act 250 law requires developers to show that their proposed developments of 10 or more housing units or commercial developments of more than 10 acres will not have "undue impacts" on water supplies (Vermont Statutes Annotated Title 10, Chapter 151, Section 6086). Arizona requires creators of any lot to show an adequate long-term water supply in order to receive subdivision permission (Arizona Revised Statutes, 45-108). States with their own environmental policy act can require that proposed developments demonstrate an adequate long-term water supply as part of the environmental impact assessment process.

State Water Law

Fresh water is a scarce resource. The purpose of state water law is to define the rights of individuals, communities, and the state to use fresh water, and to allocate water among competing uses, but not necessarily to encourage conservation.

Surface Water Law

Two main types of surface water law have evolved in the United States. In the eastern states, the riparian doctrine allows a landowner adjacent to a river or stream to withdraw and use the water. If the landowner chooses not to use the water, water rights pass with the property to subsequent landowners. Also, states allow riparian landowners to transport water to property not contiguous to the waterway. Overall, landowners along a waterway are expected to be reasonable in their use of water; for example, they are not allowed to divert or dam the waterway or reduce the water quality. The riparian system works adequately in areas where there is abundant water, little irrigation, and relatively few landowners using the water.

The appropriation doctrine applies in the drier western states to allocate water use. Water rights in the West are determined by historic use. The first guiding principle of the appropriation doctrine is "first in time, first in right." Whoever files a claim first gets first rights to use the water. A landowner does not have to own land contiguous to the river or stream, and may transport and sell water even to another watershed. Typically, a user who can show that the water will be put to a "beneficial use" receives a permit from a state water agency specifying the amount of water to which the user is entitled and what the water will be used for. In times of drought, this practice can result in a few users taking literally all of the water or all except what may be required for "minimum streamflows" to maintain wildlife habitat, leaving more recent permit holders with no water.

The second principle of the appropriation doctrine is "use it or lose it." If a water user ceases to draw water or reduces the amount used, the user may lose future rights to the water. For instance, if the holder of a water right in Kansas does not use the water for three successive years, the holder forfeits the water right. This aspect of the law creates a major obstacle to water conservation and potential water redistribution, and freezes in time antiquated water allocation schemes that may not be responsive to changing community or regional needs. The "use it or lose it" principle is especially counterproductive when it comes to irrigating farmland. Most farmers in the West still employ flood irrigation, which results in large amounts of water being lost through evaporation. Drip irrigation, though more expensive to put in place, could result in enough water conservation to supply urban needs for decades to come.

Third, water rights in the West are considered private property rights. This means that water rights—like mineral rights—can be sold separately from the rest of the property. An active market in water rights exists and water can be sold from one property to another. For example, it has been common for farmers to sell water rights to enable cities to expand.

Public Trust Doctrine

An interesting legal concept that is starting to be applied to water resources is the public trust doctrine of "public entitlement to the benefit of natural systems" (Sax 1993, 150). The public trust doctrine dates back to Roman days, and exists in the legal systems of Great Britain and the United States. It is uncodified law that says that government is responsible for holding important natural resources in trust for the public. In 1983, in *National Audubon v. Superior Court*, 658 P.2d 709 (1983), also known as *Mono Lake*, the California Supreme Court ruled that the State of California had an obligation under the public trust doctrine to oversee water use even after it was appropriated by private users. Private water users in eastern California and diversions to Los Angeles had drawn on streams feeding Mono Lake so that the natural calcium formations called tufa towers were drying up and disintegrating. Also, the low water levels in the lake enabled coyotes to raid bird nests on the islands. In short, the water diversions were endangering the natural functioning of the lake. The court ruled that private appropriators would not be allowed to seriously deplete a water resource, and long-term solutions for water use and environmental protection should be sought.

Although *Mono Lake* did not specify how the public trust should be measured, the court identified the need for the monitoring of ecological activity that produces public benefit. Such monitoring in water allocation will become increasingly necessary and difficult as competing demands for water intensify. For instance, in a situation similar to *Mono Lake*, in the early 1990s, Congress authorized the allocation of 10% to 20% of the water from California's Central Valley Project to be used for the conservation of fish habitat (Easterbrook 1996, 637).

Groundwater Law

Under the American Rule, used in the eastern states, a landowner can withdraw groundwater for beneficial uses that are reasonable on that land. Groundwater may not be transported to land not directly above the source and withdrawals may not unreasonably harm a neighbor's use of the groundwater, such as lowering the water table or reducing water pressure, and may not adversely affect a waterway or lake.

In the western states, the Conjunctive Use Doctrine holds that there is a link between groundwater and surface water use, and that water-use formulas need to manage the groundwater and surface water in a coordinated fashion to maintain adequate water supplies and water quality. For instance, conjunctive use allows alternate water supplies to be used during times of drought or high demand. However, groundwater is also considered private property, and a landowner can pump out as much as possible, even if neighbors lose their groundwater as a result (Yardley 2001, A14). Groundwater can be pumped to the surface and transported to distant sites; this is common in Arizona with the development of "water ranches" in the countryside to provide water for urban and suburban water users. Yet, since 1980, Arizona has charged groundwater users for depletion that causes ground subsidence and reduces the availability of water for future uses (Getches 1993, 131). Also in 1980, Arizona enacted a Groundwater Management Act requiring developers of new subdivisions to prove a reliable water supply for the next 100 years.

REGIONAL AND COUNTY WATER SUPPLY PLANNING

Planning for adequate, long-term supplies of high-quality water will be an increasingly important component of community and regional efforts to manage growth, especially in places experiencing rapid development and in places where water supplies are scarce. Existing and new development may pose threats of surface water and groundwater contamination at the same time that water demands from those sources are increasing.

Lack of a reliable water supply can indeed be a limit to growth. The regional or county level is ideal for water supply planning, as aquifers and watersheds typically cross multiple municipal boundaries, and both ground and surface water sources often originate in areas different from those that they serve. Texas in 2002 adopted a state water plan made up of 16 regional water plans with a time horizon of 50 years (Texas Water Development Board 2002). Kentucky requires all of its counties to have long-range water plans, and state funding has enabled several Pennsylvania counties to draft water supply plans. However, most county governments do not do water supply planning, even as part of their comprehensive planning process. Instead, water supply planning is mainly done by private water companies and public water authorities.

Five issues are central to effective water supply planning and demonstrate the close relationship between land use planning and access to sustainable water supplies:

1. *Protecting water supply sources.* Poorly planned, rapid, and excessive development can threaten water supplies through overdrafts of water, pollution runoff into surface water, and infiltration of sewage and other contaminants into groundwater. New development should be sited so as to minimize contaminant threats and limited in amount so as to keep within the carrying capacity of the water sources. Public land purchases to protect water supplies are effective yet expensive. According to the American Water Works Association, "The most effective way to ensure long-term protection of water supplies is through land ownership by the water supplier and its cooperative public jurisdictions" (The Trust for Public Land, 1997). Yet, nationwide, the median water utility owns only 2% of its watershed. Suffolk County, New York, has spent more than $100 million to acquire over 8,000 acres in

the Long Island Pine Barrens to protect fragile and high-quality underground drinking water supplies. Also, on a regional basis, transfer of development rights (TDR) has been used to protect surface water supplies in the Lake Tahoe Basin of California and Nevada, and the groundwater supplies in the New Jersey Pinelands. Through TDRs, land near important water supplies remains open as landowners receive a payment from developers who buy the development rights and move them to build at higher densities in designated growth areas.

2. *Locating water system service areas.* Public water systems are necessary to provide water for intensive residential, commercial, and industrial development, and can be used to promote compact development patterns. Reliance on public water systems can be encouraged through zoning that allows higher densities adjacent to existing built-up areas, while large-lot zoning and the strict regulation of on-site wells and septic systems will discourage the extension of water lines into farm and forest areas. Urban growth boundaries, used throughout Oregon and in several metropolitan areas around the United States, can also limit the extension of public water lines into the countryside and promote compact development (see Chapters 13 and 20).

3. *Guarding against unintended sprawl.* Unfortunately, planned water service areas are rarely coordinated with planned community growth areas, because such planning is usually done by two different entities. In many areas, water supplies are controlled by a local or regional water authority or a special water district (especially a rural water district). Special water districts are formed to provide water service to a particular location. Water authorities are created to provide water service over a wide area. The authori-

SIDEBAR 3-4
Wastewater Reuse

Wastewater reuse involves finding beneficial uses for treated wastewater from sewage treatment plants, rather than discharging it into waterways. Reused or reclaimed water is typically put through at least a secondary treatment process. In 1992, the U.S. Environmental Protection Agency set treatment standards for reclaimed water based on the anticipated level of human contact. Reclaimed wastewater, for instance, may not be used on crops intended for human consumption (Crook *et al.* 1992). Most reused water is appropriate for other agricultural, industrial, and landscaping uses, which happen to be the nation's leading consumers of fresh water. The purpose of water reuse is to conserve potable water when lower quality water will suffice.

The main obstacle to water reuse is the need to construct a second set of pipes from treatment plants to major water users, such as power plants, large farms, and residential complexes. St. Petersburg, Florida, has built a network of 260 miles of pipe to deliver reclaimed water. Tallahassee, Florida, provides reused water to 1,750 acres of irrigated crops (Florida Department of Environmental Protection 2001). Water reuse can also be successful at a more modest scale. Lagoon systems serving smaller communities and new developments can be used to spray-irrigate adjacent farm fields, parks, and golf courses with minimal additional piping. Where failing community on-lot septic systems have been replaced by lagoon and spray irrigation systems, groundwater quality has often improved due to the filtering action of soils.

Only 2% of the nation's water supply came from reused water in 1995 (U.S. Geological Survey 2002, 59). However, the reuse of water has become increasingly popular in areas with water shortages (such as Arizona, California, Florida, and Texas), which accounted for 75% of the nation's water reuse in that year. Because most of the nation's population growth over the next 20 to 50 years is projected to occur in these states, the reuse of water is likely to increase sharply as the price of treating and pumping water rises and as watering restrictions become common.

ties have broader powers than special water districts. Authorities have the power to levy taxes and fees, sell bonds, and develop land. An amazing feature of authorities is that they are not elected bodies and hence are not readily accountable to the public. Authorities undertake their own planning processes, which may not be consistent with local or county land use plans. Like most bureaucracies, authorities expand their power by expanding their size. In fact, water authorities have contributed significantly to sprawl through promoting land development in places not necessarily intended for development by communities. Other areas planned by communities for growth and development may have not sufficient water available. Ideally, water authorities and water districts should be made part of a municipal or county government to coordinate water supply planning and land use planning.

Older residential subdivisions and mobile home parks in the countryside sometimes experience failing septic systems and polluted groundwater, necessitating the extension of a public water line sometimes miles through farmland or open space to reach the development. Landowners along the water-line extension may want to hook up to the public water supply, and the public water system operators may welcome these additions to the rate base. The result is often sprawl and the premature fragmentation and conversion of agricultural land and open space. To avoid this problem, the water line can be sized to serve only the existing development with water quality problems and not take on hook-ups from new development.

4. *Water Audits.* A water audit is a study of how efficiently water is being used and the potential to conserve on water use. Cities and counties can conduct audits to save money on watering parks and landscaping and to identify leaks in the piping systems. Private landowners can benefit from better matching water use with water needs, especially in dry climates where water is scarce, irrigation is common, evaporation is high, and plants rapidly draw on water supplies. In addition, by reducing water use, audits help to decrease runoff and nonpoint water pollution (Meeks 2002, 6).

5. *Appropriate Water Pricing.* The pricing of public water also has important consequences for growth and development. Water users generally pay less than the true cost of water; that is, the price consumers pay does not reflect the cost of water source development, pumping, treatment, storage, distribution, and environmental impacts. Water users in Phoenix pay about one-sixth of the water's actual cost (National Research Council 1993, 52). These preferential water rates have helped to encourage sprawling development in the Valley of the Sun. Moreover, rates in both private and public water systems are usually based on average-cost pricing. In other words, when a new water user is added to a mature water system, the additional cost of that user's water consumption is averaged over the entire system. In effect, the average cost that the new user pays is lower than the additional or marginal cost of providing water to that user. As a result, the new user is subsidized by those already using the water system. On the other hand, in new water systems with declining average costs, when a water line is extended into the outer suburbs, water companies and public

utilities have an incentive to add as many users as possible to that line to reduce the average cost or price that the users will pay.

A clear problem is that water rates are not high enough to encourage conservation and reuse of water supplies. Traditionally, water has been priced according to the "inverted block rate" or declining price structure in which the more water the consumer uses, the lower the price per gallon. Water rates vary around the country according to available supplies and demands, but rates need to reflect the true cost of water use. Pricing blocks would also be helpful in getting farmers and other large water users to conserve and adopt water-saving measures, such as drip irrigation in the case of farming (Postel 2000, 56-57).

The Metropolitan Water District of Southern California, which serves 17 million customers, reported that in 1999, the average household consumed 163,000 gallons of water at a cost to the customer of $215, or about 0.13 cents per gallon (Metropolitan Water District 2001)! This is a typical charge for many parts of the country, and lower than some. Compare this to the normal price of more than $1 a gallon for bottled drinking water. Not included in the Metropolitan Water District's water price is the cost of pumping most of the water long distances from northern California and the Colorado River.

Water Supply Plan Objectives

Water supply plans are intended to ensure the continued ability of community water systems to provide potable water to meet current and projected future needs. A good county or regional water supply plan will have nine principal objectives. It will:

1. provide an evaluation, based on technical, managerial, and financial considerations, of

the ability of community water systems to meet projected future water demands;

2. help ensure that all systems have the long-term capacity to meet federal SDWA requirements;

3. include a source protection plan to delineate ground and surface water protection areas and public water supplies, identify potential sources of contamination within these protection areas, develop and apply watershed and wellhead protection measures to plans to keep inappropriate development away from areas that supply public water systems, and consider the purchase of lands adjacent to reservoirs and rivers to keep them undeveloped and thus protect public water systems;

4. recommend ways to deliver water from existing and potential new water systems to current and future residents in the most reliable, cost-effective, and environmentally responsible means possible;

5. encourage and implement water conservation measures;

6. help implement the water-related goals and objectives of local comprehensive plans;

7. propose future water service areas that are coordinated and consistent with the recommended growth areas of local comprehensive plans and capital improvements programs (CIPs);

8. recommend effective ways to provide water outside of community water system service areas; and

9. improve communication and coordination among municipalities and community water systems in order to facilitate continued effective water planning into the future.

In drafting the water supply plan, the county planning department should first form an advisory committee to guide the development of the plan. Public participation and citizen involvement are essential components in a community's water planning process. The next step is to compile an inventory of existing known ground and surface water sources. Much of this information should be available from the state department of natural resources or water resources board in annual water supply reports and periodic system surveys. Surface water and groundwater sources should be mapped, preferably on a Geographic Information System (GIS) system.

State agencies and public water systems in the community or region should be asked to provide information about:

- water source types (surface and groundwater) and number of sources used;

- safe yield, seasonal flow variation, and annual water use levels for each source;

- the location, capacity, current use, and age of water treatment plants, including disinfection and/or filtration systems;

- average annual and peak water use by type of use;

- the location, capacity, current use, and type of untreated and treated water storage capacity;

- maximum contaminant level or levels exceeded in treated water in last three years;

- the location, capacity, current use, age, and materials of the pumping, transmission, and distribution systems;

- existing interconnections;

- number and type of connections and population served, community served, and potential to connect to other public water systems;

- water system size (small, medium, or large), ownership, number and training of certified operators, approved operation and maintenance plans, up-to-date water supply reports;

- water system metering, rate structure, billing period, and rate schedule;

- water system annual revenues, expenses, fixed assets, long-term debts, and contingency funds; and

- emergency response plans that describe contingency procedures in the event of drought, contamination, or system breakdown, including back-up water systems.

The analysis of the inventory data and maps should compare public water system capacities with projected future water demands to determine needed system improvements or new water systems. The analysis can also be helpful in estimating potential costs of upgrading or expanding systems.

Projected future water demands for a county are made based on long-term, typically 20-year population projections. Existing average or peak daily water use is extrapolated into the future for each community water system because water use differs from system to system. Where existing populations currently served by on-lot water are projected to be served by public water, these figures are also added. A county may be served by several large- or medium-sized water systems, and dozens of small systems, many of them troubled and in need of assistance of various kinds. Counties that want to encourage compact growth patterns should recommend that their municipalities plan to provide public water to a higher percentage of development than in the past.

Water Supply Plan Recommendations

Using the analysis of the capability of the county's community water systems to meet future water needs, the planning commission and advisory committee should draft recommendations to address the following.

- *Structural, management, and financial improvements to upgrade systems.* These actions may include upgrading treatment capacity or type, adding storage capacity, modifying the planned service area, undertaking water conservation programs, and revising water pricing policies, among other actions.
- *Regional approaches to improving service, such as interconnections between water systems and joint system management.* Many small private systems with part-time personnel could benefit by sharing operators and making joint

purchases through various cooperative management strategies. Water system interconnections can be particularly helpful during times of drought, natural disaster, or contamination from spills or leakage. However, interconnections also have the potential to encourage sprawled development patterns in areas not planned for growth. For this reason, interconnections should be limited to communities within existing growth corridors and should not be encouraged in areas with important farm, forest, or other natural resources.

- *Changes to local planning, land use regulations, and infrastructure programs to promote compact growth, regulate on-lot water wells and septic systems, and encourage source-water protection.* Good land use planning and implementation will help to protect water supplies from pollution and overdraft over the long run (see also Chapter 4). This should involve cooperation and coordination with adjacent municipalities where water sources may be located.
- *New systems to serve new growth areas.* Recommendations may include the development of new public water systems to serve existing or planned new growth areas. Because new SDWA requirements make the development of new public water systems more expensive, developers may seek to avoid them. They can be encouraged through direct financial assistance and by discouraging sprawled suburban and rural development that uses on-lot wells.
- *Water conservation measures.* The EPA categorizes conservation measures according to three levels of increasing stringency. County water supply plans should recommend some combination of the following measures, depending on the availability of water in the area and the potential for drought.

Level 1 EPA measures call for public water suppliers to:

- meter all water end uses to accurately measure and charge for water used;
- control leaks and losses through the maintenance and repair of water pipes and pumping systems;
- cost and price all water supplied so that revenues adequately cover current and anticipated expenses; and
- conduct public information and education programs to encourage water conservation.

Level 2 measures feature:

- water-use audits of businesses and residences;
- retrofits of businesses and residences to improve efficiency;
- managing water pressure; and
- landscaping to minimize water use.

Level 3 measures involve:

- the reuse and recycling of water; and
- regulations on water use, such as no car washing or no watering lawns between 8 AM and 6 PM.

Wellhead Protection

Grants are available under the SDWA for municipalities and community water systems to develop watershed, aquifer, and wellhead protection plans. To date, most progress has been made on wellhead protection plans. Each state now has a wellhead protection program, approved by the EPA, to guide local governments in keeping potentially contaminating land uses and activities away from wells that provide public drinking water. These programs are now part of a state's SWAP, which addresses drinking water from both surface and groundwater sources.

Local wellhead protection programs involve five steps:

STEP 1
Form a Wellhead Protection Team

The first step in creating a wellhead protection program is to form a team that will be responsible for drafting and implementing the program. The team should consist of eight to 10 people, such as an elected official, a major water user, a developer, a planning commission member, an environmental group representative, a water system manager, an official from the conservation district, a farmer, and an attorney. If the groundwater source lies partly or wholly in an adjacent municipality, a representative of that community should be invited to participate. Guidance should be provided by a professional planner.

STEP 2
Define the Land Area to Be Protected

The team should next identify the land area to be protected. The SDWA defines the Wellhead Protection Area as:

> The surface and subsurface area surrounding a water well or wellfield, supplying a public water system, through which contaminants are reasonably likely to move forward and reach such water or wellfield.

A hydrogeologist should delineate the wellhead and aquifer protection zones, which will reflect priority protection areas. A map—preferably GIS-based—should identify three specific zones:

- *Zone I* (a circular land area of a 100- to 400-foot radius around the wellhead): Land use activities in Zone I generally pose the greatest risks to groundwater quality. For new wells, Zone I must be owned or controlled by the water supply system to prohibit activities that could contaminate the well.
- *Zone II* (the land area that contributes to a well under pumping conditions): This is considered the well's area of diversion and is greatly dependent upon local aquifer conditions and the pumping rate of the well. A circle of one-half-mile radius around the well is a default definition of this zone in the absence of a professional delineation.
- *Zone III* (the land area that contributes significant surface or groundwater to a well's area of diversion, and is typically located upgradient from the well): Zone III areas

provide recharge to the aquifer within Zone II and are larger than Zone I or II areas.

Identify Existing and Potential Sources of Contamination

After the wellhead protection zones are mapped, the team should identify existing and potential sources of contamination from all sources, including:

- residential uses, especially septic systems, the use of yard chemicals, and abandoned wells;
- commercial uses, especially gas stations, dry cleaners, junkyards, and car washes;
- transportation uses that may result in oil and gasoline runoff, spills, and road salts;
- industrial uses, especially chemical manufacturing, storage tanks, pipelines, and mining;
- agricultural uses, especially feedlots, manure storage and application, and improper storage or application of pesticides, herbicides, and fertilizers;
- institutional or public uses, especially landfills, sewage treatment plants, and golf courses; and
- hazardous wastes, especially Superfund sites, Resource Conservation and Recovery Act and Comprehensive Environmental Response, Compensation, and Liability Act Information System (CERCLIS) generators and sites, spill sites, and other hazardous waste sources (see Chapters 6 and 7).

Hazardous waste sites may be identified through various state and federal agencies, or a private vendor can provide this data in GIS format for a fee. Other potential contaminant sites, especially larger, or public ones, may be identified at the county level. More local potential contaminant sites may need to be identified through a field survey, research, or discussions with older members of the community who may have historic knowledge of illegal landfills and other potential problem sites. Known or potential sources of contamination should be mapped; again, a GIS system is ideal for this.

Evaluate Alternative Protection Tools and Techniques

Next, the team should evaluate alternative tools and techniques for wellhead protection. There is a wide variety of effective regulatory as well as voluntary techniques that a community can use to protect wellhead and aquifer areas. The major approaches that are used are as follows:

Wellhead Protection Zoning

A wellhead protection zone in the form of an overlay district can restrict the type of land uses allowed within the delineated wellhead protection areas. Restrictions can include the prohibition of certain uses or a conditional use process to ensure that new development will be properly sited to avoid polluting groundwater. The overlay district can include setback requirements for new development and buffers of trees and shrubs. For instance, Renton, Washington, has banned all new on-site septic systems in its aquifer protection zones and requires new homes and businesses to connect to central sewer systems. In one protection zone, any businesses that store more than 20 gallons of hazardous materials were given until 2003 to reduce their hazardous inventories or move out (Homsy 1997, 11).

Purchase of Land or Conservation Easements

The purchase of land or conservation easements on property can give the public direct control over land uses and activities in the wellhead protection area, particularly in Zone I. The purchase of a conservation easement is less expensive than the fee simple purchase of land, and the easement document can specify the types of land uses and activities allowed and even limit certain practices, such as pesticide spraying, that could affect groundwater quality.

On-Site Septic System Ordinance

An on-site septic ordinance can regulate the siting, maintenance, periodic clean-out, and replacement of on-site septic systems to help ensure that they function properly and do not pollute groundwater.

Wellhead Protection Sign

These signs can be placed on highways at the perimeter of wellhead protection areas to alert private landowners and the public about the location and importance of the wellhead protection area, and the need to notify authorities in the event of contaminant spills.

Remediation and Monitoring Contaminated Sites

Contaminated sites should be remediated and monitored. Remediation actions will depend upon the seriousness of the problem. Actions may include replacement of old and malfunctioning septic systems, replacement of leaking storage tanks, moving feedlots, or closing landfills. Monitoring can be done through test wells and regular testing to determine whether contaminants are migrating toward public water wells or groundwater sources.

STEP 5
Develop and Implement a Plan of Action

The wellhead protection team finally work with the community to develop and implement a plan of action, making use of a combination of the tools and techniques. A series of informational workshops and meetings will both keep the public informed and solicit input and feedback. The plan of action should include a contingency plan for how the public water system will respond to drought, other natural disaster, or emergency, such as a chemical spill.

If new wells will be developed as part of the public water system, the wellhead protection plan should incorporate them into the plan.

Effective wellhead protection involves a partnership effort, including the public water supplier, one or more communities receiving drinking water, and one or more communities where the wells are located. Effective protection requires cooperation, coordination, and creativity to meet these different needs.

Aquifer and Watershed Protection

Aquifer and watershed protection involves safeguarding much broader areas of land than wellheads, but often not with the same degree of rigor or exactness. The same five-step approach can be used to develop an aquifer or watershed protection program. An aquifer protection program can help prevent the contamination of multiple public water systems that may be located close to one another. In such a case, the costs of delineating several overlapping wellhead protection areas might not be worthwhile or necessary. Good information may already exist on the location of area aquifers. Another benefit to an aquifer protection program is that it can be used to extend protection to potential future wellhead sites before they are developed, if they lie within the same aquifer.

A challenge to the aquifer protection approach is that aquifers often underlie several different municipalities, making cooperation and coordination with neighboring communities critical. A county or regional planning commission may be helpful in getting an aquifer protection program off the ground. Where there are multiple municipalities, the tools and techniques selected to implement protection do not need to be the same, though similar programs will allow participants to use each other as resources, and so should be encouraged.

Watershed protection programs have similar benefits and challenges as aquifer protection programs, with a few differences. Watersheds include even larger areas than aquifers and have attracted the interest and involvement of county conservation districts, state water agencies, the EPA, and nonprofit watershed groups. The primary interest of all these participants is surface water quality, however, and not water supply (see Chapter 4).

LOCAL PLANNING
FOR WATER SUPPLY

Where counties have completed water supply plans, communities may incorporate inventory information, analysis, goals, and recommendations for action into the local comprehensive plan. Where no such water supply plan exists, municipalities should work with the community water systems that provide service within their boundaries and other state and local sources to compile the necessary data in the Natural Resources Inventory section of the comprehensive plan. In addition to planning for adequate future water supplies to meet the needs of consumers and industry, the local comprehensive plan should ensure the provision of an adequate future supply of water for recreation, wildlife, and energy needs. Municipalities should review their land use ordinances and revise them where appropriate to safeguard potable water supplies as well as manage local water resources for other purposes.

Inventory

Planners should gather information on and map the geology, hydrology, and watershed and aquifer boundaries within the community. Any delineated wellhead protection areas and sole-source aquifers should also be noted. Some of this information may already be available from a county or regional water supply plan. Areas with water constraints, such as locations with low water yields or high water tables, and any impaired waterways or water bodies should be identified.

It is helpful to identify the community's existing and potential large water users. Common large water users include thermal electrical generating plants, food processors, agriculture, confined animal feeding operations, electronic equipment manufacturers, chemical producers, metal and petroleum refiners, makers of paper products, golf courses, hospitals, and hotel/restaurant complexes. Also, information should be gathered and

maps drawn to show water bodies used for recreation, wildlife habitat, and energy generation. Any problems community water systems have experienced meeting SDWA requirements should be described. Finally, information on the community's public water systems and current water use should be noted as in the inventory for county water supply plans in the discussion above.

Analysis

Communities should use their 20-year population projections as a basis for projecting future water needs over the next 20 years. The number of people who should receive public water will depend upon the extent of planned growth areas and the existing and projected capacity of the public water system. Projected water needs for nonresidential uses will depend on the types of anticipated commercial and industrial users, and public and institutional users.

Planners should analyze the growth potential of the community's large water users, and the likelihood of additional large water users to locate in the community and their projected future water needs. The availability of public water together with other public utilities and services can have a significant impact on the willingness of industry and business to locate in an area. Industries are often reluctant to use groundwater because of its variability in quality and potential fluctuations in supply at certain times of the year. Public water supplies generally provide more reliable water quality and quantity.

It is useful to estimate groundwater recharge rates in rural areas to identify adequate water supplies where public water is not available. Most residences have an average water use of about 150 gallons per day (Adams County, Pennsylvania 2001). At this rate of use, groundwater yields of more than 3 GPM with the water held in storage tanks or 5 GPM without storage are adequate.

Goals and Objectives

The community should draft goals and objectives for water supply in the comprehensive plan after consultation with the larger community water systems serving the area. Goals and objectives should seek to protect surface and groundwater sources, assure that growth and development do not exceed sustainable water capacity, and encourage patterns of development that are consistent with public water supply systems. For sample goals and objectives, see Table 3-4.

Action Strategy

The Action Strategy should include tools and techniques for achieving water supply goals and objectives as well as a timetable. Water supply benchmarks should be identified and progress toward those benchmarks evaluated in an annual report on the environment. Specific action recommendations for water supply might include:

- coordinating with public water suppliers to ensure that planned future water service areas match planned future growth areas;
- adopting and implementing wellhead protection zoning for the community's public water wells;
- working with state and federal agencies, community water systems, and private land trusts and watershed associations to purchase land or conservation easements to land adjacent to public water sources;
- adopting a septic system ordinance to require the periodic clean-out, maintenance, and replacement of on-lot septic systems; and
- adopting an on-lot well ordinance to require the grouting of all on-lot wells and the proper abandonment of wells that are no longer used.

Table 3-4
Sample Public Water Supply Goals and Objectives in the Comprehensive Plan

Natural Resources	
Goal	To protect public water supplies as long-term drinking water sources.
Goal	To protect aquifer recharge areas to maintain or enhance the rate of groundwater recharge to ensure dependable future water supply.
Objective	Purchase land adjacent to the city reservoir to protect the public water supply.
Objective	Draft a wellhead area protection ordinance to protect aquifer recharge areas and groundwater supplies.
Land Use	
Objective	Discourage new development in areas that would threaten long-term public water supplies.
Objective	Promote compact development and encourage infill of vacant land and underutilized downtown sites to reduce necessary extensions of public water.
Economic Base	
Objective	Promote water supply protection and capacity enhancement to make the community attractive to new development and to sustain existing development.
Community Facilities	
Objective	Regularly test any municipally owned water supplies to ensure compliance with federal Safe Drinking Water Act standards.

Zoning Ordinance

One of the original purposes of zoning was to separate conflicting land uses. Intensive commercial, industrial, residential, and agricultural uses should be sited away from public surface and groundwater supplies. Planning and zoning should also direct development away from areas with low groundwater yields as may occur at higher altitudes, in certain geologic formations, or in arid climates.

A wellhead or aquifer zoning overlay district can be used to place additional limits on development on lands overlying public groundwater supplies. A landowner or developer would have to meet the requirements of both the overlay and the base zone. The zoning ordinance can enforce large minimum lot sizes or density standards of 25 or more acres for farm and forestry operations, and thereby promote recharge and discourage sprawl. The zoning ordinance can also limit impervious surfaces to no more than 10% lot coverage in important wellhead or aquifer recharge areas. An urban growth boundary can limit the extension of public water lines into the countryside and thus encourage compact development that can be served by public water systems. To be successful, zoning inside the growth boundary must encourage compact, intensive development, but tightly restrict development outside the boundary.

Subdivision Regulations

Subdivision regulations can help protect water supplies in several ways. First, subdivision regulations can require proof that new on-lot wells can produce a certain minimum amount of potable water and will not adversely impact water supplies on neighboring properties. Second, subdivision regulations can require developers to demonstrate a long-term adequate water supply for any development involving 10 or more dwelling units or more than 1 acre for commercial, industrial, or institutional use. Third, subdivision regulations can require new development within 1 mile of public water systems to connect to those systems as a way to limit sprawl and avoid the proliferation of private wells.

Communities with limestone or karst geology subject to sinkholes should have subdivision regulations that prohibit storm retention ponds and that do not allow stormwater to be directed toward known sinkholes or depressions.

Woodland and vegetation standards can require developers to retain or replace a fixed proportion of on-site trees of a certain dimension or in vegetative cover to reduce runoff.

Groundwater recharge can be helped by setting a limit on the area of a land parcel that can be covered by impervious surfaces.

Especially in arid climates, the subdivision regulations could require that landscaping use native vegetation, which tends to need less water than nonnative species. Subdivision regulations also could encourage homeowners and businesses to install cisterns to collect rainwater for watering lawns and gardens and washing cars. Finally, subdivision regulations that permit clustering can encourage the siting of required open space to include any wellhead or aquifer protection areas on site. Similarly, any mandatory dedication of parkland for residential subdivisions or other development can target wellhead or aquifer protection areas for preservation.

On-Site Septic System Ordinance

An on-site septic system ordinance can help protect water supplies by requiring adequate siting, maintenance, pumping, and replacement of systems. Property owners should be required to pump out on-site septic systems at least every three years. Alternatively, a municipality or county could create a local on-site septic district in which it charges each household an annual fee, and in return takes responsibility for the maintenance and replacement of on-site septic systems. Minimum lot sizes should be large enough to accommodate an on-site septic system and a replacement leach field.

On-Site Well Ordinance

An on-site well ordinance can help protect water supplies by establishing well siting, construction, water quality testing, and abandonment standards. These standards should result in the siting of properly grouted and tested wells at a safe distance from potential contamination threats.

Capital Improvements Program

Water facilities, including water treatment plants and water lines, are major infrastructure components and have a powerful influence on the location of development. The extension of public water service can promote more intensive development and even sprawl. Therefore, any municipal or county CIP should be consistent with the future land use map of the comprehensive plan and the zoning map. Where public sewer lines are planned, public water lines should be considered as well, particularly in areas with low groundwater yields.

Sometimes, multiple purposes can be served through the same capital improvement project. Communities that have, for instance, identified a need for additional parkland and that have an identified wellhead or aquifer protection area, can consider the creation of a public park that overlies part or all of these areas.

CIPs should identify potential funding sources for water system improvements, expansion, and water source protection. As mentioned above, the EPA makes grants to state revolving loan funds for the construction and upgrade of water and wastewater systems. The Economic Development Administration within the U.S. Department of Commerce makes grants to economically distressed communities for water and sewer projects. The U.S. Department of Agriculture's Rural Utilities Service offers loans and grants for water and wastewater projects in rural areas and communities of fewer than 10,000 people. Community Development Block Grant (CDBG) funds from the U.S. Department of Housing and Urban Development (HUD) can be used for water and wastewa-

ter projects. The CDBG funds can come directly from HUD or are passed through the state government's CDBG small-cities program.

WHAT TO LOOK FOR IN A DEVELOPMENT REVIEW

The proposed development should be evaluated for consistency with the comprehensive plan and CIP, and for compliance with the zoning ordinance, subdivision regulations, and any other applicable laws (see Table 3-5). The planning commission should ensure that adequate potable water will be available to the proposed development and will continue to be available to existing neighboring water users. The proposed development should not pollute ground or surface water.

CASE STUDY

CASE STUDY 3-1
New York City's Water Supply Protection Program

Several large U.S. cities rely heavily on distant water sources to meet their water demands. The development of rural lands surrounding important reservoirs not only creates competition for water supplies with these far-off cities, but also creates a serious pollution threat. The pollution may come from several sources, such as sewage treatment plants, malfunctioning on-site septic systems, farm and lawn fertilizers, pesticides, manure, and oil- and salt-laden runoff from roads.

New York City is the only large city in the U.S. that does not filter its water. In 1997 and 2002, the city was granted waivers from the EPA's Surface Water Treatment Rule, which requires drinking water systems that depend on surface water to filter the water unless strict water quality standards are met. New York City's drinking water comes from a series of 19 reservoirs in the Catskill Mountains, Delaware Valley, and east of the Hudson River in the Croton Reservoir system (see

Table 3-5
A Checklist of Water Supply Issues in a Development Review

1.	Will the proposed project use a private on-site well or a public water supply?
2.	If a private well is used, where will it be located in relation to neighboring properties, existing or planned on-site septic systems, known contaminant sites, or nearby streams or water bodies? Will required setbacks be met?
3.	Is the proposed development in a wellhead or aquifer protection area? If so, does it meet the wellhead or aquifer protection standards that have been adopted?
4.	If public water is used, how much water would the proposed project use and what is the capacity of the public water system?
5.	If private water is proposed for a large development, has an aquifer test demonstrated that planned withdrawals will not adversely impact neighboring water use?
6.	How much impervious surface does the project create? Is it within the limits of local standards?
7.	How much and what type of vegetation is proposed to be removed? Do local standards limit removal or require replacement?
8.	What are the site drainage and stormwater runoff patterns? What stormwater management techniques will be used? Do they meet local standards?
9.	What best management practices have been proposed to promote groundwater infiltration?
10.	Has the developer obtained any necessary state or federal permits?

Figure 3-4). The reservoirs supply 9 million New Yorkers with about 1 billion gallons of water each day. The watershed that feeds the reservoirs covers about 2,000 square miles. However, increased development in the watershed was threatening water quality in the early 1990s when the EPA gave New York City a choice: either build a $6 billion plant to filter its drinking water or institute a watershed protection plan to safeguard water quality by the year 2002 (Revkin 1997, 25, 27).

In 1997, New York City decided to work with the counties and towns in the watershed and pay about $1 billion to protect land near reservoirs through voluntary land purchases, improvements in farming practices, repair of failing septic systems and sewage treatment plants, and by prosecuting polluters.

In 1997, the city owned less than 4% of the land in the watershed (*ibid.*, 25). The city planned to protect more than 300,000 acres through outright

purchase or buying development rights at a cost of up to $260 million; as of 2002, more than 25,000 acres had been preserved. The protected land is intended to form a buffer around the reservoirs and along waterways. Clearly, not all of the streambanks and reservoir edges can be protected. Local land use planning and zoning are remarkably weak in the New York City watershed; some towns do not even have zoning. It is thus unlikely that local government efforts will be of much help in protecting the city's water supply.

New York City designated more than $200 million for upgrading 102 sewage treatment plants that release treated sewage into the watershed. About $35 million was spent to improve the manure management practices of dairy farmers, so that bacteria (such as giardia, crytospiridium, and Escherichia coli (E. coli)) would not enter the streams and end up in reservoirs. According to *The New York Times* (1999, A26), the city allocated $14 million for replacing failing on-site septic systems, but there are an estimated 128,000 systems in the watershed, and the city has to find them first. Meanwhile, the city has an active watershed police force that identifies and prosecutes polluters.

Despite the large amount of money New York City has spent in the watershed, there are still some hard feelings among the local residents over the intrusion of the city and its purchase of land that removed property from the local property tax rolls.

By 2000, according to a report by the New York Attorney General's Office, New York City had fallen far behind schedule in its program to upgrade the 102 sewage treatment plants that were discharging wastewater in the city's reservoirs. No construction had begun to modernize the treatment plants, and each day more than 10 million gallons of inadequately treated wastewater was mixing with city water supplies (Revkin 2000, B1). A major obstacle has been the fact that the sewage treatment facilities are owned and operated by the local governments near the reservoirs, not by New York City. The EPA could still require New York City to build a filtration plant if it is unable to get the sewage treatment plants upgraded or is too slow in completing the improvements.

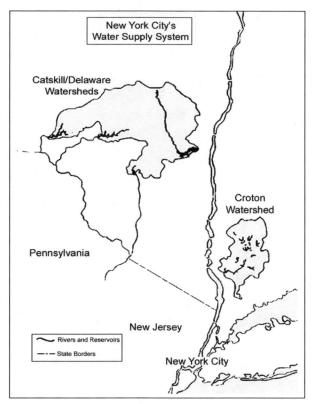

3-4   New York City's water supply system.

Source: New York City Department of Environmental Protection

4

Planning for Sustainable Water Quality

In many ways, clean water is the fuel that powers the nation's economic engine.

U.S. ENVIRONMENTAL PROTECTION AGENCY
(EPA), *LIQUID ASSETS 2000: AMERICA'S
WATER RESOURCES AT A TURNING POINT*

There's no way to treat ground water to its pre-contamination state.

LOIS EPSTEIN, ENVIRONMENTAL ENGINEER,
ENVIRONMENTAL DEFENSE FUND

Clean, fresh water is necessary for drinking, bathing, swimming, fish and wildlife habitats, irrigating crops, food processing, and a number of manufacturing processes. Clean water is first and foremost a public health issue. Reliable, long-term supplies of clean water are essential for sustainable communities and regions. In 2000, according to the EPA, about 40% of America's waterways were not fit for drinking or swimming; and about four out of every five U.S. residents were living within 10 miles of a polluted lake, river, stream, or coastal area (U.S. EPA 2000a).

Polluted water can be cleaned up. Perhaps the most dramatic example in America is Lake Erie, which in 1970 was declared "dead" because of the lack of aquatic life. Today, Lake Erie has an abundance of fish. However, the definition of clean water ultimately depends on the uses of that water. For example, water to drink must be cleaner than water to swim in, which in turn must be cleaner than water used to water lawns. In

order to clean up water, it is important to know where pollution is coming from and how these sources can be modified.

LAND USE IMPACTS ON WATER QUALITY

Land uses generate physical, biological, and chemical pollution that jeopardize water quality. Although some water pollution may occur naturally, such as eroding streambanks, most water pollution is the result of human activities.

Water pollution occurs when a chemical, physical, or biological substance exceeds the capacity of a water body to assimilate or break down that substance and harms the aquatic ecosystem or water supply. While water itself can only dilute pollutants, bacteria in the water and adjacent soils and vegetation can actually break down or absorb pollution. The assimilative capacity of water largely depends on the amounts and types of pollution, whether surface or groundwater is involved, the size and flow of the water body, and the time of year. Moving surface water is always more quickly cleansed than standing water or groundwater, because it is regularly replenished by precipitation and baseflow. Assimilative capacity is greater in the spring (with snowmelt and higher precipitation rates and higher streamflows) than in the late summer, when little rain falls and streamflows are lower.

Table 4-1
Nonpoint Water Pollution Sources

	Source	Type of Pollution
1.	Farm Fields and Grazing Land	Manure; pesticides including herbicides, insecticides, fungicides, and rodenticides; and fertilizer runoff into water bodies or groundwater. Nutrients cause algae blooms on surface water. Elevated nitrates, coliform bacteria, and pesticides enter drinking water supplies. Bare fields and overgrazed pasture and rangeland contribute to soil erosion and siltation of waterways, which harm aquatic life and reduce water quality.
2.	Logging and Harvesting	Soil erosion and siltation from logging roads and timber increase the turbidity of rivers and streams, harming fish. Loss of streamside trees reduces shade and increases water temperature, reduces water storage capacity, and destabilizes or destroys streambanks.
3.	Road Building and Construction Sites	Soil erosion and siltation from road and building construction increase the turbidity of rivers and streams, harming fish.
4.	Runoff from Impervious Surfaces	Rain and melting snow carry oil, gasoline, antifreeze, and salt into water bodies and groundwater.
5.	On-Site Septic Systems	Malfunctioning septic systems release nitrogen, phosphorus, and fecal coliform bacteria into groundwater. Even properly functioning septic systems release some pollution into groundwater.
6.	Lawns and Golf Courses	Fertilizer and pesticide runoff into water bodies or groundwater.
7.	Motor Vehicles	Sulfur dioxide and nitrogen oxide emissions cause acid rain, snow, and fog, which raise the acidity of water bodies and harm aquatic life.
8.	Mines	Acid mine drainage from mined waste and spoils leach toxic chemicals, such as sulfuric acid, into waterways.

Moving surface water receives oxygen through aeration, which enables bacteria in the water to break down additional waste. A large lake or standing body of water generally dilutes more waste than smaller bodies. The assimilative capacity of groundwater is very limited and mainly depends on the filtering capacities of overlying soil, rock, and vegetation.

Water Pollution Sources

Water pollution sources can be divided into point sources, which come from stationary and easily identifiable sites such as a sewage outfall pipe or a factory, and nonpoint sources, which come from dispersed or less identifiable locations (see Table 4-1). Nonpoint sources of pollution are often difficult to identify and control because they can be hard to see, they may be mobile or temporary, and the pollution generated may vary considerably over time. Yet, studies report that between 70% and 90% of all water pollution comes from nonpoint source pollutants (*ibid.*). There are more than 40 potential nonpoint sources of water pollution.

The EPA has identified stormwater runoff as a major source of water pollution. The 1996 National Water Quality Inventory estimated that urban/suburban stormwater runoff was a major contributing factor to the pollution of 13% of the nation's impaired rivers, 21% of impaired lake areas, and 45% of impaired estuaries. Runoff from construction sites contributed to the pollution of

6% of the nation's impaired rivers, 11% of impaired lake areas, and 11% of impaired estuaries (U.S. EPA 2000c).

In a 1998 report to Congress on the nation's water quality, the EPA found that siltation and bacteria were the most common pollutants in rivers and streams, with farm runoff and discharges from factories, sewage treatment plants, and power plants being the leading causes of pollution. In addition, the report found that nearly 16.3 million acres of lakes, reservoirs, and ponds had water quality problems, often resulting in fish consumption advisories (U.S. EPA 1998a). In lakes and ponds, nutrients from farming and heavy metals from industry were the leading sources of pollution. Of particular concern was the poor water quality in the five Great Lakes, which contain nearly one-fifth of the world's supply of fresh surface water. Among the Great Lakes states, 90% of the shorelines that were studied showed impaired water for designated uses. All of the states bordering the Great Lakes have issued advisories to limit the eating of fish from the lakes. Toxic organic chemicals and pesticides have been the leading types of pollution.

Surface Water Pollution vs. Groundwater Pollution

Some water pollution sources affect mostly surface water and some mostly groundwater. Historically, point source pollutants have been thought to contaminate mostly surface waters, yet point sources are now being recognized as major contributors to groundwater pollution. Similarly, non-point sources are now being identified as significant sources of surface water pollution, but generally have not been adequately identified as causes of groundwater pollution.

While surface water is more vulnerable to contamination, groundwater is more resistant to clean-up. Groundwater has no natural cleansing process. Groundwater pollution occurs when the contaminants from land use activities exceed the filtering capabilities of the vegetation and soils. Groundwater pollution is not as easy to detect as surface water pollution, and is harder to trace to its source (see Figure 4-1). Contaminated groundwater is 20 to 40 times more expensive to clean up than preventing pollution in the first place. Some contaminants are almost impossible to remove.

Groundwater pollution can be caused by old, poorly maintained, and improperly used septic systems; stormwater runoff; the injection of waste into wells; excess fertilizers and pesticides on farm fields; leakage from landfills and underground gasoline storage tanks; improper storage and disposal of hazardous materials; oil and gas wells; and salt water intrusion into aquifers. Groundwater pollution is a serious and growing problem in many rural and suburbanizing communities that typically rely on groundwater for drinking water supplies. In the late 1990s, hundreds of thousands of U.S. residents became sick and about 900 died each year from drinking contaminated water. More than half of the illnesses and deaths came from groundwater sources, according to the Centers for Disease Control (Homsy 1997, 10-11).

Polluting substances can enter wells by seeping through the soil and fractures in rocks down to aquifers; this is especially true in areas with carbonate geology featuring solution channels and sinkholes. In addition, polluting substances can be drawn down by the pumping action of wells and

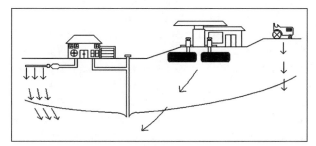

4-1 Sources of groundwater contamination.

can directly enter well water through unsealed, ungrouted, or abandoned wells.

Types of Water Pollution

Physical Pollution

Physical pollution of water includes soil erosion that causes sediment pollution of surface waters, floods that wash soil and debris into rivers and streams, and thermal heating of water by power plants and factories.

Sediment Pollution

Sediment pollution is the most common type of physical water pollution (U.S. EPA 1998a). Sedimentation makes water gritty, turbid, and unfit for drinking and swimming. Turbidity is a measure of the suspended solids in water that affect clarity; the higher the turbidity, the more "clouded" the water. Turbidity blocks sunlight to submerged aquatic vegetation, reducing the plant matter available for fish to feed on. Soil particles in water also clog fish gills and make breathing difficult. Perhaps most importantly, soil particles readily transport chemical pollutants into surface waters.

The pattern and type of land use practices greatly influence sedimentation levels. Agricultural practices, timber harvesting, and the removal of plant cover from construction sites cause the most sedimentation. Soil loss is greatest in areas with steep slopes, no vegetative cover, and along streambanks (see Figure 4-2). Plowing steep slopes and leaving harvested land bare of cover crops render land vulnerable to water and wind erosion. Overgrazing can contribute to soil erosion by removing protective vegetation. Stream channeling causes water to flow faster and increases the erosion of streambanks. Harvesting trees from steep slopes and in places with significant rainfall can contribute greatly to the siltation of rivers and streams. Construction sites involve land clearing and excavation, which expose large areas of soil to rainfall and potential runoff prob-

lems. Impervious surfaces (such as roads, parking lots, and buildings) raise the volume and speed of stormwater runoff and increase soil erosion (Figure 4-3). Sprawling patterns of development generate from five to seven times more sediment than a forest and nearly two times more sediment than compact development, according to the Chesapeake Bay Foundation (2000).

Thermal Pollution

Thermal pollution occurs naturally on hot summer days or when power plants and factories use water to cool energy equipment. Electric plants alone use an estimated 3.2 billion gallons of water each day (Owen *et al.* 1998, 214). Plants and factories emit thermal plumes into the water that can reduce the ability of the water to assimilate other kinds of pollution and raise water temperatures, which can harm or kill fish. Thermal pollution can also occur from stormwater that runs off of hot pavement into rivers and streams.

Biological Pollution

According to the U.S. EPA (1998a), biological pollution causes as many as 500,000 U.S. residents to become sick from drinking contaminated water each year. In 1997, drinking water systems distributing water to more than 10 million people violated standards for fecal coliform bacteria. That same year, the toxic microbe, *Pfiesteria piscida*, killed tens of thousands of fish in Maryland. In 1993, an outbreak of cryptospiridium (a disease-causing microbe) contaminated the drinking water supply of Milwaukee, Wisconsin, making 400,000 people sick and killing more than 50 others. (For information on public and private drinking water violations, see the Environmental Working Group in the Contacts section at the back of this book.)

Centralized municipal sewage collection and treatment systems are allowed to discharge treated wastewater into rivers and streams or through spray irrigation onto land. An estimated

4-2 Soil erosion and sedimentation along a streambank where trees have been removed.

Source: Katherine Daniels

4-3 Acres of impervious surface in a regional shopping mall parking lot increase stormwater runoff.

Source: Katherine Daniels

772 U.S. cities have combined storm and sanitary sewers that cause municipal sewage treatment plants to overflow during heavy rainstorms or snowmelts; dangerous levels of bacteria-laden sewage are then released into rivers, lakes, and estuaries, posing threats to drinking water supplies and often leading to beach closings. The EPA has estimated that it could cost as much as $46 billion to fix the nation's combined sewer overflow problem (U.S. EPA 2001).

On-lot septic systems are a significant source of fecal coliform and fecal staphylococcus bacterial contamination of groundwater. Many households with on-lot septic systems also have on-lot wells that are located close to the septic systems. In a

SIDEBAR 4-1

Potentially Deadly E. Coli Bacteria

Late summer is the time for county fairs. Rides, food, and farm animals are wonderful attractions and wholesome fun. But, in early September 1999, New York State suffered its worst outbreak of Escherichia coli (E. coli) bacteria contamination. A young girl and an elderly man died, 65 people were hospitalized, and more than 1,000 cases of poisoning were confirmed among the visitors to the Washington County Fair in Greenwich, New York.

The source was initially thought to be a nearby cattle barn. A 12-foot-deep well that stood only 83 feet away and that provided water for food vendors may have been polluted after a heavy rain swept manure from the barn area into the soil. However, a state investigation discovered that another potential source of pollution was a nearby dormitory with an on-site septic system just 20 feet from the well. A state report concluded that it was impossible to tell which of the two possible sources had actually contaminated the well water (*Times Union* 2000a, A1).

In any case, the well water was not treated with disinfectant. This fact—together with the proximity of the well to the barn and the septic drainage field, and the well's shallow depth—posed health threats that were recognized too late. In 2000, a new well water system was installed at the fair. The well was sited 260 feet away from the nearest septic system, a fence was placed around the well, and the well was equipped with a chlorination system to disinfect the water and a small filtration system (*Times Union* 2000b, B2).

The E. coli epidemic was unexpected, in part because America's water quality has largely improved since the passage of the Clean Water Act of 1972 and the Safe Drinking Water Act of 1974 and subsequent Amendments. Across the country, public water systems are required to disinfect drinking water; however, because water at most fairgrounds is provided on a temporary basis, this water is not regulated as rigorously as water systems that supply water every day. In addition, Congress has exempted some public water systems with fewer than 5,000 regular customers from the disinfection requirement because of the perceived high cost this would impose on small water systems.

1997 report to Congress, the EPA noted that about 70 million Americans—or 25% of the national population—were using some type of on-site septic system, and on-site septic systems were being used to serve 37% of new development (U.S. EPA 1997). More importantly, between 10% to 30% of all on-site systems fail each year (Rubin *et al.* 2000, 15-17).

Malfunctioning on-lot septic systems may or may not be noticeable to property owners. Many on-lot septic systems and cesspools were either improperly sited, have outlived their useful lives, are improperly used, or are not properly maintained. Even new, properly functioning systems contribute pollutants to the groundwater. Few municipalities require on-lot septic systems to be pumped out and maintained on a regular basis, and many older systems are located quite close to lakes, rivers, private wells, and even public wells. Land application of manure, septage, and sludge for farm fertilizer can also contribute to bacterial contamination of groundwater.

Chemical Pollution

Chemical pollution results from inorganic and organic sources. Inorganic chemicals are natural or man-made substances that are often toxic and do not readily break down in the environment. Organic chemicals can also be natural or man-made and toxic, but do break down in the environment.

Nutrient Pollution

Nutrient pollution includes excess nitrates, phosphates, and potassium that come from chemical fertilizers and human and animal wastes. While these nutrients are necessary for successful plant growth, excess nitrates and phosphates are prime contributors to water pollution. Nitrates in groundwater are a particular problem; concentrations of over 10 milligrams per liter are a potential health hazard to unborn children, causing oxygen deprivation and resultant mental retardation, and may also be linked to liver cancer. High levels of nitrates are also a potential health hazard for livestock, causing bovine infertility and low milk yields. Phosphates are not as readily transmitted to groundwater because they tend to bind with soil. Thus, they either remain in the soil or, where there is erosion and subsequent sedimentation in streams, contribute to the pollution of surface waters.

Sources of nutrient pollution include on-lot septic systems, sanitary sewage and package treatment plants, combined sanitary and storm sewer systems, water treatment plants, inadequate barnyard drainage, poorly constructed or maintained manure storage, unrestricted livestock access to streams, and the overapplication of fertilizer, manure, sludge, and septage to land.

Agricultural runoff is the leading source of runoff pollution in the U.S. according to the 1998 National Water Quality Inventory (U.S. EPA 1998b). Confined animal operations raise concerns about potential high levels of runoff from livestock manure, particularly where such operations are near streams or vulnerable groundwater sources. Rainstorms and flooding can worsen the potential adverse impacts. The application of manure to farm fields can be an effective and cost-efficient means of fertilizing farm fields. However, confined animal operations often occupy parcels that are too small to fully use the nutrients in the manure. Nutrients that are applied in excess of what can be taken up by plants either run off over the land surface to nearby streams or infiltrate through soil and rocks to underlying groundwater, where they can accumulate in unacceptably high concentrations.

Inorganic nitrogen and phosphorus from detergents and chemical fertilizers are major forms of nutrient pollution that can cause algae blooms as inorganic chemicals are converted to organic forms that algae plants can use. In the eutrophication of lakes, ponds, rivers, and estuaries, bacteria feed on the decomposing algae and organic nutrients from manure, sludge, and septage. This process reduces the oxygen content of the water, and causes stress on fish and other aquatic life, which depend on adequate oxygen. Land-applied sludge and septage have become common in farming areas as a supplement to commercial fertilizers, thus saving money for farmers. However, sludge and septage may contain high nutrient loads and even pathogens and heavy metals, raising concerns about potential contamination of nearby surface and groundwater sources.

Biochemical oxygen demand or biological oxygen demand (BOD) is a measure of the amount of oxygen needed by bacteria and other microorganisms to break down organic material in a body of water, at a certain temperature, and over a certain amount of time. The more organic matter there is in the water, the higher the BOD. Generally, the lower the level of dissolved oxygen, the more polluted the water and the less able the water is to assimilate additional pollution. Stormwater runoff with high nutrient loads and discharges from wastewater treatment plants and storm sewers are leading causes of eutrophication, high BOD levels, and low dissolved oxygen levels, especially in lakes and estuaries.

Natural Contaminants

Inorganic chemicals can occur naturally in soil and water or can be released into waterways through human activity. Water quality is partly influenced by geology. For example, water can range from "soft" (low in mineral content) to

SIDEBAR 4-2

Lakes and Ponds and Eutrophication

Lakes and ponds are more vulnerable to pollution than rivers and streams because moving water is better aerated and can thus assimilate more pollution. Lakes and ponds follow a cycle of slowly filling in with sediment and plants. Over the course of thousands of years, lakes and ponds mature into bogs and forests.

Nitrogen and phosphorus nutrients speed up this aging cycle to a matter of a few hundred years for lakes and a few decades for ponds through a process known as eutrophication. Nutrient-rich discharges from sewage treatment plants, farm and lawn fertilizers, and leaking septic systems can cause green algae blooms as inorganic nutrients are converted to organic nutrients. When the algae die, they sink to the bottom of the lake or pond and serve as fertilizer for weeds, including aggressive exotic weeds such as Eurasian watermilfoil. The decomposing algae and weeds use up oxygen in the water, putting stress on fish and other aquatic life. Algae and weeds also reduce water clarity and give water an odor and odd taste.

"very hard" (high in mineral content) in limestone geology. Other naturally occurring quality threats include iron, manganese, phosphorus, and sulfur. Radiation can enter water from radon gas or from uranium or radium deposits. Long exposure to radiation can cause certain kinds of cancers.

Hazardous Chemicals

Potentially toxic chemicals include an array of naturally occurring heavy metals, such as lead, copper, and zinc, and petroleum products. Coal-fired power plants are a major source of the toxic metal mercury, which mixes with water vapor and falls to earth with the rain. Mercury is the most common cause of fish consumption advisories.

According to the U.S. EPA (1999), 47 states issued 2,506 mercury advisories in 1998—an increase of almost 30% over the previous year. Minnesota led the nation with 825 fish advisories; Wisconsin was second with 447. Lead and copper still line some water supply distribution lines, exposing consumers to unacceptably high levels of these chemicals.

Pesticides (including insecticides, herbicides, rodenticides, and fungicides) can be a public health concern when they enter groundwater and waterways. Pesticides tend to bind with soil particles and are more likely to find their way into waterways through sediment transport and erosion than they are to percolate down into groundwater. Pesticides are used by homeowners, businesses, institutions, and farmers. Golf courses apply large amounts of pesticides—more per acre than any other land use. In response to growing concerns, the U.S. Golf Association has recently adopted a number of initiatives to reduce pesticide use and thus the impact it may have on surface and groundwater.

Finally, all types of chemicals, including nutrients, oil, gasoline, volatile organic compounds, antifreeze, pesticides, and road salts, are washed into surface waters through stormwater runoff. Rural, suburban, and urban runoff is difficult to control after development has occurred.

Toxic substances generated by commercial, industrial, and institutional activities can be released in chemical spills, leaks, outfalls, and dumps and contribute contaminants to waterways and groundwater. Spills occur primarily when vehicles in transit are involved in accidents and release hazardous substances. A major source of groundwater contamination is leaking underground gasoline storage tanks, which often go unnoticed until nearby wells are contaminated or until gasoline or fuel oil shows up in a nearby river or stream (see Figure 4-4). In 1990, the EPA gave owners of underground fuel tanks until December 1998 to fix leaking tanks. As of 2000, the EPA estimated that 110,000 of the nation's 750,000 under-

4-4 Abandoned gas station. Leaking underground gasoline tanks have led to the closure of many gas stations.

Source: Katherine Daniels

ground fuel storage tanks were still leaking (Zielbauer 2000, B7). Federal standards now require the approval of new underground fuel storage tanks and periodic inspection of installed underground storage tanks. Leaking hazardous waste disposal sites, sanitary landfills, and illegal dumps also continue to contribute contaminants to ground and surface water. In addition, significant direct discharge of pollutants into waterways is legally allowed through a federal permitting process under the Clean Water Act (see discussion below).

FEDERAL WATER QUALITY STANDARDS AND POLLUTION CONTROL

Water quality is first and foremost a matter of public health. Federal efforts to protect the nation's water quality are aimed at controlling and reducing water pollution and ensuring the quality of public drinking water systems. Prior to 1972, many cities and industries used rivers, lakes, and harbors

as open sewers; when the Clean Water Act was passed, only one-third of the nation's navigable waterways were considered safe for drinking or swimming. Funding programs for water and sewage treatment plant improvements, limits on industrial discharges into water bodies, and stricter federal drinking water standards have significantly improved the nation's water quality over the past 30 years. By 1998, the EPA reported that nearly two-thirds of the nation's surface waters met at least the Class B (swimmable) standard (U.S. EPA 2000b).

The Clean Water Act of 1972

The 1972 Amendments to the Federal Water Pollution Control Act, better known as the Clean Water Act of 1972, constitute the nation's primary legislation for establishing surface water quality standards, protection, and pollution clean-up (see Table 4-2). The main purpose of the Clean Water Act is "restoring and maintaining the chemical, physical, and biological integrity of the nation's waters."

The Clean Water Act is administered by the EPA, but the day-to-day regulation of water quality is mainly carried out by state water resources boards, departments of natural resources, or environmental departments. The EPA allows individual states to set quality standards for water used for purposes other than drinking. This is quite different from the Clean Air Act, under which the EPA has established national air quality standards (see Chapter 5). Still, the EPA's water quality standards program sets pollution goals and limits for individual water bodies.

The Clean Water Act is also noteworthy because it requires states to plan to maintain water quality, to protect against the degradation of high-quality waters and water bodies that already meet the swimmable and drinkable standards (see Table 4-3), and to continue to work toward the further clean-up of impaired waterways. The act also regulates the draining and filling of wetlands (see Chapter 10). Finally, the act includes provisions

Table 4-2
Clean Water Act Programs

1.	Section 201	Grants for construction of public sewage treatment plants.
2.	Section 208	State water quality standards and management plans, addressing the nondegradation of swimmable and drinkable waters and waters of "exceptional recreational or ecological significance," the identification and use of best management practices for the control of point and nonpoint pollution sources.
3.	Section 303(d)	State Total Maximum Daily Load process for prioritizing and implementing clean-up of impaired waterways. The state compiles a list of impaired waters by priority for clean-up, known as the 303(d) list.
4.	Section 305(b)	*Biennial Environmental Protection Agency Report* to Congress on the Nation's Water Quality, based on state-level data.
5.	Section 319	State plans and programs and federal loans and grants for the control of nonpoint source pollution and to publish reports.
6.	Section 402	National Pollutant Discharge Elimination System permit system for point and nonpoint sources of water pollution, including stormwater management permits and permits for confined animal feeding operations. This includes the monitoring of urban stormwater discharges into regulated streams.
7.	Section 403	Pretreatment of industrial sewage before discharge into municipal sewage treatment plants.
8.	Section 404	Wetlands permitting system for the draining and filling of wetlands (see Chapter 10).
9.	Section 503	Sewage sludge land application and disposal regulations.
10.	Section 604(b)	State water quality planning and assessment grants. Can be used for monitoring water quality and setting water quality standards.

Table 4-3
Water Quality Ratings

1.	Class A waters are suitable for public water supply, with disinfection. Quality is excellent.
2.	Class B waters are suitable for bathing, recreation, fish habitats, irrigation of crops, and other agricultural uses. Acceptable for public water supplies with filtration and disinfection. Quality is good.
3.	Class C waters are suitable for recreational boating, irrigation of crops that must be cooked before eaten, habitats for fish and wildlife, and certain industrial uses. Water quality is fair.
4.	Class D waters are suitable for supporting aerobic aquatic life and for hydropower, navigation, and some industrial uses. Water quality is poor.
5.	Class E waters carry untreated sewage or other pollutants in such concentrations that they cause a public nuisance. These waters are unfit for any use.

intended to minimize the pollution of water by requiring the pretreatment of industrial sewage, regulating the disposal of sewage sludge, and establishing planning procedures and construction grants for new and upgraded sewage treatment plants.

The National Pollutant Discharge Elimination System

Section 402 of the 1972 Clean Water Act prohibits the discharge of any pollutants into navigable waters from a point source, such as a factory or a power plant, unless the discharge has been authorized in a National Pollutant Discharge Elimination System (NPDES) permit. An individual, company, or local government can obtain a permit from the state environmental agency or from the EPA. Beginning in 1977, the EPA turned over most of the NPDES permitting, monitoring, and enforcement to the states. State discharge permits are known as State Pollutant Discharge Elimination System (SPDES) permits, or "Speedies." The permits typically run in five-year cycles.

All pollution discharge permits under Section 402 of the act must be consistent with the Section 208 state water quality management plans. Individual NPDES and SPDES permits are based on effluent guidelines that limit levels of different pollutants in wastewater. Also, the permits reflect overall water quality standards for a water body. From 1972 to 2000, the EPA and state environmental agencies issued and enforced more than 70,000 NDPES and SPDES permits (U.S. EPA 2000a).

The NPDES/SPDES permits are negotiated between the discharger and either the EPA or the state agency. The permit process has been criticized because, even if a discharger is meeting the terms of the permit, this does not mean that pollution is eliminated or even sufficiently reduced to improve water quality to drinkable or swimmable standards (Horton and Eichbaum 1991, 70-71). A permit may not require the most up-to-date pollution control technology. Also, the permit may not cover all of the pollutants released by a polluter into a waterway. Permitting is based on the type of watershed, with higher quality watersheds having more controls on permits and the highest quality watersheds not permitting any discharges. Finally, the monitoring and enforcement of the permits remains a time-consuming and expensive undertaking, and there are not always adequate personnel to do the job through the EPA or through many states.

Wastewater Treatment Construction and Planning

Wastewater treatment methods include disinfection, primary, secondary, and tertiary treatment. These levels of treatment range from the simplest to the most complex, with more polluted water requiring a greater level of treatment. Historically, communities with central sewer systems built primary treatment plants. However, secondary treatment is the minimum treatment now required under the Clean Water Act for potable water, and nearly all municipal treatment plants treat sewage to this level. By 1996, not quite two-thirds of all U.S. residents were served by secondary or tertiary sewage treatment plants (see Table 4-4).

Disinfection

All levels of wastewater treatment involve disinfection with chlorine or ozone as a final step before the release of treated effluent to waterways. Proper disinfection kills virtually all bacteria, many parasites, and some viruses.

Primary Treatment

Primary treatment involves the removal of solids and some nutrients from the water. When wastewater enters a treatment plant, it first passes through grit screens to remove large objects. The wastewater is then directed into settlement basins where organic solids either float or settle as sludge and are removed. The treated water is then disinfected and discharged into waterways, or given secondary treatment. Primary treatment removes nearly two-thirds of the solids, which

Table 4-4
U.S. Wastewater Treatment Facilities (1996)

Level of Treatment	Number of Facilities	Number of People Served (in millions)	Percent of U.S.
Primary	176	17.17	7
Secondary	9,388	81.94	31
Tertiary	4,428	82.92	31
Total	13,992	182.03	69

Source: U.S. Bureau of the Census, *Statistical Abstract of the United States, 1999*, p. 245

contain most of the chemical and biological contaminants in sewage, and a third of the inorganic nutrients.

Secondary Treatment

Secondary treatment features chemical and biological treatments to break down organic matter and remove chemicals, such as nitrogen, phosphorus, iron, and other metals. Two main secondary treatment methods may be used: the activated sludge process or the trickling filter. The activated sludge process involves the pumping of wastewater after the removal of solids to outdoor aeration basins where air is bubbled into the water to provide oxygen for microorganisms to digest the organic matter in the waste. The microorganisms and inorganic solids settle out in clarifiers at the bottom of the basins to form sludge. In the trickling filter process, wastewater is sprayed by a sprinkler onto a filter bed of stones coated with bacteria. As the wastewater trickles over the stones, the bacteria break down the organic matter, and solids are piped to a settling tank as sludge.

Sludge from the secondary treatment process is usually pumped to a sludge digester, where bacteria break it down. The sludge is later removed, dried, and either landfilled or sent to farms to be applied to land as fertilizer. Secondary treatment removes at least 80% of suspended solids and up to 90% of nutrients, such as nitrogen and phosphorus. An increasingly common secondary treatment step is nitrification/denitrification. High nitrogen loadings in surface waters have been identified as the leading cause of algae blooms and fish and shellfish die-off. The EPA has mandated lower discharge limits for nitrogen for sewage treatment plants in communities where nitrogen loadings are a problem.

Tertiary Treatment

Tertiary treatment is the most advanced form of wastewater treatment. Tertiary plants are significantly more expensive to build and operate than primary and secondary treatment plants, and they are mainly used when the receiving body of water is of a very high quality that must be maintained. One type of tertiary treatment is membrane filtration in which membranes with microscopic pores trap contaminants yet allow water to pass through. Tertiary treatment removes virtually all contaminants, including suspended and dissolved solids, chemicals, and many pathogens. It is probably the only process that is consistently effective in removing parasites, such as cryptospiridium. Another type of tertiary treatment involves carbon filtering, which is used by the Cincinnati Water Works (Swope 2000, 84). Charcoal is treated with oxygen to create tiny pores in the charcoal, which trap a variety of impurities, especially carbon-based organic chemicals, and remove odors. Wastewater that undergoes tertiary treatment is generally safe for drinking and swimming.

The construction and upgrading of wastewater treatment plants to treat municipal sewage has played a major role in improving the nation's water quality (see Table 4-4). Under Section 201 of the Clean Water Act, the EPA has given more than $30 billion in wastewater treatment grants to states and localities. Since 1972, nationwide wastewater treatment capacity has increased substantially, reaching over 42 billion gallons a day in 1996 (U.S. Bureau of the Census 2000, 586). In addition, a small but growing number of communities have separated sanitary sewers from storm sewer systems. According to the U.S. EPA (2000a), between 1972 and 2000, American governments and private industry spent more than *$1 trillion* to upgrade and expand wastewater treatment facilities.

Section 208 of the Clean Water Act requires states to conduct sewage facilities planning, which can be a powerful tool in managing the location of dense development. The location of sewage treatment plants and sewer lines is fundamental to where large and intensive developments can occur. The size or capacity of a plant to process sewage sets a limit on the outward growth of intensive development and is a key determinant of *how much* overall development a community or region can accommodate.

Nonpoint Source Pollution Control

When the 1972 Clean Water Act Amendments were passed, point sources of water pollution posed greater threats to water quality than nonpoint sources. At the beginning of the 21st century, the opposite is true, in part because the NPDES/SPDES program and the construction of wastewater treatment plants have significantly reduced point source pollution. The 1987 Amendments to the Clean Water Act added Section 319 to address the nonpoint source pollution problem. This section:

- calls for states to develop and implement plans and programs to control nonpoint source pollution;

- provides federal loans and grants for the control of nonpoint sources; and

- requires each state to prepare a nonpoint source assessment report.

Since 1990, the EPA has required an NPDES/SPDES stormwater permit on construction sites that involve clearing, grading, and excavating 5 or more acres of land (Phase I). In 1999, the EPA adopted a rule requiring an NPDES/SPDES stormwater permit on most construction sites that disturb between 1 and 5 acres of land (Phase II). Construction sites of an acre or less may require a stormwater permit if the state environmental agency or regional EPA office determines that there is potential for significant water pollution. To obtain a permit, a developer must first submit a notice of intent to disturb a site and describe the construction project, and then draft and implement a Storm Water Pollution Prevention Plan incorporating best management practices (BMPs) to minimize runoff (see Table 4-5).

Since 1990 (Phase I), NPDES permits have been required for storm sewer systems that serve 100,000 or more people, and starting in early 2003, they will be required for systems that serve fewer than 100,000 people (Phase II). An estimated 5,000 municipalities will be subject to the Phase II permitting rules. The EPA requires communities with combined sewer systems to describe the pollution discharges, demonstrate the use of at least a minimum of technologies to control the discharges, and develop long-term overflow control plans, including an estimate of square miles served by the storm sewer system, proposed BMPs, and measurable goals for each stormwater control. BMPs include detecting and eliminating illegal discharges, controlling stormwater runoff from construction sites, and preventing pollutants from entering municipal storm sewers. All cities and counties in metropolitan areas are required to adopt stormwater management ordinances to control runoff from development and redevelopment projects. The EPA has estimated that meeting these

Table 4-5
Recommended Best Management Practices for Construction Sites

Nonstructural Best Management Practices
1. Minimizing disturbance (clearing, grading, excavating)
2. Preserving natural vegetation and drainage patterns
3. Cleaning up and disposing of debris

Structural Best Management Practices	
Erosion Controls	**Sediment Controls**
1. Mulch	1. Silt fence
2. Grass	2. Inlet protection
3. Stockpile covers	3. Check dams
	4. Stabilized construction entrances
	5. Sediment traps

Source: U.S. Environmental Protection Agency (2000c)

stormwater management goals will cost up to $45 billion (U.S. General Accounting Office 2000a, 117).

The Clean Water Act does not specifically address most agricultural practices, which remain a leading cause of polluted runoff. The Natural Resources Conservation Service (NRCS) of the U.S. Department of Agriculture works with farmers nationwide to draft soil and water conservation plans and implement stream buffers, no-till farming, and other BMPs to reduce soil erosion and runoff (see Chapter 13).

A separate Coastal Nonpoint Source Pollution Control Program, Section 6217 of the Coastal Zone Act Reauthorization Amendments of 1990, addresses nonpoint pollution problems in coastal waters. Coastal areas and estuaries are especially rich in aquatic life and provide breeding grounds for fish, shellfish, and waterfowl. Section 6217 requires the 29 states and territories with approved Coastal Zone Management Programs to develop Coastal Nonpoint Source Pollution Control Programs. In this program, a state or territory describes how it will implement nonpoint source

pollution controls that conform with those described in Guidance Specifying Management Measures for Sources of Nonpoint Pollution in Coastal Waters. This program is administered jointly by the EPA and the National Oceanic and Atmospheric Administration.

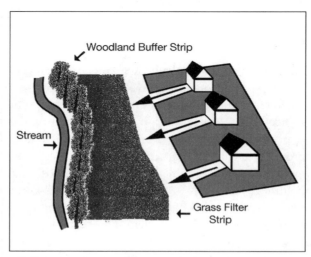

4-5 Grass filter strip and woodland stream buffer control stormwater runoff from entering stream.

SIDEBAR 4-3

Water Quality in Cost-Benefit Analysis and Risk Assessment

Economists argue that water pollution prevention and clean-up are justifiable if the benefits are greater than or equal to the costs. Water quality standards are intended to protect the public health but not to reflect the cost of pollution prevention or clean-up or to consider how many people will benefit. Strict standards could impose costs that exceed benefits in some communities or regions. On the other hand, low standards could fail to remove health hazards.

Cost-benefit analysis is designed to identify an "optimal" and "efficient" level of pollution. However, one drawback is that if pollution is permitted and water becomes degraded, it is then limited in its range of uses, such as when it falls from Class B (good quality) to Class C (fair quality, considered "impaired" under the Clean Water Act). Polluted water then becomes expensive to treat in order to meet swimmable or drinking water standards. Another drawback is that it is easier to quantify the costs of water pollution control than it is to measure in financial terms the benefits to human health, wildlife, aesthetics, and recreation. For instance, in 1994,

industries spent more than $7.6 billion on water pollution control, while governments and individuals spent more than $35 billion (Council on Environmental Quality 1996, 249), but the benefits of water pollution improvement and control were not measured.

The maximum contaminant levels set by the U.S. Environmental Protection Agency (EPA) under the Safe Drinking Water Act involve evaluations of risk assessment and risk tolerance. Risk assessment is how much harm to health and life certain levels of a contaminant are likely to cause. Risk tolerance is the maximum level of exposure people can have without experiencing health effects. As such, maximum contaminant levels may need to be reviewed periodically for health concerns and compared to the cost of stricter levels. For instance, in 2000, the EPA proposed revising the standard for arsenic levels in drinking water from 50 parts per billion to five parts per billion. About 10% of the nation's water systems have arsenic contamination problems. Most of these systems are found in small communities, and water bills would have to rise in order to meet the higher standard. The challenge is that the removal of each increment of a particular type of pollution usually costs increasingly more as standards are made more rigorous, while health benefits become harder to demonstrate.

Water Quality Monitoring and Enforcement

Monitoring water quality for drinking or swimming standards can be done through sampling at established monitoring stations at different times of the year. Both the EPA and state environmental agencies monitor water quality through hundreds of monitoring stations. Some citizens' watershed associations monitor water quality as well.

The EPA and most states have the power to enforce the Clean Water Act. The EPA has the authority to levy fines against companies, individuals, and governments that violate the Clean

Water Act. In 1999, the EPA imposed more than $20 million in criminal fines, more than $7 million in civil penalties, and more than $5 million in administrative penalties (Environmental Working Group 2000). The EPA can fine a city up to $27,500 for each spill from its sewage treatment system (Whitaker 2003, A22).

Under Section 305(b) of the Clean Water Act, states are required to submit a report to the EPA every two years on the quality of their waterways. The report features an assessment of the state's water bodies according to a range of water conditions, defined in the following ways:

- *good/fully supporting:* meeting water quality criteria and fulfilling the designated uses
- *good/threatened:* meeting water quality criteria at present, but in danger of degradation in the near future
- *fair/partially supporting:* meeting water quality criteria most of the time
- *poor/not supporting:* not meeting water quality standards
- *not attainable:* one or more of the designated water uses cannot be met because of biological, chemical, physical, or socioeconomic conditions

The Clean Water Act makes trash and waste dumping violations of the law. Ocean dumping of sewage sludge, industrial and medical waste, radioactive waste, and chemical and biological weapons have been banned under the Ocean Dumping Act of 1972 and the 1988 Amendments. Mining wastes are to some degree controlled by the 1977 Surface Mining Reclamation Act.

A number of national environmental organizations consider the enforcement of federal water quality laws a high priority. The Natural Resources Defense Council (NRDC), founded as an environmental legal firm in 1970, combines science, research, legal action, and education to support and uphold the nation's environmental laws. The NRDC has more than 400,000 members. Environmental Defense (formerly known as the Environmental Defense Fund) works with federal agencies and takes legal action to enforce environmental laws, including the Clean Water Act.

STATE WATER QUALITY PROTECTION AND CLEAN-UP

The 1977 Amendments to the Clean Water Act gave the states primary responsibility for rating the water quality of rivers, streams, and lakes. State agencies also establish water quality standards for all surface waters in the state, and these standards must be approved by the EPA. This approach is considerably different from that of the SDWA, in which the EPA establishes national standards for drinking water quality that states and local governments must meet (see Chapter 3).

Designation of Water Quality

The Clean Water Act requires state water quality standards for surface waters to include three elements:

1. *Designated uses.* The goal for all water is that it meet either Class A (drinkable) or Class B (swimmable) quality standards. Other water uses (for example, to provide life support for fish and other aquatic life or to support agriculture and boating) are also allowed. States are required to designate water bodies Class A through E.
2. *Criteria.* For certain chemicals, maximum threshold levels must be established, usually expressed as "not to exceed so many parts per million." These threshold standards are meant to protect the designated uses described above, and especially to protect people and fish from adverse health effects.
3. *Antidegradation policy.* States must not allow waters that meet the Class A or B standards to deteriorate in quality (U.S. EPA 2000a).

Special protection is provided for streams designated by the state as high quality or exceptional value waters. These waters are often smaller tributaries in higher elevations, forested watersheds, and also have important environmental characteristics such as trout fisheries. Wastewater treatment plant effluent and any other discharges to streams classified as high quality or exception value waters are permitted only if the discharge is the result of necessary social and economic development, water quality is maintained, and all existing uses of the stream are protected. These restrictions would have the effect of requiring any wastewater treatment plants in these areas to provide tertiary treatment.

Cleaning Up Impaired Waterways: Total Maximum Daily Loads

The biennial state assessments of water quality are meant to alert states, the EPA, and the public about which waters meet federal drinkable and swimmable standards and which do not. Section 303(d) of the Clean Water Act requires states to identify and create a priority list of "impaired" waterways and to implement Total Maximum Daily Load (TMDL) plans to clean up those waterways to either the drinkable or swimmable standard.

To initiate the TMDL process, a state must first identify and list by name polluted lakes, ponds, streams, rivers, and bays as "water quality limited waters," with Class C, D, or E quality water. Next, the state must rank the listed waterways for urgency of clean-up, and set a schedule for creating the TMDLs. The state then sends its list to the EPA for approval.

Each state must determine the maximum amount of pollution an impaired waterway can assimilate and still meet state and federal water quality standards for Class A or B quality water. The states must also identify and place pollution limits on the individual point sources (such as factories) and nonpoint sources (such as farm fields or timber harvests) so that maximum pollution levels are not exceeded. Finally, states are supposed to enforce the TMDL "pollution budgets" for each waterway.

As part of the process, a TMDL analysis must be done for each pollutant that is contributing to the impairment of a waterway or part of a waterway. The analysis must determine the sources of pollution and allocate to each source a certain level of that pollutant that may be discharged into the waterway. The total level of each type of pollutant from all sources must not exceed the maximum that a particular water body can assimilate consistent with federal and state water quality standards. The acceptable pollution load is thus allocated among the point sources (known as wasteload allocation) and nonpoint sources (load allocation).

The states were given between eight and 13 years to draft TMDL plans. As of 2000, most states had not begun the TMDL process, and states that had begun were short on staff and resources (National Wildlife Federation (NWF) 2000). According to a National Research Council study, as of 2001, there were "21,000 polluted river segments, lakes, and estuaries making up over 300,000 river and shore miles and 5 million lake acres. The number of TMDLs required for these impaired waters is greater than 40,000" (National Research Council 2001, 2). The study questioned whether states had the necessary scientific information to identify, assess, and reduce pollutant loadings. The Bush administration responded to the report by delaying for 18 months the requirement for states to proceed on addressing TMDLs.

If a state fails to set up TMDLs for polluted water bodies, the EPA has the authority to intervene and establish a TMDL priority list. However, the EPA itself has been slow to act on TMDLs, largely ignoring the requirement until 1997. By 2000, the EPA was under a court order or consent decree in several states to establish TMDLs (NWF 2000).

The TMDL process is key to the clean-up of impaired water bodies. Public participation in the process is required. Information on impaired water bodies and pollution sources is needed for the public to be an effective partner in decision making about the type and location of future development. If an impaired water body is cleaned up, it can be "de-listed" from the TMDL list. Clean Water Act requirements that prohibit the deterioration of the quality of the water body then take effect. The TMDL process signals a major change in water quality management away from the guesswork involved in limiting point and even nonpoint sources of pollution and toward an approach featuring scientifically supported, ambient-based water quality standards for entire waterways.

State Watershed Management

The federal government initiated the Clean Water Action Plan program in 1998 as a way to compel states to better coordinate efforts to restore watersheds that do not meet clean water standards and other natural resource goals as well as to maintain water conditions in healthy watersheds.

Clean Water Action Plans are made up of three parts:

1. A Unified Watershed Assessment, which describes the conditions in each of the state's watersheds, including those in need of restoration, preventive action, or extra protection as pristine watersheds. Section 319 of the Clean Water Act already required each state to prepare a Unified Watershed Assessment to determine where additional funding would help achieve "fishable and swimmable" waters.
2. To qualify for additional federal water quality funding, a state must put together Watershed Restoration Priorities (a list of the highest priority watersheds for restoration over the next two years).
3. Watershed Restoration Action Strategies detail the actions needed to address watershed clean-up over the next five years.

As of 2002, more than 20 states had adopted statewide watershed approaches to managing their water programs (U.S. EPA 2002). A watershed approach consists of five elements:

1. a delineation of watersheds by drainage basins;
2. assessment, planning, implementing actions, and monitoring by watershed;
3. coordination of the Clean Water Act and other regulatory programs;
4. a process for involving local governments, landowners, and the general public; and
5. evaluation of results by watershed.

States can either take the lead in watershed planning and management or else develop a locally driven partnership approach with local communities and nonprofit watershed groups. State-led watershed planning efforts have resulted in better monitoring data and assessment of problems, and greater efficiency and coordination in permitting programs (*ibid.*, 2).

One of the biggest problems that states cite is the uncoordinated timing of different EPA programs under the Clean Water Act. For instance, there is a five-year permitting reissuance cycle for SPDES and NPDES permits, a three-year water quality standards review period, and a two-year reporting cycle for water quality data to the EPA under Sections 305(b) and 303(d) listing impaired waterways and TMDLs. A coordinated reporting schedule would make all information available in the same year and would improve planning and evaluation efforts. Federal, state, and local governments must coordinate the several water clean-up and pollution prevention efforts of the Clean Water Act with the SDWA's programs to protect drinking water supplies.

State Water Quality Monitoring and Enforcement

In the 1990s, the federal government transferred most of the responsibility for monitoring and enforcing the Clean Water Act to the states. As of 1998, 45 states managed their Clean Water Act sewage treatment plant construction grants; 43 controlled the NPDES permit process; 32 regulated pretreatment of industrial waste discharged into public treatment plants; and 25 managed the Section 604(b) state water quality planning grant program (Coequyt and Wiles 2000, 9). Predictably, the level and vigor of monitoring and enforcement have varied considerably from state to state. Twenty-five states have passed audit privilege laws that enable polluters to police themselves and avoid prosecution for any violations they discover (Pear 2001, 2).

A 2000 report by the Environmental Working Group was critical of state water quality agencies. The report found that in 10 states, more than 40%

of the Clean Water Act inspections were reconnaissance inspections in which inspectors did not get out of their cars—a level of inspection the EPA deems insufficient (Coequyt and Wiles 2000, 5). From 1997 to 1999, 283 factories that had been listed as significant violators of the Clean Water Act by the EPA were not even inspected by state officials. Texas had 73 such factories, Ohio 31, and Michigan 20 (*ibid.,* 4). The report concluded: "The U.S. EPA has lost control of environmental law enforcement and, in the absence of strong federal oversight, many states have gutted environmental enforcement programs" (*ibid.,* 2).

Sierra Club Executive Director Carl Pope echoed the concerns of the Environmental Working Group when he said, "States already have a lot of power in the environmental arena, and many simply decline to use it. So we are not in favor of giving them more discretion" (Pear 2001, 18). The EPA needs to set clear guidelines and reporting standards for the states if monitoring and enforcement of the Clean Water Act is to maintain clean waters and improve the quality of the nation's impaired waterways. If the states do not do an adequate job of monitoring and enforcement, the EPA could conceivably step in to take back these functions.

Innovative State Water Quality Programs

Some states are moving ahead with innovative planning for water quality. For instance, the New Jersey Department of Environmental Protection is working with the federal government, local governments, business and industry, and concerned citizens to draft management plans for 20 watersheds. The goals are to reduce point and nonpoint pollution sources and thus protect high-quality surface and groundwater as well as clean up impaired waterways (Finucan 1999, 40). In addition, New Jersey's 1996 State Plan recommended long-term funding for the acquisition of land to protect water resources. In 1999, Oregon Governor John Kitzhaber signed an Executive Order directing the Department of Land Conservation and

Development to implement statewide planning for riparian corridors and review permitted uses in estuarine areas with the intent of speeding the recovery of coastal salmon (Johnson 1999, 56).

This land use/water quality connection is fundamental for sustainable water quality and fish habitat. The Maryland Agricultural Water Quality Cost-Share Program pays up to 87.5% of the cost to install eligible BMPs to protect water quality (Maryland Department of Agriculture 2001). There are 29 eligible BMPs, including manure storage facilities, grassed waterways, cover crops, stream buffers, nutrient management plans, and the transportation of excess manure off the farm. The maximum levels of funding range from $20,000 to $100,000. Maryland has also operated a "ReLeaf" program to pay for planting forest buffers to minimize runoff into rivers and streams (see Case Study 4-2, below). In 1995, the Massachusetts legislature passed Title 5, which requires homeowners, before they sell or expand a house, to hire a professional engineer to inspect the on-site septic system. If the system fails the inspection, the owner must fix or replace the system before the house can be sold or expanded. In the first two years of the law, about 5,400 polluting systems were detected (Daniels 1999).

COUNTY AND REGIONAL PARTNERSHIPS AND NONPROFIT GROUPS

Counties, regional governments, and nonprofits can play key roles in maintaining and improving water quality, especially when their efforts are watershed-based. Counties that have land use planning and zoning authority are in a good position to have a positive impact on water quality. These counties can adopt land development standards that reflect current BMPs, and direct growth and development away from vulnerable water bodies and waterways. Even counties that do not have this authority can provide leadership and guidance to local communities through an up-to-date comprehensive plan that addresses water quality issues and by providing technical assistance to communities.

County Conservation Districts administer a number of programs designed to reduce erosion, including reviewing and approving conservation plans for farms. The conservation districts also provide assistance to landowners interested in streambank stabilization and other soil-saving measures, such as fencing to control the access of livestock to rivers and streams. In some states, the districts also administer erosion and sedimentation control programs by reviewing and approving plans for earth-disturbing activities.

A variety of federal programs that are intended to reduce soil erosion and runoff into waterways and water bodies are administered through county or regional offices. For instance, the NRCS manages the federal Environmental Quality Incentives Program, which pays landowners to install buffer strips and other practices to reduce runoff. The county offices of the Farm Service Agency administer the federal Conservation Reserve Program. This program compensates farmers who take highly erodible cropland out of production for 10 years.

Watershed Management

Watershed management is necessary to minimize the adverse effects on water quality of runoff resulting from development and earth disturbance. In partnership with state water planning departments and nonprofit watershed associations, counties or regional planning commissions should prepare and adopt watershed plans for each watershed located within their boundaries. The plans should identify high-quality, exceptional value, and impaired waterways and water bodies as well as existing and potential sources of pollution. The plans should also present a strategy for the upgrading of water quality, including priority streams for clean-up. Pennsylvania has a state program that requires each watershed to

have a stormwater plan geared to reducing off-site flows. These plans are prepared by counties. Each municipality then must adapt its local controls to fit the framework of the watershed plan.

The EPA estimates that there are more than 3,000 private, nonprofit watershed organizations throughout the nation (Meridian Institute 2001). These watershed organizations are typically alliances of landowners, farm organizations, environmental and fish and wildlife conservation groups, elected officials, local government agencies, civic organizations, and conservation districts. Watershed alliances perform volunteer monitoring of water bodies, hold workshops and school programs, restore streambanks, plant forest buffer strips, and sponsor stream clean-up days. Berks County, Pennsylvania, has assigned segments of streams to sponsors to name and to clean up and protect. The State of Maryland has created 12 regional tributary teams covering the state to work on cleaning up and protecting waterways through demonstration projects and public education. Maryland's approach is preferable to a piecemeal approach that typifies reliance on watershed groups.

Nationwide, the League of Women Voters has taken on the issue of wellhead protection, sponsoring educational forums and workshops on the prevention of groundwater contamination in communities. Groundwater Guardians is another national group active in promoting the protection of groundwater. Sports groups such as the Izaak Walton League, Trout Unlimited, and Ducks Unlimited are active in watershed protection and restoration efforts.

Several nonprofit land trusts have become active in working with landowners and water providers to protect water quality. For example, the Society for the Protection of New Hampshire Forests has drafted two model easements in its Water Supply Land Protection Project (Society for the Protection of New Hampshire Forests 2001). Landowners and water companies can sell or donate a conservation easement to a land trust, thus placing permanent restrictions on the land (see Chapters 8 and 13). A conservation easement to protect surface drinking water supplies can ban the construction of any new buildings or structures near the surface water and require a buffer of a certain distance from the surface water for farming, forestry, or any commercial or residential uses. A conservation easement can also restrict or ban development or active uses in wellhead protection or high-yield aquifer areas.

LOCAL PLANNING FOR WATER QUALITY

Water quality strongly influences the ability of a community to sustain itself and the type and amount of development it can support. Good water quality is essential to human health, a variety of businesses, fish and wildlife, and recreational activities. Planning for water quality begins with identifying surface watersheds, groundwater aquifers, and existing and potential water pollution sources. Ideally, water quality planning should be combined with planning for water supply (see Chapter 3). Local governments should review their comprehensive plans and ordinances and revise them where appropriate to protect the quality of streams, lakes, reservoirs, wetlands, and groundwater.

Inventory

The Natural Resources section of the comprehensive plan should include information and mapping of the location and quality of waterways, water bodies, and groundwater in the community. Exceptional value and high-quality waters, Class A and B waters, public drinking water supplies, sole source aquifers, any delineated wellhead protection areas, and any impaired waterways or water bodies should be noted. Much of the water quality inventory information should be available from the state water resources board or environmental agency, the county, and community water systems.

It is important to note the location and severity of existing and potential point and nonpoint sources of water pollution. Any known hazardous waste sites and underground storage tanks should also be mapped (see Chapter 7). The impacts of existing pollution levels on drinking water, fish and wildlife habitats, recreation opportunities, and water used for other purposes in the community should be described.

Analysis

An analysis should enable local planners and the planning commission to identify strengths, weaknesses, opportunities, and threats to local water quality. For instance, an abundance of high-quality water is both a strength and an opportunity. Poor water quality is a weakness that may exist in parts of a community if, for instance, private wells have become contaminated by malfunctioning septic systems. Identifying and analyzing threats can lead to proactive strategies to avoid problems before they happen or become worse. Geographic Information Systems (GISs) are becoming a common way to identify potential sources of nonpoint pollution through land suitability analysis, development projections, and calculations of the percent of impervious surface in an area or watershed. GISs display watershed features in overlays of land uses, land cover, hydrology, watersheds, and wildlife habitats and can manipulate, analyze, and display data quickly and accurately. Maps can be produced to review proposed future land use scenarios to evaluate alternative nonpoint source impacts on water quality.

An analysis should determine the community's future water quality needs, based on projected population growth, land uses, and economic activities. Federal and state requirements, a community's values, water quality data, and projected growth in other communities in the watershed—especially upstream—must all be considered. For example, evidence of impaired water quality could lead to a determination that local ordinances should be modified to site new development more carefully and at a lower density in sensitive environmental areas, or recognition of the vulnerability of surface water to a variety of contaminants could motivate neighboring communities to work together to protect a common water resource. A community or county should evaluate how its use of water affects other communities in the watershed and vice versa. A regional, watershed approach to water planning should be encouraged. The analysis process should lead to general community goals and specific objectives for the community's water quality.

Goals and Objectives

The community should include goals and objectives for water quality in the comprehensive plan that reflect federal and state requirements as well as community desires (see Table 4-6). A general goal should be to maintain or improve surface and groundwater quality. Another goal should be to protect present and future sources of drinking water. Specific objectives should be listed in the Natural Resources, Land Use, Economic Base, and Community Facilities sections of the comprehensive plan. Development should not degrade water quality, which is essential for economic growth. Water suppliers should be coordinating water testing and protection measures with state and federal officials.

Action Strategy

The Action Strategy should present techniques and programs for achieving the water quality goals and objectives as well as a timetable. Water quality benchmarks should be identified and progress toward those benchmarks evaluated in an annual report on the environment. Specific recommendations for action might include:

- promoting partnerships between the local government and nonprofit watershed groups to educate the public and to clean up local water bodies;

- exploring state and federal funding for the separation of sanitary and storm sewers;
- working with state and federal agencies, private land trusts, and water associations on purchasing land or conservation easements to land adjacent to waterways;
- adopting a woodland protection ordinance to minimize the loss of tree cover in the development process; and
- adopting a stormwater management ordinance.

Zoning Ordinance

The zoning map should direct development away from impaired waterways and water bodies and delineated wellhead protection areas. Development permitted in these areas should be sensitively sited and required to employ BMPs, such as setbacks from water bodies of at least 100 feet, limits on impervious surface, avoidance of steep slopes, and the creation of filter strips and riparian buffers along streams and water bodies to minimize runoff.

4-6 "No dumping" sign on storm sewer to protect water quality, Seattle, Washington.

Source: Katherine Daniels

Table 4-6
Sample Water Quality Goals and Objectives in the Comprehensive Plan

Natural Resources	
Goal	To maintain and improve surface and groundwater quality.
Objective	Draft or update a community stormwater management ordinance to ensure that best management practices are being used to minimize stormwater runoff.
Objective	Sponsor a watershed group to conduct educational, clean-up, and pollution prevention activities to protect the watershed.
Land Use	
Objective	Prohibit new development or activities in areas that would threaten to pollute surface or groundwater.
Economic Base	
Objective	Promote water quality protection to make the community attractive to new development and to sustain existing development.
Community Facilities	
Objective	Ensure that local sewage treatment plants have adequate future capacity. Separate storm sewers from sanitary sewers.

Zoning should promote compact development patterns that facilitate the use of central sewer and water instead of on-site septic systems and wells, which create greater potential for contamination of groundwater. Farm and forestlands should be protected through the use of large minimum lot sizes to maintain large areas of pervious soils that readily absorb precipitation with minimal erosion and runoff. Large lot farm and forest zones also minimize the use of on-site septic systems and wells that could jeopardize water quality.

Watershed, stream, woodland, steep slope, or conservation overlay zones could be used in key areas to limit land uses or activities that could jeopardize water quality, and to require the use of BMPs where development is allowed. A floodplain overlay zone can be used to minimize development in flood-prone areas and thus protect water quality.

Using GISs, a community or county can use its existing or proposed zoning districts to produce a build-out analysis, indicating the ultimate level of development possible if all land were put to its allowed uses and densities. The build-out analysis can be used to calculate potential impervious surfaces, with an eye toward whether the zoning would allow more than 10% of the watershed to be covered in impervious surfaces—a maximum recommended percentage. A local government may then adjust zoning uses, densities, or lot coverage requirements to reduce impervious surfaces and future runoff, and thus protect water resources.

Subdivision Regulations

Subdivision and land development regulations can help protect water quality in several ways. They can require developers to use BMPs for stormwater management and flood control and to maintain or plant vegetative cover along streams and on steep slopes. The regulations can also require the siting of development away from vulnerable water resources and wetlands.

Stormwater Management Ordinance

A community can adopt stormwater management standards as part of the subdivision regulations or as a stand-alone ordinance to control the impact of development on runoff, groundwater recharge, and overall water quality. The advantage of a separate ordinance is that it can be made to apply to all earth disturbance and not just that associated with subdivisions and land development. Stormwater management provisions should include guidelines to assist developers in choosing appropriate techniques, including retention or detention basins, porous pavements, constructed wetlands, seepage pits, and swales, among others. The standard should be that post-storm runoff should be equal to or less than prestorm runoff for a 25-year storm. In limestone or karst geology, retention basins should be prohibited, and detention basins and stormwater runoff directed away from sinkholes and closed depressions.

Erosion and Sediment Control Ordinance

To further minimize runoff, local governments can enact special erosion and sedimentation ordinances that exceed the federal standards. For example, in 1998, Boise, Idaho, passed a construction site erosion ordinance to protect wetlands, the Boise River, and its tributaries. The ordinance requires developers to obtain an erosion control permit. Developers must submit a sediment, erosion, and dust control plan; a person certified by the city to implement the controls must be available at each construction site (Boise City Planning and Development Services 2000).

Woodland Protection Ordinance

Communities that want to limit stormwater runoff and erosion may choose to adopt standards that limit the removal of mature trees or require their replacement when development is proposed. Usually, a fixed percentage of trees of a certain caliper diameter at a certain height must be retained unless they are allowed to be replaced with trees of a smaller but minimum caliper size. Some developers avoid such requirements by harvesting the trees on the property before they submit a subdivision proposal. Communities can eliminate this loophole by prohibiting the clear cutting of

property within areas deemed to be important for protecting water quality, regardless of whether it is proposed for development. Communities can adopt streamside overlays that permit only selective cutting along streambanks as well as limit other uses that could jeopardize water quality. Studies have shown that mature vegetation and trees add significantly to the value of property planned for development (U.S. EPA 1998c).

Capital Improvements Program

Sewage treatment facilities and distribution systems are expensive infrastructure components and have a powerful influence over the location of development. The proliferation of on-site septic systems has posed difficulties for communities trying to establish or revise a capital improvements program (CIP). If septic systems on large lots fail, water and/or sewer lines must be extended to serve those homes and businesses, which can be very expensive. Once sewer and water lines are extended, they will promote additional development in areas not necessarily planned for growth. A CIP should be consistent with the state Section 208 sewage facilities plan, public water system planning, the future land use map of the comprehensive plan, and the zoning map. Central sewage treatment plants must maintain adequate capacity for anticipated future growth, and any combined storm and sanitary sewer systems should be separated.

WHAT TO LOOK FOR IN A DEVELOPMENT REVIEW

When a planning commission looks at a development project, it should evaluate the project for consistency with the comprehensive plan, zoning ordinance, subdivision and land development regulations, CIP, and any other applicable local laws. The potential impact of a development on water quality will depend on the size, location, and type of project as well as current environmental conditions (see Table 4-7). It is important

Table 4-7
A Checklist of Water Quality Issues in Development Review

1.	Will the proposed project use a private on-site septic system or public sewer?
2.	If a private septic system is used, where will it be located in relation to neighboring properties, any on-site wells, and nearby streams or water bodies? Will required setbacks be met? Is the site large enough to allow for a back-up system should the first septic system fail?
3.	If a public sewer is used, how much sewage will be generated and what is the capacity of the sewage treatment facility? Under Section 402(h) of the Clean Water Act, if a sewage treatment plant is in violation of its National Pollutant Discharge Elimination System (NPDES) permit, the U.S. Environmental Protection Agency may allow no new sewer hook-ups until the plant comes into compliance.
4.	Will the proposed project use private on-site wells or public water facilities? Are on-site wells required to be grouted?
5.	Do any local erosion and sedimentation control standards apply? Have they been met?
6.	What are the site drainage and stormwater runoff patterns? What best management practices have been proposed to reduce pollution from runoff?
7.	Will there be discharges into streams or other surface water?
8.	Has the developer obtained any necessary state or federal permits?

to keep in mind the cumulative impact of multiple new developments on water quality. That is one reason why regular testing of private and public water supplies and waterways is strongly recommended.

CASE STUDIES

The following case studies describe attempts to protect groundwater quality in greater Austin, Texas—one of America's fastest growing regions in the 1990s—and efforts in Maryland to protect the water quality of rivers and streams that feed into the Chesapeake Bay—one of the world's largest estuaries.

CASE STUDY 4-1
Barton Springs and Austin, Texas

Protecting water quality can be accomplished through a combination of land and water regulations and land purchases. However, in Texas, as in every state, private landowners have the right to use groundwater under their property. Barton

Springs lies southwest of Austin, the burgeoning capital city of Texas. High-tech industries, led by Dell, have spurred rapid population growth and sprawling development patterns through much of Travis County. The Barton Springs watershed covers over 360 square miles and the aquifer supplies well water to 45,000 people. In 1987, the Texas legislature created the Barton Springs/Edwards Aquifer Conservation District to prevent contamination and regulate the amount of water pumped out of the aquifer. In 1992, a Save Our Springs ordinance was passed by the City of Austin to limit the amount of new impervious surface to between 15% and 25% of any tract over the Barton Springs aquifer. In 1998, Austin voters approved a $65 million bond issue to purchase sensitive lands and conservation easements in the Barton Springs contributing and recharge zones. The U.S. Fish and Wildlife Service has declared the Barton Springs salamander a rare and endangered species, and is drawing up rules to protect the salamander's habitat by limiting development density, capturing potentially harmful runoff in ponds, and preserving streamside flora.

In contrast, neighboring Hays County does not have any regulations to limit development over the Barton Springs Aquifer, and yet Hays County contains twice as much of the aquifer as Travis County.

CASE STUDY 4-2
The Maryland Stream ReLeaf Program

Riparian forest buffers are the most cost-effective way to reduce nonpoint source pollution, by filtering sediment and stormwater before they reach waterways. According to the EPA, an acre of riparian forest buffer can remove an estimated 21 pounds of nitrogen each year for 30 cents a pound. By comparison, it costs wastewater treatment plants in the Washington, D.C., area about $3 to $5 a year to remove a pound of nitrogen (U.S. EPA 1998c).

The Chesapeake Bay is one of the world's largest estuaries, where fresh water and salt water combine to provide a rich breeding ground for shellfish and water fowl. In 1900, the Chesapeake Bay was a world leader in the production of oysters, and Chesapeake Bay blue crabs still support a major industry. However, yields of crabs and oysters have declined sharply in recent decades, and the water quality of the bay has suffered in that same period.

In 1983, a unique compact was forged among three states in the Chesapeake Bay watershed (Maryland, Pennsylvania, and Virginia), the District of Columbia, and the federal government to protect the waters of the Chesapeake Bay. Loss of forest cover and resulting impervious surfaces can reduce water quality. In the Baltimore-to-Washington, D.C. corridor, the amount of forest cover declined from about 50% of the land area in 1975 to 37% in 2000 (Maryland's Tributary Teams 2000).

In 1996, Maryland adopted a riparian forest buffer initiative, called the Stream ReLeaf program, to create, coordinate, and monitor streamside forest buffers with landowners and communities. The buffers serve several purposes, including the filtering of sediment and runoff, protection of wildlife habitat, streambank stabilization, flood control, regulating water temperature, and provision of recreational greenways.

The program set a goal of creating 600 miles of forest buffers along streambanks by 2010. By 2000, 209 miles had already been planted, restored, or conserved. The Maryland Department of Natural Resources used a GIS to target rivers and streams with high nutrient loadings, low order streams, and unforested streambanks for tree planting. The GIS is able to track the location of stream forest buffers, the size and tree species in the buffer, funded projects, and conserved buffers.

Funding for the program comes from the Chesapeake Bay program, the EPA, the U.S. Forest Service, the federal Conservation Reserve Enhancement Program, and state buffer incentive money.

5

Planning for Sustainable Air Quality

I said, "What's a first stage smog alert?"
"Avoid driving, avoid strenuous activity,"
   Wells answered.
Harp said, "Avoid breathing."

JOHN MCPHEE, *THE CONTROL OF NATURE*

Air is a resource that we take for granted because it is everywhere around us, and because we involuntarily breathe several times each minute. But, since the 1970s, there has been a heightened public awareness of the quality of the air we breathe. The term smog—combining the words smoke and fog—is widely familiar. Hazy smog reduces visibility and the enjoyment of scenic vistas, and damages clothing, buildings, crops, and trees. During the summer months, news media in major cities often broadcast smog alerts to keep the elderly and those with respiratory problems indoors and to warn others to avoid physical exertion.

The American Lung Association estimates that air pollution in the U.S. accounts for about 60,000 premature deaths each year. In addition, dirty air can increase the effects and frequency of illnesses, such as asthma attacks, chronic bronchitis, emphysema, lung cancer, and circulatory problems.

Perhaps the most powerful images of the vulnerability of the air we breathe have come from the photos of earth from outer space: a lonely blue ball shrouded in white wisps of atmosphere. The atmosphere—what we call the air—is made up of several different gases. Nitrogen makes up about

80% of the total; oxygen 16%; and traces of argon, helium, carbon monoxide, carbon dioxide, methane, ozone, and sulfur make up the remaining 4%.

The atmosphere serves several purposes. It provides necessary oxygen for humans and animals to breathe and carbon dioxide for plant respiration. The atmosphere, with the help of the sun and gravity, regulates climate through the hydrologic cycle. The atmosphere redistributes important nutrients, such as nitrogen and phosphorous, back to the earth. The carbon cycle enables the atmosphere to provide a warm protective shield against the cold of space. This phenomenon, commonly known as the "greenhouse effect," holds in some of the sun's warmth as it reflects off the earth's surface. Also, the natural ozone in the stratosphere blocks most of the sun's ultraviolet rays that can cause skin cancers, cataracts, and genetic mutations. The makeup of the atmosphere can change over time, causing climate and temperature fluctuations and long-term changes. The primary source of climate change in a human time frame is air pollution.

SOURCES OF AIR POLLUTION

Not all air pollution is caused by humans. Volcanoes can spew enormous amounts of fine gray ash that can travel thousands of miles and remain suspended in the atmosphere for months. Meteorites have hit the earth with the force of atomic bombs; it is thought that 65 million years ago, a huge meteorite may have blown soil and rock into the atmosphere and thereby blocked the sun's rays, lowered global temperatures, and drove the dinosaurs into extinction. Forest and brush fires touched off by lightning strikes can generate smoke that travels hundreds of miles, but most natural disasters occur infrequently and produce minor amounts of air pollution.

Since the Industrial Revolution began in the late 18th century, human-generated air pollution has presented far more problems than natural sources. The Industrial Revolution was based on the burning of nonrenewable fossil fuels, such as coal to drive steam engines and oil to fuel internal combustion engines. When burned, these fuels generate particles of soot, and toxic substances such as mercury. These fuels also release sulfur, nitrogen, and carbon, which then mix with air and water vapor to produce several types of pollution, including sulfur dioxide (acid rain), nitrogen oxides (smog), carbon monoxide, and carbon dioxide (greenhouse gas).

There are several ways to describe the sources of air pollution. Mobile sources feature motor vehicles, airplanes, lawn mowers, and leaf blowers. Motor vehicles alone cause about one-third to one-half of all air pollution (Stephenson 2002, 2). Stationary direct sources include factories, municipal and private incinerators, power plants, fireplaces, wood-burning stoves, home furnaces, gas stations, dry cleaners, sewage treatment plants, and landfills. Indirect sources are stationary sources to which people must travel, such as shopping centers and sports stadiums. The U.S. Environmental Protection Agency (EPA) differentiates between major sources of air pollution and area (small) sources. Out-of-region sources, such as acid rain, are carried into a region by winds from other regions or states, and are beyond local or regional control.

Air, like water, has an ability to assimilate pollution. Air pollution occurs when the assimilative capacity is exceeded. The ability of an airshed—a local or regional air supply—to assimilate pollution can be estimated as a coefficient of ventilation, a measure of horizontal and vertical mixing potential. The coefficient of ventilation is found by multiplying the height of the mixing layer of air and the mean wind speed through the mixing layer. The coefficient of ventilation will vary over time and space, depending on precipitation levels, temperature, and the capacity of land, vegetation, and water to collect and absorb air pollution. A computer model can estimate and predict both assimilation and air pollution levels based on weather conditions.

Concentrations of air pollution vary according to the following circumstances:

- *The amount and rate of pollution released by local stationary and mobile sources:* The more pollution and the faster it is released, the greater the concentration of air pollution.

- *The form of the pollution* (gas, evaporating liquid, and particulates (solids)): Gases are more apt to rise and be carried away. Liquid and solid sources are apt to remain local.

- *The prevailing wind direction and speed:* The stronger the upper level and surface winds, the faster and farther pollution is dispersed. Also, areas downwind from concentrations of air pollution have less precipitation.

- *Climate:* Warm, humid air will hold more pollution than cold, dry air. Air pollution normally rises with warm air and dissipates horizontally with wind. For instance, in summertime in Los Angeles, a 1-degree rise in temperature raises the risk of smog by an estimated 3%.

- *Topography:* Thermal inversions are common in the western United States where cities, such as Los Angeles, Portland, and Salt Lake City, have been built close to mountain ranges. A thermal inversion occurs when cooler air close to the ground is trapped under a ceiling of warmer air. Polluted air cannot rise to disperse, and smog, in particular, can become dangerously concentrated. There is a risk of severe health effects if certain conditions converge, such as dense population, industrial area, valley, fog, and thermal inversion.

- *Vegetative cover:* Trees and other plants help absorb and filter air pollution. Cities with little greenspace create "heat islands" that trap dust as the temperature rises.

Once air is polluted, it is not easy to clean up, unlike polluted water that often can be treated and purified. Wind can help to dissipate dirty, stagnant air, but polluted air does not recognize political boundaries. It is not limited to a single community or region and can travel hundreds of miles. The best known example of moving air pollution is the acid rain caused largely by coal-fired electrical plants in the Midwest that falls hundreds of miles away on the northeastern states.

TYPES OF AIR POLLUTION

Nitrogen Oxide

Nitrogen oxide (NOx) is a reddish brown gas that comes mainly from the exhaust of cars, trucks, and buses, and from factory smokestacks. Nitrogen dioxide (NO_2) is a main ingredient in smog, which can reduce visibility and cause lung damage, bronchitis, and asthma attacks. Nitrogen dioxide can also combine with water vapor to form nitric acid, which falls from the sky as acid rain. Damage to trees and lakes from acid rain is well known. Nitrogen dioxide also raises the level of nitrates in drinking water. Nitrogen oxides can also damage bays and estuaries; for instance, nitrogen oxides from motor vehicles have caused algae blooms in the Chesapeake Bay that threaten aquatic life (Stephenson 2002, 5).

Sulfur Dioxide

Coal-fired electrical plants, paper and metal factories, and the burning of gasoline are the primary sources of sulfur dioxide (SO_2). This toxic gas can harm lungs and reduce visibility as well as damage or kill plants by interrupting photosynthesis. Sulfur dioxide also interacts with water vapor to form sulfuric acid, which returns to earth as acid rain. Sulfuric acid can erode stone buildings, metal, rubber, and plastic.

Lead

Lead (Pb) is a heavy metal that, when airborne, can cause developmental disabilities in children, neurological problems, and cancer. It is also harmful to wildlife. Airborne lead pollution can result from peeling paint, lead smelters, and the manufacture of lead storage batteries. Since 1973, lead emissions have been greatly reduced in the U.S., due in large part to the phasing out of lead from gasoline, completed in 1995.

Carbon Monoxide

Carbon monoxide (CO) is a colorless, odorless gas that is poisonous to humans. Carbon monoxide is a by-product of the internal combustion engine, and about 90% of carbon monoxide comes from motor vehicles. Carbon monoxide reduces the ability of blood to deliver oxygen to the body's cells, muscles, and tissues. It can also exacerbate lung and circulatory problems. In large amounts, without ventilation, carbon monoxide is fatal.

Particulates

Particulates (PM-10) come in the form of microscopic dust, soot, smoke, and tiny bits of minerals, such as asbestos, that combine with water droplets in the air. PM-10 refers to particles less than or equal to 10 micrometers in diameter (a human hair has a diameter of about 70 micrometers). Particulates emanate from fireplaces, smokestacks, processing plants, farm fields, cars, buses, and diesel trucks. Particulates are the primary cause of haze that reduces visibility. More importantly, particulates are the leading air pollution health threat in America, causing nose and throat irritation, respiratory ailments such as asthma, and premature death. Both the elderly and children are especially vulnerable to particulate pollution.

Ozone

Ozone (O_3) is a poisonous form of oxygen created by nitrogen oxide and hydrogen compounds (also known as volatile organic compounds (VOCs)). VOCs easily escape into the air from internal combustion engines, factories, paints, solvents, glues, fireplaces, and wood stoves. VOCs include toxic chemicals such as benzene, ethylene, formaldehyde, toluene, methyl chloride, and methyl chloroform. VOCs can cause cancer and a variety of other serious ailments. Ozone reacts with sunlight to produce photochemical smog. The resulting brownish haze is difficult to see through, and smog fills the lungs with a burning sensation. Smog can cause serious lung ailments and damage to crops, trees, and other plants. In addition, smog corrodes fabrics, rubber, and building materials, and leaves behind a film of grime.

May through September is the ozone smog season in most of the nation's major metropolitan regions. Air quality will vary with the weather conditions. Smog problems increase along with warmer temperatures, higher humidity, and less wind to dissipate the smog.

Ozone-Depleting Chemicals

In the stratosphere, 6 to 31 miles above the earth, ozone occurs naturally and helps to block ultraviolet rays that can produce skin cancers, cataracts, and genetic mutations, and reduce crop yields. The loss of upper-level ozone has been a health problem in many parts of the Southern Hemisphere, and has been traced to chlorofluorocarbons (CFCs) and other chemical gases used in air conditioners, refrigerators, aerosol sprays, and in the production of plastic foam. CFCs release chlorine, which destroys ozone in the upper atmosphere. The production of CFCs and other ozone-destroying chemicals were targeted for drastic reductions under the international Montreal Protocol of 1987.

Toxic Chemicals

Toxic chemicals pose serious health threats to humans and other living organisms. Toxic chemicals that are often released into the air include mercury from coal-fired power plants, perchloroethylene from dry cleaning shops, and dioxin from the incineration of medical wastes.

Carbon Dioxide

Carbon dioxide (CO_2) is the major "greenhouse gas" to which the recent worldwide rise in average temperatures has been attributed. Climate warming in turn can change ocean levels, weather patterns, and the functioning of ecosystems. The U.S. produces more carbon dioxide emissions than any other country, generating about one-quarter of the world's annual total (U.S. Energy Information Agency 2001). Although, carbon dioxide makes up a very small proportion of the earth's atmosphere (about .036%), the concentration of carbon dioxide is increasing at a rate of about half a percent a year (Hawken *et al.* 1999, 236).

FEDERAL AIR QUALITY LEGISLATION

Air is a common property resource. No one owns the air, so no one has an incentive not to pollute it. In the first half of the 20th century, air pollution from cars, factories, trash burning, heating systems, and electrical utilities increased because there were no requirements or incentives to limit emissions.

Governments in America employ two kinds of air quality standards. Ambient air quality standards refer to the maximum allowed level of pollutants in the air in order to protect human health, property, and the natural environment. Emissions standards relate to the amount of pollution a factory, car, or truck is allowed to release into the environment. The EPA, states, and metropolitan regions are responsible for maintaining and improving air quality. Governments, businesses, and individuals are all responsible for air pollution emissions.

THE CLEAN AIR ACT AND THE 1970 AND 1977 AMENDMENTS

Federal air quality legislation began in 1955 with the Air Pollution Control Act, which provided funds to states to control air pollution. The original Clean Air Act of 1963 gave states more funds and help with cross-boundary pollution. The 1965 Motor Vehicle Air Pollution Control Act enabled the federal government to set emission standards for new vehicles. The 1967 Air Quality Act gave additional funds to states and required that they establish air quality control regions.

Under the Clean Air Act Amendments of 1970, the EPA sets National Ambient Air Quality Standards (NAAQS) that cities, states, and metropolitan regions are required to meet or else draft plans to come into compliance. Ambient air simply means the surrounding open air as opposed to air inside a building. Primary air quality standards are designed to protect human health (see Table 5-1). Secondary air quality standards are established to maintain visibility, limit the erosion of buildings, and avoid serious damage to plant and animal life (see Table 5-1). These standards apply to six "criteria" pollutants: (1) nitrogen dioxide; (2)

Table 5-1
National Primary and Secondary Ambient Air Quality Standards

Pollutant	Primary Standard	Secondary Standard
Carbon Monoxide	10 milligrams per cubic meter (9 parts per million (ppm))—maximum 8-hour concentration. 40 milligrams per cubic meter (35 ppm)—maximum 1-hour concentration not to be exceeded more than once a year.	No secondary standard
Lead	1.5 micrograms per cubic meter averaged over 3 months not to be exceeded more than once a year.	Same as the primary standard
Nitrogen Dioxide	100 micrograms per cubic meter (.053 ppm)—annual arithmetic mean.	Same as the primary standard
Ozone	160 micrograms per cubic meter (.08 ppm)—concentration not to be exceeded for 8 hours. Maximum 3-year concentration not to be exceeded more than once a year	Same as the primary standard
Particulates	50 micrograms per cubic meter annual geometric mean 150 micrograms per cubic meter—maximum 24-hour concentration not to be exceeded more than once a year. (New additional standards) 15 micrograms per cubic meter—annual. 65 micrograms per cubic meter—24-hour concentration not to be exceeded more than once a year.	50 micrograms per cubic meter—annual geometric mean 150 micrograms per cubic meter—maximum 24-hour concentration not to be exceeded more than once a year
Sulfur Oxides	80 micrograms per cubic meter (.03 ppm)—annual arithmetic mean. 365 micrograms per cubic meter (.14 ppm)—maximum 24-hour concentration not to be exceeded more than once a year.	1,300 micrograms per cubic meter (.5 ppm)—maximum 3-hour concentration not to be exceeded more than once a year

Note: All measurements of air quality are corrected to a reference temperature of 25 degrees Celsius and to a reference pressure of 760 millimeters of mercury (1,013.2 millibars).
Source: U.S. EPA, 40 C.F.R. Sections 50.4–50.11.

sulfur dioxide; (3) lead; (4) carbon monoxide; (5) particulates; and (6) ozone.

Each of the six criteria pollutants can interact with the others in ways that heighten the effects of any one pollutant. Air pollution also increases the moisture in the air, which has occurred with the heavy use of motor vehicles in the desert setting of greater Phoenix.

The EPA has divided each state into air quality control regions with air quality monitoring stations (see Figure 5-1). Each region has an air qual-

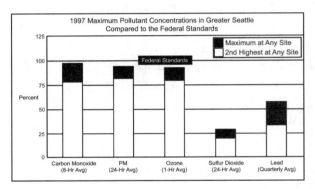

5-1 Air pollution measurements, greater Seattle, Washington, 1997.

Source: City of Seattle

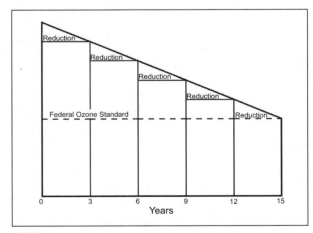

5-2 Clean Air Act pollution emission reduction budgets.

ity rating for each of the six major criteria pollutants. The ratings are I, II, and III. Rating I indicates the worst quality air, falling short of the federal standards; Rating II meets the federal standards; and Rating III is the cleanest air. The EPA monitors air quality regions for compliance with standards or nonattainment, but an area with a rating of III could slip to a rating of II by absorbing more air pollution and still not violate the federal air quality standards.

The EPA has rated nonattainment areas according to the severity of the pollution. For political and financial reasons, the worse the pollution, the longer time the nonattainment area has to reach the federal air quality standards. For instance, there are five levels of smog pollution and associated time lines for clean-up (see Figure 5-2):

- *marginal:* a three-year clean-up schedule
- *moderate:* a six-year clean-up schedule
- *serious:* a nine-year clean-up schedule
- *severe 1:* a 15-year clean-up schedule; and *severe 2:* a 17-year clean-up schedule
- *extreme:* a 20-year clean-up schedule

Under the 1970 Amendments, the EPA sets air pollution emissions standards for new stationary sources of pollution, such as electrical utilities and factories, and for mobile sources, such as cars and trucks. The states are responsible for inspecting, monitoring, and setting emissions standards for pollution sources existing as of 1970. Existing sources of air pollution may exceed the national standards so long as the NAAQS are met. Each state is allowed to make its own decisions on how best to regulate existing sources to meet the ambient air quality standards through State Improvement Plans (SIPs). This process is described in the section on State Air Quality Management Plans.

Efforts to control motor vehicle emissions include minimum efficiency standards for new cars, cleaner burning engines, cleaner fuels, and vehicle inspection and maintenance. In the early 1970s, car makers were required to install catalytic converters, which reduce emissions by turning incompletely burned gasoline into carbon dioxide, nitrogen, and water. At first, leaded gasoline hindered the effectiveness of the converters, but this problem was resolved when auto makers pressured oil companies into producing unleaded gasoline. By 1975, five years after the Clean Air Act became law, unleaded gasoline was available to enable catalytic converters to function properly.

Corporate Average Fuel Economy (CAFE) standards were first enacted in the 1970s to set fuel efficiency requirements for a vehicle manufacturer's entire fleet of cars and trucks. The 1977 Clean Air Act Amendments emphasized reducing motor vehicle pollution by requiring inspections and maintenance in 70 cities and several states where carbon monoxide and ozone standards had not been met.

THE 1990 CLEAN AIR ACT AMENDMENTS

In 1990, Congress passed a mammoth set of Amendments to the Clean Air Act, featuring:

1. new requirements for SIPs to improve air quality and to prevent deterioration in air quality (see the section entitled "State Air Quality Management Plans");
2. a requirement for state and metropolitan transportation plans that conform to state air quality improvement plans;
3. sanctions against states and regions that do not meet attainment levels or do not show progress toward attainment;
4. continued and expanded motor vehicle emission controls;
5. air pollution control technology requirements;
6. requirements for air pollution permits;
7. air pollution offsets;
8. a process to identify and reduce toxic air contaminants; and
9. trading of air pollution credits.

Transportation Plans

Metropolitan areas are required to establish Metropolitan Planning Organizations (MPOs), which have the responsibility to plan for transportation projects. There are 341 MPOs across the nation. Each MPO must adopt a transportation planning process that will maintain the region's air quality or move the region toward attainment of federal air quality standards in three-year intervals (42 U.S.C.A. Section 7511a(g)). The transportation plans have three elements:

- *20-year Regional Transportation Plan (RTP):* must be consistent with both the state transportation plan and state air quality improvement plan, especially the emissions budgets
- *Three-year Transportation Improvement Plan (TIP):* essentially an update of the regional plan, which must also be consistent with the state TIP and the state air quality improvement plan and emissions budgets. (In California, TIPs cover seven years and are updated every two years; in Georgia, TIPs cover six years and are updated every two years.) The three-year plans must show that any increase in vehicle miles traveled and vehicle trips will not jeopardize the improvement of air quality. The three-year plans include specific transportation projects recommended for federal funding and projects to be paid for entirely with state, local, or private money. The plans may include techniques such as High Occupancy Vehicle (HOV) lanes; surcharges to parking fees; van pools; and employer-based, trip-reduction programs, such as flex time and carpools. Areas with severe pollution can even impose traffic restrictions. For example, in the early 1990s, Denver allowed on the road only cars with even-numbered license plates on one day and cars with odd-numbered license plates on the next.
- *Individual transportation projects:* Undertakings such as new roads, bus, and rail lines

SIDEBAR 5-1

Atlanta, Air Quality, and the Georgia Regional Transportation Authority

Greater Atlanta, Georgia, has become the new poster child for sprawl, replacing Los Angeles. The Atlanta region now stretches for 110 miles from north to south across 13 counties and contains about 3.2 million people, resulting in the lowest population density of America's largest metropolitan areas at 1,370 people per square mile (Firestone 1999, 22). This spread-out settlement pattern forces a heavy reliance on motor vehicles and thwarts the use of mass transit. Atlantans drive an average of 34.9 miles a day to and from work—the longest commute of any major city—and spend an average commuting time of 31 minutes each way (Ehrenhalt 1999, 22). In 1999, Atlantans spent an average of 53 hours stuck in traffic, tied with Seattle drivers for the longest delays in the nation, behind only Los Angeles drivers (Schrank and Lomax 2001, 38). Mass transit in the suburban counties is sorely lacking. For instance, until 2002, Gwinnett County, with more than 522,000 residents, had no mass transit.

In July 1998, the EPA withheld federal highway funds from 13 Georgia counties because the air quality of greater Atlanta had fallen below federal standards for smog-inducing ozone. In 1999, Atlanta experienced 69 smog-alert days—a local record (Firestone 1999, 22). In addition, Atlanta's cars and trucks were emitting 250 tons a day of smog-producing nitrogen oxide, a level roughly 36 tons more than the Clean Air Act allows (Ehrenhalt 1999, 21). The EPA gave greater Atlanta until 2005 to reduce nitrogen oxide pollution.

In response, the state legislature created the Georgia Regional Transportation Authority (GRTA, pronounced *greta*). The GRTA has the power to block highway projects and major construction, such as regional malls, which would attract traffic. The GRTA can also push for the construction of mass-transit alternatives. Based on the GRTA and a state plan to improve air quality, the EPA lifted the ban on federal highway funds in July 2000, but the construction of new roads has been stalled by legal wrangling between the state and environmental groups (Firestone 2001, A18). Atlanta and its neighboring counties have a strong incentive to clean up their air. The metro region has been eyeing federal funds to help pay for a proposed outer-ring interstate 35 miles from downtown Atlanta. The new highway has an estimated price tag of $5 billion. Yet, if built, the new highway could foster more sprawl and automobile dependence.

Atlanta is hardly the only metro area with air quality that falls short of federal standards. Houston and Los Angeles lead the nation in smog (ozone) pollution. Yet, the EPA has not withheld highway funds from those areas and has granted them time extensions to meet the federal air quality standards. In this sense, the EPA has made an example of Atlanta.

must be listed on both the RTP and the TIP, and must be consistent with the state transportation plan and the state TIP and the state air quality improvement plan in order to quality for federal funding (see Figure 5-3).

Sanctions

Failure to reduce pollution according to state emissions budgets can potentially lead to penal-

ties and intervention by the EPA. The 1990 Clean Air Act Amendments allow the EPA to withhold federal funds for new highway and industrial construction in areas with air quality below the federal standards. For example, in 1999, the EPA threatened to withhold federal highway funds from the Dallas-Fort Worth metropolitan region unless ozone levels were reduced. The message is that either regions work to improve air quality, or

SIDEBAR 5-2

California's Crackdown on Motor Vehicle Emissions

California has long been a trend-setter in air quality standards. California passed air quality legislation in 1968, two years before the Clean Air Act Amendments of 1970. The U.S. EPA has long granted California a waiver from federal air quality standards, as long as the state's standards exceed the federal standards.

In 1998, the California Air Resources Board set emissions standards for cars, trucks, and buses that were about twice as stringent as the federal standards. Manufacturers who do not meet these emissions standards face stiff fines. Also, beginning with the 2004 models, diesel cars and trucks must meet the same standards as those for gasoline-powered vehicles (Bradsher 2000, B5).

California had gone so far as to require that by 2003, 2% of all cars and trucks sold must produce zero emissions; these vehicles must run on electricity or fuel cells that do not produce carbon dioxide. Another 2% must be low-emission hybrid vehicles that combine gasoline power and electric batteries, and another 6% must be super low-polluting vehicles that also rely mainly on electricity and fuel cells (Pollack 2001, A10). But California dropped these requirements when it became clear that auto makers could not deliver enough low- and super-low-emission vehicles.

In 2002, California became the first state to authorize standards on carbon dioxide emissions from motor vehicles (Hakim 2002, A14). By law, the California Air Resources Board will set standards to achieve maximum feasible reductions of this greenhouse gas.

In 2003, Honda Motors began selling hydrogen fuel cell cars to the City of Los Angeles (*Money* 2003). Cars powered by hydrogen fuel cells that produce energy through an electrochemical process. There are no moving parts and little noise. The fuel cells split hydrogen into electrons to make electricity and protons, which make water and heat as by-products. There is no combustion and hence no air pollution. The new vehicle technologies can reduce overall pollution emissions, but they are not a panacea. For each solution, there are some drawbacks, such as batteries made with heavy metals or the need for electricity to charge batteries or produce hydrogen.

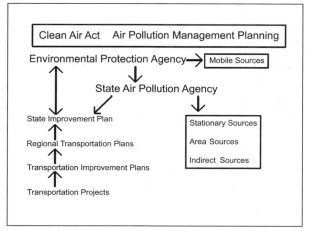

5-3 Clean Air Act air pollution management planning.

federal sanctions will create the incentive for the regions to act. In 1999, the EPA also cited nine other metropolitan areas for serious ozone levels: Atlanta, Baltimore, Chicago, Hartford, Houston, Milwaukee, greater New York City, Philadelphia, and Washington, D.C. If the states and regions do not draft acceptable plans for improving ozone levels, the EPA may draft plans for them.

The 1990 Amendments also gave the EPA the power to levy fines against violators of the Clean Air Act without having to go to court. In 2000, the EPA settled a record $93.2 million air pollution case with plywood manufacturer Willamette Industries. Willamette had avoided installing pollution-control equipment to reduce the emission of

SIDEBAR 5-3

The Energy, Air Quality, and Water Quality Link

With the passage of the Clean Air Act Amendments in 1990, the U.S. Environmental Protection Agency (EPA) gave gasoline producers the choice of adding ethanol or the chemical methyl tertiary butyl ether (MTBE) to oxygenate gasoline. This reformulated gasoline would enable engines to burn gasoline more thoroughly and thus reduce carbon monoxide emissions. The oil companies chose to use MTBE in most cases because it was more easily available. The EPA then required nine metropolitan regions with smog problems to use higher amounts of MTBE to reduce air pollution.

Unfortunately, the EPA did not test MTBE adequately before recommending its use. MTBE is now suspected of being a carcinogen. Because MTBE does not break down quickly and readily dissolves in water, it is very difficult to clean up. Also, small quantities of MTBE can contaminate large drinking water supplies with a bad odor and a taste like turpentine. By the late 1990s, MTBE had been detected in as many as 9,000 wells throughout the nation (Perez-Pena 1999, B6). As many as one-fifth of the nation's urban wells may be affected. Leaking underground gasoline storage tanks, powerboats and jet skis on lakes and rivers, and stormwater runoff that carries automobile residues are common sources of MTBE.

MTBE from leaking gasoline storage tanks contributed to the contamination of seven public wells in Santa Monica, California; most of the city's wells were shut down in 1996 (DePalma 2001, 1, 13). The city then successfully sued oil companies for $22 million to pay for clean-up. California Governor Gray Davis ordered that MTBE be phased out altogether in that state by 2002.

VOCs that react with nitrogen to create smog. In the settlement, Willamette agreed to pay an $11.2 million civil penalty, spend $8 million on environmental projects, and invest $74 million in new emissions-control equipment (Wald 2000a, A12).

Motor Vehicle Emission Controls

Building on the 1970 and 1977 Amendments, the 1990 Clean Air Act Amendments contained several provisions aimed at reducing air pollution from motor vehicles. Catalytic converters on cars were first required in the 1970s. Starting in 1990, catalytic converters had to work for 100,000 miles and cars must have dashboard lights and under-the-hood systems to show whether the converters are functioning effectively to control pollution.

The 1990 Amendments called for more stringent inspection and maintenance programs than had been required under the 1977 Amendments.

However, the 1990 Amendments did not change the CAFE standards, which were first enacted in the 1970s. In 2002, the average miles per gallon standard was 27.5 based on a combination of city and country driving. For light trucks and sport utility vehicles (SUVs), the standard was only 20.7 miles per gallon, even though light trucks and SUVs produce more pollution per vehicle than cars. About half of all motor vehicles sold in America in 2000-2002 were light trucks and SUVs.

According to the U.S. EPA (2000a), the average gasoline-powered car in 1997 generated 606 pounds of carbon monoxide, 80 pounds of hydrocarbons, 41 pounds of nitrogen dioxide, and 10,000 pounds of carbon dioxide. Buses and heavy trucks pollute much more than cars do, and the 1990 Clean Air Act Amendments required truck and bus makers to modify their diesel engines to reduce most particulate emissions and to improve fuel efficiency. The 1990 Amendments also mandated that diesel fuel have less sulfur content.

Gasoline refiners have to reformulate gasoline sold in smoggy areas to contain less volatile

SIDEBAR 5-4

Radon Gas: A Persistent Toxic Substance

Radon is a naturally occurring substance that is released as a colorless, odorless gas from decomposing uranium or radium in rock. The radioactive gas can seep into the basements of homes and buildings. Radon has been identified as the second leading cause of lung cancer (after smoking), contributing to an estimated 7,000 to 30,000 deaths each year (U.S. Environmental Protection Agency (EPA) 2001a). It may take several years of exposure to radon gas for lung cancer to develop, but for people who smoke and are exposed to high levels of radon, the risk of lung disease is increased.

Radon is common in the Rocky Mountain states, along the northern tier of the Plains and the Midwest, and in the northeastern states, particularly Pennsylvania, New Jersey, and New England. Radon exists in millions of homes and buildings. City, county, and state health departments are creating maps of radon levels. There are often wide variations in radon levels within a single city or county, and radon readings can vary over time. In 1988, the U.S. Surgeon General recommended that all homes in the United States be tested for radon in the indoor air. That same year, Congress passed the Indoor Radon Abatement Act, which provided federal funding and technical assistance to states with the goal of making indoor air as free of radon as the ambient air outdoors. The EPA recommends that all homes below the third floor be tested for radon, and has set a standard of no more than four picocuries of radon per liter (U.S. EPA 1999a). Radon levels can be reduced for a few hundred to a few thousand dollars by adding a ventilation system to remove indoor air and bring in outside air.

organic contaminants, such as benzene (a known carcinogen). In congested areas with cold weather, refiners were required to sell oxyfuel (gasoline with more oxygen to burn cleaner and reduce carbon monoxide). In heavy pollution areas, gas stations must install devices on gas pumps to catch gasoline fumes. In addition, all gasoline was required to contain detergents to prevent the build-up of engine deposits and keep engines running smoothly and burning fuel more thoroughly. Finally, the 1990 Amendments promoted alternative, cleaner burning fuels, such as alcohol, ethanol, and liquified natural gas, through federal subsidies to producers.

Air Pollution Control Technologies

The 1990 Clean Air Act Amendments required new air pollution sources and modifications to air pollution sources in areas that meet air quality standards to install Best Available Control Technology (BACT). These technologies are determined on a case-by-case basis, and can be combined with air pollution offsets (see below) for Prevention of Significant Deterioration (PSD) in the region's air quality. The best available technology may change over time and can vary across regions.

As of 2000, most large urban areas in America did not meet one or more federal air quality standards (Moore 2001). In nonattainment areas, major new stationary sources of air pollution that would emit 100 or more tons per year of any pollutant and major modifications to existing sources must install technologies to achieve the Lowest Achievable Emissions Rate (LAER). Like BACT, the LAER involves a case-by-case analysis of required technology and can vary over time and from place to place. LAER requirements can be combined with pollution emissions offsets to achieve the necessary no-net increase for air pollutant levels. Existing stationary sources in nonattainment areas must install Reasonable Available Control Technology. These technologies are established by individual states on a case-by-case basis.

Air Pollution Permits

The 1990 Amendments require large, existing stationary polluters, such as factories and power plants, to obtain and pay for a pollution permit. This requirement is similar to the National Pollutant Discharge Elimination System/state discharge permits approach used under the Clean Water Act for discharges into waterways. Permits are issued by the states, and the EPA can step in to issue or revoke a permit if a state does not perform its duties. The permit indicates the level of pollutants currently being released, the allowable level of pollutant emissions, and actions the polluter is taking to reduce the pollution. Polluters are responsible for regularly monitoring their own emissions and reporting any violations.

The permit system is a one-stop process that covers all types of air pollution that may emanate from a power plant or factory. Permit applications and permit information are a matter of public record, and can be obtained from a state or regional air pollution control agency or the EPA. Planners, businesses, and citizens can readily find out where the major polluters are located and what they are emitting into the air.

Air Pollution Offsets

An offset is a way to achieve an improvement in air quality while allowing a change in sources of air pollution. Take the case of a company located in a nonattainment area that wants to expand production or change a production process in a way that will increase the emission of one of the six major air pollutants. This change will be allowed only if there is an offset—a reduction of the pollutant by an amount somewhat greater than the proposed increase—somewhere else in the region. An offset can come from reductions inside the company or from another company in the area. An offset will keep the region on track toward the attainment of federal air quality standards. The 1990 Amendments allow companies to trade offsets. In a nonattainment area, the required offset is often a reduction of as much as 1.5 tons of pollution emissions for each ton of emissions from a new facility (Moore 2001, 4). This is just one example of how the Clean Air Act is more stringent on development in nonattainment areas than in areas that currently meet the federal clean air standards. Because of this uneven regulation, the Clean Air Act creates an incentive to build in areas that already meet clean air standards.

Toxics

The 1990 Amendments gave the EPA responsibility for setting standards for 189 hazardous air pollutants and reducing toxic emissions over a 10-year period. Exposure to toxic air pollution can cause cancer, respiratory problems, and neurological damage. As of 1999, Texas, with its prominent petrochemical industry, led the nation in the amount of toxic air emissions (Yardley 1999, A22). The EPA must identify and regulate major and area (small) sources of toxic emissions, including gas stations, chemical factories, dry cleaners, coal-fired power plants, auto paint shops, and print shops. Once a toxic source type is identified, the EPA requires applications for approval of new plant construction and alterations. Also, the EPA requires testing, monitoring, record keeping, and reporting by the companies generating or using the toxic substance (see Chapter 7). If a company wants to increase toxic emissions, it will have to offset the increase by reductions elsewhere in the company or by purchasing a reduction credit from another company, as noted above.

In 1989, the EPA's 33/50 program encouraged companies to voluntarily reduce their emissions of 17 toxic chemicals, such as benzene, mercury, and cadmium, by 33% by 1992 and 50% by 1995. A total of 1,135 companies responded with a 34% reduction in toxic emissions—a decrease of more than 500 million pounds by 1992 and further reductions by 1995 (Easterbrook 1996, 205). As of 2000, the EPA had set regulations for airborne emissions of more than 300 toxic chemicals.

The 1990 Amendments also created the Chemical Safety Board to investigate accidental releases of hazardous air pollutants, much as the National Transportation Safety Board investigates train and plane crashes.

The 1990 Amendments marked a departure from the 1977 Amendments that had based acceptable amounts of hazardous pollutants on tolerable risk levels. Instead, the 1990 Amendments mandated that maximum achievable control technology be used to combat the major industrial sources of toxic air pollution. The link between human health and best available technology will continue to evolve over time as more scientific information is gathered and analyzed and new technologies are developed.

Tradable Air Pollution Credits

The 1990 Clean Air Act Amendments established a cap-and-trade market mechanism to set a national limit on pollution emissions and allocate pollution allowances among polluters. Polluters who exceed their annual allowance must buy "pollution credits" from polluters who emit less than their allowance. Thus, polluters have an incentive to reduce emissions, both to save money and to earn it through trading credits. The more businesses reduce pollution, the more they lower their costs of production, and hence become more efficient and competitive.

In the 1980s, the federal government used the cap-and-trade approach to decrease lead in gasoline by requiring petroleum refineries to purchase a lead-pollution permit in order to add lead to gasoline. The refineries could then trade these permits among themselves, so that a refinery that reduced the use of lead below the permitted level could sell its remaining allowance to other refineries that were still exceeding their permitted levels. Thus, refineries had an incentive to produce unleaded gasoline and simply sell the lead-pollution permits for cash. Lead in gasoline was eliminated in 1995.

The 1990 Amendments built on the success of the market approach to removing lead from gasoline. In drafting the 1990 Clean Air Act, economists convinced Congress that it would be cost-effective for large polluters, such as coal-fired electrical utilities and major industrial plants, to buy and sell air pollution credits as a way to reduce sulfur dioxide emissions—one of the major ingredients in acid rain. Companies that reduce their emissions below federal allowances can earn a tradable credit for each ton of sulfur dioxide below the federal standards. The credits can be sold to other plants anywhere in the United States, enabling them to exceed their emission limits.

The federal government auctions off credits or makes credit grants each year. The goal is to reduce the number of credits issued so that the price of the remaining credits rises, creating an incentive for industry to reduce or eliminate their emissions over time. In 1993, air pollution credits began trading on the Chicago Board of Trade. Some environmental groups purchased credits and simply retired them forever, thus reducing the total amount of allowable sulfur dioxide emissions. The goal was to cut the 1990 level of sulfur dioxide emissions in half by 2005. Through the trading of pollution credits, industrial companies achieved this reduction about six years ahead of time and also saved electrical consumers a few billion dollars. The price of pollution credits in 2000 was about $140 to $150 per ton of sulfur dioxide. The EPA and state air quality agencies can monitor smokestack emissions with sensors that are linked to government computers. Thus, the government can determine the amount of pollution credits a company is due or must buy to come into compliance.

Still, tradable credits are not without shortcomings. The credits were based on pre-1990 levels of sulfur dioxide emissions, so the largest polluters received the largest pollution allowances. For instance, the majority of sulfur dioxide emissions come from coal-fired plants built before 1970, which, in many cases, use high-sulfur coal. For political reasons, more than 300 of these old coal-fired generating plants were required to meet only local air quality standards under the 1970 Clean Air Act. This meant that older plants, which were emitting most of the sulfur dioxide, were allowed to operate without having to invest in new pollution-control technology as long as the owners did not make major renovations or additions to their plants. But any new or substantially upgraded electrical-generating plants must install best management practices (BMPs) and meet strict emissions standards under what are known as the New Source Review Rules. As of 2001, these older generating plants were producing more than half of America's electricity and the majority of the carbon dioxide, nitrogen oxide, sulfur, and mercury emitted by all types of electrical plants (Greider 2001, 28). In 2002, the EPA changed the New Source Review Rules by allowing older electrical-generating plants and refineries to modernize without adding the latest air pollution control devices.

Sulfur dioxide trading does not affect the other main cause of acid rain: nitrogen oxide. In 1999, eight northeastern states (Connecticut, Delaware, Massachusetts, New Hampshire, New Jersey, New York, Pennsylvania, and Rhode Island) began an emissions trading program to reduce nitrogen oxides with results that are encouraging. Regulators from each state set 1999 emission allowances at about half of 1990 emissions levels. Each state received a share of allowable emissions credits that were then divided among power plants and major industrial sites. Companies that hold their nitrogen oxide emissions below their allotted level are free to sell the difference in credits to companies that exceed their levels. For the main smog-producing period of May through September 1999, total nitrogen oxide emissions were about 175,000 tons—less than half the 1990 emissions and 20% less than the allowed 218,000 tons. Businesses are finding it cheaper to reduce emissions than to continue to pollute. Further reductions of nitrogen oxide emissions are planned by lowering the allowable level of emissions.

PROGRESS AND CONTINUING CHALLENGES IN SOLVING AIR POLLUTION PROBLEMS

From 1970 to 2000, America's overall air quality improved as emissions of the six criteria pollutants fell by 29% (U.S. EPA 2001b, 1). The number of air quality alert days in major cities declined by half to fewer than 300 per year. However, the cost of achieving improvements in air quality has been high—about $636 billion from 1972 to 1994 (Council on Environmental Quality (CEQ) 1996, 249). Even so, the EPA estimated that, between 1970 and 1990, the 1970 Clean Air Act and the 1977 Amendments produced net money-equivalent benefits of $13.7 to $21.7 *trillion* (U.S. EPA 1997). These figures include health benefits, enhanced longevity, greater visibility, and reduced soil damage. The EPA also projected that by 2010, the 1990 Clean Air Act Amendments would create about $4 of benefits for every $1 spent on pollution controls. The Amendments would extend the lives of 23,000 Americans each year, avoid more than 1.7 million asthma attacks each year, and save 4.1 million lost work days in 2010 alone (U.S. EPA 1999b).

Despite the improvements in the average quality of the nation's air, the U.S. EPA (2001b, 5) reported that 62 million U.S. residents were living in counties that did not meet the NAAQS for at least one of the six principal pollutants. Yet, if ozone concentrations based on an eight-hour standard are used (rather than the 24-hour measure), 122 million Americans were living in places that did not meet all six air pollution standards in 1999.

A continuing and widespread air pollution problem is motor vehicle emissions, which are likely to increase because of:

- population growth;
- rising numbers of motor vehicles;
- increased number of trips and vehicle miles traveled (VMT);
- greater congestion; and
- continued sprawling development patterns, which mean longer driving trips in both time and distance.

As traffic delays mount, motor vehicles will idle longer and be caught in stop-and-go patterns. The idling and starting of engines contribute more to air pollution than moving traffic.

Nitrogen Oxide

Motor vehicles and industries were the main reasons why the 2000 level of nitrogen oxide pollution—the main contributor to ozone and smog—was 20% higher than the 1970 level (*ibid.*, 4). Over those 30 years, the nation's population grew by more than 50 million people, the number of cars nearly doubled, and VMT soared by 143% (*ibid.*, 1). Nitrogen oxide emissions from electrical utilities were 23% higher in 1996 than in 1970 (CEQ 1996, 282). Nitrogen oxide continues to be a major contributor to acid rain (see Case Study 5-1, below).

Sulfur Dioxide

In 2000, sulfur dioxide emissions that cause acid rain were 44% lower than the 1970 level (U.S. EPA 2001b, 4). The wider use of smokestack scrubbers and gas bags, along with the shift from high-sulfur to low-sulfur coal, accounted for much of the reduction in sulfur dioxide emissions. Moreover, in 2000, sulfur dioxide emissions were 30% less than in 1990 and below the federally allocated level for industry emissions (U.S. EPA 2000b, 16; 2001b, 2). These figures suggest that the emissions trading program begun in 1992 has had a positive effect on air quality. Another indicator of improving air quality is the declining acidity of precipitation in the eastern United States, from a pH reading of 4.43 in 1985 to 4.55 in 1995 (U.S. EPA 2000b, 289).

Lead

Airborne lead pollution has been almost eliminated, dropping by 98%—from 220,869 tons in 1970 to less than 4,000 tons in 2000—after lead was phased out of gasoline (U.S. EPA 2001b, 4; U.S. Bureau of the Census 2001, 216).

Carbon Monoxide

There have been great strides in reducing carbon monoxide pollution from automobiles, even as the number of motor vehicles and miles traveled increased. The EPA reported that carbon monoxide emissions dropped by 25% between 1970 and 2000, and much of this reduction can be attributed to better fuel economy (U.S. EPA 2001b, 4).

Particulates

Between 1970 and 2000, emissions of particulates (PM-10) fell by 88%, according to the U.S. EPA (*ibid.*). Gasoline and diesel engines, dust from roads, burning coal, and burning wood remain major sources of particulates. After the energy crisis of the 1970s and through the 1990s, many people who moved to the country chose to heat their homes, at least in part, with wood. The amount of timber harvested for firewood more than tripled, from a billion cubic feet in 1977 to more than 3.1 billion cubic feet in 1994 (CEQ 1996, 32). Burning wood produces much more particulate pollution and carbon dioxide than burning oil or natural gas. Several local governments have had to curb the use of wood stoves and fireplaces under certain weather and pollution conditions. Smaller particulates of 2.5 microns (PM-2.5) are still of considerable concern because of their ability to lodge in the lungs and cause damage. In 2004, the EPA will begin to regulate PM-2.5 particulate emissions (Wald 2002, 39).

Ozone

Ground-level ozone concentrations decreased by 44% 1970 and 2000, but ozone levels showed little improvement after 1990 (U.S. EPA 2001b, 4). Ozone in the southern and north central regions has worsened since 1990, according to the EPA. For example, in 1999, nearly half of Texas's 19 million inhabitants were living in areas that did not meet federal standards for ozone (Yardley 1999, A22). On the positive side, in 2001, Denver became the first city in the nation to improve its air quality to "clean air status" under the federal Clean Air Act, for ozone. As recently as 1977, Denver was ahead of only Los Angeles for worst urban air quality (Stein 2001, 1). In 2004, the EPA is scheduled to tighten the ozone standard from 125 parts per million over a four-hour period to 80 parts per million over an eight-hour period (Wald 2002, 39).

Toxic Air Pollution

The 1990 Amendments, industry cooperation with the EPA's 33/50 early compliance program, and a ban on burning toxic substances in municipal incinerators have resulted in notable reductions of toxic emissions. The EPA reported that emissions of toxic air pollutants decreased as a whole by about 23% from 1990 to 1996 (U.S. EPA 1999e, 2).

In California, annual toxic releases into the air fell by more than 80% from 1988 to 1997. Much of California's reduction was attributed to the state's 1986 "right to know law" (Proposition 65) that requires companies to report their releases of toxic chemicals or else face fines of $5,000 per day for each person not warned (*The Economist* 2001a, 62). Companies responded both by making the necessary disclosures and by lowering emissions. Still, nationwide in the late 1990s, motor vehicles were the source of more than half of toxic air emissions, and contributed up 90% of the carbon monoxide found in urban air (*ibid.*). Also, the incineration of medical waste and other toxic substances by private firms is a short-term response to the need to dispose of toxic waste. The EPA estimates that as many as 20 million rural residents burn trash in their backyards. Trash burning contributes to particulate pollution and carbon dioxide emissions as well as to toxic releases. Recycling and landfilling trash are better ways to handle most trash.

Substituting nontoxic materials, recycling, tighter regulations on burning, or a combination of tighter regulations with tradeable permits can further reduce toxic emissions.

Coal-fired, electrical-generating plants are the leading source of airborne mercury pollution. According to the Natural Resources Defense Council (2000, 41), power plants release 98,000 pounds of mercury into the air each year, but there are no federal regulations on mercury emissions from these plants. High levels of mercury in fish have been detected in the Northeast, downwind from the coal-fired plants of the Midwest. Mercury can damage the nervous system and is fatal in large doses. The long-term solution is to phase out coal-fired plants in favor of natural, gas-fired plants, or develop "clean coal technology" that sharply reduces mercury emissions.

Ozone-Depleting Chemicals

While most air pollutants have local or regional impacts, some have global effects. One such example is ozone-depleting chemicals. Emissions of most chemicals that destroy high atmospheric ozone have declined dramatically since the 1987 Montreal accord that called for a phasing out of these chemicals. America's releases of three types of CFCs—the main cause of ozone depletion—fell from 202 million metric tons in 1990 to 41 million metric tons in 1999 (U.S. Bureau of the Census 2001, 217). Worldwide, the production of ozone-depleting chemicals has fallen by 90% from the 1987 level and at a modest cost (Dunn and Flavin 2002, 48).

Carbon Dioxide

Carbon dioxide is the major greenhouse gas that contributes to global warming and is associated with other air pollutants. The U.S. has not established standards to reduce carbon dioxide emissions, even though a reduction in carbon dioxide emissions would also lower emissions of particulates, ozone, and nitrogen and sulfur oxides (Dunn and Flavin 2002).

Power plants produced almost 40% of America's carbon dioxide emissions in 2000, and they released 25% more carbon dioxide in 2000 than in 1990. The Clean Air Act requires the EPA to review and update standards for power plant emissions every eight years, but the EPA has not done this for a long time. Meanwhile, carbon dioxide emissions from cars, trucks, buses, and trains rose by 23% in the 1990s. Carbon sinks—farmlands and forests where carbon is naturally absorbed—took up 18% less carbon in 2000 than in 1990 (Revkin 2003, A1, A17).

The Kyoto Protocol of 1997, signed by 163 countries, called for industrialized countries to set limits on the emission of carbon dioxide and other greenhouse gases from cars, power plants, and industry, but the U.S. Senate failed to ratify the Kyoto Protocol. The U.S. would have to reduce greenhouse gas emissions by 600 million tons by 2012, a level 7% below 1990 emissions. The Senate felt that the cost of compliance would be too high. In 2001, President George W. Bush officially declined to support the Kyoto Protocol. Interestingly, the Kyoto Protocol would set up internationally tradeable pollution credits, similar to the pollution credits the U.S. has used to reduce sulfur and nitrogen dioxide emissions from factories and power plants in the United States. Also, several American companies have set their own targets for reducing greenhouse gases (Dunn and Flavin 2002, 43).

STATE AIR QUALITY MANAGEMENT PLANS

The relationship between the EPA and the states is meant to be a partnership, and somewhat flexible in meeting the NAAQS. The state air quality improvement plan process was established under the 1970 Clean Air Act Amendments, and revised under the 1977 and 1990 Amendments, as a way to compel states to help maintain and improve air quality.

The EPA requires states to submit air quality management plans, known as SIPs, for review and approval. SIPs are designed to enable states to meet, maintain, and enforce the NAAQS. MPOs were created under the 1990 Clean Air Act Amendments to enable local residents and planners to have input into what federally funded projects are needed. The states and the MPOs must show that their growth strategies and investments in transportation are consistent with the SIP and do not exceed SIP emissions targets for mobile air pollution sources. State plans must include land use and transportation controls, if necessary, to meet federal air quality standards. Otherwise, states and regions cannot spend federal funds on highway or transit projects that would create or worsen air quality problems. Several MPOs with air quality problems have modeled the level of emissions from different land uses in an attempt to determine alternative land uses that would enable the region to meet or maintain compliance with air quality standards (Stephenson 2002, 9).

Required elements of SIPs include:

- A review of proposed major, new stationary sources of air pollution, such as factories or power plants. There must be recommended limits on emissions from each single source. Each source may produce a different mix of pollution.

- A review process for large, new indirect pollution sources that would attract mobile sources of pollution (cars, trucks, and airplanes). Indirect sources include shopping centers, airports, highways, and sports stadiums.

- Designation of air quality maintenance areas and air quality improvement areas.

- Air quality maintenance plans, which explain how the state will maintain air quality and prevent "significant deterioration" in areas that meet the national air quality standards.

- Plans to improve air quality in "nonattainment areas" that currently do not meet the national air quality standards.
- Rules for the six criteria pollutants and emissions standards for hazardous air pollutants.
- Land use and transportation connections.
- Motor vehicle emission and fuel standards.
- How state environmental policy conforms with the Clean Air Act.

SIPs are used by state environmental agencies in reviewing the potential air quality impacts of large development proposals. These proposals may involve a stationary direct source (such as a new factory) or a stationary indirect source that attracts large amounts of traffic (such as a shopping mall). The SIP process must involve the public through hearings and opportunities to comment. To improve air quality in nonattainment areas, the SIP must include:

- a modeling of the air quality and pollution emissions in a region;
- determination of the level of emissions that will still result in attainment of the federal standards;
- the amount of emissions from mobile and stationary sources;
- a timetable of emissions reductions in moving toward attainment; and
- the allowable emissions "budgets" each year.

Reducing pollution emissions in parts of the nation where the economy and population are growing is a challenge. Take, for example, a growing region with an emissions level that is x tons of sulfur dioxide above the federal standard. In year three, because of economic growth, the level of emissions would be expected to increase to $x+y$ tons of sulfur dioxide above the federal level. Therefore, to meet the federal sulfur standard in year three, the region must reduce sulfur emissions by $x+y$ tons to comply with the federal air quality standards.

Administration, Monitoring, and Enforcement

The EPA has made grants to states to draft SIPs, and the states and the EPA share responsibility for administering, monitoring and enforcing the Clean Air Act. The EPA and the states have dozens of air quality monitoring stations. The EPA also operates a continuous emissions monitoring program, which requires owners of facilities that emit sulfur dioxide and nitrogen oxides to regularly test their pollution control and submit reports of emissions levels. A state may prevent the construction of a major highway or electrical-generating plant if the pollution it generated would cause the area or state to violate one or more national air quality standards. The EPA may also veto certain major construction projects. A state air pollution agency can fine a company for violating air pollution standards, as can the EPA.

In the 1990s, there was a shift in the control of environmental programs from the federal government to the states (see Chapter 4). As of 1998, all 50 states were responsible for the review of new sources of air pollution under the Clean Air Act. Forty-six states managed the program to prevent significant air quality deterioration, and 41 states operated the new air pollution source performance standards and the national emissions standards for hazardous air pollutants (Coequyt and Wiles 2000, 9).

A developer of a large project, such as a factory, must obtain two permits from the state environmental agency: an Air Pollution Control Permit to Construct and Operate the factory and an Indirect Source Air Pollution Control Permit for allowed parking capacity. The permits may include conditions that the developer has to meet to ensure compliance with the air quality standards. The developer should follow the direction of the state Air Pollution Control Division in performing an air quality impact assessment of the projected emissions from the factory, and from car and truck traffic traveling to and from the factory. The likely impact of these emissions is then compared to the NAAQS. If the air quality in the air pollution control district currently meets national standards, the proposed development cannot degrade the air quality beyond a certain percentage of the remaining "clean air capacity" (also known as PSD increments). The air quality impacts of the proposed factory are compared to the available PSD increments for nitrogen oxides, particulate matter, carbon monoxide, and sulfur dioxide.

Each state is also responsible for monitoring and identifying major air polluters. However, Coequyt and Wiles (2000) found that state inspectors failed to inspect 560 large factories listed as high priority violators between 1997 and 1999. Half of the uninspected factories were in five states—Ohio, Indiana, Wisconsin, Illinois, and Michigan—each with a high concentration of polluting, coal-fired power plants. The EPA's Office of Inspector General (1998, 1) reported "enforcement audits disclosed fundamental weaknesses with state identification and reporting of significant violators of the Clean Air Act." The report cited states as not reporting significant violators to the EPA and cited the regional EPA offices for not pressing the states for compliance with the law. The report recommended that the EPA reinforce its compliance monitoring strategy. The state's role in monitoring and enforcing the Clean Air Act is delegated from the federal government, and the federal government could take back that authority.

The EPA has levied stiff fines on air polluters, yet has been reluctant to exercise its powers to dramatically limit local and regional development in order to meet the federal air quality standards. The EPA apparently fears curbing economic growth and incurring the political wrath of congressional representatives, the business community, and voters. Also, the seemingly arbitrary enforcement of the Clean Air Act in withholding federal highway funds from greater Atlanta and not from greater Los Angeles or Houston does not engender faith in the EPA.

The Clean Air Act experience demonstrates that it is one thing to pass a law and another to see that it is properly carried out, particularly when authority for carrying out much of the program is delegated from one level of government to another. In sum, air quality improvement will continue to vary from state to state and among air quality management districts within the states. The overall trend in air quality in the U.S. is positive, but much work remains to be done.

Two of the greatest needs in air quality improvement are minimizing sprawling land use patterns and instituting more efficient and coordinated transportation systems. America's sprawling metropolitan areas have increased dependence on automobiles and trucks, and made less-polluting and energy-conserving mass transit less feasible and less attractive. Some critics of the Clean Air Act contend that businesses have been forced to stay away from cities with air pollution problems and settle in the outer suburbs instead. Yet, dispersed businesses only worsen the air quality problems through dependence on the automobile and highway congestion.

The EPA has begun to recognize that sustainable land use patterns incorporating mass transit can be effective in reducing vehicle trips, VMT, and air pollution (U.S. EPA 1999h). State air pollution control agencies can:

- quantify the emissions reductions from sustainable land use patterns in SIPs;
- adopt implementing measures in SIPs to bring about sustainable land use patterns; and
- document emissions reductions from sustainable land use patterns that support the conformity of RTPs with SIPs.

Metropolitan areas can pursue sustainable land use policies that promote transit-oriented development, mix residential and commercial development, encourage pedestrian-oriented neotraditional design, target infill development and redeveloping downtowns, and discourage suburban outward sprawl. These efforts would create greater opportunities for efficient mass transit (see Case Study 5-2, below).

LOCAL PLANNING FOR AIR QUALITY

The comprehensive plan must establish the linkage between air quality, land use, and transportation systems. The plan should then show how proposed future development and transportation systems will impact local air quality in relation to federal air quality standards and the SIP. A municipal or county comprehensive plan must also be coordinated with any RTPs drafted by the MPO.

Inventory

The Natural Resources Inventory section of the comprehensive plan should contain information on local and regional air quality, including weather and topography, any local air pollution problems, and both major and area (small) sources of air pollution, especially toxics. The inventory should also include information on growth patterns and transportation networks as they affect air quality.

Planners can contact their state air pollution control agency for information about air quality reports and the SIP. Also, the EPA publishes a regular *State Air Pollution Implementation Plan Progress Report.*

The state air quality office can provide air quality reports for particular regions that indicate major sources of pollution and whether the community is located in a region that meets or does not meet federal air quality standards. In urban areas, it is a good idea to map ambient air quality at different air quality monitoring stations and to note areas that do not meet air quality standards.

Analysis

The analysis should note whether the proposed comprehensive plan is consistent with the state's SIP and any regional MPO plan. Alternative ways

to meet the air quality requirements of these plans should be evaluated.

Goals and Objectives

This section should spell out general goals and specific objectives for maintaining or improving air quality to meet federal standards and to comply with the SIP and any regional MPO plan. The comprehensive plan should express one or more air quality goals and specific objectives supporting these goals (see Table 5-2).

Action Strategy

The Action Strategy should present techniques and programs for achieving the air quality goals and objectives as well as a timetable. Air quality benchmarks should be identified and progress toward those benchmarks evaluated in an annual report on the environment. Specific recommendations might include the following:

- Adopt mixed-use zoning in the downtown to promote residential development near commercial development, to reduce commuting times, and to encourage alternatives modes of transportation to the car.
- Identify infill sites within the city that could be developed.
- Add 10 miles of bicycle lanes over the next five years.
- Add HOV lanes to encourage carpooling.
- Explore funding for the creation or expansion of mass-transit systems.
- Approve only new or expanding businesses that are consistent with the SIP, RTP, and TIP.
- Publish annual air quality reports for the region, especially information on industrial and motor vehicle emissions.

Zoning Ordinance

One of the original purposes of zoning was to separate conflicting land uses, such as keeping smoke-belching factories out of residential neighborhoods. New industries that emit air pollution

Table 5-2
Sample Air Quality Goals and Objectives in the Comprehensive Plan

Natural Resources	
Goal	To maintain (or "to improve and maintain") local and regional air quality.
Objective	Support efforts to reduce regionally generated air pollutants from residential, industrial, and transportation uses—in particular, emissions from vehicles and wood- and coal-burning stoves.
Economic Base	
Objective	Promote air pollution control measures to make the community attractive to new development.
Land Use	
Objective	Promote compact development as a way to reduce air pollution by decreasing automobile dependence and increasing the feasibility of mass transit. Encourage infill of vacant land and underutilized downtown sites.
Transportation	
Objective	Promote the use of mass transit and alternative modes of transportation to reduce air pollution.

should only be permitted to locate in commercial or industrial zones, away from population centers and natural resource zones. Zoning ordinances typically include setback requirements from property boundaries, in part to promote air circulation. Some zoning ordinances have additional standards for vegetative screening, earth berms, and buffer areas, which can be used to reduce the impacts of air pollution on neighbors.

Zoning can also enhance air quality where governments are serious about creating more compact development that reduces car trips and commuting times, and enhances the feasibility of mass transit. To promote compact development, zoning ordinances must allow mixed-use residential and commercial developments at a fairly high density. At a county or regional level, zoning that tightly limits the number of dwellings allowed on open land outside of established settlements will help control the growth of automobile-dependent sprawl.

Subdivision Regulations

Subdivision and land development regulations can further the protection of air quality as part of the development process. The subdivision ordinance can require that a large percentage of trees

above a certain size be maintained or replaced on a site to help absorb and filter air pollution, provide shade (which lowers ground-level temperatures in the summer), and generate oxygen. Many subdivision ordinances require developers of large residential subdivisions to dedicate parkland or fees in lieu of parkland. Parkland may include bicycle paths and walking trails for alternative modes of transportation.

Capital Improvements Program

The location, type, and timing of public infrastructure greatly influence where and when commercial, industrial, and residential developments are built, which in turn affects air quality. If a goal of the comprehensive plan is to promote compact development, this should be reflected in the capital improvements program (CIP). The program should include an explicit policy of concurrency, stating that no development can occur until adequate public facilities (schools, sewer, water, roads, police, and fire service) are in place. The concurrency policy will reduce sprawl and VMT, but only if zoning is strict outside of developed areas. Otherwise, developers will choose to build in the countryside and contribute to automobile-

Table 5-3
A Checklist of Air Quality Issues for a Development Review

1.	What are the size, location, and land uses of the proposed development?
2.	Will the development generate a large amount of air pollution or attract a large amount of motor vehicle traffic?
3.	What transportation modes are available to provide access to the proposed project?
4.	Will the proposed project cause traffic congestion?
5.	How would the proposed development project affect the State Improvement Plan or current air pollution levels?
6.	Would the proposed project cause a deterioration of air quality?
7.	Is an environmental impact statement required by the federal, state, or local government?
8.	Has the developer obtained any necessary state or federal permits?

dependent sprawl and air pollution. A smoother flow of cars and a better mix of transportation modes can also reduce air pollution. Cities and metropolitan counties can explore adding HOV lanes, additional mass-transit systems, and the creation of bicycle and walking paths.

WHAT TO LOOK FOR IN A DEVELOPMENT REVIEW

A proposed development should be evaluated according to the current comprehensive plan, zoning ordinance, subdivision and land development regulations, CIP, and any other applicable local laws. The location of the proposed use in relation to existing and planned development can influence the future growth of an area, modes of transportation, traffic congestion, and overall air quality (see Table 5-3). The sketch plan stage of a larger subdivision or land development review is a proper time to investigate the likely air pollution impacts and possible modifications or mitigation to minimize air pollution. Planners should be aware of the potential cumulative impact of several small, new developments on transportation systems and air quality. While proposed subdivisions are not normally denied based on the potential of air quality impacts, these impacts can be mitigated through

better project design and transportation improvements. Large developments should be reviewed through an environmental impact process (see Appendix).

Planners should contact the state environmental agency's Air Pollution Control Division if there is any question about air quality impacts. A state environmental agency typically may use a computer model of expected air pollution impacts of a development and may suggest alternative technologies to control air pollution emissions. Communities and regions with decision-making control over development should review the findings and permits of the state environmental agency, especially if a state review under a State Environmental Policy Act is conducted. Local governments may disagree with the findings; however, increasingly, state and federal regulators are exercising the final say over whether to approve or deny a proposed development based on air pollution criteria.

CASE STUDIES

The following case studies illustrate the ongoing air quality problems from acid deposition, and how greater Portland, Oregon, recognized the land use/transportation/air quality connection and responded with a combination of more compact development and mass transit to maintain air quality while allowing growth.

CASE STUDY 5-1
Acid Deposition and Federal and State Air Quality Standards

Acid rain is better known among scientists as acid deposition, which includes not only acid rain but also acidic snow, fog, particulates, and gases. Acid deposition is formed through the interaction of sulfur dioxide and nitrogen oxides with sunlight and water vapor. Acid deposition contains both sulfuric acid and nitric acid. Due in part to the prevailing southwesterly winds, New York and the Northeast have been the recipients of acid deposition caused by air pollution from the Midwest.

Ironically, acid deposition has fallen into a regulatory purgatory, as federal regulators have failed to decide whether acid deposition is air pollution or water pollution. A 2000 study by the General Accounting Office reported that, while the 1990 Clean Air Act succeeded in reducing sulfur emissions from factories and power plants, nitrogen oxides—released by these sources as well as from motor vehicles—have continued to be a major source of acid deposition. Acid levels in most lakes tested in the Adirondack Mountains of northern New York increased during the 1990s (Dao 2000, A1). As of 2000, an estimated 500 lakes in the Adirondacks were "dead"—they no longer supported aquatic life. According to the Albany *Times Union* (2000, A12), by 2040, as many as half of the region's 2,800 lakes and ponds could share a similar fate.

Acid levels are measured on a logarithmic pH scale ranging from 0 to 14; the lower the number, the higher the acid content. Acidic readings range from 0 to 5.6, neutral measurements can vary from 5.6 to about 9, and basic or alkaline is 9 to 14. The log scale means that water with an acidity reading of 4.0 is 10 times more acidic than water with a 5.0 reading. Clean rain has an acidity of 5.6. Many

parts of the northeastern United States have acid rain readings of 4.4.

Damage to crops and trees and the disappearance of fish in lakes and ponds in the Northeast have been attributed to acid deposition. Just as alarming, acid deposition can reduce phytoplankton at the bottom of the food chain. Acid deposition increases the rate at which mercury leaches out of rocks and soil, and can cause mercury poisoning in water and fish. Children are especially vulnerable to mercury, which can reduce intelligence and bring on erratic behavior. According to neurotoxicologist David Carpenter, "Almost every New York lake has some mercury in fish. When mercury exceeds the safe limit [.002 milligrams per liter in New York], steps need to be taken by the state to ensure people don't eat the fish" (Cappiello 1999a, A1). Statewide, New York has a warning not to eat more than one meal of fish per week. Neighboring Vermont has issued an advisory against eating any fish caught in the state because of potential mercury contamination (*ibid.*, A7).

The 1970 Clean Air Act allows states to set air quality standards that exceed the federal standards. For example, in 1999, New York took steps to reduce the pollution emissions from 32 in-state power plants that contributed to acid deposition. The state mandated a sulfur dioxide emission level by 2007 of half the level of the federal standard, and a reduction in nitrogen oxide emissions of 25% below the federal standard. Moreover, the cuts in nitrogen oxide would apply to year-round emissions, unlike the federal requirement for nitrogen oxide reductions in the summer months only. As a result of the new, more stringent emissions standards, New York power plants will have to invest in expensive pollution filter systems.

However, coal-fired power plants in the Midwest contribute many times the amount of emissions responsible for acid deposition as New York plants. For example, in 1998, New York produced 313,606 tons of sulfur dioxide and 102,000 tons of nitrogen oxide; Ohio generated 1.4 million tons of sulfur dioxide and 515,882 tons of nitrogen oxide (Cappiello 1999b, A1).

In 1999, New York State and the EPA began legal action against several midwestern and southern utilities that had made improvements to old coal-fired power plants that did not comply with the BMP requirements. Late in 2000, Virginia Electric Power Company settled out of court with New York State and the EPA. The company agreed to spend $1.2 billion over 12 years to reduce emissions of sulfur dioxide, nitrogen oxides, and particulates by 70% through upgrading eight power plants (Perez-Pena 2000, A1). As part of the settlement, the company cannot sell any tradable air pollution credits to other utilities. Then-EPA Administrator Carol Browner commented, "This is the single greatest air pollution reduction ever achieved from a utility" (*ibid.*) The settlement also marked the first time that a state has sued a polluter in another state under the Clean Air Act. Late in 2000, the EPA and the State of New York reached an agreement with Cinergy Corporation of Cincinnati, Ohio, to spend $1.4 billion over 12 years to cut sulfur dioxide and nitrogen oxide emissions from 10 coal-fired power plants (Archibold 2000, B10).

The ongoing struggles over acid deposition demonstrate the need for a federal role to ensure the right of each region of the nation to clean air and clean water. Allowing one region to deposit its air pollution on another region is contrary to the spirit of the Clean Air Act. The federal government should require that pre-1970 coal-fired power plants be phased out or substantially upgraded within a few years. In fact, in 2000, the EPA conducted a cost-benefit analysis of reducing acid rain that estimated the benefits from fewer respiratory illnesses, cleaner water, and greater visibility at $60 billion; and the costs of upgrading power plants at just $5 billion (U.S. EPA 2000d, 45)

CASE STUDY 5-2
The Land Use, Air Quality, and Transportation Study in Portland, Oregon

Interstate 5 runs the length of Oregon and passes through the center of its largest city, Portland. In 1989, state highway engineers proposed a new interstate highway that would connect Interstate 5 south of Portland around the west side of the city to Interstate 5 on the Washington side of the Columbia River.

A citizens' group, concerned about the sprawl-inducing effects of the new highway, opposed the interstate link. In the early 1990s, 1000 Friends of Oregon (a land use organization formed to monitor Oregon's 1973 State Land Use Law) became involved in the highway dispute. However, 1000 Friends took a broader than usual approach to the highway controversy. They joined with transportation and architectural consultants to undertake a $1 million study of the connection between air quality, alternative modes of transportation, and different land use patterns in greater Portland.

In 1994, Portland released its *Land Use, Transportation, Air Quality Connection* report. The study showed that building more highways around Portland would lead to more automobile-dependent sprawl and increased air pollution. Part of the problem was that Portland sits between the Coast Range and the Cascades, which rise up to 12,000 feet. It is not uncommon for inversions to occur, in which stagnant cold air becomes trapped under warm air and pollution concentrations build up. The study's conclusions helped put an end to the west side interstate.

The study also featured the transit-oriented development (TOD) designed by New Urbanist architect Peter Calthorpe (1993). TODs combine a European-style transit system and the traditional U.S. small town—what he described as a revival of the "street-car suburb," popular in the early 20th century. Calthorpe designed compact, high-density "nodes" at intervals along the rail lines, with the transit stations serving as the centers. In places without existing rail lines, buses could be used, or new light-rail lines could be built. TODs include a core area of about a quarter-mile radius, and a secondary area that extends outward for an additional quarter mile. Within this bounded area, development occurs at a full range of densities—houses, apartments, and commercial space within walking or biking distance of a transit line and an easily accessible town center at the transit hub. The compact design of TODs help keep the surrounding landscape open. The study noted that mass transit is more environmentally benign and more energy efficient than the use of the personal automobile (Major 1994, 16). To help reduce VMT, the study proposed expanding into the western suburbs the light-rail system that had served Portland's eastern suburbs since 1986. In September 1998, the west side light-rail line was opened, linking Hillsboro to downtown Portland.

The TOD concept became a reality in 1998 when ground broke on Orenco Station, near the west side light-rail line (see Figure 5-4). The 206-acre site is scheduled to have 1,800 dwelling units, pocket parks, and a commercial district with three-story buildings—all within walking distance of the rail station. A ride to downtown Portland takes just 35 minutes. Orenco Station is effectively a new town, but one that fits into the region.

The 2040 plan of Metro, greater Portland's regional elected government, has identified 35 centers with potential for TODs, which link main streets and transit corridors. These centers will occupy about one-fourth of the metropolitan area and contain about half of the region's people.

Greater Portland has made the decision to limit urban expansion to 2040 to no more than 18,000 acres. Over that time, the population is expected to increase by as many as 750,000 people to about 2 million. If mass transit were not available, the region would choke on traffic congestion and air pollution. In the late 1990s, an estimated 40% of trips to downtown Portland were made by mass transit. Downtown Portland, unlike many U.S. urban centers, is a thriving place.

Several U.S. cities have taken note of the success of Portland's light-rail system. Light-rail commuter lines now exist in 20 metropolitan areas and are being proposed in another 40, including greater Minneapolis-St. Paul; the City of Charlotte and Mecklenburg County, North Carolina; Atlanta; Miami; and Phoenix (see Chapter 16).

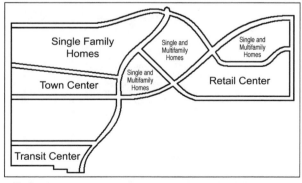

5-4 Layout of Orenco Station, near Hillsboro, Oregon.

Source: Pacific Realty Associates, LP, www.orencostation.com. Used by permission.

6

Planning for Solid Waste and Recycling

Waste is a wholly human concept.
STEVE BREYMAN, DIRECTOR OF THE ECOLOGICAL
ECONOMICS, VALUES AND POLICY PROGRAM,
RENSSELAER POLYTECHNIC INSTITUTION
(*TIMES UNION* (ALBANY, NY) 2000, B1)

In some instances, large companies may want to take their trash across state lines because they can dispose of it cheaper than here in New York.
JANET MATHEWS, DIRECTOR,
NEW YORK LEGISLATIVE COMMITTEE
ON SOLID WASTE MANAGEMENT
(*TIMES UNION* (ALBANY, NY) 1999, A6)

We live in a society that places a premium on convenience. Many of the products we consume and most of the packaging we use have a useful life span of only a few weeks. Quick disposal then becomes a priority, usually through weekly trash collection. For the ordinary consumer, what happens to the trash after it is removed is often a case of "out of sight, out of mind." As a result, America has often been called the "throw-away society" because of the tendency not to reuse or recycle products and packaging.

Solid waste consists of municipal garbage and industrial waste. Disposing of solid waste is a matter of public health. If allowed to accumulate, household garbage and industrial waste can soon become a breeding ground for a variety of pests and generate polluted runoff into waterways and groundwater. In addition, the smell and sight of rotting garbage are offensive. However, disposing of solid waste is not cheap, and the cost of disposing of solid waste has been increasing despite greater recycling efforts. In 2000, solid waste costs nationwide were more than $38 billion (U.S. Bureau of the Census 2002, 221).

THE CHALLENGE OF SOLID WASTE

Americans generate more municipal solid waste per person than any other country (Dernbach 2002, 9). In 2000, Americans produced nearly 232 million tons of municipal garbage, of which about 30% was recycled, 55% was dumped into landfills, and 15% was incinerated (U.S. Bureau of the Census 2003, 219). The encouraging news is that municipal garbage generated per person in America held steady at about 4.5 pounds per day between 1990 and 2000. However, more important than weight is the sheer volume of garbage, which is growing at a rate of 2% to 4% a year. At this rate, the size of the waste stream will double over the next 16 to 30 years.

Disposal of Municipal Solid Waste

Despite the closing of many municipal landfills, overall landfill capacity has not changed much, because new, larger regional landfills are handling more solid waste, and big private trash haulers, such as Waste Management and Browning Ferris, have expanded their operations. The states with the most number of landfills in 1999 included Alaska (322), California (188), Texas (181), Florida (95), Georgia (76), and Virginia (70). *BioCycle* magazine reported that eight other states had less than 10 years of landfill capacity at then-current rates of disposal (Goldstein and Madtes 2001, 42). Thus, the siting of new landfills will be an important land use issue for states and communities in the near future.

A compelling argument can be made that a community or region should be responsible for safely disposing of its own waste, but disposal should be seen as a last resort. Unfortunately, in the short run, disposal is often cheaper than recycling or reuse. Tipping fees at municipal landfills are much lower in America than in Japan or Germany, for instance, and manufacturers do not include the costs of disposal in the price of their products. If the costs of disposal were included in the price of products, prices would be higher and consumers would buy fewer products. Moreover, consumers would have an incentive to buy products that could be recycled, thus lowering the need to dispose of as many products.

Reduction, Reuse, and Recycling

Reduction

The reduction of solid waste depends on effective consumer education, regulations, and incentives that stress the importance of purchasing longer lasting products and consuming less. This need not result in a reduced standard of living. Authors Paul Hawken, Amory Lovins, and L. Hunter Lovins go so far as to assert that "90% to 95% reductions in material and energy are possible in developed nations without diminishing the quantity or quality of services that people want" (Hawken *et al.* 1999, 176).

The federal government could help reduce solid waste by banning certain kinds of packaging that are not biodegradable. Packaging makes up about one-third of all municipal solid waste, and packaging refuse has more than doubled since the 1960s. Reducing the use of plastics in packaging would be a good place to start. Plastics make up about one-third of the volume of municipal solid waste. Plastics take hundreds if not thousands of years to break down. While it is possible to recycle most plastics, some plastics, such as styrofoam, are not easily recycled. In a highly publicized action, the McDonald's company switched from styrofoam to cardboard to package its take-out hamburgers.

Incentives and regulations can compel manufacturers to use fewer inputs. Companies that can use each other's by-products could be grouped together in eco-industrial parks—a pilot project that the U.S. Environmental Protection Agency (EPA) is pursuing—based on success in Denmark. Manufacturers could also be required to take back and recycle their products, which would create an incentive to create longer lasting products that use fewer inputs in the first place.

Reuse

Reuse is the next best strategy to reducing the overall consumption of goods. Reuse means that a product can be used again with little or no processing. Donating old clothes to the Goodwill or taking shopping bags back to the grocery store are two examples of reuse. Boxes are durable and can be used more than once. One possibility would be to establish a waste exchange to match buyers and sellers. One person's waste is another's raw material.

Recycling

Recycling is the reuse of materials to make new products. By reducing the need to harvest, mine, and process virgin materials, recycling conserves wood, minerals, oil, energy, and water. For example, recycled aluminum cans use about 95% less energy in processing than new aluminum cans, because making aluminum is a very electricity-intensive process. Recycling also reduces the emission of greenhouse gases—especially carbon dioxide—as reprocessing is less energy-intensive than original processing. Recycling saves on landfill expenses and litter clean-up costs, cuts pollution, and creates jobs (as many companies manufacture with recycled materials). For instance, according to The GrassRoots Recycling Network report, *Wasting and Recycling in the United States,* industries that manufactured with recycled materials employed 103,413 people in 10 northeastern states as of 2000 (Institute for Local Self-Reliance 2000).

Recycling programs depend on the willingness of consumers and businesses to participate, on regulations that require recycling, and on making recycling convenient. Raising tipping fees at landfills creates another incentive to rein in consumption and to reuse and recycle, although this could lead to an increase in illegal dumping. On average, Americans pay about $31 a ton to dump garbage, compared to $300 to $400 a ton in Germany and Japan (Ackerman 1997; Hawken 1993, 72).

Creating Markets for Recycled Materials

The economics of recycling work better for some materials than for others. One issue is the cost of separating recyclables by color of glass or type of plastic. Another is the price of competing virgin materials, such as newsprint and cardboard, which discourage recycling efforts. Critical to the success of any recycling program is the existence of a strong and reliable market for the recycled raw materials and finished products. Yet, prices for recycled raw materials can be very volatile. Government subsidies for wood and paper products from the national forests and tax depreciation for oil and forest products companies have helped to keep the prices of products from virgin materials artificially low. This in turn discourages reuse and recycling and encourages waste. For example, governments are big buyers of paper products. To help create stronger markets for recyclables, governments at all levels can institute procurement practices that favor the purchasing of products made from recycled materials, such as recycled paper.

Some states—notably California, Utah, and Minnesota—have created recycling market development zones that offer a package of incentives for recycling businesses. The incentives include low-interest loans, product marketing assistance, permit streamlining, property tax reductions, and a consistent supply of material from local municipalities. Still, several recycling needs and challenges remain for developing recycling businesses and physical processes. For instance, most plastic and paper packaging is difficult to recycle, and more could be done to recycle yard waste and food waste. Yard waste in the form of grass cuttings, leaves, and discarded Christmas trees can account for up to as much as 20% of municipal garbage. Burning yard waste is no longer an option in urban and suburban areas because of the air pollution it would produce. Instead, yard waste is often dumped in landfills. Yard waste can be returned to the land through composting. Yard waste is piled up and, over several months, microorganisms turn it into a form much like dirt. The compost is then sold or given away to gardeners and farmers.

The EPA estimated that in 1999, Americans threw out more than 21 million tons of food, which accounted for about 14% of the nation's total municipal solid waste (Leroux 1999). The recovery rate for food waste was a paltry 2.4%. The U.S. Department of Agriculture puts the amount of food wasted that year at 48 million tons, more than twice the EPA's estimate (*ibid.*). Food scraps and leftovers can be added to yard trimmings and wood chips to make rich compost, and the food decomposes more quickly and with less odor than in a landfill. Food processors and restaurants are beginning to do just that. Also, household backyard composting is a possibility in suburbs and more rural areas.

Some recycling practices are controversial. About 130 million tons of sludge are created each year from sewage and water treatment plants

(Miller 1998). Slightly more than half of this sludge—also known as "biosolids"—is spread on farmlands, forestlands, and other lands. The application of sludge as fertilizer on farmland may run a number of risks. Sludge may contain heavy metals that can be taken up by crops and livestock and passed on to humans. Even if sludge is tested before application, heavy metals can build up in the soil over time. It is important to note that sewage treatment plants pay farmers to take the sludge. Some food processing companies have stated that they will not purchase crops grown on fields to which sludge has been applied. In 1992, the EPA banned the dumping of sewage sludge into oceans and coastal waters to protect seashore recreation, marine life, and the fishing industry. If sludge cannot be recycled onto land, then the two remaining alternatives are to burn it or to bury it.

Recycling and reuse of products and packaging is not a total solution to solid waste. The amount of material that consumers, businesses, and governments use will have to decrease in the long run. Continuous disposal of products means that manufacturers of those products must obtain raw materials from the earth to make new products. Many raw materials, such as aluminum and other metals, are nonrenewable.

SOLID WASTE: THE FEDERAL RESPONSE

In 1976, Congress passed the Resource Conservation and Recovery Act (RCRA), which tied the disposal of municipal solid waste to the protection of water supplies under the Clean Water Act. Subtitle D of RCRA empowered the EPA to set minimum national standards for the states to follow in issuing permits for new, existing, or expansions of public or privately owned and operated solid waste landfills. These landfills may accept nonhazardous waste, including household waste, septic tank waste, nonhazardous sludge, and commercial and industrial solid waste.

The Resource Conservation and Recovery Act

The EPA evaluates state permitting programs for compliance with the minimum national standards, but allows the states some flexibility in how they allow landfill operators to meet the standards. States may enact landfill regulations that are stricter than the federal standards.

RCRA minimum standards apply to:

- *The location of landfills:* Landfills must be kept away from steep slopes, wetlands, sinkholes, airports, public drinking water supplies, and natural hazards such as earthquake fault zones and floodplains.
- *Operating procedures:* Daily compacting and covering of waste with soil is required. Access is restricted in order to prevent illegal dumping. Stormwater runoff and air emissions must be controlled. Landfills may not accept 55-gallon drums filled with liquid waste.
- *The design of liners:* Liners must minimize the leaching of pollutants into groundwater. The liner design the EPA prefers is a plastic liner over a 2-foot layer of clay. There should also be a leachate collection system to capture and treat leachate.
- *Groundwater monitoring systems:* These systems are required to detect leakage from landfills. Groundwater sampling and analysis must be conducted twice a year.
- *Corrective action:* If a leak from a landfill is detected, there must be clear procedures to correct it.
- *Closure of a landfill and post-closure monitoring and maintenance:* After the landfill stops accepting waste, a final cover of a synthetic liner (at least 2 feet of clay and topsoil and vegetation) must be placed over the landfill to keep liquids from leaking into or out of the site. For 30 years after closure, the owner/operator must maintain the final cover, monitor groundwater and landfill

gas, and perform general maintenance of the site. After 30 years, new permanent structures may be built on top of the landfill site.

- *Financial assurance:* The landfill operator must demonstrate the financial capacity to undertake corrective action, if needed, and to pay for the closure of the landfill and post-closure monitoring and maintenance (40 C.F.R. Chapter 1 Part 258).

In 1978, there were an estimated 20,000 landfills in the United States. However, RCRA's stricter landfill regulations resulted in the closure of thousands of landfills that could not meet the new safety standards. In 1986, the first national listing of municipal landfills found 7,683 active sites. The 1996 EPA listing reported 3,091 active municipal landfills, which declined to 2,216 municipal landfills in 1999 (U.S. EPA 2002a; Goldstein and Madtes 2001, 51).

Full Cost Accounting

The EPA encourages municipalities to use Full Cost Accounting to help local officials and the public recognize and compare the direct and indirect costs of solid waste management and disposal. These costs include:

- acquisition of equipment and materials;
- siting and construction of facilities;
- collecting, processing, and marketing recyclables;
- transportation;
- operation and maintenance of facilities (e.g., transfer stations, landfills, and materials recovery facilities);
- clean-up of illegal dumping sites;
- landfill closure and post-closure monitoring;
- program promotion; and
- administration (U.S. EPA 1996a).

Full Cost Accounting provides a complete picture of municipal solid waste management costs on a continuous basis. This method can lead to better negotiating positions if municipalities contract out their waste hauling to a private company, or it can lead to better decisions by municipalities if they handle their own waste. Full Cost Accounting can also help municipalities determine the value of recycling, and whether to use a regional landfill or incinerate garbage.

The "Pay-As-You-Throw" Program

The EPA has taken the lead to reduce waste and promote recycling by sponsoring a "pay-as-you-throw" program, nicknamed PAYT. Traditionally, communities have charged households for garbage service as part of the property tax bill, or private companies have charged a flat monthly fee, regardless of the volume or weight of garbage collected. In a PAYT program, a municipality or private waste hauler bases the fees on the volume, type, or pounds of garbage the household generates. Garbage disposal can be charged according to the size or number of containers, by the type of garbage identified by bag tags, or by weight. Communities that participate in this pricing strategy typically reduce their waste by 14% to 27% and increase recycling by 32% to 59% (Hui 1999). As of early 1999, more than 4,000 communities serving 27 million people were using PAYT programs, including San Jose, California; Seattle, Washington; and Austin, Texas.

PAYT is an excellent example of the adage "Think globally, act locally." PAYT programs help to reduce greenhouse gas emissions from the methane gas created by landfills. The EPA predicts that if 200 more communities with populations of 100,000 adopted PAYT pricing, the reduction of greenhouse gas emanating from landfills would be the equivalent of taking 2.8 million cars off the road.

Federal Efforts to Reduce, Reuse, and Recycle Solid Waste

In the 1970s, the EPA thought that adequate waste disposal could be achieved by landfilling or burning garbage. In 1990, Congress passed the Pollution Prevention Act, which marked a sharp departure from the end-of-pipe or end-of-smoke-

SIDEBAR 6-1

Landfill Gas to Energy

Compacted garbage in landfills breaks down slowly because it does not have much oxygen. A by-product of degrading garbage is landfill gas, made of approximately half methane gas and half carbon dioxide. Methane is a powerful greenhouse gas that is 21 times as effective at trapping heat as carbon dioxide. As trash decays, these gases are emitted into the air, adding to global warming. Landfill air emissions produce about 40% of America's human-generated methane, or 10% of the nation's global warming chemical emissions.

The build-up of methane gas within a landfill can pose a significant risk of fire; under the 1990 Clean Air Act Amendments, larger landfills must collect and burn off landfill gases to destroy trace volatile organic compounds (U.S. Environmental Protection Agency (EPA) 1996b). In a "controlled" landfill, a piping system collects the landfill gas and channels it to a collection point. There are two options: either flare off the gas or use the gas as an energy source. The methane gas can be used as fuel for nearby businesses, shipped into natural gas distribution lines, or used on site to generate electricity in natural gas turbines.

In 1994, the EPA began a Landfill Methane Outreach Program to reduce landfill gas emissions. As of 2001, more than 325 landfill gas-to-energy projects were in operation in the United States. That year, the projects prevented the release of 15.1 million metric tons of carbon equivalent, comparable to taking 12.2 million cars off U.S. roads for one year (U.S. EPA 2002b).

stack control of pollution or the acceptance of solid waste as a valid output. The act set a priority on pollution prevention that "reduces the amount of any hazardous substance, pollutant, or contaminant entering any waste stream or otherwise released into the environment prior to recycling, treatment, or disposal" (P.L. 101-508, 42 USC 13101-13109). Moreover, "pollution that cannot be prevented should be recycled ... pollution that cannot be prevented or recycled should be treated in an environmentally safe manner ... and disposal or other release into the environment should be employed only as a last resort and should be conducted in an environmentally safe manner" (*ibid.*). The Pollution Prevention Act set an emphasis for decreasing the amount of waste through the "three Rs"—reduce, reuse, and recycle. The federal government has mandated that the paper it buys (and that others must use in submitting grant requests) must contain at least 30% recycled material (Easterbrook 1996, 117). Since 1991, the EPA has coordinated federal agency efforts to use recycled or recyclable products whenever possible.

There is considerable debate about the percentage of garbage that the United States could recycle. The EPA believes that 40% or more of municipal solid waste could be recycled. Forty-six states have established goals to recycle 20% to 70% of municipal waste, and most call for cities and towns above a certain size to have curbside recycling. However, in densely populated Japan, as much as 90% of solid waste is recycled. The Japanese have a higher rate of recycling in part because they have less space to put waste.

STATE SOLID WASTE DISPOSAL PROGRAMS

States have primary authority for the siting of landfills and trash incinerators. Most states have followed the EPA's policy of "integrated waste management," featuring reducing the sources of waste, recycling, and landfilling or burning waste with recovering some energy. Several states have set waste-reduction targets and recycling goals, strengthened by mandatory recycling programs. In 1999, 48 states had programs to collect and compost yard waste. Minnesota led the nation with 431 local programs. At least 21 states ban yard waste from landfills altogether, requiring that it be composted instead. A number of states have also banned certain materials from landfills, such as car batteries, tires, and yard trimmings (Chertow 2002). Returnable container laws in 11 states require sellers of bottles and cans to offer a deposit on returnables. This has worked well to reduce litter and solid waste, and lower the cost of solid waste disposal. In 1995, the State of Wisconsin banned all paper from its landfills (Hawken *et al.* 1999, 185), which created a strong incentive for households, businesses, and governments to recycle paper.

LOCAL AND REGIONAL SOLID WASTE DISPOSAL OPTIONS

Counties and municipalities today have four options for the disposal of solid waste:
1. bury the garbage in a local landfill;
2. ship it to a regional landfill;
3. ship it to a landfill in another state; or
4. incinerate it.

Each option has both advantages and drawbacks.

Local Landfills

The burying of waste in local landfills is convenient for waste haulers and is a relatively inexpensive process. Decomposing garbage in landfills can produce commercial quantities of methane gas for local use.

Environmental concerns and community opposition can be impediments to creating new landfills. Landfills can and often do have negative impacts on the immediate surroundings. Pungent odors, flies, vermin, and frequent heavy truck traffic do not make for good neighbor relations. A large landfill can have a visual impact on a neighborhood. Garbage can blow onto neighboring properties. Landfill leachate can leak into groundwater, polluting drinking water supplies and posing health hazards. Although municipal landfills are not supposed to take hazardous waste, they can end up with household products that contain hazardous chemicals as well as lawn pesticide and herbicide containers. Air pollution in the vicinity of landfills has been linked to health problems, and the EPA has a program to monitor emissions from landfills. Finally, the siting of new landfills often raises heated debate over issues of environmental justice. Specifically, is the landfill being located near low-income residents or certain minority groups?

Regional and Out-of-State Landfills

Regional landfills can be sited away from population centers where there will be less opposition and less environmental impact. However, the price of burying garbage is likely to rise as regional landfills are sited farther away from population centers where the garbage is generated. When an old municipal landfill reaches capacity and is closed, a new landfill site often cannot be found nearby. This means that garbage must be transported to a landfill farther away. The attractiveness of this option depends in large part on energy costs. For example, New York City's huge Fresh Kills landfill—the world's largest landfill—was closed to municipal waste in March 2001. Transporting the 13,000 tons of daily household garbage out of New York City to alternate sites will cost an estimated $622 million over five years (Lipton 2000, A1). If energy costs rise, transporting the garbage will become more expensive. Most of the garbage will be carried by trucks, causing more air pollution, more traffic congestion, and wear and tear on roads and bridges. According to one estimate, there could be up to 700,000 more garbage truck trips *each day* across the Hudson River bridges (*ibid.*, B3).

Some communities with large, dense populations are removing their solid waste by rail. Napa County, California, relies on rail to move its solid waste to landfills outside of the county (Merrill 1999). Even the ecologically conscious Seattle, Washington, sends its garbage by double-decker rail cars across the state line to be buried in Oregon.

Yet, there are very real concerns about relying on out-of-state landfills. What would happen if those states used up their landfill capacity or decided they didn't want to take any more out-of-state waste? In 2000, a federal judge ruled that Virginia could not block garbage coming in from New York and other states. The judge said that garbage imports constituted interstate commerce, which only the federal government has the power to regulate.

Economically distressed rural areas are often tempted to take the waste of others, but sometimes rural areas cannot handle their own waste. For instance, the municipal landfill of the small town of Haines, Alaska, was shut down, forcing the town to send its garbage to the State of Washington! (Lende 1999). Illegal dumping of trash remains a problem in many rural areas, either by local people or from out-of-town sources. For example, from 1996 to 2000, Pride (Personal Responsibility in a Desirable Environment)—a program involving the federal government, the State of Kentucky, and local volunteers—identified and mapped 1,996 dumps in southeastern Kentucky, of which 377 have already been cleaned up (Clines 2000, A18). Breathitt County even offered a $5 reward for any appliance reclaimed from a dump or creek and was overwhelmed with 5,000 rusting appliances in a matter of three days! Still, state and local enforcement of solid waste disposal laws is crucial to ensuring environmental quality in the long run.

Incinerating Trash

About one out of every seven tons of municipal trash in America goes up in flames. Trash incinerators can generate electricity by producing steam to turn turbines as the trash is burned. The revenues from the sale of electricity can cover much of the cost of incinerating the garbage. Trash incinerators are typically large enough to handle a regional waste stream, and, like regional landfills, can be sited away from population centers. Incinerators also save on landfill space. Yet, burning garbage does not destroy garbage; it only changes the form

from a solid to a lesser solid (fly-ash) and gas. Even smokestack scrubbers and gas traps do not eliminate pollution; the remaining toxic fly-ash must be disposed of, and some particulates, carbon dioxide, sulfur dioxide, and nitrogen oxides are released. Incineration of medical waste sends toxics such as dioxin into the air. Trash incinerators, like the coal-fired electrical plants mentioned in Chapter 5, have tall smokestacks that send air pollution high into the atmosphere where the prevailing winds will carry the pollution out of the local area.

In the 1970s, the EPA required states to ban burning at municipal landfills. This ban, along with the high cost of building incinerator facilities, has made recycling and landfills more acceptable options. Yet, many rural dwellers still burn their trash in their backyards.

Local Efforts to Reduce Solid Waste

Mandatory recycling programs exist in many cities and states. In 2000, there were more than 9,000 curbside recycling programs serving nearly 134 million Americans (U.S. Bureau of the Census 2003, 220) (see Figure 6-1). Millions of people also recycled at work. Recycling has worked fairly well for aluminum cans, other metal containers, glass bottles, newsprint, plastics, cardboard, and paper (see Table 6-1). For example, in 1998, nearly half of all metals used in America came from recycling (Gardner and Sampat 1999, 45) (see Figure 6-2). Paper and wood make up nearly half of the weight of all garbage (Ince 1996). Newspaper recycling has been popular in households, and paper recycling has been popular for businesses, governments, and educational institutions. Reclaimed wood can be used for building materials or as firewood, wood chips, or paper. However, the EPA anticipates that paper and wood waste will increase faster than the population in the near future (Franklin Associates, Ltd. 1997).

Paper recycling is especially important because the initial production of paper involves huge amounts of water and energy as well as the release

Table 6-1
U.S. Municipal Solid Waste and Recycling by Type (2000)

Material	(in millions of tons)		
	Generation	Recovery	Percent Recovered
Paper	86.7	39.4	45.4
Glass	12.8	2.9	22.7
Metals	13.5	4.6	34.1
Aluminum	3.2	0.9	28.1
Plastics	24.7	1.3	5.3
Yard	27.7	15.8	57.0
Other Wastes (Food, Rubber, Textiles, Wood)	61.9	4.1	6.6

Source: U.S. Bureau of the Census, *Statistical Abstract of the United States: 2002* (2003), p. 220

6-1 Curbside recycling by households is required in many communities.

Source: Katherine Daniels

6-2 Scrap metal recycling.

Source: Katherine Daniels

of large amounts of toxic chemicals into the air and water. Pulp processing and paper manufacturing use more water per ton of output than any other industry in America, whereas recycled paper uses only 10% to 40% of the energy needed to manufacture new paper (Abramovitz and Mattoon 2000, 108). According to the Worldwatch Institute, "U.S. pulp and paper factories have one of the highest pollution intensities, or emissions per value of output, of the 74 industrial sectors monitored by the government's Toxic Release Inventory" (*ibid.*).

Food recycling and reuse holds considerable promise. In 1993, the Intervale Foundation, a non-profit organization, began working with the Chittenden County, Vermont, Solid Waste District to produce compost from food waste. About 10,000 tons of organic material are mixed into farm soil each year. The composting facility is now privately and profitably operated, restoring soil and reducing the amount of waste that goes to landfills. Because of dense settlement patterns, backyard composting may be difficult in cities. San Francisco, California, however, began a food waste recovery program in the early 1990s called "The Fantastic Three." The city provided 2,800 households with three 32-gallon bins—one for garbage, a second for recyclables, and a third for food waste. Nearly half of the food "waste" was ultimately recycled or composted, about double the usual rate. Much of the food that enters the waste stream is still safe for human consumption. Caterers and restaurants have plenty of leftovers. Social service agencies and organizations can use this food, thus reducing solid waste costs and the costs to taxpayers of operating social support programs. San Francisco's Food Bank has successfully redistributed over 500 tons of edible food each year from more than 600 donating companies.

Local governments can grant property tax breaks to start-up recycling firms to help reduce their costs. Alternatively, local governments can include these firms in incubator programs in which the companies operate in low-rent space for

---

SIDEBAR 6-2
Eco-Industrial Parks

An eco-industrial park employs the principle of a closed loop in which the waste from some producers is turned into the raw materials and energy for another producer. The often-cited example of an eco-industrial park is in Kalundborg, Denmark. The industries in the park recycle and share resources, as one company's waste becomes another's raw material. The businesses include a coal-fired power plant, an oil refinery, a wallboard manufacturer, and a pharmaceutical company. The power plant transmits excess steam for heat to the refinery and the drug maker. The oil refinery sells natural gas to the wallboard company and to the power plant. The refinery recovers sulfur dioxide to sell to a chemical company outside the industrial park. Also, steam heat from the power plant is used to heat nearby homes and commercial greenhouses, and heat from the refinery warms the water for a local fish farm (Hawken 1993, 62-63).

The U.S. Environmental Protection Agency operates a small eco-industrial park pilot program to encourage demonstration projects.

---

18 months to two years, and receive training in marketing, accounting, and finance. The EPA offers grants to start up recycling businesses.

LOCAL PLANNING FOR SOLID WASTE DISPOSAL, REUSE, AND RECYCLING

Waste management is typically the third biggest expense for communities after schools and roads. A municipality or county should establish long-term waste management goals and strategies that are consistent with state requirements. Pricing based on volume or weight of garbage generated can create a powerful incentive to reduce waste and increase reuse and recycling. Many communities and private haulers have set a limit on the size of trash containers; any trash exceeding that size involves an extra cost to the household or business. However, higher disposal fees may also lead to more illegal dumping, so additional policing and enforcement may be needed. In the long run, separating waste, recycling, and composting can be more cost effective than most landfilling and incineration, and much healthier for the environment and community residents.

Inventory

Planning for the disposal of solid waste is often overlooked as part of a traditional comprehensive plan. The Community Facilities section of the comprehensive plan should indicate the location of municipal and regional landfills and remaining capacity, where private waste haulers dispose of solid waste, and where solid waste is recycled. Also, any neighborhoods or districts not covered by solid waste or recycling service should be noted. Finally, the inventory should show total and per capita waste generation and recycling by type and percentage of waste.

Analysis

An analysis includes population projections to determine future needs for solid waste disposal and recycling. The analysis should also suggest ways to achieve additional recycling. If the analysis indicates that landfill capacity will be reached within the planning period, the community should evaluate different local and regional disposal options, using Full Cost Accounting. This evaluation will help to identify the advantages and disadvantages of each option.

Goals and Objectives

The Community Facilities section of the comprehensive plan should express goals to reduce solid waste, to dispose of solid waste safely and responsibly, and to increase the reuse and recycling of solid waste. The Community Facilities section and other sections of the comprehensive plan should contain objectives to achieve these goals (see Table 6-2).

Table 6-2
Sample Solid Waste Goals and Objectives in the Comprehensive Plan

Community Facilities	
Goal	To reduce solid waste, to dispose of solid waste safely and responsibly, and to increase the recycling of solid waste.
Objective	Support efforts to reduce locally and regionally generated solid waste from residential, commercial, industrial, and public places.
Objective	Monitor the remaining capacity of existing landfills and identify future local landfill sites or regional landfill facilities.
Economic Base	
Objective	Promote cost-effective solid waste disposal and recycling programs.
Land Use	
Objective	Keep landfills away from sensitive environmental areas, such as steep slopes and wetlands.
Objective	Encourage compact development to make solid waste and recycling pick-up easier and cheaper.
Objective	Separate areas designated for future growth away from any potential landfill sites.
Natural Resources	
Objective	Protect air quality by avoiding the use of incinerators to dispose of solid waste.

Action Strategy

The Action Strategy should present techniques and programs for achieving the solid waste and recycling goals and objectives as well as a timetable. Solid waste reduction and recycling benchmarks should be identified, and progress toward those benchmarks evaluated in an annual report on the environment. Specific recommendations might include:

- Start the recycling of yard waste through composting at the local or regional landfill.
- Price the disposal of garbage by volume.
- Conduct a Geographic Information System analysis of potential landfill sites within the community or region.
- Allow recycling businesses in commercial and industrial zones.
- Explore funding for the creation or expansion of recycling businesses.
- Require the local government and encourage the local school district to purchase paper with at least a 30% recycled content.
- Explore the feasibility of a landfill gas-to-energy project.

Zoning Ordinance

A fundamental purpose of zoning is to separate conflicting land uses in order to protect public health and safety. Landfills are one of the classic Locally Unwanted Land Uses. Communities that do not want a landfill in their jurisdiction can simply not list them as permitted uses in the zoning ordinance. Other communities may want to identify rural areas with parcels of at least 20 acres in size where a landfill might be appropriate. In those areas, the zoning ordinance can list landfills as a conditional use. Industrial zoning could be allowed next to a landfill to take advantage of landfill methane gas as an energy source. Incinerators can either be zoned out of a community or else may be permitted as a conditional use in rural places well away from residential areas. However, incinerators should not be viewed as a long-term solution to solid waste disposal. Zoning can encourage recycling by allowing recycling, collection stations, and composting businesses in industrial zones and certain commercial zoning districts. Zoning can also allow the use of composting in these zones as well as in large-lot residential areas.

Nuisance Ordinance

One way to discourage the build-up of garbage on a property is through a locally adopted nuisance ordinance. The ordinance can specify that derelict cars or household appliances may not be placed in the front yard, and that garbage in the front yard must be removed within 24 hours. Violation of the ordinance should carry a fine. A nuisance ordinance can help to maintain community appearances and minimize threats to public health.

Subdivision Regulations

The creation of a landfill must meet federal and state regulations for construction and operation. Developers should have received the necessary state and federal permits. Local subdivision and land development regulations should require the developer to conduct a full environmental impact assessment (see Appendix). Subdivision and land development regulations can encourage recycling in the construction, renovation, and replacement of buildings. For new construction, the regulations could require that any scrap wood be recycled. The regulations could also require that if more than 5% of a building is renovated, the developer must recycle the materials removed from the building. Similarly, for any demolition of buildings, the materials must be recycled. These recycling requirements can be formalized in a developer agreement in which the developer agrees to the recycling requirements and will post a bond to ensure that the recycling will be done.

Capital Improvements Program

The capital improvements program (CIP) should reflect the goals and objectives of the Community

Table 6-3
A Checklist of Solid Waste and Recycling Issues in a Development Review

1.	What types of solid waste will the proposed development generate?
2.	Will the proposed development rely on a public or private solid waste hauler?
3.	Where will solid waste be disposed of or recycled?
4.	How will the level of solid waste generated by the proposed development affect the capacity of local landfills?
5.	If a landfill, incinerator, recycling, or collection facility is proposed, is the site located a safe distance from population concentrations?
6.	If a landfill, incinerator, recycling, or collection facility is proposed, is it allowed in the particular zone? Are setbacks and buffers from property lines met?
7.	If a landfill is proposed, does the area geology and hydrology minimize potential contamination of groundwater and surface waters?
8.	Has the developer obtained any necessary state or federal permits?

Facilities section of the comprehensive plan in planning for the management and recycling of solid waste. Landfill capacity and future needs, siting of new or expanded solid waste facilities or incinerator facilities, and recycling and composting facilities are all important considerations, and decisions should be guided by Full Cost Accounting for each option.

A CIP can be used to describe proposals for a new landfill, expansion of an existing landfill, construction of an incinerator, or development of recycling facilities—the timing, cost, and financing arrangements. The location of any of these disposal or recycling facilities is crucial to future growth of a community or region, and should be coordinated with the future land use map and zoning ordinance.

What to Look for in a Development Review

A proposed development should be evaluated according to the current comprehensive plan, zoning ordinance, subdivision and land development regulations, CIP, and any other applicable local laws. In reviewing a proposed residential, commercial, or industrial development, renovation, or demolition, planners should ask how solid waste will be disposed of or recycled (see Table 6-3). Residential developments in urban and suburban areas should allow for easy curbside recycling. Large-lot residential areas should enable on-site composting. The proposed siting of a regional landfill can raise heated emotions. A landfill can take up several acres and emit a pungent smell over a wide area. Local residents often resent the importation of garbage from outside the community. State environmental agencies often play a major role in deciding the location of new landfills. However, local planners may also be asked to evaluate the alternatives to landfills, such as an incinerator, expanded recycling, or alternative landfill locations. Local planners may want to contact the regional EPA office for advice. First and foremost is the appropriateness of the site: geology, hydrology, aquifers, surface waters, wetlands, and existing and planned development must be considered.

7

Planning for Toxic Substances and Toxic Waste

The most alarming of all man's assaults upon the environment is the contamination of air, earth, rivers and sea with dangerous and even lethal materials.
RACHEL CARSON, *SILENT SPRING*

Times Beach, Missouri, has no residents today. The town was founded in the 1920s when people could buy a piece of real estate near the Meramec River as part of a subscription to the *St. Louis Sun Times* newspaper. Times Beach grew into a town of 2,400. It was a common practice to use oil in the process of resurfacing streets. Unfortunately, oil can soak up toxic chemicals. In 1982, a flood struck Times Beach, revealing the presence of severe dioxin contamination. The town was evacuated, the Federal Emergency Management Agency (FEMA) bought up all of the real estate, and a massive clean-up began.

Dioxin makes up a class of 75 organic chemicals that contain chlorine. Dioxin is found in polyvinyl chloride plastic, paper bleaches, pesticides, and chlorinated solvents. Seven types of dioxin are highly toxic, producing birth defects and cancer, and attacking the immune system. Dioxin does not break down easily, accumulates in the food chain—especially in fat tissue—and can migrate long distances.

It took several years and millions of dollars to remove thousands of tons of contaminated soil from Times Beach. The remediation effort culminated in a controversial, U.S. Environmental Pro-

tection Agency (EPA)-mandated burning of the soil. The disappearance of Times Beach as a town alerted Americans to the serious, even deadly, health threats from exposure to toxics. Nonetheless, on September 11, 1999, the State of Missouri opened a state park on the spot where Times Beach had once stood.

THE CHALLENGE OF TOXIC SUBSTANCES AND HAZARDOUS WASTE

It is a common saying among toxicologists that there are no hazardous substances until people are exposed to certain levels of concentration. Another way to say this is that anything in a sufficiently large enough amount can hurt you. Toxic substances do not quickly or easily break down in the environment; in rather small quantities, they can pose severe health threats including cancer, respiratory and neurological damage, birth defects, miscarriages, and even death. Some toxic substances occur naturally, such as the heavy metals arsenic, cadmium, chromium, copper, lead, mercury, and zinc. Radioactive nuclear waste from nuclear power stations, the manufacture of atomic weapons, and hospital x-ray equipment involve human manipulation of natural substances such as uranium.

Human-made, or synthetic, toxic substances include:

- medical waste, often from contaminated polyvinyl chloride (PVC) plastics used in intravenous tubes and blood bags, among others; and

- about 500 chemical compounds, mainly from the group of synthetic organic chemicals known as organochlorines, including polychlorinated biphenyls (PCBs), chlordane, dioxin, solvents, fungicides, pesticides, industrial degreasers, and chlorofluorocarbons (CFCs).

Since World War II, there has been explosive growth in the production of synthetic toxic substances, from about 1 billion pounds in 1945 to about 400 billion pounds in 2000 (U.S. Bureau of the Census 2001, 220). Toxic substances may purposely be released onto land or into air or water (such as in the application of pesticides) or by mistake (such as in a chemical spill caused by a train accident). Toxic contamination of groundwater and surface water drinking supplies is a particular concern because large populations may be exposed for long periods without their knowledge. Even when toxic contamination is detected in groundwater, it may be difficult or impossible to clean up. Toxic substances can enter the food chain, killing fish and decimating other wildlife. Soil poisoned by toxic substances is unfit for human habitation and the production of crops and livestock. Toxic releases into the air can turn deadly, as was revealed after thousands of people in Bhopal, India, were killed or injured in 1984 by a release of toxic gas by the American-based Union Carbide company.

Spills of hazardous materials usually occur during their transport, such as chemical spills in freight train crashes and derailments, and truck accidents. If spills are not contained and cleaned up quickly, pollutants can run off into rivers, streams, and lakes, and leach into groundwater. When these spills happen near cities and towns, they can pose hazards to public health and force local residents to be evacuated. Sometimes haz-

---

SIDEBAR 7-1

Rachel Carson and *Silent Spring*

Rachel Carson is often hailed as the founder of the modern environmental movement because of her 1962 book, *Silent Spring*. Carson sounded the alarm that pesticides such as dichlorodiphenyltrichloroethane (DDT) were devastating wildlife and the environment. Large birds, especially eagles and condors, ingested DDT through their prey; a side effect was a thinning of eggshells, causing the eggs to break prematurely and killing the chicks. DDT also traveled up the food chain to humans and was detected in mothers' milk. Carson warned that pesticides in food and drinking water could interact with each other and cause cancer in humans. *Silent Spring* led to the federal ban of DDT in 1972. The number of endangered large birds has since made a dramatic recovery, and the bald eagle—America's national symbol—may soon be taken off the endangered species list. However, DDT is still used on crops overseas that are then imported to the United States.

---

ardous materials are released into the air or water from industrial plants and utilities. For example, at times, nuclear plants vent radioactive steam; chemical plants emit high concentrations of toxic chemicals into the atmosphere; and the contents of leaking storage tanks, barrels, and dumps can seep into waterways and groundwater.

TOXIC WASTE DISPOSAL

Toxic waste is very difficult to recycle, and disposal requires careful handling and long-term monitoring. Roughly 80 million pounds of hazardous waste are disposed of in the United States each year (U.S. Bureau of the Census 2001, 220). In the past, most hazardous wastes were dumped in wells, mine shafts, landfills, vacant lots, ravines, wetlands, sewers, ditches, along rural roads, or placed in steel drums. Moreover, many toxic dump sites have been abandoned and the contents not fully assessed.

There are five ways to dispose of toxic waste:

1. burial;
2. deep well injection;
3. incineration;
4. fly-ash storage; and
5. storing in liquid form in containers.

Each method has drawbacks.

Simple burial in municipal landfills is not allowed because hazardous waste can leak into the groundwater. Private landfills, licensed to accept toxic waste, must have clay or plastic liners as well as in-ground monitors to detect leakage. The siting of toxic waste dumps is a very controversial, political issue. No one wants to be exposed to toxic waste, yet some local governments may see a dump site as a source of tax revenue and jobs. Rural areas and places with concentrations of low-income residents and minorities are often vulnerable to both legal and illegal hazardous waste dumping. Private waste dump operators are attracted to the countryside because land is fairly cheap and there are relatively few people who would be exposed should there be a spill or leak. Illegal dumping will probably continue in rural areas because there is an abundance of territory in which to dump waste without immediate detection.

Deep well injection runs the risk of putting toxic waste into aquifers used for drinking water or irrigation. Incineration of toxic waste raises the possibility of air pollution and dispersing toxics over a large area. For example, burning medical waste, especially contaminated plastic ware, releases dioxins into the atmosphere. Fly-ash must be kept from interacting with rain so that the remaining toxins in the fly-ash do not wash off into groundwater or surface water. If toxics are kept in secure containers, these containers must be stored somewhere and monitored for leakage.

Storage of toxic liquids in metal containers is vulnerable to corrosion and leakage over time,

especially when the containers are buried in the ground. Storage of nuclear waste presents special problems. In 1998, the federal Department of Energy became the "owner" of all commercial nuclear waste and hence responsible for disposing of it. The amount of nuclear waste will increase for years to come based on recent trends (Council on Environmental Quality 1996, 328). Until additional nuclear disposal capacity is added, especially for high-level waste, thousands of tons of nuclear waste will continue to accumulate in containers at commercial reactor sites. After 14 years and $4.5 billion in studies, the U.S. Department of Energy in 2002 proposed storing much of the nation's nuclear waste under Yucca Mountain, Nevada (Wald 2002, A1, A19). However, nuclear waste has a "half-life" (i.e., stays dangerous) for about 10,000 years. Opponents of the Yucca Mountain plan have raised a number of arguments, from seismic activity that could cause leaks, to corrosion of containers, to a terrorist attack.

Hazardous waste is difficult, but not impossible, to recycle. Only an estimated 3.5% of hazardous waste generated in the United States is reused or recycled, although as much as 20% could be, according to some experts. Europeans regularly reprocess nuclear waste for fuel in power plants, and the Netherlands operates a hazardous waste exchange whereby companies can bring in and take away hazardous substances for reuse. Syracuse, New York, also has a hazardous waste exchange. However, the recycling of toxic chemicals that have been used to manufacture products, such as dioxins in PVC pipe or PCBs in electrical transformers, is rare. Therefore, the primary challenges become how to reduce the generation of toxic waste and how to safely dispose of it.

One way to reduce toxic waste is to raise the cost of using toxic substances and disposing of toxic waste through the imposition of an environmental tax, as discussed in Chapter 2. According to Lois Gibbs, founder of the Citizens' Clearing House for Hazardous Wastes, "When the cost is

SIDEBAR 7-2

Toxic Nightmares: Rocky Flats and Woburn

Two of the best-known cases of toxic waste pollution occurred at the nuclear arsenal at Rocky Flats, Colorado, and in the dumping of chemicals over a drinking water aquifer by the W. R. Grace Corporation and Beatrice Foods at Woburn, Massachusetts.

The Rocky Flats Nuclear Weapons plant, located 15 miles northwest of Denver, produced triggers for nuclear bombs from 1952 until it was shut down in 1989. The U.S. Department of Energy operated the plant with the Rockwell International Corporation on the 6,300-acre property. In 1989, U.S. Environmental Protection Agency (EPA) investigators found thousands of cubic meters of radioactive and chemical waste, including plutonium and uranium, carbon tretrachloride, trichloroethylene (TCE), and tetrachloroethylene (perc). The waste was scattered over 134 individual sites that were subsequently designated for clean-up. Chemicals had been dumped on the ground, other waste was stored in corrodible steel drums, and groundwater was contaminated. The Department of Energy hired the Kaiser-Hill Company to do the clean-up work, which began in 1996 and is expected to take 10 years to complete. For its role in the illegal dump-

ing, Rockwell International was fined $18.4 million (Pankratz 1997). However, Rocky Flats is only one of many polluted sites that produced nuclear arms. Closing and cleaning up these sites will cost an estimated $147 billion (Janofsky 1999, A7).

In Woburn, a suburb north of Boston, an epidemic of leukemia among children was traced to two corporate sites during a protracted legal battle between eight families of the dead children and W.R. Grace and Beatrice Foods. From the 1950s to the 1970s, the toxic industrial solvents TCE and perc were dumped or placed in corrodible drums on the site of the two industrial plants. The chemicals seeped into groundwater that served as part of Woburn's public drinking water supply. Children are more vulnerable than adults to exposure to hazardous waste, and several developed leukemia. A multiyear legal battle followed in which the families sought damages from the companies that owned the plants, and eventually settled out of court with W.R. Grace and lost the case against Beatrice.

Later, the EPA successfully sued the two companies for clean-up costs, but clean-up was not so easy to achieve. As Jonathan Harr explained in his book *A Civil Action*, "the EPA unveiled a reclamation plan that would take fifty years to complete and would cost an estimated $69.4 million, the largest and most costly environmental cleanup in New England" (Harr 1996, 491).

high enough, corporations will decide to recycle wastes, reclaim materials, substitute nontoxics in their products and eventually change their processes of production" (Dowie 1995, 134).

Toxic substances highlight the challenge of risk assessment: setting exposure and maximum tolerance standards that are scientifically accurate and that everyone can trust. Should certain substances be banned altogether or can humans tolerate trace amounts? Where is that tolerance threshold, or does the tolerance vary from person to person?

Risk assessment is an inexact science. The EPA has established tolerance levels for toxic substances, which are reviewed from time to time. The dilemma is that strict tolerance levels may burden industry and local governments, but liberal tolerance levels may expose many people to serious and unnecessary harm. Sometimes the EPA declares a substance unsafe and bans further production, such as dichlorodiphenyltrichloroethane (DDT) and PCBs. It is commonly believed that all chemicals licensed for use in the United States have been tested by the federal government for safety. In fact, the great majority of licensed chemicals have been tested only by the manufacturer, and information about hazards often comes to light only after the chemical has been used for years. Risk assessment and tolerance levels are a good example of the precautionary principle, which holds that it is wise to restrict or ban certain substances that may cause harm even though scientific evidence is not yet conclusive.

Brownfield Remediation

The EPA defines brownfields as "abandoned, idled, or underused industrial and commercial facilities where expansion or redevelopment is complicated by real and perceived contamination" (U.S. EPA, Brownfields Home Page 2001). Brownfield sites range in size from abandoned corner gas stations to defunct factory complexes. Estimates vary on the number of brownfields, but across American there may be more than 500,000 sites (Eisen 2002, 457). Rehabilitating brownfields for commercial, industrial, and residential space provides an excellent example of how environmental quality is fundamental to economic improvement. Brownfields often have good access to transportation networks, sewer and water facilities, and population concentrations. Former industrial sites have been developed into technology parks, new manufacturing and warehousing operations, museums, restaurants, parks, marinas, and housing through new construction as well as the rehabilitation and adaptive reuse of existing buildings.

In 1994, the U.S. Conference of Mayors cited brownfield clean-up as their top priority. In the mayors' report, *Recycling America's Land*, "187 cities estimated that more than 550,000 jobs could be created on former brownfields sites" (U.S. Conference of Mayors 1997). Redevelopment would also bring in an estimated $878 million to $2.4 billion in tax revenues each year (*ibid.*). The mayors argued that recycling brownfields was essential for attracting new business investment, new jobs, and new places to live. Bringing people back to the cit-

ies would revive old neighborhoods, and slow or reverse population loss to the suburbs.

FEDERAL ACTION ON TOXIC SUBSTANCES

In the early 1970s, Congress embarked on more than a decade of legislation to identify toxic substances and regulate their manufacture, transportation, use, and disposal. There are four main laws that regulate the manufacture and use of pesticides and industrial chemicals, track the release of toxic chemicals, and encourage recycling and reuse of toxics:

1. the Federal Insecticide, Fungicide, and Rodenticide Act (FIFRA) (or the Federal Environmental Pesticide Control Act);
2. the Toxic Substances Control Act;
3. the Emergency Planning and Community Right-To-Know Act; and
4. the Pollution Prevention Act.

The Federal Insecticide, Fungicide, and Rodenticide Act

The FIFRA Amendments of 1972 (also known as the Federal Environmental Pesticide Control Act) requires manufacturers of these chemical pesticides to register them with the EPA before they are distributed (7 USC Section 136 *et seq.*). The pesticides also must be labeled, stored, handled, and applied according to certain standards. For example, farmers who use pesticides are required to get training in the application of pesticides and to keep detailed records of their use.

The Toxic Substances Control Act

In 1976, Congress passed the Toxic Substances Control Act, which allows the EPA to obtain information from private companies on new and existing chemicals, and to control or in some cases ban the manufacturing, distributing, importing, and processing of toxic chemicals (15 USC Sections 2601-2629). One of the early results of the Toxic Substances Control Act was the EPA ban on the use and production of PCBs, cancer-causing chemicals found in many industrial processes. However, the procedures for controlling or banning a toxic substance can take years to complete. Legislation by Congress to control or ban a substance is a quicker solution. There are more than 60,000 chemicals in use in America, and only a few of them have been tested for their effects on humans and the environment (Dernbach 2002, 26).

The Emergency Planning and Community Right-to-Know Act

The Emergency Planning and Community Right-To-Know Act of 1986 (42 U.S.C. 11001 *et seq.*) was passed by Congress in response to the 1984 accidental toxic chemical release in Bhopal, India, that killed several thousand people. The act was designed to help local communities protect public health and safety and the environment from chemical hazards. The EPA can obtain information from private companies on new and existing chemicals under the 1976 Toxic Substances Control Act. The Emergency Planning and Community Right-to-Know Act goes a step further in requiring companies that manufacture, use, or store hazardous materials to keep records on the location, quantity, use, and release of those materials into the air, land, or water.

The 1986 act requires the EPA to issue an annual Toxic Release Inventory. The 2000 Toxic Release Inventory contained information on the manufacture, use, transportation, treatment, and emissions of more than 650 toxic chemicals. The inventory was compiled from 91,500 forms submitted by some 23,500 industrial facilities (U.S. EPA 2002a). The inventory reported that 7.1 billion pounds of toxic substances were released into the environment, and 3.4 billion pounds—nearly half of the emissions—came from metal mining operations. Manufacturing operations placed second, with toxic releases of about 2.3 billion pounds, or almost one-third of all emissions. Electrical-gener-ating facilities were third, with nearly 1 billion pounds in toxic releases.

The Emergency Planning and Community Right-to-Know Act also set up planning procedures for state and local governments to follow in response to hazardous materials (haz-mat) spills. Each state is required to appoint a State Emergency Response Commission, divide the state into Emergency Planning Districts, and appoint a Local Emergency Planning Committee for each district. The local committees should include firemen, health officials, community groups, industrialists, government officials, media, and emergency managers. Each city and county must have an office of emergency management, so if a haz-mat spill occurs, the response can be coordinated from that office. It is important to note that the state and local governments bear a responsibility only to contain a haz-mat spill; it is up to the person, company, or government agency that created the spill or owner of the property to pay for the clean-up of the spill.

FEMA operates a number of special programs to support state and local government emergency management agencies and Native American tribes to prepare for and respond to emergencies involving chemical weapons stockpiles, radioactive materials, and other hazardous materials. There is a growing concern that haz-mat emergencies may eventually result from acts of terrorism.

The Pollution Prevention Act

The 1990 Pollution Prevention Act created the EPA Office of Pollution Prevention and Toxics to promote the reduction, reuse, and recycling of toxic chemicals and waste in general. Businesses must report to the EPA the amounts of toxic substances that they treat, dispose of, recycle, reuse, or release into the environment. The Office of Pollution Prevention and Toxics is responsible for administering the Emergency Planning and Community-Right-to Know Act, the Toxics Substances Control Act, and the Toxic Release Inventory.

Convention on Persistent Organic Pollutants

In 2001, the United States signed the Convention on Persistent Organic Pollutants (POPs) to ban the production of 10 POPs (McGinn 2002). These substances are highly toxic, do not break down easily, and bioaccumulate in the food chain. POPs include dioxins and furans, PCBs, DDT, and certain pesticides. Some POPs are known carcinogens; others disrupt the reproductive system in humans and wildlife.

Oil Pollution Act

Although the Clean Water Act prohibits the discharge of oil and 300 other substances in harmful amounts into surface and groundwater, Congress passed the Oil Pollution Act of 1990 (33 U.S.C. 2702 to 2761) to strengthen the ability of the EPA to prevent and respond to catastrophic oil spills. The Oil Pollution Act was enacted in response to the huge oil spill caused when the oil tanker *Exxon Valdez* hit a reef in Alaskan waters in 1989. However, oil spills can also occur when an oil storage tank ruptures or in oil truck accidents.

The act spelled out new rules to reduce the number oil spills and quantity of oil released. The act also established the Oil Spill Liability Trust Fund financed by a tax on oil to clean up spills when the responsible party is unwilling or unable to do so. Owners of oil storage facilities, oil barges, and tankers must provide the EPA with plans stating how they will respond to major spills. The act also requires state contingency plans as part of a National Contingency Plan to respond to large spills on a regional basis. States may impose additional liabilities, fines, and penalties on parties responsible for oil spills.

More than 8,000 oil spills were reported in U.S. waters in 2000 (U.S. Bureau of the Census 2003, 217). While most spills involve fewer than 100 gallons, large spills of more than 100,000 gallons cause serious damage to aquatic life and coastal environ-

ments. From 1990 to 1999, the oil industry spent an estimated $17 billion to comply with the Oil Pollution Act (American Petroleum Institute 1999).

The Resource Conservation and Recovery Act

Congress passed the Resource Conservation and Recovery Act (RCRA) in 1976 and the Hazardous and Solid Waste Amendments in 1984 to regulate the disposal of hazardous waste (42 USC Sections 6901-6991). The purpose of these laws was to create a "cradle-to-grave" tracking system for hazardous substances, from their manufacture to their disposal. In this way, Congress hoped that all hazardous substances would be accounted for and properly disposed of, and random dumping would be eliminated.

RCRA and its 1984 Amendments gave the EPA the power to do the following:

- Identify, define, and list hazardous wastes.
- Ban the land disposal of dioxin, PCBs, and other toxic synthetic chemicals. Instead, they must be neutralized and stored in drums or else incinerated.
- Set standards for keeping records on the manufacture, use, and disposal of hazardous wastes.
- Set standards for how private firms handle, package, and transport hazardous waste.
- Set standards for the operation of hazardous waste disposal sites by private firms, and require treatment of hazardous wastes prior to disposing of them in private, licensed landfills. Hazardous waste disposal sites must have impermeable clay or plastic liners, and in-ground monitors to detect any leakage. Disposal sites must be covered in dirt each time hazardous waste is dumped to minimize airborne exposure. Toxic waste may not be dumped in municipal landfills.
- License private waste disposal companies through a Hazardous Waste Permit Program.
- Inspect private waste disposal sites.

SIDEBAR 7-3

Cleaning Up Leaking Underground Fuel Storage Tanks

Leaking underground fuel storage tanks are a leading cause of groundwater pollution in the United States. In 1984, Congress amended the Resource Conservation and Recovery Act of 1976 to direct the U.S. Environmental Protection Agency (EPA) to set up a program for the removal or replacement of leaking underground fuel storage tanks. In 1988, there were an estimated 3 million underground fuel storage tanks, each with a capacity of 1,100 gallons or more. The EPA gave tank owners 10 years to comply with the new regulations. By 2001, the number of underground storage tanks had fallen to 750,000, though an estimated 150,000 were operating illegally and probably leaking (U.S. EPA 2003).

The EPA has turned over most of the monitoring and enforcement of the leaking underground storage tank regulations to the states. Congress set up a Leaking Underground Storage Trust Fund with $1.3 billion, but has allowed the EPA to use only the interest from the fund (about $70 million a year). Moreover, the EPA can spend that money only to clean up spills, and not to find, remove, or replace leaking tanks (Zielbauer 2000, A1, B7). In 2000, the EPA estimated the costs of assessing and cleaning up abandoned and unregistered underground storage tanks at $450 million, half of which would be paid by the states (U.S. EPA 2000, 31).

There are commercial databases available for known underground leaking storage tanks and where tanks have been removed. This information can be used to create a Geographic Information System database to help in planning the location of future development and public and private water sources.

- Impose fines and penalties for violations.
- Set standards for state hazardous waste management programs, though the implementation of these programs is largely controlled by the states (40 CFR Section 272).

In 1985, the EPA closed 1,100 of the nation's 1,600 licensed toxic waste disposal sites because the operators had not installed wells to monitor for groundwater contamination, or the operators lacked insurance or adequate assets to cover the cost of paying for future problems emanating from the sites. Landfills to handle toxic and radioactive waste are in short supply. There are only a handful of such sites around the country, mainly in Texas, New Mexico, Utah, and Idaho. In 1994, President Clinton issued an executive order directing federal agencies not to concentrate pollution in general, and toxic waste sites in particular, in minority neighborhoods.

Under RCRA, the EPA has set up a leaking underground storage tank program to identify and remove these threats to groundwater. The EPA approves state programs for regulating underground storage tanks, and the states are primarily responsible for carrying out the programs.

Unlicensed dumping of toxic waste is considered a felony under both RCRA and the Clean Water Act. For instance, in 1999, a developer was convicted of having asbestos waste dumped in several places in New Haven, Connecticut. The maximum penalties included a $2 million fine and up to 34 years in prison (*The New York Times* 1999a, 51). That same year, a man who dumped water contaminated with oil from a New Jersey truck repair shop into a storm drain that emptied into the Hackensack River faced up to 10 years in jail and $150,000 in federal fines (*The New York Times* 1999b, B7).

Comprehensive Environmental Response, Compensation, and Liability Act

In 1978, a huge toxic dump was discovered at Love Canal near Niagara Falls, New York. The dumping of toxic substances there had begun in the 1920s; but in the 1940s and 1950s, the Hooker Chemical Company buried over 20,000 metric tons of hazardous waste, including dioxin and a witch's brew of more than 80 other chemicals. The City of Niagara Falls bought the property from Hooker, and about 800 single-family homes, 240 apartments, and a school were built on top of the dump site. Over the years, toxic waste seeped into basements and bubbled up into yards. Residents experienced miscarriages, birth defects, cancer, and other illnesses, until finally the contaminants were discovered. Eventually, most of the homes were purchased by the government, the residents were relocated elsewhere, and the school was closed at a total cost of $250 million (Gibbs 2001, 4).

The Love Canal disaster alerted policy makers to the reality that RCRA, though designed to regulate the manufacture and disposal of toxic waste, did not address the pressing need to clean up large hazardous waste sites and to establish liability to pay for clean-up. The Comprehensive Environmental Response, Compensation, and Liability Act of 1980, better known as CERCLA, or the Superfund law, was passed by Congress in response to Love Canal and the growing awareness that there were potentially thousands of toxic waste sites throughout the nation (42 USC Sections 9601-9675).

CERCLA gave the EPA the authority to identify hazardous waste sites, to maintain a National Priorities List of the most polluted sites (also known as "Superfund" sites), to recover clean-up costs from those responsible for the dumping, and to clean up abandoned sites. In cleaning up sites, the EPA was empowered to bill individual states for 10% of the cost on private land and 50% on public land. The strict liability provision of CERCLA makes all previous and current owners or waste dumpers liable for clean-up costs, even if a person or company purchased a property without knowing that it contained hazardous waste. Also, the "joint and several" clause of CERCLA allows the EPA to make one company or individual liable if others cannot be found or if others have no money to pay for clean-up costs. Not surprisingly, businesses and local governments have been reluctant to purchase and rehabilitate property on which any hazardous waste was dumped. Yet, the redevelopment of less contaminated "brownfields" is crucial to the economic health of cities and older suburbs as well as to curbing sprawl. If brownfields can be successfully rehabilitated for new businesses, jobs, and housing, there would be less demand for building in the outer suburbs and countryside, and less development of farmland, woodland, and wildlife habitat.

A Superfund of $1.6 billion was initially set up to pay for the clean-up of abandoned toxic waste sites and to track down the businesses, government agencies, and individuals liable for dumping the hazardous substances. From early on, it was clear that billions of dollars of federal money would be needed to adequately clean up the many Superfund sites. In 1986, the Superfund Amendments and Reauthorization Act placed another $8.5 billion in the fund. The Superfund also receives revenues from state matching funds and recovers the cost of clean-ups from polluters. From 1986 to 1995, a Superfund tax was imposed on the sale of petroleum products and corporate income. Since then, the nation's taxpayers have had to shoulder an increasing burden of the cost of Superfund clean-ups.

By 1996, the EPA had identified 12,781 hazardous waste sites in need of clean-up, not including 17,000 hot spots on military bases. In 2001, there were more than 1,200 hazardous waste sites on the National Priorities List, but only 739 sites had been cleaned up, at a cost of more than $10 billion, or about $25 million per site (Probst and Konisky 2001). Costs ranged from an average of $140 million for a "mega" clean-up site to an average of $12 million for a "nonmega" site (*ibid.*, xxv). To clean up all of the hazardous sites identified by the EPA, including sites on federal lands, would

SIDEBAR 7-4

Hazardous Waste and the New Information Economy

An emerging concern about the New Information Economy is the use of toxic substances (solvents, acids, and heavy metals) in manufacturing computers and related equipment. Since California's Silicon Valley arose as a major computer manufacturing region, 23 former chip-making plants have been declared Superfund hazardous waste sites (O'Meara 2000, 127). Moreover, given the accuracy of Moore's Law (Gordon Moore from Intel Corporation), of the doubling of transistors per integrated circuit every couple of years, many computers rapidly become obsolete. In 1998, businesses, governments, and individuals retired 20 million computers; only 2.3 million were recycled and 600,000 resold or donated (Schuessler 2000,

G1). The rest were sent to landfills. Yet, computers contain lead, mercury, chromium, and arsenic, which can leak into the environment. The National Recycling Coalition has predicted that, between 2000 and 2007, 500 million computers will become obsolete (*ibid.*).

Several computer makers have internal recycling programs. Gateway offers rebates on new computers when customers turn in old ones for recycling. For a small fee, IBM enables customers to ship old computers to a recycling center. Hennepin County, Minnesota, has operated an electronics recycling program since 1992 (*ibid.*). However, the U.S. Environmental Protection Agency has been reluctant to require businesses to take back and recycle their consumer electronics products. By contrast, European Union countries and Japan are requiring electronics companies to take back and recycle obsolete consumer products.

cost an estimated *$750 billion* (*ibid.*). In some cases, as much as 60% of the clean-up costs have gone for litigation expenses against the polluters. CERCLA provides no money for the victims of hazardous waste dumping who suffer losses in property values, illness, and the loss of loved ones.

An EPA investigation of a Superfund site consists of three parts:

1. a remedial study;
2. a feasibility study; and
3. a five-year review to evaluate the progress in cleaning up the site.

In the remedial investigation, the EPA personnel assess the environmental risks posed by the hazardous waste. Are the risks high, moderate, or small, and is clean-up needed sooner or later? The feasibility study involves the selection of clean-up strategies, based on an engineering evaluation and cost estimates. The EPA may take any of several "removal actions" to contain Superfund sites. The EPA may order the fencing off of a polluted site so that no access is allowed for additional

dumping and to minimize the chances of exposing the public. The EPA may require the covering of contaminated soils with clay and the installation of impervious liners and pumps to collect runoff and leachate. The EPA can also ban the use of a contaminated water supply, provide a new water supply for nearby residents and businesses, or evacuate the contaminated area, as in the case of Times Beach, Missouri. The EPA may also pursue remedial actions, such as washing contaminated soil, removing the contaminated soil, or treating polluted water, to rehabilitate a site for future commercial, residential, or public use.

From 1993 to 2000, the EPA was involved in more than 6,400 actions to remove hazardous waste that posed direct threats to public health and the environment (Mintz 2002, 448). Nonetheless, the environmental agency has come under heavy criticism for its slow progress in implementing the Superfund law. The quality of the EPA's five-year reviews of the clean-up actions has also been criticized as less than thorough

SIDEBAR 7-5

A Toxic Clean-up Dilemma

General Electric (GE) is one of America's largest and most successful companies. Between World War II and 1976, GE legally discharged 1.3 million pounds of toxic polychlorinated biphenyls (PCBs) into the Hudson River at factories in Fort Edward and Hudson Falls in upstate New York (Johnson 2001, A1).

PCBs were first developed in 1929 and were hailed as a miracle chemical because they do not burn and do not dissolve in water. PCBs, like dichlorodiphenyltrichloroethane (DDT), belong to the group of persistent organic compounds that are highly toxic, accumulate in the food chain, and do not easily break down. PCBs, which often came in an oil-like yellow liquid, were used in a variety of manufacturing processes. GE used PCBs in making electrical insulators and capacitors, until the chemical was banned by Congress after passage of the Toxic Substances Control Act of 1976.

GE's releases of PCBs contaminated sediment along a 40-mile stretch of the Hudson River. In the 1980s, the U.S. Environmental Protection Agency (EPA) identified this area as one of the nation's largest Superfund sites, but, surprisingly, decided not to compel a clean-up action at that time. Fishing was banned in the upper Hudson from the late 1970s until 1995, and an advisory against eating fish from the Hudson still applies for children and women of childbearing age.

In 2000, the EPA ruled that GE must dredge up and dispose of about 2.6 million cubic yards of contaminated sediments that contain some 100,000 pounds of PCBs (*ibid.*). GE contended that the river's flow has flushed out significant quantities of PCBs and will continue to do so. The company argued that dredging the contaminated sediments would actually release more PCBs into the river water, disrupting the river ecology, recreation, and commerce. GE will have to spend an estimated $460 million to dredge out several PCB hot spots and dispose of the PCB-tainted sediment.

The PCB problem is not confined to the Hudson River, but has arisen in many areas. For example, in Monroe County, Indiana—home to the City of Bloomington—the Westinghouse Company used PCBs in making electrical equipment and, in 1977, PCBs were discovered in a local landfill. In 1985, the EPA ordered the PCBs to be incinerated. A local citizens' group, Coalition Opposed to PCB Ash, fought the incineration as well as a toxic dump proposal. In 2000, the EPA built a $5.8 million treatment plant to clean the water flowing from the landfill (Hinnefield 2001, 1).

(Probst and Konisky 2001, xxvii). Questions have been raised about the degree of remediation needed, about whether to burn or bury hazardous waste, and about future uses of dump sites. Environmentalists worry that the EPA has favored the incineration of toxic waste. Burning not only releases toxic substances into the atmosphere, but the remaining ash typically contains heavy metals, dioxin, and chlorine compounds. The ash must then be buried in hazardous waste dumps. Finally, the exemption of oil and petroleum waste from CERCLA requirements has kept many potentially hazardous waste sites outside of EPA jurisdiction (Mintz 2002, 450).

Brownfield Remediation

Imagine the following scenario: You are the head of a company that purchased an old industrial site and built a new factory. You won the support of your shareholders and the community. Then government workers took soil samples and determined that the property had high levels of hazardous waste. Although your company did not create the hazardous waste, your company bears the liability and cost for clean-up under CERCLA, the Superfund law. Until the turn of the 21st century, this was a nightmare that kept many businesses from rehabilitating abandoned industrial areas in cities, older suburbs, and some rural areas.

Mining and Toxic Waste

Mining was probably America's first significant source of hazardous waste, and is still one of the leading sources of toxic releases into the environment, according to the annual Toxic Release Inventory (U.S. Environmental Protection Agency (EPA) 2002a). Hard-rock mining methods today involve a variety of toxic chemicals, such as cyanide to separate gold ore from rock as well as mercury and sulfuric acid. Some mine wastes, such as the tailings from lead and uranium mines, are highly toxic. Acid mine drainage can pollute surface water and groundwater, contaminate drinking water supplies, kill fish, and poison soil.

There are more than 100,000 coal, metal, and nonmetal mines in the United States, but there are also an estimated 500,000 abandoned mines. Monitoring mines once they have been shut down is critical. For instance, The Iron Mountain mine, which produced copper for 100 years in northern California, has been closed since the 1960s. However, the mine has continued to leach sulfuric acid and heavy metals into nearby streams and the Sacramento River. According to the EPA, "As recently as five years ago, this site dumped the equivalent of 150 tanker cars full of toxic metals into the Sacramento River each day during winter storms" (*The New York Times* 2000, 32). The Iron Mountain mine has been declared a Superfund site, and the EPA expects to spend more than $800 million to treat the acidic water draining from the mine, but full clean-up may never be achieved. The Mineral Policy Center, a nonprofit group, estimates that the cost of treating and removing toxic waste at the nation's abandoned mines could range from $32 to $72 billion; the EPA has estimated that cost at up to $35 billion or more (Mineral Policy Center 1997; U.S. EPA 2000).

Brownfield sites show a moderate amount of contamination from hazardous waste, but not high enough levels to be placed on the EPA's priority list for the Superfund program. Still, brownfields may pose a threat to public health.

Four Elements of Brownfield Redevelopment

The successful redevelopment of brownfield sites depends on:

- a reliable assessment of the contamination;
- risk-based clean-up standards;
- limits to future clean-up liability; and
- financial incentives for redevelopment of brownfields.

Brownfield redevelopment occurs as a partnership between public regulatory and funding agencies on the one hand, and private investors, developers, and neighborhood groups on the other.

Reliable Assessment of the Contamination

Lending institutions routinely require an assessment of the possible existence of hazardous waste, leaking underground storage tanks, or asbestos before they will issue a commercial loan involving the purchase of real estate. This process is known as due diligence. If a lender were to make a loan on a property with hazardous waste, the borrower could at some future date be held liable for cleaning up the waste and default on the loan. Prior to 1996, a lender who foreclosed a loan on a property with hazardous waste could have been held liable for the clean-up.

There are two levels of environmental assessment, both of which should be performed by a professional engineering firm. A Phase I Environmental Site Assessment is an investigation into the current and previous ownership and uses of a property. People with knowledge of the property should be interviewed, and databases of hazardous waste sites maintained by the EPA and the state environmental agency should be reviewed. A site inspection is then conducted to look for indications of buried hazardous waste, leaking underground storage tanks, discarded drums with chemical waste, signs of hazardous waste contamination, and asbestos in buildings. If evidence of hazardous waste or a history of past use of hazardous materials on the property is discovered, it must be reported to the state environmental agency and the EPA, followed by a more in-depth Phase II Environment Assessment.

A Phase II assessment involves the taking of soil and water samples and laboratory testing according to EPA standards. Soil samples will include shallow soils to detect spills and soils below 4 feet to determine underground leakage. Samples of surface water may be taken and monitoring wells may be installed to test for groundwater contamination. If hazardous waste is found, the EPA and the state environmental agency should be notified. They will then determine the necessary remediation actions before any development can proceed. If hazardous substances are found during either assessment, a company or individual can either avoid purchasing the contaminated property or enter into an agreement with the state to specify clean-up procedures and the future use of the property to minimize liability.

Risk-Based Clean-up Standards

Stringent clean-up standards, in which brownfields are expected to be fully restored to 100% "clean" levels, can discourage voluntary clean-up and redevelopment of brownfields because of the high cost. Assumptions about potential health risks may overstate the actual impact of the contaminants on the public and future on-site workers and residents. Many states are allowing the intended use of a property to guide the level of clean-up necessary to protect public health and the environment. For instance, a contaminated property that will be used for a warehouse with a concrete floor will not have

the same risks to human health that a playground or residential use would pose.

Limits to Future Clean-up Liability

The federal government allows individual states to oversee the clean-up of abandoned industrial sites and the recovery of clean-up costs. As of 2002, the EPA had entered into agreements with 18 states, giving the states the power to set clean-up criteria and methods (Johnson 2002, 16). States can grant relief from liability under the Superfund law to companies and investors that redevelop lightly to moderately polluted properties. States and developers can enter into a Prospective Purchase Agreement that spells out the conditions of clean-up before the developers actually purchase a property and any remediation takes place. These conditions can include risk-based standards, which allow different levels of clean-up based on different uses.

In 1996, Congress limited the liability of lenders who make loans for brownfield redevelopment or foreclose on mortgages on brownfield sites. In 2002, Congress passed the Small Business Liability Relief and Brownfields Revitalization Act, which removed the unlimited liability feature of CERCLA for owners of brownfields in order to encourage redevelopment of the sites (Eisen 2002). In addition, as of 2002, 40 states had initiated voluntary clean-up programs; as long as the landowner cleans up the hazardous waste, no financial penalty or liability is assessed. Typically, a developer approaches state and local officials with a proposal to investigate, remediate, and redevelop a brownfield site. Ideally, the developer and the local government will elicit public input and assure the public that the redevelopment is consistent with neighborhood and community-wide plans.

Financial Incentives for Redevelopment of Brownfields

Cleaning up brownfields can be expensive. Both the federal government and several state govern-

SIDEBAR 7-7

Notice of Intent to Redevelop a Brownfield Property

Pursuant to North Carolina Statute 130A-310.34, the CK Land Development, Inc. has filed with the North Carolina Department of Environment and Natural Resources [DENR] a Notice of Intent to Redevelop a Brownfields Property in Charlotte, Mecklenburg County, North Carolina. The property consists of tax parcels 123-041-14 through 123-041-21, which total 2.84 acres. Environmental contamination exists on the Property in groundwater and soil. CK Land Development, Inc. has committed itself to make no other use of the Property than for shops, offices and residences. The Notice of Intent to Redevelop a Brownfields Prop-

erty includes: (1) a proposed Brownfields Agreement between DENR and CK Land Development, Inc. which in turn includes (a) a legal description of the Property, (b) a map showing the location of the Property, (c) a description of the contaminants involved and their concentrations in the media of the Property, (d) the above-stated description of the intended future use of the Property, and (e) proposed investigation and remediation; and (2) proposed Notice of Brownfields Remediation.

The full Notice of Intent to Redevelop a Brownfields Property may be viewed at _____. Written public comments may be submitted to DENR within 60 days of this Notice. Written requests for a public meeting may be submitted to DENR with 30 days of this Notice at _____.

Note: The above notice appeared in *The Charlotte Observer* on March 26, 2000 in a slightly different form.

---

ments have been willing to pay large sums for clean-up. Since 1993, the EPA has funded national and regional brownfield clean-up and redevelopment projects through grants to states, cities, and towns (U.S. EPA 2002b). The grants have enabled communities to assess and inventory brownfield sites as a first step toward redeveloping those properties. The EPA's Brownfield Assessment Demonstration Pilots program offers state and local governments up to $200,000 for the assessment of contaminated sites and to test the effectiveness of clean-up and redevelopment efforts. By 2002, the EPA had funded 590 demonstration projects.

The City of Baltimore has used an EPA grant to set up a Geographic Information System (GIS) identifying available vacant and underutilized properties, about half of which are brownfields. The city's planning department has successfully used a GIS to help developers find, assess, and redevelop properties. The EPA has claimed that the grants have led to the creation of more than 5,000 jobs, with each dollar of grant funds leveraging $25

in public and private investment in redevelopment projects, totaling over $1 billion (Ryan 1998, 22).

The EPA has also established a revolving loan fund to lend money to cities and towns, which in turn lend these funds to developers interested in redeveloping brownfields. By 2002, 129 projects had been selected for $129 million in loans (U.S. EPA 2002b). In 2002, Congress authorized $1.25 billion over five years in grants to state and local governments for brownfield remediation (*The New York Times* 2002, A10). Although this level of funding is modest compared to the overall need, it indicates that Congress recognizes the importance of brownfield remediation.

State Efforts in Brownfield Remediation

Since 1995, the EPA has turned over to the states considerable responsibility for the identification, monitoring, and redevelopment of brownfields. By 2001, 47 states had enacted legislation establishing brownfield clean-up goals and extending protection to property buyers from future liability involving prior contamination. Though details vary from state to state, new provisions generally include simplified development permitting procedures, government grants and low-interest loans, and corporate income tax credits for redeveloping brownfield sites. For instance, Colorado offers developers a state income tax incentive of up to $100,000 for cleaning up brownfield sites (Salkin 2002, 278). Several states have also compiled lists of brownfield sites in addition to the Superfund sites identified by the EPA.

The State of New Jersey has posted its brownfield sites on an interactive Internet system. Maps show brownfield locations by county and municipality, whether a brownfield is in an economic incentive zone, the proximity of a brownfield to transportation networks, and brownfield sites that are being marketed for redevelopment (see njgeodata4.state.nj.us/i-map/brownfields/default.htm).

Pennsylvania has led the nation in the redevelopment of brownfields. The state's brownfield laws, passed in 1995, cut through regulatory red tape by setting statewide clean-up standards, and offering landowners and developers immunity from liability for previous contamination (Pennsylvania Department of Environmental Protection 2003). In addition, Pennsylvania offers grants to local governments and nonprofits for brownfield assessment.

Pennsylvania's Land Recycling and Environmental Remediation Standards Act goes beyond current EPA regulations by establishing three risk-based standards. The standards help officials to determine the level of clean-up necessary before development can begin and to identify appropriate redevelopment projects. The first category involves background standards, which indicate the level of contamination that is unrelated to releases on site, such as soils with naturally occurring levels of a heavy metal. Second, statewide health standards apply to soil and water, and reflect the level of exposure expected from the proposed land use on the redeveloped site. Third, site-specific standards

relate to the amount of contamination that occurred from previous activities on the property. By 2002, more than 1,100 sites had been cleaned up. The State of Pennsylvania had made $53 million in grants and loans, and more than 30,000 jobs had been created (Pennsylvania Department of Environmental Protection 2003).

LOCAL PLANNING FOR HAZARDOUS SUBSTANCES AND TOXIC WASTE

The use and disposal of hazardous substances raise important issues for local planning. First, what should the role of the public be in making decisions about the location of industries that manufacture or use toxic substances? While some people may feel that scientific issues are beyond the understanding of the general public, an informed public is the foundation of a democratic society and community-level decision making about the environment. Second, the siting of industrial plants that use or dispose of toxic waste is often controversial and contentious. These plants are classic Locally Unwanted Land Uses. They are seen as necessary for modern industrial life and hence have to go somewhere. Yet, in the past, many of these plants had been located near low-income and minority neighborhoods. While these plants offer jobs and tax base, they may affect an area far beyond a single community. The siting of these plants may involve decisions by communities, regions, states, and the federal government.

Inventory

Planners must keep accurate and up-to-date records of hazardous waste landfills, Superfund and brownfield sites, toxic substances stored and used in the community, and any toxic spills or leaks, in order to plan for safe future growth and development. Municipal and private landfills and mining sites, both those currently in operation and those that have been closed, should also be identified and described. The EPA maintains a database of Superfund sites. The state environmental agency may have similar databases on toxic sites in a GIS format. Commercial vendors also have such data. Specifically, information should be provided on RCRA generators and sites; Superfund sites (known as Comprehensive Environmental Response, Compensation, and Liability Act Information System (CERCLIS) sites); brownfields; underground storage tanks; leaking underground storage tanks; oil and gas pipelines; and National and State Pollution Discharge Elimination System permits that involve point sources (pipe outfalls) from which toxic waste is discharged into rivers, lakes, and streams, and others.

Private companies that already report to the federal government on contaminants—used, manufactured, or stored on site—can be required to provide this information to the local government. This is especially prudent for drafting haz-mat and other local emergency response plans, and for wellhead protection planning (see Chapter 3).

Analysis

Information on the location, size, and types of contaminated sites will suggest the responses that are needed and where to plan for growth. Progress in the clean-up of any Superfund sites and brownfield sites should be noted. Potential for brownfield remediation should be evaluated. Threats to public water supplies from nearby use and storage of hazardous substances and contaminated sites should be analyzed. The adequacy of haz-mat and emergency response plans should also be assessed.

Goals and Objectives

The planning commission should draft goals and objectives for managing hazardous substances and toxic waste as well as remediating contaminated sites (see Table 7-1). The Community Facilities and other sections of the comprehensive plan

---

SIDEBAR 7-8

Chemical Exposure and Local Governments

Children are especially vulnerable to the adverse health effects of hazardous substances. Local governments and school districts can minimize or eliminate pesticide use in school buildings, on playgrounds, and in public parks. At a minimum, local governments and school districts should provide advance warning and signage when school grounds, parks, and classrooms are going to be treated. Eleven states use a registry system through which private companies inform residents who want to know when pesticides are going to be sprayed in their neighborhood. Several communities also require treated properties to be posted for 24 hours after pesticide applications.

Information on the incidence and location of cancer cases in a region should be available from the county or state environmental agency. For instance, in 1999, the State of New York published county maps of cancer rates for the three most common cancers: breast, colorectal, and lung. In 2000, the state released county maps of four rarer cancers: thyroid, brain, bladder, and kidney. The next stage will be to produce neighborhood-level maps of cancer cases to identify cancer clusters. Finally, an attempt will be made to link the location of potential toxic sources with cancer clusters.

---

should address the storage, disposal, and recycling of hazardous waste.

Action Strategy

The Action Strategy should present techniques and programs for achieving the hazardous waste goals and objectives as well as a timetable. Hazardous release and clean-up benchmarks should be identified and progress toward those benchmarks evaluated in an annual report on the environment. Specific recommendations might include the following:

Table 7-1
Sample Hazardous Waste Goals and Objectives in the Comprehensive Plan

Community Facilities	
Goal	To use and store hazardous substances responsibly, to dispose of hazardous waste safely, and to increase the recycling of hazardous materials.
Objective	Organize an annual household hazardous waste pick-up day within the community.
Land Use	
Objective	Keep hazardous waste landfills away from sensitive environmental areas, such as steep slopes, thin soils, and wetlands.
Objective	Separate areas designated for future growth from any potential hazardous waste landfill sites.
Natural Resources	
Objective	Protect air quality by avoiding the use of incinerators to dispose of hazardous waste.
Objective	Protect drinking water supplies and air quality from contamination through releases of toxic substances.

- Inform the county Emergency Management Agency of the location of any wellhead protection areas, which should be given priority consideration for protection in the event of a hazardous materials spill.
- Post signs with spill response contact numbers on roads at the boundaries of wellhead protection areas.
- Apply for federal and state funding to assess the condition of brownfield sites for potential redevelopment.
- Locate new businesses that use, store, manufacture, or dispose of hazardous substances in heavy industrial zones with long setbacks from neighboring properties.
- Require new development within 1 mile of a landfill to connect to a public water system.

Zoning Ordinance

Many communities do not want a hazardous waste landfill in their jurisdiction. The local zoning ordinance can state that they are not permitted uses in any zoning district. Remote rural communities may want to identify sparsely settled areas with suitable geology where a hazardous waste landfill might be appropriate. In those areas, the zoning ordinance could list such landfills as a conditional use, subject to the applicant conducting a thorough environmental impact assessment. Although the local elected governing body may approve the landfill as a conditional use, state and federal approval and licensing will also be necessary. Hazardous waste incinerators can either be prohibited through the zoning ordinance or permitted only as a conditional use in rural places well away from residential areas; however, incinerators should not be viewed as a long-term solution to hazardous waste disposal. Again, state and federal approval will be necessary.

Heavy industry that would manufacture, use, store, or dispose of hazardous substances can be limited to heavy industrial zones where surface and groundwater are unlikely to be impacted.

The zoning ordinance can encourage the redevelopment of brownfield sites by allowing for a wide array of uses, depending on the necessary level of clean-up for each use. Also, promoting the adaptive reuse of existing buildings, rather than requiring demolition, can minimize development expenses and protect historic buildings.

Table 7-2
A Checklist of Hazardous Substance and Toxic Waste Issues in a Development Review

1.	What is the size, location, and use of the proposed project?
2.	Is the proposed project allowed in the particular zone?
3.	Are setbacks and buffers from property lines met?
4.	What hazardous substances will be used, stored, or disposed of on the site?
5.	What are the land uses on the adjacent properties?
6.	What is the geology and hydrology of the site? What are the potential on- and off-site impacts to water quality?
7.	Where are public water supplies located in relation to the site? Does the site minimize potential contamination of these supplies?
8.	How does the proposal fit with community hazardous material and emergency response plans?
9.	Has the developer obtained any necessary state and federal permits?

Subdivision Regulations

The subdivision ordinance can require buffering berms and vegetation between hazardous waste disposal sites and neighboring properties or between brownfield sites slated for redevelopment and adjacent properties. Stormwater runoff should be contained on site. Vegetation, swales, and retention basins should be used.

Capital Improvements Program

The capital improvements program (CIP) should address hazardous waste landfill capacity and future needs, siting of new or expanded hazardous waste facilities or incinerator facilities, and recycling facilities. The location of any of these disposal or recycling facilities should be coordinated with the location of current and future public drinking water supplies, and existing and future planned development areas. New developments within 1 mile of a hazardous waste facility should be required to use public water systems rather than private wells. In addition, new or upgraded public infrastructure may be needed to promote the redevelopment of brownfield sites.

What to Look for in a Development Review

A proposed development should be evaluated according to the current comprehensive plan, zoning subdivision and land development regulations, CIP, and any other relevant ordinances. In reviewing a proposal for a development that could generate, store, use, or transport hazardous materials, planners should consider how the toxic materials will be handled and disposed (see Table 7-2). If a proposed development will generate large amounts of waste, participation in a recycling program could be required as a condition of approval. Pretreatment of hazardous wastes and connection to a public sewer system is highly recommended and may be required by state or federal law. Proposed projects that involve the use, storage, or disposal of toxic chemicals should be kept away from drinking water supplies and wellhead protection areas (see Chapter 3). If a project that involves the use, manufacture, or disposal of toxic substances is approved, planners should make sure that the owners of the business comply with the toxic release reporting requirements of the Emergency Planning and Community Right-To-Know Act.

Planning for
Natural Areas

8

Protecting the Nation's Landscape Treasures

In wildness is the preservation of the world.
                                    HENRY DAVID THOREAU

Americans ought to keep expanding the land preservation system while the purchase price remains affordable.

                                    GREGG EASTERBROOK,
                    A MOMENT ON THE EARTH (1996, 434)

America is blessed with a variety of outstanding, irreplaceable natural landscapes that include wilderness areas, wild and scenic rivers, vistas, geologic formations, and cultural and historic landscapes. These national treasures—along with state, regional, and locally significant landscapes—provide important recreational, ecological, and educational values as well as related economic activity. Moreover, these special landscapes link America's past, present, and future. Careful planning, management, regulation, and land acquisition are needed to ensure that future generations can also enjoy and benefit from these special landscapes. Federal, state, and local governments as well as private landowners and private nonprofit groups, have been active in protecting these landscapes. Partnerships are often forged to stretch available funding and to engender cooperation among landowners, local residents, visitors, and government officials.

THE CHALLENGE OF LANDSCAPE PROTECTION

Decisions about how to use America's outstanding natural landscapes have important implications for the economies and environments of nearby communities and regions. This is especially true in the western states, where the federal government owns more than half of the land area of Alaska, Arizona, Idaho, Nevada, Oregon, Utah, and Wyoming, and large amounts of California, Colorado, New Mexico, and Washington. A 2000 study by the World Wildlife Fund and the Natural Resources Defense Council (NRDC) reported that from 1967 to 1997, rural western counties with more than 10% of their land protected and roadless—wilderness, national parks, and national monuments—showed a 46% higher increase in jobs and a 27% greater increase in incomes than other rural western counties (NRDC 2001, 11). The study suggested that in the counties with more protected land, growth in service-related jobs, especially tied to tourism, were able to more than offset the decline in employment in timber, ranching, and mining. Commercial recreation areas are often tied to natural features, such as beaches, lakes, mountains, or wilderness. Recreation businesses can contribute significantly to local economies. In 1996, outdoor recreation generated $40 billion in revenue and provided almost 800,000 full-time jobs (Lerner and Poole 1999).

The National Park Service faces three challenges in its role as a manager of many of the America's landscape treasures. First, the number of visitors to the national parks has soared since 1970, reaching a record 286 million visitors in 1998 (Janofsky 1999, 1). The crowds of visitors are jeopardizing the ability of the National Park Service to keep some parks in their natural conditions. The National Park Service has estimated that more than $3.5 billion in infrastructure improvements and repairs are needed at the national parks, monuments, and wilderness areas (*ibid.*). Second, tracts of privately owned land or "in-holdings" within national parks, and especially within national seashores and national preserves, could be developed for residential or commercial uses with negative impacts on the wildlife, ecosystems, and scenic values of Park Service lands. Another threat is the development on private lands and in communities adjacent to national parks (Howe *et al.* 1997). The Park Service has found that:

> "The loss of biodiversity at the species level in national parks of the American West was directly correlated with both the size of the parks and their age . . . rais(ing) the specter of long-term depletion of the national park's [sic] ecological assemblages and functions . . . This raised new questions about how the 'sea' of surrounding land was being managed as well as the viability of any biodiversity conservation strategy focused primarily on protected area refugia" (Duane 1999, 225).

National parks, national forests, state parks, state forests, and local parks are popular recreational areas for many Americans, and often act as magnets for second homes and retirement homes, condominium complexes, and commercial recreation facilities. The type and amount of recreation can have significant impacts on the environment. For example, the large majority of western ski areas are on U.S. Forest Service (USFS) lands. Ski areas are built in areas with sensitive environments, including steep slopes, thin soils, and narrow streams and headwaters. Soil erosion,

pollution of headwaters, and destruction of wildlife habitats are potential problems. Equally problematic are adequate water supplies and sewage disposal. Ski areas often use large amounts of water to make snow, in large part because they prefer the consistency and reliability of man-made snow to natural snow. Also, the excessive use of fireplaces in ski areas can cause air pollution. Ski areas attract thousands of visitors for a day, a weekend, or a week-long stay, virtually turning a rural environment into an urban one. Colorado, for example, has more than 10 million skier days a year at its ski resorts. Nationally, skiers logged an estimated 53 million skier-days in 2000 (U.S. Environmental Protection Agency (EPA) 2000, 42).

Beginning in the late 1990s, ski areas throughout the United States sought to expand the number of ski trails as well as add more residential and commercial development to create four season resorts with a village atmosphere. In 2000, several environmental groups formed the Ski Area Citizen's Coalition and rated 51 ski resorts in 10 western states (Janofsky 2000, 46). Only nine resorts received an A for environmentally friendly business policies; seven resorts received a B; 14 a C; 11 a D, and 10 an F.

The main rating criteria included:
- avoiding expansion of developed skiing acreage into undisturbed forest;
- avoiding commercial and residential development on undisturbed lands;
- avoiding water degradation;
- protecting wildlife habitat;
- reducing traffic and emissions; and
- conserving energy and water.

Encouragingly, 160 ski areas in 31 states have adopted a set of environmental principles agreed upon by state, federal, and ski industry representatives (Janofsky 2000).

FEDERAL PLANNING FOR PROTECTING THE NATION'S LANDSCAPE TREASURES

The federal government owns more than 635 million of America's 2.2 billion acres, mainly in the western states and Alaska (U.S. Bureau of the Census 2003, 211). Most of these lands are managed by the USFS or four agencies in the Department of the Interior:

1. the Bureau of Land Management (BLM);
2. the Bureau of Reclamation;
3. the National Park Service; and
4. the U.S. Fish and Wildlife Service (FWS).

At the beginning of the 20th century, the federal attitude toward the natural environment was mostly utilitarian. Landscapes could be useful to humans if they were properly managed. In a few instances, areas of unique natural beauty or geologic or historic value gained protection as national parks, but other federal lands were managed primarily for the production of timber, minerals, and livestock. Since the 1960s, the federal government has been taking on a greater stewardship role, and natural resource production has become more balanced with recreation, wildlife, and watershed management.

Wilderness Areas

The USFS, founded in 1905, is an agency within the Department of Agriculture. The USFS is responsible for managing 191 million acres in 155 national forests in 40 states. The national forests cover about one-quarter of all public lands, and more than 160 million acres are located in the western states and Alaska. The USFS is required to draft management plans for each forest that incorporate the principle of "multiple use-sustained yield." The multiple uses include timber harvesting, watershed management, recreation, grazing, wildlife habitats, and wilderness areas. Some of these uses may conflict with each other, and balancing them is no small challenge. Sustained yield means that these multiple uses should remain productive at some minimum level far into the future.

The Wilderness Act of 1964 allows Congress to designate parts of national forests as wilderness areas in which commercial timber operations and permanent roads are banned. Wilderness areas must be managed for the preservation of their wilderness character, which the act defines as:

> ". . . areas where the earth and its community of life are untrammelled by man, where man himself is a visitor who does not remain. And wilderness is further defined to mean an area of undeveloped federal land returning its primeval character and influence, without permanent improvements or human habitation, which is protected and managed so as to preserve its natural conditions" (16 USC Section 1131(a)).

Since the 1960s, about 34 million acres of national forests have been protected as part of the wilderness system. Other wilderness areas are managed through the Department of the Interior, including national wildlife refuges managed by the FWS, parts of national parks under the National Park Service, and some lands managed by the BLM. The single largest area of wilderness was set aside when the Alaska National Interest Lands and Conservation Act of 1980 preserved about 56 million acres (Egan 2000, A14). By 1996, the Council on Environmental Quality (CEQ) had listed more than 103 million acres in the National Wilderness Preservation System (CEQ 1996, 260).

In 2001, as one of his last acts in office, President Bill Clinton issued an order—The Roadless Area Conservation Rule—designating an additional 58.5 million acres of national forests in 39 states as "roadless areas." This designation made these lands effectively off limits to timber harvesting, mining, and grazing, and qualified them for possible future addition to the wilderness system (Jehl 2001, A1, A12). The new roadless areas would result in a total of more than 92 million acres of national forest, almost half of the national forest acreage, being protected from development.

Shortly after taking office, President George W. Bush modified the Clinton order by allowing a case-by-case amendment of the rules on roadless areas and the timber harvest ban (*ibid.*, A1). Adding land to wilderness areas—either through a change in the designation of federal lands or through the federal purchase of land—is controversial, particularly in the western states, where the federal government already has huge land holdings. On the other hand, conservation biologists warn of the rising pressures on ecosystems and argue for the expansion of wilderness areas to protect wildlife habitats, especially of large carnivores (see Chapter 9).

National Parks and Monuments

The National Park Service was created in 1916 and manages more than 83 million acres in 385 separate units, including 57 national parks, national seashores, national monuments, national recreation areas, national preserves, and national rivers and trails (Seelye 2002, A23). Many of the larger sites are found in the western states and Alaska, while smaller sites—often with historic significance—are more common in the eastern U.S. Examples of Park Service lands include Grand Canyon National Park in Arizona, the Canaveral National Seashore in Florida, Gettysburg National Military Park in Pennsylvania, and the Tallgrass Prairie National Preserve in Kansas. The creation of a national park requires an act of Congress and the president's signature, but national monuments can be declared by the president without congressional approval on lands that are already in federal ownership. National seashores and preserves are created by Congress.

The role of the Park Service is "to conserve the scenery and the natural and historic objects and wildlife therein as will leave them unimpaired for future generations" (39 USC Section 535). In other words, Park Service lands are to be maintained mostly as natural environments. In the national parks, for instance, no hunting is allowed, but a

limited amount of grazing is permitted, as is mining, under very strict conditions. These activities are not supposed to conflict with the goal of maintaining the natural environment.

Since the 1970s, the Park Service has worked with state and local governments and private landowners to discourage incompatible development on private in-holdings within lands managed by the Park Service. Techniques have included zoning, acquisition of conservation easements, and, most recently, management agreements. A conservation easement is a voluntary sale or donation of development rights by a landowner to a government agency or a qualified, private nonprofit organization. Management agreements are less formal than conservation easements. Management agreements between private landowners and the Park Service have proved successful in the Santa Monica Mountains National Recreation Area in California and along the New River Gorge National River in West Virginia.

Since the early 1980s, there has been more cooperation among federal, state, and local governments, nonprofit groups, and private landowners on protecting unique landscapes. The National Park Service has introduced the concept of "partnership parks" in which there is little or no federal acquisition of land, but management cooperation involving the Park Service, state and local governments, nonprofits, and private landowners. This effort allows for the protection of larger areas than would be possible with just federal land acquisition. Examples include National Heritage Areas and Corridors, such as the Illinois and Michigan Canal Heritage Corridor, formed in 1984.

The Bureau of Land Management

The BLM manages about 262 million acres, or nearly half of all federal lands (BLM 2002). Most BLM lands are in Alaska, and nearly all the rest are in 11 western states. As the population in the West has grown over the last half century, BLM lands have become increasingly important for recreation uses and as cultural and historic attractions. The Federal Land Policy Management Act of 1976 requires BLM lands, like the national forests, to be managed according to the principle of "multiple use-sustained yield" for a variety of uses, including timber harvesting, recreation, mining, wilderness preservation, fish and wildlife habitat, and livestock grazing.

The BLM operates a National Landscape Conservation System that consists of National Conservation Areas, including some wilderness areas, and 17 National Monuments. The National Conservation Areas are designated by Congress and cover more than 13 million acres, including the California Desert Area, Gunnison Gorge in Colorado, and Red Rock Canyon in Nevada. During his two terms in office, President Clinton used the Antiquities Act of 1906 to designate five new national monuments and expand another, covering a total of 3.1 million acres. Monument status means that these federal lands cannot be developed or logged, but can continue to be grazed and used for recreation. Included in the new monuments are more than 300,000 acres of California's giant sequoias—the world's largest trees—that can grow to 40 feet in diameter and 300 feet tall. The largest of the new monuments is the 1.7 million-acre Grand Staircase-Escalante National Monument in southern Utah.

Wild and Scenic Rivers

The Department of the Interior oversees the national Wild and Scenic Rivers system, enacted by Congress in 1968, except in the national parks, where the Department of Agriculture is responsible for their management. As of 2000, almost 11,000 miles of waterways in 36 states were included in the system. Designated rivers may not be dammed or diverted, and commercial and industrial uses of the riverbanks are prohibited. Any other development must abide by federally determined acreage, setback, and frontage limitations.

An additional 60,000 miles of rivers could qualify for the Wild and Scenic Rivers system. To be added to the system, a river must be free flowing, and neither diverted nor channeled. The riverbanks must contain historic sites or important natural features, such as scenic areas, geological formations, and wildlife habitats. A river may be classified as one of three types, and different stretches of the same river can be classified differently:

1. A "wild river" is free of dams and is generally inaccessible except by trail. Waters are unpolluted and shorelines primitive, representing America's natural past.
2. A "scenic river" is free of dams but is accessible in places by roads. Shorelines are largely primitive and undeveloped.
3. A "recreational river" may have undergone some diversion or water impoundment in the past. The river is readily accessible by road, and shorelines may have experienced some development.

An act of Congress or an act of the legislature of the state or states through which the river flows is needed to bring a river into the Wild and Scenic Rivers system. State-level legislation means that the state or states will manage the river at no cost to the federal government, subject to the approval of the Secretary of the Interior.

American Heritage Rivers

In 1997, President Clinton launched the American Heritage Rivers Initiative to help communities with historically "working rivers" protect the water quality and natural habitats of their rivers as well as restore historic buildings, spur new commercial and residential development, and foster local recreation and arts activities along waterfronts. In 1998, 14 rivers were selected as American Heritage Rivers, including the Connecticut River in New England, the St. Johns River in Florida, the Upper Mississippi River from Minnesota to Missouri, and the Willamette River in Oregon. Each heritage river has a designated "River

Navigator" who helps communities receive better access to technical and financial assistance from federal agencies. Whereas the Wild and Scenic Rivers Act is designed to protect remote and undeveloped rivers, the American Heritage Rivers approach emphasizes economic development and environmental, historic, and cultural protection for working rivers. The program highlights the important link between a quality built environment and a quality natural environment.

National Heritage Areas

The National Heritage Area program was begun in 1984 as a way to promote partnerships among federal, state, and local governments and the private sector to conserve cultural resources and historic landscapes. As of 2000, Congress had created 18 Heritage Areas in 16 states. A Heritage Area can be local (such as America's Agricultural Heritage and Partnership in Iowa) or regional (such as the Blackstone River Valley National Heritage Corridor in Massachusetts and Rhode Island).

For each area, Congress designates a "management entity"—a local government, nonprofit, or federal commission to coordinate the operation of the Heritage Area. The management entity drafts a management and protection plan for projects in the Heritage Area, such as a visitor's guide, walking trails, or rehabilitation of historic buildings. The National Park Service provides technical assistance as well as financial support for a few years following the creation of the Heritage Area. A Heritage Area remains privately owned and no federal land use regulations are imposed. The manager of the Heritage Area sponsors tours, interpretive programs, museums, and festivals as "heritage tourism" to promote understanding of the area's natural, cultural, and historic significance.

National Trails System

The National Trails System Act of 1968 had the goal of creating 25,000 miles of trails. Although this figure has not yet been reached, the act was instrumental in buying land to create the Pacific Crest Trail on the west coast and to secure land in public ownership alongside the Appalachian Trail, which stretches from Georgia to Maine (Bryson 1999, 112).

The Land and Water Conservation Fund

The federal Land and Water Conservation Fund, established in 1965, has been a major source of funding for the purchase of natural environments. The fund receives royalties from federal offshore oil and gas leases in the continental shelf. These revenues have been used to add land to the national parks, national forests, and the National Wildlife Refuge System (see Chapter 9). As of 2000, the Land and Water Conservation Fund had helped to preserve almost 7 million acres in 38,000 park, recreation, and wildlife habitat projects (National Park Service 2001).

The annual allocation of Land and Water Conservation funds is divided as follows: 40% for federal land acquisition and 60% for state projects. To receive funding, a state must draft a Comprehensive Outdoor Recreation Plan for approval by the Department of the Interior, describing how the state will spend the federal money to meet its outdoor recreation needs. The federal funds may be used to cover half the cost of purchasing or improving recreational land, and must be matched by funds from state and local governments and nonprofit groups. Land acquired with Land and Water Conservation funds must remain forever in outdoor recreation use. Much of the money to states has gone to expand state parks, which now cover about 10 million acres.

While Congress may authorize up to $900 million a year from the fund for acquisitions, funding has not yet been close to that level, averaging slightly less than $150 million a year. By 2000, Congress had authorized a total of more than $2 billion to federal agencies and $3 billion in matching grants to state and local governments for the

Sierra Club Sues Hawaii Over Tourism Funding

All states advertise their recreation opportunities in the hope of attracting out-of-state visitors. In January 2000, the Sierra Club filed suit against the State of Hawaii, alleging a violation of the state's environmental review law. The Sierra Club claimed that Hawaii had not done an environmental impact assessment at the same time that the state authorized $114 million for the Hawaii Tourism Authority to promote tourism.

About 7 million visitors a year come to Hawaii, and tourism is the state's leading industry. Argued Jeff Mikulina, director of the Sierra Club's Hawaii Chapter, "An environmental assessment would tell us whether Hawaii's physical and natural infrastructure can handle more tourists . . . drinking our water, using our electricity, generating sewage and garbage, and filling our beaches" (McDowell 2000, Section 5, 3). Hawaii's volcanic islands feature fragile environments with steep slopes, extensive coastlines, and limited amounts of fresh water. Hawaii's State Land Use Plan, begun in 1961, has resulted in the designation of most parts of the islands as conservation lands and agricultural areas where development is strictly controlled. The State of Hawaii currently requires that developers apply for and obtain as many as 18 permits for building in conservation areas.

purchase of private lands. State and local governments provided another $3.3 billion in matching funds (*ibid.*).

In 2000, Congress responded to public pressure for more funding for land conservation by passing the Land Conservation, Preservation, and Infrastructure Improvement Act. The act created a trust fund of $12 billion that can be spent only on land conservation projects between 2001 and 2006. Funding for the Land and Water Conservation Fund increased to $540 million a year; $154 million was provided for urban and historic preservation; $400 million for coastal programs under the National Oceanic and Atmospheric Administration; and almost $300 million for additional federal land acquisition. Also, a total of $680 million was authorized for the construction of new facilities on federal lands, especially at the heavily visited national parks (U.S. Department of the Interior 2000). Said Representative Norm Dicks (D-Washington), who worked on the legislation, "This is, by far, the greatest increase in conservation spending in the history of the country" (Holmes 2000, A14).

STATE PROGRAMS TO PROTECT LANDSCAPE TREASURES

State governments have a number of agencies and programs involved in the protection of important landscapes. The leading types of agencies are the departments of state parks and natural resources. There are about 10 million acres of state parks in the United States, many of which contain important scenic, geologic, historic, and wildlife resources. Every state has one or more programs designed to protect specific natural landscapes, such as floodplains, wetlands, or coastal zones. Many state programs designate and protect state scenic rivers and byways, and purchase conservation lands for wildlife and watershed protection.

In the 23 states west of the Mississippi River, there are some 400 million acres of state trust lands. These lands were given to the states by the federal government. They are supposed to be managed to produce income for the good of society. Most of these lands are rural and can be managed for timber harvesting or grazing. Yet, the cultural, historic, and wildlife habitat resources on these lands are often significant.

More than 20 state governments have State Environmental Quality Review Acts that require state agencies to perform reviews of state projects or approvals that would affect the environment, including water and air quality and important scenic, geologic, historic, and wildlife resources.

Areas of Critical State Concern

The identification and protection of areas of critical state concern can be an effective way to protect important open lands, fragile environments, and natural hazards of statewide significance, such as wildlife habitats, wetlands, and coastal areas. The designation of critical areas is proactive state planning, which puts communities, landowners, and developers on notice that sensitive environmental areas may not be developed.

Four of the leading examples of areas of critical state concern are the New Jersey Pinelands, areas designated under Florida's 1972 land use law, the Lake Tahoe region between California and Nevada, and New York's 6 million-acre Adirondack Park. The Pinelands—known for its cranberry bogs, cedar swamps, and small villages—covers a seven-county area of more than 900,000 acres in southern New Jersey, overlying one of the largest aquifers along the east coast. In 1978, the United States Congress passed legislation calling for the protection of the Pinelands; in 1979, the State of New Jersey responded by setting up the Pinelands Commission. The commission then drafted a comprehensive plan that designated most of the Pinelands as a "preservation" area with very limited development. The plan also included a "protection" area where more development could occur. A crucial part of this plan was a transfer of development rights (TDR) program, established in 1983, to compensate landowners in the preservation area and to move potential development into the protection area. As of 2000, more than 19,000 acres of land had been preserved through the TDR program (Brennan *et al.* 2000).

Under Florida's 1972 land use law, the state government may declare up to 5% of the state as critical areas. Regulations are drafted and responsibility shared by the state and local governments (Healy and Rosenberg 1979, 134-144). Most of the critical areas have involved wetlands and coastal areas. The protection of critical areas was strengthened by the passage of Florida's Growth Management Act in 1985, which requires local governments to draft comprehensive plans consistent with statewide goals.

The Lake Tahoe Regional Planning Agency was jointly established in 1969 by California and Nevada. A prime concern of the agency is regulating development so that runoff from septic systems and roads does not pollute Lake Tahoe, known for its clarity and deep blue color. The lake and the surrounding scenic vistas are major tourist attractions. In the 1980s, the agency evaluated all lands within the 207,000-acre basin and set categories for how much impervious surface would be allowed to cover a property. The agency also established a quota of about 300 new dwellings per year. In 1987, the agency created a TDR program to allow the transfer of underused impervious surface from one property to another. Also, TDR can be used to enable property owners to remove existing structures. The agency's TDR program was unsuccessfully challenged as a taking under the 5th Amendment in 1997 (Pruetz 1997, 12-13; *Suitum v. Tahoe Regional Planning Agency* (U.S. Supreme Court 96-243)). Also, the agency's use of a 32-month moratorium on development from 1981 to 1984 while it drafted a new comprehensive plan was deemed not to be a "taking" of private property by the U.S. Supreme Court (*Tahoe-Sierra Preservation Council v. Tahoe Regional Planning Agency*, No. 00-1167 (Lucero and Soule 2002, 4-7)).

New York's Adirondack Park is a combination of 40% state-owned land and 60% private land. The state land is generally off limits to development—even logging—according to a clause placed in the state constitution in 1895 that these lands be kept "forever wild." Since 1973, the private lands have been regulated by the Adirondack Park Agency, except for development within designated hamlets where local control is exercised as well. The Adirondack Park Agency has established six zones: hamlet, industrial, moderate intensity, low intensity, rural use, and resource management. Any development proposal in each of these zones must receive a permit from the agency before construction can commence. The resource management zone covers more than 1 million acres of privately owned land and allows only one dwelling per 42 acres (Healy and Rosenberg 1979, 187). The power of the Adirondack Park Agency has caused considerable controversy and resentment among local landowners. On the other hand, the Adirondacks are one of the premier recreation areas in the Northeast, with hundreds of lakes and several mountains above 4,000 feet, and logging is still a viable industry.

Acquisition of Land and Conservation Easements

Since the late 1980s, many states—often with voter approval—have substantially increased expenditures for buying environmentally significant open space, land for parks, farmland, buffers for drinking water sources, and natural areas. In 1988, California voters approved $776 million in bonds to protect natural areas, farmlands, and the Pacific coastline. Twelve years later, California voters approved more than $4 billion in state bonding for purchasing land for parks to protect watersheds, drinking water supplies, and coastal areas. In 1990, the Florida legislature earmarked $3 billion for the Preservation 2000 Initiative, which resulted in the purchase of about 900,000 acres of environmentally sensitive lands and riparian areas. In 1999, the Florida legislature repeated itself by passing the $3 billion Florida Forever measure for natural land purchases over the next 10 years (Beatley 2000, 13).

In 1992, Colorado voters passed a citizens' initiative, earmarking $35 million a year in state lottery proceeds for the Colorado Open Space program to purchase parklands, natural areas, wildlife habitat, and conservation easements on farm and ranchlands. In 2001, voters allowed the State of Colorado to borrow up to $115 million against future lottery proceeds in order to speed up the purchase of these lands. The Pennsylvania legislature enacted a statewide Key '93 program to purchase parklands and natural areas; the program was launched with $50 million and receives about $10 million a year from the state real estate transfer tax. New York voters in 1996 passed a $1.5 billion Environmental Bond Act to be used in part to purchase natural areas and open space in keeping with the state's open space plan. In 1999, Environmental Bond funds helped to purchase land and conservation easements on a 144,000-acre tract of private land in the Adirondacks (see Chapter 14). In 2000, the Georgia legislature approved $30 million for open space preservation, and Ohio voters approved $25 million for farmland preservation.

All told, in 1998 through 2002, voters across America approved more than 500 local and state ballot measures containing more than $20 billion for public land acquisition and so-called "smart growth" programs (Land Trust Alliance 2002a). Commenting on the overwhelming support for these ballot measures, Russ Shay of the Land Trust Alliance observed, "Clearly, people are tremendously concerned about what their communities will look like in the future, and they are very willing to invest their tax money to protect parks, farms, forests, and fields" (Land Trust Alliance 2002b).

LOCAL AND REGIONAL ACQUISITION OF OPEN SPACE

Many communities have chosen land acquisition as a powerful addition to the comprehensive planning and land use regulation process. The acquisition of land and conservation easements helps to clarify where development should or should not go. It is a way to keep sensitive environmental features from being developed while providing open space, air and water quality, parklands, trails, and recreational benefits. Land acquisition can help a community maintain a balance between development and open land, keep its options open for the future, and minimize the need for costly public infrastructure investments to serve development.

Public Efforts to Protect Special Landscapes

Land acquisition is often necessary because of impending development pressures and because zoning and other land use regulations are either politically vulnerable or unacceptable. Simply put, zoning is not permanent; it can and often is changed through the political process. Moreover, strict zoning often faces opposition from landowners, which can quickly block public land conservation efforts. One way around the opposition is the purchase of open space and environmentally important lands by county, township, and city governments. These purchases are usually voluntary between the government agency and landowners. Eminent domain can be used if the government agency pays "just compensation" (an amount often determined by a judge) to the landowner and puts the land to a public use, such as a park. However, eminent domain often stirs up fears among landowners of the government taking their land and at a price that may be too low.

Purchases of land and conservation easements by local governments can be expensive, running into millions of dollars (see Table 8-1). For instance, in March 1999, voters in Sarasota County, Florida, passed an increase in property taxes to cover the cost of up to $53 million in bonds to purchase an estimated 36,000 acres of environmentally sensitive lands (Thomson 1999, 1). Also, governments typically must obtain the approval of voters. Yet, outright purchase is preferable if the government wants to minimize the development

of certain fragile lands and actively manage them for recreation or nature preserves. Conservation easements are especially attractive for protecting working farms and forestlands that also have environmentally important features.

Local opposition to public land acquisition typically focuses on tax increases and the loss of property tax base, as public lands and most lands held by nonprofit organizations are exempt from property taxes. However, several studies have shown that permanently preserved land tends to increase the value of nearby private land (Lerner and Poole 1999), which expands the tax base. In addition, most residential development today requires a greater expenditure in public services than it generates in property tax revenues (Daniels and Bowers 1997, 55). In the long run, land preservation can end up costing residents less than they would pay to provide public services to developed land.

Greenways and Trails

Greenways and trails are an excellent way to provide access to special landscapes and create linkages within and between communities. Greenways and trails are linear open space areas through woods, fields, and along highways, rail or utility corridors, and waterways. While trails typically provide for public access, greenways may or may not. Greenways and trails can link residential areas with schools, parks, and commercial areas to minimize the use of cars. The creation of regional trails and greenways can be a catalyst for counties and municipalities to undertake other beneficial regional planning efforts such as water planning, habitat conservation, floodplain management, and recreation plans. Efforts to create trails and greenways have generally enjoyed widespread public support. Funding to buy land to create greenways has come from federal Land and Water Conservation funds, some state programs, many communities, and several nonprofit organizations.

Table 8-1
A Sample of Local Land Preservation Ballot Measures Passed in 2000

Jurisdiction	Funding Amount	How Financed	Funds to Purchase
Boulder County, Colorado	$80.8 million	Bonds	Open Space
Golden, Colorado	$26.42 million	Bonds	Open Space
Longmont, Colorado	$60 million	Sales Tax Use Tax	Open Space
Alachua County, Florida	$29 million	Bonds	Open Space + Watershed Protection
Broward County, Florida	$400 million	Bonds	Parkland
Leon County, Florida	$400 million	Sales Tax	Open Space
Volusia County, Florida	$40 million	Property Tax	Open Space
Bernalillo County, New Mexico	$25 million	Property Tax	Open Space, Watershed + Historic Site Protection
Greensboro, North Carolina	$34.2 million	Bonds	Open Space + Parkland
Raleigh, North Carolina	$16 million	Bonds	Parkland
Wake County, North Carolina	$15 million	Bonds	Open Space + Watershed Protection
Beaufort County, South Carolina	$40 million	Bonds	Open Space
Austin, Texas	$13.4 million	Bonds	Open Space + Parkland
San Antonio, Texas	$65 million	Sales Tax	Watershed Protection
Seattle, Washington	$26 million	Property Tax	Open Space + Parkland

Source: Land Trust Alliance (2002a)

Trails offer a variety of recreational and even commuting options, such as walking, running, biking, and horseback riding. Many communities have taken advantage of established rights-of-way along utility corridors to create trail networks. Waterways make especially attractive locations for trails because of their scenic and recreational qualities and because most other types of development are not permitted within floodplains. Abandoned railroad corridors make excellent rails-to-trails projects because of the established rights-of-way and linkages among neighboring communities. At least 700 rails-to-trails projects have been developed nationwide (Daniels 1999, 232). The federal Transportation Efficiency Act for the 21st Century (TEA-21), passed in 1998, requires 10% of its surface transportation funds to be set aside for transportation enhancements such as greenways and trails (Platt 2000, 20).

Greenways along waterways provide important buffers to keep development at a distance from water resources, to intercept and filter stormwater runoff, and to receive floodwaters and thus protect built-up areas. Greenways along highways help to absorb fumes, exhaust, noise, and bright lights. Greenways also break up monotonous roadsides and can reduce the number of curb cuts for commercial or residential areas. Greenways can provide important wildlife habitat corridors and promote a variety of recreational pursuits, such as boating, canoeing, fishing, and bird watching. Oregon's Willamette River Greenway, which runs more than 100 miles from Eugene to Portland, began through state legislation in the mid-1970s. In rural areas, no new development is allowed within 100 feet of the river; in urban areas, the greenway provides a walking trail, adding to the local quality of life. The Willamette Valley is a major farming region, and the greenway helps to filter runoff before it reaches the river. The Willamette River Greenway has been credited with significantly improving the water quality of the Willamette River.

In 1990, Maryland created a Greenways Commission to foster and connect green corridors across the state. More than 900 miles of greenways had been established by 2000, with many more miles in progress (*ibid.*, 19). In 1991, the New York legislature created the Hudson River Greenway Conservancy to work with local communities to coordinate the efforts of local governments and nonprofit groups in developing trails on both sides of the Hudson River (from Battery Park in New York City 150 miles north to the confluence of the Hudson and Mohawk Rivers). To date, the greenway has helped to build or improve more than 60 miles of trails. In 1998, Florida took the lead among states in the creation of a statewide greenway system including recreational trails. The system will connect natural areas and landscapes to support the "ability of these ecosystems to function as dynamic systems" (Florida Department of Environmental Protection 1998, 11).

Boulder, Colorado, has spent millions of dollars since the early 1980s to buy up a 20,000-acre greenbelt that separates the city and Boulder County as well as preserves city land above the 5,870-foot mark (Daniels 1999, 76). In 1999, voters in Mecklenburg County, North Carolina, approved a $20 million bond to purchase land for greenways in the Mountain Island Wake watershed. In 1995,

voters in the metropolitan region of Portland, Oregon, passed a $135 million park and open space bond to purchase up to 6,000 acres of greenway corridors and parkland (*ibid.*, 233). Greater Chattanooga, Tennessee, is creating a 75- to 100-mile riverside greenway and trail system (Beatley and Manning 1998). Greater Indianapolis, Indiana, already has a network of more than 175 miles of greenways and trails (Indy Greenways 2001).

The San Francisco-based Greenbelt Alliance not only drafted a greenbelt plan for the greater San Francisco Bay Area, but also has worked with local governments to help preserve 600,000 acres of greenspace (Platt 2000, 21). The Trust for Public Land (TPL) has been working with landowners and local governments on the creation of a 180-mile greenway along Georgia's Chattahoochee River (*ibid.*, 19). The Washington, D.C.-based Conservation Fund has a goal to help create a nationwide network of greenways connecting natural areas, historic sites, parks, and open spaces. Through its American Greenways Program, the fund makes small seed grants for local greenway efforts and serves as an information clearinghouse on the development of greenways.

Private Nonprofit Efforts to Protect Special Landscapes

Since the early 1980s, when the Reagan administration made deep funding cuts in the Department of Interior, the Land and Water Conservation Fund, and the EPA, private nonprofit organizations have grown both in number and in their land protection efforts. At the same time, these organizations have grown as a result of frustrations with the rapid pace of growth in many communities and the ineffectiveness of local planning to protect important landscapes and natural resources. These organizations include land trusts, river and watershed protection groups, sports groups, and private wildlife preserves. Often, local groups have sprouted up to complement larger and better financed national organizations.

Private, nonprofit groups have applied for and received from the Internal Revenue Service (IRS) a tax-exempt "charitable organization" status under Section 501c(3) of the Internal Revenue Code. As a charitable organization, a nonprofit may accept donations of land, conservation easements, and money, and donors may claim donations as income tax deductions. However, nonprofits are not allowed to endorse candidates or engage in partisan politics.

Nonprofits have stood out for their creativity in accomplishing land protection projects both on private land and in conjunction with government agencies to expand public land holdings. Innovations have included the purchase of land involving several funding sources; gifts of land from companies, families, and individuals; the purchase and donation of conservation easements; joint purchases of land or easements with government agencies; land trades; mitigation banking; candidate conservation agreements; and the attraction of "conservation buyers" who are willing to purchase land and sell or donate conservation easements.

Land Trusts

Land trusts work directly with private landowners to preserve land and sometimes act as intermediaries between landowners and government agencies who share a common interest in keeping the land intact. Land trust staff and volunteers often have a good understanding of the extent of sensitive lands and wildlife habitats in a region and the need to protect large blocks of land and migration corridors to maintain ecosystems.

Land trusts began in 1891 when the Trustees of Reservations was formed in Massachusetts. By 1960, there were about 400 land trusts nationwide, but the numbers soared in the 1980s and early 1990s in response to cuts in federal land protection funding. By 2003, there were more than 1,200 land trusts, with at least one land trust in every state, according the Land Trust Alliance, a national orga-

nization devoted to promoting the creation and development of land trusts. The alliance serves as a clearinghouse of information about land trust practices, publishes a variety of books and reports, and sponsors an annual national conference.

Many land trusts are located in the densely populated Northeast where public lands are rather scarce. However, land trusts have become popular in California, Colorado, and the Midwest where development pressures have become intense. Some land trusts operate nationally, such as The Nature Conservancy (TNC) and the TPL. Some have a statewide focus, such as the Vermont Land Trust, which has preserved nearly 400,000 acres, and the Montana Land Reliance, which has preserved more than 360,000 acres (Vermont Land Trust 2002; Montana Land Reliance 2002). Many land trusts have a regional presence: the Maine Coastal Heritage Trust has preserved more than 60,000 acres of the state's shoreline and islands; the Peninsula Open Space Trust has preserved more than 40,000 acres on the San Francisco, California, peninsula; and the Brandywine Conservancy has preserved more than 25,000 acres in the Brandywine River Valley of southeast Pennsylvania and northern Delaware (Wright 1998, 84; Peninsula Open Space Trust 2002; *Farmland Preservation Report* 2000). All told, as of 2002, land trusts had protected more than 6 million acres nationwide.

The larger land trusts have professional staff and increasingly are using a Geographic Information System (GIS) to identify and evaluate important environmental areas and resource lands, and to monitor properties they own or on which they hold conservation easements. Moreover, land trusts have become serious players in local and regional land use planning efforts; there are many examples of public-private easement purchases and other partnership efforts involving land trusts and government agencies (Endicott 1994).

Most land trusts are small and locally focused. They are often are staffed by volunteers and have generally preserved no more than a few thousand acres. The shortcomings of most land trusts are a lack of staff and financial resources, and the ability to create only "islands" of protected land, often amid encroaching development. Islands of preserved land are often insufficient to protect entire ecosystems or special landscapes. In any easement donation or purchase, the land trust takes on a long-term responsibility for monitoring the property to ensure that the landowners abide by the terms of the easement. Monitoring takes time and staff and is expensive; most land trusts ask easement donors to give a "stewardship endowment" to help pay for monitoring. A shortage of funds means that a land trust will be forced to rely on easement donations rather than pursuing easement purchases.

Conservation Easement Donations

The main technique that land trusts use to protect land is the donation of conservation easements. Some larger land trusts are able to purchase conservation easements either at full value or in a bargain sale of part cash and part donation. (For an example of a conservation easement sale, see Figure 13-1.) Many federal agencies have also acquired conservation easements by purchase or donation, including the National Park Service, the FWS, the Natural Resources Conservation Service, the Farm Service Agency, and the USFS. Several state conservation agencies also have programs to acquire conservation easements.

Many landowners love their property and do not want to see it become part of the built environment. However, the rising value of real estate in recent decades has put pressure on families wanting to keep land in the family. Transferring land intact to heirs has become more difficult. Federal estate taxes began at 37% on estates valued at more than $1 million in 2003. The personal exemption from the estate tax rises to $3.5 million by 2009. There will be no estate taxes in 2010, but in 2011 the estate tax returns at 2001 rates and exemptions.

One way for a landowner to reduce the value of an estate is to donate a permanent conservation easement to a land trust. The permanent conservation easement is a legal contract restricting the use of the land to open space, and possibly farming or forestry uses (see Table 8-2). The easement is signed by the landowner and the land trust and recorded at the county courthouse. The easement "runs with the land," meaning that it applies to future owners as well as the landowner who donates the easement. The land trust that holds the conservation easement has a legal responsibility to monitor the property and enforce the terms of the easement. Monitoring should consist of an annual on-site visit and written report. Monitoring is an excellent way to maintain a good relationship with landowners.

The value of a conservation easement is determined by a professional appraiser in a written appraisal. The value is the difference between the estimated fair market value of the property if it were sold today and the estimated value of the property subject to the restrictions of the conservation easement.

There are several potential tax benefits from donating a permanent conservation easement. The landowner may use the value of the easement as an income tax deduction, subject to certain limits as defined in Section 170(h) of the Internal Revenue Code (see Table 8-2). There may be estate tax benefits, depending on the size of the landowner's estate. A few states offer state income tax credits for people who donate a conservation easement on their land. For instance, Colorado will refund up to $20,000 in state income taxes for an easement donation (Salkin 2002, 278). Finally, in some states, the landowner may receive a reduction in the assessed value of the property for property tax purposes. For instance, the Maryland Environmental Trust, a state agency, has the authority to grant a 13-year property tax abatement for any property on which it receives a conservation easement donation.

Table 8-2
Valuing the Donation of a Conservation Easement

Example: 90 Acres of Natural Area: Open Land, Forest, and Wetland
$500,000 Appraised Fair Market Value $240,000 Appraised Value Restricted to Open Space and Wildlife Habitat $260,000 Appraised Conservation Easement Value
Income Tax Savings
Landowner's Adjusted Gross Income = $80,000
30% of Adjusted Gross Income is the maximum deduction for one year, but the landowner can spread the donation over six years. Depending on income, a landowner may not be able to use the entire donation as an income tax deduction.
$24,000 = Maximum one-year deduction
$24,000 x 6 = $144,000 maximum deduction over six years, assuming a constant income of $80,000 a year. (Note: The landowner cannot use $116,000 of the donation, and it is lost.)
Total income tax savings = about $50,000
Estate Tax Savings
Estate Value Reduction = $260,000. Actual estate tax savings will depend on size of the landowner's estate and year of settlement.
Property Tax Savings
Vary from state to state and even community to community. In some cases, there may be no property tax savings.

Some landowners feel that they cannot afford to donate an easement but want to find a way to keep most of their land intact while getting some cash out of a portion of their land. On occasion, land trusts have been involved in "limited development" projects in which a few to several house lots are subdivided and excluded from the easement while the remaining open land is included. Land trusts need to be careful when considering a limited development project. They need to ask themselves: Will the project really further the conservation purposes of the land trust, or is the landowner trying to use the conservation easement on part of the property to increase the value of the house lots that can be sold? As a general rule, the fewer house lots and less land area kept out of the easement, the more likely that the land conservation purposes of the easement will be achieved.

Developers have become interested in placing conservation easements on open and often fragile lands as part of overall development designs. The open land can add value to the houses, apartments, or office space, even though the tax benefits to developers are often very small. Land trusts or local governments must be careful in deciding whether to accept an easement on a small portion of a developed area, and, again, should determine whether the preservation of the land really furthers its larger conservation goals. Landowners should be aware that if they try to claim an easement as an income tax deduction on the open part of their property, the IRS may reduce the value of the easement if it can be proven to increase the value of the developed portion. This is known as "private inurement." If local regulations require that open space be provided as a condition of approval, the IRS may deny an income tax deduction on an easement donation as well.

Ad-hoc Citizens' Groups

Not all land protection takes place through government agencies or formal private organizations. Ad-hoc citizens' groups are often formed to try to protect a property with scenic views, wildlife habitat, or other natural features that are threatened with development. These last-ditch efforts often fail because development permission has already been granted by the local government, or citizens are unable or unwilling to scrape together the funds to take the case to court or to buy the property outright.

"Ad-hoc" in Latin literally means "toward this" or "for this purpose," reflecting the specific interest of a group. One shortcoming of ad-hoc groups is that they are often formed around a single issue; once that issue is resolved, the groups disband. This is reactive planning. Yet, several nonprofit organizations began as ad-hoc groups and evolved into land trusts or land use watchdog organizations. As such, many ad-hoc groups are serious "players" in the land use and environmental decisions made in their communities. For instance, in 1991, plans to dam the Locust Fork River in Alabama brought on a crisis that compelled a group of citizens to form the Friends of the Locust Fork River. The Friends were able to defeat the dam and have kept the Locust Fork a free-flowing river. The Friends evolved into a nonprofit organization, currently with about 900 members, and undertake public awareness programs, river clean-up days, and recreational outings on the river.

National Land Conservation Organizations and Private Foundations

There are several national organizations that actively seek to protect landscapes with local, regional, or national significance. These organizations participate in debates over environmental legislation; enter lawsuits against government agencies, polluters, and developers; and fund the preservation of important land and water environments. These national organizations typically have large amounts of money, and their land acquisitions can have major impacts on local communities. Local planners should be aware of these organizations and forge a working relationship with them, just as with state, local, and regional land trusts. Information on how to contact these and other national environmental organizations is listed in the Contacts section at the end of the book.

The Sierra Club is the nation's oldest environmental organization, founded in 1892 by the pioneering conservationist John Muir. Unlike many other environmental groups, the Sierra Club does not have a nonprofit status because of its lobbying efforts and political involvement. The Sierra Club also takes legal action. The Sierra Club has been instrumental in protecting some of America's greatest natural treasures, such as the Grand Canyon. There are state and regional Sierra Club chapters that are active in state and local land conservation issues.

The Wilderness Society was formed in 1935 to preserve, protect, and expand wilderness areas. The Wilderness Society does economic and ecological evaluations of federal policy, purchases property for wilderness, and takes legal action to protect wilderness areas (see Table 8-3).

The Nature Conservancy, formed in 1951, has protected more than 12 million acres of land in the United States, and more than 80 million acres overseas (TNC 2002). TNC owns and manages almost 1,500 nature preserves worldwide. The Trust for Public Land, founded in 1972, protects land for greenways and recreation areas, urban parks, water quality, scenic vistas, and historic and working landscapes. As of 2002, the TPL had helped protect more than 1.4 million acres in 45 states.

The Conservation Fund was established in 1985 to protect land and water resources. The fund seeks to "conserve open space, parklands, water resources, wetlands, wildlife and waterfowl habi-

Table 8-3
America's 15 Most Endangered Natural Lands Identified by the Wilderness Society (1999)

1.	Arctic National Wildlife Refuge, Alaska
2.	Cascade Crest, Washington
3.	Copper River Delta in Chugach National Forest, Alaska
4.	The Everglades, Florida
5.	Grand Canyon National Park, Arizona
6.	Greater Yellowstone region of Wyoming, Montana, and Idaho
7.	Klamath Basin, California/Oregon border
8.	North Woods, Maine
9.	Medicine Bow and Routt National Forests, Wyoming/Colorado border
10.	The Mojave National Preserve, California
11.	Okefenokee National Wildlife Refuge, Georgia/Florida border
12.	Owyhee Canyonlands, Idaho
13.	Sierra Nevada Old-Growth Forest, California
14.	The Sonoran Desert, Arizona
15.	Southeastern Wilderness, Utah

Source: The Wilderness Society (1999)

tat in cooperation with others." As of 2002, the fund had helped to protect 3.4 million acres at a cost of more than $400 million (The Conservation Fund 2002). In 1998, the fund worked with land trusts and state governments to preserve some 200,000 acres in the northern forests of New York, Vermont, and New Hampshire (see Chapter 14). The Conservation Fund also works with developers to demonstrate that sensitive development design is good for business and can enhance community character.

American Rivers was founded in 1973 with a mission to increase the number of rivers protected through the National Wild and Scenic Rivers System. American Rivers works with government agencies and local watershed organizations to restore wildlife habitat and water quality, and has helped to protect more than 22,000 miles of river and more than 5.5 million acres of riverside lands,

an area about equal in size to the State of Vermont (see Table 8-4) (American Rivers 2001).

There are several private foundations that actively support land trusts and national land conservation organizations. These foundations are important sources of funding, and the competition for their grants is intense. Leading foundations that support land conservation efforts include:

- The Doris Duke Foundation
- The Ford Foundation
- The W. Alton Jones Foundation
- The John D. and Catherine T. MacArthur Foundation
- The Andrew W. Mellon Foundation
- The David and Lucille Packard Foundation
- The Pew Charitable Trusts
- The Rockefeller Foundation
- The Surdna Foundation
- The Robert W. Woodruff Foundation

Table 8-4
America's 10 Most Endangered Rivers (2001)

	River	States Included
1.	Missouri River	Missouri, Kansas, Iowa, Nebraska, South Dakota, North Dakota, Montana
2.	Canning River	Alaska
3.	Eel River	California
4.	Hudson River	New Jersey, New York
5.	Powder River	Wyoming, Montana
6.	Mississippi River	Minnesota, Wisconsin, Illinois, Iowa, Missouri, Kentucky, Tennessee, Arkansas, Mississippi, Louisiana
7.	Big Sandy River	Kentucky, West Virginia
8.	Snoqualmie River	Washington
9.	Animas River	Colorado, New Mexico
10.	East Fork Lewis River	Washington

Source: American Rivers (2001)

The Doris Duke Foundation, for instance, has provided more than $13 million in support of TNC's land preservation efforts in Rhode Island and New Jersey. The Mellon Foundation has contributed significantly toward the preservation of battlefield sites. The Packard Foundation has provided $175 million for the purchase of conservation easements in California.

Many local and regional foundations also support conservation projects within their vicinity. For example, the Freeman Foundation in Vermont has been a major contributor to the Vermont Land Trust. The William Penn Foundation in Philadelphia and the Oxford Foundation in Oxford, Pennsylvania, have provided substantial funding for the Lancaster Farmland Trust.

LOCAL PLANNING FOR LANDSCAPE TREASURES

Communities are recognizing that both long-term residents and newcomers appreciate the open space, wildlife habitats, scenic vistas, and water quality protection that natural landscapes provide. At the same time, there are demands on the land for working farm, forestry, and mining uses, and for residential and commercial uses. Striking a balance among the natural environment, working landscapes, and the built environment is one of the biggest challenges that local governments face. As much as possible, it is advisable to keep these three areas separate to minimize conflicts. Balance requires cooperation and long-term commitment from politicians, landowners, the building industry, land conservation groups, and the public at large. Politicians both within and across jurisdictions will have to agree to protect certain important environmental features and implement effective regulations, incentives, and land acquisition programs. Landowners and developers must be able to live with the regulations and incentives. Land conservation groups can help to supplement public funds for land conservation and land protection efforts. The public will need to support the politicians and spending programs at the ballot box.

Table 8-5
Sample Special Landscapes Goals and Objectives in the Comprehensive Plan

Natural Resources	
Goal	To protect important and unique natural and historic landscape features that provide aesthetic, recreational, educational, and economic opportunities.
Objective	Put an open space bond measure on the ballot.
Objective	Nominate unique natural features for state or federal designation and protection.
Community Facilities	
Objective	Complete a community open space plan.
Objective	Add additional lands to community and regional parks, greenways, and trails.
Economic Base	
Objective	Protect important and unique natural landscape features that are important to local tourism and recreation businesses, and to the quality of life of local residents.
Land Use	
Objective	Keep commercial recreational development away from unique natural landscape features, such as ridgelines and viewsheds.
Objective	Encourage compact development to avoid the loss or degradation of important and unique natural landscape features and vistas.

Inventory

The comprehensive plan should include an inventory and maps of the environmental treasures of the community, including their location, type, and importance. These treasures might be environmental features recognized at the federal, state, regional, or local levels, such as mountain ridges and other geologic formations, scenic vistas, historic and cultural landscapes, parks, and scenic rivers and highways. Information sources include the state environmental department or department of natural resources; the state historic preservation office; and the state transportation department, TNC, and local land trusts. It is also a good idea to survey local residents and land conservation groups to ask them what they consider the community's landscape treasures. The planning commission can also undertake a viewshed analysis to identify scenic vistas in the community that are worthy of protection.

Analysis

The analysis should rank natural and cultural landscapes for their importance. The analysis should also use the community's future population projection to evaluate potential impacts on special landscapes and to estimate the need for future parks, recreation areas, and trails. This analysis should be the basis for the goals and objectives, the Action Strategy, and in drafting the future land use map and the zoning map.

Goals and Objectives

The comprehensive plan must set realistic goals and objectives for special landscapes (see Table 8-5). The overall goal should be to protect important landscape features that have aesthetic, recreational, educational, and economic value. Other goals and objectives should be identified in the Natural Resource, Community Facilities, Land Use, and Economic Base sections of the plan. From these goals and objectives should come specific strategic actions.

Action Strategy

The Action Strategy should present techniques and programs for achieving the special landscape goals and objectives as well as a timetable. Landscape protection benchmarks should be identified and progress toward those benchmarks evaluated in an annual report on the environment. Specific recommendations might include the following:

- Explore the use of zoning overlay districts to protect sensitive environmental features, such as scenic rivers and highways, ridgelines, and viewsheds within in-holdings and adjacent to important public landscapes.
- Explore state and federal funding for the purchase of environmentally sensitive lands and conservation easements.
- Create partnerships with nonprofit groups for the preservation of important and unique natural and cultural resources.
- Add acreage to the county and municipal park systems to include sensitive environmental areas over the next five years.
- Discuss creating a regional trail network with neighboring municipalities and counties.

Zoning Ordinance

Some communities use conservation zoning to limit the amount of development that can occur on private land in an attempt to protect natural features. Typically, conservation zoning employs a large minimum lot size, such as 10 acres, for each house that can be built. Yet, even this type of zoning must leave a landowner with a viable economic use of the property. Courts may vary in their interpretation of when a conservation zoning ordinance goes too far and results in an unreasonable loss of economic use.

The success of large-lot zoning often depends on the minimum lot size that is required. For example, a conservation zone with a 5-acre mini-

mum lot size will simply encourage the subdivision of land into 5-acre "estates" and "ranchettes." The larger the lot size, the more likely the zoning will keep land in contiguous open blocks that are beneficial to wildlife and plant life, and provide open space for the community. Public officials often hope that timber and agricultural zones with large minimum lot sizes of 40 acres or more will also help to protect natural features and habitats.

If a community or county uses large-lot zoning, it is a good idea to offer landowners preferential property taxation. Because landowners are limited in the number of lots they can sell, and because they are providing a public service in keeping their land mostly open, the property tax burden should not be so high as to force them to sell land to pay the taxes.

Alternatively, a community can promote lower development densities through density-based zoning, such as one building lot per 10 acres, but the building lot can be no more than 2 acres in size. Siting standards in the zoning ordinance can require minimum setbacks from scenic rivers and roads.

Zoning overlay districts are a common tool used to protect significant environmental areas that have public value. An overlay zone is a special zoning district created to protect a specific resource, such as a scenic corridor. These resources often have irregular boundaries that do not coincide with private property lines. The overlay zone is drawn on the zoning map on top of a base zone—such as a residential zone or an agricultural zone—to include the selected features for protection and thereby create a double zone. A landowner who proposes to develop property in a double zone must meet the provisions of both the base zone and the overlay zone.

Take, for example, an area that has a base zone R-1 single-family, but part of the area lies within the viewshed of a scenic highway. A scenic viewshed overlay zone "SV" could be placed on top of part of the R-1 zone to create tighter building restrictions, such as requiring that all new buildings be at least 100 feet from the highway and have landscaping. The proposed development would have to meet the zoning requirements of both the R-1 zone and the SV zone.

An overlay zone can be applied on top of any base zone. Often, the overlay zone will span two or more bases zones. Overlay zones can be used to protect a variety of the following environmental features: mountain ridges and unique geologic formations; areas with steep slopes (greater than 15% slope); wetlands; floodplains; scenic rivers, highways, and viewsheds; historic and cultural landscapes; aquifers, wellhead areas, and watersheds; historic buildings and districts; and important plant and wildlife habitats.

Subdivision Regulations

A growing number of communities are adopting mandatory dedication standards for parks, open space, and trails in their subdivision and land development ordinances. Developers of residential subdivisions are required to set aside land or fees in-lieu-of-land for these amenities. Developers can be required to set aside land for parks, trails, and greenways where communities have identified desired future locations of trails and greenways in a specially adopted open space plan. An adopted open space plan has the advantage of facilitating the interconnection of multiple individual trail and greenway segments.

The subdivision and land development ordinance is important for regulating developments proposed near significant natural features. The ordinance should include standards for an environmental impact assessment (EIA) for major residential subdivisions, and commercial and industrial projects of more than 1 acre. Stormwater runoff should be contained on site as much as possible through vegetation, swales, and retention basins. Roads and impervious surfaces should be tightly controlled. The subdivision ordinance can require

buffering berms and vegetation to protect neighboring special landscapes.

Capital Improvements Program

The capital improvements program (CIP) should be used to direct growth and development away from environmentally and culturally important landscapes. Major roads, schools, and extensions of sewer and water systems should generally be kept out of these areas in order to discourage intensive growth and development that would degrade the quality of these landscapes. A CIP may include funding for the public acquisition of privately held, environmentally important lands or the public purchase of conservation easements to those lands. Land and easement purchases are often expensive, require long-term financing, and hence are considered capital investments. Such land preservation is sometimes referred to as "green infrastructure," and can be as important as traditional infrastructure, such as sewer and water facilities, for attracting economic development and providing a good quality of life in a community.

What to Look for in a Development Review

A proposed development should be evaluated according to the current comprehensive plan, zoning ordinance, subdivision and land development regulations, and any other relevant ordinances. Planners should check any development proposal with a map or database of significant natural, cultural, and historic sites in the community. If the development is likely to have an adverse impact on these sites, the development may need to be scaled down or reconfigured to provide needed protection. For larger developments, an EIA should identify potential conflicts with sites of importance to the community (see Table 8-6). The better a development fits ecologically and blends in aesthetically with the natural and cultural environment, the more of an asset it will be to the community.

Table 8-6
A Checklist of Natural and Scenic Environment Issues in a Development Review

1.	What are the size, location, and land uses of the proposed development?
2.	Is the proposed development allowed in the particular zone?
3.	Are setbacks and buffers to property lines met?
4.	How close is the proposed development to any important natural sites and environmental features?
5.	Is the proposed development within a scenic viewshed?
6.	Will trail linkages and greenways be provided consistent with a local or regional open space plan?
7.	Are conservation easements being donated to a government agency or private nonprofit organization to protect open space?
8.	How can the proposal be modified to protect important on-site or nearby natural features?
9.	Has the developer obtained any necessary state or federal permits?

9

Planning for Wildlife Habitat

Certainly extinction is natural . . . [But] scientists predict that between now and 2030, the earth will lose between a quarter and a third of all existing species. And this is in absence of life to replace them.
EDWARD LAROE, NATIONAL BIOLOGICAL SERVICE

Preserve plants, animals and natural communities that represent the diversity of life on Earth by protecting the land and waters they need to live.
FROM THE MISSION STATEMENT OF
THE NATURE CONSERVANCY (TNC)

Metropolitan areas, dominated by a mix of built environments and working landscapes, make up over one-fifth of the land area of the lower 48 states. The working landscapes of farms, ranches, and forests make up about two-thirds of the nation's land area, but there are significant areas of native plant and wildlife habitat within the working landscapes. Easily half of the United States can be considered native habitat in varying degrees of quality. Programs to protect important plant and wildlife habitats have been created by federal, state, and local governments as well as private sector interest groups. An overarching question is whether these programs can protect enough land and habitat for plant and animal species to sustain entire ecosystems. Also important is keeping development away from sensitive environments such as wetlands, floodplains, steep slopes, and coastal areas that are more suited to wildlife than humans. Although habitat destruc-

tion is the most widely recognized cause of wildlife loss, air and water pollution, diseases, and invasive species that compete with native plants and animals also pose major threats to wildlife.

PRESSURES ON WILDLIFE HABITAT

At the turn of the 21st century, plant and animal species worldwide are becoming extinct at a rate not seen since the disappearance of the dinosaurs 65 million years ago. Over the last 100 years, some 70 vertebrate and 200 plant species have become extinct in North America (The Wildlands Project 2001). In passing the Endangered Species Act (ESA) in 1973, Congress recognized that "various species have been rendered extinct as a consequence of economic growth and development untempered by adequate concern and conservation." Moreover, Congress stated that threatened and endangered species "are of aesthetic, ecological, educational, historical, recreational, and scientific value to the Nation and its people." Biologists take these statements a bit further in noting that certain species, such as frogs and salamanders, act as "indicator species" of the health of local and regional ecosystems—not just for wildlife, but for humans as well.

The United States has more than 200,000 native species of plants and animals (about 10% of the world's known species), and contains 21 of the world's 28 different types of ecosystems (Stevens 2000, A16). More than 1,200 species of plants and animals in the U.S. are listed as threatened or endangered, and wildlife habitat dwindles as the nation's population continues to grow. In 1991, a U.S. Environmental Protection Agency (EPA) Science Advisory Board study warned of a high risk of habitat loss and species extinction in America (U.S. EPA 1991). As of 2000, most of the nation's ecosystems had suffered losses of three-quarters of their original area (Stein *et al.* 2000).

The outward growth of metropolitan areas is increasing the interaction between humans and wildlife. Consider greater Miami eating into the Everglades, Los Angeles creeping up the San Gabriel Mountains, greater Denver stretching along the Front Range of the Rockies, and Seattle expanding toward the Cascades. Author Mike Davis notes that there were nine mountain lion attacks reported in metropolitan fringe areas of California from 1986 to 1995—the first since 1909 (Davis 1999, 244). Large animals are usually the first species driven out by suburban sprawl, but sometimes they linger in their former habitats. Deer frequently invade suburbs looking for something good to nibble on. Bear rummage in garbage cans. Many animals, like squirrels, raccoons, pigeons, and skunks, have a way of finding ecological niches in which they can survive and even thrive around humans.

BIODIVERSITY, LANDSCAPE ECOLOGY, AND WILDLIFE HABITAT

Ecologists and biologists speak of biological diversity or biodiversity as a measure of the variety of plant and animal species, the populations of each species, the interaction among those species, and the overall health of an ecosystem. Species variety and populations provide choices in food and habitat selection, insulating ecosystems with high biodiversity against major disturbances caused by disease, fire, heavy rainfall, or drought. The higher the level of biodiversity, the more resilient the ecosystem is. High biodiversity in turn creates very productive environments that generate substantial environmental services, such as climate moderation, nutrient recycling, water purification and recharge, oxygen production, and assimilation of waste and pollutants. Yet, habitats with low biodiversity—such as cattail marshes, woodland pools, and sand plains—may support species of plants and animals that are not found in habitats that are species rich.

Loss of biodiversity can occur when the variety of species declines, the population of one or more species decreases, or habitats become fragmented and there is less interaction among species. It is often difficult to predict the effects of reduction or loss of a particular species on an ecosystem. Loss of biodiversity may lead to changes in an ecosystem that may be subtle or profound. For example, Dutch elm disease has wiped out most of the elm trees in the eastern United States. Most of the trees were planted in the late 19th century as shade trees along streets and as windrows in farm fields. The loss of the elm trees is mostly aesthetic. By contrast, the eradication of traditional deer predators, especially mountain lions and wolves, has meant a sharp increase in deer numbers, and a deer herd management problem in much of the United States. Deer hunting has become essential for keeping the number of deer under control. If not "harvested," the number of deer would skyrocket, exceeding the carrying capacity of the countryside. Already, each year, hungry deer destroy millions of dollars of farmers' corn, consume backyard gardens, and cause thousands of highway accidents.

In the mid-1990s, Reed Noss and two other biologists reported on the condition of more than 400 specific American ecosystems. They found that declines in biodiversity had left 30 ecosystems critically endangered, with a loss of more than 98% of species; 58 endangered ecosystems had declines of 85% to 98% of species; and 38 threatened ecosystems had lost 70% to 84% of species (Noss *et al.* 1995, 1). Most of the loss in biodiversity occurred in the Northeast, South, Midwest, and California—areas with significant population and development. Terrestrial ecosystems made up 57% of the losses, wetlands ecosystems 33%, and aquatic ecosystems 10%.

Loss of biodiversity can result from:

- direct habitat destruction (such as filling wetlands; plowing, overgrazing, or paving grasslands; fragmenting habitats and migration routes with roads; and siting sprawled and scattered development);
- qualitative changes that degrade habitat (such as the transition from a forest to a tree farm); and
- the invasion of nonnative plants, insects, diseases, and animals.

Ecosystems are not static—the mix of plants and animals in an ecosystem can and does change over time—but the rate and degree of change are important. Ecosystems proceed through stages, called successions, from a pioneer stage of rocks and lichens until they reach the forest stage, also known as the climax stage. For example, the Douglas fir forests of the Pacific Northwest are called late succession forests. As ecosystems, these forests took a long time to evolve through a natural cycle of fire and regeneration to a climax stage.

Noss *et al.* called for ecosystem conservation as a necessary complement to species-level conservation. Yet, scientists cannot accurately estimate how much of an ecosystem must be maintained to support ecosystem processes or a certain number of species. Environmental planner Timothy Beatley has argued that more "proactive, bolder, and larger-scale conservation strategies" are needed to protect and preserve biodiversity, and that "biodiversity preservation must be redefined as [human] self-preservation" (Beatley 2000, 5, 8).

Landscape Ecology

Landscape ecology is the study of how multiple ecosystems fit together into a mosaic of a regional landscape. Eugene Odum, who coined the term "ecology," speaks of a patchy landscape of human and natural systems (Odum 1997, 60). The patch size and shape are important for determining what kinds of species are able to live there. To biologists and ecologists, a key concept in maintaining biodiversity and ecosystem health is critical mass. A critical mass is the minimum area of land or water needed to support a healthy number of a species and species types. A concern among biologists, ecologists, and planners is the degree of resilience of natural environments to disruption, either from a natural event (such as fire, flood, or heavy rainfall) or from human intrusion (such as hiking, all-terrain vehicles, forestry, farming, or residential and commercial development). Resilience is likely to be greater where there is a critical mass of plant and animal species.

Most wildlife conservation problems arise from loss of habitat. In general, for a decline of 70% of ecosystem area, about one-third of the species will be lost. However, large animals, especially carnivores, need a large critical mass of land. For instance, the U.S. Fish and Wildlife Service (FWS) estimates that a single grizzly bear needs 17,510 acres (Easterbrook 1996, 381). Also, many animals are territorial both in defending their space and in their reluctance to move. This territorial imperative can make some species especially vulnerable to habitat loss.

The loss of critical mass can happen in different ways. A natural event, such as flood or fire, can devastate a large area, destroy habitat, and isolate or kill numerous animals. However, natural habitats will regenerate from the effects of such events. Human actions, on the other hand, are more likely to encroach permanently on habitat, resulting in the loss of a critical mass of habitat and the disappearance of certain species of plants and animals that cannot acclimate to the change.

The transformation of a forest into a suburban residential subdivision, filling wetlands to create cropland, and clear cutting commercial forests all reduce the necessary critical mass of land for habitats and species. The development of roads, houses, and commercial areas causes fragmentation of wildlife habitat into smaller and often unsustainable sizes. Wildlife nesting and feeding grounds and migration corridors are often bisected or destroyed. Development also brings pollution from stormwater runoff, pesticide use, soil erosion, illegal dumping, and accidental spills, which can destroy habitat and kill wildlife. Roads are especially harmful to wildlife, as cars and trucks often kill or injure animals trying to cross roads. The 380,000 miles of roads in the national forests (about eight times as many miles as in the nation's interstate system), which were built primarily to provide access for mining and logging, create edges, bisect contiguous blocks of land, increase soil erosion, and expose large areas to invasive plants and insects.

As people settle near or next to natural areas, there are edge effects. Edge effects occur where two ecosystems overlap in what is called an ecotone, an area of transition from one biological community to another. The edges of two ecotones can support a rich diversity of species, to some extent including the species of the neighboring ecosystems. For instance, an ecotone can usually accommodate a large number of species in fields between hedgerows and tree rows, but human encroachment can create a different type of ecotone. The edge of natural areas can become exposed to pesticides and herbicides sprayed on lawns. Dogs, cats, and children foray into the edge of the natural area, and hunt small animals and trample plants. Nonnative plants may start to intrude into the edge as well. This is common along roadways where long-distance trucks can carry the seeds of plants several hundreds of miles. Some plants and animals can thrive in the edge, such as thistle, squirrels, and sparrows, but as more of an area becomes developed, the ecosystem changes. Edges become less clearly defined, wildlife habitats become fragmented, migration becomes more difficult, and some species become locally extinct (Lidicker 1999, 333-343). Through

the planning process, communities should seek to protect distinct natural edges.

The protection of wildlife migratory routes and corridors that connect wildlife habitats is emerging as a necessary planning strategy for migratory species and to provide access to water. Isolated species run the risk of losing genetic diversity. Inbreeding is bad for animals just as it is for humans. Most mammal species require a population of about 500 animals to remain genetically healthy. The corridors approach often meshes nicely with the creation of greenways along rivers and streams to protect water quality and keep development away from floodplains and wetlands. Questions worth asking include: Are wildlife corridors enough? And, if so, how wide and how long do the corridors have to be? Will they connect to core habitat areas, breeding and feeding grounds, and water supplies?

Finally, while there is often special concern for the larger and more threatened species, such as the California Condor and the grizzly bear, the loss of flora and fauna on the lower end of the food chain may actually be more important for the health of ecosystems and regional landscapes.

Bioregionalism

A bioregion is a distinct collection of plant and animal ecosystems that function in certain ways and have particular needs for survival. Temperature and precipitation primarily determine most bioregions, with elevation, soils, watersheds, and microclimates as contributing factors. According to the National Geographic Society, the United States contains nine major land bioregions and eight water bioregions (see Table 9-1). There may be several bioregions within a single state and more than one bioregion within a county. A bioregion may consist of up to several local ecosystems with differing types and numbers of plants and animals.

The concept of bioregionalism has two components: the protection of native plant and animal species from nonnative species, and

Table 9-1
Land and Water Bioregions of the United States

Land Bioregion	Where Mainly Found
Tundra	Alaska
Boreal Forests	Alaska
Tropical Forests	Hawaii
Hardwood and Mixed Hardwood and Softwood Forests	Eastern U.S.
Softwood Forests	Southeast, Pacific Northwest, Southern Rockies
Grasslands	Great Plains
Wet Grasslands	Florida Everglades
Coastal Scrub and Grasslands	Southern California
Desert	Desert Southwest, Eastern Oregon

Water Bioregion	Where Mainly Found
Arctic Rivers and Lakes	Alaska
Temperate Lakes	Midwest
Temperate Rivers	Eastern U.S., Midwest, Great Plains, Pacific Northwest
Rivers without Outlet to Sea	Great Basin
Subtropical Rivers	Southern Florida, Southern Texas
Seasonally Dry Rivers and Lakes	Southwest, Great Plains

Source: Adapted from U.S. Forest Service (1993)

maintaining native habitat in the face of development pressures.

Some native plants thrive in particular microclimates and cannot simply be replanted to other locations. Travelers both intentionally and unwittingly introduce exotic plants, seeds, insects, and even animals to the United States that can overtake native species. The nonnative kudzu vine was introduced in the South in the 1940s and has vigorously proliferated. In the 1990s, the zebra mussel emigrated to the U.S. in the hulls of ships, and spread throughout the Great Lakes and smaller lakes such as Lake Champlain and Lake George, New York. This fresh-water mussel has done billions of dollars of environmental and property damage, including clogging water supply and power plant intake pipes, cutting swimmers with its sharp shells, and absorbing nutrients needed by other aquatic life.

The Asian long-horned beetle arrived in America in 1996 and has the ability to literally eat trees from the inside out. The beetle has no known predator and is becoming a serious problem. Infected trees have been cut down, and pesticides will probably have to be used (Stout 2000, 28). Fire ants with their nasty stings arrived in Alabama from South America in the 1920s. They have since spread throughout the Southeast. Mosquitoes carrying the potentially deadly West Nile virus killed seven people and sickened 55 in greater New York

City in 1999; by 2002, the virus had been reported in 44 states, in more than 3,000 cases, causing 241 deaths (National Biological Information Infrastructure 2003).

These pest invasions are made more acute by the fact that increased air travel and international trade have brought distant parts of the globe close together. In 1999, invasive plants and animals cost the United States an estimated $123 billion (McNeil 2000, 254). As exotic plants and wildlife displace native species, entire ecosystems may be affected and natural environmental processes disrupted. One emerging strategy is to concentrate habitat and species protection efforts on so-called "hot spots" where there are large numbers of plant and animal species. For example, California and Hawaii have the greatest diversity of plants and animals of all the states, and the largest number of threatened and endangered species. Both states have inspection personnel at entry points checking for exotic plants and, in the case of Hawaii, exotic animals as well. The area along California's Pacific coast to about 100 miles inland has the highest concentration of plant and animal diversity in the United States. This is also the area where most of California's 34 million people live and where millions more could be living by 2025.

FEDERAL EFFORTS TO PROTECT WILDLIFE HABITAT

The federal government has a variety of programs aimed at protecting plant and wildlife habitat. Federal agencies have taken steps toward managing entire ecosystems rather than just isolated parcels of land or individual species. First, coordination among federal agencies has improved. The Interagency Ecosystem Management Task Force, composed of members from the federal agencies that influence natural areas, sees its role as: "To restore and maintain the health, sustainability, and biological diversity of ecosystems while supporting sustainable economies and communities . . . the ecosystem approach integrates ecological, eco-

nomic, and social factors that affect a management unit defined by ecological—not political—boundaries" (Interagency Ecosystem Management Task Force 1995). This kind of cooperation is fundamental for forging a more holistic view of the role of the natural environment, and leads to better data collection (see Table 9-2), coordination of efforts, and more effective program innovations.

In 1993, the Council on Environmental Quality (CEQ) drafted a set of principles for preserving biodiversity in federal management programs and National Environmental Policy Act (NEPA) environmental impact reviews:

- Take an ecosystem view. Sites do not exist in isolation but as part of local and regional ecosystems.
- Protect communities and ecosystems. Look beyond individual species to the community and ecosystem relationships, and natural processes that sustain the species.
- Minimize habitat fragmentation. Connected habitats allow for a wider distribution of species than isolated pockets.
- Promote native species, and native biological and genetic diversity.
- Protect rare and ecologically important plants and animals, especially "keystone" species.
- Maintain or mimic natural ecosystem processes.
- Restore ecosystems, communities, and species.
- Monitor for biodiversity impacts. Be willing to learn and manage adaptively as a substitute for lack of information (CEQ 1993, 18).

The Endangered Species Act

The ESA of 1973 has become perhaps the most far-reaching environmental law in America. It applies to all land in the United States, both public and private, and an estimated 70% of threatened and endangered species live on privately owned lands (U.S. FWS 1998). The ESA prohibits any willful

Table 9-2
Federal Information Sources Related to Wildlife Habitat

Program	Sponsor	Coverage
National Wetlands Inventory	Department of the Interior U.S. Fish and Wildlife Service (FWS)	Information on wetlands resources
Gap Analysis	U.S. Geological Survey (USGS) Biological Resources Division	Maps of vegetation, terrestrial vertebrates, and endangered species
Biomonitoring of Environmental Status and Trends	USGS Biological Resources Division	Temporal and geographic trends in contaminants that may threaten fish and wildlife
North American Breeding Bird Survey	USGS Biological Resources Division	Long-term trends in bird populations
Waterfowl Breeding Population and Habitat	Department of the Interior U.S. FWS	Estimates of breeding numbers and habitat
Status and Trends	USGS Biological Resources Division	Data on biological populations and habitats
Public Land Statistics	Bureau of Land Management (BLM)	BLM natural resource management programs
National Stream Quality Accounting Network and Hydrologic Benchmark Network	USGS	Trends in water quality; trends in waters that have little human influence

Source: Council on Environmental Quality, *Annual Report, 1996* (1996), pp. 387-388

"taking" of threatened or endangered species. Taking is defined as killing, hunting, harming, capturing, or collecting a threatened or endangered species, or destroying its habitat. Violations of the ESA may be met with stiff penalties. The Secretary of the Interior may levy fines ranging from $500 to $25,000, and the Justice Department may impose fines of $25,000 to $50,000 and up to 12 months in jail. Any citizen may file suit against any person, business, or agency for violations of the ESA.

The U.S. FWS and the National Marine Fisheries Service are responsible for administering the ESA. It is the job of both agencies to identify plants and animals that are threatened or endangered with extinction, and to ensure that private and government actions do not harm these species. The agencies are charged with identifying critical habitat areas, and drafting and implementing recovery plans that will enable a threatened or endangered species to recover to a sustainable population. The FWS may also reintroduce species into former habitat, such as the release of wolves into Yellowstone National Park in the early 1990s.

The Secretary of the Interior may declare a plant or animal species endangered if the species "is in danger of extinction throughout all or a significant portion of its [habitat] range." A threatened species "is likely to become an endangered species within the foreseeable future" (ESA Section 3, PL 93-205). Specifically, a species must be at risk for at least one of the following reasons:

- the destruction or threatened destruction of habitat;

Table 9-3
Listed Threatened and Endangered Species
by Top Ten States and Territories (2003)

State	Number of Species Listed
Hawaii	312
California	283
Florida	100
Alabama	90
Tennessee	83
Texas	81
Puerto Rico	75
Virginia	55
Georgia	54
Arizona	54

Note: A species can be found in more than one state.

Source: U.S. Fish and Wildlife Service (2003a)

- overuse of the species for commercial, scientific, educational, or recreational purposes;
- disease or predation;
- lack of regulations to prevent a decline in population; and
- other natural or man-made factors threatening survival.

As of 2002, there were 1,070 animals and 746 plants listed as threatened or endangered in the United States (U.S. Bureau of the Census 2003, 223). The number of threatened and endangered species has more than tripled since 1980. In 1999, Hawaii had the most listed species at 308, followed by California, and Florida (see Table 9-3). Alaska and Vermont tied for the fewest listed species at only six each.

The Secretary of the Interior must publish the intention to list a species as threatened or endangered in the *Federal Register*, and a public comment period is advertised. The secretary then identifies "critical habitat"—a critical mass of land and water composed of public or private holdings, or both—necessary for the survival and recovery of the threatened or endangered species. The critical habitat designation also involves a public comment period and may include public meetings to solicit comments. As of 2003, critical habitats had been designated for 999 species in 564 recovery plans (U.S. FWS 2003b). Finally, the FWS and National Marine Fisheries Service must draft and implement species recovery plans. So far, just over half of all threatened or endangered species have recovery plans.

The FWS has about 7,000 employees who, in addition to drafting recovery plans, are responsible for the nation's wildlife refuges, and for monitoring and enforcing the ESA. Recovery plans consist of an evaluation of the condition of a particular species, the designation of critical habitats that are generally off limits to development, and other goals and actions that will promote the recovery of species numbers. According to the National Wildlife Federation (NWF), only seven species have recovered to the point of being "delisted," but more than 350 listed species of plants and animals have achieved stable numbers or are improving (NWF 2001).

The FWS has the authority to give emergency endangered status to a plant or animal species for a period of 240 days. During that interval, the service can begin the regular process for listing the species as endangered. The service did this, for example, in early 2000 in the case of the California tiger salamander in Santa Barbara County. The purpose of the emergency rule is to prevent a species from becoming extinct by affording it immediate protection while the normal listing process is being followed (U.S. FWS 2000).

The FWS and the National Marine Fisheries Service are also charged with ensuring that the actions of other federal agencies do not jeopardize threatened or endangered species. For instance, the FWS is often the lead agency in NEPA reviews of federal projects that could affect threatened or endangered species habitat. From 1979 to 1992, there were more than 145,000 federal interagency consultations under the ESA, but only 69 federal projects were canceled (*ibid.*).

Many landowners fear that they will lose the ability to use or sell their land as they wish if their land is declared a necessary habitat for rare and endangered species. For example, responding to the emergency protection given to the tiger salamander, Santa Barbara County, California, rancher Jim Campbell said, "I've seen exactly one [tiger salamander] in my 65 years here. It's the way they [the FWS] can shut you down with so little information. They treat you like a criminal on your own land" (Sternold 2000, A14). Some private landowners opposed to the ESA have even advocated a policy of "Shoot, Shovel, and Shut Up" to avoid the risk of having threatened or endangered species found on their property.

There have been only a few cases in which a court ruled that a taking of private property had occurred under the ESA. In the 1997 case of *Bennett et al. v. M. Spear* (U.S. Supreme Court 95-813, March 19, 1997), ranchers were restricted from drawing irrigation water in order to protect two rare and endangered species of fish. The U.S. Supreme Court reversed two lower court decisions and ruled unanimously that enforcement of the ESA had caused the ranchers unreasonable economic harm. However, in 2000, a federal court ruled that 170,000 acre-feet of Rio Grande water must be used to support the habitat of the rare and endangered silvery minnow (*The Economist* 2000, 25). This lack of legal consistency will only heighten the controversy surrounding the ESA.

Arguments over the federal ESA and the wetlands filling and dredging permit process of Section 404 of the Clean Water Act were largely responsible for the backlash of property rights laws that have been adopted in 18 states since the early 1990s. These laws require governments to compensate landowners if a new regulation reduces the value of property by more than a certain percentage. These laws are contrary to U.S. Supreme Court rulings that have supported regulations that reduce but do not remove all economic value of a property.

Shortcomings of the ESA

The ESA has two major shortcomings:

1. It is reactive, rather than proactive, serving as an emergency-room type of treatment for species that have been allowed to decline to the brink of extinction; and

2. It is not comprehensive; that is, the targeting of specific species and their habitats tends to overlook the need to protect entire ecosystems and biodiversity in general.

In 1995, the National Academy of Sciences released a study of the performance of the ESA. The study reported, "There is no doubt that [the ESA] has prevented the extinction of some species and slowed the decline of others" (National Academy of Sciences 1995, 3). Furthermore, the study supported the listing of species and subspecies of plants and animals: "The committee concludes that the ESA's inclusion of species and subspecies is soundly justified by current scientific knowledge and should be retained" (*ibid.*, 5). The report cited the protection of habitats as crucial, but found that recovery plans needed to be drafted and implemented more swiftly:

"Because habitat plays such an important biological role in endangered species survival, some core amount of essential habitat should be designated for protection at the time of listing a species as endangered as an emergency stop-gap measure . . . Despite increased attention from Congress, recovery plans are developed too slowly and recovery planning remains handicapped by delays in its implementation, goals that are sometimes not scientifically supported, and the uncertainty of its application to other federal activities. No recovery plan, however good it might be, will help prevent extinction or promote recovery if it is not implemented expeditiously" (*ibid.*, 5,6).

SIDEBAR 9-1

Gap Analysis Program

In the 1990s, the U.S. Geological Survey began a Gap Analysis Program (GAP) to provide regional assessments of the conservation status of native plant and vertebrate species. The GAP includes:

- mapping of the vegetative land cover of the U.S. by remote-sensing satellite imagery and geographic information systems (GIS);
- GIS maps with layers of predicted distributions of vertebrate species, land ownership, and management status; and
- documenting the gaps in biodiversity in vertebrates and vegetative land cover types in areas managed for long-term maintenance of biodiversity.

This information can be used by federal, state, and local government agencies and private land trusts to set priorities in plant and wildlife protection, such as identifying additional land to acquire, designating rare or endangered species habitat areas, or adopting changes in land management. A GAP has been completed in several states, and some local governments and private land trusts are using a GAP in their land acquisition strategies. For example, the Coastal Georgia Land Trust is using GAP information to map priority areas for conservation. The trust has also used GIS layers from counties and the state regional development center to evaluate individual parcels.

GAP information can be updated every few years to monitor progress toward species conservation goals.

SIDEBAR 9-2

The Wildlands Project

In 1991, the Wildlands Project, a nonprofit organization, was formed by conservation organizations, conservation biologists, and concerned citizens to look 100 years into the future to identify what needs to be done to protect the ecological integrity and biological diversity of North America. At the heart of the Wildlands Project is an effort to create large interconnected areas of wilderness to promote the recovery of wild lands in which native plant and animal species can thrive.

Specific protection goals include connecting wildlife corridors, buffering wildlife areas from human development, reducing habitat fragmentation, and controlling the invasion of exotic spe-

cies. In addition, the Wildlands Project sponsors research and educational programs about the importance of biodiversity.

In describing his support for the Wildlands Project, noted biologist Paul Ehrlich said, "The Endangered Species Act, although the best act of its sort in a major nation, is inadequate to protect the precious biological resources of North America" (The Wildlands Project 2001). Adds eminent Harvard Professor E.O. Wilson:

"The Wildlands Project is bold and comprehensive ... Unless we expand the area of conservation of wild environments, and design their shape and connections in accordance with the principles of conservation biology, many more American species will go extinct even in the reserves already set aside." (*ibid.*).

SIDEBAR 9-3

Fisheries and Extinction

Ocean fish have long been thought to have good ability to recover from heavy harvesting by commercial fishermen. As of late 2000, no ocean fish had been listed as rare and endangered under the Endangered Species Act, although in 1999 the anadromous chinook salmon had been listed in the Puget Sound region of Washington State. However, a 2000 study of North American ocean fisheries reported that 82 species and stocks are at risk of extinction (Musick *et al.* 2000). As much as 90% of some species have already been lost. The study cited three "hot spots" in U.S. waters—the Puget Sound of Washington State, the northern coast of the Gulf of Mexico, and parts of south Florida—where fishing has decimated stocks and species (see Figure 9-1).

Professor John A. Musick, lead author of the study, commented, "Now we're beginning to realize we can drive these fish out of existence" (Balzar 2000, A5). Species cited as at risk included five species of sharks; five species of anadromous sturgeon; and popular food fish, such as the Atlantic cod and Atlantic halibut.

Environmentalists would prefer to see long-range land conservation strategies implemented that would provide adequate, sustainable, and diverse habitats through a combination of large core areas connected by wildlife corridors with buffered land areas or transition areas adjacent to human developments.

To create and maintain both core areas and corridors will require a mix of land acquisition and regulations. Wildlife managers agree that it is preferable to own the land to be managed rather than rely on other landowners. The federal government makes grants to states through the Cooperative Endangered Species Conservation Fund for land acquisition and planning. Increased funding for the acquisition of wildlife refuges under the federal Land and Water Conservation Fund would help expand protected habitats. Many state departments of natural resources are active in purchasing land for wildlife habitats, but land use regulations that protect wildlife habitats on private lands will be crafted mainly by local governments.

Habitat Conservation Plans

Provisions for Habitat Conservation Plans (HCPs) were added to the ESA in 1982 to clarify where development would be allowed and where habitats should be protected (Section 10(a)(1)(B) of the ESA). An HCP is a voluntary contract for large-scale ecosystem management, usually between the federal government and private landowners. The FWS usually takes the lead role in negotiating HCP agreements. HCPs also involve state and local governments in their planning, regulation,

9-1 Fish farm, Puget Sound, Washington. Farm-raised fish are being grown in response to dwindling natural fish stocks. However, farm-raised salmon may cause disease and genetic problems for wild salmon, which are listed as an endangered species in the Pacific Northwest.

Source: Katherine Daniels

and funding. Developers were concerned that environmentalists were using the ESA to block their projects, while environmentalists argued that the act allowed for government intervention too late and on areas too small to be effective.

HCPs designate critical habitats that are essential to the survival and recovery of threatened and endangered species and hence are off limits to development. At the same time, HCPs identify lands where development is allowed. An HCP may apply to a single species or several species. A plan may cover a small amount of land or up to thousands of acres, and can influence forestry, ranching, farming, and urban and suburban development patterns. HCPs for large areas can run to more than 1,000 pages. HCPs are typically set up for 30, 50, or 100 years, and are approved by the Secretary of the Interior or the Secretary of Commerce.

In an HCP, the developer agrees to minimize the "take" of listed and as yet unlisted endangered species to the maximum extent possible. The developer in turn receives an "incidental take permit" from the FWS and "No Surprises" treatment, which absolves the developer of responsibility for habitat and species conservation on land designated for development as long as a recovery plan for the species is in place (see Case Study 14-2). A further incentive is the "safe harbor agreement," which gives a private landowner, who voluntarily "creates, restores, or improves" threatened or endangered species habitat to a certain biological standard, freedom from future ESA regulations if a new threatened or endangered species is attracted to the property.

In agreeing to the HCP contract, the developer avoids jeopardy with the law and gets assurances that no additional land or funding will be required in the future to protect endangered species on the owner's property. The HCPs may allow development to occur on habitat if the development is offset by the protection, restoration, or relocation of threatened and endangered plants and animals elsewhere. For example, the International Paper Company agreed to relocate 16 pairs of the endangered red cockaded woodpecker from its forestlands in southeast Georgia to an actively managed habitat area in southwest Georgia (NWF 1999).

A strength of the HCP approach is that it is a negotiated compromise that avoids costly and time-consuming litigation. It is a departure from the more common adversarial "command and control" approach to environmental regulation in which the government sets strict standards and then monitors activities and enforces the law. The HCP approach was remarkably popular under the Clinton Administration as a way to try to strike a balance between property development and the protection of wildlife habitats. From 1982 to 1993, only 14 HCPs were implemented. However, as of 2002, there were more than 400 HCPs covering 16 million acres, including one-tenth of the commercial forestland in the Pacific Northwest (U.S. FWS 2002).

One of the uncertain impacts of the ESA is the listing of species that are affected by urban and suburban development. For instance, in 1999, the FWS listed the chinook salmon in the Puget Sound. The potential impact on development in and around fast-growing Seattle has not been made clear. Federal agencies must review thousands of federally funded or permitted development projects each year to determine their impacts on the salmon (Wortman 2002, 9). Will an HCP be required for the entire Puget Sound? Will massive public purchases of riparian and coastal lands be needed to minimize pollution? From a planning standpoint, the chinook listing underscores the need to promote compact urban form in order to protect and sustain regional biodiversity.

The National Wildlife Refuge System

The FWS manages the National Wildlife Refuge System to "preserve, restore, and enhance in their natural ecosystems all species of animals and plants that are threatened or endangered . . . [to]

perpetuate the migratory bird resource . . . [and to] provide recreational experiences oriented toward wildlife." The system was started in 1903 and now contains 530 wildlife refuges and game ranges, covering more than 93 million acres. Funding for the acquisition of wildlife refuges has come from the federal Land and Water Conservation Fund (see Chapter 8), and from the Migratory Bird Hunting Stamp Act and the Pittman-Robertson Act. At the beginning of the waterfowl hunting season, hunters must purchase a Migratory Bird Hunting Stamp, the proceeds from which are used to purchase and maintain wildlife refuges. The Pittman-Robertson Act of 1937 placed an excise tax on the sale of sporting guns and ammunition. Revenues from this tax are dispersed to the states to purchase wildlife habitat and to conduct research and management (Owen *et al.* 1998).

One of the best known yet least visited refuges is the Arctic Wildlife Refuge in northern Alaska. The refuge is a breeding ground for caribou, a summer habitat for migratory birds, and a year-round home to the musk ox. Since the discovery of oil on Alaska's north slope and the construction of the trans-Alaska oil pipeline in the 1970s, oil companies have been pressuring Congress to open the Arctic Wildlife refuge for energy exploration.

The National Wildlife Refuge System Improvement Act of 1997 clarified that hunting, fishing, wildlife observation and photography, or environmental education and research are allowed in the refuges only if they are compatible with the conservation of species in the refuge. The act placed responsibility on the Secretary of the Interior to maintain the "biological integrity, diversity and environmental health of the system . . . for the benefit of present and future generations of Americans."

National Estuarine Research Reserves and Marine Sanctuaries

Estuaries are remarkably rich wildlife breeding grounds in waters where fresh water and saltwater mix. Most of the nation's fish breed in estuarine waters and they are popular locations for birds and waterfowl. The National Oceanic and Atmospheric Administration (NOAA) in the Department of Commerce manages the National Estuarine Research Reserves, covering 427,000 acres of estuaries in 21 reserves (CEQ 1996, 261). NOAA also operates the National Marine Sanctuary Program, which was authorized in the Marine Protection, Research and Sanctuaries Act of 1972. Fourteen national marine sanctuaries protect more than 11,000 square miles of ocean and coasts (*ibid.*).

The sanctuaries are selected for their biodiversity, ecosystem stability, and cultural heritage. For example, the Florida Keys National Marine Sanctuary encompasses the entire marine ecosystem of the islands, including the world's third-largest barrier reef. The Hawaiian Islands Humpback Whale National Marine Sanctuary protects whale habitat in the shallow waters of Hawaii. Sanctuaries may be designated by the Secretary of Commerce, subject to review by Congress, or by an act of Congress. Funding for the program has been in the range of $11 to $14 million a year. With more than half of all Americans living within 100 miles of the coast, the pressures on marine habitats from development and water pollution are intense and are likely to increase. The strength of the sanctuaries approach is that it attempts to protect entire ecosystems rather than just specific species.

Wildlife Incentives Program

The Wildlife Habitat Incentives Program (WHIP) was created under the 1996 Farm Bill to provide cost-share money to landowners who improve wildlife habitat. Four types of habitat were targeted:

1. upland grasslands, shrub and scrub lands, and forests;
2. wetlands and salt marshes (including those that are newly created or enhanced), wild rice beds, and winter flooding of crop fields;
3. riparian and in-stream habitats that can benefit from tree plantings to stabilize stream-

banks, fencing out livestock, and alternative watering facilities; and

4. rare and endangered species habitats.

WHIP is a voluntary program that provides cost-share payments to landowners through five to 15-year agreements to undertake habitat development activities. Since the WHIP actively began in 1998, landowners have enrolled more than 1.6 million acres as of 2002 (Natural Resources Conservation Service (NRCS) 2002). Most of the acreage has involved upland habitats, while one-fifth of the acreage includes rare and endangered species habitats. The WHIP is administered by the NRCS of the U.S. Department of Agriculture. Local planners can coordinate with County Conservation District offices to encourage landowner participation in the WHIP, targeting those areas identified as important wildlife habitat in the local comprehensive plan.

The Bureau of Land Management

The grazing of privately owned livestock on public lands administered by the Bureau of Land Management (BLM) in the West has been allowed since the Taylor Grazing Act of 1934. Ranchers pay a fee called an Animal Unit Monthly (AUM) based on the rangeland feed consumed by a cow and calf over a month. The level of the AUMs has been hotly debated because the rates are below the cost of renting private rangeland for grazing. The BLM has been criticized for allowing its rangeland to be overgrazed by cattle. This reduces habitat and food available for native wildlife. Also, cattle trampling streambanks have caused soil erosion and stream sedimentation, and cattle defecating in streams have further reduced water quality and fish habitat.

Grasslands Reserve Program

The 2002 Farm Bill created the Grasslands Reserve Program (GRP) to protect grasslands that are important wildlife habitat, especially for migratory waterfowl. These grasslands are mainly found in the Upper Midwest states of Iowa, Minnesota, and North and South Dakota. Landowners may voluntarily sell either term conservation easements on their land for 10 to 30 years, or perpetual easements. For land under conservation easements, no disturbance of the land, such as plowing, is allowed. Congress authorized $254 million for the GRP over five years and expects to protect up to 2 million acres (Ducks Unlimited 2002).

STATE PLANNING FOR WILDLIFE HABITAT

Forty-six states have state-level endangered species acts (excluding Alabama, Utah, West Virginia, and Wyoming, as of 2002). Several states have created their own lists of threatened and endangered plants and animals, separate from the federal list. For example, Vermont has only six species of plants and animals on the federal list, but 195 species on the state list (Vermont Natural Resources Council 2000). Certain native species may be found over a wide range for the nation as a whole, but in dwindling numbers in particular states. Developers can be required to take steps to protect important habitat of state-listed species.

TNC has been working with many state environmental agencies to identify and compile biological diversity and habitat types in a computer data bank. Ecosystems can then be rated according to their rareness and fragility. These ratings can be fed back into the local and county comprehensive planning process to identify areas that should be protected from development. This information could also be useful in drafting an environmental impact statement under NEPA or one of the state environmental protection acts. Sometimes, state agencies are reluctant to release site-specific data about rare and endangered species for fear of poaching or intentional damage. A persistent local planner may be able to persuade the state agency to share the data on the condition that it not be revealed to the public.

A few states have mandated that local governments proactively plan for the protection of plant and animal habitats. Florida's 1972 Environmental Land and Water Management Act gives the state government the power to declare up to 5% of the state as "critical areas" of statewide importance. Such areas may include wildlife habitat, and local governments must draft regulations to protect these areas or the state will do it for them. Oregon's 1973 State Land Use Act requires city and county governments to draft comprehensive plans that include 19 statewide goals that carry the force of law. Local comprehensive plans must be approved by the state for compliance with all of the goals. Goal 5 requires local governments to "conserve open space and protect natural and scenic resources," such as "fish and wildlife areas and habitats" and "wilderness areas." Moreover, "fish and wildlife areas and habitats should be protected and managed in accordance with the Oregon Wildlife Commission's fish and wildlife management plans." (Oregon Department of Land Conservation and Development 1985, 7).

The State of Massachusetts has produced a BioMap indicating areas that are considered crucial to the state's rare and endangered species. The map designates over 1 million acres of core habitats for 246 plant species and 129 animal species. The map also identifies nearly 1 million additional acres that can serve as buffers between the core habitats and developed areas. Local planners can use the map as a guide for land conservation as well as where to direct development (www.state.ma.us/dfwele/dfw/nhesp).

State fish and game departments set hunting and fishing seasons, stock waterways with fish, and manage wildlife refuges. State forestry departments regulate forest practices and thus have a direct effect on wildlife habitats and watersheds. State environmental agencies make judgments about protecting wildlife habitats in administering wetlands permits as part of the Clean Water Act. States may include provisions for protecting wildlife habitats in drafting coastal zone management plans (see Chapter 11), and may require the protection of wildlife habitats in state environment protection acts as part of state and local government environmental impact assessments (EIAs) of proposed developments.

Some states protect plant and animal habitats in state parks, in state refuges, and through the purchase of land and the purchase of conservation easements on private lands. For example, the Great Outdoors Colorado program, started in 1992 through a citizens' initiative, receives tens of millions of dollars each year in state lottery proceeds to purchase parklands, natural areas, wildlife habitats, and conservation easements to farm and ranchlands. An extra benefit of the state funding programs is that they encourage local governments to plan for the protection of plant and animal habitats and to raise local funds to participate in land and conservation easement acquisition efforts.

Nonprofit Organizations and Wildlife Habitat Protection

Private nonprofit organizations have long been active in preserving land for wildlife habitat. There are several well-known national organizations as well as hundreds of local land trusts active in purchasing land, conservation, and partnering with government agencies.

Environmental Organizations and Land Trusts

The National Audubon Society

Founded in 1905, the National Audubon Society has 550,000 members in 508 chapters around the United States. Named for the naturalist and artist John James Audubon, the National Audubon Society owns and operates 100 wildlife sanctuaries and nature centers. The National Audubon Society is most closely associated with bird watching. It is interesting to note that "birders" spend more money on their hobby than hunters and fishermen combined.

The National Wildlife Federation

Founded in 1936, the NWF is the nation's largest member-supported conservation organization, with more than 4 million members and 46 state affiliate organizations. The purpose of the federation is to draw together individuals, private groups, businesses, and government to protect wildlife, wilderness, and environmental quality. The NWF works with Congress on federal wildlife issues, occasionally takes legal action, and emphasizes environmental education to stimulate public interest in the management of wildlife resources.

The Nature Conservancy

Founded in 1950, TNC is the leading private protector of wildlife habitats and natural areas. TNC owns more than five million acres in nearly 1,400 preserves in all 50 states. Around the world, TNC has preserved more than 12 million acres, often transferring land it has purchased to state and local governments (TNC 2001, 30). TNC also enters into voluntary habitat management agreements with private landowners and local governments. In the early 1990s, TNC completed what was at the time the largest single private land conservation project in the United States by acquiring a conservation easement on the 502-square-mile Gray Ranch in New Mexico (*ibid.*, 29).

TNC has initiated a National Heritage Inventory in partnership with state environmental agencies in almost every state. The inventory is a data bank of the location, type, importance and scarcity of indigenous ecosystems, and their plant and animal species. In 2000, TNC identified six priority protection areas for rare and endangered species: Hawaii, San Francisco Bay, Southern California, the Mohave Desert, Southern Appalachia, and the Florida Panhandle.

Preservation Tools

In addition to the acquisition of land and conservation easements, a number of land trusts have undertaken limited development in which a land-owner agrees to donate or sell development rights to the land trust and retains the right to develop a portion of the land at a density below what the zoning would allow. Limited development should be used sparingly. If several limited developments are built in an area, low-density sprawl might result, with negative impacts on nearby wildlife habitats. Several land trusts are becoming active in mitigation banking for wildlife habitats, wetlands, and natural areas (see Chapter 10).

A good example is The Center for Natural Lands Management based in southern California, where development pressures are intense. In the late 1990s, the center acquired the 123-acre Manchester property on the southwestern edge of the City of Encinitas in San Diego County. The site contains several threatened and endangered plant species associated with sage scrub and maritime chaparral, and the endangered California gnat-catcher. The center then established the Manchester Mitigation Bank, the purpose of which is to sell credits to developers to mitigate for habitat losses associated with their nearby developments. The Manchester reserve also has hiking trails for recreational opportunities (Center for Natural Lands Management 2001).

Sports Groups

Hunters and fishermen play an important role in support of the protection of wildlife habitats, wetlands, and the natural environment. Ducks Unlimited, Trout Unlimited, the Izaak Walton League, and rod and gun clubs, among other sportsmen's organizations, have a strong interest in protecting wildlife habitats, primarily watersheds, wetlands, streambanks, and forests. For example, Trout Unlimited will stock streams with fish and stabilize streambanks to minimize erosion and sedimentation that could harm fish.

One group that straddles the hunting and conservation camps is the Rocky Mountain Elk Foundation, founded in 1984. The foundation acts to protect elk and other wildlife habitats, but is not

SIDEBAR 9-4

Species Conservation in San Diego County, California

San Diego County, California, has more rare and endangered plant and animal species than any other county in the United States. From 2000 to 2020, the county is projected to add more than *1 million* inhabitants and 408,000 new housing units (San Diego Association of Governments 2000). If current development trends continue, 600,000 more acres will be developed over those 20 years. If compact, environmentally sensitive development patterns based on transit-oriented development can be achieved, development will consume only 200,000 acres. The compact, "smart growth" scenario is aimed at saving wildlife habitat, farmland, and open space while reducing traffic congestion and improving air quality. The county government intends to work with 18 cities within the county to put the smart growth strategy into practice.

The smart growth scenario features a conservation plan designed to protect 85 plant and animal species and their habitats. The plan sets aside 172,000 acres, stretching from the Mexican border north to the San Dieguito River Valley and east from the Pacific Ocean to national forestlands. The plan includes lands within the City of San Diego and 10 other cities as well as San Diego County lands. As of 2000, about 22,000 acres had been preserved.

The goal is to provide a regional open space and habitat preservation system. This can be achieved by combining the habitat protection of the smart growth plan with the more than 160,000 acres protected through a Habitat Conservation Plan (HCP) in northern San Diego County. In the mid-1990s, federal, state, and local governments and private developers agreed upon a HCP to protect the endangered coastal gnatcatcher. The county reserved 82,000 acres of state and federal land; the State of California and local governments purchased 27,000 acres of private land for $300 million, and developers agreed to set aside 63,000 acres in exchange for being able to develop elsewhere (Natural Resources Defense Council 1997, 38).

opposed to hunting. The foundation has more than 100,000 members in 41 states and seven Canadian provinces, and has conserved or enhanced habitat on some 2.9 million acres (Rocky Mountain Elk Foundation 2001).

LOCAL PLANNING FOR PLANT AND WILDLIFE HABITAT

Local governments have traditionally had little direct involvement with plant and wildlife protection, but this is rapidly changing. It is becoming clear that local planning efforts can influence the size, location, and quality of wildlife habitats on private land. Local planning and land acquisition programs also can complement the habitat protection efforts of state and federal governments and private nonprofit groups. One of the shortcomings of the comprehensive planning approach is that it has a time horizon of no more than 10 to 20 years. This is not enough time to take a truly long-term view of a community or region. A particular problem for plant and wildlife protection is that successive comprehensive plans can easily result in what can be called "death by halves" (i.e., in the first 20-year comprehensive plan, half of the community may be planned for development; the next comprehensive plan for the following 20 years may slate half of the remaining open land for development; and so on). Eventually, what little habitat remains becomes so limited and fragmented as to be unable to sustain certain plant and wildlife communities.

Table 9-4 lists six principles for wildlife habitat protection. Planners can incorporate these princi-

Table 9-4
Biological Principles for Local Habitat Protection

1.	Maintain large, intact areas of native vegetation needed to support animal wildlife by preventing fragmentation through development.
2.	Set priorities for species and habitats to support and improve the numbers and diverse locations of those species.
3.	Protect critical landscapes and regulate the use of vegetation in new developments to minimize the invasion of exotic plants.
4.	Identify and protect wildlife corridors to connect habitats and provide uninterrupted movement.
5.	Protect rare species habitats and ecological processes in those habitats.
6.	Balance the opportunity for recreation by the public with the habitat needs of wildlife.

Source: Adapted from *Managing Development for People and Wildlife: A Handbook for Habitat Protection by Local Governments*, The Great Outdoors Colorado Trust Fund (1997)

ples into goals, objectives, and implementation strategies.

Because wildlife are mobile, planning efforts should be coordinated with neighboring communities. Intergovernmental agreements are a good way to coordinate the location and pace of future growth. These agreements can address future annexations of land by cities, sensitive areas of regional significance, regional wildlife corridors and trail systems, and the funding of land and conservation easement acquisition programs.

Inventory

An inventory and mapping of plant and animal species types and numbers, and the location, extent, and quality of habitats, should be compiled. Rare and endangered plant and animal species and their habitats are especially important to note. The state fish and game department, land grant university, biology departments of local colleges and universities, hunting and fishing groups, and even inventories by local, state, and national nonprofit organizations can be helpful.

Analysis

Wildlife habitats are usually identified on maps as a combination of core home territory and corri-

dors for migration. Priorities should be set for the wildlife species that are of most concern, especially threatened and endangered plants and animals. Habitats should then be ranked in priority with the largest and most intact as the most valuable. The analysis should evaluate minimum habitat needs necessary to sustain healthy populations of wildlife. It may be necessary to consult with a botanist and a wildlife biologist in conducting the inventory, especially in analyzing the data on rare and endangered species and their habitats. The analysis will be helpful in drafting the future land use map, such as delineating core wildlife habitats and migration corridors where development should be kept to a minimum.

Goals and Objectives

The comprehensive plan should set goals and objectives that promote the protection of important plant and animal habitats (see Table 9-5). Objectives to achieve the goals should be included in the Natural Resources, Economic Base, and Land Use sections of the comprehensive plan. From these goals and objectives should come specific recommendations for strategic actions.

Table 9-5
Sample Plant and Wildlife Protection Goals and Objectives in the Comprehensive Plan

Natural Resources	
Goal	To maintain populations of all native species by preserving habitats and ecosystems necessary to support viable populations of these species.
Goal	To minimize human impacts that harm the number and distribution of native species.
Objective	Cooperate with state and federal agencies and other local governments as well as nonprofit groups and private landowners, to protect important plant and animal habitats.
Objective	Monitor the type and number of plant and animal species and changes to their habitats over time.
Economic Base	
Objective	Protect important plant and animal habitats that are important to local tourism and recreation businesses.
Land Use	
Objective	Locate developments away from important plant and animal core habitats and migration corridors.
Objective	Encourage compact development to avoid the loss or degradation of important habitats.
Objective	Explore the use of Voluntary Environmental Agreements with landowners and developers to protect wildlife habitats.

Action Strategy

The Action Strategy should present techniques and programs for achieving the wildlife protection goals and objectives as well as a timetable. Wildlife habitat retention benchmarks should be identified and progress toward those benchmarks evaluated in an annual report on the environment. Specific recommendations might include the following:

- Use zoning overlay districts to protect plant and animal habitats.
- Explore state and federal funding for the purchase of plant and animal habitat areas and conservation easements.
- Create partnerships with nonprofit groups for the preservation of important habitat areas.
- Add 200 acres of nature preserves to the county park system over the next five years.
- Discuss habitat protection efforts with neighboring municipalities and counties.
- Require major subdivisions to include wildlife corridors, where appropriate.

- Participate in HCPs, where appropriate, to balance habitat protection with economic growth.

Zoning Ordinance

Local planners and governments can use the zoning ordinance in several ways to protect wildlife habitat (see Table 9-6). First, communities should use zoning to promote compact growth and reduce the fragmentation of habitats. Second, a common zoning technique is a wildlife habitat overlay zone, applied over the base zone. Summit County, Colorado, has a habitat protection overlay zone that "seeks to fully protect wildlife habitats within the wildlife overlay zone from significant adverse affects of development" (Summit County, Colorado, 1994).

The overlay zone can also be a multipurpose conservation zone that protects sensitive areas, such as floodplains, wetlands, and steep slopes, along with wildlife habitats. Overlay zones should spell out the permitted density of development in an area and minimum setbacks for development from wildlife habitat. For example, along a river or stream corridor, a setback of 100 feet is fairly common, such as along much of Oregon's Willamette River Greenway. These buffer lands can help protect wildlife corridors and habitats by keeping houses separate from migration routes and core habitat areas. Finally, communities can require most, if not all, proposed development in an overlay zone to be treated as a conditional use.

Large minimum lot sizes or very low development densities in farming and forestry areas can help protect wildlife by limiting the fragmentation of habitat and exposure to domestic animals, people, and vehicles. For example, several western and midwestern counties use a 40-acre minimum lot requirement for new dwellings. Oregon counties have designated about 16 million acres of farm and ranchlands in agricultural zones of 40 to 320 acres, and 10 million acres of forestland in "timber conservation zones," which have minimum lot sizes of 40 to 160 acres. Other communi-

ties across the country use a low-density standard of one dwelling per 25 acres, with the dwelling placed on a lot of no more than 2 acres.

Subdivision Regulations

Subdivision regulations can be used in many ways to minimize the impacts of new development on wildlife habitat areas (see Table 9-6). A certain percentage of a tract proposed for development can be required to remain open space. Proponents of cluster development have argued that clustering homes on part of the site while leaving a significant amount of open space will foster compatibility with wildlife. The problem is that when people move to the countryside, they bring dogs, cats, and kids with them. Dogs are frequently unleashed, cats are hunters by nature, and kids like to roam. For these reasons, clustering is not the ideal approach to wildlife protection (see Chapter 19 for an in-depth discussion of cluster development). In general, the fewer people living near wildlife habitat, the fewer the conflicts. For

Table 9-6
Wildlife Habitat Protection Tools

Regulations	Financial Incentives
Conservation Zoning	Preferential Property Tax Assessment
Habitat Overlay Zoning	Transfer of Development Rights
Agricultural Zoning	Purchase of Development Rights
Cluster Zoning	Fee Simple Acquisition
Adequate Public Facilities Ordinance	Limited Development
Urban or Village Growth Boundary	Land Trades
Subdivision and Land Development Ordinance	Conservation Easement Donation
Tree Regulations	
Developer Agreements	
Ridge and Steep Slope Ordinance	
Intergovernmental Agreements	
Mitigation Agreements	

this reason, we do not advocate the use of clustering or density bonuses near important wildlife habitat, but rather setbacks together with very low-density development.

The subdivision regulations could include the mandatory dedication of parkland or open space to buffer wildlife habitats near the new development. A steep slope requirement can limit the removal of vegetation in steep areas that support wildlife. Floodplain regulations can restrict development along river and stream corridors, which are also prime habitat areas.

Subdivision regulations can include provisions for the protection, replacement, or cutting of trees and vegetation, which wildlife use for food and cover. Tree regulations have been gaining in popularity. Some prohibit the removal of trees above a certain height or diameter; others require the replanting of trees removed in the land development process. Landowners sometimes attempt to circumvent this requirement by clear cutting their properties prior to submitting a land development or subdivision proposal. Such actions can be avoided by requiring that a certain percentage of a property be planted or replanted. Vegetation regulations specify the types of plants that may be removed or planted. For instance, most regulations favor native trees, shrubs, and grasses, which provide the best habitat for native wildlife and which reduce the likelihood of the introduction of aggressive nonnative species.

The removal or clear cutting of existing trees and shrubs may be prohibited along wildlife corridors and streams and in steep slope areas. Vegetation may also be required to create buffers between developed areas and wildlife habitat, especially ponds and streams. Fencing may be necessary to separate developed areas from wildlife habitats. Limiting access to wildlife areas, especially by motorized vehicles, can be very important in the protection of habitats.

One of the greatest threats to wildlife habitats and mobile animals is new roads. The roads are often built to specifications of 24 feet or more across. They fragment habitats and create a setting for road kill. Shorter, narrower roads and streets can help protect wildlife.

Capital Improvements Program

The location, capacity, and timing of public facilities can have important consequences for wildlife protection. The phasing of development through an adequate public facilities ordinance reduces leapfrog development that can quickly fragment and destroy habitats. The adequate public facilities ordinance reflects the principle of concurrency: developments cannot be built until there are adequate public facilities (schools, roads, sewer and water, fire and police protection) to service those developments. Urban growth boundaries can also be an effective way to phase growth and limit the extension of sewer and water lines into the countryside.

Financial Incentives for Protecting Wildlife Habitats

Financial incentives for protecting wildlife habitats include preferential property tax assessment, purchase of conservation easements, fee simple acquisition, and land trades (see Table 9-6). Local governments can reduce property tax assessments on specific private lands that have high-quality wildlife habitats. This results in lower property taxes as a way to encourage landowners not to sell their land for development. If a local government uses such an incentive, there should be a provision to recapture the foregone property taxes if the land or part of it does become developed. A property tax stabilization contract can be used in which a landowner agrees not to develop the property for a certain number of years in return for preferential property tax assessment.

Local governments can purchase development rights to land with wildlife habitats. Local governments may also have to develop partnerships with private land trusts to put together enough funds

Table 9-7
A Checklist of Plant and Wildlife Habitat Issues in a Development Review

1.	What are the size, location, and land uses of the proposed development?
2.	Is the proposed development allowed in the particular zone?
3.	Have setbacks and buffers from property lines been met?
4.	Are there any known rare and endangered plant or wildlife species or habitats on or adjacent to the proposed development site?
5.	Is part of the development site in a wildlife corridor?
6.	Has the developer conducted an environmental impact assessment on the proposed development site?
7.	Could the impact on plant and wildlife habitat be reduced through a different design or siting?
8.	Has the developer obtained any necessary state or federal permits?

to purchase development rights. Fee simple acquisition of wildlife habitats is more expensive than purchasing development rights, but gives the local government more control over the management of the property. Land trades between government agencies and private developers have been popular, especially in western states. The developers acquire land that is more suited to development, and the government agencies take title to lands that fit with existing holdings to create larger, more viable wildlife habitats.

What to Look for in a Development Review

A proposed development should be evaluated according to the current comprehensive plan, zoning, subdivision and land development regulations, and any other relevant ordinances (see Table 9-7). Properly crafted subdivision regulations enable the local government to ask the developer to provide an EIA of the impacts of the proposed development on wildlife. If the proposed develop-

ment is above a certain size and near known wildlife habitats, the planning commission may want to contact the state department of fish and game (or wildlife) for comments.

Of particular concern is the presence of any threatened or endangered plant and animal species. Planners should check their maps and databases of the whereabouts of these species. If these species are found to be on the proposed development site, the applicant will have to work with state and federal agencies through the ESA. Also, local and state officials have an interest in preventing populations of plants and animals from declining to levels that would trigger the application of the ESA.

Finally, the planning commission should assess the cumulative impact of the proposed development, together with existing development, on wildlife habitats. Issues of critical mass, edge effects, migration routes, and fragmentation are important to identify and evaluate.

10

Planning and Managing Wetlands

The national goal of no net wetlands losses still has not been met.

U.S. DEPARTMENT OF AGRICULTURE
(USDA) NEWS RELEASE, JANUARY 9, 2001

Wetlands are vital natural resources that provide a variety of environmental services: flood protection, erosion control, stormwater absorption, filtering of sediment and pollutants, aquifer recharge, fish and wildlife habitats, carbon sinks, and open space. Wetlands hold enormous amounts of carbon and thus are important in regulating climate as well as recycling carbon. Wetlands act as a buffer between land and waterways, and stabilize shorelines. Wetlands remove significant amounts of biological oxygen demand (BOD), which leaves more oxygen available for fish and wildlife. By acting as reservoirs or sponges, wetlands accumulate and then slowly release the water they retain, either into streams and rivers or into groundwater to recharge aquifers. This process is especially helpful in maintaining water supplies during times of drought. Wetland ecosystems provide essential habitats for waterfowl, beavers, muskrats, fish, shellfish, cranberries, wild rice, and small organisms at the bottom of the food chain. Many of the federally listed threatened and endangered species rely on wetlands for their survival. Wetlands serve as stopover spots for migrating birds and waterfowl, and provide valuable recreational benefits, as evidenced by the more than $600 million a year that hunters spend harvesting waterfowl (Dennison and Berry 1993).

Wetlands vary in their size, location, type, plant and animal species, and value to the environment. Wetlands can be identified according to three criteria:

1. *Plant life:* Wetlands support special hydrophytic plant communities, such as Brook-Side Alder, Royal Fern, and switchgrass;

2. *Surface water:* Wetlands are subject to permanent or periodic flooding or wet soils at a depth of 18 inches for at least a week during the growing season; and

3. *Soils and groundwater:* Wetlands contain wet (hydric) soils, that are poorly drained and have a high water table (less than half a foot from the surface for at least one week of the growing season (Cowardin 1979).

There are two general types of wetlands: inland and coastal. Inland wetlands are referred to as fresh-water or palustrine wetlands, and are found along rivers and streams (riparian wetlands), in depressions surrounded by dry land in the Midwest (prairie potholes), in areas of high water tables that reach to the earth's surface (fens), and where soils are made wet for a season or longer by precipitation (bogs) (see Figure 10-1). Coastal wetlands are known as tidal or estuarine wetlands. They are found along the Atlantic, Pacific, Alaskan, and Gulf coasts.

PRESSURES ON WETLANDS

Historically, most Americans viewed wetlands as swamps, wasteland, or cheap land that could be drained, dredged, filled, and either farmed or developed for residential, commercial, or industrial purposes. About 53% of the original wetlands in the lower 48 states—about 117 million acres—have been filled in. Fresh-water wetlands account for 95% of all wetland losses, and more than three-fourths of the fresh-water wetland losses have been for agricultural uses (Platt 1996, 437). Twenty-one states have lost more than half of their original wetlands. In the major farming states of California, Illinois, Iowa, Missouri, and Ohio, roughly nine-tenths of the original wetlands are gone, mostly to cropland (Council on Environmental Quality 1996, 304-305). In addition, more than 1 million acres of wetlands have been dredged to become open water (Platt 1996, 437). About 100 million acres of wetlands remain in the United States, of which about 20 million acres are isolated wetlands and are not part of navigable waterways.

Suburban and Exurban Sprawl

As people and development spread farther into the countryside and along coastal areas (see Chapter 11), wetlands are often disturbed or filled. On the one hand, it is important for new development to be sited a certain minimum distance—usually 100 feet—from a wetland. On the other, the drawing of water from wells can deplete nearby wetlands, and wetlands can be polluted by effluent from on-site septic systems.

10-1 Fresh-water wetland, Albany County, New York.

Source: Katherine Daniels

Valuing the Environmental Services of Wetlands

In the last quarter of the 20th century, wetlands became recognized as valuable resources, performing environmental services that by some estimates are worth tens of thousands of dollars per acre each year (Maltby 1986). It is important to accurately value wetlands to help a local, state, or federal government agency determine whether a wetland should be filled. Wetlands do not necessarily work in isolation; they filter water across a watershed. Moreover, as wetlands become fewer and farther between, entire wildlife migration routes can be threatened. Waterfowl stop to feed and rest at regular intervals along their routes; however, when wetlands at key intervals are lost, flocks may not be able to bridge the distance to the next wetland. Destruction of wetlands results in the release into the atmosphere of large amounts of carbon dioxide and methane gases, which contribute to global warming (Bridgham *et al.* 1995). Weighing the dollar value of the environmental services of a wetland and the potential value as developed real estate is not easy. However, if cost-benefit analysis is going to be used in the decision-making process, the benefits of wetlands and the cost of their destruction must be estimated.

FEDERAL WETLANDS PROTECTION EFFORTS

As of 2001, almost 70% of the remaining wetlands in America were privately owned (Ducks Unlimited 2001, 13). Federal wetlands protection efforts feature the regulation of the dredging and filling of wetlands, land acquisition, and a combination of voluntary financial incentives and agreements with landowners.

Section 404 Federal Wetlands Permits

Section 404 of the Clean Water Act Amendments of 1972 and 1977 established a permit process for the review of projects that would involve the dredging or filling of wetlands (33 U.S.C. 1344). The Clean Water Act defines wetlands as "areas that are inundated or saturated by surface or groundwater at a frequency and duration sufficient to support a prevalence of vegetation typically adapted for life in saturated soil conditions." However, the differing interpretations of this definition and the actual identification and delineation of wetlands have created shifting standards, uncertainty, and considerable friction between landowners and state and federal agencies.

Section 404 is administered by both the Army Corps of Engineers and the U.S. Environmental Protection Agency (EPA). The Corps of Engineers derives its authority from Section 10 of the Rivers and Harbors Act of 1899, which gives the Corps responsibility for any action that affects the course, location, or condition of the waters of the United States. The EPA drafts guidelines for the Corps to follow in administering Section 404 permits, and the EPA may override a Corps decision (Section 404(b)(1)).

Section 404 referred to dredging and filling "in the waters of the United States," leaving it unclear whether this meant all waters or only navigable coastal and riparian waters. In 1986, the Army Corps of Engineers began regulating the dredging and filling of isolated fresh-water wetlands under the Section 404 permit review process. In 2001, the U.S. Supreme Court rescinded federal authority over these isolated wetlands, ruling that the jurisdiction of the Corps applies only to wetlands that are part of "navigable waters" (*Solid Waste Agency v. United States Army Corps of Engineers*, No. 99-1178). The court upheld the right of states to regulate isolated fresh-water wetlands because they do not involve interstate commerce. As much as one-fifth of the nation's wetlands—about 20 million acres—are isolated fresh-water wetlands, and the continuing loss of these wetlands has been cited as a threat to migratory birds and drinking water supplies.

The Corps of Engineers has issued two types of wetland permits: nationwide and individual. Indi-

vidual permits tend to involve large development projects where compliance with other federal laws and regulations must be reviewed. Most Corps permits used to be called nationwide permits and referred to 40 categories, including impacts of wetlands filling on navigation, flood control, utilities, and highway crossings. From the 1970s until 1996, nationwide permits allowed for the filling of up to 10 acres of isolated wetlands. Environmentalists claimed that developers used this permit to fill too many wetlands and to avoid the expense of the longer and more intensive individual permit review. A 1996 lawsuit by the Natural Resources Defense Council compelled the Corps of Engineers to reduce the threshold size for nationwide permits from 10 to 3 acres and to reassess this standard. In 2000, the Corps of Engineers adopted a much stronger standard, requiring a project that would fill more than half an acre of wetland to be reviewed as an individual permit.

To receive an individual permit, the Corps must determine whether the applicant's project is in the public interest and complies with a variety of federal laws including the National Environmental Policy Act (NEPA); the Coastal Zone Management Act (CZMA); the Marine Protection, Research, and Sanctuaries Act; and the Endangered Species Act (ESA). Under NEPA, the Corps must consider alternative sites for the proposed development project. The EPA may also review any permit application submitted to the Corps and may prohibit permits in certain wetlands. Obtaining an individual permit can take up to several months, but nearly all applications are approved. Yet, conditions are attached to about half the permits granted, and many applications for individual permits are withdrawn before they are processed (see Table 10-1).

Section 401 of the Clean Water Act requires a landowner to obtain a state Section 401 certification before the landowner can acquire a Section 404 permit from the Corps of Engineers. The Section 401 certification stipulates that the state has

Table 10-1
Section 404 Approval Process for Federal Wetlands Permit

1.	At a preapplication meeting between the U.S. Army Corps of Engineers district office and landowner, the conceptual design of the project is discussed, and the Corps makes suggestions about improving the design of the project and on-site or off-site mitigation measures. This meeting is similar to a sketch plan meeting between a subdivider and a local planning commission.
2.	Landowner submits a formal application to the district office. Project manager reviews application, including whether the Corps has jurisdiction. Public notice published and public comment period of 15-30 days begins. A public hearing may be held.
3.	Project manager decides whether the activity meets one of the 40 nationwide permit categories. If so, project manager makes a recommendation to grant or not to grant a permit to the district engineer who sends the applicant a letter verifying approval or denial of the permit. A letter granting a permit may include specific conditions about construction, best management practices, and mitigation.
4.	If the project will have major impacts, the district engineer may require an individual permit, which involves a more detailed review. The review invokes the National Environmental Policy Act, Section 404(b)(1), calling for the consideration of practicable alternatives to the proposal, a determination of public interest, and compliance with other federal resource protection laws.
5.	The Environmental Protection Agency has the power to veto a permit granted by the Corps, but this has happened very rarely.
6.	The district office bears the responsibility for monitoring and enforcing the terms of the nationwide and individual permits.

done a preliminary review of the project. If the wetland to be filled is in a coastal area, a landowner must also provide evidence that the proposed project complies with the state Coastal Zone Management Program before a Section 404 permit will be issued.

Section 404 allows individual states to approve general permits for minor dredging and filling actions that affect a half-acre or less of wetlands. These permits are processed through the state department of natural resources or environmental conservation. General state permits make up the large majority of wetlands permits. For example, in fiscal 1995, about 60,000 permit applications to dredge and fill wetlands were submitted nationwide; over 50,000 involved general state permits with little or no federal review. The average time for the general permit reviews was 17 days (Perciasepe 1995).

An important concern is monitoring and enforcing the terms of the permits. The Corps of Engineers investigates about 5,000 alleged violations of Section 404 permits each year (U.S. Army Corps of Engineers 2001). If a violation is found, the Corps can issue a cease and desist order. Remediation of the violation may involve voluntary compliance by the landowner or legal action.

Wetlands Mitigation

In deciding whether to issue a permit, the Corps must consider the water dependency of the proposed project, and proposed mitigation efforts designed to minimize or replace the loss of water quality, wildlife habitat, and recreational use from dredging or filling. When evaluating water dependency, the Corps must determine whether the particular use can be sited away from the wetland. For example, a marina requires access to water; a restaurant does not. Mitigation involves minimizing the environmental impacts of dredging or filling the wetland on fish and wildlife, recreation, flood damage prevention, water supply and quality, navigation, and public safety. Key issues for on-site mitigation include the wetland site characteristics, appropriate filling procedures, the location of any fill, materials used as fill, and the control of fill materials.

Section 404 guidelines allow for off-site mitigation, defined as the "restoration of alternative degraded sites"; that is, if a development project will unavoidably dredge or fill a wetland, the developer can submit a mitigation plan along with the 404 permit application. The developer can restore a wetland, construct a new wetland elsewhere, or pay a third party (such as a land trust) to do the work. In 1989, President Bush declared a policy of no net loss of wetlands—a policy that has been maintained by subsequent presidents. In the 1990s, mitigation became very popular among developers as a way to obtain a 404 permit. Between 1993 and 1998, the Corps gave permission for the filling of 63,144 acres of wetlands in exchange for 72,542 acres of created or restored wetlands (*Realty Times* 2000). Yet, a National Academy of Sciences study noted that the Army Corps did not track or verify whether the mitigation had actually been completed (National Academy of Sciences 2001). Moreover, the study reported that from 1987 to 1996, the rate of loss of wetlands was about 58,000 acres a year.

Off-site wetlands mitigation is decided on a case-by-case basis. It is important that the mitigation create, restore, or protect a wetland of equal size and quality to the wetland being lost, and preferably in the same watershed. It is possible for constructed wetlands to function as successful ecosystems, but some constructed wetlands have been known to fail where sites are poorly chosen. A 2001 report by the National Academy of Sciences found that artificial wetlands do not come close to recreating the functions of a natural wetland (*ibid.*). The report also contended that the Army Corps of Engineers has done little monitoring of developers' compliance with constructed wetlands requirements. Constructed wetlands alter the existing soil,

hydrology, and plant life in an area. This in turn affects the larger ecosystem, creating new wildlife habitat while displacing existing habitat. A cheaper, quicker, more beneficial, and more successful solution is to restore wetlands that have been previously drained or filled (Hunt 1998).

For long-term protection of restored or constructed wetlands, a developer can be required to donate a conservation easement to a land trust or government agency on the new or restored wetland mitigation site. The developer should be required to provide a stewardship fund to the land trust or government agency for proper long-term monitoring and maintenance of the wetland.

A mitigation bank can be set up by a government agency, a land trust, or other private, nonprofit organization to preserve wetlands through the sale of mitigation credits to developers seeking a 404 permit (40 CFR Part 1508.20 and 40 CFR Part 230). A mitigation bank can be established on public or private land, and can involve an agreement or partnership between a government agency and a private organization. The mitigation banks will either have already created or restored wetlands and banked mitigation credits or will use the payment from the developer to create or restore additional wetlands. Thus, mitigation banking relieves the developer of having to physically create mitigating wetlands as part of the development proposal. This can speed the development approval process. Moreover, a mitigation bank may consist of large parcels with more valuable wetland resources that those slated to be dredged or filled, and the larger wetlands can be better managed and protected. As of 2001, more than 700 mitigation banks across the nation had been approved.

A state agency or local government should review and certify a nonprofit organization's ability to maintain a new or restored wetland, consistent with state and federal statutes. A private organization or government that is proposing to create a mitigation bank must submit a prospectus to the Corps of Engineers. A mitigation bank proposal

SIDEBAR 10-1

Constructed Wetlands for Wastewater Treatment

There is a growing interest in using constructed wetlands for wastewater treatment, especially in rural areas that do not have access to central sewer systems. Unlike "enhancement" wetlands that attempt to serve the many functions of natural wetlands, wastewater treatment wetlands attempt to replicate the plants, soils, and microorganisms found in natural wetlands to remove contaminants from municipal or private residential, commercial, or industrial wastewater.

Constructed treatment wetlands come in a variety of sizes to meet the needs of a few residences, individual businesses, or large subdivisions. Constructed wetlands can work well for secondary and tertiary wastewater treatment. The City of Davis, California, has incorporated wetlands with ponds and lagoons to receive stormwater and tertiary-treated wastewater. The water is then further cleansed before being released into the Sacramento River (Beatley 2000, 15-16). Treatment wetlands are also being used to handle dairy wastewater, stormwater runoff, and even acid mine drainage. As of 2001, more than 500 wastewater and stormwater treatment wetlands have been built around the United States.

Treatment wetlands usually feature either subsurface flow or a free-water surface wetland, although it is possible to combine both types in a single treatment system. A free-water system most resembles a natural wetland, and the wastewater flows over the soil at a shallow depth. In subsurface flow systems, wastewater is run through a channel or cell containing gravel or crushed rock. There is a lining or barrier at the bottom of the wetland to limit seepage. The flow rate is regulated so that untreated water does not rise to the surface. Plants filter out the contaminants, and microorganisms digest organic material, all of which settle to the bottom of the wetland as sludge. The treated water is then held as surface water or used as spray irrigation onto land (often farmland).

The effectiveness of a constructed treatment wetland depends on the design, operation, pollutant types and loadings, and climate. A well-designed and managed wetland can remove about 80% to the biological oxygen demand, nitrogen, phosphorus, and suspended solids in wastewater (Moshiri 1993). One limitation to treatment wetlands is they are unable to remove heavy metals, which can gradually accumulate in the sediment. However, their use for rural and residential uses makes heavy metals less of an issue. Most treatment wetlands are found in the warmer climates of the United States, where freezing temperatures that would interfere with the treatment function of the wetland are rare or brief.

Attractive features of treatment wetlands are little odor, low maintenance and operating costs, aesthetic benefits, and wildlife habitat. On the other hand, liability remains an important concern for homeowners' associations, municipal treatment operators, and owners of private systems. Wetlands should be fenced to keep out small children and trespassers. Periodically, the sludge from the bottom of the wetland needs to be removed and properly disposed of to minimize odors and the build-up of heavy metals.

that involves filling wetlands to create cropland is made to the Natural Resources Conservation Service (NRCS). The public has an opportunity to comment on a proposed mitigation bank.

A proposal to create a mitigation bank needs to describe:

- the physical wetlands aspects of all the sites to be included in the bank;
- a method to determine mitigation credits at the sites and debits from wetlands to be filled by the developers seeking 404 permits;
- management and maintenance of the wetlands in the mitigation bank; and
- reporting and monitoring policies.

In sum, a landowner proposing to develop a wetland has three choices:

1. build at a certain distance from the wetland (e.g., no closer than 100 feet);
2. purchase wetlands mitigation credits from a mitigation bank and then fill and develop the wetland; or
3. apply for a permit to fill a wetland and agree to create a new wetland somewhere else.

Federal Wetlands Acquisition, Incentives, and Restoration

Most fresh-water wetlands have been filled for agricultural purposes. Two federal acts are designed to discourage the conversion of wetlands for farming. The Swampbuster provision of the 1985 Farm Bill made farmers who plow up wetlands ineligible for federal farm subsidies. The 1990 Farm Bill created the Wetlands Reserve Program, administered by the NRCS within the USDA, to protect privately owned wetlands and adjacent farmlands from development. The program has three voluntary strategies:

1. cost-sharing agreements with landowners to restore existing wetlands in which the federal government pays 75% of the cost;
2. the purchase of 30-year term conservation easements at 75% of the value of a permanent

easement and with the federal government paying 75% of the cost of restoration; and

3. the purchase of permanent conservation easements along with the federal government paying 100% of the cost of restoring the wetland.

By 2001, more than 1 million acres of wetlands had been protected through the Wetlands Reserve Program (NRCS 2001a). The 2002 Farm Bill authorized an additional $1.5 billion for the program and raised the acreage enrollment cap to 2.275 million acres (Ducks Unlimited 2002).

The Conservation Reserve Enhancement Program, begun in 1996 and managed by the NRCS, makes payments to farmers to plant riparian buffers of trees and grass near rivers and streams, and to restore wetlands. This helps to reduce soil erosion, improve water quality, and provide wildlife habitat. Farmers and ranchers voluntarily enter 10- to 15-year contracts, and state money can be used to match federal funds. By 2002, 368,000 acres in 20 states had been enrolled (Farm Service Agency 2002).

In 1989, Congress passed the North American Wetlands Conservation Act to provide federal cost-share grants to implement the North American Waterfowl Management Plan. The purpose of the plan is to restore, protect, and manage wetlands for migratory birds and other wildlife. Federal grants are matched by state and local governments and nonprofit organizations on a dollar-for-dollar basis. As of 2002, more than 8.5 million acres of wetlands had been restored in more than 900 projects in the U.S., Canada, and Mexico, at a total cost of $1.3 billion (Ducks Unlimited 2002).

The U.S. Fish and Wildlife Service (FWS) administers the Coastal Wetlands Planning, Protection, and Restoration Act of 1990. In the eight years through 1998, the service made $52 million in grants to 24 states for the conservation of more than 87,000 acres of coastal wetlands. States, local governments, and nonprofits have contributed matching funds and are responsible for the management of the wetlands. For example, in fiscal 1999, a $940,000 federal grant helped the Alabama Department of Conservation and Natural Resources purchase forested wetlands in the Mobile-Tensaw Delta adjacent to Mobile Bay—one of the largest wetland ecosystems in the United States (U.S. FWS 1998). The FWS also maintains a National Wetlands Inventory that includes wetlands data available in digital map form and viewable over the Internet. As of 2002, the inventory included nearly the entire nation. Like the NRCS soil survey maps, the wetlands inventory maps are not meant for regulatory use.

The EPA's State Wetlands Grants Program offers grants to states, tribes, and local governments for wetlands restoration and protection projects. Grant funds can be used for wetlands conservation plans, creating or updating a wetlands database, physically restoring wetlands, and ecological monitoring and assessing wetlands. A total of $15 million was available in fiscal 2000.

Finally, federal Land and Water Conservation Funds have been used to purchase wetlands to create wildlife refuges.

While the data are not conclusive, government and private wetlands protection efforts point to progress in reducing the annual amount of wetlands loss. In the 1980s, about 80,000 acres of wetlands on nonfederal land were converted each year (NRCS 1999). According to the National Resources Inventory conducted by the NRCS, between 1992 and 1997, about 32,600 acres of wetlands were lost each year (NRCS 2001b). However, in its 1998 Water Quality Inventory, the EPA found that wetlands were being lost at a rate of about 100,000 acres per year (U.S. EPA 2000, 1).

The large difference in annual loss of wetlands reported by the two federal agencies reveals a fundamental lack of clarity and consensus on what constitutes a wetland: wet soils, a quarter-acre bog, or land that floods periodically. For instance, the 1987 Corps of Engineers *Wetlands Delineation Man-*

ual for wetlands identification has been called "unreadable" (Easterbrook 1996, 439). In the midst of this controversy, the "no net loss" policy, however well intended, has little meaning. The lack of a clear definition of wetlands has caused widespread concern among landowners who fear that their land will be declared unbuildable. The Clinton Administration took a large step to relieve farmers' concerns by ruling that 53 million acres of farmland that had been created from wetlands before 1985 would be considered "prior converted wetlands" and not be subject to the regulations of Section 404.

STATE WETLANDS MANAGEMENT

State governments, through their departments of natural resources or the environment, have been active in identifying and delineating wetlands and in the review of wetlands permits. Many states have published handbooks on identifying and delineating wetlands. Like many other federal programs, wetlands regulation is being gradually shifted to state control. For example, in 1994, New Jersey gained formal control of the Section 404 permit program within its borders. States have long exercised review of proposed development of wetlands through the CZMA, Section 401 of the Clean Water Act, and Section 404 review of general permits for filling or dredging small wetlands of less than half an acre in navigable waters. Also, the federal government and individual states can regulate wetlands under the ESA if rare and endangered species are found in a wetland (see Chapter 9), or under the Safe Drinking Water Act if the wetland influences surface drinking water (see Chapter 3). Some states have even declared certain wetlands to be of statewide importance and hence worthy of extra protection. For instance, in 1988, the Maine legislature passed a Natural Resources Protection Act establishing state regulatory authority over wetlands.

The size of nonnavigable wetlands under state authority varies from state to state. For example,

SIDEBAR 10-2

Big-Time Wetlands Restoration: The Florida Everglades

The Florida Everglades is a swampy region at the southern end of Florida that has shrunk from 4,000 square miles to about 2,700 square miles due to water diversions, farming, and development (McCormick 1995). Still, the Everglades remains the world's second largest wetland and is famous as the habitat for alligators, the American crocodile, and many species of fish and water birds. The landscape is a mix of saw grass, open water, clumps of trees, and mangrove forest. The Everglades are best thought of as "a river of grass"—a description that conservationist Marjorie Stoneman Douglas used as the subtitle of her famous book, *The Everglades*. The Kissimmee River empties into Lake Okeechobee, and the overflow from the lake supplies the Everglades, where the water flows at a gentle rate of about 2 feet per minute. The unique and diverse ecology of the region became widely recognized when 2,190 square miles of the Everglades were declared a national park in 1947.

Ironically, in 1948, after two hurricanes had put much of south Florida underwater, Congress directed the Army Corps of Engineers to drain half a million acres south of Lake Okeechobee, and the Kissimmee River was rerouted in a series of canals, levees, and pumping stations. About 1.7 billion gallons of fresh water a day—or about four-fifths of the fresh water supply—were diverted from the Everglades and out to sea, to the detriment of native fish, plants, and wildlife (*The New York Times* 2000, A28). The main beneficiaries of the water control projects were sugar cane growers and the inhabitants along Florida's south Atlantic coast. Besides the loss of water, agricultural and urban runoff have created water pollution problems. Invasive species pose additional threats to native species.

In 2000, Congress agreed to work with the State of Florida to restore the Everglades. The estimated cost would be nearly $8 billion over 36 years, with the federal government covering most of the expense, but the State of Florida also contributing (Schmitt 2000, A21). Part of the project would involve returning the Kissimmee River to much of its old winding course. However, the centerpiece would be the construction of huge reservoirs to store rainfall and then release the water into the Everglades through redesigned canals. The water storage proposal is an attempt to satisfy the water demands of sugar cane producers and urban residents, while providing an adequate water supply to the Everglades ecosystem.

in Michigan, the state has authority over the filling and development of nonnavigable wetlands of 5 or more acres; wetlands of less than 5 acres are under local control. In New Hampshire, the state reviews all wetlands proposals that would impact more than 3,000 square feet; projects affecting 3,000 to 20,000 square feet are treated as minor projects; and those above 20,000 square feet are considered major projects and also require a review by the Army Corps of Engineers.

A number of states have drafted State Wetland Conservation Plans to integrate and expand wetland protection and management programs. A main thrust of these plans is educating landown-

ers and the general public about the importance of wetlands. Voluntary stewardship is part of the plans in Texas and Maine. Tennessee maintains a list of priority wetlands for acquisition and/or restoration.

Maryland has both tidal and a nontidal wetlands programs. State tidal wetlands are those below mean high water; private wetlands are those above the mean high water line and in private ownership. Mitigation is required for unavoidable impacts, with a preference toward on-site mitigation (Maryland Department of the Environment 2002). The nontidal wetlands program protects isolated wetlands by requiring a 25-

foot buffer from proposed developments. The buffer requirement increases to 100 feet for nontidal wetlands of state concern. The nontidal wetlands program also requires mitigation for any wetland losses. Finally, the nontidal wetlands program provides for the development of watershed management plans, which can be used as a basis for regulatory decisions to protect wetlands (*ibid.*).

LOCAL PLANNING FOR WETLANDS

Even though there are state and federal requirements governing the development of wetlands, local governments should be prepared to take an active role in protecting wetlands. This is especially true given the 2001 U.S. Supreme Court decision limiting the authority of the Army Corps of Engineers to regulate wetlands only in navigable waters. Also, some states regulate only large, nonnavigable wetlands. For example, New York State regulates isolated wetlands of 12.4 or more acres, leaving the local governments to regulate smaller, isolated wetlands; however, many local governments do not regulate the development wetlands at all.

Local wetlands provide a variety of important environmental services, and local governments should identify important wetlands in determining the location, type, and density of future development through the comprehensive planning process. The comprehensive plan serves as the legal basis for local zoning and subdivision regulations to protect wetlands.

Inventory

Local governments should identify wetlands as part of the Natural Resources Inventory section of the comprehensive plan. National wetlands maps and Geographic Information System databases are available from the FWS. NRCS county soil survey maps identify hydric soils, some of which include wetlands. State environmental agencies and many county planning offices have wetlands maps as well. Local mapping of smaller wetlands not included in the state or federal databases should be encouraged.

Analysis

A land suitability analysis will indicate limitations for development in areas with wetlands or hydric soils. Wetlands can be evaluated and rated for significance by size and by the environmental services they provide, such as wildlife habitat or aquifer recharge. Potential for wetlands mitigation and banking should also be assessed.

Goals and Objectives

Local planning officials should draft goals and objectives to protect wetlands as part of the comprehensive plan (see Table 10-2). The protection of wetlands should be listed as a goal in the Natural Resources section of the comprehensive plan. Objectives to achieve this goal should be included in the Economic Base section, given the valuable benefits and economic activity that arise from wetlands. Also, the Land Use and the Community Facilities sections should have objectives to direct development away from wetlands.

Action Strategy

The Action Strategy should present techniques and programs for achieving wetland protection goals and objectives as well as a timetable. Wetland protection benchmarks should be identified and progress toward those benchmarks evaluated in an annual report on the environment. Specific recommendations might include the following:

- Use a zoning overlay district to protect large, contiguous areas of wetlands.
- Explore the use of constructed wetlands for wastewater treatment.
- Explore the creation of a wetlands mitigation bank with private nonprofit organizations.
- Protect wetlands through outright purchase and the purchase of conservation easements.

Table 10-2
Sample Wetlands Goals and Objectives in the Comprehensive Plan

Natural Resources	
Goal	To protect important wetlands that provide water recharge, flood protection, wildlife habitat, aesthetic, and educational benefits.
Objective	Adopt local wetlands protection standards for isolated fresh-water wetlands, and all wetlands of less than half an acre in navigable waters.
Economic Base	
Objective	Protect wetlands that are important to local hunting, fishing, and birding businesses.
Land Use	
Objective	Direct development away from important wetlands.
Community Facilities	
Objective	Avoid locating growth-inducing community facilities near wetlands.

Zoning Ordinance

The main purpose of local regulations that affect wetlands is to control land uses near wetlands to ensure that they do not discharge pollutants and sediment into the wetlands, to ensure that proposed buildings are set far enough from wetlands so that high water tables and hydric soils do not flood basements, and to minimize the dredging and filling of wetlands.

A setback requirement from the edge of identified and delineated wetlands is appropriate in the zoning ordinance (e.g., no dwellings may be erected within 100 feet of a wetland of more than 1 acre). Some communities use a wetlands protection overlay zone to direct development away from areas with large amounts of wetland where on-site septic systems could cause water pollution and on-site wells could dry up the wetlands.

An overlay zone may be specific for the protection of wetlands or may be a multipurpose conservation zone that protects a range of natural features, including wetlands. For instance, riparian wetlands are typically protected through a floodplain overlay zone. Other zoning standards include limiting development density and hence the likely impacts of development on wetlands. This can be done through rural residential zoning in 3- to 5-acre minimum lot sizes, density and siting standards, or agricultural or forestry zoning in 20-acre or more minimum lot sizes.

Local governments may choose not to allow the dredging and filling of wetlands, even where the state or federal government would permit it. For example, in the famous Wisconsin case of *Just v. Marinette County*, the court upheld a county wetlands protection zoning ordinance with this opinion: if you pay swamp prices, you get swamp uses (*Just v. Marinette County*, 210 N.W. 2d 761, 1972).

Farming, forestry, and residences create runoff carrying pesticides, herbicides, fertilizers, manure, and sediment. Communities can work with cooperative extension agents to make sure that farmers, foresters, and rural homeowners are educated about integrated pest management so as to minimize the use of pesticides near wetlands.

Subdivision Regulations

The subdivision and land development ordinance should spell out conditions under which on-site septic and wells are acceptable; otherwise, central sewer and water can be required. Stormwater runoff should be contained on site as much as possible through vegetation, swales, filter strips, and retention basins. Roads and impervious surfaces should be strictly controlled to minimize runoff into wetlands. The subdivision ordinance should require buffering berms, filter strips, and vegetation between development and nearby wetlands.

For large developments, the subdivision ordinance should require the developer to conduct an environmental impact assessment, including an evaluation of likely impacts on wetlands (see Appendix). Wetlands mitigation requirements should be spelled out in the subdivision ordinance unless the state standards are considered adequate. The ordinance should also allow constructed wetlands as wastewater treatment systems according to specific design and management standards.

Capital Improvements Program

Local planning officials should use the capital improvements program (CIP) to direct growth and development away from large wetlands or groupings of smaller wetlands. Major roads, schools, and extensions of sewer and water systems can generally be kept out of these areas in order to discourage intensive growth and development. If appropriate, the CIP could include plans for constructed wetlands to service the community, its schools, or other public uses.

The CIP could include funding programs for the public purchase of wetlands or the acquisition of conservation easements. Partnering with land trusts and sports groups could be pursued. For instance, since 1937, Ducks Unlimited has helped protect more than 1.5 million acres of America's wetlands (Ducks Unlimited 2001, 8).

What to Look for in a Development Review

What a community can look for in a development review involving wetlands depends on the goals and objectives in the comprehensive plan and, more importantly, the standards and requirements spelled out in the zoning and subdivision regulations and other relevant ordinances (see Table 10-3). The existence and size of wetlands on the property and on adjacent properties should be ascertained. The design of the proposed development project for mitigating impacts to wetlands on site and on neighboring properties should be assessed. Finally, it is important to review any wetlands permits the developer has received from the relevant state agency or Army Corps of Engineers.

Table 10-3
A Checklist of Wetlands Issues in a Development Review

1.	Are there wetlands on or adjacent to the site proposed for development?
2.	Is the proposed development allowed in the particular zone?
3.	Are the minimum distances of proposed buildings, on-site septic systems, and wells from wetlands met?
4.	Should the applicant be required to conduct an environmental impact assessment, including impacts on wetlands?
5.	Is filling, dredging, or drainage of part or all of a wetland proposed?
6.	Is there a wetlands mitigation plan?
7.	Will stormwater runoff from the proposed project affect nearby wetlands? How will this be mitigated?
8.	If a wetland is proposed for treating wastewater, has the design of the wetland been reviewed by the municipal or county engineer?
9.	Has the developer obtained any necessary state or federal wetlands permits?

CHAPTER

11

Coastal Zone Management

Housing construction is booming along the Atlantic and Gulf Coasts, especially on barrier islands, where exposure to storms and the rising sea is greatest.
      USA TODAY, JULY 27, 2000, P. 4A

To conserve, protect, where appropriate develop and where appropriate restore the resources and benefits of all coastal shorelands, recognizing their value for protection and maintenance of water quality, fish and wildlife habitat, water-dependent uses, economic resources and recreation and aesthetics.
      STATE OF OREGON,
      GOAL 17: COASTAL SHORELANDS

The coastal zone can be defined in a number of ways (Beach 2002, iii). Broadly, the coastal zone may be thought of as the area within 50 miles of sea coasts and the Great Lakes. This definition includes counties that have ocean and Great Lakes shorelines, which account for 17% of America's land area. Alternatively, coastal watersheds—the area draining into coastal waterways—cover 13% of the nation's land. Finally, individual states narrowly define the coastal zone under the federal Coastal Zone Management Program as 3 miles out to sea and up to 1,000 yards inland from the mean high tide. Some states have expanded the area designated as coastal zone. In California, for instance, the coastal zone is up to 3 miles from shore and as far as 5 miles inland.

America's coastal areas have remarkably rich and diverse land and water resources. Coastal waters include bays, estuaries, marshes, lagoons, and ocean or Great Lakes waters stretching from the high water mark to a mile or more offshore.

Coastal lands have "a direct and significant impact on coastal waters" (16 U.S.C. Section 1453(a)) and include more than 72,000 miles of shoreline (U.S. Environmental Protection Agency (EPA) 1998a). These shorelines vary from headlands and pocket beaches along the Pacific coast to coastal wetlands in Louisiana to the rocky coast of Maine, and include such varied ecosystems as the coral reefs and mangrove swamps of Florida and the bluffs and coastal plains along the Great Lakes as well as dunes, mud flats, forests, farmlands, and built-up cities and towns.

Estuaries are coastal water bodies where fresh water and salt water meet. These unique, oxygen-rich environments support aquatic life that provides essential links in the food chain. The nation's 90,000 square miles of estuaries provide the main spawning grounds for more than three-quarters of America's commercial fish and shellfish, and more than four-fifths of the recreational fish catch (U.S. EPA 2001a). Salt marshes and tidal wetlands offer important waterfowl habitat and migratory flyway stops. In addition, estuaries provide temporary or permanent habitat for about three-fourths of the nation's threatened and endangered species (Restore America's Estuaries 2002).

About one-third of all Americans visit coastal areas each year, making over 900 million trips and spending some $44 billion (U.S. EPA 2000a). Beaches are popular recreation spots for swimming, surfing, and sunbathing. Sport fishing, boating, snorkeling, and scuba diving are also popular pastimes. Commercial fishing and shell fishing harvest more than 10 billion pounds a year (*ibid.*). Publicly owned coastal areas include 10 national seashores and national recreation areas under the authority of the National Park Service, parts of the National Wildlife Refuge System under the management of the FWS, several coastal military installations, and state and local parks and beaches.

THE CHALLENGE OF COASTAL ZONE MANAGEMENT

Population Growth and Development

Coastal areas have absorbed much of America's population growth and development over the past two centuries. Today, most Americans live within 100 miles of the ocean or Great Lakes, and 14 of America's largest cities hug the coast (Beach 2002, 1). Moreover, the majority of the nation's population growth to 2050 is expected to continue to concentrate in coastal areas, especially in California, Florida, and Texas (*ibid.*, 2). Nationwide, if current development trends continue, more than one-quarter of America's coastal acreage will be developed by 2025—a sharp increase over the 14% developed in 1997 (*ibid.*, 5).

In 2001, the EPA rated the general condition of the nation's coasts between poor and fair (U.S. EPA 2001b, xviii). Many coastal wetlands have been dredged and filled to make farmland, residential space, and commercial sites, such as ports, marinas, and offices. Increased impervious surfaces direct polluted stormwater runoff to coastal waters, threatening aquatic life (Beach 2002, 8). Industrial, residential and agricultural uses along waterways leading to the ocean and Great Lakes have acted as both point and nonpoint sources of coastal water pollution, contributing toxic substances and nutrient loadings, which result in algae blooms. Estuaries are especially vulnerable to toxic pollution from urban stormwater runoff, factories, and sewage treat-

ment plants, because the configuration of estuaries limits tidal flushing action that could help to aerate water and assimilate pollution (U.S. EPA 2000b). Estuaries also receive rivers and streams at their dirtiest downstream point. In addition, upstream water withdrawals slow streamflow, and hence cleansing and flushing action. Estuaries are prone to nutrient pollution from stormwater runoff from farm fields, forestry operations, on-site septic systems, air pollution, and sewage treatment plants. The National Pollutant Discharge Elimination System program allows almost 20,000 industrial and municipal discharges into estuarine waters each year (Svarney and Barnes-Svarney 2000, 431).

Managing Coastal Recreation

Coastal recreation activities involve going to a beach or lakeshore to swim, surf, snorkel, fish, or simply sunbathe. About one-third of all Americans visit coastal areas each year, and hotel/motel development and second-home development have been strong in coastal communities. The development of hotels, motels, and second homes has heightened the competition for coastal lands and created a number of pollution problems.

A 2000 EPA report examined the environmental impacts of several kinds of commercial recreation, and found that the degree of hotel use was the main factor in energy and water consumption. Coastal recreation used the most water and had the highest biological oxygen demand and total suspended solids release rates. Coastal recreation also had the highest energy use for transportation because of the distance traveled and high number of trips, estimated at nearly 1 billion in 2000 (U.S. EPA 2000a, 42). Car trips to coastal recreation areas and the use of motor boats produced more air pollution than other types of recreation. Visitors to coastal areas tend to eat in restaurants and generate large amounts of municipal waste (*ibid.*).

Improving Water Quality

A particular challenge facing residents of estuarine watersheds, such as the Chesapeake Bay region, is how to accommodate new population growth and development while improving, not just maintaining, water quality. Water quality—Class A (drinkable) and Class B (swimmable) waters—is essential to the commercial success of waterside-related businesses and communities. Experts agree that when more than 10% of a watershed is converted to impervious surfaces, water quality problems become chronic (Beach 2002).

Residential and commercial developments too close to the shoreline contribute to beach erosion. As Ian McHarg pointed out in *Design With Nature*, the first and second line of dunes are very fragile and should not be built upon, whereas the back dune area with its scrub timber can actually accommodate a fair amount of development (McHarg 1971, 7-13). Low-lying and sandy barrier islands are particularly vulnerable to storm damage. When upstream dams block sediment flow to beaches and storms wash away sand, state and local governments face spending millions of dollars each year on sand to replenish beaches (Jehl 2001, 14).

Motor boating and sailing are usually organized around marinas and boat clubs. This concentration of activity can increase the stress on the local environment. Proper pumping out of wastes and disposal of garbage are important to maintain water quality. The dredging of wetlands to create or expand marinas should be carefully controlled to limit impacts to wildlife and water quality.

Waterfront Redevelopment

Many of America's urban waterfronts were first developed as commercial and industrial districts. Public access to the waterfront has long been limited in urban areas as water-related businesses (e.g., oil terminals, warehouses, and lumber yards), and shipping and railroad networks have taken precedence over public recreational needs. However, with the decline of heavy manufactur-

ing, many urban waterfronts have become blighted and underused. Recent waterfront renewal efforts have become the focus of urban redevelopment in many coastal cities. Success stories of revitalization range from Boston's Quincy Market to Baltimore's Inner Harbor to Seattle's Pike Street Market area.

FEDERAL PLANNING AND MANAGEMENT OF COASTAL RESOURCES

The federal role in the management of coastal areas and resources is largely spelled out in three laws: the Coastal Zone Management Act (CZMA) of 1972 (PL 92-583, 16 U.S.C. 1451 *et seq.*), the Marine Protection Research and Sanctuaries Act of 1972 (better known as the Ocean Dumping Act) (PL 92-532), and the Coastal Barrier Resources Act of 1982 (PL 97-348).

The Coastal Zone Management Act of 1972

Congress passed the CZMA to address the rising threats to coastal areas:

> "The increasing and competing demands upon the lands and waters of our coastal zone occasioned by population growth and economic development ... have resulted in the loss of living marine resources, wildlife, nutrient-rich areas, permanent and adverse changes to ecological systems, decreasing open space for public use, and shoreline erosion" (16 USC Section 1451 ©).

The CZMA is a nationwide effort to provide federal funding, guidelines, and technical help for the 30 coastal and Great Lakes states (and five territories) that voluntarily agree to draft plans and manage development in their coastal areas. The act is administered by the National Oceanic and Atmospheric Administration (NOAA), which was created through the Marine Protection Research and Sanctuaries Act of 1972.

The purpose of the CZMA initially seems very broad and even contradictory, in allowing states to provide for industrial and commercial development, public beach access, mineral and energy resource extraction, the protection of cultural and natural landmarks, waste disposal, and the harvesting of fish and shellfish. State plans must include:

- The boundaries of the coastal zone, both the extent of the zone into the water and onto land. The zone extending 3 miles into the water from mean high water mark is the same for all states. Each state sets the inland extent of the coastal zone. For example, California designated a minimum 1,000 yards inland from the Pacific shore, but up to 5 miles in undeveloped areas.

- Land and water uses permitted in the coastal zone, and priority uses in different areas of the zone. States also must create a system to resolve conflicts among competing uses.

- Identification of areas of planning concern, including an inventory of sensitive environmental areas, such as habitats of rare and endangered species, flood and landslide hazard areas, and a designation of areas of particular concern, such as "transitional or intensely developed areas where reclamation, restoration, [and] public access . . . are especially needed; and those areas especially suited for intensive use or development" (38 *Federal Register* 33046, November 29, 1973).

- A description of state controls to implement the coastal zone plan, including direct regulation by the state or local regulation with state standards and review, and the acquisition of land, water, and buildings through condemnation, fee simple purchase, or purchase of conservation easements.

- An inventory of public access to beaches and waters and plans for public acquisition.

- Coordination of federal, state, regional, and local government agencies in administering

federal water and air pollution laws, especially permits for filling wetlands.

The state plans must also take into account national interests in the siting of large development, such as electrical generating plants, national seashores, harbors and ports, interstate highways, and military installations. The national interest also includes fisheries; prime farmland; mineral resources; and historic, scenic, and cultural sites. Finally, any federal agency activity, whether inside or outside the coastal zone, must be consistent with the CZMA if it affects natural resources, land uses, or water uses in the coastal zone (Godschalk 1992, 110). This means that federal decisions must be consistent with the state plans and that, remarkably, the state plans take precedence over federal decisions.

Congress passed the Coastal Zone Act Reauthorization in 1993. Section 6217 requires each state with an approved coastal zone management plan to develop a Coastal Nonpoint Pollution Control program, which must then be approved by NOAA and the EPA. Congress authorized funding for the creation of nonpoint coastal pollution control programs in 1999.

The Marine Protection Research and Sanctuaries Act of 1972

The Marine Protection Research and Sanctuaries Act, often referred to as the Ocean Dumping Act, was enacted by Congress to meet America's obligations under the Convention on the Prevention of Marine Pollution by Dumping signed in 1972 by 80 countries. The act bans the ocean dumping of high-level radioactive waste and nuclear, chemical, and biological weapons. A 1988 Amendment banned the dumping of sewage sludge, industrial waste, and medical waste, and all municipal dumping operations by the end of 1991. A 1992 Amendment established a program within the EPA to monitor coastal water quality and pollution sources.

The Marine Protection Act also established the Office of Coastal Zone Management within NOAA to provide grants and technical assistance to states in implementing the CZMA. The Marine Protection Act created a marine sanctuaries program, analogous to the Wilderness Act program, through which NOAA can designate certain coastal and ocean regions off limits to development. As of 2000, 18 National Marine Sanctuaries have been established in 15 states and are managed by NOAA. In late 2000, President Clinton created the nation's largest nature preserve under the waters of the northwestern Hawaiian Islands. The 84 million acres of the Northwestern Hawaiian Islands Coral Reef Reserve contain almost 70% of the nation's remaining coral reefs (Associated Press 2000, A27). The preserve forbids oil and gas drilling or changes to the seabed or coral. Fishing is allowed to continue, but only at 2000 harvest levels.

Coastal Barrier Resources Act of 1982

Barrier islands in the Gulf of Mexico and off the Atlantic coast are low-lying, sandy stretches of land that provide important wildlife habitats. Many of the islands are still undeveloped. Barrier islands are ever shifting as sand is washed away from the ocean-facing side and redeposited on the leeward side. Barrier islands are especially vulnerable to storms and hurricanes. For instance, barrier islands along the North Carolina coast were hit by hurricanes in the 1990s. Storm surges and beach erosion brought down several dozen houses. The construction of structures to hold sand and the replacement of dunes and beaches with new sand can minimize damage to barrier islands. However, a key protection component is more stringent setback requirements. In fact, 13 states have already adopted special setback requirements from beaches for new construction. North Carolina includes an erosion setback in its Coastal Area Management Act.

Of America's 1.6 million acres of barrier islands, about 53% (840,000 acres) are in public ownership or are under private protection, another 29% (454,000 acres) have been designated as part of the Coastal Barrier Resources System, and another 18% (287,000 acres) are privately held and unprotected (Platt 1996, 433). The Coastal Barrier Resources Act of 1982 was designed to keep both private and publicly owned barrier islands largely undeveloped. The act set up the Coastal Barrier Resources System, under the management of the National Park Service to designate certain barrier islands for protection. In order to discourage development, the Coastal Barrier Resources System made the owners of designated barrier islands ineligible for the National Flood Insurance Program (NFIP), federal sewer and water funds, federal road and bridge money, and federal funds for beach restoration. However, local regulations may still allow development on islands within the Coastal Barrier Resources System.

National Estuarine Reserve and National Estuary Program

Estuaries are remarkably rich spawning grounds for fish, shellfish, other aquatic life, and waterfowl. There are three kinds of estuaries:

1. a *positive estuary* is where the rate of evaporation from the surface is less than the volume of fresh water entering the estuary from rivers, streams, and direct land drainage;
2. a *neutral estuary* has a rate of evaporation equal to the rate of incoming fresh water; and
3. an *inverse estuary* has little or no fresh water entering and is often cut off from the sea in tidal pools.

Section 315 of the CZMA authorized the Secretary of Commerce to establish the National Estuarine Reserve Research System and gave the secretary the power to "acquire, develop, or operate estuarine sanctuaries, to serve as natural field laboratories in which to study and gather data on the natural and human processes occurring within the estuaries of the coastal zone," and to "acquire lands to provide access to public beaches and other public coastal areas of environmental, recreational, historical, aesthetic, ecological, or cultural value" (16 U.S.C. Section 1461, 1972). The Estuarine Reserve Research System is managed by NOAA and offers cost-sharing money for land acquisition and management on a 50-50 matching basis to the states with laws that protect estuarine resources. As of 2000, the system covered 25 estuaries (U.S. EPA 2000b).

The National Estuary Program was created in 1987 under Amendments to the Clean Water Act. The purpose of the program is to identify, restore, and protect important estuaries by involving federal, state, and local government agencies and the general public. For each estuary in the program, a Comprehensive Conservation and Management Plan is drafted and specific actions taken to address restoration and protection. As of 2002, there were 28 estuaries in the program nationwide (U.S. EPA 2002a). The EPA administers the National Estuary Program and provides grants and technical assistance to local governments, watershed groups, and private citizens who are responsible for carrying out the actions. For instance, the estuary program in Buzzards Bay in southeastern Massachusetts has identified nutrients, pathogens, contaminated seafood, and habitat loss as major management issues. The program has implemented beach testing and stormwater analysis, and has compiled an inventory of coastal wetlands. The program published a brochure for landowners and local officials about land use options to manage nitrogen inputs.

The Great Lakes Program

The five Great Lakes contain about 18% of the world's fresh water. In 1972, the United States and Canada created the Great Lakes Program to restore and maintain the chemical, physical, and biological integrity of the lakes. The American effort—known as the Great Lakes National Program—is administered by the EPA and has an annual budget of about $15 million (U.S. EPA 2002b). The focus of the Great Lakes Program was initially to construct and upgrade sewage treatment plants in order to reduce nutrient loads, especially phosphorous. Recently, the program has adopted an ecosystem approach aimed at restoring and protecting the health of the entire 200,000-square-mile drainage basin. The program added minimum water quality standards and has worked to coordinate the efforts of many state and local governments within the basin (Beatley *et al.* 2002).

Coordinating Federal Coastal Protection Efforts

Coordination of federal coastal protection efforts is an ongoing challenge because of the confusing number of federal laws and agencies involved in the management of coastal resources.

- Coastal flood management is administered by the Federal Emergency Management Agency (FEMA), through the NFIP, the Flood Disaster Protection Act, and the Stafford Disaster Relief and Emergency Assistance Act.
- Coastal wildlife habitats are managed by the U.S. Fish and Wildlife Service in wildlife sanctuaries and through the Endangered Species Act.
- Coastal wetlands development is regulated by the Section 404 permitting program of the Clean Water Act administered by the Army Corps of Engineers and the EPA. Also, the Department of Agriculture's Swampbuster Program of the 1985 Farm Bill discourages the filling of wetlands for farming, and the Wetlands Reserve Program of the 1990 Farm Bill enables the Natural Resources Conservation Service (NRCS) to purchase conservation easements on farm wetlands. The NRCS also has programs for wetlands restoration.
- Coastal water quality standards and control of nonpoint pollution are the responsibility of the EPA through the Clean Water Act and the Safe Drinking Water Act.

- The National Park Service manages national seashores and national parks in coastal areas as well as barrier islands through the Coastal Barrier Resources System created under the Coastal Barrier Resources Act.
- The planning and management of the coastal zone and estuary protection are the responsibility of NOAA under the CZMA and the National Estuary Program.

Performance of Federal Coastal Protection Programs

Evaluations of the performance of the CZMA have been sketchy. Environmental Geography Professor Rutherford Platt contends that the act has improved the management of coastal areas, especially through the passage of new state laws, regulations such as setbacks from coastlines for new development, and land acquisition (Platt 1996, 418). Environmental Planning Professor Timothy Beatley and co-authors agree that, compared to the pre-1972 era, "coastal development patterns and practices are more respectful of protecting coastal resources and reducing exposure of people and property to coastal risks" (Beatley *et al.* 1994, 127). The application of coastal development controls has varied considerably among the states. NOAA has not required specific measures, such as setbacks for new developments to reduce erosion, or minimum planning performance standards. Beatley *et al.* argue for a stronger system of monitoring state performance and compliance with the goals of the CZMA (*ibid.*).

Yet, development along parts of the Atlantic and Gulf coasts has been particularly heavy since the mid-1990s. Despite being hit by five hurricanes in the space of three years, landowners along North Carolina's coastal areas and Outer Banks have shown a desire to hold onto their properties and keep rebuilding if necessary. Second-home development in coastal areas has continued to grow, and much of this development is not well sited. A 2000 study prepared for FEMA predicted that "within the next 60 years approximately 25% of homes located within 500 feet of the coast (excluding those located in most urban centers) will fall victim to the effects of erosion. Erosion-induced losses to property owners during this time are expected to be half a billion dollars annually" (Heinz Center 2000, Foreword). The study estimated that about 1,500 homes a year will be lost to erosion over the next 60 years, at an annual cost to the federal government of $80 million or more (*ibid.*, 3, 4). Also, experts are predicting an increase in storm activity between 2000 and 2020, in part caused by global warming, that will take a toll on development in the coastal zone (see Chapter 12).

Water quality remains a problem in many coastal areas. Outbreaks of the toxic algae *Pfiesteria* killed tens of millions of fish in Maryland's portion of the Chesapeake Bay in 1997 and along the North Carolina coast in 1991 and 1995. The EPA's 1998 National Water Quality Inventory reported that over 15,000 square miles of the estuarine water of the lower 48 states had chronic water pollution problems, mainly from nutrients, bacteria, and toxic organic chemicals. The most common pollution sources were industrial plants, urban runoff and storm sewers, and municipal sewage treatment plants. The EPA also reported that 12% of the shoreline miles assessed had impaired water quality, mainly from bacteria, turbidity, and excess nutrients (U.S. EPA 2000c, 1).

Public access to beaches has become a major problem, as populations increase and most coastal areas remain privately owned. Moreover, public beach closings because of polluted runoff and sewage carrying fecal coliform bacteria are fairly common in the summer months when stormwater runoff is heavy and rainstorms cause sewers and drains to overflow, sending raw sewage into coastal waters. The sewage carries a variety of bacteria, viruses, protozoa, and parasites that can cause illnesses ranging from diarrhea to hepatitis. Beach contamination can last for several days after each overflow. In 2000, there were 11,270 beach closings or advisories, and more than half of the beach closings were in California (Whitaker 2001, A16). In 2000, Congress amended the Clean Water Act to require states to develop water quality standards for pathogens that cause infectious diseases in coastal recreational waters and to set water quality standards for public beaches. The Beach Environmental Assessment and Coastal Health Act of 2000, better known as the Beach Bill, also offered grants to states to perform regular testing of water quality at beaches and to notify the public of health hazards.

A 2000 study by the National Academy of Sciences reported that pollution from nitrogen and phosphorus fertilizers was killing marine life and harming marshlands in one-third of the nation's coastal areas. For instance, scientists have identified an enormous "dead zone" of 7,500 square miles of oxygen-depleted water that stretches from the mouth of the Mississippi River into the Gulf of Mexico. The study identified as major problem areas estuaries where water moves slowly and the coasts of nine states: California, Florida, Louisiana, Maryland, Massachusetts, New York, North Carolina, Texas, and Washington. The study warned that the situation would worsen unless strong actions were taken (National Academy of Sciences 2000).

Federal coastal land and water protection programs need to be more clearly consistent with each other. In 2000, President Clinton issued an executive order directing the EPA, the Commerce Department, and the Department of the Interior to improve the coordination of the federal coastal protection programs. The EPA, for example, must review permits for discharges into coastal waters and waterways that feed into coastal areas, and determine whether new coastal zone land use controls are needed (Lacey 2000, A12). State coastal protection plans and local land use ordinances need to be better coordinated with the federal programs. State and local governments, landowners,

developers, and the general public could benefit from "one-stop shopping" for information on federal flood insurance, coastal zone management development and protection plan requirements, water quality, and coastal and wetlands protection funding opportunities.

STATE AND REGIONAL COASTAL PROTECTION PROGRAMS

Several states have enacted land use management programs to protect coastal resources in keeping with the federal CZMA. California, North Carolina, Oregon, and Hawaii have taken the CZMA the most seriously and have devoted considerable personnel and state funding to manage coastal resources (see Case Study 11-1, below). By contrast, the Great Lakes states have generally lagged. Oregon, Maryland, and California (see Case Studies 11-1 and 11-2, below) have gone beyond the federal standards and incorporated coastal planning into statewide programs as well as local land use planning.

Oregon's Pacific coast varies from sandy beaches, to jutting headlands, to the rock "haystacks" of Cannon Beach, to estuaries where rivers and streams from the Coast Range empty into the ocean. Coastal areas are used for fishing, boating, logging, and tourism. About one-third of the Oregon coast is state parkland, and the public has the right of access and use to all dry sand beaches—both public and private. Oregon's 1973 State Land Use Act led to the adoption of 19 statewide planning goals, which carry the force of law. Counties and municipalities are required to incorporate these goals into their comprehensive plans and zoning ordinances. Four of the goals relate to the protection of coastal resources: estuarine resources, coastal shorelands, beaches and dunes, and ocean resources (Oregon Revised Statutes, Chapter 197).

Goal 16: Estuarine Resources. "To recognize and protect the unique environmental, economic, and social values of each estuary and associated wetlands; and to protect, maintain, where appropriate develop, and where appropriate restore the long-term environmental, economic, and social values, diversity and benefits of Oregon's estuaries."

Goal 17: Coastal Shorelands. "To conserve, protect, where appropriate develop and where appropriate restore the resources and benefits of all coastal shorelands, recognizing their value for protection and maintenance of water quality, fish and wildlife habitat, water-dependent economic uses, economic resources and recreation and aesthetics. The management of these shoreland areas shall be compatible with the characteristics of the adjacent coastal waters."

Goal 18: Beaches and Dunes. "To conserve, protect, where appropriate develop and where appropriate restore the resources and benefits of coastal beach and dune areas; and to reduce the hazard to human life and property from natural or man-induced actions associated with these areas."

Goal 19: Ocean Resources. "To conserve the long-term values, benefits, and natural resources of the nearshore ocean and the continental shelf" (Oregon Department of Land Conservation and Development (ODLCD) 1985).

For each goal, the local government must first conduct an inventory of the appropriate resources. Areas that are suitable for water-dependent uses, such as boat ramps and aquaculture, must be identified. In general, development must be limited to existing urban areas or built-up rural areas. Sensitive coastal areas with natural hazards, wetlands and wildlife habitat must also be identified, and must generally be designated for long-term protection. Finally, the ODLCD reviews the local plans for compliance with the statewide goals. The ODLCD monitors development activity along the coast; every five years, the ODLCD reviews local plans to ensure continuing compliance with the statewide goals.

Land Trusts and Coastal Area Protection

Several land trusts are active in preserving coastal lands for their scenic beauty and wildlife habitat. The Nature Conservancy (TNC) and the National Audubon Society are acknowledged national leaders. However, several regional land trusts have preserved thousands of coastal acres. For instance, the Low Country Conservancy in South Carolina has worked with state and local governments to protect 150,000 acres in the Ashepoo/Combahee/Edisto Basin (Beach 2002, 15).

Big Sur in Monterey County on California's central coast is world famous for its stunning views of rocky coastline and steep hills dropping into the ocean. The Big Sur Land Trust was founded in 1978 and has preserved more than 30,000 acres from Big Sur to the Carmel Valley and north to the Elkhorn Slough. In addition to acquiring conservation easements, the Big Sur Land Trust has purchased land and then transferred it to the State of California. A noteworthy example of this public-private partnership began in 1993 when the Big Sur Land Trust used a grant from the 1990 California Wildlife Protection Act to initiate the purchase of the 1,300-acre Point Lobos East Ranch, adjacent to the Point Lobos State Reserve. In 2002, the Big Sur Land Trust partnered with TNC and the State of California to purchase the 10,000-acre Palo Corona Ranch. The ranchland connects several state parks and a federal wilderness area, creating a 70-mile corridor for wildlife migration and human recreation (TNC 2002, 61).

Land trusts as private nonprofit groups are allowed a limited amount of lobbying and may not endorse political candidates; however, land trusts may take legal action. In 1999, the Bolsa Chica Land Trust won a case to protect environmentally sensitive habitat area on the southern California coast. The Appeals Court also struck down the approval of the California Coastal Commission (CCC) to permit development on the condition that habitat area would be recreated elsewhere (*Land Use Law and Zoning Digest* 1999, 11).

SIDEBAR 11-1

Protecting the Chesapeake Bay

The Chesapeake Bay is America's largest estuary, with a watershed that covers 64,000 square miles and contains 15 million people in Maryland, Pennsylvania, Virginia, and the District of Columbia. The Chesapeake Bay has long been famous for its oysters and blue crabs. However, the oyster harvest has sharply declined to fewer than 500,000 bushels a year, far from its peak in the early 1900s of 20 million bushels annually (Clines 2000, A18). Crabs, too, have become harder to find. Over recent decades, considerable residential and commercial development has occurred adjacent to the bay. Meanwhile, farms in the watershed have focused on intensive livestock operations and the production of feed corn, contributing to nutrient runoff that enters the bay.

Maryland's Coastal Zone Management Program was approved by the federal government in 1978. However, it quickly became apparent that the coastal program alone would not be sufficient to stem the deterioration of the bay's water quality. In the early 1980s, the Chesapeake Bay was placed on the U.S. Environmental Protection Agency (EPA) list of impaired waters, in part because of low levels of dissolved oxygen.

In 1980, Maryland and Virginia established the Chesapeake Bay Commission to cooperatively manage the bay and coordinate land and water resource planning to improve the bay's water quality. Pennsylvania and Washington, D.C., joined the commission a few years later. In 1983, Maryland, Pennsylvania, Virginia, the District of Columbia, and the EPA entered into the historic Chesapeake Bay Agreement, aimed at improving the water quality and restoring aquatic life in the bay.

Since 1984, Maryland's Critical Areas law has required new development within 1,000 feet of the high tide to meet standards designed to miti-

gate adverse effects on water quality and wildlife habitat. Also, Maryland requires retention of a large portion of vegetation and replantings of vegetation in new developments to intercept runoff. Maryland has also promoted tree planting along riparian areas to absorb runoff before it reaches streams and is washed into the bay (see Chapter 4). Since 1997, Maryland's "Smart Growth" laws have created incentives for more compact development and land preservation to limit sprawl. According to the Chesapeake Bay Foundation (CBF)—a private, nonprofit organization working to improve the bay's water quality—sprawl causes five to seven times more sediment and phosphorus runoff than a forest, and nearly twice as much sediment and nitrogen runoff as compact development (CBF 2000b).

In recent years, federal and state governments have been spending about $150 million a year to reduce nitrogen, phosphorous, and toxic pollution, and to restore water grasses and fish passageways (*ibid.*). While reductions in nitrogen and phosphorus nutrients have been achieved, a looming threat is the likely further increase in population within the Chesapeake watershed. In June 2000, the three states, the District of Columbia, and the EPA revised the Chesapeake Bay agreement to include specific antisprawl goals: to reduce the loss of farmland and forestland by 30,000 acres by 2012, and to permanently preserve 20% of the watershed land by 2010 (*ibid.*).

In 2000, the CBF rated the bay at 28 out of a possible 100. According to CBF President William C. Baker, "Today's Bay is in somewhat better shape than the Bay of 15 years ago . . . We'll never see a Bay that is as pristine as that which John Smith saw . . . But . . . we can take the Bay's health to at least a score of 40% by the year 2010, and we would hope, with added effort, to reach a score of 50%" (CBF 2000a). Yet in 2001, the bay's rating slipped back to 27 out of 100.

LOCAL PLANNING FOR COASTAL RESOURCES

Although much attention is focused on the role of federal and state governments in managing coastal resources, local government planning and land use controls are very important. Local governments make the day-to-day decisions about development that both individually and cumulatively affect the environmental quality of the coastal zone.

Local communities should recognize that as more people move to the coast, they bring development, drive up land values, and heighten the financial and development expectations of landowners. This situation makes regulatory approaches to managing coastal land politically more difficult and also raises the cost of purchasing coastal land for public use or purchasing conservation easements to keep private lands in large blocks. Nonetheless, a local comprehensive plan and land use controls should address stormwater runoff, beach erosion, exposure to storms, dredging of wetlands, and developments on fragile coastal lands.

Inventory

Communities should conduct an inventory and assessment of coastal resources in the Natural Resources Inventory section of the comprehensive plan. The state's coastal zone management plan, state department of natural resources, and the coastal zone office of NOAA should be able to provide ample information on local coastal zone resources. The county planning office or regional planning agency office should also have useful information. Beaches, headlands, estuaries, tidal wetlands, dunes, soils, slopes, wildlife habitat, water bodies, and water quality should be included in the inventories and mapped.

Analysis

The land suitability analysis should indicate priority sites for water-dependent uses as well as sensitive lands. Future growth and development should be directed away from coastal areas in general, and specifically areas subject to natural hazards and with limited potential to support development.

Goals and Objectives

The comprehensive plan must set realistic goals and objectives for the coastal zone (see Table 11-1). Economic base objectives must recognize the need for maintaining and improving coastal resources, which are essential for continued economic activ-

Table 11-1
Sample Coastal Resources Goals and Objectives in the Comprehensive Plan

Natural Resources and Environmental Analysis	
Goal	To protect important and unique coastal resources and features that provide aesthetic, recreational, wildlife, and educational opportunities.
Objective	Cooperate with state and federal agencies, local governments, nonprofit groups, and private landowners to protect important and unique coastal areas.
Economic Base	
Goal	To protect important and unique coastal resources and features that are important to local tourism and recreation businesses, and to the quality of life of local residents.
Land Use	
Objective	Direct development away from natural hazards and sensitive environments in coastal areas, such as steep slopes, dunes, beaches, and wetlands.

SIDEBAR 11-2

Local Planning and Coastal Storms

Coastal areas are notorious for their vulnerability to natural hazards (see Chapter 12). Godschalk *et al.* surveyed 403 coastal communities about land use controls aimed at mitigating the effects of hurricanes and coastal storms (see Table 11-2) (Godschalk *et al.* 1989). Zoning and subdivision regulations were the most commonly used protections, often combined with a comprehensive plan. Especially creative techniques included evacuation plans, shoreline setbacks, dune protection, hazard area ordinances, and transfer of development potential out of hazardous areas.

Godschalk *et al.* asked the communities what they perceived as the most effective coastal protection techniques. The 10 leading responses were special hazard area ordinances, impact fees or special assessments, dune protection regulations, location of public structures to minimize risk of storm damage, shoreline setback regulations, acquisition of undeveloped land in hazard areas, acquisition of damaged buildings in hazard areas, evacuation plans, transfer of development potential from hazardous to nonhazardous sites, and the location of capital facilities to reduce or discourage development in hazardous areas (Godschalk *et al.* 1989). These responses reflect a desire to limit development in coastal areas with exposure to natural hazards.

ity and quality of life. Land use objectives should feature minimizing development in fragile coastal environments. From these goals and objectives should come specific strategic actions.

Action Strategy

The Action Strategy should present techniques and programs for achieving the coastal resources goals and objectives as well as a timetable. Coastal resource protection benchmarks should be identified and progress toward those benchmarks evaluated in an annual report on the environment. Specific recommendations might include the following:

- Use zoning overlay districts to protect sensitive environmental features, such as floodplains, wetlands, headlands, and viewsheds.
- Explore state and federal funding for the purchase of environmentally sensitive lands and conservation easements.
- Create partnerships with nonprofit groups for the preservation of important coastal areas.
- Explore the use of financial incentives, such as transfer of development rights, to reduce development in hazardous areas.

Zoning Ordinance

Communities can adopt either a conservation zone or a coastal overlay zone to limit and appropriately site development in coastal areas. Either zone can be used to protect areas with slopes of greater than 15%, wetlands, beaches and dunes, and scenic viewsheds. A key feature to include is a deep setback from beaches, dunes, and the mean high tide. This will place buildings on firmer ground and protect them from storm surges. In some cases, a limited development of fewer building lots than the zoning would allow, together with the sale or donation of a conservation easement, can produce a minimum of intrusion on significant environmental features. It is important to note that the famous U.S. Supreme Court *Lucas* case involved the invalidation of zoning provisions that would have deprived the landowner of all reasonable use of a beachfront property (*Lucas v. South Carolina Coastal Council*, 112 S. Ct. 2886 (1992)). While zoning is one way to limit the development of fragile environments, it will not be able to ban all development. Ordinances must be carefully crafted in keeping with the goals and

Table 11-2
Development Controls in Coastal Communities

	Development Control	Number of Communities Using	Percentage of Total
1.	Zoning Ordinance	354	87.8
2.	Subdivision Ordinance	347	86.1
3.	Comprehensive Plan or Land Use Plan	340	84.4
4.	Evacuation Plan	272	67.5
5.	Shoreline Setback Regulations	218	54.1
6.	Capital Improvements Program	216	53.6
7.	Location of Public Structures and Buildings to Reduce Storm Damage Risk	185	45.9
8.	Dune Protection Regulations	152	37.7
9.	Location of Capital Facilities to Reduce or Discourage Development in Hazardous Areas	126	31.3
10.	Public Acquisition of Undeveloped Land in Hazardous Areas	118	29.3
11.	Special Hazard Area Ordinance	109	27.0
12.	Hazard Disclosure Requirements in Real Estate Transactions	103	25.6
13.	Recovery and Reconstruction Plans and Policies	87	21.6
14.	Transfer of Development Potential from Hazardous to Nonhazardous Sites	84	20.8
15.	Hurricane or Storm Component in Comprehensive Plan	80	19.9
16.	Construction Practices Seminars	62	15.4
17.	Public Acquisition of Development Rights or Scenic Easements	56	13.9
18.	Preferential Property Assessment or Reduced Property Taxation	44	10.9

Source: Godschalk *et al.* (1989); Beatley *et al.* (1994)

objectives of the comprehensive plan to demonstrate that limitations on development are a matter of public health, safety, and welfare.

Subdivision Regulations

On-site septic use should be very limited in coastal areas because of the potential for sewage to leach into water bodies. Wells should also be limited because of the threat of salt-water intrusion. The subdivision ordinance should spell out conditions under which on-site septic systems and wells are acceptable. Otherwise, central sewer and water can be required, such as through an adequate public facilities ordinance. Stormwater management and vegetative cover are essential to minimize runoff into water bodies. Roads and impervious surfaces should be strictly controlled. The subdivision ordinance can require buffering berms and vegetation between developed areas and estuaries or tidal wetlands. Finally, for larger developments, an environmental impact statement describing and analyzing

**Table 11-3
A Checklist of Coastal Resource Issues in a Development Review**

1.	Is the proposed development consistent with a state-approved local coastal zone plan?
2.	Is the proposed development consistent with the zoning ordinance and subdivision regulations? Does it meet the setback, height, and bulk coverage requirements?
3.	Is the development located on beaches, dunes, or cliffs, or is it set back a safe distance away?
4.	What are the land uses on the adjacent properties?
5.	Will the development require any public infrastructure investment?
6.	Does the proposed development have a stormwater management plan and an erosion and sedimentation control plan?
7.	Are any wetlands proposed to be dredged or filled?
8.	Is public access to beaches preserved?
9.	Has the developer obtained any necessary state or federal permits?

potential effects on coastal resources should be required (see Appendix). Impacts on soil erosion, runoff, water quality and supply, wildlife habitat, and natural hazards in particular should be addressed.

Capital Improvements Program

Local planning officials should use the capital improvements program (CIP) to direct growth and development away from largely undeveloped shorelines. Major roads, schools and other public buildings, and extensions of sewer and water systems should generally be kept away from these areas in order to discourage intensive growth and development. Capital spending may be needed to maintain public beaches and marinas, and to acquire land or conservation easements to provide public access to the shore and to keep sensitive wetlands, headlands, and dunes from becoming building sites.

What to Look for in a Development Review

A proposed development should be evaluated according to the current comprehensive plan, zoning ordinance, subdivision and land development

regulations, CIP, and any other relevant ordinances. Proposed development in the coastal zone must be closely scrutinized because of the potential environmental impacts and risks to human life and property (see Table 11-3). Developments should be set back a safe distance from beaches to avoid storm surges and to protect from high winds. Minimizing stormwater runoff and erosion from building sites is important to protect the quality of waterways that empty into the ocean, and hence the quality of water along the shore.

CASE STUDIES

California stands out for its variety of planning programs for the sustainable use of coastal resources. In the early 1970s, the state established a Coastal Commission to oversee development in coastal areas through a permit development system, working with local governments to improve planning and increase public access to the coast. The California Coastal Conservancy has actively acquired shoreline property as well as funded local government and nonprofit land conservation efforts in the coastal zone.

CASE STUDY 11-1
The California Coastal Commission

The CCC was created by a statewide referendum—Proposition 20—in 1972 and made permanent by the legislature in 1976. The purpose of the commission is to oversee development along California's 1,100 miles of Pacific coast by promoting public access to the coast, protecting sensitive coastal and marine resources, and ensuring that residential, commercial, industrial, and public developments in coastal areas are properly planned and constructed. The CCC defines the coastal area as all lands below mean high tide and 3 miles out to sea, and generally about 1,000 yards inland. The inland area is usually less than 1,000 yards in urban places and may be up to 5 miles in undeveloped stretches.

The CCC, along with the San Francisco Bay Conservation and Development Commission (BCDC), administers the CZMA in California, requiring each of the 73 cities and counties in the coastal zone to draft a local coastal program for review and approval by the regional commissions and the state Coastal Commission. The CCC has 16 members, 12 of whom are voting members appointed by the governor and legislature, and four are cabinet secretaries. The CCC appoints an executive director who, as of 2000, had a staff of 115. The CCC has a Strategic Plan and holds meetings three or four times a month. The CCC also has six regional commissions, each with six local officials and six appointed members.

Each local government coastal program must include a land use plan, maps, zoning ordinances, and other plan implementation measures. The regional commissions and the CCC review each local coastal program every five years to ensure that it is consistent with the Coastal Act and to consider amendments to local programs. Once a local program is approved, local governments make their own decisions about whether to approve developments in coastal areas. These decisions can be appealed to the regional commission and the CCC.

The regional commissions and the CCC also issue permits for development in tidal and submerged lands. These permit decisions supersede local zoning, subdivision, and building permit actions. In 1996-7, the regional commissions and the CCC issued a total of 1,299 permit-related decisions (CCC 1997, 16). Permit approvals have been granted for about nine out of 10 development applications, but the commissions often attach specific conditions to the permits. Enforcement of permits and conditions is an ongoing challenge because of the large number of developments approved each year and limited CCC monitoring staff.

The CCC and the BCDC have the authority to review federal actions that could affect California's coastal resources, such as oil and gas leases, military installations, and the filling of wetlands under Section 404 permits issued by the Army Corps of Engineers. The CCC also reviews all port master plans and amendments. The CCC has drafted a Coastal Nonpoint Source Water Pollution Control program, under amendments to the CZMA.

The CCC has been aggressive in its efforts to provide more public access to the California coast, and works with the California Coastal Conservancy and the State Lands Commission to implement the Coastal Access Program. In 1987, the Coastal Commission became embroiled in a famous U.S. Supreme Court case (*Nollan v. California Coastal Commission*, 483 U.S. 825) over public access to the coast. The Nollans sought permission to replace a smaller house with a larger one in the coastal zone, and the commission conditioned approval on the Nollans giving public access to the beach. The Nollans appealed to the California courts and eventually to the U.S. Supreme Court. The court found in favor of the Nollans, stating that there was no clear link between the permit to build and the required public beach access, and that the access sought was out of proportion to the proposal to build a house. Ironically, the CCC already had gained many miles of public beach access in just this way, but most of the agreements for beach access expire in 2002 to 2004.

The CCC has raised the awareness of the coast as a critical environmental area. The development permit process has discouraged poor projects and improved other projects, such as by requiring buildings to be sited so as not to block scenic views of the coast. The review and approval of local coastal plans by the regional commissions and the CCC have no doubt raised the quality of planning and land use controls in coastal communities and counties. Despite the *Nollan* decision, the CCC has helped increase public access to the coast in a state where coastal real estate is at a premium. However, with California's population expected to increase by as many as 18 million between 2000 and 2025, both the regional commissions and the CCC will have their hands full in reviewing development permit applications, ruling on local coastal plan amendments, and protecting coastal resources.

CASE STUDY 11-2
The California Coastal Conservancy

The California Coastal Conservancy was created by the California legislature in 1976 to purchase, protect, restore, and enhance coastal resources and to work with local governments, other state agencies, nonprofit organizations, and private landowners. As of 2000, the conservancy had spent more than $200 million on more than 700 projects along California's coastline. The conservancy has a staff of 50 and an annual budget of nearly $40 million. The conservancy coordinates its efforts with the CCC and the BCDC. The conservancy has no regulatory authority; instead, it was created as a separate agency from the CCC to work directly with landowners and land trusts in public-private partnerships.

The goals of the conservancy include:

- *To improve public access to the coast by acquiring land and easements and building trails and stairways.* For example, beach access projects have been completed in Mendocino, Los Angeles, Orange, San Diego, Santa Cruz, and Sonoma Counties. Stairways and trails have been built in Los Angeles, San Luis Obispo, and Santa Barbara Counties.

- *To protect coastal wetlands, streams, and watersheds.* Projects include the Los Angeles River Plan, Santa Ana River Mouth in Orange County, Del Sol Vernal Pools in Santa Barbara County, and the Santa Clara River Watershed in Ventura County.

- *To restore urban waterfronts for public use and coastal dependent industries.* Examples include the Pier 1 Plan and Pier 7 public access in San Francisco and Spud Point Marina in Sonoma County.

- *To acquire and hold environmentally sensitive lands for public access, open space, and habitat protection.* These include the North Bank acquisition in Sonoma County, the Seadrift Lots acquisition in Marin County, and the Suisun Marsh acquisition in Solano County.

- *To protect agricultural lands.* In the early 1980s, the conservancy made grants to the Marin Agricultural Land Trust that enabled the trust to purchase easements on several thousand acres of farm and ranchland in Marin County.

The California Coastal Conservancy brings financial muscle to the protection of coastal resources as a complement to the CCC's regulatory approach. This model has been copied by Maryland, which created the Maryland Environmental Trust—a state agency—to preserve land resources to complement state land use planning and regulatory actions.

12

Planning for Natural Hazards and Natural Disasters

We're seeing a clash between development and natural [beach] erosion, and erosion will ultimately win—unless a hurricane gets you first.

GERED LENNON, CITY COUNCILMAN,
FOLLY BEACH, SOUTH CAROLINA
(ULLMANN 2000, 5A)

It used to be we'd never see a house or structure when we were on a fire, but these days it's rare that you have a fire where you're not trying to save buildings and people.

BOBBY KITCHENS, U.S. FOREST
SERVICE (USFS) (MILLOY 2000, A10)

Hurricane Floyd was the largest storm to hit the Atlantic coast in the 20th century. Spanning hundreds of miles across and packing winds of over 100 miles per hour, Floyd charged ashore in mid-September 1999. In just two days, Floyd poured more than 20 inches of rain on low-lying eastern North Carolina. Rivers and streams surged over their banks, killing 48 people, 2.5 million chickens, 500,000 turkeys, and 100,000 hogs. The floodwaters swamped 209 sewage treatment plants, scores of farm manure lagoons, and chemical and fertilizer plants. The resulting murky, contaminated brew polluted drinking water for 40,000 people and threatened to spread deadly diseases in the form of tetanus, typhoid, and cholera (Firestone 1999a, A22). Property damage exceeded $6 billion. More than 30,000 homes were flooded, as were hundreds of businesses and thousands of cars.

The loss of wildlife and the harm to coastal commercial fisheries were also severe.

Floyd had brought the 500-year flood and the worst environmental disaster in the history of North Carolina (Firestone 1999b, A1, A23), but Floyd was the fifth hurricane to slam into the state over a three-year period. Some people claimed that Floyd was a symptom of global warming, which is thought to produce more frequent and violent storms. To others, Floyd was just plain bad luck or, in the language of the insurance business, an act of God.

THE CHALLENGE OF PLANNING FOR DISASTER-RESISTANT COMMUNITIES

Natural disasters include floods, wildfires, hurricanes, tornadoes, snow and ice storms, avalanches, downpours, landslides, beach erosion, earthquakes, wildfires, drought, and volcanic eruptions. In an average year, natural disasters affect millions of Americans and cause more than $26 billion in damage throughout the United States (Mileti 1999). Natural disasters demonstrate time and again the folly of people who think they can subject nature to their will, or build wherever they want to with impunity. While not all losses of property and life can be avoided, careful planning for the location, type, and durability of development in and near hazard-prone areas can reduce losses and speed recovery.

Large Natural Disasters

Large natural disasters such as Hurricane Floyd pose special challenges to sustainable environmental planning. Yet, most of the annual losses from natural disasters occur in small, local events. It is difficult to predict where natural disasters will happen, for how long, and at what intensity. Their impacts are often swift and brutal. Cleanups are slow. Memories of disasters fade, and it can be difficult to convince people to prepare for catastrophes that may not occur again in their lifetimes. Mitigation programs, building retrofits, and development restrictions are often expensive and unpopular without a clear threat. The benefits of such efforts accrue gradually over time as the effects of disasters are reduced.

The number of serious natural disasters has been increasing over the last 20 years. In the 1980s, the federal government declared fewer than 25 federal disaster areas each year. In the 1990s, the number rose to more than 40 each year (Burby *et al.* 1999, 254). Moreover, the risk of damage from natural disasters will likely increase over the next several decades because most of the nation's population growth is expected to continue to be concentrated in states that have historically high exposure to natural hazards—especially California (earthquakes, wildfires, and landslides), Florida (hurricanes and wildfires), North Carolina (hurricanes), and Texas (hurricanes and tornadoes). Most of the easily developable areas in these states are already built up, forcing new development onto more hazardous terrain. Continued suburban sprawl in metropolitan areas will heighten the vulnerability of people and property to natural disasters. As more people choose to live in coastal areas in low-lying, flood-prone areas, and in places subject to earthquakes, wildfires, and landslides, greater property damage and loss of life will occur. Sensitive natural environments should act as

boundaries to suburban growth; not respecting these boundaries can and will lead to trouble.

Floods

Over the past 100 years, floods have caused more loss of life and property damage in the United States than any other type of natural disaster. More presidential disaster declarations are made for floods than for any other natural hazard. Each year, floods do more than $1 billion worth of property damage, and often result in the loss of human life. The 1993 floods in the Missouri and Mississippi River systems killed at least 50 people, left thousands homeless, caused an estimated $16 billion in damage, and cost the federal government about $5.5 billion (Platt 1996, 418). In the 20th century, more than 10,000 Americans died in floods. It is also significant to note that property damage from floods became much more costly in the latter half of the 20th century as America's population increased and more development took place near sea coasts and waterways.

Wildfires

Wildfires are part of nature's cycles and serve important functions in ecosystems. Forests, chaparral, and prairies are often set ablaze by lightning strikes. These fires burn off competing trees, grasses, and shrubs, and provide better access to nutrients and sunlight for the remaining and rejuvenating vegetation (e.g., the ponderosa pine cannot reproduce without fire). Although over $126 million was spent trying with little success to control wildfires in Yellowstone National Park in 1988, the forest grew back all the more healthy, and the wildlife is thriving (Wright 1998, 159). The chaparral of southern California regularly catches fire and later comes back to life. The Konza Prairie, owned and managed by Kansas State University, is periodically subject to controlled burns. Controlled burns have been used successfully. From 1996 to 2000, there were 31,200 federally approved burns (Wilkinson 2001, 16), but the controlled burn that got out of hand in Los Alamos, New Mexico, in the spring of 2000 burned more than 400 homes and nearly 50,000 acres. Still, in recent years, the majority of America's wildfires have been caused by careless people or arsonists (*The Economist* 2000, 25).

Wildfires pose severe threats to property and human life because of their size and the swift pace at which they can spread. The number of wildfires that have destroyed over 1,000 acres increased from 25 in 1984 to about 80 a year in the late 1990s (Jehl 2000, A1). In the 1990s, wildfires did $3.2 billion in damage to homes and property (Janofsky 2000, A18). The USFS has estimated that 39 million acres of national forest in the western states are at high risk of catastrophic wildfires (U.S. General Accounting Office (GAO) 1999, 3).

Drought

Drought is an abnormally dry climatic condition caused by a lack of rain or snowfall. Droughts are part of the natural climate cycle. In an average year, about 10% of the United States suffers from drought conditions (*The Economist* 2002, 29). Droughts can cause billions of dollars in damage to crops and livestock, threaten drinking water supplies, and hurt water-related businesses such as ski areas. Droughts also raise the risk of wildfires. There are two options for dealing with droughts: emergency response and water management. Emergency response features water use advisories and restrictions on water use (see Chapter 3). Water management emphasizes water storage in reservoirs and aquifers, and interconnections between public water systems, in addition to water conservation measures, such as low-flow showerheads, low-flush toilets, and minimum watering of lawns. The federal government has several drought-related programs, most of which involve crop and livestock payments to farmers and ranchers who have suffered drought-related losses. The most relevant one for western planners is the snow survey and water supply forecasting program operated mainly by the Natural Resources Conservation Service (NRCS).

Violent Storms

The hurricane season in the United States runs from mid-August into October. Hurricanes form off the west coast of Africa and travel eastward across the Atlantic. Areas vulnerable to hurricanes include the Atlantic coast from Florida to New England, and the Gulf coast from Florida to Texas. In the 1990s, these coastal areas experienced considerable development that is often at risk from hurricane damage (see Chapter 11). Hurricanes are measured by wind velocity, but the rain from hurricanes combined with ocean storm surges can also bring flooding to coastal areas. To some degree, hurricanes can be tracked; ultimately, where they will strike and with what force cannot be predicted with great accuracy. Hurricane Andrew, which hit South Florida in 1992, destroyed thousands of homes and caused $16 billion in damage.

While about a dozen hurricanes occur in an average year in the United States, there are usually about 1,100 tornadoes (U.S. Bureau of the Census 2003, 223). Tornadoes are formed by severe, "supercell" thunderstorms when an updraft of air turns into a spinning air column with powerful force. Most tornadoes occur in the spring in the Great Plains and Midwest when warm, moist air flowing in from the Gulf of Mexico slides under cool, dry air. Texas, Oklahoma, and Kansas suffer the most tornadoes. Even in the southeastern states and southern California, tornadoes are not uncommon (Davis 1999, 157). Homes without basements and mobile homes especially pose risks to inhabitants in areas subject to tornadoes.

Tornadoes are rated according to the Fujita Scale (or F-scale). A common weak tornado (F-0 or F-1 on the Fujita Scale) has winds from 40 to 112 miles per hour. A strong twister rates F-2 or F-3 and has winds from 113 to 206 miles per hour, while a rare, violent tornado in the F-4 and F-5 rating packs winds from 207 to 318 miles per hour (*ibid.*, 159). Tornadoes often strike with very little warning, and it is difficult to predict the extent of the damage, particularly for strong and violent tornadoes. Given the observed phenomenon of global warming, violent storms are likely to occur more frequently and become more destructive in their intensity.

Coastal Erosion

Each year, the Army Corps of Engineers and individual states and communities spend tens of millions of dollars replacing sand on coastal beaches. Normally, sand is naturally replenished by local streams that flow into the sea. However, numerous dams have blocked the downstream movement of sand, thus depleting the ocean beaches. Attempts to limit coastal erosion with seawalls actually accelerate erosion, and groins—structures extended out into the sea bed—may keep sand from shifting for only a short while. Coastal erosion is caused by storms and, especially along the Atlantic and Gulf coasts, by rising sea levels. The average annual erosion rate on the Atlantic coast is 2 to 3 feet a year; on the Gulf coast, the average erosion rate is 6 feet a year. Major storms can erode as much as 100 feet inland in a single day (Heinz Center 2000, 5).

About 41 million people were living in a county on the Atlantic or Gulf coast in 2000. Moreover, from 1993 to 1999, these counties grew almost 50% faster than the rest of the nation (*USA Today* 2000, 16A). This increased development activity was driven by a strong demand for second homes and retirement homes. Also, a considerable amount of new development occurred on barrier islands—constantly shifting, fragile strips of low-lying land, vulnerable to hurricanes, storm surges, and beach erosion. The loss of beaches and the incursion of seas mean that coastal ecosystems and thousands of homes, second homes, and commercial establishments are put at risk of damage and destruction.

Landslides

Landslides are sudden descents of earth, rock, and debris that currently cause between $1 and $2 billion in property damage and more than 25 deaths each year (U.S. Geological Survey (USGS) 2002). Most landslides are in fact mudslides; water-saturated soils become too heavy and plunge down bluffs, hillsides, and mountain slopes. Landslides can be caused by intense rainfall, rapid snowmelt, earthquakes, or volcanic eruptions. Landslides are most likely to occur when there are weak clay soils on steep slopes, or fill has been added to steep slopes to reduce the degree of slope. A swollen river or stream at the base of a hill can eat away earth and rock, producing a landslide.

Human actions can also contribute to the conditions that make landslides happen. For example, a road cut at the base of a hill can destabilize the hillside. For this reason, retaining walls are often used along interstate highways that run through hilly terrain. Depositing fill on top of a hill can also have a destabilizing effect. The combination of loading the top of the hill and cutting away at the bottom creates maximum instability. Other human actions that contribute to landslides include clear cutting of forests, or removal of vegetation on steep slopes or upgradient from steep slopes. The west coast is especially vulnerable to landslides because of heavy winter rains combined with construction on hillsides and forest clear cutting. The east coast and narrow valleys in Appalachia have experienced numerous landslides because of a combination of clay soils, steep slopes, and rainstorms and snowmelt.

Potential damage from landslides can be minimized through land use planning and building mitigation measures, preparedness and public warnings, and emergency response programs. Since the mid-1970s, the USGS has operated the National Landslides Hazards Program to conduct research and to respond to landslide disasters. For instance, the USGS drafted three types of maps to improve landslide mitigation, preparedness, and response in greater Seattle:

1. a landslide inventory map of the Regional Transit Authority route corridors;
2. a map of landslide susceptibility; and
3. landslide probability maps, involving rainfall and earthquakes.

Land Subsidence

Land subsidence can occur naturally as well as from mining activities (see Chapter 15) or water withdrawals. Natural land subsidence occurs where there are sinkholes and closed depressions in the ground. Sinkholes are common in limestone and carbonate geology, and can suddenly open up and literally swallow buildings, tractors, cars, and people. Sinkholes are direct conduits to the underlying groundwater. Closed depressions may become sinkholes if they receive too much stormwater. A first step is to identify areas vulnerable to land subsidence. For instance, the State of Pennsylvania has produced maps of sinkholes and closed depressions, and shares the maps with local governments.

Avalanches

An avalanche is a sudden release of snow in mountainous areas. The force of an avalanche is similar to a flash flood—a powerful wall of rapidly moving snow and debris that flattens virtually everything in its path. Avalanches are fairly common in Alaska and occasionally occur in the Rockies, Sierra Nevadas, and the Cascade Range; in some rare cases, they happen in the Appalachian Mountains. Avalanches are a particular threat near ski resorts. In 2000, Alaska suffered 33 major avalanches, which caused an estimated $16 million in damage to houses and cars and killed two people (McFadden 2000, B5). Avalanche areas and incidents should be noted on local and regional hazardous area maps as part of a Natural Resources Inventory. Some avalanches are predict-

able. The State of Alaska has even bombed or dynamited avalanche areas to release snow before the build-up can strike without notice. Avalanche warnings should be posted to keep people out of harm's way. An avalanche overlay zone may be a good idea to restrict development from mountainous areas with a history of avalanches.

Earthquakes

In October 1989, Americans switched on their television sets to watch the third game of the World Series between the Oakland Athletics and the San Francisco Giants. Suddenly, the upper decks of San Francisco's Candlestick Park began to sway. An earthquake measuring 6.9 on the Richter scale had struck. The game was canceled without serious incident, but other parts of the Bay Area were not so fortunate. A span of the Oakland Bay Bridge collapsed as did Oakland's Cypress Freeway. Many apartment buildings in San Francisco's Marina district were severely damaged and some caught fire. In all, 67 people were killed and the bill to repair the damage reached $7 billion.

However, the Loma Prieta earthquake that hit San Francisco pales in comparison to the 1994 Northridge quake in greater Los Angeles, which took 72 lives, injured 9,000 people, and caused an estimated $42 billion in damage, making it the single costliest natural disaster in American history (Davis 1999, 7). Freeways buckled, 25,000 people were made homeless, and an estimated 5,600 schools were damaged; federal disaster relief came to $13 billion (*ibid.*, 11, 47).

It is difficult to predict where a quake will strike, when it will hit, and the magnitude of the quake. Earthquakes occur most frequently along the west coast, and earthquakes in California are a daily event (see Figure 12-1). Major earthquakes hit San Francisco (1906) and Alaska (1964), but the most powerful quakes recorded in the continental United States were along the New Madrid Fault in Missouri in the winter of 1811 and 1812. Western earthquakes are more localized, whereas midwestern and eastern quakes are felt over large areas. The New Madrid quakes shook buildings up to 1,000 miles away! The Federal Emergency Management Agency (FEMA) estimates that 40 states are at moderate to high risk for earthquakes.

FEDERAL PLANNING FOR NATURAL DISASTERS AND HAZARD MITIGATION

FEMA is the leading federal agency for responding to natural disasters and planning to minimize damage from natural hazards. FEMA was formed in 1979 "to reduce loss of life and property and protect our nation's critical infrastructure from all types of hazards through a comprehensive, risk-based, emergency management program of mitigation, preparedness, response and recovery" (FEMA 2001). FEMA is mostly thought of in its role of providing financial and material relief to victims of federally declared disaster areas. Between 1990 and 2000, FEMA spent $25 *billion* to help people rebuild their communities after natural disasters struck (FEMA 2000a). However, as important as disaster relief is, FEMA also operates

several programs to improve state and local planning efforts to prepare for disasters and minimize the loss of property and lives.

Hazard Mitigation Assistance Programs

The Stafford Disaster Assistance and Emergency Relief Act of 1973 enables the federal government to contribute up to 75% of the cost of hazard mitigation measures. These include both predisaster and postdisaster assistance. Predisaster financial and technical assistance is available for the drafting of disaster preparedness plans for hazard mitigation, hazard warnings, rehabilitation, and recovery. Postdisaster assistance involves providing food, clothing, shelter, and financial help to disaster victims. In addition, the act provides for property acquisition and the cost of relocating the former property owners.

Mitigation Assistance Program

FEMA makes grants to states to draft comprehensive hazard mitigation plans, which serve as the basis for actions to avoid and minimize damage and to speed disaster clean-up and relief. There are three categories within the program:

1. the State Hazard Mitigation Program;
2. the Hurricane Program for hurricane-prone states; and
3. the Earthquake Program for states subject to seismic hazards.

To improve planning for natural hazards before disasters strike, Congress passed the Disaster Mitigation Act of 2000, which requires states and communities to draft hazard safety and mitigation plans in order to be eligible for Hazard Mitigation Grant Program funds. There are two levels of plans that the states can draft, and the plans must be approved by FEMA. A Standard State Plan must:

- describe the process used to create the plan;
- present risk assessments and evaluations of natural hazards;
- include a mitigation strategy for reducing losses identified in the risk assessment;

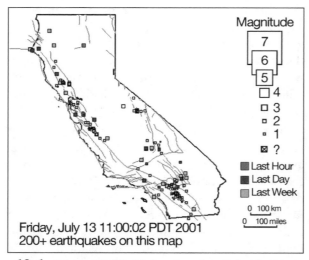

12-1 Map of California earthquakes, July 13, 2001.
Source: U.S. Geological Survey

- spell out the state process for supporting and coordinating local mitigation plans; and
- formulate a mitigation plan maintenance process for monitoring, evaluating the progress of, and updating the state mitigation plan.

An Enhanced State Mitigation Plan includes all of the elements of the Standard State Plan, but shows that the plan is integrated with other state and regional planning programs as well as FEMA programs.

States with an approved Standard State Plan at the time of a disaster declaration qualify for 15% more in Hazard Mitigation Grant Program funds. States with an approved Enhanced State Mitigation Plan qualify for 20% additional funding. The act provides grants to state and local governments to draft the plans, and emphasizes increased planning coordination between state and local governments (Steinberg and Burby 2002, 23). All states were supposed to have an approved mitigation plan by August 2002. All local governments were supposed to have an approved Hazard Mitigation Plan by November 2003 in order to be eligible for federal mitigation funding and assistance.

The Hazard Mitigation Grant Program is available to state and local governments, Native American tribes, and certain nonprofit organizations within a presidentially declared disaster area. The grant program is intended to reduce or eliminate losses from future disasters. Projects include purchasing and relocating buildings from hazard-prone areas, strengthening buildings to protect against future damage, raising buildings above the 100-year flood level, and drafting local and state ordinances and standards to protect new buildings from damage. Up to 15% of FEMA's disaster funds can be spent on the Mitigation Grant Program, with FEMA paying up to 75% of any one project. Grant recipients must fund the other 25%, and Community Development Block Grant funds from the U.S. Department of Housing and Urban Development may be used for that purpose.

Technical Assistance Programs

FEMA offers three mitigation technical assistance programs that support state and local hazard mitigation planning efforts before a disaster occurs, and provides advice on construction, engineering, and floodplain management improvements after a disaster has struck:

1. the Hazard Mitigation Technical Assistance Program;
2. the National Earthquake Technical Assistance Program available in 45 states; and
3. the Wind and Water Technical Assistance Program.

FEMA administers the National Hurricane Program and publishes hurricane evacuation maps based on data from the National Weather Service's National Hurricane Center. FEMA also undertakes studies of evacuations from hurricanes and damage risk analysis.

Project Impact

In 1997, FEMA created Project Impact to encourage communities and businesses to cooperate in preparing for natural disasters and thus reduce property losses and loss of life. FEMA estimates that for every dollar spent in damage prevention, two dollars are saved in repairs (FEMA 2000a). Project Impact involves four steps:

1. *Formation of a Disaster Resistant Community Planning Committee.* The committee should have broad representation from the public, businesses, and local government, especially the planning department.
2. *Risk assessment.* The committee identifies which natural disasters threaten the community, and specific buildings and areas that are vulnerable. Geographic Information System (GIS) mapping through the local planning department can be very helpful. The committee should ask: Where in our community is flooding most likely? Are we vulnerable to sustained winds of 70 miles per hour or more? Are we at risk for an earthquake?

3. *Setting priorities and taking action.* The committee should set short- and long-term priorities for buildings that should receive disaster mitigation, the type of mitigation measures needed, and funding sources. The committee should also review and suggest revisions to local building codes, if necessary. Also, structures in high-risk locations, such as floodplains or hilltops, should be protected. Systems and buildings that usually have high priority for structural improvements include utility and transportation systems (especially roads and bridges), hospitals, and police and fire stations. In addition, efforts to strengthen the structures of houses and commercial buildings in high-risk locations should be undertaken.

4. *Keeping the public informed and involved over the long term.* Preparedness and planning for natural disasters require attention and vigilance over the long run. This is especially true in growing communities, where increasing numbers of people and their property face risk of a natural disaster. A disaster-resistant community planning committee can, at a minimum, provide an annual report of conditions and progress in disaster mitigation.

By 2000, nearly 200 communities and more than 1,100 businesses were involved in Project Impact. For example, Deerfield Beach, Florida (on the southeast Atlantic coast) is a growing city of 50,000. Since the early 1920s, Deerfield Beach has been hit by at least seven major hurricanes, including one that killed more than 2,000 people. The city adopted the Project Impact approach and was able to form a public-private partnership with local businesses. The city relocated critical public services into a single disaster-resistant building, retrofitted a school to serve as a safe shelter in times of disaster, and began a home-retrofitting program to enable residences to withstand hurricane-force winds (FEMA 1999a).

Floods and Floodplains

FEMA defines a flood as "a general and temporary condition of partial or complete inundation of normally dry land areas from overflow of inland or tidal waters or from the unusual and rapid accumulation or runoff of surface waters from any source" (FEMA 2001). There are three main types of flooding: shallow river flooding, flash floods, and coastal flooding. Shallow-river flooding typically occurs in the early spring when rainstorms and melting snow cause rivers to overflow their banks. These floods are common in most northern states. Heavy downpours from thunderstorms produce flash floods, such as in the narrow valleys of Appalachia and the canyons of the Southwest. These storms result in swift, powerful walls of water that can sweep away virtually anything in their path. Coastal flooding varies in location, season, intensity, and impact. The hurricane season of late summer and early fall in the southeast and Gulf coast states can produce strong tidal surges. On the Pacific coast, winter and spring storms cause mudslides and beach erosion. In the Northeast, winter storms frequently cause beach erosion.

Flood hazard areas consist of two parts. The floodway consists of the channel of the waterway and the normal area of a 1% flood, and indicates where destructive flooding will most likely occur. The perimeter zone or flood fringe defines the outer edge of the floodplain, which will experience back-up water or occasional moving water. Most flood hazard areas are defined as the area submerged by the highest flood likely to occur over a 100-year period, known as the 100-year floodplain (see Figure 12-2). Yet, the 100-year flood standard is not foolproof. For instance, in 2001, the Mississippi River produced its fourth 100-year flood within just eight years (Grunwald 2001, B1).

Some 94 million acres, or about 7% of the United States, are located within 100-year floodplains (FEMA 1994). European settlers preferred to build cities and towns close to waterways, which provided drinking water, water power for mills, and a means of transportation. Often, homes and businesses were built in floodplains. Floodplains absorb and dissipate floodwaters as well as provide important wildlife habitat. However, in the 17th, 18th, and 19th centuries, the extent and function of floodplains and the changes in river courses were not well understood. People who were flooded out typically repaired the damage or built new homes and businesses on the same site. This resistance to resettlement away from floodplains still remains, often abetted by federal flood insurance and disaster aid as well as local planning and zoning.

Floodwaters increase in speed and volume as more impervious surface is added upstream, contributing additional stormwater runoff into waterways. The location of industrial buildings in floodplains increases the risk of chemical pollutants leaking into waterways during flood events. The channeling of rivers and streams destroys wetlands along rivers and streams, reducing the ability of waterways to absorb floodwaters. About 6% of the nation's rivers have been straightened for shipping or to protect developments and farmlands in floodplains, especially along the Mississippi River (McNeil 2000, 183).

Floodplains often have highly fertile soils for farming because of the rich deposits of silt. However, floods can sweep chemical fertilizers, manure, and pesticides into waterways. In the

1990s, the State of Vermont banned the farming practice of spreading cow manure during the winter because spring runoff routinely washed tons of manure into rivers and streams.

For years the construction of flood control dams and levees was seen as the best way to minimize flood damage. However, flood control dams are expensive and have submerged thousands of acres behind them. Levees require maintenance and can break, which happened along the Mississippi River in the flood of 1993, with disastrous results. Levees, like channelization, displace natural floodplains, increasing downstream flooding.

Federal Flood and Floodplain Programs

In 1968, Congress passed the National Flood Insurance Program (NFIP), which was followed by the Flood Disaster Protection Act of 1973 and the National Flood Insurance Reform Act in 1994. The federal approach to reducing flood losses has two main components:

1. the identification of flood hazard areas; and
2. the availability of federal flood insurance for homeowners and business owners in communities that have adopted and enforced a floodplain management ordinance to reduce risks to new construction in Special Flood Hazard Areas (within the 100-year floodplain).

To identify flood hazard areas, FEMA has produced:

- Flood Hazard Boundary Maps that show the likely extent of flooding in the flood fringe district;
- Flood Insurance Rate Maps that show the NFIP rates according to locations in the floodway and flood fringe district;
- Flood Boundary and Floodway Maps; and
- Special Flood Hazard Areas maps indicating lands that generally have a 1% chance of being flooded in any given year, also known as the 100-year flood, or base flood. Put another way, these lands are likely to be flooded once every 100 years. In inland

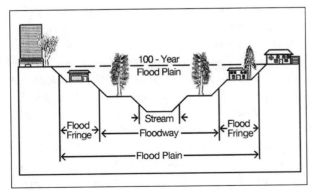

12-2 Floodplain with 100-year floodway.

areas, these maps identify both the floodway and the flood fringe. Along coasts, the maps indicate high hazard areas where a 3-foot breaking wave will reach during a 100-year storm. The Special Flood Hazard Area maps are the basis for the federal flood insurance and flood management programs.

FEMA has come under criticism for not updating flood hazard and boundary maps on a regular basis. As of 2000, about one-third of the flood maps were more than 15 years old. Waterways change course, and upstream and upslope development can increase flooding; hence, the old maps do not always accurately indicate up-to-date flood risks (Razzi 2000, 108). New technologies, such as GIS and remote sensing, are now being used to update maps. Good maps are essential for effective local land use planning as well as informing property owners and prospective buyers of flood risks and potential losses.

The National Flood Insurance Program

FEMA administers the NFIP through the Federal Insurance Administration and the Mitigation Directorate. Community participation in the NFIP is voluntary, but if a community does not adopt a floodplain management ordinance, property owners in the floodplain are not eligible for federal flood insurance. Also, federal grants and loans are not available for property acquisition or construction in the 100-year floodplain. If the president declares a community a disaster area and the community is not a participant in the NFIP, federal funds cannot be granted for the permanent repair or reconstruction of buildings in the 100-year floodplain. Individuals would still be eligible for disaster relief unrelated to building repair and replacement.

About 19,000 communities—nearly all of those eligible—have chosen to participate in the NFIP. A community can apply to join the NFIP through a resolution of the local governing body, filling out an NFIP application form, and passing a local floodplain management ordinance. The application is then sent for review and approval at one of FEMA's 10 regional offices. Through the NFIP, FEMA works with communities on a four-step approach to floodplain management:

1. *Mitigation:* actions and techniques to minimize potential flood damage to existing buildings;
2. *Risk reduction:* keeping most new construction out of identified and mapped floodplains;
3. *Prevention:* promoting land use planning and building codes that reduce the likelihood of flood damage to buildings; and
4. *Preparedness:* making communities able to respond to flood disasters.

The Flood Disaster Prevention Act of 1973 required flood insurance for any building or personal property in a 100-year flood area before a lending institution could make a loan to the owner. Any written property appraisal for lending purposes, such as a mortgage or a construction loan, must indicate whether any part of a property is located in the 100-year floodplain. Communities that do not participate in the NFIP are not eligible for federal funding, such as Small Business Administration grants and loans, financing through a Federal Deposit Insurance Corporation or Federal Savings and Loan Insurance Corporation guaranteed lender, or federal hazard mitigation grants.

The NFIP adopted the "Write Your Own Program" in 1983 to permit private insurance companies—as well as the Federal Insurance Administration—to write, sell, and service the Standard Flood Insurance Policy. Private insurers are paid for writing policies and processing claims, but the federal government is responsible for covering property losses. As of 1995, FEMA and private insurance companies held nearly 3 million policies on about $200 billion worth of properties in floodplains (Platt 1996, 427).

The rates for federal flood insurance vary according to the community status: Emergency Phase or Regular Phase. The Emergency Phase is the first step in joining the NFIP. A community in this phase may or may not have a Flood Hazard Boundary Map, but lacks a local floodplain management ordinance. A community in the Regular Phase has a Flood Insurance Rate Map, a Flood Insurance Study, and an adopted and implemented floodplain management ordinance qualifying the community for federal flood insurance coverage. As of 2000, the regular annual flood insurance premium for $100,000 of coverage was about $300 (FEMA 2000b). Insurance coverage was limited to a maximum of $250,000 for a home and $100,000 for the contents of the home, or $500,000 for nonresidential structures and $500,000 for the contents of the structures.

A community may still allow the construction of buildings within the 100-year floodplain and in coastal high hazard areas according to a local floodplain management ordinance that meets the standards of the federal Standard Flood Insurance Policy. In turn, building owners are required to purchase federal flood insurance. Yet, amazingly, less than one-quarter of the eligible buildings in 1999 were covered by federal flood insurance policies (FEMA 1999b). This low rate of property owner participation has meant a low amount of insurance premiums to cover federal disaster relief. A community must enforce its floodplain management ordinance or else FEMA can place a community on probation or revoke its participation in the NFIP. However, these enforcement actions have rarely been taken.

To meet the minimum FEMA requirements, local regulations must mandate that the lowest floor of any new building be at or above the 100-year flood level. Also, usually fill is not allowed in the floodway or flood fringe, and development may not occur in the floodway. The NFIP Community Rating System offers discounts of 5% to 45% off property owners' insurance premiums if the community has adopted additional floodplain management measures beyond the minimum federal requirements. Additional local measures may include public information programs, floodplain mapping and more rigorous management regulations, elevating structures in the floodplain (notice the many houses on stilts along the North Carolina coast), strengthening structures against floods, and acquisition and relocation of structures in the floodplain. Some states and communities have prudently chosen to prohibit all new development in floodways to minimize the risk of property losses and the loss of life.

The NFIP has come under criticism for allowing people who own property in floodplains to file damage claims more than once. The Congressional Budget Office has estimated that eliminating repeat claims for property replacement under the NFIP would save about $1 billion over 10 years (*USA Today* 2000, 16A). Also, people can apply for flood insurance after a flood has already damaged their property. A generous loophole allows a community to apply and be accepted into the NFIP within six months of a federal disaster area declaration, and receive federal funds to repair and rebuild structures in the 100-year floodplain. This loophole hardly encourages proactive planning to keep development away from floodplains. Arguably, once the damage has occurred, property owners in floodplains should either move or be left to take their chances on future flooding damage. Otherwise, American taxpayers will continue to subsidize those who purchase federal flood insurance and knowingly choose to live and work in floodplains (Burby *et al.* 1999, 247-258).

Greenways to Mitigate Flood Damage

There is a growing interest in linking flood hazard mitigation with the ecological restoration of floodplains. Floods replenish habitat for fish and wildlife. Wetlands that are periodically flooded don't dry up and hence are better able to absorb floodwaters and filter contaminants. Agricultural soils benefit from the siltation action of floods. Floods also tend to keep away invasive plants and maintain native plant species. Wildlife and energy professionals, policy makers, and the public are increasingly moving away from structural solutions to flooding problems. There is also a growing movement to remove larger dams from some rivers to return fish runs and restore wetlands and floodplains. State and local governments, nonprofit organizations, businesses, and citizens' groups can comment on the relicensing of dams by the Federal Energy Regulatory Commission. Overall, the joining of floodplain restoration and flood hazard mitigation makes sense as part of a watershed management plan, not just a community-by-community or county-by-county planning effort.

FEMA's Flood Mitigation Assistance program makes grants through the states to communities to buy up floodplains for permanent greenways. All purchases are made on a voluntary basis; local governments cannot use their powers of eminent domain. The riparian greenways create buffers between waterways and built-up areas, and filter runoff from built-up areas before it reaches the waterways. For example, Lincoln County, Montana, used a Flood Mitigation Assistance Grant to purchase 30 acres of floodplain to act as a buffer between Parmenter Creek and the local high school and a housing subdivision. "The land will be left in a natural state, allowing the annual runoff from Parmenter Creek to continue to spread out and dissipate naturally," said Rick Weiland, Director of FEMA Region VIII. "If the area had been developed, it might have meant trying to control the water by forcing it into a restricted channel, which would have posed a significant flood threat" (FEMA 1999c).

Some states and communities have used FEMA grants to demolish structures in floodplains to avoid future property damage and risks to human life. This is a particularly effective use of FEMA funds, as many communities would not otherwise be able to undertake this task. After the 1993 floods in the Midwest, FEMA and state governments spent hundreds of millions of dollars to buy up and take down almost 13,000 houses and busi-

nesses damaged by floodwaters or likely to be damaged by future flooding (Jehl 2001, A1). As of 2000, FEMA and the State of North Carolina had authorized $254 million to "retire" 4,200 homes damaged by flooding from Hurricane Floyd. Said then-FEMA director James Lee Witt, "Every dollar we spend saves $2 or $3 in future losses" (*Planning* 2000, 30).

Wildfires

From 1993 to 1999, the federal government spent an estimated $2.9 billion responding to wildfires (Janofsky 2000, A18). In 2000, Congress responded to the widespread outbreak of wildfires in the western states with an appropriation of $1.8 billion to increase the federal government's firefighting capacity (*The New York Times* 2000, 39). As more people choose to settle in the outskirts of the rural-urban fringe, the risk of wildfires escalates. The USFS has estimated that 40 million Americans live in areas close to wild lands, much of them forested. In California and Colorado alone, as many as 3 million people live in that suburban-wilderness interface where there is at least a moderate risk of wildfires (Jehl 2000, A16).

The USFS and the Bureau of Land Management (BLM) are the two main federal agencies that deal with wildfires. Both agencies draft fire-preparedness plans and estimate funding needs to respond to wildfires before the fire season begins. In both agencies, forest management plans and practices have long emphasized fire suppression. Unfortunately, this only builds up the number of trees for a larger conflagration sometime later. Commenting on the wildfires of 2000 that burned more than 7.5 million acres, Jerry Williams, stationed with the USFS in Montana, noted, "A healthy forest has 60 to 70 trees per acre. Instead, we have 600 to 700 trees per acre here . . ." (Milloy 2000, A10). Approaches to reduce the risk of wildfires include discouraging development in forested areas, using firebreaks around homes, using nonflammable roofing materials, and thinning trees. Yet, according to the GAO, thinning trees and reducing underbrush on the nation's 39 million most fire-prone acres would cost $725 million a year for 12 years (*The New York Times* 2000, 26).

The USFS and the BLM have entered into numerous agreements with other federal, state, and local fire-fighting organizations. The National Interagency Fire Center, a consortium of federal agencies, is based at Boise, Idaho, and mobilizes fire-fighters and equipment to respond to wildfires.

Coastal Erosion

The National Flood Insurance Reform Act of 1994 called for an assessment of coastal erosion and property losses along the nation's sea coasts and Great Lakes shoreline. A 2000 study prepared for FEMA predicted that "within the next 60 years approximately 25 percent of homes located within 500 feet of the coast (excluding those located in most urban centers) will fall victim to the effects of erosion. Erosion-induced losses to property owners during this time are expected to be half a billion dollars annually" (Heinz Center 2000, Foreword). An estimated 350,000 buildings are located outside major cities and within 500 feet of

the open ocean and Great Lakes. Over the next 60 years, about 1,500 homes each year will be lost to erosion (*ibid.*). The estimated cost to the NFIP will be $80 million or more each year (*ibid.*, 3-4). Some of these heavy property losses are expected to come from changing weather patterns. Experts are predicting an increase in storm activity between 2000 and 2020, in part caused by global warming. Also, according to the EPA, a 1-foot rise in the sea level along the Atlantic and Gulf coasts is likely by 2050, and possibly as soon as 2025 (U.S. EPA 2001) (see Figure 12-3).

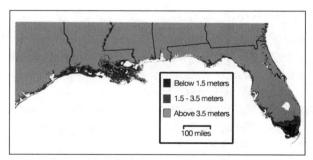

12-3 Low-lying coastal areas in the southeastern United States.

Source: U.S. Geological Survey

The coastal erosion study urged FEMA to develop erosion hazard maps that indicate the location of coastal areas subject to erosion. Currently, FEMA's flood insurance rate maps do not provide property owners or prospective buyers with information about erosion risks, nor do FEMA's flood insurance rates reflect the cost of expected erosion losses in coastal areas. The study recommended a doubling of the flood insurance rates in coastal areas that have erosion risks. The study found that while more development was occurring in erosion-prone coastal areas, the NFIP had both positive and negative effects. The insurance program was in effect subsidizing risk and thus not discouraging people from building in erosion-prone areas. On the other hand, the planning and building standards required by the flood insurance program had positive results:

> "Development density in several of the high-risk coastal areas studied . . . increased by more than 60 percent over the last 20 years. Roughly 15 percent of this increase appears attributable to the influence of the National Flood Insurance Program. However, the building standards and floodplain management requirements that are part of the program have reduced flood and erosion damage per structure by roughly 35 percent. Thus, for development after 1980, the program has lowered damage by about 25 percent below the level that would have occurred without the program." (Heinz Center 2000, 3)

Earthquakes

The National Earthquake Hazards Reduction Act of 1977 (PL 95-124) established the National Earthquake Hazards Reduction Program, a joint effort of FEMA, USGS, the National Science Foundation, and the National Institute of Standards and Technology. The activities of the earthquake reduction program include:

- identifying earthquake hazards;
- developing earthquake-resistant design and construction standards;

- developing plans for earthquake mitigation, preparedness, and response to earthquake events; and
- educating the public about earthquake hazards.

FEMA shoulders the overall responsibility for earthquake planning and coordinates the earthquake damage reduction efforts with other federal agencies. Through state, county, and city emergency management offices, FEMA coordinates state and local earthquake mitigation, preparedness, and response measures. The USGS identifies and evaluates areas with earthquake potential, assesses risks of earthquakes, and issues earthquake predictions. The USGS and state geologists from the Central United States Earthquake Consortium have mapped earthquake risks related to the New Madrid seismic zone in Arkansas, Illinois, Indiana, Kentucky, Mississippi, Missouri, and Tennessee. The National Science Foundation funds research on the impacts of earthquakes, and improvements to the design and durability of buildings and structures to withstand earthquakes. The National Institute of Standards and Technology tests earthquake-resistant design and construction, and advises on national earthquake building standards and state and local earthquake-related regulations.

Communities should determine the likelihood and possible intensity of earthquakes and possible locations. Earthquake incidents should be mapped for location, intensity, and dates. Seattle experienced two major earthquakes in the 20th century: a quake measuring 7.1 on the Richter Scale in 1949 and a 6.5 quake in 1965. The USGS began a program in the late 1990s to map the major faults of the Seattle region, and earthquake hazards such as the risk of liquefaction (mudflows) and landslides (USGS 2000). The retrofitting of buildings in greater Seattle to withstand earthquakes was credited with limiting property damage to only $2 billion and avoiding any loss of life when a quake of 6.8 on the Richter scale hit in February 2001.

Local land use plans and capital improvements plans should be coordinated with state and local emergency management plans for earthquake mitigation, preparedness, and response. This way, new development can be directed away from areas of high earthquake risk, and public infrastructure (roads, bridges, and major public buildings) can be upgraded to withstand most quakes. For example, since 1993, New York City's Metropolitan Transportation Authority has made seismic-resistant retrofits part of its renovation of bridges (Chang 2000, A27), but retrofitting thousands of existing buildings carries an enormous price tag. Earthquake insurance, unlike federal flood insurance, is very expensive, running to several thousand dollars a year in California.

Volcanic Eruptions

In 1980, Mount St. Helens—a 9,677-foot volcano in southern Washington State—erupted with the force of an atomic bomb, killing 57 people and devastating an area of 200 square miles. Mount St. Helens blew more than 1,300 feet off its top, leaving an 8,363-foot peak. Mudflows choked Spirit Lake and the Toutle River. Volcanic ash rained on Portland, Oregon as well as on places dozens of miles to the east. In 1982, Congress created the 110,000-acre Mount St. Helens National Volcanic Monument. Slowly, the land is coming back to life.

American volcanoes are found in northern California (Mt. Shasta and Mt. Lassen), Oregon (Mt. Hood), Washington (Mt. Rainier), Alaska (Mt. Trident), and Hawaii (Kilauea). Eruptions produce ash, lava, and toxic gases, and often mudflows. The USGS is producing maps of mudflow hazards and volcanic ash hazards, and educational materials for local officials and educators. State and local emergency management plans, including evacuation plans, are prudent within several miles of a volcano.

STATE PLANNING FOR NATURAL DISASTERS AND HAZARD MITIGATION

Several state agencies are directly involved in planning for natural disasters and the mitigation of natural hazards. State emergency management agencies are responsible for drafting and updating Hazard Mitigation Plans, which identify areas of the state at risk for natural disasters and recommend actions to reduce risks of damage and loss of life. The plans are also used to evaluate proposed projects in presidentially declared disaster areas for receipt of federal funds under the Hazard Mitigation Grant Program. The State Hazard Mitigation Officer coordinates the Mitigation Plan and the Mitigation Grant Program between FEMA and local governments.

North Carolina, for instance, requires all cities and counties to have an approved Mitigation Plan in order to qualify for state funds in the event of state-declared disasters (North Carolina Department of Emergency Management 2002). Local governments are directed to include the following in their plans:

- Hazard Identification and Analysis, in terms of type, frequency, strength, and likely location of occurrence. A multihazard map of the community, especially showing flood-prone areas, is required.

- Vulnerability Assessment of any vulnerable residential, commercial, industrial, and public structures, and an estimate of the potential cost of damage to those structures. Identify and map any vulnerable populations, structures, or areas—especially those that have experienced repeated damage over the years. Conduct an inventory of projected population and development in vulnerable areas if current development trends continue. Estimate the potential future damage costs.
- Community Capability Assessment featuring an inventory of the community's existing and proposed policies, programs, and ordinances that may affect vulnerability to natural hazards. Determine the community's technical and fiscal capabilities to implement hazard mitigation efforts.
- Community Goals that support or hinder hazard mitigation efforts and determine the need to modify goals or adopt new goals for hazard mitigation.
- Mitigation Strategy including a list of new or revised goals, objectives, plans, capital improvement programs, and zoning and subdivision ordinances to mitigate hazards. Involve the public in the process. Draft a Hazard Mitigation Plan for local adoption by the community's governing body. Provide for regular review and updating of the plan.

Nearly all eligible states have drafted land use plans and regulations as part of the Coastal Zone Management Act. Nineteen of the 30 coastal states consider erosion risks in reviewing proposals for new construction near the shore, but the majority of land use regulations are under the authority of local governments. Here, implementation is spotty. Better coordination in the control or mitigation of coastal erosion is clearly needed. Longer setbacks for new construction from beaches and shorelines and no development on the ocean side of barrier islands are prudent regulations to minimize the risk of storm and erosion damage.

Although Utah has not experienced a major earthquake in over 150 years, the chances of a powerful quake sometime in the future are fairly high. In response, Utah has approved a state earthquake building code, and created the Utah Seismic Safety Commission to advise on earthquake safety and draft a long-range plan for earthquake safety.

State emergency management agencies coordinate emergency services; contingency planning; evacuation planning; and local, state, and federal government responses to natural disasters and releases of hazardous materials (so-called haz-mat incidents; see Chapter 7). State emergency management agencies also work with city and county emergency management agencies to educate the public about preparing for and mitigating impacts of natural disasters.

Some states require local governments to include hazard mitigation elements in their local comprehensive plans, and these communities are making the greatest improvements in safety (Steinberg and Burby 2002, 22). California mandates local plans to address earthquake safety and a variety of other natural hazards. Florida and North Carolina require local comprehensive plans to identify and mitigate hurricane hazards.

LOCAL PLANNING FOR NATURAL DISASTERS AND HAZARD MITIGATION

Natural disasters are unavoidable, but their damage can be minimized through careful local land use planning with state and federal assistance. Only if planners and politicians strictly limit the amount and location of development in hazardous areas and require high construction standards will the chances of major damage be effectively reduced. Unfortunately, most local governments do not include planning for natural hazards and disasters in their comprehensive plans to minimize development in those areas, nor do local building codes and subdivision regulations require that hazard mitigation features be included in new construction, much less in strengthening existing buildings.

Local governments can adopt a separate hazard mitigation plan or combine hazard mitigation planning with the comprehensive plan. A section on natural hazards in the comprehensive plan can alert citizens to the risks of building in hazardous areas and serve as the basis for land use regulations to minimize development in those areas. Some hazardous areas attract development because of scenic views or remoteness, such as mountainsides, ridgetops, and beachfront sites; however, not all land can or should be built upon. Good local planning minimizes the loss of life and property both on site as well as downstream and downslope. Areas subject to natural hazards are usually either unbuildable or should be developed for only very low densities and low-impact uses. Major public services should not be sited in such hazardous areas.

Inventory

An inventory and mapping of past natural disasters as well as current hazard-prone areas are essential in drafting the comprehensive plan. State environmental agencies have data on the location and intensity of past natural disasters and hazard-prone areas. FEMA maps should be viewed with care. As much as one-third of federal flood insurance claims come from property outside of high-risk flood areas. The location, magnitude, and date of each flood should be mapped.

Local planning offices should map areas at risk of wildfires; landslides; land subsidence; and earthquake or volcanic activity according to location, topography, vegetation, and proximity to existing development. Steep slopes can be estimated from NRCS county soil survey maps and USGS topographic maps.

Analysis

The data collected in the inventory should enable the community and qualified consultants to assess the potential for damage in hazard-prone areas. This will be helpful in drafting the future land use map of the comprehensive plan, indicating where new development should or should not be encouraged. Future growth and development should be directed away from hazard-prone areas as much as possible.

Goals and Objectives

The comprehensive plan must set realistic goals and objectives for hazard-prone areas and responses to natural disasters (see Table 12-1). The local emergency management office should be asked to help draft the goals and objectives. Two general goals in the Natural Resources section should be to protect property and lives from exposure to natural hazards, and to respond quickly and effectively to natural disasters. Objectives to achieve these goals should emphasize cooperation with state and federal agencies in planning and emergency response.

Action Strategy

The Action Strategy should present techniques and programs for achieving the natural hazards and disasters goals and objectives as well as a timetable. Hazard prevention and disaster response benchmarks should be identified and progress toward those benchmarks evaluated in an annual report on the environment. Specific recommendations might include the following:

- Use zoning overlay districts to protect hazard-prone features, such as floodplains, steep slopes, sinkholes, and wildfire areas.
- Explore state and federal funding for the purchase of hazard-prone lands and conservation easements.
- Create partnerships with nonprofit groups for the preservation of hazard-prone areas.

Table 12-1
Sample Natural Disaster Response and Hazard-Prone Areas
Goals and Objectives in the Comprehensive Plan

Natural Resources	
Goal	To respond swiftly and effectively to natural disasters and to protect local residents and their property from natural hazards.
Objective	Cooperate with state and federal agencies on emergency management response planning.
Objective	Monitor the condition of hazard-prone areas over time.
Land Use	
Objective	Keep development away from natural hazards and sensitive environments, such as steep slopes, sinkholes, dunes, beaches, floodplains, wetlands, and fault lines.
Community Facilities	
Objective	Avoid locating community facilities in hazard-prone areas.
Objective	Upgrade and retrofit community facilities to minimize potential damage from natural disasters.
Transportation	
Objective	Ensure that transportation networks are adequate to withstand natural disasters and to evacuate residents in case of a natural disaster.

- Explore the use of financial incentives, such as transfer of development rights, to reduce development in hazardous areas.
- Locate public buildings away from hazardous areas.
- Review fire service and building codes and strengthen them if necessary.
- Add a flood warning district of land adjacent to the flood fringe.

Zoning Ordinance

Understanding development limitations and risks is important for communities in drafting zoning regulations to guide the location and design of development. Most commercial, residential, industrial, and institutional land uses are not suited to hazard-prone areas. In areas with the most severe building constraints, such as steep slopes over 25%, communities may choose to prohibit all development. In other areas prone to hazards, zoning should allow only very low densities and should include siting standards with appropriate setbacks from waterways, wetlands, steep slopes, and coastal areas.

A conservation zone or an overlay zone can be used to limit development in hazard-prone areas, such as areas with slopes of greater than 15%, floodplains, seismic activity areas, fire-prone areas, beaches and dunes, and areas that are likely to experience sinkholes. Development and fill in floodplains should be prohibited in order for the community residents to obtain the lowest cost federal flood insurance and the highest protection from flood damage. In coastal areas with a history of hurricanes, a key feature to include is a long setback from beaches, dunes, and the mean high tide. This will protect buildings from storm surges and place buildings on firmer ground.

The City of Sanibel, Florida, is a barrier island off Florida's Gulf coast and is connected to the mainland by a causeway. The city was concerned that if growth and development continued without limit, there could be serious problems in evac-

SIDEBAR 12-3

National Model Building Codes

There are three national model building codes:
1. **BOCA (Building Officials and Code Administrators International, Inc.):** BOCA's National Building Code has been adopted as law by many communities and states in New England and the Upper Midwest. BOCA, 4051 West Flossmoor Road, Country Club Hills, IL 60478-5795, (708) 799-2300.
2. **SBCCI (Southern Building Code Congress International, Inc.):** SBCCI develops the Standard Building Code, which has been adopted by many southern states. SBCCI, 900 Montclair Road, Birmingham, AL 35213, (205) 591-1853.
3. **ICBO (International Conference of Building Officials):** ICBO develops the Uniform Building Code used in many western states. ICBO, 360 Workman Mill Road, Whittier, CA 90601, (800) 423-6587 x3227.

uating the island during a hurricane. As a precaution, the city changed its zoning to reduce the number of dwelling units allowed and hence to set a limit on the number of people who would need to be evacuated (City of Sanibel 1997).

Building Codes

Local officials should ensure that existing and new buildings meet building codes. It is also wise to retrofit major public buildings to withstand major storms. However, often storm events are more destructive because of the large number of poorly sited or inadequately constructed buildings. For instance, when Hurricane Andrew struck Florida in 1992, considerable property damage was attributed to poorly constructed houses that did not meet local building codes. Finally, local emergency management offices should coordinate with state emergency offices on plans for evacuation and

emergency shelter facilities. To minimize potential flood damage, the City of Sanibel, Florida, adopted a building code requiring the first floor of a home to be 14 feet above sea level (Hampson 2000, 4A). Major commercial buildings must be built or retrofitted to withstand hurricane-force winds.

Salt Lake County, Utah, which includes Salt Lake City and more than 1 million people, passed an ordinance that requires a study of geologic hazards before a building can be built in areas identified as most at risk for earthquakes. Many major buildings, including fire stations, hospitals, and hundreds of schools, have been strengthened or replaced with earthquake-resistant structures. The San Francisco Office of Emergency Services has helped train about 9,000 citizens for emergencies, especially earthquakes, in their neighborhoods. The city also required exterior decorations to be removed from many buildings, fearing that in the event of a quake the decorations could fall, harming pedestrians. In 1995, New York City changed its building code to include seismic-resistant designs in new buildings and major renovations of older buildings. One such design—base isolation—involves the installation of rubber pads under large buildings to cushion the effects of shaking.

Subdivision Regulations

Subdivision and land development regulations should address development in hazard-prone areas through standards for sewage disposal, water supply, roads, stormwater management, vegetative cover, and an environmental impact assessment (EIA). On-site septic systems should be limited in hazard-prone areas, especially on steep slopes, floodplains, and sinkholes, because soils in these areas are usually unsuitable for septic systems and because of the potential for sewage to leach into surface water and groundwater. Wells also should be limited. At the same time, it makes little sense to extend central sewer and water service and public roads that would encourage development into hazard-prone areas.

Stormwater management and vegetative cover are essential to minimize runoff into areas prone to sinkholes and off of steep slopes. Any permitted development in the floodplains should have a certain percentage of vegetative cover to absorb water and hold the soil. The subdivision ordinance can require buffering berms and filter strips to control runoff. Finally, for larger developments, a developer should be required to submit an environmental impact statement describing and analyzing potential risks of developing in a hazard-prone area (see Appendix).

Capital Improvements Program

Local planning officials should use the capital improvements program (CIP) to direct growth and development away from hazard-prone areas. For instance, it has been common for sewage treatment plants to be located in floodplains close to waterways. Treatment plants should be elevated wherever possible to avoid flooding that would wash raw sewage into waterways. Similarly, water treatment plants should be retrofitted or sited so as to minimize the likelihood of flood damage. Other major public capital investments, such as schools and roads, should be kept away from hazard-prone areas. Existing public buildings should be retrofitted to withstand potential hazards. Public acquisitions of greenways and parklands are appropriate capital expenditures in floodplains, along coastlines, and in areas with steep slopes.

What to Look for in a Development Review

A proposed development should be evaluated according to the current comprehensive plan, zoning ordinance, subdivision and land development regulations, CIP, building code, and any other applicable local laws. A rule of thumb in reviewing development plans in hazard-prone areas is "an ounce of prevention is worth a pound of cure." Developers and landowners should be required to indicate any hazard-prone areas on a map and describe them (see Table 12-2). Local and state building codes should require strict construction standards for new buildings and renovations.

Table 12-2
A Checklist of Hazard-Prone Areas Issues in a Development Review

1.	What are the size, location, and land uses of the proposed development?
2.	Is the proposed development allowed in the particular zone?
3.	Does the proposed development meet the setback, height, and basic coverage requirements?
4.	Are there any hazard-prone areas on the property or on adjacent properties?
5.	What are the land uses on the adjacent properties?
6.	Has the developer conducted an environmental impact assessment?
7.	Would public infrastructure need to be extended to serve the proposed project?
8.	What steps has the developer taken to minimize potential damage from natural disasters both on site and downstream or downslope?
9.	Has the developer obtained any necessary state or federal permits?

Planning for Working Landscapes

13

Planning for Sustainable Working Landscapes: Farmland and Ranchland

To preserve farmland and ensure the long term economic viability of agriculture in Michigan for present and future generations.

MISSION STATEMENT OF THE MICHIGAN
FARMLAND AND COMMUNITY ALLIANCE,
AN AFFILIATE OF THE MICHIGAN FARM BUREAU

For many communities, preserving open space and farmland is integral to planning for and managing growth.

U.S. GENERAL ACCOUNTING
OFFICE (GAO) 2000, 10

Farmers and ranchers own most of the privately held land in the United States, about 930 million acres (see Figure 13-1), or more than 40% of the entire nation (Natural Resources Conservation Service (NRCS) 2001) (see Table 13-1). Farmland and ranchland are renewable natural resources that have the potential to produce food and fiber year in and year out. However, the productivity of these lands can decline or disappear if they are overused, abandoned, polluted, or converted to housing subdivisions, office complexes, and shopping malls. Working agricultural landscapes provide a rich variety of environmental services: wildlife habitat, groundwater recharge, air pollution and carbon dioxide absorption, and scenic viewsheds, among others.

13-1 Farmers and ranchers own most of the privately held land in America, about 930 million acres.

Source: Lancaster County, PA, Agricultural Preserve Board

279

Table 13-1
Ownership of Land and Land Uses
in the Lower 48 States (1997)

Land Uses	Acreage (in millions of acres)
Cropland	375.0
Conservation Reserve Program	32.7
Developed Land	105.4
Forestland	399.0
Pastureland	119.6
Rangeland	403.1
Other Rural Land	56.3
Total Private Land	1,491.1
Federal Land	402.2
Water Areas	50.8
Total Land and Water Areas	1,944.1

Source: Natural Resources Conservation Service, *National Resources Inventory, 1997* (Revised) (2001)

Agriculture is a big industry and is the backbone of many rural economies. In 2000, American farmers produced $194 billion in food and fiber, and the United States exported $51 billion worth of farm products and imported $39 billion (U.S. Bureau of the Census 2003). Nationwide, the average farm size is nearly 500 acres. Though there are nearly 2 million farms, many farms can be called "hobby farms" because they produce less than $10,000 a year in gross sales, and the owners rely mainly on off-farm jobs. The top 750,000 commercial farms produce about 90% of all farm output.

At the beginning of the 20th century, about one out of every three Americans—roughly 25 million people—lived on farms. A hundred years later, fewer than 5 million people lived on farms, or less than 2% of the nation's population. The reason for the changes? Leading the way were scientific breakthroughs in crop yields thanks to hybrid seed varieties, fertilizers, pesticides, and herbicides. Mechanization in the form of tractors, combines, and milking machines enabled one person to do the work of many. Livestock production increased through better breeding and nutrition, resulting in more quickly marketable meat and greater milk production per cow. Expensive public irrigation projects combined with subsidized water for farms boosted crop output. Also important were the federal farm credit system to help finance farm operations, the Land Grant university system to conduct research, and the Cooperative Extension Service to transfer information to farmers.

Advances in agriculture have enabled greater production on less acreage, reducing the need for farmland even as America's population more than tripled in the 20th century. In fact, the biggest problem that American farmers face is low commodity prices because of overproduction of corn, soybeans, wheat, and milk.

Since the 1930s, federal farm programs have been aimed at providing a safety net for farm income. The government has provided deficiency payments to make up the difference between the market price for certain commodities (corn, soybeans, wheat, and cotton) and the "parity price," which reflects a reasonable return for farmers. Federal farm payments have been important for keeping farmers in business and keeping farmland in farm use. However, because the payments are mostly based on volume of production, the larger farms have reaped most of the subsidies. In fact, the top 10% of farms receive two-thirds of the subsidies, while two-thirds of all farmers receive no subsidies at all. About half of all farm subsidies go to farmers in just six states: Illinois, Iowa, Kansas, Minnesota, Nebraska, and Texas (Lugar 2002, A15).

CHALLENGES TO MAINTAINING WORKING AGRICULTURAL LANDSCAPES

The Business of Farming and Ranching

Farmers and ranchers face five challenges in maintaining their operations: profitability, the safe and environmentally sound management of their operations, passing the farm or ranch on to the next generation, resisting the temptation to sell land for development, and the protection of farmland from conflicting land uses and conversion to nonfarm development.

Profitability

Farming and ranching, first and foremost, are businesses. Businesses change over time, and owners need to innovate and adapt. If farmers and ranchers can earn a decent living, they usually will stay on the land. Typically, the farm or ranch is the largest single asset the family owns. The land serves as a bank account, an insurance policy, and a retirement fund. Sooner or later, every farmer or rancher faces three choices of what to do with the land:

1. sell it to the highest bidder, often for development;
2. pass it on to a family member through sale, gift, or will; or
3. sell it to another farmer or rancher.

Which choice the landowner makes will depend on several factors, including:

- age, health, and financial circumstances of the owner;
- whether any children want to take over the farm or ranch;
- the amount of development pressure;
- the number of farms and ranches nearby; and
- personal goals and values.

The trend toward fewer and larger commercial farms is likely to continue; this is especially true for dairy and livestock production and for farms growing corn, soybeans, wheat, and cotton. Yet, the number of small commercial farms is increasing. These farms typically raise vegetables, fruits, nursery crops, and horses for niche markets. Caught in the middle are the traditional family farms with annual gross sales of $40,000 to $250,000. They are facing a financial squeeze that will force some farmers to expand, some to become producers for niche markets, and others to leave farming.

Safe and Environmentally Sound Management

Farmers and ranchers have often found themselves at odds with environmentalists. Most farmers and ranchers pride themselves on being good stewards of the land. Yet, the level of stewardship varies from farm to farm and from ranch to ranch. Farms and ranches are major sources of soil erosion and water pollution. Good management of soil, water, manure, and chemicals can increase agricultural productivity as well as sustain a quality environment for local residents and wildlife. Ultimately, protecting the farmland base, profitable farming, and environmentally responsible farming methods are all necessary for sustainable agricultural operations.

Farming is a leading source of water pollution (see Chapter 4). Minimizing soil erosion and carefully applying pesticides, fertilizers, and manure are essential to protect the quality of surface and groundwater. Careful use of irrigation sources is necessary to sustain long-term water supplies (see Chapter 3). Agriculture has great potential for water conservation. For instance, the replacement of flood irrigation with surge irrigation (which alternates between crop rows) and drip irrigation (used successfully in Israel) could cut agricultural water needs by more than half. Good management of soil and water resources costs money, and often federal or state funding is available to cover some of the farmer's costs. Soil and water management pay dividends in long-run land productivity.

About 480 million pounds of pesticides and 460 million pounds of herbicides are sprayed on crops each year, and some of these chemicals have caused drinking water problems in several states (U.S. Environmental Protection Agency (EPA) 1997). Integrated pest management (IPM) is a good way to reduce and tailor the amount of pesticides used to respond to pest problems, rather than try to use them on a preventive basis. The county cooperative extension service can assist farmers with the development of IPM plans.

Water utilities have begun to offer financial incentives to farmers to improve water quality downstream. The New York City watershed program is paying farmers in the Catskill Watershed to clean up barnyards and reduce runoff that could pollute city reservoirs. Otherwise, the EPA has threatened to require New York City to build a $6 billion water filtration plant (see Chapter 3). In addition, all over the nation, nonprofit watershed organizations are working with farmers and other landowners on source water protection for wildlife and drinking water.

It takes several hundred years for nature to create just 1 inch of topsoil. Soil losses in some places are alarming. For instance, about half of the rich prairie topsoil in Iowa—the nation's second leading farm state—has washed or blown away over the last 150 years (Eisenberg 1999, 31).

Soil erosion occurs from natural wind and rain erosion, and disturbance of the earth by humans and livestock, which speeds up the erosion process. Soil exposed during plowing or after harvesting corn is vulnerable to wind erosion. Rainstorms can wash soil into rivers and streams where it can pose serious threats to drinking water supplies and aquatic life. Pesticides, herbicides, chemical fertilizers, and livestock manure can bind to soil particles and wash into waterways, ponds, and lakes. This runoff can contaminate drinking water, cause eutrophication (algae blooms) in ponds and lakes, and poison fish. Soil erosion also increases the release of carbon into the atmosphere, adding to the greenhouse effect and global warming.

Soil erosion rates depend on the type of soil, slope, microclimate, and vegetative cover. Grasslands typically have lower erosion rates than cropland, especially if the cropland is plowed up to grow row crops such as corn. The general standard for measuring soil erosion is call tolerance or "T." In most cases, cropland can withstand the loss of up to 5 tons per acre per year without experiencing a major loss in productivity. Scientists use the Revised Universal Soil Loss Equation to calculate the rate of soil loss (see Table 13-2).

Passing on the Farm

The average age of America's farmers and ranchers is about 55 years old (U.S. Department of Agriculture (USDA) 1999a). This means that in the first two decades of the 21st century, millions of acres of farm and ranchland will change hands. What happens to that land will have long-term effects on working landscapes, environmental quality, and communities throughout the United States.

In suburban areas and near rural resorts, the increased value of farmland as potential development land has made passing the farm to the next generation more difficult because of heavy estate taxes. Sometimes, heirs must sell the land, usually

Table 13-2
Revised Universal Soil Loss Equation

A = RKLSCP
where
A = average annual soil loss in tons per acre
R = rainfall erosivity index
K = soil erodibility factor
L = slope length
S = slope
C = cropping factor
P = conservation practices factor

for development, in order to pay the estate taxes. The 2001 federal tax law provided substantial estate tax relief, and the sale or donation of conservation easements can also lower the value of a farm or ranch for estate tax purposes (see below).

Resisting the Temptation to Sell Land for Development

With each passing year, more people come to live in the countryside and commute to their urban or suburban jobs. The price of farmland for farming is generally much lower than it is for housing lots and commercial sites. Farmland typically sells for $1,000 to $3,000 an acre, while house lots fetch $30,000 to $50,000 or more per acre. Commercial sites can run into hundreds of thousands of dollars per acre. As development pressures mount, farmers become tempted to sell lots for development or else sell the entire farm for development. When farmland is subdivided and developed, the land base becomes fragmented and land prices increase. The remaining farmers have a harder time finding land to rent or buy to expand their operations. Conflicts with nonfarm neighbors tend to increase. Also, property taxes rise as new residents demand more public services—schools, roads, police, fire protection, and central sewer and water facilities. Farm-support businesses have fewer customers and may be forced to close. Some remaining farmers may reduce investments in their farms as they perceive the sale of their land for development to be inevitable. This "Impermanence Syndrome" means that the local agricultural industry has become unstable and is likely headed for a decline (Coughlin and Keene 1981).

Protecting Farmland from Conflicting Land Uses

Farming today is an industrial activity that is not compatible with most residential development. Farmers apply chemicals that can drift onto neighboring properties. Dust from plowing can blow onto adjacent properties. Livestock farming generates large amounts of manure, and the unpleasant odors can cross property boundaries. Farm machinery and large trucks from food processing firms can produce loud noise as well as slow local traffic.

Residential developments also cause conflicts for farms. Nonfarm neighbors may complain about smells, dust, and noise, and even take farmers to court. Farmers often mention trespassing and vandalism as problems. Also, nonfarm developments may compete with farms over local water supplies that farmers rely on for irrigation and watering livestock.

In Chapter 9, we discussed the importance of a critical mass of land to support wildlife habitat and plant species, and the threat to habitats from the fragmentation of the land base. Critical mass in the working landscape means that a minimum number of acres and farms or ranches are needed to sustain the local agricultural industry. For example, at a county level, there usually needs to be more than 50,000 acres of farmland to keep the farm support businesses profitable and thus maintain farming as a local industry over the long run (Daniels 2001). Like wildlife, once farming leaves a community, it is nearly impossible to bring it back in any significant way. While the increasing popularity of niche markets, such as small truck farms and horse operations, helps keep farmland in production, these farms will not provide as much open land or sustain as many support businesses as will large dairy, grain, vegetable, fruit, and cattle enterprises. This is not to say that the amount of farm and ranchlands should be rigidly fixed, but it is important for communities to avoid the fragmentation of the working landscape and to support their local agricultural industry. Ultimately, the protection of farmland in metropolitan areas will succeed only if America's cities and older suburbs can be redeveloped to accommodate much of the nation's anticipated population growth (see Chapter 18).

Farmland Loss

Good quality farmland is a limited resource. Prime farmland has highly productive soils, a

Table 13-3
Farmland Capability Ratings

Soils Class	General Slope	Erosion Factor	Limitations*
Class I (Prime)	Slight	Slight	Few limitations that would restrict use
Class II (Prime)	3%–8%	Moderate	Some limitations; use conservation practices
Class III (Statewide Importance)	8%–15%	High	Many limitations; use special conservation practices
Class IV	15%–25%	Severe	Many limitations; very careful management required
Class V			Very low productivity; pasture, range, woodland, wildlife uses
Class VI			Severe limitations; few crops, pasture, woodland, wildlife uses
Class VII			Very severe limitations; no crops, use only for range, pasture, wildlife
Class VIII			Most limited; use only for range, woodlands, wildlife, aesthetics

* There are four subclasses that describe particular soil limitations: "e" for erosion, "w" for wetness, "i" for internal soil problems, and "c" for climate. For example, a Class IIe soil is at risk for erosion and a Class IIIw soil has poor drainage or a high water table.

Source: U.S. Department of Agriculture, Natural Resources Conservation Service, 1999

slope of 8% or less, adequate rainfall or access to irrigation, and requires less fertilizer and erosion control than nonprime farmland. Prime farmland is rated as Class I or II by the NRCS (see Table 13-3). Agricultural soils of statewide importance are rated Class III; some unique soils, such as for orchards, are rated Class IV. The United States has about 330 million acres of prime farmland, of which 211 million acres were used for crop production in 1997 (NRCS 1999). Development is drawn to prime farmland because it is the easiest land to develop, and the greatest losses in acreage are in the metropolitan areas where the farmlands are both productive and close to markets.

Approximately 16% of the nation's prime farmland is located within metropolitan areas. Yet, this land produces about one-quarter of the nation's food (Daniels and Bowers 1997). Counties adjacent to metropolitan counties contain another fifth of the nation's prime farm ground and produce approximately one-third of total farm output. Thus, about half of the nation's 600 leading agricultural counties are either within or adjacent to major metropolitan areas. In rural counties surveyed by the GAO in 2000, 45% said that loss of farmland was a major concern, and 59% responded that maintaining at least some land in farming was a high priority in planning for the future (U.S. GAO 2000, 133).

The 1997 National Resources Inventory reported that an average of 645,000 acres a year of prime farmland were converted to development between 1992 and 1997 (NRCS 2001). However, adding in rangeland and pastureland pushes the annual total conversion of farmland to 1.28 million acres a year between 1992 and 1997. State- and county-level information on farmland acreage is provided in the Census of Agriculture, published every five years. However, the Census of Agriculture numbers are based on sampling and surveys, and do not suggest to what uses the farmland is converted.

From a national perspective, the loss of farmland to other uses is not yet a threat to America's overall food supply. Yet, the amount of farmland acres lost and the rate of loss at the national level do not give an accurate picture of what is happening at the regional or local level. There are a number of key agricultural areas that produce a large proportion of America's food, and many of these areas are experiencing strong development pressures. The Central Valley of California is the nation's premier source of fruits and vegetables, but by the year 2040, urban sprawl could convert 1 million acres of valley farmland. Already, commuters to the San Francisco Bay Area and Silicon Valley are settling in the Central Valley 80 miles away (American Farmland Trust (AFT) 1995). The Grain Belt—from western Ohio through Indiana, Illinois, Missouri, Iowa, and Minnesota—is the leading corn and soybeans region. Parts of this region were identified by AFT as being among the 10 most threatened farming areas (AFT 1996). New York and Pennsylvania are leading dairy states, but they have large populations that are leaving central cities and moving into the countryside. Florida and Texas with important farming industries continue to attract new residents.

FEDERAL PLANNING FOR FARMLAND PROTECTION

The federal government has provided relatively little direction for state and local governments in planning for farmland protection. According to a 2000 report by the GAO, there is no general federal policy on the preservation of farmland (U.S. GAO 2000, 10). The Farmland Protection Policy Act of 1981 directed federal agencies to avoid projects that would convert prime farmland. So far, most of the federal projects have involved highways. A weakness of the act is that it does not give private citizens any authority to oppose the federal projects. Few, if any, projects have been denied because of the act. The GAO study commented that the act has been "ineffective" and a "toothless tool" because federal agencies can convert farmland with impunity (*ibid.*, 135-136). In fact, federal spending on highways and sewer and water facilities, along with the federal home mortgage interest subsidy, have encouraged the conversion of millions of acres of farmland to suburban development.

In 1996, Congress created the Farmland Protection Program to make grants to state and local governments and land trusts to buy conservation easements (development rights) to farmland. The initial $35 million in funding helped to leverage state and local funds that resulted in the preservation of about 67,000 acres according to AFT (AFT 2002, 9). To build on this success, in the 2002 Farm Bill, Congress authorized $985 million over 10 years for farmland preservation grants (*Farmland Preservation Report* 2002a, 1). State and local governments apply for the federal funds through the state office of the NRCS. The national office of the NRCS then decides how the grant funds will be allocated.

FEDERAL SOIL AND WATER CONSERVATION PROGRAMS

Federal Soil Management Programs

In 1982, slightly more than 3 billion tons of America's soil were blown or washed away; by 1997, erosion losses had dropped to 1.9 billion tons (NRCS 1999). The reasons for the dramatic improvement can be traced to a combination of federal programs and the efforts of private landowners.

The 1985 Farm Bill contained three path-breaking provisions for soil conservation. First, the federal government required owners of 120 million acres of highly erodible land to draft conservation plans by 1990 and implement those plans by 1995. Second, the Sodbuster clause made farmers who plowed up highly erodible soils ineligible for federal farm subsidy payments. Third, the Farm Bill created the Conservation Reserve Program (CRP), which pays farmers a per-acre fee not to grow crops on highly erodible land for 10 to 15 years. As of 2000, landowners had placed about 36 million acres into the CRP, which is managed by the Farm Service Agency of the USDA. Most of this land is in the Midwest and Great Plains. The CRP has the added benefits of increasing wildlife habitats, restoring wetlands, and improving air quality. Through fiscal 2001, the CRP had cost a total of about $16 billion (NRCS 2000). In the 2002 Farm Bill, Congress reauthorized the CRP, expanded the allowable acreage in the program to 39.2 million acres, and added $1.5 billion in funding (*Farmland Preservation Report* 2002a, 3).

In their efforts to reduce soil erosion and the use of chemicals, many farmers have adopted no-till practices, planting seeds in slits in the soil without plowing. Cropland planted using no-till practices more than tripled from 14 million acres in 1989 to almost 43 million acres in 1996 (Council on Environmental Quality (CEQ) 1996, 312).

Other helpful practices include:

- contour farming (plowing around hills rather than up and down them) to minimize soil erosion and runoff;
- strip-cropping and grass strips to intercept runoff;
- mulch-till (leaving crop residues rather than plowing them under) to reduce soil erosion;
- winter cover crops (such as rye grass) that fix nitrogen in the soil and reduce wind erosion and runoff;
- terraces on steeper slopes of 10% to 25% to reduce runoff;
- grassed waterways to intercept soil before it washes into streams;
- riparian buffers and filter strips of grass and trees to intercept and trap runoff; and
- shelter belts and windbreaks of trees and shrubs to reduce wind erosion and provide wildlife habitat.

The Conservation Reserve Enhancement Program, begun through the 1996 Farm Bill, makes payments to farmers to plant former cropland in trees and grasses to create riparian buffers and restore wetlands. This helps reduce soil erosion, improve water quality, and provide wildlife habitat. Farmers and ranchers voluntarily enter into 10- to 15-year contracts, and state money can be used to match federal funds in some cases.

The Environmental Quality Incentives Program (EQIP) of the USDA—also created in the 1996 Farm Bill—provides financial, technical, and educational help for landowners to install filter strips, riparian tree buffers, and management plans to address soil erosion and water quality problems. The NRCS received more than 57,000 requests for EQIP assistance in 1997 alone. As of 2000, there were 35 million acres enrolled in the program. Payments to landowners are limited to $10,000 a year or $50,000 for the length of a five- to 10-year contract. Congress reauthorized the EQIP program at $9 billion in the 2002 Farm Bill (*Farmland Preservation Report* 2002a).

Federal Water Management Programs

Agriculture is the leading user of water in most states. Farming and ranching use 85% of America's groundwater each year to grow crops and feed livestock. In the Great Plains and the Southwest, access to water is the difference between productive agricultural land and wasteland. Given the high rate of population growth in the Southwest, the competition over water will become more intense in the future.

The National Resources Inventory reported that between 1982 and 1997, the amount of irrigated farmland in the western states declined by 1.5 million acres, but irrigation in the East increased by 1 million acres. Severe and prolonged droughts may lead to concerns about surface and groundwater withdrawals in areas that rely on irrigation. For example, the Ogallala Aquifer underneath western Texas, Oklahoma, and Kan-

**Table 13-4
Conservation Programs of the
Natural Resources Conservation Service
of the U.S. Department of Agriculture**

Conservation Farm Option
Conservation Plant Materials Center
Conservation Technical Assistance
Environmental Quality Incentives Program
Farmland Protection Program
Forestry Incentives Program
Grazing Lands Conservation Program
Resource Conservation and Development
Rural Abandoned Mine Program
Snow Survey and Water Supply Forecasting
Soil Surveys
Watershed Protection and Prevention Operations
Watershed Surveys and Planning
Wetlands Reserve Program
Wildlife Habitat Incentives Program

Note: For more information on these programs, contact the local Natural Resources Conservation Service office; see also NRCS in the "Contacts" section.

sas has about 50 years of water remaining at current irrigation rates (Purdy 1999, 30). The Ogallala is a deep aquifer that is not much replenished by rainfall in a region that averages no more than 20 inches a year.

There are several farming practices that should be encouraged to reduce water pollution. The county conservation district and the NRCS can provide technical assistance. Streambank fencing to keep cows out of rivers and streams can be extremely helpful in lowering pollution from manure. Grass waterways in fields can intercept runoff that may contain chemicals or manure. Balancing manure application with the ability of land to absorb it is crucial. On large farms where manure is stored in pits and lagoons, manure is commonly applied on land in large doses a few times a year. More frequent and smaller applications would give the land better ability to absorb the nutrients and minimize runoff and groundwater pollution. Manure management plans drafted by a certified agronomist are required for large

livestock farms, and are recommended for smaller livestock operations as well, especially on small acreages.

Wetlands on farms and ranches vary from prairie potholes in the Midwest to marshes, swamps, and bogs on the east and west coasts and in the South. Wetlands can be important for migratory wildlife and water recharge, and serve as buffers against flooding. However, in the past, millions of acres of wetlands were filled or drained to create cropland and pastureland. Despite the federal "no net loss of wetlands" policy, the loss of wetlands on farms continues. The National Resources Inventory reported that from 1992 to 1997, about 36,000 acres of wetlands a year were lost to agricultural uses, although 30,000 acres of wetlands were created each year.

The Wetlands Reserve Program was created by the 1990 Farm Bill and had protected more than 1 million acres of privately owned wetlands and adjacent farmland by 2002. The program has three voluntary strategies:

1. cost-sharing agreements with landowners to restore wetlands in which the federal government pays 75% of the cost;

2. the purchase of 30-year term easements at 75% of the value of a permanent easement and with the federal government paying 75% of the cost of restoration; and

3. the purchase of easements in perpetuity with the federal government paying 100% of the cost of restoring the wetland.

The 2002 Farm Bill authorized another $1.5 billion for the Wetlands Reserve Program (*Farmland Preservation Report* 2002a, 3).

Federal Rangeland Management

Federal rangelands in the western states are often used for grazing cattle or sheep. Some federal rangeland is within national forests or national parks, but the large majority is on land managed by the Bureau of Land Management (BLM). BLM lands generally have low productivity potential for agriculture, and so are used for rangeland. Like the national forests, BLM lands are supposed to be managed according to the principle of "multiple use-sustained yield." These uses include rangeland, recreation, mining, timber production, fish and wildlife habitat, industrial development, and wilderness areas.

The BLM has been criticized for favoring livestock grazing over other uses. In 1996, of the rangeland managed by the BLM, 39% was rated in fair condition and 14% in poor condition (CEQ 1996, 318). Overgrazing has been cited as a major cause of the expansion of deserts in the West. Overgrazing depletes native grasses and vegetation, and leads to soil erosion from wind and rain. Cattle trampling streambanks adds sedimentation to streams and destroys rich wildlife habitat. Cattle defecating in streams also degrade water quality and fish habitat.

The BLM has also been criticized for subsidizing the cattle and sheep industries. The BLM in 1999 charged $1.35 per Animal Unit Monthly for one cow plus a calf or five sheep to graze on BLM lands for a month. The comparable private grazing rate is anywhere from $5 to $12 a month. More importantly, only a small percentage of the U.S. cattle supply is raised on BLM land, leading some to wonder if the environmental damage is worth the cost.

STATE FARMLAND PROTECTION PROGRAMS

Farmland protection programs are found in every state. Most states have passed enabling legislation that allows county and municipal governments to use a variety of planning tools, such as agricultural zoning, purchase of development rights (PDRs), and transfer of development rights (TDR) to help protect farming areas. States can enhance local efforts by offering farmland owners with property tax incentives, legal protection, and PDRs to keep their land in farming.

Preferential Property Taxation

Forty-nine states offer preferential assessment on farmland by assessing the land for tax purposes at its use-value as farmland, rather than its "highest and best use" as potential residential, commercial, or industrial development property. Thus, the farmer's property tax bill is much less than what it would be if the farm were assessed as a development property. There are three varieties of preferential assessment:

1. simple preferential assessment, in which a landowner voluntarily enrolls the land and can withdraw the land at any time without a penalty;

2. preferential assessment with a "roll-back" provision (also known as deferred taxation) to recapture tax benefits along with an interest penalty if farmland is withdrawn from the preferential assessment program or sold for development; and

3. preferential assessment based on a contract that lasts for 10 to 25 years.

Preferential farmland assessment programs alone have not been very successful in keeping farmland from being developed. The tax breaks are small compared to the prices that developers routinely offer farmers. Many farmers have benefited from preferential taxation as they wait to sell their farms for development. Moreover, because eligibility requirements are often minimal (e.g., 10 acres and at least $1,000 a year in gross farm sales), preferential assessment programs have been widely abused by land speculators and hobby farmers who earn nearly all of their income off the farm. In these cases, the property tax break is subsidizing the speculator's holding costs while the land appreciates in value, or is subsidizing the hobby farmer's rural lifestyle. Preferential assessment programs need to be reworked to target tax benefits to commercial farm operations that contribute significantly to the local and regional farming industry.

Most states require local governments to conduct a new assessment of property value about every five years, which usually results in increased assessments. While use-value taxation of farmland in growing communities provides some protection against soaring tax bills based on highest and best use, the property tax rate may still rise to pay for additional public services demanded by the growing population. Preferential assessment does not place a limit on the property tax rate. In most places, the tax rate consists of two parts: the real estate tax and the school tax. School taxes make up half to three-quarters of the local tax burden. As more people move into an area, and new schools must be built, the school tax can increase sharply. The State of New York has addressed the school tax issue by giving a credit against state income taxes to farmers based on the amount of school taxes they pay.

Preferential assessment is an important ingredient in a package of farmland protection programs. It makes sense to link preferential assessment to land zoned for farming as is done in Maryland and Oregon. Preferential assessment is also important for farmers who sell development rights or donate conservation easements. They want some assurance that if they preserve their land for farming, they will not eventually be taxed off the land. Harford County, Maryland, even exempts preserved farmland from the county property tax (Daniels and Bowers 1997, 98).

Right-to-Farm Laws

A right-to-farm law is designed to reduce conflicts between farmers and nonfarm neighbors. Often, people from urban and suburban areas move to the countryside to enjoy the open spaces and what they perceive as a safer and cleaner way of life. However, most farming operations involve heavy machinery and chemical sprays, and many others raise livestock and handle large amounts of manure. Newcomers are not accustomed to the noise, dust, odors, and slow-moving farm machin-

ery on local roads. In some cases, newcomers have tried to enact nuisance ordinances that would restrict farming activities to certain times of the day. In other cases, nonfarm neighbors have taken farmers to court over farming practices.

Right-to-farm laws exist in every state, except Iowa. Some local governments have enacted their own right-to-farm laws as well. The laws generally mean that a farmer cannot be found to create a nuisance if the farmer is following standard farming practices. Right-to-farm laws do not make farmers exempt from state and federal pollution and safety laws. In some states, farmers may be vulnerable to legal challenges if they attempt to dramatically expand their operations, such as from 150 dairy cows to 900, or if they change the type of operation, such as from grain farming to hogs.

Right-to-farm laws do not prohibit a neighbor from taking a farmer to court. Michigan acted to minimize the vulnerability of farmers to frivolous nuisance suits by allowing a judge to require the neighbor to pay the farmer's court costs and attorney's fees if the judge rules against the neighbor's complaint (Daniels and Bowers 1997, 91). Right-to-farm laws have not been widely tested. They are sure to come under more scrutiny in the future given the changing perceptions of what a farm is and what a standard farming practice is (see Case Study 13-1, below). On the one hand, farmers must operate their farms as good neighbors; on the other, people who move to the countryside need to be aware that farming is a business and, in most cases, the farmers were there first.

Agricultural Districts

Agricultural districts are a voluntary way to offer farmers limited protection without using land use restrictions such as zoning. The provisions of agricultural districts vary somewhat from state to state. However, in general, farmers must enroll a certain minimum amount of land, usually 500 acres, and receive approval from a local township

Table 13-5
Leading State Programs in Farmland Preserved (2002)

State	Acres Preserved	Dollars Spent (in millions)
California	15,400	$18.2
Connecticut	28,393	$82.8
Delaware	64,830	$67.3
Maryland	198,276	$286.0
Massachusetts	50,664	$126.0
New Jersey	89,392	$265.8
Pennsylvania	224,406	$450.4
Vermont	96,000	$38.0

Source: *Farmland Preservation Report* (2002b), p. 3

or county government. The benefits of a district may include:

- use-value property tax assessment;
- exemption from local nuisance laws that would restrict normal farming practices;
- greater protection from eminent domain actions by governments;
- exemption from sewer- and water-line assessments;
- limits on the extension of public sewer and water lines, and major highways into the district; and
- eligibility to apply to sell development rights to a county or state government.

Farmers in 21 states have enrolled about 30 million acres in agricultural districts. Most districts are formed in rural areas under little development pressure, rather than close to cities and suburbs where development pressures are intense. No penalties are levied if and when a farmer withdraws land from an agricultural district, except that roll-back taxes may be due. Agricultural districts make the most sense when combined with agricultural zoning and preferential property tax programs. In this way, the farmers in agricultural districts pay lower property taxes and get some protection from nonfarm development.

Purchase of Development Rights

PDR is a voluntary transaction in which a farmer receives a cash payment in return for signing a contract, called a deed of easement, that restricts the use of the land to farming or open space. Most sales of development rights are permanent, though a deed of easement may specify a certain term, such as 30 years. PDR programs have gained in popularity since the first one was created in Suffolk County, New York, in the 1970s. As of 2002, 24 states, dozens of counties, and several townships had enacted PDR programs (see Tables 13-5 and 13-6). Forty-nine states allow local governments to spend public dollars to acquire development rights to private property. In smaller states, such as in New England and Delaware, statewide PDR programs have not involved local funding. In larger states, state PDR funds have been used to match local funds, creating an incentive for the creation of county and township PDR programs.

In America, a landowner actually owns a bundle of rights to the land. These rights include water rights, air rights, mineral rights, the right to sell the land, the right to pass it along to heirs, the right to use the land, and the right to develop it.

Table 13-6
Leading Counties in Farmland Preserved (2002)

	County	Acres Preserved
1.	Lancaster County, Pennsylvania	55,000
2.	Montgomery County, Maryland	54,871
3.	Chester County, Pennsylvania	44,452
4.	Sonoma County, California	41,688
5.	Carroll County, Maryland	39,668
6.	Baltimore County, Maryland	38,183
7.	Marin County, California	34,092
8.	Harford County, Maryland	33,006
9.	Burlington County, New Jersey	31,548
10.	Berks County, Pennsylvania	30,873

Note: Includes farmland preserved by state and local governments and private land trusts.

Source: *Farmland Preservation Report* (2002c), p. 2

Any one of these rights can be separated off from the bundle and sold, donated, or otherwise encumbered. When landowners sell development rights to a local or state government, they give up only the right to develop their land. The landowners retain all other rights and responsibilities that go with land ownership, such as the right to sell the property and the responsibility for property taxes. Despite the government's investment in the land, it remains private property and no public access is allowed. However, landowners must practice good stewardship, and the property will occasionally be visited and inspected by the agency holding the development rights. Preserved farms can be passed on to heirs or sold, though the restrictions spelled out in the deed of easement also apply to future landowners.

The value of the development rights is determined by an appraisal, based on comparable sales of farms with development rights to determine a market value, and sales of farms with no remaining development rights to determine a restricted agricultural value. The difference between the market value of the subject farm and the restricted agricultural value is the value of the development rights (see Table 13-7).

The development rights payment is taxed as a capital gain. This means that a seller can deduct any basis (cost of buying the farm plus improvements minus depreciation) in the farm ($170,000 in Table 13-7) from the payment to determine the taxable capital gain.

Selling development rights enables the farmer to get cash out of the land without actually having to sell the land. The cash payment can help in expanding the farm operation, establishing a retirement fund, and passing the farm on to the next generation. The sale of development rights reduces the value of the farm for federal estate tax purposes and thus can help in passing the farm on to heirs. Finally, many farmers love their land and never want to see it converted to nonfarm uses.

PDR programs can be expensive. Communities and counties will have to decide whether they want to spend millions of dollars to preserve farm-

Table 13-7
Example of Purchase of Development Rights

400-Acre Farm	$1,200,000	Appraised Fair Market Value
	$700,000	Appraised Value Restricted to Farming or Open Space
	$500,000	Appraised Development Rights Value and Cash Paid
Subtract	$170,000	Landowner's Basis in Farm
		(Basis is the Cost of the Land and Buildings Plus Improvements Minus Depreciation)
	$330,000	Taxable Capital Gain
	Gains Tax Due at 20% Federal and 5% State = $82,500	
	Net Return on Sale of Development Rights = $417,500	

land. In areas with heavy development pressure, farmers have sold development rights for more than $10,000 an acre. At that cost, governments can save little farmland. Instead, the preserved farmland will likely become "islands" of open land amid a suburban landscape. On the other hand, there may be no compelling reason to spend public money to preserve farmland that is remote from development. Areas of moderate growth pressure are ideal for PDR programs because the costs to the public are reasonable, yet PDR prices are usually high enough to interest farmers.

PDRs are attractive because they offer a more permanent solution than zoning and provide private landowners with compensation in return for giving up the right to develop. Thus, PDR programs avoid the 5th Amendment takings challenge that can hamper agricultural zoning. However, PDR programs can make agricultural zoning more palatable because they offer compensation to landowners for restrictions and, in turn, owners of preserved farms recognize the need to protect their borders from nonfarm development.

A PDR program makes sense if large blocks of several hundred acres or more can be preserved. Such sizable areas help to reduce land use conflicts by keeping development at a distance and

SIDEBAR 13-1

Land Trusts and Farmland Preservation

In the 1990s, private land trusts started to expand their land-saving role by preserving significant amounts of farmland. Nearly 100 land trusts nationwide list farmland preservation as one of their goals. Land trusts may buy a perpetual conservation easement (development rights), accept donations of conservation easements, or do a bargain sale involving part cash payment and part donation. The Marin Agricultural Land Trust has preserved more than 30,000 acres in Marin County, California, just north of San Francisco. The Vermont Land Trust has worked closely with the State of Vermont to help preserve more than 80,000 acres. The Colorado Cattleman's Land Trust (CCLT), created in the early 1990s, is a fascinating example of ranchers forming their own land trust to work on preserving land with their fellow ranchers. The CCLT has preserved over 130,000 acres of ranchlands, primarily through the donation of conservation easements (*Farmland Preservation Report* 2001, 7).

channeling development to appropriate locations. For example, PDR programs can help to create urban and village growth boundaries (see Figure 13-2). As more farmland is preserved, it is more likely that farm-support businesses will remain in operation and sustain agriculture as a local and regional industry. Finally, many PDR programs require that a farm have a soil and water conservation plan in place before the development rights are purchased.

LOCAL PLANNING FOR FARMLAND PROTECTION

The guiding document in any farmland protection effort should be the county or township comprehensive plan. Yet, some plans do not even mention farmland protection or the importance of farming to the community. Farmland protection can be a key ingredient in managing and directing community growth over the next 20 years or more. Members of the farm community should be included in the comprehensive planning process through appointment to the planning commission, by serving on a citizens' advisory committee, or participating in public hearings on the plan.

If agriculture is part of the local economy, it should be discussed in the Natural Resources Inventory and Economic Base sections of the local comprehensive plan. In the past, many local governments listed farmland as "vacant" on their current and future land use maps. This indicates an intention to see this land developed into nonfarm uses. In reality, farmland is "developed" land; farmers make substantial investments in the land to maintain and enhance its agricultural productivity. Local governments must make a conscious decision whether they want agricultural operations to be part of the future of their communities. Above all, it is essential that local governments not confuse farmland protection with open space protection. Farming is a business that does provide open space. But to keep the land open, farming must provide farmland owners with a decent income.

Inventory

The first step in the comprehensive planning process is to identify agricultural resources, including the number of farms, acres in farming, location of farms, land ownership patterns, soil quality, types of agriculture, the annual value of farm production, and agriculture-related employment and any agriculture-related businesses in the community. Most of this information is available at the county and state levels from the Census of Agriculture. State departments of agriculture publish annual reports on county farming. The state land grant university and the county cooperative extension service can also be of help.

The NRCS of the USDA has published soil surveys of most counties in the United States. The NRCS has digitized many of these surveys for use in Geographic Information Systems (GISs). County and municipal property tax maps can also help to identify farm parcels receiving preferential property tax assessments and parcels enrolled in agricultural districts. Many tax maps are being digitized as well. Lancaster County, Pennsylvania, has digitized an orthophoto layer that shows buildings and is keyed to the property tax assessment layer to

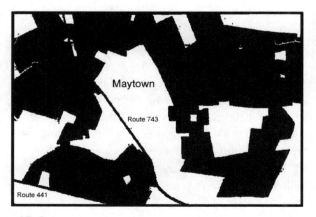

13-2   A block of 3,000 acres of preserved farmland around the village of Maytown, Lancaster County, Pennsylvania.

Source: Agricultural Preserve Board, Lancaster County, Pennsylvania

identify land uses. This allows parcels assessed as farmland to be easily identified. Additional GIS data layers might include sewer and water lines, waterways, roads, and the location of nonfarm development. These data indicate potential conflicts between farms and nonfarm development as well as where it makes sense for future development to be located to minimize conflicts.

Finally, the inventory could include a survey of farmers that asks whether they are interested in staying on the farm or passing it on to the next generation. Farmland protection does not work without the support of at least a sizable segment of the farming community. If farmers in a community or region do not see a future in farming, there is no way the public can force them to continue farming.

Analysis

Communities and regions must determine how much of a farming industry there is to protect. Many local governments, especially in rapidly suburbanizing areas, decide to undertake a farmland protection program when there are only a few remaining farms. In these cases, the best that can be done is to protect some open space that will give a feel for what the area was like when it was rural. However, this is very different from protecting a working landscape (Daniels and Bowers 1997).

The Land Evaluation and Site Assessment (LESA) system, developed by the U.S. Department of Agriculture, can be used to identify high-quality farmland with long-term viability for agricultural production (see "A Note on Rezonings and the Land Evaluation and Site Assessment System," below).

The location, size, and types of farm operations will suggest the potential for farmland protection and the appropriate techniques to use. Ideally, a community will have large, contiguous farms that are separated from residential and commercial areas. These farms should be identified on a map as the community's high-priority farmlands. In

these cases, agricultural zoning of at most one dwelling per 25 acres and PDR are valid farmland protection options. Increasingly, however, situations are common in which nonfarm residences are scattered throughout farming areas and few farms are contiguous to other farms. Agricultural zoning will be a tough sell in these places because farmers can see the increased value of their land for development. PDR may not work effectively because farming and developing areas are not clearly separated.

Goals and Objectives

The comprehensive plan should state realistic goals and objectives for agriculture and farmland in the Natural Resources, Economic Base, and Land Use sections (see Table 13-8). In particular, agriculture should be recognized as a valid form of economic development, providing incomes, jobs, and tax base.

Action Strategy

The Action Strategy should present techniques and programs for achieving the farmland and farming goals and objectives as well as a timetable. Farmland protection and farm support benchmarks should be identified and progress toward those benchmarks evaluated in an annual report on the environment. Specific recommendations might include the following:

- Create a farmland protection package of techniques including: financial incentives, such as use-value property taxation; land use restrictions, such as agricultural zoning; and economic development programs to help farmers earn a decent living and afford to keep farming.
- Require commercial livestock operations to be located in agricultural zones and new farm buildings to have long setbacks from neighboring properties.
- Conduct a build-out scenario showing the number of nonfarm dwellings that could be

Table 13-8
Sample Goals and Objectives for Farmland and the Farming Industry in the Comprehensive Plan

Natural Resources	
Goal	To encourage the sustainable use of valuable agricultural land while maintaining environmental quality.
Objective	Promote the development and use of soil and water conservation plans and practices on agricultural land.
Objective	Coordinate with state governments on right-to-farm laws, agricultural districts, and use- value property tax assessment.
Economic Base	
Goal	To promote the development of individual farming businesses and the growth of agriculture as a local industry.
Objective	Revise the zoning ordinance to allow farm stands on farms and bed-and-breakfast operations. Pursue funding for the creation of farmer's markets in nearby cities and villages.
Land Use	
Goal	To avoid conflicts between farm operations and nonfarm development.
Objective	Use the zoning ordinance to separate areas designated for future growth from commercial agricultural areas.

built in farming areas under the current zoning.

- Explore local, state, federal, and private land trust funding for preserving valuable agricultural lands.

Zoning Ordinance

Agricultural zoning is a widely used technique for protecting farmland. The purposes of agricultural zoning are to protect high-quality soils, to separate conflicting farm and nonfarm land uses, to slow the conversion of farmland to other uses, and to prevent the fragmentation of the farmland base into parcels too small to farm.

It is important to differentiate between effective agricultural zoning that protects farmland from development and weak agricultural zoning that allows numerous nonfarm residences. Many communities employ what they call agricultural-residential or rural zoning; but typically these zones have 1- or 2-acre minimum lot sizes that fragment the land base, permit many new homes in the

countryside, and raise land prices. These zones are really rural residential zones that will eventually lose most of the farms. The State of Oregon has addressed the demand for rural residences by allowing counties to designate rural residential zones with 3- to 5-acre minimum lot sizes on lower quality soils away from commercial farming areas. Some other local governments allow the clustering of houses and the retention of some open space, including farmland, in an attempt to maintain rural character (see Chapter 19). However, clustering cannot protect commercial farm operations.

Effective agricultural zoning regulations strictly control:

- the land uses allowed in the zone;
- the number and size of new farm parcels;
- the number, size, and siting of nonfarm parcels allowed; and
- setbacks for farm buildings from property lines.

Outright permitted uses should include farm buildings and structures (but not large, confined

SIDEBAR 13-2

Agricultural Economic Development

Most local governments overlook the potential of agricultural-related economic development. More jobs are created in processing and transporting farm products than on the farm, and there is considerable potential for linking farmers directly with consumers. Some possibilities include:

- community-supported agriculture in which non-farmers buy shares in what a farmer produces
- farm markets and stands, and U-pick operations
- farm festivals and farm vacations at bed-and-breakfast operations
- wineries
- organic produce
- local value-added food manufacturing, such as bakeries
- direct delivery of milk
- greenhouse produce

The more profitable farming is, the more likely farmland will stay in production. Local zoning ordinances and land development and subdivision regulations should balance support for these enterprises with standards to ensure that they are operated in environmentally friendly ways.

---

animal feeding operations (CAFOs)) and farm houses that will not be subdivided off the farm. A few California counties use exclusive farm zones in which only farm-related development is allowed. Conditional use review should apply to large projects such as airports, landfills, or CAFOs. A thorny issue for many local governments is whether to allow golf courses in agricultural zones. Golf course developments typically bring additional residential development. At a minimum, golf courses should be allowed only as conditional uses, and probably not at all in agricultural areas where livestock are prevalent.

There are three main types of agricultural zoning:

1. large minimum lot size;
2. fixed area ratio; and
3. sliding scale.

Several major agricultural counties in California and the Midwest employ minimum lot sizes of 40 acres or more. Oregon has required all of its counties with commercial farming operations to zone farmland for minimum lot sizes of at least 40 acres and as large as 320 acres. These large lot sizes discourage nonfarm buyers and help to maintain a critical mass of farmland to support farm-related supply, processing, and transportation businesses. Counties and communities that use minimum lot sizes of 5 or 10 acres do not protect commercial agriculture, but instead cause more land to be taken out of farming than is necessary, and run the risk of having the zoning invalidated by the courts as an "exclusionary" form of residential zoning.

Fixed-area ratio zoning is density-based, such as one dwelling per 25 acres with the dwelling sited on a lot of no more than 2 acres. In this case, if a landowner owned 125 acres, the landowner would be allowed to subdivide five 2-acre building lots, and would retain 115 acres for the farm operation. Fixed-area ratio zoning is used effectively in many townships in Lancaster County, Pennsylvania. It has an advantage over the minimum lot size approach in that it maintains larger farm parcel sizes.

Sliding scale agricultural zoning permits nonfarm dwellings based on the sizes of existing parcels and not on a fixed ratio. For example, a sliding scale might allow one additional dwelling on parcels of 2 to 25 acres, another dwelling on 25.1 to 60 acres, another dwelling on 60.1 to 100 acres, and another dwelling on farms above 100 acres. In this case, the sliding scale limits the total number of new nonfarm dwellings subdivided from a farm above 100 acres to no more than four.

Siting standards should require that nonfarm residences be sited on lower quality soils and in locations where they will not conflict with neighboring farm operations.

Sliding scale zoning tends to be used in areas where land has already been fragmented into fairly small parcels. While sliding scale zoning may be more politically acceptable than large-lot zoning, it may be seen to unfairly benefit rural lot owners over large farm owners.

With fixed area and sliding scale zoning, local governments must set up a system to keep track of the nonfarm lots created and the number of remaining nonfarm lots that can be subdivided off the farm. This tracking system can be done on computer and cross-referenced with notes on subdivision plans.

Setbacks for farm buildings from property lines and for nonfarm residences from property lines are both important for limiting conflicts between neighbors. Setbacks can vary from a few hundred feet to a quarter of a mile for farm buildings; the longer setback is recommended for CAFOs that produce large amounts of manure and odors. Setbacks for nonfarm residences should be at least 100 feet, and screening in the form of trees, shrubs, and earth berms is recommended to intercept dust, odors, and noise from neighboring farm operations.

People who are contemplating a move into an agricultural area should be forewarned about what a working farm landscape means. Some local governments have added a nuisance disclaimer to the agricultural zoning ordinance, such as:

> "All lands within the Agricultural Zone are located in an area where land is used for commercial agricultural production. Owners, residents, and other users of this property or neighboring property may be subjected to inconvenience, discomfort, and the possibility of injury to property and health arising from normal and accepted agricultural practices and operations, including but not limited to, noise, odors, dust, the operation of machinery of any kind, including aircraft, the storage and disposal of manure, the application of fertilizers, soil amendments, herbi-

cides, and pesticides. Owners, occupants, and users of this property should be prepared to accept such inconveniences, discomfort, and possibility of injury from normal agricultural operations, and are hereby put on official notice that the state 'Right to Farm Law' may bar them from obtaining a legal judgment against such normal agricultural operations." (Warwick Township, Lancaster County, Pennsylvania).

Some farmers oppose agricultural zoning because they fear it restricts their ability to sell land for development. However, agricultural zoning provides commercial farmers with a stable land base and a minimum of intrusion of nonfarm development. Moreover, agricultural zoning is critical to the success of PDR and TDR programs. Once a farmer has sold development rights, the farmer does not want to see dozens of new houses built next door. Many local government officials are concerned about potential legal challenges based on 5th Amendment "takings" if they "downzone" land to agricultural use. However, agricultural zoning is legal and defensible if it is tied to the goals, objectives, inventory, and analysis of the comprehensive plan, furthers a public purpose, is reasonable, and does not remove all economic use of the property.

A Note on Rezonings and the Land Evaluation and Site Assessment System

Ruling on requests to rezone farmland to a nonfarm use is often difficult for local governing bodies. The LESA system was developed by the NRCS in 1983 to help local communities identify lower quality farmland for future development and to protect highly productive farmland with long-term economic viability on a case-by-case basis. The LESA system consists of two parts:

1. a land evaluation rating of the quality of land for farming; and
2. a site assessment rating of the surrounding economic, social, and geographic features that measure development pressures on the farm and that indicate farm viability.

Table 13-9
Determining the Land Evaluation Score Based on Soil Productivity

Soil Class	Corn Yield in Bushels Per Acre for Soil Class Divided by the Highest Soil Class Yield	Ratio	Times 100	Land Evaluation Rating
I	150/150	1.00	100	100
II	130/150	0.87	100	87
III	110/150	0.73	100	73
IV	100/150	0.67	100	67
V	70/150	0.47	100	47
VI	50/150	0.33	100	33
VII	45/150	0.30	100	30
VIII	0/150	0.00	100	0

Sample 300-acre farm has 80 acres of Class I soils, 180 acres of Class II soils, and 40 acres of Class III soils

80 acres × 100 rating = 8,000
180 acres × 87 rating = 15,660
40 acres × 75 rating = 3,000
26,660

26,660 points divided by 300 acres = 88.81 Land Evaluation Score

Both the land evaluation and the site assessment ratings include several factors and point scores (see Tables 13-9 and 13-10). When the points for each factor are added up, they produce a total score for a farm. This total is then compared to a threshold level. If the total points are below the threshold, development tends to be appropriate; if the total points are above the threshold, the land should remain in farm use.

Information for the land evaluation process is available from a county soil survey. Land capability ratings indicate potential for crops, such as the yield of corn in bushels per acre. Information for the site assessment rating can be gathered from U.S. Geological Survey quad maps, the current land use map of the comprehensive plan, the zoning map, a map of local sewer and water lines, and the county conservation district and county extension office.

The site assessment score is then added to the land evaluation score to give an overall score for the property (251.81 in Table 13-10). The planning commission or elected officials must then set a threshold level of points to help decide whether the property should be protected or developed. The threshold in Table 13-10 is 175 points. The farm scored 251.81 points, indicating a valuable property for farming that should not be developed.

The LESA system has the advantages of being objective, numerically based and flexible. There is often some trial and error involved in setting the point scores and weights, however. Especially important is how farmland quality (land evaluation) is weighted against development potential (site assessment). The original NRCS handbook weighted farmland quality one-third of the total

Table 13-10
Land Evaluation and Site Assessment System for Sample 300-Acre Farm

	Site Assessment Factors	Weight Assigned	Sample Farm Points	Total of Points Times Weight Assigned	Maximum Possible Points
1.	Percentage of land in agriculture within 1.5 mile radius	20.0	9	18.0	20
2.	Percentage of land in agriculture adjacent to farm site	1.5	8	12.0	15
3.	Percentage of farm site in agriculture	1.5	9	13.5	15
4.	Percentage of farm site zoned for agriculture	2.0	10	20.0	20
5.	Distance from city or village	1.5	8	12.0	15
6.	Distance to public sewer or water	1.5	5	7.5	15
7.	Size of farm vs. average farm size in county	2.5	8	20.0	25
8.	Road frontage of site	1.5	8	12.0	15
9.	Farm support services available	1.5	8	12.0	15
10.	Historic, cultural, and environmental features on farm site	1.0	6	6.0	15
11.	Consistency with county plan	1.0	15	15.0	15
12.	Consistency with municipal plan	1.0	15	15.0	15

Site Assessment Subtotal	163.0	200 Maximum
Land Evaluation Subtotal	88.81	100 Maximum
Total Points Possible		300 Maximum
Threshold Points for Development		175 or below
Total Actual Points		251.81
Recommendation: Do not rezone farm to nonfarm uses		

Source: Adapted from the *National Agricultural Land Evaluation and Site Assessment Handbook*, U.S. Department of Agriculture (1983); Daniels and Bowers, *Holding Our Ground* (1997), p. 79

potential 300 points and development potential two-thirds. However, local officials could put a heavier weighting on farmland quality, such as 150 points out of 300 total points, to balance the protection of high-quality soils against other factors. Since 1983, many communities have modified the LESA system by adding or removing factors and weightings to use the system in ranking applications for the purchase of development rights, evaluating rezoning proposals, and compiling an inventory of viable farmland in the comprehensive plan.

Subdivision Regulations

There are two types of development projects that affect agricultural areas:

1. farm-related buildings; and

2. the subdivision and development of house lots and commercial and industrial sites.

Farm-related buildings most often involve worker housing; the construction or expansion of barns and confinement buildings for livestock; and the construction of machinery sheds, silos, feed bunkers, greenhouses, and manure storage facilities. Some types of farm-related buildings are treated as accessory uses and do not involve a subdivision review.

Many states do not allow local governments to directly regulate farm-related buildings. Still, the construction of animal confinement structures and manure storage facilities may have implications for stormwater management and groundwater and surface water quality, and should be reviewed according to the local land development regulations.

An environmental impact assessment (EIA) is appropriate for the proposed construction or significant expansion of a CAFO (see Appendix). Similarly, an EIA should be done for any proposed major residential subdivisions in farming areas. At a minimum, the subdivision ordinance can require buffering berms and vegetation between residences and commercial farm operations.

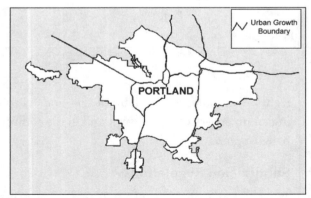

13-3 The Metropolitan Service District growth boundary of greater Portland, Oregon.

Source: Portland Metro

Capital Improvements Program

Communities should use the capital improvements program (CIP) to direct growth and development away from commercial farming areas. Major roads, schools, and extensions of sewer and water systems can be kept out of farming areas—especially land zoned for agriculture and agricultural districts—in order to discourage intensive residential and commercial development.

Urban and Village Growth Boundaries

An important element in protecting farmland is accommodating development in a compact style that minimizes sprawl. Perhaps the single best technique for promoting compact development is the Urban Growth Boundary and its smaller variation, the Village Growth Boundary. A growth boundary is intended to separate land designated for growth and development from land identified for rural and resource uses. A growth boundary is based on an agreement between a city and county or city and surrounding townships. The agreement designates a boundary line outside a city or village that includes enough buildable land within the boundary to support development over the next 10 to 20 years, based on population projections and land use needs to support that population (see Figure 13-3). The agreement stipulates that urban services, especially sewer and water lines, will not be extended beyond the growth boundary. Thus, the CIP is crucial to keeping infrastructure within the growth boundary. The boundary may be reviewed for needed changes every five years or so.

Outside the boundary, the land should be zoned at very low densities, such as for farming or forestry. Oregon cities and counties have done just that. Otherwise, if rural zoning allows a house every acre or two, residential development will simply jump over the growth boundary and sprawl across the countryside. Inside the boundary, moderate to high densities should be allowed in order to create compact developments.

America's first growth boundary was established by the City of Lexington and Fayette County, Kentucky, in the 1950s. In the 1970s, the State of Oregon mandated that its 36 counties and 236 cities agree on growth boundaries. In the 1990s, 22 growth boundaries were voluntarily created in Lancaster County, Pennsylvania (see Figure 13-4). Also in the 1990s, a dozen cities in northern California voted to adopt 20-year growth boundaries. By 2000, nearly 80 cities around the nation had adopted formal growth boundaries or urban service areas that have much the same effect on limiting sprawl and the extension of public services (Burby *et al.* 2001, 475-490).

Transfer of Development Rights

TDR is another method local governments can use to protect farmland yet provide the landowner with financial compensation. TDR is a way to move development potential from one parcel of land to another. By contrast, PDR results in the retirement of development potential.

A municipal or county government creates a market in TDRs through the comprehensive planning process, and particularly through careful

13-4 Urban growth boundary separating residential development and farmland in Manheim Township, Lancaster County, Pennsylvania.

Source: Katherine Daniels

zoning and location of infrastructure. The local government first identifies, maps, and zones areas for long-term protection called "sending" areas. The local government then issues development rights "credits" to landowners in the sending areas. Next, the government identifies, maps, and zones "receiving" areas that are suitable for development, and requires developers who want to build at increased densities in the receiving area to first purchase development rights credits from landowners in the sending areas. The prices of development rights are determined through negotiations between developers and landowners, just as in a private market.

In order for the TDR market to operate effectively, the number of development rights credits that the local government gives to landowners in the sending area must correlate closely with the increased development potential the government allows on parcels in the receiving areas. The increased development potential must be great enough to motivate developers to purchase TDRs. Generally, densities within receiving areas must be allowed to increase by one to two units per acre to make TDRs work.

More than 100 counties and municipalities have adopted TDR programs to protect farm and forestlands, scenic areas, historic properties, and wetlands (Pruetz 1997). TDRs enable local governments to do the following:

- Increase density in designated growth areas to make full use of public infrastructure and minimize sprawl.
- Let private developers pay landowners for TDRs, so that public money is not needed. This means that a TDR program is cheaper for taxpayers than a PDR program.
- Compensate landowners for restrictions placed on their land, thus avoiding the takings issue of the 5th Amendment.
- Preserve over time a significant amount of land. At the same time, channel new development into growth areas. This can help the

local government achieve a balanced growth strategy.

TDRs work best in places where working landscapes and natural areas are clearly separated from existing and planned development areas. This enables the creation of distinct sending and receiving zones. However, there also must be an active real estate market and a growing population to ensure that developers are willing to purchase TDRs and to build more intensively in the receiving areas. TDRs do not work well in rural areas with little development pressure; they work best in communities with receiving areas that are served by public sewer and water.

There are two major types of TDR programs. Mandatory programs have dual zones: a separate sending area and a separate receiving area. Mandatory TDRs depend on downzoning to at most one dwelling per 20 acres in the sending area and bonus zoning in the receiving area to create landowner incentives to sell TDRs and developer incentives to buy TDRs. Voluntary programs involve a single zone for both sending and receiving TDRs. In the single zone, landowners have the choice between developing some or all of their land—usually according to fairly permissive zoning of between 2- and 5-acre minimum lot sizes, or selling some or all of the development rights to other landowners or developers. The single-zone TDR program can lead to a large number of rural residences amid farming areas. Transfers within a single zone are more of a limited development technique that preserves some open space. The mandatory, dual-zone approach is clearly preferable for managing growth and protecting important farmland.

Montgomery County, Maryland—a suburban area north of Washington, D.C.—has operated the nation's most successful TDR program to preserve farmland. Since 1982, the county has preserved over 42,000 acres in more than 6,000 transactions. The county first created a 90,000-acre sending area by downzoning the land from one dwelling unit per 5 acres to one dwelling unit per 25 acres. The county then issued landowners one transferable development rights credit for every 5 acres of land they owned. At the same time, the county designated receiving areas in which developers could build one extra dwelling unit per acre by purchasing one transferable development rights credit. Initial TDR prices in Montgomery County were about $3,000 per TDR credit; more recently, the average is between $50,000 and $60,000 per TDR credit (Johnston and Madison 1997, 370).

When TDRs are transferred from a property in the sending area, a permanent conservation easement is placed on the deed, restricting development to agricultural and open space uses. However, a landowner need not sell all TDRs. Some can be retained to develop the land in the sending area at the allowed zoning.

TDR programs have not enjoyed as much popularity as PDR programs because of the complexity in establishing well-defined sending and receiving areas. In receiving areas, residents may oppose having the density of development increase. Landowners may be reluctant to have their property placed in a sending area because of the uncertainty of the market value of their TDRs. However, a TDR program can be used together with a PDR program, as Montgomery County, Maryland, has done since the early 1990s. Farmers can decide whether to sell development rights to developers in the form of TDRs or to the county government as PDRs.

What to Look for in a Development Review

A proposed development should be evaluated according to the current comprehensive plan, zoning ordinance, subdivision and land development regulations, CIP, and any other relevant ordinances. The planning commission should ask about the size, location, and type of any proposed farm structures (see Table 13-11). Especially if the development involves a CAFO, the commission should investigate whether the proposed project

Table 13-11
A Checklist of Farm-Related and Nonfarm Development Issues in a Development Review

1.	What are the size, location, and land uses of the proposed development?
2.	Is the proposed development a farm-related development or a nonfarm development that involves farmland?
3.	Is the proposed development allowed in the particular zone?
4.	Are setbacks and buffers from property lines met?
5.	What are the land uses on the adjacent properties?
6.	Have nonfarm dwellings been sited on the least productive soils and away from active farming?
7.	How will sewer and water service be provided?
8.	For confined animal feeding operations, how will manure be managed? How will potential water quality impacts be mitigated?
9.	Has the developer obtained any necessary state or federal permits?

could create problems for neighbors. If the answer is yes, a determination must be made about whether these problems can be remedied through the design of the project. If the proposed project involves the construction or expansion of livestock facilities, the planning commission should ask how the manure will be handled. If the expansion will qualify the farm as a CAFO, the landowner will be required to draft a "nutrient" (manure) management plan and obtain a permit from the state environmental agency. The planning commission should also require a stormwater management system for any proposed CAFO.

Nonfarm development proposals in farming areas are common. The size, type, and location of these proposals are important to consider. Proposed nonfarm developments should be checked for proper setbacks from property lines and how sewage and water will be provided. The extension of sewer and water lines into farming areas should be discouraged, as this infrastructure will only increase development pressure on nearby farms.

Finally, the planning commission should determine if any state or federal funds or approvals are involved in the development project. In some states, governors have issued Executive Orders requiring state agencies to minimize the conver-

sion of prime farmland. Likewise, the federal Farmland Protection Policy Act of 1981 called for the USDA to review proposed federal projects that could result in the conversion of prime farmland. These projects may also be subject to review under the National Environmental Policy Act environmental impact statement process.

CASE STUDY

CASE STUDY 13-1
Confined Animal Feeding Operations

One of the most emotional environmental issues that has emerged in the working landscape over the past 20 years is CAFOs. The economics of livestock and dairy farming have resulted in lower profit margins per animal or gallon of milk. Farmers have responded by increasing the size of herds or going out of business. For example, nationwide between 1993 and 1998, the number of farms raising 500 or fewer hogs decreased by 104,000, while the number of farms producing more than 2,000 hogs grew by more than 2,300 (Purdy 1999, 29).

CAFOs are defined as having 1,000 or more animal units, with a unit equal to 1,000 pounds. This translates to at least 1,000 head of cattle, 2,500 hogs, or 30,000 chickens. These large complexes can produce as much waste as a small city, yet they are not required to have wastewater treatment plants. Instead, the manure is most often stored in lagoons until it can be pumped out and spread on farmland, usually two or three times a year. However, the volume of manure can easily exceed the ability of the land to absorb the nutrients for crops. Rainfall can wash manure off fields into groundwater and surface water. Burst lagoons caused large fish kills in North Carolina in the mid-1990s. Torrential rains from Hurricane Floyd flooded dozens of hog manure lagoons in North Carolina in 1999, contaminating water supplies and causing enormous clean-up problems.

The 1972 Clean Water Act exempted nonpoint sources of pollution, such as runoff from farm fields, from the federal National Pollutant Discharge Elimination System (NPDES) permit program. Since then, livestock farming has changed dramatically, especially in the size of the operations. Many livestock farms raise thousands of cattle or hogs, or millions of chickens, each year.

In 1994, the U.S. Second Circuit Court of Appeals ruled that large farms are point sources of pollution under the 1972 Clean Water Act and must obtain an NPDES discharge permit (*Concerned Area Citizens for the Environment v. Southview Farms* 34 F.3d 14 (2d Cir 1994)). The defendant in the case, Southview Farms, a large dairy operation in western New York, had a manure lagoon with a capacity of 6 million gallons. The spreading of the manure from the lagoon resulted in the pollution of neighboring wells and streams. In 2002, the EPA began requiring CAFOs to apply for an NPDES permit, draft and implement a manure management plan, and submit an annual report. Nationwide, about 15,500 farms will be affected (U.S. EPA 2002). CAFO operators can apply for EQIP funding from the federal government to improve their conservation and nutrient management practices.

Some local governments have moved to limit the size or location of livestock operations. Rice County, Minnesota, limits the size of feedlots to 750 animal units. A variance could allow a maximum of 1,500 units on a farm (Daniels 1999, 249). Elkhart County, Indiana, took a different approach by establishing three agricultural zones; two allow CAFOs and one does not. In Illinois, new large livestock operations may face setback requirements of up to a half a mile from the nearest residence. Increasingly, the burden will be on livestock farmers rather than nonfarmers to be good neighbors.

14

Planning for Sustainable Working Landscapes: Forestry

The forests are the "lungs" of our land, purifying our air and giving fresh strength to our people.

FRANKLIN D. ROOSEVELT (LITTLE 1997, 15)

Harvests cannot exceed growth if forests are to continue providing healthy fish and wildlife habitats, clean and pure drinking water, and scenic beauty.

MIKE DOMBECK, FORMER HEAD,
U.S. FOREST SERVICE (USFS) (JEHL 2000, A24)

Forests are highly valuable renewable resources and diversified ecosystems that provide a variety of environmental services in addition to paper and wood products. Most of America's water supplies begin as rain and snowmelt runoff from forests. Forests have a great ability to absorb rain and snowmelt, and thus protect watersheds by limiting flooding and filtering runoff. Trees control soil erosion and sedimentation in rivers and streams by holding soils in their root system and soaking up precipitation. Trees serve as carbon sinks by taking in carbon dioxide and releasing oxygen, thus mitigating global warming. Trees also filter air pollution, intercepting dust and soot as well as ozone and carbon monoxide from cars and industry. It would cost billions of dollars nationwide for machines to filter this much air. Trees moderate temperatures by providing shade and windbreaks. Forests provide crucial wildlife habitat and offer a range of recreational experiences, from hunting to hiking. Timber harvesting is an impor-

tant part of the working landscape in many rural communities and some suburbanizing areas.

A forest is defined as land that has at least 10% of its area in trees (Smith *et al.* 2001). More than 740 million acres—about one-third of the entire United States—is covered in forests (U.S. Department of Agriculture (USDA), USFS, 2001) (see Figure 14-1). About one-third of these forests are publicly owned as state forests, national forests, national parks, public parks, and Bureau of Land Management (BLM) lands, mainly in the western states and Alaska (see Figure 14-2). There are about 484 million acres of privately owned forests in the lower 48 states. Most of these forests are concentrated in the Midwest, East, and South (see Table 14-1).

Old-growth forests are climax ecosystems that include mature trees that have never been harvested. Old growth generally produces the most board feet per harvested tree and is highly prized by timber companies. However, only 5% of the nation's original old-growth forests remain (Little 1997, 132). Old-growth forests cannot be viewed as renewable resources, as they cannot be replaced within a few decades. The old growth that remains is primarily in the Pacific Northwest, northern California, and Alaska. Second- or third-growth forests grow on land that has been cut over once or twice already. These trees are typically smaller than old-growth trees. Commercial timber companies also plant seeds and sprouts to

Table 14-1
Forestland in the Lower 48 United States by Region and Ownership (2000)
(in millions of acres)

Region	Private	National Forest	Other Public Forest	Total
North	129	13	22	164
South	201	15	4	220
Rocky Mountains	38	91	14	143
Pacific Coast	116	51	52	219
Total Acres	484	170	92	746

Note: There are about 22 million acres of national forest in Alaska, or a total of 192 million acres of national forest nationwide.

Source: U.S. Bureau of the Census (2003)

reforest land, and to create pine plantations like crops in rows, usually in the Southeast.

PRESSURES ON FORESTS

Pressures on forests come from several directions. First, the demand for wood and virgin paper products is likely to continue to grow, despite increases in recycling. The volume of timber products consumed rose from about 12.5 billion cubic feet in 1976 to almost 17 billion cubic feet in 2000 (U.S. Bureau of the Census 2003, 543). New homes contain an average of 10,000 board feet of lumber and are being built at a rate of more than 1.5 million a year. Meanwhile, the paperless office that computers and the Information Age were supposed to create has yet to become a reality. In 1997, each American used an average of 335 kilograms of paper and paperboard, and accounted for about 30% of world consumption of these products (Abramovitz and Mattoon 2000, 102).

Second, there is a growing demand for wilderness areas, wildlife habitats, and recreation activities in the national forests that compete with the use of these lands for timber production. In 1980, about 15% of the nation's timber came from national forests, mainly in the Pacific Northwest. In 1994, the Northwest Forest Plan reduced harvests in the national forests in Oregon and Washington to comply with a court order to protect the

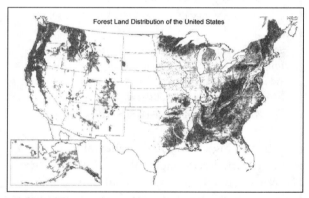

14-1   Forest cover of the United States.

Source: U.S. Forest Service

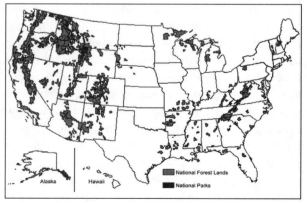

14-2   National forests of the United States.

Source: U.S. Forest Service

rare and endangered northern spotted owl. As of 2000, national forests accounted for less than 5% of the nation's timber production (Jehl 2000, A24). In addition, in 2001, President Clinton designated 58.5 million acres of national forests as roadless areas and off limits to logging. President George W. Bush has tried to modify the Clinton rule to allow for case-by-case amendments of the rules on roadless areas and the timber harvest ban.

Third, metropolitan areas will continue to expand into the countryside, resulting in the conversion of woodlands to housing sites, shopping malls, and office parks. According to the National Resources Inventory, from 1992 to 1997, more than 6 million acres of woodland were cleared for building sites, mainly in metropolitan areas (Natural Resources Conservation Service (NRCS) 2001). In 1973, roughly 37% of greater Washington, D.C., was forested; however, in 1997 trees covered only 13% of the region (*U.S. News and World Report* 1999, 48, 50). The National Audubon Society estimated that in the late 1990s, an average of 50 acres of forests were cut down every day in greater Atlanta (Montaigne 2000, 60). American Forests, a tree conservation organization, used satellite Landsat images and Geographic Information System (GIS) maps to show that, from 1962 to 1998, land in the Puget Sound area of Washington State with less than 20% tree coverage increased from 25% to 57%, and land with more than 50% coverage fell from 42% to 27% (*ibid.*). Moreover, few cities or suburbs have restrictions on tree cutting or requirements for the planting or replacement of trees in their subdivision regulations.

Many cities have become "heat islands." Their temperatures rise during the day and stay warmer at night because of the huge amount of paved surface and the lack of tree cover. The warmer the temperature, the more air conditioning is used. Suburbs are now starting to become heat islands as well. In the 13-county Atlanta metropolitan area from 1973 to 1998, nearly 350,000 acres of for-est were cleared—most often for development—raising city and surrounding area temperatures (William and Bruce 1999).

Fourth, pressures to develop forestland for vacation homes, retirement homes, resorts, or rural residences exist in some rural areas. As with farmland, millions of acres of privately owned forestland are going to change hands in the first 20 years of the 21st century. Many owners of family-held industrial forests and nonindustrial forests are nearing retirement age or have already retired. Decisions about transferring land within the family or selling the land for development will have important consequences for local communities. The Pacific Forest Trust has estimated that about 9 million acres, or one-fourth of the private forests in the Pacific Northwest, are at risk of conversion to nonforest uses (Pacific Forest Trust 1998, 3).

Major timber companies are primarily interested in earning a profit for their shareholders. These companies usually have a real estate development division that keeps a close eye on the nonforest value of company holdings. If the price of land rises above what the land is worth for producing wood and paper, selling to a developer will be an attractive option. For example, in the late 1990s, the St. Joe Paper Company decided to develop 800,000 acres of forestland it owns in the Florida Panhandle; this area features a growing number of vacation homes but also has an abundance and diversity of wildlife. The sale of 500,000 acres in the late 1980s by a single timber company in the northern forest of Vermont, New Hampshire, New York, and Maine raised public concern that huge areas could be opened up to second-home development. This concern sparked the creation of the federal Forest Legacy Program (see Case Study 14-1, below).

The USFS has noted that "[p]arcelization of private ownerships will continue to be a management challenge with landscape-level planning becoming more difficult and habitat associated with edge effects becoming more plentiful because of increased fragmentation of forest cover" (USDA, USFS 2000a, 2). When forestland is subdivided into residential and recreational lots, surrounding land values increase, further reducing the attractiveness of harvesting timber over a large area. As more lots are created, there are more likely to be conflicts between timberland managers and neighbors over noise, herbicides, pesticides, and slashburn. As more people move to forested areas, the risk of forest fires rises as well. Finally, as more forestland is converted to housing sites, a critical mass of available timber may be lost, making harvesting uneconomic and resulting in the closure of local mills.

Fifth, forests are vulnerable to insects, diseases, and acid deposition in the form of acid rain, snow, and fog. A 1993 USFS report found that the volume of tree deaths increased by 24% between 1986 and 1991, "in all regions, on all ownerships, and for both hardwoods and softwoods" (Powell *et al.* 1993, 2). In the Smoky Mountains, nearly all of the Fraser fir trees have been damaged by acid rain and the balsam wooly adelgid, a type of moth (Bryson 1999, 93; Little 1997, 39). The American chestnut was virtually wiped out between 1904 and the early 1930s by an Asian fungus. Many of the Red Spruce on Camel's Hump in Vermont have been harmed or killed by acid deposition, which leaches away soil nutrients (Little 1997, 20, 24). Ponderosa pine in southern California continue to suffer ozone injury from motor vehicle-generated smog (*ibid.*, 60). Since arriving in America in 1869, gypsy moths have stripped the leaves from about 60 million acres of trees in the East and Midwest, and continue to do significant damage (*ibid.*, 119). Finally, there is evidence that global warming is raising temperatures enabling non-native beetles to invade and destroy forests in Alaska (Egan 2002, 1).

Sixth, each year fires burn millions of acres of forest (see Chapter 12). Fires caused by human negligence and arson cause more damage than fires that occur naturally through lightning strikes. Forest fires are part of a natural forest cycle. Fires clear underbrush and return nutrients to the soil. However, the dominant federal and state forest management policies have been to suppress forest fires, even though these policies may in fact add to the build-up of undergrowth that will more readily ignite in dry years.

Seventh, competition from foreign timber can affect the economics of domestic forest production. Imports of lower priced foreign timber can undersell American-produced timber, causing some U.S. timber mills to fall idle and motivating some large timber owners to sell forestland for development.

Finally, certain forestry practices can reduce the value of forests in providing a variety of environmental services. Timber harvesting and the construction of logging roads, especially on steep slopes, can cause soil erosion and the siltation of rivers and streams, and can fragment and destroy wildlife habitat. The use of chemical herbicides and pesticides in forests can contaminate water supplies and harm humans and wildlife. The USFS has been criticized for continuing to allow large clear cutting in the national forests.

FOREST TYPES

There are two types of private forests: industrial and nonindustrial. Industrial forests are owned by timber companies, have access to lumber and paper mills, and are generally found in large, contiguous blocks. These managed forests are usually more productive, with a higher amount of wood per acre than nonindustrial forests. Industrial forestry requires a long-term investment in land, trees, mills, and equipment. Just as a local farming industry needs a critical mass of farms and farmland to sustain farm support businesses, the forest industry requires ownership of or access to a certain minimum number of harvestable trees in order to keep local lumber and paper mills operating. Newly planted commercial forests take from

20 to 40 years or more to reach harvestable size, depending on the species. The primary industrial forestry areas are the Pacific Northwest, northern California, the Alaskan coast, the upper Midwest, the Southeast, and the northern tier of New York, Vermont, New Hampshire, and Maine. The most productive forests are in the South and the Pacific Northwest.

There are nearly 10 million owners of private forestland in America, and most private forestlands are in parcels of less than 50 acres (Richardson 2000, 175). These nonindustrial forests are owned by rural residents, owners of second homes, farmers, and others. Nonindustrial forests made up slightly more than half of all private timberland in 1996, and produced 73% of all hardwood harvested that year (USDA, USFS 2001, 3). As part of the 1996 Farm Bill, Congress created the Forestry Incentives Program, managed by the NRCS, to improve management of nonindustrial private forests for future timber harvesting and environmental protection. The Forestry Incentives Program provides funds for tree planting and timber stand improvement.

Climate, soil, location, and elevation determine the location of forest types. Eastern hardwood forests make up just over half of all timberland in the lower 48 states. There are several kinds of eastern hardwood forests. The oak-hickory forest is the most common, found from southern New England throughout the South and into the Upper Midwest. These woods are often used to make furniture. Maple-beech-birch forests are the next most common, found mainly in the North Central and Northeast regions where they are known for their splendid fall colors. Oak, gum, and cypress forests are found exclusively in the South. Elm-ash-cottonwood forests are typically found on bottomlands in the North Central and Northeast regions. Aspen-birch forests take over after other species are harvested; these forests produce pulpwood and provide important habitat for deer.

Eastern softwood forests are the most important source of forest products in the South and Southeast, where longlash-slash and lobolly-short leaf pine forests are dominant. These pines are used for paper pulp, chip board, and some furniture. Spruce-fir and white-red-jack pine forests are found in the Northeast. Spruce-fir forests produce pulpwood for paper, and jack pine forests are harvested for saw logs.

Softwoods make up about 85% of the forests in the western states. Douglas fir, the most abundant and commercially important timber species, is prized as structural lumber. Ponderosa pine is a major source of lumber from the Rocky Mountains and the Southwest, and lodgepole pine is mostly found in the Rocky Mountains. Fir-spruce forests grow at medium to high elevations, particularly in California. Hemlock-sitka spruce forests are most common in the Coast Range of western Oregon and Washington and along the Alaskan coast. Western hardwoods consist mainly of three species: California oaks, aspens in the Rockies, and red alder in the Pacific Northwest.

FEDERAL FORESTLAND PROGRAMS

Managing the National Forests

The federal government has primarily influenced the use of the nation's forestlands through the management of the National Forest System. America's national forests contain about 192 million acres in 155 national forests in 39 states (see Figure 14-2). The large majority of national forestlands is located in the western states and Alaska. The national forests were created under the Organic Act of 1897, which defined the purposes of the forests as "securing favorable conditions for water flows and a continuous supply of timber." The planning and management of the national forests is authorized in three federal laws: the Multiple Use-Sustained Yield Act of 1960, the Forest and Rangeland Renewable Resource Act of 1974, and the National Forest Management Act of 1976.

The 1960 act set forth the concepts of multiple-use and sustained yield, which have since been the guiding principles for the management of the national forests. The act requires the use of national forests to be balanced among managed timber harvesting, recreation, wildlife habitat, wilderness, watershed protection, and soil conservation. By striking the right balance, forest managers may sustain the flow of wood products and recreational and environmental benefits indefinitely without exhausting the forest resources.

The Forest and Rangeland Renewable Resource Act of 1978 called for the USFS to make projections of timber resources and the demand for timber from the national forests. Since 1974, the USFS has published four reports on the condition of the nation's forests (USDA, USFS 2001). Amendments to the National Forest Management Act added requirements to the Renewable Resource Act for land and resource management plans (LRMPs) that indicate how the various uses of each forest will be balanced. These plans must include a regional element that balances timber harvests based on their productive capacities with a forest's ability to provide recreation, wildlife habitat, wilderness, and watershed protection. The LRMPs are used for identifying and evaluating proposed timber harvests. The National Forest Management Act also affirmed the legality of clear cutting on national forestlands.

Citizens have input into the LRMPs in determining planning objectives, inventorying the forest resources, assessing current management, identifying alternative management strategies, and selecting a management approach. After a management plan is approved by the USFS, citizens can participate in monitoring and evaluating the plan. Citizen participation is very important in areas such as the Oregon Coast Range, Idaho, and western Montana, where much of the local economy is dependent on the timber industry and forest recreation activities.

About half of the land area of national forests is authorized for logging, and the USFS has constructed more than 370,000 miles of logging roads to give private timber companies access to timber stands (Bryson 1999, 47). There are also hundreds of mines, oil and gas wells, condominiums, and 137 ski areas on national forestlands (*ibid.*, 46). By contrast, about 34 million acres, or 17% of national forestlands have been designated as wilderness areas where logging and development are not allowed.

The USFS has been criticized for favoring timber harvesting over recreation activities and soil, water, and wildlife conservation. Especially in the western states, the sale of federal timber to private timber companies is very important in keeping local mills operating. The USFS has also been criticized for subsidizing timber companies in the form of road construction and for selling timber harvest rights to private companies at well below the value of the timber. In fact, the USFS typically loses money on its timber harvest contracts, not even counting the investment it makes in logging roads (O'Toole 1997). According to the Wilderness Society, between 1989 and 1997 the USFS lost an average of $242 million a year, or a total of more than $2 billion (Bryson 1999, 48). If the USFS sold the harvesting rights at market value, considerably fewer trees would be harvested in the national forests.

The USFS does not pay property taxes to local governments on national forestlands within their jurisdiction. Instead, the USFS makes "payments-in-lieu-of–taxes," known as PILTS. The PILTS are based on the annual revenues produced from the harvesting of timber, grazing, or recreation uses. Often, the PILTs system creates an incentive for local communities to encourage timber harvesting. This is similar to local communities encouraging development to expand the property tax base. In both cases, there may be long-term negative environmental impacts.

Forestland Preservation

The federal government has had a very limited role in the protection of privately held forestland, but this role is increasing because of the mounting development pressures on private timberlands. In 1990, Congress enacted the Forest Legacy Program, which allowed the USFS to purchase permanent conservation easements on forestland, purchase forestland, or make grants to states for acquisitions of forestland or easements (see Case Study 14-1, below). To qualify for the Forest Legacy Program, a state forester must draft an assessment of need—identifying forestlands with important commercial timber or riparian or ecological values that are threatened by development—for approval by the USFS. A state must provide at least 25% of project costs. As of 2001, the Forest Legacy Program had resulted in the purchase of conservation easements on more than 200,000 acres in 15 states (Pacific Forest Trust 2001). The 2002 Farm Bill authorized another $60 million for the program.

STATE FORESTLAND PROGRAMS

State involvement in the management of private forestlands has mainly focused on forest practices acts and preferential taxation for forestlands.

State Forest Practices Acts

Private forests, like the national forests, often contain the headwaters of rivers and streams, and are the best land cover for minimizing stormwater runoff and soil erosion. Thus, careful management of private forests is important for maintaining water quality for drinking-water supplies and wildlife habitat. About three-quarters of the states have enacted forest practices laws to regulate the management of private forestland (Fischman 2002, 336). These laws are intended to ensure the regeneration of forests; to provide some environmental safeguards for soils, water, and wildlife; and to prevent nuisances that would harm neigh-

boring landowners or the general public. A timber harvest plan and permit are usually required before a harvest can occur. Most states regulate timber harvesting practices through required replanting of harvested sites, required disposal of slash, and road construction standards that minimize erosion and sedimentation in waterways. Some states have restrictions on logging on steep slopes and near streambanks, limits on clear cutting, and protection for important wildlife habitats and wetlands.

Forestry practices often raise heated debate because of the trade-off between harvesting methods and environmental damage. There are three general ways to harvest timber: clear cutting, selective cutting, and high grading. Clear cutting involves the removal of nearly all of the trees in a specific area. From an industry standpoint, this practice is attractive if the trees are of similar age and diameter. For instance, in the Southeast, pine trees are typically raised in a monoculture "plantation" on private land. The trees reach maturity at the same time and are harvested together. Clear cutting is necessary for some species, such as Douglas fir, that will not grow in the shade of other trees. However, clear cutting destroys wildlife habitat and scenic and recreational values, and creates downstream flooding and pollution problems. Runoff from clear-cut sites can lead to siltation of rivers and streams and destroy fish spawning grounds. Some state forest practices acts require harvesters to leave a screen of trees along public roads to mask, at least somewhat, the ugliness of the stumps and tangle of slash left behind by clear cutting. Similarly, a row or two of trees may be required to be left along a streambank to stabilize soils and prevent erosion.

Selective cutting makes sense in a forest where the trees have a mix of ages and "pole sizes" (diameters). Selective cutting is well suited to hardwoods (e.g., oak, ash, maple, and cherry) because individual trees are often valuable for making furniture.

Table 14-2
Riparian Management Areas for Logging in Oregon

Stream Type	Type F (Fish Use Stream)	Type D (Domestic Water Use Stream)	Type N (All Other Streams)
Large Stream Average annual flow of >10 cubic feet per second	100 feet	70 feet	70 feet
Medium Stream Average annual flow of >2 but <10 cubic feet per second	70 feet	50 feet	50 feet
Small Stream Average annual flow of 2 cubic feet per second or less	50 feet	20 feet	Specific Measures

Source: Oregon Department of Forestry (1994)

On the other hand, gaining access to and harvesting individual trees is usually more difficult and expensive than clear cutting. Selective cutting does not mean just taking the trees with the highest market value. In many cases, a forest stand needs to be thinned—not only of some mature trees, but of small, low-value trees as well. This selective cutting enables the remaining trees to grow faster, healthier, and straighter. Selective cutting is often associated with sustainable yield forestry and balancing timber harvesting with recreation, wildlife, and soil and water conservation. Selective cutting generally has much less impact on wildlife and the environment than clear cutting, especially on steeper slopes and near streams.

High grading is a form of selective cutting in which loggers harvest the best trees and leave the lower quality trees. This practice, though not as disruptive as clear cutting, can reduce the health of the forest and defeat the purpose of sustainable yield, especially in an even-aged forest. High grading can involve taking one species at a time, such as high-value oak, which diminishes the diversity of the remaining forest. High grading can also mean the cutting of all trees above a certain pole size.

High grading and clear cutting can be attractive to forest products companies because the market for wood tends to operate on boom and bust cycles. When market prices are high, cutting as many logs as possible looks like a good strategy.

Model State Forest Practices Laws

Some states have innovative forest practices laws. California requires landowners and loggers to file a timber harvest plan with the Department of Forestry. The department then forms a harvest plan review team and meets with members of the state Fish and Game Department and Water Quality Agency to discuss potential impacts. These meetings are open to the public, and the public can submit written comments to which the Department of Forestry must respond in writing. Finally, the California Environmental Quality Act—the state's version of the National Environmental Policy Act, also applies. The Department of Forestry must assess the cumulative impacts to the environment that the harvest plan might generate (Harris 1997, 184, 198).

The Oregon Forest Practices Act establishes specific riparian management area widths for streams of different sizes and uses (Oregon Revised Statutes Chapter 629) (see Table 14-2). Loggers must meet vegetation retention and water quality protection standards within riparian management areas.

The State of Maryland enacted a far-reaching forest conservation law in 1991. The primary pur-

SIDEBAR 14-1

Third-Party Certification: A Voluntary Approach to Sustainable Private Forest Management

The Forest Stewardship Council was created in 1993 to operate a third-party certification program to identify wood products that come from sustainably managed forests. Forest products companies may voluntarily cooperate with the certification program, which informs consumers about wood that has been produced in an environmentally responsible fashion. Consumers can put their money where their values are by purchasing wood products from certified forests. According to the council, at the beginning of 2000, there were 64 certified sustainable forests in the United States, covering nearly 4 million acres. A big breakthrough for forest certification was the decision by Home Depot, America's largest lumber retailer, to sell only lumber from certified forests, beginning in 2002. The cooperation of enlightened forest companies and enlightened wood products retailers shows that good forestry can also mean good business.

The Certified Forest Products Council and Scientific Certification Systems maintain lists of certified wood products suppliers for consumers to contact (see Contacts in the back of this book). SmartWood, a program of the Rainforest Alliance, certifies salvaged and recycled wood from buildings being torn down. This, in turn, helps to reduce the amount of wood send to landfills.

pose of the law is to minimize the loss of forestland to development, and thus limit the potential for runoff and silt entering the Chesapeake Bay watershed. The law defines a forest as 100 trees per acre with 50% or more of the trees with a diameter of 2 or more inches. The law applies to forestland on the site of any proposed public or private development of over 40,000 square feet. All Maryland counties, except two, were required to draft local forest conservation ordinances. The ordinances require that before development can occur, the landowner must:

- identify and delineate forest stands;
- have a forest management plan drafted by a professional forester, including measures for erosion and sedimentation control, the retention of as much existing forest as possible, and a plan for planting trees and shrubs for runoff control;
- draft a two-year maintenance and monitoring plan; and
- protect the forest through a conservation agreement or other long-term agreement

(e.g., a property tax reduction is available for landowners who enter into a 15-year forest conservation management agreement).

The law also allows for off-site mitigation, which may involve the planting of street trees in a nearby city or village or replanting a forest. Any new plantings must use native species, and new forests must include over- and understory trees and shrubs. The idea is to plant a forest, not a park. For timber harvests on more than 5,000 square feet of land, the landowner must have an erosion and sedimentation plan drafted by an approved forester, and best management practices approved by the local conservation district.

To date, most of the developments reviewed under the forest conservation ordinances have occurred in Montgomery, Prince Georges, and Charles Counties. Between 1992 and 1997, Montgomery and Prince Georges Counties retained and planted more acres of forest than were cleared for development. In Charles County, which is about 65% wooded, slightly more acres were cleared than retained or planted in trees. Maryland developers have said that they were receiving prices 10% to 15% above average for house lots next to forests and streambank forest buffers (U.S. Environmental Protection Agency 1998).

State Forestland Protection Programs

Because timber takes decades to reach maturity, forestland—even more than agricultural land—requires preferential property taxation to protect it from rising property taxes as well as encroaching development. Even with selective cutting practices, a forest may not yield a harvest every year. Commercial timberland normally sells for under $1,000 per acre, much less than what the land could be worth for residential sites, second homes, or resort areas. States use three approaches for the preferential taxation of forestland:

1. exempting timberland from property taxes for a certain length of time;
2. assessing the land at its use-value as timberland, not based on its "highest and best" use as potential residential or commercial property; and
3. combining use-value assessment with a yield tax on timber at the time it is harvested.

It makes sense to combine preferential taxation for forestland with forestry zoning to protect the forest from nonforest development, minimizing potential conflicts and property tax increases. Oregon, for instance, has required counties with commercial forestry operations to zone the land for very large minimum lot sizes of 40 to 160 acres. This discourages nonforestry buyers and helps to maintain a critical mass of forestlands to support commercial timbering. Forest landowners in Oregon's timber conservation zones may apply for use-value property taxation, and harvested forestlands must be restocked for use-value assessment to continue. The deferred taxes must be repaid if the land is sold for a nonforest use. Forest landowners in these zones are exempt from nuisance ordinances that would limit standard forest practices.

Fifteen states have purchased development rights to preserve working timberlands through the federal Forest Legacy Program. More often, states have occasionally purchased development rights to private forestland for watershed protection or wildlife habitat, usually through their department of natural resources or environmental conservation.

LAND TRUSTS AND THE PROTECTION OF FORESTLAND

Several land trusts have been active in acquiring conservation easements to timberland either through purchase or donations to protect wildlife habitats, drinking water supplies, and scenic and recreational sites, or even to ensure responsible harvesting of timber. The sale of easements by owners of family-held forests can provide cash and estate tax benefits to enable the transfer of land within the family to the next generation (see Chapter 13). The donation of an easement can provide income tax and estate tax benefits. In addition, landowners gain the satisfaction of knowing that their land will not be converted to nonforest development. A conservation easement on forestland may or may not permit commercial harvesting of timber. Conservation easements that do permit forestry usually require the landowner to prepare a forest management plan, which must be approved by the land trust or government agency holding the easement, before any timber harvesting can begin. It is recommended that a professional forester draft the management plan and oversee any harvests and road building, because these activities must comply with the conservation easement as well as state forest practices laws.

The Society for the Protection of New Hampshire Forests was founded in 1901 and has since helped to protect more than 1 million acres of New Hampshire forestlands through the purchase and donation of conservation easements and outright land purchases. The society also owns and man-

Forests and Carbon Sequestration

Carbon sequestration is the storage of carbon. Forests are well-known carbon sinks because they absorb carbon dioxide and release oxygen into the atmosphere, thus helping to regulate global warming. An acre of trees can absorb about 10 tons of carbon dioxide a year (Little 1997, 205). Selective cutting of forests can result in an annual net storage of carbon, whereas clear cutting creates a net carbon release into the atmosphere, contributing to global warming. The 1997 Kyoto Protocol of the United Nations Framework Convention on Climate Change, signed by 164 countries, but not the U.S., is intended to reduce greenhouse gases that contribute to global warming. The primary mechanism to achieve reductions is the establishment of an international trading system in carbon credits. This trading system is similar to the sulfur air pollution trading credits used in the United States (see Chapter 5). Carbon-generating businesses, such as energy, utility, and manufacturing companies, will need to buy carbon credits or significantly reduce their output of carbon. The purchase and protection of timberlands is one way that these businesses can help to reduce overall greenhouse gas emissions, especially carbon dioxide.

ages more than 30,000 acres in over 100 forest preserves. The Vermont Land Trust (VLT) holds conservation easements on more than 100,000 acres of forestland. The VLT has often joined with state agencies, private foundations, and other conservation groups to preserve large tracts of forestlands in northern Vermont (see Case Study 14-1, below).

The Pacific Forest Trust in Boonville, California, has preserved more than 25,000 acres through conservation easements in California, Oregon, and Washington, and has consulted on conservation practices on more than 750,000 acres (Pacific Forest Trust 1999, 2001). In its *Annual Report, 1998*, the trust described its forest stewardship principles:

"While the easements cover varied forest types and conservation objectives, all those lands will stay in family ownership and productive use for ranching, recreation, and timber harvest. Among the very significant natural resources protected is habitat for threatened and endangered species such as coho salmon, steelhead, marbled murrelet, northern goshawk, greater sandhill crane, and peregrine falcon. Valuable old-growth and riparian forests, wetlands, and streams are conserved. Second-growth forests will be managed for native biodiversity and sustainable production of forest products" (Pacific Forest Trust 1999, 3).

The Pacific Forest Trust has taken the lead in drafting conservation easements and advising forest landowners to include forest practices that will attract buyers of carbon credits to forestlands, as established under the 1997 Kyoto Protocol. Purchases of carbon credits will make sustainable forestry that much more profitable. In 2000, the Pacific Forest Trust completed its first sale of carbon credits to the Green Mountain Energy Company (Pacific Forest Trust 2000).

LOCAL PLANNING FOR FORESTLANDS

Forest areas can be an important part of a rural community's identity and economy. The value of forestry for timber production and environmental and recreational purposes should be identified. Growth and development should be directed away from high-priority forest areas. Trees are also important in urban and suburban areas where an urban forestry program of tree plantings and maintenance can benefit the urban environment.

Inventory

The inventory of forestlands should include information and GIS mapping on existing forest cover; watersheds; timber suitability ratings for soils; endangered or threatened plant or animal habitat; and existing industrial, nonindustrial, and public forest locations. Additional information should be provided identifying tree species and current forest practices. The value of timber production and the location of mills and any forest-related businesses in the community should be described.

The state department of forestry, cooperative extension service, state land grant university, and the NRCS can provide maps and information on forests. Private forest companies may also offer information.

Analysis

The analysis should use the future population projection of the comprehensive plan and Land and Water Suitability Analysis to evaluate the likely impacts of potential growth on the community's forestlands and local economy. The analysis should also suggest alternative scenarios to accommodate growth. Current forest practices and identified adverse environmental impacts should also be evaluated and approaches to mitigate them discussed. High-priority forestlands for timber, recreation, and environmental services should be identified for protection. Statewide, national, and international trends in timber production should be examined for ways in which they could affect the local forest economy and use of forestlands.

Goals and Objectives

The chief goal for forestlands should be to protect large contiguous blocks of land to maintain a critical mass of trees that will both keep existing mills in operation and provide continual environmental and recreational benefits. The Natural Resources, Economic Base, and Land Use sections of the comprehensive plan should provide objectives for limiting nonforest development and protecting the environment (see Table 14-3).

Action Strategy

The Action Strategy should present techniques and programs for achieving the forestland goals and objectives as well as a timetable. Forest protection benchmarks should be identified and

Table 14-3
Sample Goals and Objectives for Forest Resources in the Comprehensive Plan

Natural Resources	
Goal	To encourage the sustained yield management of forests for timber resources, recreational uses, and environmental services.
Objective	Monitor the impacts of timber operations on the environment, including water quality, noise levels, and important wildlife species habitats.
Economic Base	
Objective	Promote replanting and selective cutting practices to maintain the economic value of forest resources over time.
Land Use	
Objective	Keep commercial timber operations away from sensitive environmental areas, such as steep slopes, thin soils, watersheds for drinking water, and wetlands.
Objective	Separate areas designated for future growth from existing commercial timber sites.

progress toward those benchmarks evaluated in an annual report on the environment. Specific recommendations might include the following:

- Apply forest zoning to a critical mass of commercial timberland.
- Encourage forest owners to seek third-party certification that their timber is produced sustainably.
- Explore local, state, federal, and private land trust funding for preserving valuable forestland for wildlife habitat, watersheds, scenic and recreational uses as well as timber supplies.

Zoning Ordinance

Zoning can be an effective tool to protect commercial forestlands by separating working forests from potential conflicting residential and commercial land uses. Several counties in Oregon have created Timber Conservation zones for forestlands capable of producing 50 or more cubic feet per acre per year of Douglas fir, the main commercial species. Minimum lot sizes range from 40 to 160 acres in remote regions and where much of the land is owned by commercial timber companies. In addition to forestry, the Timber Conservation zones allow some commercial recreation, grazing of livestock, and a limited number of nonforestry residences in areas of lower soil productivity and away from commercial timberlands. There are about 13 million acres in Timber Conservation zones in Oregon, which cover about one-fifth of the entire state.

Some counties in California have created Timber Production Zones (TPZs), which designate lands for timber production and exclude all other uses. Landowners sign an agreement to keep the land in forest use and receive property tax reductions. A landowner may petition the county to remove land from the TPZ, but permission may be granted only after a public review; even then, the landowner must keep the land in forest use for another 10 years. TPZs have kept the price of for-

estland affordable for timber harvesting by discouraging nonforest buyers (Cromwell 1984, 158).

Some suburban communities have enacted ordinances banning the clear cutting of timber, citing loss of privacy with fewer trees, threats to drinking water supplies and wildlife habitats, increased flood damage, and reduced property values (Revkin 1997, B1). Others have prohibited clear cutting within buffer strips, along streams and public roads, or near sensitive wildlife habitats.

Subdivision Regulations

Forest-related activities will be subject to state laws regulating forest practices. Where state standards are weak and communities are not preempted from adopting their own forest protection standards, they may do so in the subdivision regulations. The subdivision ordinance can require buffering berms and vegetation between residences and commercial forest sites. Developers can be required to retain a certain percentage of trees of a certain size, to replace trees destroyed during construction, and to plant trees on site, particularly along roads, in parking lots, along streambanks and on steep slopes. Any tree ordinance should ensure that utility rights-of-way are kept free of trees.

Capital Improvements Program

Local planning officials should use the capital improvements program (CIP) to direct growth and development away from commercial forestlands and sensitive forest environments. Major roads, schools, and extensions of sewer and water systems should be directed away from such areas to discourage intensive residential and commercial development. Communities may elect to spend public funds to preserve forestlands for parks, trails, or working forests as part of the CIP.

What to Look for in a Development Review

A proposed harvest or development should be evaluated according to the current comprehensive plan, zoning ordinance, subdivision and land

Table 14-4
A Checklist of Forestry-Related and Nonforestry-Related Issues in a Development Review

1.	Does the zoning allow the proposed project? Are setbacks and buffers from property lines met?
2.	What is the area of tree cover on site? Are there areas of old growth or trees of more than 100 years old?
3.	What harvesting rates and practices are planned?
4.	Will new roads be built or existing roads widened? What measures will be taken to reduce erosion potential?
5.	What are the land uses on adjacent properties?
6.	What will be the impact on water quality and supply? How will these impacts be mitigated?
7.	What will be the impact on wildlife and recreation? How will this be mitigated?
8.	Are there planned buffer strips along streams, roads, or property lines? Is there planned woodland retention and replacement?
9.	Has the developer obtained any necessary state or federal permits?

development regulations, CIP, and any other applicable local laws. A planning commission should focus on the potential impacts of proposed timber-related development or proposed nonforestry development on both commercial forestry and the forest environment. For projects related to industrial forestry, the planning commission should focus on the potential environmental impacts (see Table 14-4). For proposed nonforestry developments, such as residential subdivisions, the main concern is the conversion of forestland next to active logging operations.

CASE STUDIES

Forestland protection requires cooperation from state, federal, and local governments and private land trusts as well as landowners who want to see their land remain available for timber harvesting and other purposes. Case Study 14-1 describes the efforts to maintain the forestland base in the northernmost tier of the Northeast. Case Study 14-2 illustrates the use of a Habitat Conservation Plan (HCP) under the Endangered Species Act (ESA) to enable forestry to continue, but with some areas set aside for habitat to support rare and endangered species. Case Study 14-3 illustrates the trade-offs between timber harvesting and protection of the spotted owl in the Pacific Northwest.

CASE STUDY 14-1
The Northern Forest Initiative

Note: This case study was originally developed for the National Governor's Association and is used by permission (see Daniels 2001).

In the early to mid-1980s, large tracts of forestland in remote areas of northern New York and New England were sold, potentially for second-home and commercial development. Local and state officials became alarmed and pressed Congress to initiate the Northern Forest Lands Study to assess the current conditions and future uses of the 26 million-acre region of forestland that stretches from the Adirondack Mountains of New York across northern Vermont, New Hampshire, and Maine. The region is larger than all of the national parks in the lower 48 states put together. About 80% of the land is privately owned, and most of the public land is in the Adirondack Mountains of New York.

Northeastern forestry operations have come under greater competition from operations in the southeastern U.S. as well as overseas. This competition has placed more pressure on the companies to sell or develop their land for nonforestry uses. Some 70 million people live within a day's drive of the northern forest region, providing a ready market for vacation and retirement homes. Still, in 2000, the region's forest industry supported nearly 250,000 jobs and an impressive $33 billion in economic activity.

The Northern Forest Study, published in 1994, emphasized the purchase of conservation easements to private forests as the best way to keep this land from being developed for nontimber uses. Even before the Northern Forest Study was completed, Congress passed the Forest Legacy Program in 1990 to give the USFS the authority and funding to purchase permanent conservation easements on forestland, purchase forestland, or make grants to states to purchase easements and forestlands. The northern forest became a major focus of the Forest Legacy Program in the 1990s. The federal government purchased 39,000 acres in the northern forest for $24 million, or about $600 an acre. At the same time, New York, Vermont, New Hampshire, and Maine appropriated more than $200 million to buy more than 520,000 acres. Meanwhile, private, nonprofit groups bought conservation easements on about 1 million acres of forestland. In 1999, the State of New York completed its single largest forest conservation project by paying the Champion International Corporation $24.9 million for conservation easements on 110,000 acres and the outright purchase of 29,000 acres in the northwestern Adirondacks. The conservation easements allow timber harvesting as well as public access for recreation. The purchased lands were added to the state-owned lands and will not be available for timber harvesting.

Also in 1999, Champion International sold 133,000 acres of heavily cut-over forestland in northeastern Vermont to a coalition of land conservation groups, including the Conservation Fund, the U.S. Fish and Wildlife Service (FWS), the Richard King Mellon Foundation, the Freeman Foundation of Vermont, the VLT, and the State of Vermont. The Champion land was the largest single landholding in the State of Vermont and featured 26 natural heritage sites, 15 lakes and ponds, and 33 miles of riverbanks (Revkin 1998, B5). The Conservation Fund purchased 106,000 acres of the property and sold 84,000 acres subject to a conservation easement to the Essex Timber Company of Boston, and another 16,500 acres to the Vermont Agency of Natural Resources. The FWS purchased 27,000 acres from Champion to add to the Silvio Conte National Wildlife Refuge.

In 2001, the New England Forestry Foundation—a private conservation group based in Groton, Massachusetts—paid over $28 million for a single conservation easement on 762,192 acres in northern Maine (Adams 2001, A2). The area includes 85 lakes and 2,000 miles of shoreline. The landowners—the Pingree family—will continue their timber business, which is certified for ecologically sensitive forest management practices.

In sum, there are many organizations and state governments working for the protection and stewardship of the northern forest. The Northern Forest Alliance—a collection of 33 forestry and conservation groups in the region—keeps a close watch on what happens in the northern forest and advocates sustainable management of the forest for both the economy and the environment.

Case Study 14-2
The Headwaters Forest

The Pacific Lumber Company, based in the coastal rainforest of Humboldt County in northern California, was purchased by the Murphy family in the 1920s. The company owned nearly 200,000 acres of timberland, and the Murphys practiced selective cutting of giant redwoods (Harris 1997, 26). Many of the trees were more than 500 years old, stood more than 200 feet tall, and were up to 12 feet in diameter. In the mid-1980s, Pacific Lumber was taken over by the Houston-based Maxxam Corporation for $900 million through the sale of high-interest "junk" bonds. To pay off the bonds, Pacific Lumber tripled the rate of harvest to sell more wood. The selective cutting policy was abandoned in favor of clear cutting, and Pacific Lumber became the largest private logger of redwoods in the United States (Nieves 1999, A12; Harris 1997).

The company's track record as an environmental steward has been far from exemplary. In 1995, Pacific Lumber was cited for violating the ESA by destroying habitat of the marbled murrelet, a small bird (*The New York Times* 1999, A24). From 1996 to 1999, Pacific Lumber was cited for 128 violations of California forestry rules; in 1998, the California Department of Forestry temporarily suspended Pacific Lumber's logging permit because of the violations (*ibid.*, A12). Pacific Lumber has also been sued by environmental groups for violations of the Clean Water Act and for threatening spotted owl and salmon habitats.

In 1999, the State of California and the federal government purchased 10,000 acres of redwoods from Pacific Lumber for $480 million, more than half the price that Maxxam had paid for all of Pacific Lumber just 15 years before. The Headwaters Forest was created from this land purchase and is now a public preserve that includes part of the remaining 3% of the nation's original redwood forests that have not been logged (Nieves 1999, A1). As part of the settlement, Pacific Lumber agreed to a 50-year HCP that affects how the company harvests timber on its remaining 211,000 acres of forestlands (see Figure 14-3). The company will be able to log about 179 million board feet and received "no surprises" guarantees, meaning the company will not be held liable if new threatened or endangered species are found on its land (see Chapter 9).

The Pacific Lumber case underscores two important issues: the need for enforcing sustainable forest practices on private land, and the potentially high cost of preserving unique timberlands.

CASE STUDY 14-3
The Spotted Owl Controversy

The struggle between those who earn their livelihood from cutting timber and those who want to preserve old-growth forests reached a crescendo in the 1990s over the northern spotted owl (*Strix occidentalis caurina*). The owl is found in late-successional and old-growth forests of western Washington and Oregon and in northwestern California, where it roosts in trees during the day and hunts at night. Environmentalists view the bird as an indicator species of the health of the forest ecosystem; timber interests see the forests as their liveli-

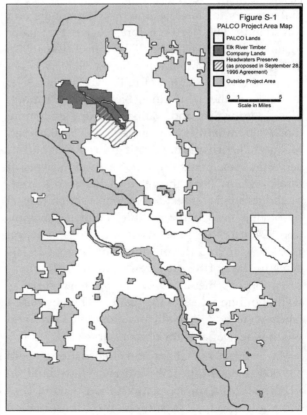

14-3   Map of the Pacific Lumber Habitat Conservation Plan, 1999.

Source: Foster Wheeler Environmental, used by permission.

hood. In June 1990, the FWS declared the spotted owl a threatened species. The ruling affected logging on both private and public land. In Oregon, an estimated 90% of spotted owl nests are on federal land, where the ESA requires the protection of habitat to enable the spotted owl to recover in numbers. On private land, the act prohibits "take," defined as the harming, killing, or capturing of a threatened or endangered species.

Sweet Home, Oregon, is a small community in the state's lush Willamette Valley. Through the 1980s, the Sweet Home district of the Willamette National Forest—one of the most productive forests in the National Forest System—produced about 86 million board feet of lumber each year. After the spotted owl was declared a threatened species, the timber harvest plunged and the lumber mills in Sweet Home suffered. In 1991, the Sweet Home Chapter of Communities for a Great Oregon took the federal government to court over the spotted owl. The case was finally decided in 1995 in favor of the federal government, and specifically in support of the ESA prohibition against significant habitat modification or degradation (*Babbit v. Sweet Home Chapter of Committees for Oregon* 63 U.S.L.W. 4665 (1995)).

In 1993, President Clinton held a forest summit meeting in Portland, Oregon. From that meeting, President Clinton set up a Forest Ecosystem Management Assessment Team to identify options to resolve the spotted owl controversy; in 1994, Option 9 was adopted through the environmental impact statement process. Option 9 lists three general management categories on federal land:

1. species habitat with no harvesting;
2. species habitat with thinning or light harvesting possible; and
3. harvesting areas that limit most logging within 2,000 acres of a spotted owl nest, prohibit logging within 70 acres of a nest, and require loggers to leave 15% forest cover.

The Northwest Forest Plan of 1994 sought to protect species habitat by ending logging on millions of acres of timberland managed by the USFS and the BLM. Meanwhile, about $1 billion in federal funding was offered for job training and to create new jobs for displaced forest workers. In 1994, the Oregon Department of Forestry identified spotted owl nest trees on private land and designated a minimum 70-acre core area around the trees for protection. In addition, approval from the Oregon Department of Forestry is needed if the harvest will occur within one-half mile of a nesting tree. The landowner must draft a harvest plan with the minimum core area. In most cases, timber harvesting within the core area is not allowed. Moreover, because a landowner's harvest plan may not comply with the federal ESA, approval from the FWS is also recommended. For instance, Oregon's 70-acre minimum core area may not provide sufficient owl habitat for breeding pairs (Oregon Department of Forestry 1994).

The spotted owl controversy is by no means settled. In 1997, the U.S. Supreme Court ruled that farmers in southern Oregon could sue the federal government for lost property value caused by the ESA. A few weeks later, the Oregon Supreme Court ruled that the Boise Cascade Corporation, a major timber company, was entitled to government compensation for loss of property value caused by logging restrictions to protect the spotted owl (Brinckman 1997).

CHAPTER

15

Planning for Mining

Mining itself may only occur for a few years, but the legacy of that activity is likely to be evident for much longer.
LAWRENCE J. MACDONNELL
(MACDONNELL AND BATES 1993, 79)

Mines produce a variety of minerals, metals, and aggregates that are used in everyday products and in the construction of buildings, roads, and bridges. America's mined resources are worth more than $150 billion a year, and the value of finished products from the nation's mines and quarries is nearly $400 billion a year (U.S. Bureau of the Census 2001, 704). America's major metals include iron, copper, gold, silver, molybdenum, lead, and zinc. Leading nonmetal minerals include phosphate for making fertilizers and detergents, and coal for making steel and generating electricity. Aggregates—crushed stone, gravel, and sand— are used to make roads, bricks, concrete, glass, lime for soil treatments, and many other products. At least 100 metric tons of sand and gravel aggregates are used to build an average single-family house (Wernstedt 2000, 77).

America is the world's most mineral-dependent country. Each American consumes about 20 tons of new metals each year (Brooke 1998, 18). In 1993, the United States became a net importer of nonfuel minerals for the first time; in 2000, U.S. imports of nonfuel minerals exceeded exports by $29 billion (U.S. Geological Survey 2001). Meanwhile, American mining companies have been investing in overseas mines, partly because of stricter environmental laws in America and partly because of untapped resources in other countries.

There are more than 100,000 active metal and nonmetal mines in the United States. Coal mining is centered in Kentucky, Ohio, Pennsylvania, and West Virginia in the East; and in Montana, Utah, and Wyoming in the West. Hard-rock metal mines are found mainly in the western states, and are usually operated by large mining companies. The mining of aggregates is most common in New England, the upper Midwest, along the west coast, and the Southwest. Aggregate mining varies from small, family-operated gravel and sand pits to large, privately owned corporate rock quarries (see Figure 15-1). Unlike the farming industry, a mine can profitably exist without other mines nearby, though the more mines in an area, the greater the likelihood of support businesses.

Mines contain nonrenewable mineral and aggregate resources in finite amounts. Mines are

15-1   Quarry site, Fishkill, New York.
Source: Katherine Daniels

vulnerable to depletion over time as well as to changing prices for minerals and extraction costs. Economic supply describes the amount of a resource that is financially attractive to recover. For instance, a mountainside may contain traces of gold but not enough to attract a company to pay to open a mine and dig out the gold. How long a mine remains open depends on the market prices for minerals and aggregates, the physical supply of the minerals or aggregates, and the cost and rate of extraction. Prices of minerals and aggregates change over time because of new mining technologies, new discoveries of deposits, and the substitutions of one material for another.

The regulation and development of mines and quarries is often a confusing mix of federal, state, and local laws, permits, and ordinances. Mine operators generally need to meet federal Clean Air Act and Clean Water Act standards as well as mine safety and reclamation standards. In some cases, state agencies may impose additional standards, and can approve a mining permit in spite of local opposition. County and township governments may attempt to regulate the location of mines and quarries, the hours of operation, and the design of the mine or quarry site.

THE CHALLENGES OF MINERAL AND AGGREGATE MINING

Environmental, Economic, and Social Impacts

Mining significantly disturbs the environment, through deep mining, open-pit mining (copper and quarrying), or strip-mining off topsoil and digging out ores, coal, or aggregates. Mine operators, planners, elected officials, and the public must address five main concerns:

1. the safe operation of the mine for workers;
2. environmental impacts on nearby residents and the community;
3. the reclamation of mined land after the mine has come to the end of its economic life;

4. increasing competition among different users for lands that contain minerals and aggregates; and
5. economic and social effects on the community.

Mine Safety

Mining is dangerous work. In 2000, 38 miners died in coal mines, and 47 miners died in accidents at metal and aggregate mining sites (Associated Press 2001, A24). Deep mining has long posed threats for respiratory disease, such as black lung disease in coal miners, and loss of life from mine cave-ins. Open-pit mines generate large amounts of dust and particulates that can cause respiratory trouble. Blasting can harm hearing. All types of mining involve the operation of heavy machinery. The federal Mine Safety and Health Administration and the Occupational Safety and Health Administration in the Department of Labor set safety standards for mine workers.

Environmental Impacts of Mining

Mining may impact nearby residents and their property in many ways. Noise from explosives blasting rock and the operation of heavy mining equipment, stamping mills, and trucks can easily disturb the peace and quiet of a neighborhood as well as reduce the value of surrounding property. Vibrations from blasting can damage nearby homes and buildings. Air pollution from dust and particulates and the smelting of ore pose health threats. Mining can affect the level of the water table—either lowering it so that neighboring wells dry up, or raising it so that flooding is a problem.

Acid mine drainage from either surface mines or underground mines can pollute surface water and groundwater. Acid drainage occurs in places where rock and soil contain high levels of iron sulfides (pyrites) that break down into water-soluble sulfuric acid. This acid contaminates drinking wells, kills fish in streams, and pollutes soils so that vegetative growth is stunted. Other mining-related impacts may include: water pollution from mine tailings and ore processing; soil erosion and sedimentation from loss of topsoil; surface subsidence or collapse; destruction of plant and wildlife habitat; and the sight of huge piles of mine tailings, also known as slag. For instance, it is common for a ton of rock to be processed for less than an ounce of some metals, such as gold. Some tailings are highly toxic, carrying elements of arsenic, cadmium, chromium, copper, cyanide, lead, mercury, or radioactive uranium. In all, American mines generate more than 2 billion tons of solid and liquid waste each year.

Hard-rock mining in the West uses large amounts of water to process ore. The wastewater is pumped to holding ponds where the tailings settle out. The water can then be used again for processing. Chemicals used in processing, such as cyanide to leach out gold from ore, can be stored in leakproof ponds and continually recycled and reused. Catch basins and sediment barriers can control siltation from running into streams. However, on a number of occasions, cyanide has spilled into rivers and streams, killing large numbers of fish and wildlife, and even some humans. One such disaster happened in 1992 at a Summitville, Colorado, gold mine where toxic wastewater from a cyanide gold-leaching operation leaked into the Alamosa River, killing virtually all of the fish and aquatic life along a 17-mile stretch. The mine owners declared bankruptcy and left the country, leaving taxpayers with a $150 million clean-up bill (Egan 2001, 1, 16).

Aggregate mining may cause air pollution from particulates; noise pollution from heavy earthmoving equipment, heavy truck traffic, and blasting; sediment in streams, changes in stream channels, and the level of the water table; and soil erosion. Sand and gravel, being sedimentary deposits, are often found in floodplains and river channels, and are extracted with bulldozers, front-end loaders, tractor scrapers, and draglines. Streambank spawning beds and wildlife habitat may be destroyed in the process. Crushed stone is quarried by drilling and blasting rock and then scooping stone with power shovels or bulldozers. Heavy trucks are used to haul sand, gravel, and stone.

Across the country, there are some 500,000 abandoned mines (U.S. General Accounting Office 1996). The western United States is dotted with hundreds of ghost towns that were originally built around mines. Abandoned quarries are common in the eastern U.S. Abandoned mines can pose serious environmental hazards. Pennsylvania contains about one-third of the nation's abandoned mines, including more than 250,000 acres of abandoned surface mines, 2,400 miles of streams polluted with mine drainage, over 7,000 abandoned oil and gas wells, widespread subsidence problems that threaten the stability of buildings on the surface, mine fires (78 were reported burning in 1999), and numerous slag heaps that leach acid drainage into water. The Pennsylvania Department of Environmental Protection (DEP) has estimated the cost of cleaning up these environmental problems at $15 billion (Pennsylvania DEP 1999).

The State of Pennsylvania has identified many abandoned mines on a Geographic Information System (GIS). Conservation districts and nonprofit watershed groups also identify abandoned mines and work on ways to reclaim them. These sources of information are important for local governments in their comprehensive planning decisions about where new development should or should not be located.

Mined Land Reclamation

Mined land reclamation is desirable for aesthetic reasons as well as for the health and safety of neighboring residents and communities. Reclamation can remediate pollution and safety hazards, stabilize land subsidence, and return mined land to beneficial uses. Reclaimed pits and quarries have been converted to housing sites, office parks, golf courses, grazing lands, forestlands, parks, recreation lakes, and wildlife habitats. Another possibility is "remining," in which an old mine reopens subject to an agreement that the operator will reclaim a certain number of acres for each new acre mined. Thousands of abandoned mines have yet to be reclaimed.

Competition for Land with Mineral and Aggregate Deposits

The increasing competition for lands with minerals and aggregate deposits is drawing local governments into debates about whether mines and quarries should be developed, and, if so, where these activities should occur. As more Americans move farther away from central cities into the exurbs and rural areas, they come into greater contact with mining and quarrying operations. Proposals for new mines and quarries are often met with local opposition. Nearby homeowners, farmers, ranchers, and tourist enterprises may raise concerns about a loss in property value and quality of life from the spillover effects of the mining operations. On the other hand, as more land is developed for housing and commercial uses in the exurbs and rural areas, less land is available for mining and quarrying.

Socio-economic Impacts of Mining on the Community

Hard rock and large surface mining operations are known for creating "boom and bust" cycles in rural communities. Typically, a new mining operation will foster a sudden demand for housing, schools, and other public services that the community may find difficult to meet. Later, when the mining declines or ends, much of the population may leave and local businesses may close. Rural mining towns, like timber towns, often lack the economic diversification that could protect them from downturns in the mining industry.

FEDERAL MINING REGULATIONS

Mining is regulated by the federal government mainly through the General Mining Law of 1872, the Surface Mining Control and Reclamation Act, and the Clean Water Act.

Mining Operations and Reclamation Standards

The General Mining Law of 1872 today applies to hard-rock minerals such as copper, gold, molybdenum, or silver (MacDonnell 1993, 71). The law allows individuals and companies to buy mining claims on federal land for $2.50 to $5 an acre without any obligation to pay royalties to the government for the minerals extracted. According to geographer Jack Wright, "Between 1994 and 1996, the government sold 2,701 acres of Western public lands containing $15.8 billion in minerals for $13,095" (Wright 1998, 109). This amounts to nothing short of a whopping subsidy to mining companies. As of 2002, there were thousands of privately owned mines operating on federal land. Proposals for new or expanded mining operations on federal land require a National Environmental Policy Act review. Mining companies must draft plans for developing a mine and rehabilitating the mined land once mining stops. On both public and private land, mining operations may come into conflict with the Endangered Species Act through the actual or potential destruction of rare and endangered species habitats.

In 1977, Congress passed the Surface Mining Control and Reclamation Act. The act was intended to encourage deep mining, which is environmentally less harmful than strip mining, though more expensive and potentially less safe for workers. The act created the Office of Surface Mining Reclamation and Enforcement to require mine operators to fill in excavations, replace topsoil, and return the land to its original contours. Mining companies must post a bond to guarantee that the reclamation will be done once the mine ceases operation. If the company does not do the reclamation work, the state can use the bond to pay to have it done. Mining companies may also be fined if they do not reclaim mine sites.

The act set up the Abandoned Mine Reclamation Fund to reclaim mined lands abandoned before 1977. The fund receives revenues from a fee of $.35 per ton of surface coal and $.15 per ton of deep coal mined. The fund has paid for more than $1 billion worth of reclamation projects, involving more than 2,000 mines. The fund can also be used to respond to emergencies such as mine fires, mine drainage, and subsidence.

America has among the largest coal reserves of any country in the world. Coal provided for 22% of the nation's energy needs in 2000, and coal-fired electrical plants accounted for more than 56% of all electricity generated in the U.S. (U.S. Bureau of the Census 2003, 566). The 1977 Strip Mining Act does not appear to have slowed coal production. In 2000, the U.S. produced a record 1.07 billion tons of coal, up more than 28% from the 1980 level (*ibid.*). More than 60% of coal production in 2000 came from surface mines and slightly less than 40% from underground mines. Eastern mines produced slightly more than mines in western states. However, production from western surface mines has been increasing because utilities are demanding more western coal, which is lower in sulfur than eastern coal.

Mining can destroy wetlands, especially in scooping out sand and gravel. Aggregate mining companies must obtain permits from the Army Corps of Engineers under Section 404 of the Clean Water Act (see Chapter 10). Because a mine is potentially a point source of water pollution, mine operators also must acquire a National Pollutant Discharge Elimination System (NPDES) permit from the U.S. Environmental Protection Agency (EPA) or state environmental agency if materials from mining are to be discharged into bodies of water.

Federal Clean-up Assistance

The EPA makes grants to states under Section 104(b)(3) of the Clean Water Act to improve water quality through acid mine drainage remediation technologies. The EPA also makes grants under Section 319 of the Clean Water Act for cleaning up nonpoint pollution sources, including mine drainage. Acid mine drainage can be treated with crushed limestone to neutralize the acid.

The Natural Resources Conservation Service (NRCS) administers the Watershed Protection and Flood Prevention Act, which can be used to treat mine drainage through passive means, such as wetlands. Through the Rural Abandoned Mine Program, the NRCS provides technical and financial assistance to landowners who voluntarily enter five- to 10-year contracts to reclaim abandoned coal-mined lands or treat acid mine drainage. The Bureau of Land Management (BLM) operates the Abandoned Mine Lands Cleanup program, and has identified 9,400 abandoned mines on land it controls. The BLM has worked with state governments to clean up abandoned mines and to prosecute mining companies for violations of toxic waste dumping under the Comprehensive Environmental Response, Compensation, and Liability Act (the Superfund law) (see Chapter 7).

STATE MINING REGULATIONS

State environmental agencies have the primary responsibility for implementing the Clean Water Act and the Safe Drinking Water Act. These agencies issue NPDES/State Pollutant Discharge Elimination System permits for mines and monitor mining activities that might threaten waterways or public drinking water supplies. State environmental agencies (such as in Maryland and Pennsylvania) or separate state mining agencies (such as in New York and Virginia) issue permits to develop or expand mines and also review reclamation plans. In drafting mining permits, state agencies are concerned about controlling runoff, erosion, and sedimentation; use of chemicals; air and water quality; and impacts on wetlands (Wernstedt 2000, 80). In many states, state mining agencies have the power of preemption over local regulations that affect mining operations.

LOCAL PLANNING FOR MINERAL AND AGGREGATE RESOURCES

Mineral and aggregate resources can be an important part of a community's economy. The comprehensive planning process can help a community identify these resources and direct development away from them. Sometimes communities will have to make difficult choices about whether to allow the extraction of minerals or aggregates at a particular site.

Inventory

Mineral and aggregate resources sites should be identified as part of the Natural Resources Inventory of the comprehensive plan. The inventory should include the location, type, size, quality, and status of existing and potential resources. Mineral and aggregate sites should be mapped, preferably on a GIS system. The GIS database should include abandoned mines and quarries, as well. Information may be obtained from the state mining agency and the geology department of the state land grant university.

Analysis

The possible expansion of existing mineral and aggregate resources sites and the potential development of new sites should be evaluated to determine whether and under what conditions they should be allowed to be mined. Considerations include the proximity of groundwater and surface drinking water supplies and impacts on fish and wildlife habitats. The proximity to existing development and the impacts that could occur from mining should also be assessed. Likewise, proposed growth areas that are near to existing or potential mineral or aggregate sites should be evaluated for possible impacts from mining. High-priority future mineral or aggregate sites should be protected from competing or conflicting on-site and adjacent land uses.

Goals and Objectives

Goals and objectives for mineral and aggregate resources will vary from community to community. Some suburban communities may not want to see the development of mines and quarries, while many rural communities may welcome the economic activity that comes from mining and quarrying. In any case, it is important to safeguard the health and welfare of the community's residents. Mining goals and objectives should be spelled out in the Natural Resources, Economic Base, Land Use, and Transportation sections of the comprehensive plan (see Table 15-1).

Action Strategy

The Action Strategy should present techniques and programs for achieving the mineral and aggregate goals and objectives as well as a timetable. Benchmarks should be identified and progress toward those benchmarks evaluated in an annual report on the environment. Specific recommendations might include the following:

- Locate mines and quarries in Heavy Industrial zones with long setbacks from neighboring properties.
- Adopt a wellhead protection program to protect aquifer recharge areas from mining and aggregate operations.
- Note noise, traffic, and releases of toxic materials listed in the EPA's Toxic Release Inventory in an annual report on environmental quality.
- Explore state and federal funding for reclaiming abandoned mines and quarries.

Zoning Ordinance

Mineral and aggregate resources are not found everywhere. Residential and commercial development, if not carefully located, can preclude the development of valuable mineral and aggregate

Table 15-1
Sample Goals and Objectives for Mineral and Aggregate Mining in the Comprehensive Plan

Natural Resources	
Goal	To encourage the development of valuable mineral and aggregate resources while maintaining environmental quality.
Objective	Monitor the impacts of mining operations on the environment and nearby residents, including air and water quality and noise levels.
Economic Base	
Objective	Promote the development of mineral and aggregate resources in ways that do not detract from the attractiveness of the community for other businesses.
Land Use	
Objective	Keep mining and quarrying operations away from sensitive environmental areas, such as steep slopes, thin soils, wetlands, sole source aquifers, and important surface waters.
Objective	Separate areas designated for future growth from potential mineral and aggregate extraction sites.
Transportation	
Objective	Ensure that road and rail networks are able to safely transport mineral and aggregate products through the community.

resources. Once a potential mineral or aggregate site is paved over, it will not likely be developed.

Often, mines and quarries are proposed in rural or urban fringe communities with little or no zoning. This can leave local residents little chance to review the proposed projects except at a state-level hearing or through a court challenge. A community can use zoning to require the location of mineral and aggregate operations in a specific mining district. For instance, Loudoun County, Virginia, limits mining and quarrying to a Mineral Resource-Heavy Industry zone (Wernstedt 2000, 80). A mining district can include:

- large minimum lot sizes, such as 20 acres or more for the development of a mine;
- long setbacks from neighboring property lines and surface water sources, such as from 300 feet to a quarter of a mile; and
- restrictions on hours of operation, noise levels, vibration standards, and frequency of blasting.

Another way to handle mines and aggregate sites is to make them conditional uses in rural farming and forestry zones. A conditional use affects an entire community, and mining and aggregates can have off-site impacts, such as heavy trucks traveling through the community. The conditional use process means that the local elected officials must make a ruling, and that the burden of proof for meeting safety and other standards is on the mine or quarry operator. It is generally a mistake to make mining and aggregate extraction a special exception. Special exceptions are not meant to exclude certain land uses; rather, special exceptions are designed to allow uses that affect only the immediate neighborhood and whose impacts can rather easily be minimized through limits on activities or proper development design.

Some communities use a "floating zone" for mine and quarry development. A floating zone may or may not appear on the zoning map but may be used wherever community officials decide it is appropriate. The floating zone approach is generally not a good way to site developments that can involve major off-site impacts. The rezoning or conditional use process makes more sense, and involves greater public scrutiny.

Subdivision Regulations

The local subdivision ordinance can require buffering berms and vegetation between mining operations and neighboring properties. The subdivision ordinance should require that stormwater runoff be contained on site as much as possible. Vegetation, swales, and retention basins should be used. Developers may be required to construct new roads or make road improvements with mine development or expansion, as heavy trucks can do considerable damage to roadbeds. Proposed new residential subdivisions in the vicinity of mining operations that would rely on groundwater could be required to have aquifer tests first to determine whether there is sufficient potable water to meet anticipated needs.

Capital Improvements Program

The capital improvements program (CIP) should be used to keep public growth-inducing infrastructure away from mineral and aggregate operations. An impact fee might be provided for in the land development regulations to make mine and quarry operators help pay for the wear and tear on local roads from heavy trucks. Because mining can occur in a boom or bust cycle, providing the right level of public utilities and services can be difficult. In a mining boom, an influx of new residents can overtax local services; when the bust occurs, many residents leave and the tax base declines sharply, leaving the remaining residents to pay for infrastructure. Planners in such communities should promote diversification of the local economy to smooth out the swings of the boom and bust cycle.

What to Look for in a Development Review

A proposed project should be evaluated according to the current comprehensive plan, zoning ordinance, subdivision and land development regulations, and any other applicable local laws. Proposals to develop or expand mines and quarries should include an environmental impact assessment (see Table 15-2). The assessment should address issues of noise, traffic, geology, potential for landslides and subsidence, water quality and supply, wildlife habitat, and proximity to existing and planned development. The mine or quarry operator should provide a reclamation plan. The operator should also present any necessary state and federal permits.

The design of a mining site should minimize runoff, noise, air pollution, and vibration. Areas of potential future mine expansion should be noted. Proposals for residential, commercial, and industrial development that could affect existing mining operations should include measures such as setbacks, berms, and vegetation to screen noise and dust and to absorb runoff. Potential traffic congestion from mining operations may require additional traffic lights and even new road configurations.

Table 15-2
A Checklist of Mineral and Aggregate Resource Issues in a Development Review

1.	What are the location, size, and proposed land uses of the mineral or aggregate project?
2.	Is the proposed mineral or aggregate development allowed in the particular zone? Are setbacks and buffers from property lines met?
3.	What are the land uses on the adjacent properties?
4.	Has the developer conducted an environmental impact assessment as required in state, federal, or local regulations?
5.	What will be the impacts on air and water quality, water supplies, earth subsidence, slope stability, and wildlife habitat? Is the proposed development designed to minimize these impacts?
6.	How will toxic substances and tailings will be handled and disposed of?
7.	How much truck traffic will be involved and what routes will be used?
8.	What will be the impacts of noise and vibration on nearby residential and commercial properties? Is the proposed development designed to minimize noise and vibration?
9.	Has the developer obtained any necessary state or federal permits? Has the developer provided a reclamation plan?

Planning for
the Built Environment

16

Transportation Planning and the Environment

Today, Oregonians drive more than 25 billion miles a year; that's 40 percent of Oregon's energy use. Without any change in Oregonians' driving habits, the state's projected growth in population will mean at least a 30 percent increase in yearly auto travel over the next two decades. This huge increase in auto travel threatens to diminish Oregon's quality of life.

OREGON OFFICE OF ENERGY

We are realizing that we can't just build more highways to get out of congestion.

JOHN FRECE, AIDE TO THEN-MARYLAND
GOVERNOR PARRIS GLENDENING
(*CHRISTIAN SCIENCE MONITOR,* JAN. 20, 1999, 5)

Planners have traditionally focused on how land use patterns and densities generate commuting, freight, and shopping trips, and how these land use patterns can be served by a mix of transportation modes—from cars and trucks to buses, trains, subways, bicycles, foot, boats, and airplanes. However, over time, it has become evident that transportation modes vary enormously in their financial costs, the built environment patterns they help create, their use of energy, and in their effects on air and water quality. How well these transportation modes function individually and as an "intermodal" network greatly determine the safety, convenience, sense of community, economic competitiveness, and environmental quality of a community or region.

Transportation is not just a matter of getting from here to there. Transportation systems form the circulatory system—the veins and arteries—of a region and determine how that region connects to the outside world. In the words of noted architect Kite Singleton, "Transportation is the single most important factor in creating urban form in the U.S. today" (Singleton 2000). The private automobile has been the overwhelming passenger transportation mode of choice, while trucks have reaped most of the dollars spent on freight transport. Yet, motor vehicle traffic congestion is clogging the arteries of many of America's metropolitan regions and releasing large amounts of air pollution. These regions depend heavily on motor vehicles because of sprawling, low-density suburbs that make mass transit unfeasible.

TRANSPORTATION PLANNING CHALLENGES

Energy-Efficient Transportation Systems and Land Use Patterns

The challenge for planners is to create the conditions for viable intermodal transportation systems and to manage the demand for different modes. Communities and regions need to develop and support energy-efficient transportation systems and land use patterns that enable the safe and convenient movement of people and freight (see Table 16-1). Greater transportation efficiency means a reduction in energy use, less pollution, less use of nonrenewable fossil fuels, and less expense for businesses, governments, and individuals. Transportation accounts for about two-thirds of America's oil consumption (Dernbach 2002, 37). Reduced energy use would decrease America's expenditures for imported oil, which accounts for more than half of the oil consumed in the U.S. Energy-efficient land use patterns enable more modes of transportation to be financially viable, providing more choices for passengers and freight haulers, and promoting an intermodal network.

Table 16-1
Energy Efficiency of
Different Transportation Modes

BTUs* Per Passenger Mile		
Car	Bus	Light and Heavy Rail
5,338	3,822	1,122

*BTU = British Thermal Unit, or the amount of energy needed to heat a pound of water 39.2 degrees Fahrenheit by 1 degree.

Source: Newman and Kenworthy (1999), p. 76

16-1 Traffic delays result in the use of billions more gallons of gasoline and add to air pollution.

Source: Katherine Daniels

Overemphasis on Highway Construction

Highway construction alone has not been able to solve traffic congestion problems. A study of traffic conditions of 68 urban areas in 1999 reported that the annual average delay per person increased from 11 hours in 1982 to 36 hours in 1999 (Shrank and Lomax 2001, iii). Moreover, the periods of traffic congestion have increased from about five hours a day to seven hours a day. In 1999 alone, traffic delays resulted in the consumption of 6.8 billion additional gallons of fuel and 4.5 billion hours stuck in traffic, at a total estimated cost of $78 billion (*ibid.*) (see Figure 16-1). As of 2000, there were 217.3 million registered motor vehicles in the U.S. and 281 million people; however, the number of vehicles registered was increasing at a rate faster than the population growth (Wald 2001, A12).

Spending on roads will continue to be popular and will likely absorb most of the future dollars spent on transportation because that is how most people have become accustomed to travel and because the highway lobby is politically powerful. Furthermore, federal and state gasoline taxes are earmarked for road construction and repair. In 2001, the Federal Highway Administration made more than $26 billion in grants to state and local governments from the federal highway trust fund, while Federal Transit Administration (FTA) grants for mass transit totaled just over $7 billion (U.S. Bureau of the Census 2003, 672). State gasoline taxes raised more than $30 billion in 2000; in 1998, state and local highway debt stood at nearly $90 billion, more than double the debt level in 1985 (*ibid.*, 673).

In 1999, the American Highway Users Alliance—a private group made up of motorists, truckers, and insurance and oil companies—issued a report naming the top 167 intersections across the nation in need of improvement. The report proposed that expanded road capacity, synchronized traffic lights, computerized routing systems, reversible commuter lanes, and moveable traffic barriers would maintain a better flow of traffic, shorten traffic delays, save energy, reduce air pollution, and save lives. The report highlighted what are considered the nation's 18 worst traffic bottlenecks. Four of the top bottlenecks were in greater Los Angeles, another four were in greater Washington, D.C., and three were in greater Atlanta. To some degree, the bottlenecks were inevitable. As Steve Haynes of the American Automobile Association told *The New York Times* (1999, A37), "The number of automobiles and trucks on the highways has grown dramatically in the past 30 years, but the miles of new road has only increased very, very slightly."

Often, road networks laid out in the 18th and 19th centuries are not capable of handling large traffic volumes or high-speed traffic. For instance, in Loudoun County, Virginia—a suburbanizing area west of Washington, D.C.—semirural Gum Springs Road carried 7,500 vehicles a day in 2000, more than double the traffic load in 1995 (Rein 2000, A22). Also in 2000, in Spottsylvania County, Virginia (southwest of Richmond), almost 30,000 cars and trucks a day crossed the intersection of Brock Road, a two-lane winding road with no shoulder, double the traffic level of 10 years previous (*ibid.*, A1). These growing exurban areas experience a disproportionate share of the nation's more than 40,000 annual traffic fatalities (Lucy 2000, 14). Even if these roads were widened or additional roads built, there is no guarantee that traffic congestion would be alleviated.

Ring roads—circular roads around cities or villages—and limited access bypasses have gained in popularity as a way to relieve traffic congestion in downtowns, increase traffic speeds, and service growing suburban areas. Several metropolitan areas either are building ring roads or have them on the drawing board. Raleigh, North Carolina, has one ring road and is building a second ring road ranging from 12 to 25 miles from the downtown. Three other North Carolina cities—Charlotte, Greensboro, and Wilmington—have ring roads proposed or under construction. Houston has three ring roads and is planning a fourth. Greater Nashville, Tennessee, is seriously considering a 185-mile ring road 35 miles from downtown to accommodate drivers who in 1998 traveled an average of 36.1 miles per day (Kreyling 2000, 4). Greater Atlanta wants to build a second ring road about 35 miles from the downtown at an estimated cost of $5 billion.

Many smaller communities are exploring the construction of bypasses around their communities. Recent increases in traffic, especially truck and commuter traffic, have brought considerable noise, pollution, and gridlock. John D. Edwards, Jr., traffic expert, warns, "In many cases, bypasses have been built to serve relatively small through-traffic volumes and principally for the enhancement of suburban real estate values. When that happens, the public loses twice; we pay for unneeded infrastructure, and we cause deterioration of existing businesses and infrastructure" (*ibid.*, 7).

The construction of ring roads and bypasses can open up vast amounts of rural land to low-density residential development and commercial strips. Close to existing development, ring roads and bypasses can destroy neighborhoods and displace residents—burdens that often fall heavily on low-income and minority populations.

Traffic expert Anthony Downs (1999, 955) warns that ring roads and bypasses may not provide a solution to peak-hour traffic loads: "The most important thing to understand about peak-hour traffic congestion is that once it has appeared in a region, it cannot be eliminated or even substantially reduced."

In addition, building or improving highways to relieve congestion might be short-lived in areas where populations are projected to grow substantially. Finally, building more roads or High Occupancy Vehicle (HOV) lanes to increase speeds can increase air pollution. As cars exceed 35 miles per hour, emissions of hydrocarbons and nitrous oxide rise, and then soar above 60 miles per hour.

Interstate Highway System

Prior to 1950, most suburbs extended only a few miles outside of central cities. In 1956, Congress approved the construction of the 43,500-mile interstate highway system, which transformed both the urban and suburban landscape. The highways ran from the heart of downtowns—where thousands of buildings were sacrificed to make way for the new roads—out to the suburbs, where commuters could live and still reach jobs in the central city or, eventually, in other suburbs. Suburban shopping centers, office parks, industrial plants, and secondary roads sprouted up near interstate interchanges. The interstates reduced the cost of transporting goods; provided safe, convenient access for employees and shoppers; and helped to increase America's dependence on the automobile.

From 1970 to 1990, America's population grew by 31%; however, the amount of developed land in metropolitan areas increased by 74%, and the number of vehicle miles traveled (VMT) by U.S. residents jumped by 93%, or three times the rate of population growth (U.S. General Accounting Office (GAO) 2000, 12). Highways, cars, and trucks promoted a more dispersed settlement pattern, enabling people to live farther from work and shopping, and resulting in the greater consumption of land per person. By 1990, more U.S. residents were living in suburbs than in central cities, and more commuting trips were being made between suburbs rather than from suburbs to the inner city.

The building of the interstate highways also marked a major shift in public transportation investment policy in favor of private motor vehicles and reliance on cheap and plentiful gasoline. Jane Holtz Kay reported that "between World War II and the mid-1960s, the nation had spent a meager $1.5 billion for local public transporta-tion, an average of $75 million a year, while doling out $51 billion a year to motor vehicles" (Kay 1997, 254). By the 1980s, the maintenance bill for interstates was placing a heavy burden on state transportation departments. Between 1983 and 1993, America's road mileage increased by only 1% to 3.9 million miles (Orsbon 1997, 3). Meanwhile, the number of cars and VMT steadily increased. In many metropolitan areas, the pace of traffic slowed, travel times lengthened, and cars spewed more air-polluting exhaust. Over the same 10 years, federal spending on mass transit averaged a meager $2.5 billion a year, a small fraction of highway spending nationwide (*ibid.*). State highway officials estimated that highways needed $31 billion a year in federal funds just to maintain highways in their current condition (*ibid.*).

Motor vehicle manufacturers and car and truck drivers have enjoyed tremendous federal and state subsidies through public road construction and gasoline prices that do not reflect the air and water pollution costs generated by driving. Transportation planner Reid Ewing estimated in 1997 that a price of $6 per gallon for gasoline would reflect the true environmental and road construction costs of driving (Ewing 1997, 107-126). By comparison, public subsidies for bus, rail, and subway systems are quite small. The lack of adequate subsidies has placed an enormous handicap on these alternate transport modes in competing with the public road system and the private automobile. Land use attorney Robert Freilich makes the argument in favor of subsidies to mass transit (Freilich 1999, 308). He reasons that mass transit is a public good, much like schools and police and fire services. We don't make public schools or police or fire pay their way, so why should public transportation be expected to break even? The point is that mass transit provides an essential service while reducing air pollution and highway congestion and promoting compact development.

Mixing Motor Vehicles and Mass Transit

Cars and trucks can provide individuals and businesses with flexibility and widespread access. Moreover, motor vehicles will likely be the dominant transportation mode of choice for years to come. Nonetheless, a recent trend among planners, politicians, and the public has been a growing interest in expanding mass-transit options for moving people; reorienting regional land use patterns to accommodate future growth; and reducing car dependence, traffic jams, and air pollution. The interest in mass transit seems to be a case of "back to the future." From 1900 until just after World War II, mass transit in the form of buses, trolleys, and railroads was the dominant mode of transportation in America. Transit ridership peaked at 23.4 billion trips in 1946 (Layton 2000, A12), but by 1972, transit ridership reached a post-World War II low of 6.5 billion trips (U.S. GAO 2000, 12). Transit accounted for 12.6% of all work trips in the U.S. in 1960, but by 2000, transit's share of work trips had fallen to about 5%. Yet, in 2000, transit ridership reached 9.4 billion trips, a 45% increase over the 1972 figure (Layton 2001, 27). Automobiles made up 69.5% of work trips in 1960 and a dominating 87% in 1995 (U.S. Department of Transportation (DOT) 1995, 231; Armas 2002). Just over three-quarters of all commuting trips in 2000 were made by single drivers (Armas 2002).

Significantly, passenger ridership on mass transit grew at a faster rate than VMT between 1996 and 2001, according to the Surface Transportation Policy Project (STPP) (STTP 2002). A number of metropolitan areas are making substantial investments in transit as the best alternative to road construction and to accommodate growing populations. For example, in greater Washington, D.C., transportation projects scheduled to the year 2025 favor spending $40 billion on mass transit and $36 billion on roads (Layton 2001, B1, B27).

Encouraging Alternative Modes of Transportation

Bicycle and pedestrian travel can be healthy ways for people to travel around a community. Bicycle lanes along roads, streets, and trail networks can promote bicycle use. However, the popularity of walking—other than for exercise—has fallen, in part because of sprawling development and in part for safety reasons. According to the STPP, the number of pedestrian trips fell by 42% between 1980 and 2000. In 1997 and 1998, U.S. residents made only 6% of trips on foot, but nearly 11,000 pedestrians were killed in those years, accounting for 13% of all traffic fatalities (STPP 2000b). Part of the problem is poorly designed development that does not include sidewalks, crosswalks, or traffic calming devices to slow motor vehicles. Another problem is the need for fairly dense, mixed-use developments that make possible walking to shopping, recreation areas, and work. Such developments can be very attractive to empty nesters and senior citizens.

Context-Sensitive Solutions

Transportation projects can have major impacts on the appearance, operation, and choice of transport modes. State departments of transportation as well as city, town, and county highway departments need to recognize community goals and meet transportation service and safety standards. Historic preservation, traffic calming, wider sidewalks, retention of street trees, parking, and bridges are common concerns. Context-sensitive transportation projects—from rebuilding main streets to installing bicycle paths to installing light rail lines—should be done with a minimum of disruption to the community and the environment. Public involvement in the planning and design of transportation projects is key.

FEDERAL APPROACHES TO TRANSPORTATION PLANNING

Intermodal Surface Transportation Efficiency Act

Congress heralded a new direction in transportation planning with the passage of the Intermodal Surface Transportation Efficiency Act (ISTEA) (pronounced *ice-tea*) of 1991 (Public Law 102-240). Prior to ISTEA, federal transportation money was spent largely on highway construction and improvement projects based on where the federal government wanted to spend the money, including many congressional pork barrel projects. ISTEA combined new highway construction, mass transit, and intermodal projects as a solution to both traffic jams and air pollution. At the same time, ISTEA established a transportation planning system that gives states and metropolitan areas a major say in what federally funded transportation projects are needed.

The central goals of ISTEA are:

- to make transportation investments more responsive to local and regional needs, and to give greater state and local control over those investment decisions;
- to maintain existing transportation systems and the efficient operation of those networks;
- to improve intermodal integration;
- to integrate transportation planning with air quality planning, specifically to minimize transportation-related fuel consumption and air pollution; and
- to require state departments of transportation to make cost estimates of alternatives to every road project.

Metropolitan Planning Organizations

Under ISTEA, every metropolitan area with a population of more than 50,000 must have a designated Metropolitan Planning Organization (MPO) in order to qualify for federal transportation funding. Metropolitan regions are determined by the federal Office of Management and Budget, and are generally made up of one or more counties with at least one county having 50,000 or more residents. Counties that are adjacent to metropolitan "core" counties and have a high rate of commuting to the core counties are included in defining a metropolitan region.

In 2001, there were 341 MPOs ranging from small metropolitan areas to multistate authorities (Stephenson 2002, 1). Members of MPOs are appointed through the local and county governments in a metropolitan region. The purpose of MPOs is to receive broad public input on transportation issues, set regional transportation priorities for both the short- and long-term, draft transportation plans, and identify specific projects. MPOs should:

- analyze the performance of the region's transportation systems and trends in the use of different modes;
- make projections of future land use, travel demands, and performance of transportation systems;
- involve the public and local government agencies that are affected by transportation decisions; and
- draft a 20-year Regional Transportation Plan (RTP) and a three- to five-year Transportation Improvement Plan (TIP) with specific highway projects that also reflect air quality considerations.

MPOs are required to draft a long-range RTP to guide land development and transportation investment over the next 20 years. MPOs need to determine what types of future development patterns should be encouraged or improved to enhance the feasibility of multimodal and intermodal transportation systems and improvements. In addition, MPOs should determine how future development and transportation systems can enhance the quality of life, protect the environment, and sustain economic vitality in the region. MPOs should then ascertain the financial requirements needed to create the desired systems and improvements, and how to obtain the necessary financial resources.

Transportation Improvement Plan

Each MPO is also responsible for drafting a short-range TIP, which includes transportation projects to be implemented over a three- to five-year period (Dittmar *et al.* 1999, 51-56). The TIP must include major investment studies in transportation corridors, environmental justice issues, and air quality impacts as well as transportation alternatives to the automobile, such as pedestrian- and bicycle-oriented systems, and the protection of wetlands, wildlife habitats, and open space. The TIP should identify both federal and nonfederal sources of funds for transportation projects, and how that money will be spent over several years to complete the listed projects. Especially important are capacity-expanding projects and travel demand management efforts that form a congestion management system. Travel demand management is a way to balance transportation use among different modes to improve efficiency and minimize delays.

The TIP must show how the short-range plan meets the requirements of ISTEA and the how the specific recommended projects are consistent with the region's 20-year transportation plan, the state transportation improvement program, and the State Improvement Plan (SIP) for improving air quality.

Coordination with State Transportation Planning

The Clean Air Act Amendments of 1990, together with ISTEA, link transportation planning to land use planning in a "continuous transportation/air quality planning process," and require a plan for achieving reductions in air pollutants. The U.S. Environmental Protection Agency (EPA) may deny highway projects if a state does not submit a SIP to maintain and improve air quality. Transportation projects and Transportation Control Mea-

sures listed in an MPO's TIP must be consistent with the SIP (see Chapter 5). Transportation Control Measures may include such actions as imposing or increasing highway tolls to discourage motor vehicle use, employer-based trip reduction plans, HOV lanes, and public transit. MPOs must provide detailed air quality projections based on computer modeling of VMT, vehicle speed, and emissions for the entire metropolitan area and for specific transportation corridors.

State departments of transportation are responsible for drafting the State TIP, which contains a list of transportation projects recommended for federal funding. Each state governor approves the State TIP and submits it to the Federal Highway Administration and the Federal Transportation Administration for approval. These federal agencies then disburse funds to the states.

ISTEA provided $155 billion over six years for state and regional transportation projects. About $2.6 billion of the money allocated to the states went to fund a variety of transportation enhancement projects—from the rehabilitation of old train stations to creating bicycle paths from abandoned rail corridors, to purchasing conservation easements along scenic highways. However, the large majority of ISTEA funds were spent on the construction of new highways and the repair of older roads and bridges. Part of this funding bias reflects the orientation of state departments of transportation. Moreover, in recent years, states have had to cover a larger share of the maintenance of the interstate highway system.

Overall, ISTEA did little to change the mix of transportation modes in America. In 1996, motor vehicles accounted for nearly nine out of 10 miles traveled (Council on Environmental Quality 1996, 359). The number of passenger miles logged on highways increased by 16% from 1990 to 1996. Over the same time period, mass-transit passenger miles were virtually unchanged and rail miles fell by 15%, while airplane travelers registered a 24% increase. Federal and state transportation spending priorities will change only when local and regional transportation priorities lead the way toward a better balance among motor vehicle travel, mass transit, and alternative transport modes.

Transportation Equity Act for the 21st Century

The Transportation Equity Act for the 21st Century (TEA-21) was passed in 1997 to continue intermodal transportation programs and to fund transportation construction projects begun under ISTEA. TEA-21 authorized almost $200 billion in funding. Like ISTEA, TEA-21 provided money for many bicycle and pedestrian projects (at about $630 million a year) as well as a total of $42 billion for mass transit (STPP 2000a) but, like ISTEA, most of the TEA-21 money has gone for highway repair and construction. The Congestion Mitigation and Air Quality funding portion of TEA-21 supports the concept of extending and widening highways to reduce congestion and motor vehicle emissions. Often, the new highway construction is in the form of ring roads around major urban centers and roads connecting the new growing suburbs to the greater metropolitan road network. While the interstate highways fostered suburban sprawl, now additional roads are needed to service the sprawl that the interstates created. Yet, it remains to be seen whether new road construction will actually alleviate traffic congestion or reduce air pollution.

TEA-21 added requirements for MPO TIPs to identify and evaluate the distribution of costs and benefits from transportation projects, based on race, ethnic background, and income. This is an attempt to strengthen the role of environmental justice in the transportation planning process begun under ISTEA. The goal is to ensure that low-income people and minorities are not unfairly disadvantaged and share in the benefits of transportation projects by gaining better access to mobility and less exposure to air and noise pollution.

Following up on planning for environmental justice, in fiscal 2000, the U.S. DOT launched the Transportation and Community and System Preservation Pilot (TCSP) program. Through this program, the U.S. DOT makes grants to state and local governments and MPOs to stimulate planning that would improve transportation efficiency and also reduce the environmental impacts of transportation systems, ensure efficient access to jobs, avoid costly future public infrastructure investments, and encourage private investment to support these goals. The TCSP program had $120 million available through fiscal 2003, and in the first funding round, 84 out of 292 applications were funded (U.S. GAO 2000, 28). Clearly, the public demand for creative transportation solutions is strong and all levels of government are responding.

REGIONAL APPROACHES TO TRANSPORTATION PLANNING

Many metropolitan areas are facing substantial population increases between 2000 and 2020 along with the threat of increasing traffic congestion and reductions in air quality. ISTEA and TEA-21 were aimed primarily at expanding the supply of highways in an attempt to accommodate more motor vehicles. Metro area planners have three alternatives to simply building more roads:

1. Intermodal networks can combine motor vehicle use with a variety of mass-transit systems and expanded bicycle and pedestrian traffic.

2. Mass transit in the form of light rail and buses can move greater volumes of passengers through a transit corridor more quickly than cars.

3. Travel demand management seeks to smooth out traffic flow to increase the efficiency of transportation systems. This can be achieved by raising the price of driving through higher tolls at rush hour and increasing parking costs, or by providing safe, reliable, convenient, and cost-effective alternatives to the car.

Intermodal Transportation

The intermodal concept encourages metropolitan areas to link different transportation networks (e.g., buses and light rail, buses and subways, bicycles and buses, airports and light rail, boats and buses, walking and buses, or cars and trains) so that people and goods move more smoothly. However, if travel is to be successfully split among a number of modes, settlement patterns need to incorporate a mix of housing, stores, and offices at a fairly high density to make mass transit feasible and to encourage walking and bicycling. Many suburbs lack the minimum density of seven to eight units to the acre needed to make mass transit feasible (Pushkarev and Zupan 1977). In his study of edge cities—suburban places built around office parks and shopping malls on the periphery of major urban areas—Joel Garreau cited a rough consensus among transportation experts that it would take 30 million square feet of office space (about 700 acres) to make a light-rail line feasible in an edge city (Garreau 1991, 131).

Because most commuting trips are between suburbs, mass-transit solutions will have to target the suburbs as well as downtowns. University of California Professor Robert Cervero (1998, 440-441) warns:

> "Transit investments that are out of kilter with how our cities and regions grow do nobody any good. Running trains and buses that fail to draw people out of drive-alone cars does little to relieve traffic congestion, conserve fuel, or reduce pollution. The best prescription for filling trains and buses, and winning over motorists to transit, is to find a harmonious fit between transit systems, and the cities and suburbs they serve. This is the core lesson of the transit metropolis."

The flexibility of the car in making numerous stops in a nonlinear trip pattern will be beat only if transit-oriented developments (TODs) can provide a variety of commercial services and employment opportunities within walking distance of transit lines and housing. A rule of thumb in planning transit stops is that most U.S. residents will not walk more than a quarter of a mile if they can help it (Fulton and Calthorpe 2001).

Bicyclists and pedestrians, like mass-transit riders, rely on fairly dense development patterns. Sidewalks and footpaths greatly increase opportunities for walking. The *ZPG Reporter* (Zero Population Growth 2000, 6) reported that, in 1999, only 0.6% of all trips in the U.S. were by bicycle. Just recently, buses and trains have begun to install special equipment to carry bicycles. Bicycle transportation is sometimes perceived as less than safe because of the need to compete for road space with cars and trucks. Bicycle paths that are separate from roads provide the highest degree of safety and can be integrated into larger development designs. Marked bicycle lanes also provide a measure of safety.

Light Rail, Transit-Oriented Developments, and the Centers and Corridors Strategy

A pattern of transportation corridors that link distinct mixed-use residential and commercial centers is emerging as a solution to congested highways and air quality concerns. Much of the attention for the centers and corridors strategy has focused on the construction of mass-transit bus and light-rail systems. However, the strategy can also make motor vehicle transportation more efficient by reducing the need to use cars and hence lowering the demand for road space. Buses, trolleys, and light rail can move more people more rapidly through a transportation corridor than motor vehicles. These transit lines also encourage compact TOD within walking distance of transit stops. More than 40 major U.S. cities are studying or planning to add commuter light-rail lines to connect the inner city and suburbs. Buses and trolley lines have worked well in helping to revive downtown San Diego. In anticipating the need to accommodate as many as 1 million new residents from 2000 to 2020, San Diego County is planning to extend the trolley line eastward and promote mixed-use TOD within one-quarter mile of the transit corridor (San Diego Association of Governments 2000).

Light Rail

Light rail generally runs at grade, on the same level as motor vehicles and pedestrians. Light rail gives a smooth ride, can make frequent stops, and can operate at speeds of up to 55 miles per hour. The trains produce little pollution and can carry a moderate number of riders. Light-rail systems may compete with motor vehicle traffic where roads intersect. Installing light rail typically requires the acquisition of rights-of-way, and the cost is higher than for bus systems. Portland, Oregon, demonstrated that light rail could successfully attract large numbers of passengers when integrated into a system of centers and transit corridors (see Figure 16-3). In the process, development has been directed to downtown Portland and to hubs along the light-rail lines. Portland actually reduced the number of downtown parking spaces available, thus lowering automobile dependence and alleviating air pollution. TOD, such as Orenco Station west of Portland (see Case Study 5-2) or the 130-acre new town center under construction in Gresham (east of Portland) are being built at fairly high densities to promote walking and bicycling as well as transit ridership (Ehrenhalt 2000, 12).

Architect Peter Calthorpe helped design Portland's TOD approach as a version of the streetcar suburb of the early 20th century. A TOD features a core area of about a quarter-mile radius and a secondary area that extends an additional quarter mile out. Within this bounded area, development occurs at a fairly high density, focused on an easily accessible town center at the transit hub (see Figure 16-2). Portland light-rail official G.B. Arrington has estimated that developers in the region have invested more than $2.3 billion in projects near the light-rail lines. Moreover, "There's been an evolution in the comfort level of the development community about doing development around transit stations. We now use light rail as a tool to direct growth" (*ibid.*).

The success of the Portland, Oregon, light-rail system won the attention of many other metropolitan areas that have either built their own light-rail systems or are seriously pursuing light-rail lines (see Table 16-2). The Dallas Area Rapid Transit (DART) in automobile-dependent Dallas, Texas, began a light-rail system in 1992, and by 2002 boasted 44 miles of track, 34 stations, and more than a dozen light-rail transit villages under construction or in the planning stages (DART 2003). Daily ridership topped 40,000 passengers.

Denver followed the example of Dallas, and in the late 1990s, private businesses contributed $2.5 million toward a $40 million new light-rail spur line (Kansas City 2000, 5). Nationwide, according

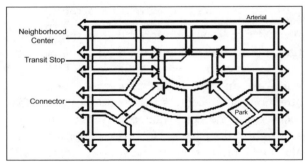

16-2 Transit-oriented development. The primary impact zone is an 800-foot radius around a transit station. Here, retail and office space and some dense residential development are recommended. Bicyclists and pedestrians can access the transit station and the commercial district of the primary zone. The secondary impact zone extends out a quarter of a mile—the maximum distance that most Americans are willing to walk. Within the secondary impact zone, a mix of single- and multifamily residential development, parks, and schools are recommended. The tertiary impact zone stretches from a quarter of a mile to half a mile. Residential development is less dense in the tertiary zone than in the secondary impact zone.

Source: City of Austin, Texas

Table 16-2
Advantages of Transit-Oriented Developments

Measures	Results
Vehicle Trips	18% reduction in auto trips
Vehicle Miles Traveled (VMT)	12% less total VMT in morning peak
Travel Time	18%–28% reduction on network
Air Quality	Deterioration of air quality slowed
Land Use	Less land needed for roads and lower public cost of development
Pedestrian Traffic	Promotes greater pedestrian movement
Reverse Commuting	Promotes greater access to jobs for commuters from cities to suburbs, aids in the welfare-to-work process

Source: Federal Transit Administration, *Building Livable Communities with Transit* (1999), p. 3

16-3 Light-rail train and automobile sharing the street in Portland, Oregon.

Source: Katherine Daniels

to the North American Light Rail Industry (2000), as of early 2000, there were 18 light-rail systems in operation (Table 16-3) and an additional 40 light-rail systems proposed or in development. Some of the metropolitan areas studying light rail include such automobile-dependent places as Albuquerque; Phoenix; Houston; Atlanta; Minneapolis/St. Paul; Kansas City, Missouri; Orlando; Indianapolis; Cincinnati; San Antonio; Colorado Springs; and the Raleigh-Durham-Chapel Hill region. In 2000, the FTA received 400 applications from cities for federal money to create new light-rail systems; in response, the FTA has changed its matching funds formula from 80-20 federal-state to 50-50, in order to stretch the federal dollars (Kay 2000, 15). However, applications for developing light rail continue to exceed the available funding.

In 2000, voters in Phoenix approved a 0.4% sales tax for expanded bus service and the construction of 24 miles of light-rail lines to connect Phoenix with Mesa and Tempe. Slated to open in 2006, the light-rail project will operate in a separate lane at street level, and is expected to help reduce car traffic and promote more compact development along the light-rail route. Seattle is investing up to $12 billion to build a 23-mile light-rail system from Sea-Tac Airport north to the University of Washington area. The line is proposed to have 16 stations, and each station is envisioned to serve as a center of mixed-use residential and commercial activity. Yet, much of the growth in greater Seattle is occurring to the east away from the light-rail line. It is far from certain whether the light-rail system will be able to keep pace with Seattle's growing population. From 1990 to 2020, the population of greater Seattle is expected to increase by 50%. Even if the proposed system of 125 miles of light rail and 81 miles of commuter rail is built, traffic congestion is expected to increase by 240%. Almost half of the freeway network is projected to operate under congested conditions (Nelson 1999).

Atlanta's Metropolitan Area Rapid Transit Authority (MARTA) began a major TOD in the northern suburb of Buckhead in 2000 as part of its effort to improve its traffic and air quality problems. MARTA will lease out 51 acres and provide $81 million in financing for the construction of 4.8 million square feet of office, retail, and residential space near Lindbergh station (Kreyling 2001, 6). The California legislature, in the mid-1990s, enacted a Transit Village Development Planning Act of 1994 to promote the creation of TOD (White and Jourdan 1997, 9). The act allows local governments to adopt transit village plans to create mixed-use developments around transit stations. The act also authorizes state transportation funding and streamlined permit processing as incentives.

Commuter Rail and Heavy Rail

Commuter rail and heavy rail are also important transit options. Many U.S. cities have commuter rail service. Commuter rail involves trains that run on tracks that are shared with freight trains. Unlike light rail, commuter rail runs on rights-of-

Table 16-3
Metro Areas with Light-Rail Systems (2000)

Baltimore
Boston
Buffalo
Cleveland
Dallas
Denver
Hudson-Bergen, New Jersey
Los Angeles
Newark, New Jersey
New York City
Philadelphia
Pittsburgh
Portland, Oregon
Sacramento
Salt Lake City
San Francisco
San Jose
St. Louis

Source: North American Light Rail Industry, www.lightrail.com (2000)

SIDEBAR 16-1

A Tale of Two Rivals

Los Angeles and San Francisco have long been fierce rivals in sporting competitions, but their transportation planning and network operations provide a stark contrast. Los Angeles' sprawl and automobile dependence are legendary and not well suited to mass transit. The Metropolitan Transportation Authority (MTA) of Los Angeles County is the region's Metropolitan Planning Organization (MPO) and is charged with providing bus, subway, and light-rail service to the county's 20 million inhabitants and 89 cities. Unfortunately, the MTA has been the butt of jokes in the national press and on city streets (Dittmar *et al.* 1999, 16). Despite having a nearly $3 billion annual budget, the MTA has been plagued with cost overruns in the construction of a 400-mile light-rail system. As of 1999, the subway system had not been completed and was costing a whopping $330 million a mile. The existing bus system is seriously overcrowded (*ibid.*, 17-18). Both short-term and long-range transportation planning and implementation appear to be lacking.

The Metropolitan Transportation Commission (MTC) of the San Francisco Bay Area was created by the state legislature as a separate regional planning agency to fund and coordinate transit services provided by a dozen other local and regional agencies. The MTC functions as the region's MPO and has the power to approve or disapprove transportation projects; it has even overruled the state transportation agency, Caltrans, on proposed highway projects. In effect, the MTC operates as an oversight agency to minimize local transit rivalries and to direct funding as needed, according to the regional Transportation Improvement Plan (TIP). The MTC has emphasized transit projects ahead of highway projects in the TIP, as a better way to serve the Bay Area's 7 million residents and more than 90 cities. The MTC has used a small portion of its federal Surface Transportation Program funds to make grants to counties to undertake transportation and land use planning. The MTC has used Transportation Equity Act for the 21st Century funds to award grants to local transit agencies for traffic calming, transit-oriented development, and main street revitalization—all of which reduce auto travel and improve air quality (*ibid.*, 36).

---

way that are separate from roads and streets. Commuter rail is diesel powered and takes longer trips than light rail, allowing passengers to travel intrastate and interstate. Also, commuter rail can serve lower suburban densities. Commuter rail and park-and-ride lots are common for intermodal connections in suburban areas.

Heavy rail has an exclusive right-of-way with a third rail power source. The Bay Area Rapid Transit (BART) system in greater San Francisco is an example of heavy rail; in 2000, voters in Santa Clara County, southeast of San Francisco, approved a $6 billion ballot measure to build a rail system to connect to BART as well as to expand light rail and the bus system in the San Jose area (The Brookings Institution 2001). In 2000, Florida voters approved an amendment to the state constitution requiring the construction of a high-speed rail network connecting the state's five largest cities. Heavy rail can operate above or below grade at high speed, has the capacity to carry thousands of passengers, and generates little pollution. On the other hand, heavy rail depends on high densities and can be very expensive to install.

Railroad passenger service is typically underfunded compared to highways and airports, which are heavily subsidized. The federal Amtrak system has repeatedly been threatened with budget cuts and curtailed operations. Passenger rail service provided by Amtrak can be an important link for intercity or long-range commuting. For towns that have rail lines but no passenger service, it may be worthwhile to ask Amtrak to add at least a whistle-stop once or twice a week. This can be a way to provide access for tourists, especially bicyclists. Amtrak has already made such arrangements with tourist towns in Vermont.

ALTERNATIVE TRANSPORTATION MODES

Alternative transportation systems to the car and truck are important for creating a multimodal and intermodal transportation network that enables people to have a variety of reliable transportation choices and reduces energy use and air pollution. Communities and regions should examine the potential for a variety of modes, including bus, light rail, ferry boats, heavy rail, bicycle, and foot. For example, the bus system in Ames, Iowa (a college city of 50,000), recorded more than 3 million bus trips in 1999. Dozens of metro areas are developing light-rail systems. Ferry boats carry commuter traffic in greater New York, San Francisco, and Seattle. Communities along New York's Hudson River are exploring reinstating ferry connections to serve both commuters and tourists. In 1997, Austin, Texas, adopted a Bicycle and Pedestrian ("bike and ped") program to integrate these modes into the transportation system. The program features creating wide curb lanes, trails, sidewalks, and crosswalks along with 33 miles of new bike lanes. In addition, more bike racks are being built around the city and traffic light bicycle sensors are being installed at major intersections. Moreover, the "bike and ped" program has been joined with efforts to establish a network of greenbelts throughout the city and region.

ISTEA and TEA-21 Funding for Alternative Modes of Transportation

ISTEA created a source of funding for bicycle and pedestrian travel as well as historic preservation and environmental improvements. Projects quali-

fying for funding include pedestrian and bicycle trail systems, landscaping and scenic easements along highways, and the preservation of historic bridges. Projects receive bonus points if they are located within state-designated heritage areas, where there are significant cultural and historic resources. Ten percent of TEA-21 funds have been available for similar transportation enhancement projects, using matching state and local funds. Under TEA-21, a proposed project must fit into a historic, scenic and environmental, or pedestrian or bicycle category. These projects may include:

- acquisition of scenic easements, and scenic or historic sites;
- scenic or historic highway programs, including landscaping and control and removal of billboards;
- the rehabilitation and operation of historic transportation buildings, structures, and facilities;
- archaeological planning and research;
- establishment of transportation museums;
- mitigation of water pollution caused by highway runoff;
- reduction of wildlife fatalities caused by motor vehicles and maintenance of connected habitats;
- construction of paths and trails for pedestrians and bicyclists; and
- preservation of abandoned railroad corridors.

The National Rails to Trails Conservancy has been very active in working with local communities to transform old rail beds into bicycle and pedestrian paths. While many of these paths are used chiefly for recreation, some may also be used for commuting. There are an estimated 700 rails-to-trails projects in use nationwide (Daniels 1999, 232). The development of these trails has been a popular and important part of regional intermodal transportation plans. The City of Burlington, Vermont, used federal funds to help turn an abandoned rail line into a paved trail extending

SIDEBAR 16-2

Energy, Transportation, and the Internet

The Internet has already produced major changes in how people communicate, work, shop, invest, and entertain themselves. The Internet and related businesses have been a driving force in America's New Information Economy. Improved access to information and knowledge has played a role in boosting the nation's productivity. In fact, in 1997 and 1998, the American economy grew by 9% and energy consumption increased only slightly (*The Economist* 2000, 11).

In 2000, more than 16.5 million Americans worked at home at least one day a month, many of them computer and Internet users (Hafner 2000, G1). People who work at home and commute to the main office a few days a week are known as "telecommuters." Substituting e-mail conversations for face-to-face visits and on-line shopping for trips to the store can save energy. The telecommuting trend is increasing, and "facilitating an ever more spatially dispersed economy which in turn is causing metropolitan areas to become larger, more dispersed, and less densely populated" (Office of Technological Assessment 1995, 1). However, the energy savings in less commuting may be canceled or outstripped by the longer commutes when people do travel to the main office.

SIDEBAR 16-3

Airport Planning and Development

Intermodal transportation is important for connecting passengers and freight to the outside world. Air travel is essential for economic development in the New Information Economy, both to move passengers and to ship high-valued freight. Air travel literally soared in the 1990s, with the number of passengers flying from U.S. airports climbing from 465 million in 1990 to 614 million in 1998, a 32% increase (U.S. Bureau of the Census 2001, 650). Yet, air transportation is often overlooked by local and regional planners because airports tend to be controlled by separate airport authorities that do their own planning and development in conjunction with the Federal Aviation Administration (FAA). However, the location and size of airports have enormous implications for sprawl, transportation, and neighborhood impacts. Airports near city centers pose noise, air pollution, and on-the-ground traffic congestion problems for nearby neighborhoods. Moreover, these airports have little space to expand without tearing down buildings. Yet, environmental impact reviews, lawsuits, and political wrangling can extend the time from planning to construction for several years, if not indefinitely.

The construction of new airports in the countryside can encourage sprawling development patterns. Denver's new airport, built in the early 1990s, is jokingly referred to as being half-way to Nebraska, more than 15 miles east of downtown. Development has followed in the airport's path. Kansas City, Missouri's airport is 12 miles from downtown and has been a catalyst in the region's low-density sprawl (Daniels 1999, 116). There has been considerable growth in air traffic at smaller regional airports as people try to avoid the larger, more congested airports.

from the downtown waterfront to more than 7 miles north.

The funding of enhancement activities and alternative transportation modes is one way to encourage context-sensitive development. Context-sensitive highway design is needed to integrate transportation systems into the natural and built environments. For years, the American Association of State Highway and Transportation Officials' *A Policy on Geometric Design of Highways and Streets* (2001) has dominated highway and street construction thinking. However, new and redesigned roads based on this so-called "Green Book" often harm scenic, historic, or environmentally sensitive areas by widening roads, removing curves to increase speed limits, removing trees and stone walls, and replacing old bridges. In 1997, the Vermont Agency of Transportation adopted new highway design standards that are more sensitive to local character and allow transportation officials flexibility in establishing the width of roads and bridges (Myerson 1998). Eugene, Oregon, allows new local roads to be 20 feet in width, compared to the 28-foot width in the "Green Book"; narrower roads tend to cause drivers to slow down, and the less pavement means less runoff, particularly in Eugene where annual rainfall approaches 50 inches. In 1997, Connecticut began to allow bridges to be narrower than the recommended 28 feet wide to maintain a more human scale in keeping with the surroundings (Cho 1998, 36).

Assessing Transportation Needs to Manage Transportation Demand

Level of service is the current standard used in traffic impact studies for determining the capacity of a road intersection compared to its current level of use. A level of service study uses a grade scale from A (excellent) to F (failing) to indicate the amount of time a vehicle must wait to move through an intersection. Ratings of D and F indicate highly congested intersections with larger volumes of traffic than they were designed for.

Traffic loads are typically taken from mechanical traffic counters and sometimes by human observers. In addition, states often maintain databases of accident locations. The data indicate intersections and road segments with histories of numerous accidents that can be ranked for eventual improvements. Although some high-accident sites are related to congestion, others stem from hazardous road configurations, such as too many curb cuts or short sight distance for vehicles turning out into traffic. Overall, the level of service standard is skewed toward car and truck travel rather than multimodal travel along corridors. The level of service approach needs to be revised to evaluate how alternative transport modes and land development patterns can alleviate motor vehicle congestion.

Traffic impact studies are the basis for determining needed on-site and off-site traffic improvements, such as traffic lights, turn lanes, and road widenings as part of the subdivision and land development process. A number of communities have adopted adequate public facilities ordinances stating that development permission will not be granted unless public facilities are in place to serve a proposed development. A traffic impact study can help a community determine whether a proposed development will comply with a local adequate public facilities ordinance. However, traffic impact studies have tended to focus solely on roads and highways. Instead, traffic impact studies need to be recast as transportation impact studies, which work out multimodal solutions, including transit, bicycle and pedestrian opportunities, and safety issues. When tied to an adequate public facilities ordinance and a capital improvements program (CIP), transportation impact studies have the potential to influence transportation networks and the location, timing, and character of development at a specific site as well as for entire neighborhoods.

Travel Demand Management

States and metropolitan areas can explore a variety of measures to manage the demand for transportation, especially for space on highways. These approaches can make motor vehicle traffic flow more smoothly, discourage driving, or encourage the use of alternate modes of transport. Ways to discourage driving include raising gasoline taxes, raising the price of highway tolls during rush hours, increasing parking fees, and decreasing the number of parking spaces. Several states offer transponders for drivers to place in their cars for automatic charging of tolls. This reduces waiting times to pass through tolls, and hence less idling and air pollution. Intelligent streets and highways with sensors can be tied to car-borne computers to alert drivers of traffic jams and map out alternative routes.

There are several creative ways to encourage the use of alternative modes of transport. TEA-21 allows employees to receive up to $100 a month tax-free in employer-paid transit benefits. In 1991, the State of Washington passed a law requiring companies employing more than 100 workers to offer them a program of commuting alternatives. Options can range from free parking for vanpools and carpools to encourage ride sharing to a cash payment as an alternative to a free car parking space. Several cities have developed commuter trip reduction programs and match workers with vanpools and carpools. Employers can offer flextime so workers can avoid rush hours and help reduce peak traffic flows, and telecommuting can minimize the number of trips between home and the office. California has mandated that companies in smog-prone areas that employ 50 or more people must charge their workers a market price for parking or give them an equivalent amount of money for alternative means of commuting (Hawken *et al.* 1999, 41-42). Austin, Texas, created a program—Ozone Action Days—that offers free bus rides for cyclists to encourage bicycling and intermodal transportation.

Communities can dedicate HOV lanes or reverse commuting lanes for buses and carpooling, and can build park-and-ride lots at transit stops. Mixed-use and compact residential developments can also be encouraged through the zoning ordinance.

Getting people to live closer to their work, schools, and shopping would go far toward reducing car trips and encouraging mass transit. Maryland's Live Near Your Work program, an element of Maryland's smart growth legislation, offers grants of up to $3,000 to people who buy homes near their work. The Federal National Mortgage Association (Fannie Mae) has created a location-efficient mortgage option for people who buy a home near shopping and public transit. Fannie Mae figures the transportation savings as part of the income needed to qualify for the home loan (Natural Resources Defense Council 2000, 7).

Planning for Neighborhood Roads and Streets

Big arterial road projects, such as freeways, ring roads, and bypasses, tend to capture the majority of attention in transportation planning, but the network of local and collector streets that connect motor vehicle traffic to arterials significantly influence traffic flows. To achieve a smooth flow, minimize driving trips, and maximize the potential for pedestrians and bicycle use, a grid street pattern is more effective than the all-too-frequent suburban use of cul-de-sacs. Alleys reduce on-street parking, and narrower local streets can promote slower speeds and greater safety. A well-integrated system of local streets, sidewalks, and bicycle and pedestrian paths that link specific sites, neighborhoods, and districts give local residents access to homes, parks, schools, shopping, transit stops, and jobs. Interconnected neighborhoods benefit nondrivers, such as children and the elderly as well as parents who are not needed to drive them everywhere.

Traffic Calming

Decreasing the number of cars on local roads by providing other transport choices is one approach to reducing congestion. Another is to allow cars to use the neighborhood collector and local streets, but on the neighborhoods' terms. Many communities have adopted traffic-calming measures as a way to use physical design to slow and divert traffic. Pedestrian and bicyclist safety and the reduction of accidents are the priorities with traffic calming, but noise reduction and a certain aesthetic appeal in landscaping along streets can also be accomplished. Traffic consultant Cynthia Hoyle defines traffic calming as "environmentally compatible mobility management" (Hoyle 1995, 9). According to planner Reid Ewing, "The places that are doing traffic calming are some of the most livable" (Knack 1998, 12), such as Montgomery County, Maryland, and Austin, Texas.

Traffic-calming devices are designed to control the speed of traffic or to reroute traffic, and are not meant for major arterial roads where moving large volumes of traffic at high speed is the goal. On collector and local streets, speed control devices include speed bumps and humps, rumple strips, raised intersections, textured crosswalks, angled slow points, planters, chicanes or bends in the road, road-narrowing "neckdowns," roundabouts, and traffic circles. Traffic diversions involve one-way streets, cul-de-sacs, or even closing off streets. Traffic diversions have played a key role in helping to create "defensible space" in which community residents guard against crime and promote revitalization (Newman 1995, 149-55). On the other hand, traffic diversions can have the effect of displacing rather than reducing traffic congestion and may also separate rather than interconnect neighborhoods. In many cases, traffic calming offers an acceptable alternative to diverting traffic. Care should be taken that garbage trucks, ambulances, and fire trucks can gain ready access to properties.

Traffic calming should be done with citizen involvement as part of a neighborhood or community transportation planning effort. Traffic calming dovetails nicely with the New Urbanism designs for mixed-use and pedestrian-oriented urban development and redevelopment. Motor vehicles are accepted, but they are not allowed to dominate the landscape.

LOCAL PLANNING FOR TRANSPORTATION

Local transportation planning should involve coordination and consistency among city and county comprehensive plans and CIPs. If local governments are part of a metropolitan area, their plans and programs should be consistent with the TIP of the MPO. To make mass transit viable, local governments will have to adopt comprehensive plans, zoning and subdivision ordinances, and CIPs that encourage more compact, transit-supportive development. Areas for higher density, mixed-use development near transit stations and corridors can be designated on the future land use map of the comprehensive plan.

Inventory

The transportation element of the comprehensive plan should begin with an inventory and mapping of the different modes of transport, including the type, location, capacity, level of use, and condition of each transportation mode. Any problems with the current transportation system (e.g., sites with a high number of traffic accidents, low level of service ratings, the physical condition of roads and bridges, and low mass-transit ridership) should be identified. The state department of transportation or the MPO should have the necessary information. Planners should be aware of proposed transportation projects in their own community, in neighboring communities, throughout the region, and in the State TIP. Municipalities should also ask the public for their ideas and concerns about transportation as part of a community needs assessment survey.

Analysis

The analysis should use projections of future populations and the information on identified transportation problems to evaluate the community's transportation network and its ability to meet projected transportation needs. The viability of developing new transportation modes, such as bike paths or light rail, should be explored as well as the potential for intermodal links. Possible transportation demand management tools as well as compact growth forms should also be evaluated.

Geographic Information System (GIS) mapping and evaluation will become increasingly helpful in making the link between transportation systems and land use planning. For instance, the EPA has been testing GIS-based planning software called Smart Growth INDEX that analyzes the potential impacts of transportation projects on land use, air quality, and traffic congestion. The software can evaluate a variety of transportation and land use scenarios to assist in the drafting of local or regional comprehensive plans.

Goals and Objectives

The overriding goals should be to promote intermodal and multimodal transportation systems to improve transportation efficiency and transportation options in the community (Table 16-4). These goals should be linked to specific objectives in several other chapters of the comprehensive plan.

Table 16-4
Sample Transportation Goals and Objectives in the Comprehensive Plan

Transportation	
Goal	To provide safe, reliable movement of people and goods through intermodal and multimodal transportation systems.
Objective	Coordinate local transportation plans with the Metropolitan Planning Organization Transportation Improvement Plan, the State Transportation Improvement Program, and State Improvement Plan for air quality.
Objective	Promote the development of alternative modes of transportation to the car and truck, especially mass transit, and bicycle and pedestrian paths.
Objective	Provide safe streets, and keep roads and bridges in good repair.
Objective	Improve transportation links with neighboring communities.
Economic Base	
Objective	Promote intermodal transportation systems to make the community attractive to new development.
Land Use	
Objective	Plan according to transportation corridors to manage growth and create more efficient transportation systems.
Objective	Encourage infill of vacant land and underutilized downtown sites to minimize sprawl and facilitate mass-transit options.
Natural Resources	
Objective	Promote the use of mass transit and alternative modes of transportation to conserve energy and reduce air pollution.

Action Strategy

The Action Strategy should present techniques and programs for achieving the transportation goals and objectives as well as a timetable. Transportation benchmarks should be identified and progress toward those benchmarks evaluated in an annual report on the environment. Specific recommendations might include the following:

- Adopt mixed-use zoning and adaptive reuse of buildings in the downtown to reduce commuting times and encourage alternative modes of transport.
- Add bicycle lanes, paths, and routes that connect the places where people live, work, shop, and entertain themselves.
- Add HOV lanes to encourage carpooling.
- Explore funding for the creation or expansion of mass-transit systems.
- Study the feasibility of developing park-and-ride sites for commuters, connected with the bus system.
- Install traffic-calming devices in predominantly residential neighborhoods

Zoning Ordinance

Effective zoning promotes a land use pattern that is conducive to the creation and use of a variety of transport modes. Mixed-use zoning and adaptive reuse of buildings can promote TOD, and greater pedestrian and bicycle traffic, as can denser development in general. In urban and suburban corridors where transit is available, the local zoning ordinance should include a Transit Overlay District. This overlay district could extend from one-quarter to one-half mile around an existing or proposed transit stop, and require mixed uses, fairly high density, and pedestrian connections. Zoning incentives for high-density development might include reduced parking requirements or placing off-street parking behind buildings, reduced setbacks or zero lot lines, and higher floor area ratios of built area to lot size.

Some states permit municipalities to adopt an "official map" that lays out the community's desired future street network. Developers must build streets that are consistent with the official map. Yet, relatively few municipalities use this important transportation planning tool. Instead, developers build too many cul-de-sacs and isolate development from existing road networks.

Subdivision Regulations

Subdivision and land development regulations should ensure safe, reliable transportation access to new developments. Subdivision regulations can require narrow street widths, interconnected streets, and the use of traffic-calming devices. Developers proposing large developments should be required to provide a traffic impact study to determine the type and extent of impacts on road networks and other transportation systems. The subdivision ordinance should spell out ways to encourage transit use, such as adding a bus stop. The subdivision regulations can also require transportation impact fees for traffic improvements, and require the mandatory dedication of parkland, which can include bicycle and pedestrian trails. The regulations can also require the development of bicycle and pedestrian paths to connect residential developments to schools, parks, and shopping. Sidewalks can be required as well. In general, cul-de-sacs should be discouraged, except where the topography makes thru-roads prohibitively expensive. The subdivision regulations can promote the use of alleys with garages placed behind the houses. Alleys reduce curb cuts and on-street parking needs, and serve as additional paths through neighborhoods. Subdivision regulations can replace minimum parking requirements with maximum parking space allowances. Some states, such as Pennsylvania, allow local governments to adopt an "official plan" map of a future road network with which future developments must comply.

Table 16-5
A Checklist of Transportation Issues for a Development Review

1.	What are the size, location, and uses of the proposed development?
2.	What modes of transportation will provide access to the proposed development?
3.	What is the capacity of nearby roads?
4.	What is the record of traffic accidents near the proposed development?
5.	Is a traffic impact study required? Impact fees?
6.	What transportation investments do the subdivision regulations require the developer to make?
7.	How does the proposed development fit with the community's capital improvements program? With the Metropolitan Planning Organization's Transportation Improvement Program?
8.	Will new roads be built? If so, how will they connect with existing roads?
9.	Is there an official map of proposed local roads? Does the proposed development meet local standards for siting, grading, road layout, width, and other factors?
10.	Has the developer obtained any necessary state or federal transportation-related permits?

Capital Improvements Program

The Transportation and Land Use sections of the comprehensive plan are crucial for drafting a realistic CIP. Coordinating land use planning and transportation planning is essential for creating an orderly, efficient community and region. The community will want to spend its transportation funds to provide access to places where growth is desired and where dense development already exists. The key to effective future transportation systems will be choices among and connections between transport modes. Beyond building and repairing roads and bridges, local governments can build park-and-ride lots, bicycle and pedestrian paths, and bus and light-rail systems to better manage traffic. Parking and transportation impact fees can be used to generate revenue and pay for road improvements. Communities should consider alternatives to new parking structures, and not permit new ground-level parking lots.

What to Look for in a Development Review

When a planning commission looks at a development project, it should evaluate it for consistency with the comprehensive plan, zoning ordinance, subdivision and land development regulations, CIP, and any other applicable local laws. Assessing the impact of a proposed development on highway traffic capacity and other transport modes is a necessity (see Table 16-5). Although the review of transportation impacts and design may be time consuming, large developments in particular, once built, will influence the location and type of transportation systems, land use patterns, energy use, air quality, impervious surface coverage, and the overall efficiency of the community's transportation system for a long time to come.

CASE STUDIES

The following case studies illustrate how two metropolitan areas have recognized the limits of relying upon motor vehicles for future transportation needs. Kansas City and Charlotte have begun planning processes to develop more extensive mass-transit systems and coordinate new development in more compact centers and corridors. However, overcoming the traditional emphasis on road construction has not been easy.

CASE STUDY 16-1
Kansas City, Missouri

Metropolitan Kansas City, Missouri, is one of the most sprawling regions in the nation. In 1950, greater Kansas City had a density of 5,665 people per square mile. By 1990, the density had fallen to just 1,397 people per square mile (Singleton 2000). As a result, dependence on the automobile soared. However, a proposal to build a new interstate-type ring road several miles outside of downtown Kansas City was scrapped in the late 1990s. Public officials and concerned citizens pointed to the high cost of the ring road as well as the potential for the road to induce further sprawl.

In November 1999, Kansas City, Missouri, voters approved a $0.01 sales tax that would raise an estimated $67 million a year for infrastructure improvements, including mass transit. The city's planners recommended a four-step process to promote transit:

1. Either select a fixed guideway route for rail or bus transit that does not involve interference from cars and trucks, or else decide not to build a mass-transit system (fixed guideway transit systems provide an assurance of future service because the routes are not easily changed).
2. Draft a detailed land use plan and economic development strategy based on the route and transit mode. For example, TOD reduces the need for parking in commercial areas, allowing for more compact development.
3. Finalize the choice of a fixed route transit mode and technology.
4. Create a plan for funding and a timetable for implementation.

The Kansas City transit plan called for relying on mass transit as both an urban and suburban development and redevelopment tool. Within a quarter-mile of each transit stop, the plan recommended higher densities of commercial and residential development to encourage ridership. Transit stops should be intermodal centers that link a number of transport modes. Transit should extend to regional centers where there are shopping malls and higher density housing; and transit should provide access to community centers where there are professional offices, retail outlets, and lower density housing. Finally, park-and-ride centers should be built in outlying suburban areas to enable suburbanites to use the multimodal transportation system.

Meanwhile, citizens in greater Kansas City formed the Regional Transit Alliance to advocate in favor of mass transit. Many cities with effective transit systems have such organizations, made up of transit riders, business owners, and concerned citizens from a variety of neighborhoods and interest groups.

CASE STUDY 16-2
Transportation Planning in Mecklenburg County, North Carolina

Charlotte and adjacent Mecklenburg County are located in the south central region of North Carolina. Since 1980, Charlotte has grown into a major financial center. According to the U.S. Bureau of the Census, from 1990 to 1998, the Charlotte metropolitan region grew by an estimated 220,000 people to 1,162,000, a 19% increase. It was clear that roads alone were not going to solve the region's transportation needs. In 1999, the joint Charlotte-Mecklenburg planning commission set forth a transportation vision for the region, summarized as follows:

Where Are We Today?

Charlotte-Mecklenburg is still an automobile-dominated community. A low density, suburban land use pattern and a resulting dependence on automobiles have created widespread congestion throughout the County.

Some major road improvement projects have recently been completed to relieve some of the congested areas. However, our community is growing and is expected to gain more than 230,000 persons in the next 20 years. This growth will mean economic development for Charlotte-Mecklenburg but it will also mean more road congestion. It is clear that we cannot continue to do business as usual. We must look to our future and coordinate our transportation decisions with our vision for land use, including the provision for alternative means of transportation to the automobile.

**Where Are We Going and
How Will We Get There?**

The land use and transportation future for Charlotte-Mecklenburg has been clearly defined in the Committee of 100's Transportation and Land Use Vision for the Charlotte Metropolitan Area. The Vision calls for a transportation system built around a "centers and corridors" development pattern whereby the most intensive development occurs along the five main corridors of the economic centers of the region. Roadway, transit, bicycle, and pedestrian systems will then be developed to serve and reinforce the development pattern.

Implementation of this vision will occur through the 2015 Transportation, the Transportation Improvement Program (TIP), and the Analysis for Fixed Guideway Transit. The 2015 Transportation Plan addresses all forms of transportation and provides local elected officials with a guide on which to base future transportation investment decisions. The Analysis for Fixed Guideway Transit is a guide for future mass transit, including recommendations for the potential of High Capacity Transit (light rail), HOV Lanes, and further expansion of the Charlotte bus system (Charlotte, North Carolina 2001).

In 2002, the Charlotte Area Transit System planners produced a Corridor System Plan, which recommended major investments in mass transit, including 28 miles of bus rapid transit using some exclusive busways, 21 miles of light rail with overhead electric lines, and 29 miles of commuter rail (Charlotte Area Transit System 2002, 5). By 2025, planners expect the regional mass-transit system to serve more than 200,000 daily riders, compared to 50,000 in 2002. The cost of building the system is $2.9 billion, with half of the funds coming from the federal government. The other half will be split between the State of North Carolina and greater Charlotte.

17

Planning for Energy

Our aging power grid is not able to meet the needs of the information age.

Carl Guardino, President, Silicon Valley
Manufacturing Group (Edwards 2000, 7L)

70-80 cents of every energy dollar immediately leaves the community.

Rocky Mountain Institute,
Community Energy Workbook, 1995

Energy provides the power and mobility for modern lifestyles. Energy comes from a variety of sources and goes into a wide range of uses—from transportation to manufacturing to heating and lighting to running computers. Americans have largely taken for granted inexpensive and plentiful energy supplies, but the era of cheap energy appears to be waning. Land use patterns have a strong influence on transportation systems and energy use. Sprawled patterns require more energy and rely heavily on private motor vehicles. Compact development encourages walking, biking, and mass transit as options to driving. Thus, a major energy choice for communities and regions is how to mix a variety of transportation systems and maintain energy use and pollution levels within acceptable standards (see Chapter 16). Equally important is for communities to determine where their energy will come from and at what cost. Energy prices, supplies, and sources change over time. Energy conservation (using less energy) and energy efficiency (reducing energy waste) can stretch energy supplies and promote economic development. For instance, new commercial, residential, and public buildings and alterations to existing buildings can be required to meet energy efficiency standards and to achieve greater energy conservation.

AMERICA'S ENERGY CHALLENGES: PRODUCTION, CONSUMPTION, EFFICIENCY, AND CONSERVATION

The challenges for homeowners, businesses, and governments are how to secure long-term energy supplies, become more energy efficient, conserve on the use of energy, and reduce energy-related pollution. Not only do energy efficiency and conservation stretch household budgets, increase business profits, and hold down tax increases, they also buy time for the development of alternative, more environmentally friendly energy sources, such as hydrogen and solar energy, to enable a smoother transition away from nonrenewable energy.

Energy Production

Communities and regions must decide how much of their energy needs they should produce for themselves, how much to rely on imported energy, and how much energy can be saved through conservation and greater energy efficiency.

Different sources of energy have different environmental impacts. Renewable energy sources (e.g., solar, wind, biomass, water, and geothermal power) provide a small fraction of America's energy needs. Yet, they generate much less air and water pollution than nonrenewable oil, natural gas, and coal.

Renewable energy sources also reduce America's dependence on imported energy supplies.

Communities and regions are often faced with decisions over the location of new electrical-generating facilities that are needed to power economic growth. These facilities, however, may generate air pollution and require large amounts of water for cooling. It is also important for cities and counties to plan for energy emergencies that may occur from natural disasters or from the cut-off of imported energy supplies.

Energy Consumption

America's energy appetite continues to grow. In 2000, Americans consumed 16% more energy than in 1990 and 25% more than in 1980, as measured in British thermal units or the amount of energy needed to heat 1 pound of water at 39.2 degrees Fahrenheit by 1 degree (U.S. Bureau of the Census 2003, 563). Industrial uses accounted for nearly 40% of overall energy use, followed by transportation at 27%, residential uses at 21%, and commercial uses at 16% (*ibid.*). Petroleum, natural gas, and coal provided 84% of America's energy needs. Oil accounted for 97% of the energy used for transportation. Such heavy reliance on nonrenewable energy sources is not sustainable in the long run, in part because Americans import most of the oil they consume.

Energy Efficiency

On the positive side, America's energy use has become more efficient. Advances in energy-saving technology reduced the amount of energy needed to produce a unit of output by 36% in 1998 compared to 1970, while the size of the nation's economy more than doubled (Belsie 1999, 4). Over the same time period, improvements in building heating and cooling technologies resulted in savings of almost $33 billion and 60 million fewer metric tons of carbon emissions (U.S. Department of Energy (DOE) 2000, 5).

Energy Conservation

A reduction in energy consumption can mean financial savings for individuals, families, businesses, and communities. Most communities import a large majority of the energy they consume. The less energy imported, the more money remains in the community. Moreover, conservation is usually the least expensive solution to energy needs, especially compared to the cost of building new electrical-generating facilities. However, three interrelated trends do not bode well for energy conservation: demographics, personal tastes and preferences, and technology.

Overall energy consumption rose in the 1990s as America's population increased by 32 million people. The U.S. Bureau of the Census is projecting a nationwide increase by 2025 of another 55 million people, which will put further demands on energy supplies (U.S. Bureau of the Census 2001, 13). Since 1990, more Americans have been living in suburbs than in central cities. This decentralized pattern of development means more reliance on cars and longer commuting distances (Myerson 1998, c6). The number of two-income families has increased, often compelling the use of two cars for commuting. Also, sales of gas-guzzling Sport Utility Vehicles and minivans boomed in the 1990s and early 2000s, increasing energy consumption.

As suburban populations grow, Americans are showing a desire for larger houses. Between the early 1970s and 1999, the average size of a new house increased in size from 1,600 square feet to 2,260 square feet, even though the average family size decreased from 3.6 to just three people (Rozhon 1999). The cost of heating and cooling increases with the greater house size. Yard sizes have increased as well (Meck 2000). Larger yards mean more energy to mow the lawn, leaf-blow the leaves, and snow-blow the snow.

Technology often creates new demands for energy. In 1970, fewer than 40% of the nation's homes had central air conditioning. By the late 1990s, more than 80% of homes had central air (*ibid.*). America's population growth over the next 20 years is expected to be concentrated in three states: California, Florida, and Texas. Given the hot summers in these states, the demand for air conditioning and electricity will surely rise. In addition, more homes now have dishwashers, washers, dryers, microwave ovens, multiple television sets, audio equipment, and other electrical gadgets. A new energy-intensive technology is the computer and its peripheral equipment. While estimates vary, computers may be using as much as 13% of the nation's electricity (Edwards 2000, 7L).

The design of developments can also affect air pollution as well as energy conservation. Already, many urban downtowns are heat islands with summer temperatures several degrees higher than suburban and outlying areas. For instance, according to the Lawrence Livermore National Laboratory, Los Angeles could reduce summer temperatures by 4 degrees Fahrenheit by planting about 10 million trees and using lighter colored materials on rooftops (Lawrence Livermore 2001). The decrease in temperature would reduce ozone levels by about 10% as well as save $175 million in air-conditioning costs.

Finally, community recycling programs are another way to reduce energy use (see Chapter 6). Recycling involves much less energy than processing virgin natural resources.

AMERICA'S ENERGY SOURCES

The U.S. mainly relies on five sources of energy: coal, petroleum, natural gas, nuclear, and hydropower. Each energy source has advantages and disadvantages in its production, use, and environmental impacts.

Coal

America has among the largest coal reserves of any country in the world. In 2000, coal production reached a record 1.07 billion tons and provided 22% of the nation's energy needs. Coal-fired electrical plants accounted for more than 56% of all electricity generated in the U.S. (U.S. Bureau of the Census 2003, 566).

Deep mining and strip mining of coal scar landscapes and cause acid mine drainage, which pollutes soil and water (see Chapter 15). Burning coal emits particulate air pollution as well as nitrogen dioxide and sulfur dioxide (the primary ingredients in acid rain) and carbon dioxide (the leading greenhouse gas) (see Chapter 5). Nationwide, power plants produce about 115 million tons of potentially toxic coal ash each year. So far, coal ash has been disposed of in landfills, settling ponds, and even strip mines; about one-third of all coal ash is recycled into building materials (Jehl 2000a, A1). Cleaner coal-burning technologies are needed, but the pollution impacts of coal burning are not easy to remediate.

Oil

Americans relied on oil for 40% of their energy needs in 2000 (U.S. Bureau of the Census 2003, 566). Petroleum products are convenient to use in motor vehicles and for home heating, and, adjusted for inflation, oil was cheaper in 2000 than in 1980 (*ibid.*, 569). However, extracting, transporting, and refining petroleum into gasoline creates air and water pollution. Massive oil spills—such as the 1969 oil platform blow-out off Santa Barbara, California; and the multimillion-gallon spill from the *Exxon Valdez* in Prince William Sound, Alaska, in 1989—can devastate wildlife and foul coastlines. The burning of gasoline and diesel fuel in motor vehicles is a prime contributor to air pollution (see Chapter 5).

Production of crude oil in the U.S. has been declining fairly steadily since 1970, while imports have nearly tripled. In 1970, the U.S. produced 9.64 million barrels a day and imported 3.42 million barrels a day. In 2001, domestic crude oil production was 5.8 million barrels a day, and imports stood at 9.1 million barrels a day (*ibid.*, 571). By 2020, according to the U.S. DOE (2000, 30), the U.S. will be importing 64% of the 25 million barrels it consumes each day. According to the British Petroleum Statistical Review of World Energy, the United States in 2002 had *11 years* of proven oil reserves if it were to provide for all of its own oil needs (*The Economist* 2002, 102).

On average, in the 1990s, America imported more than $50 billion worth of oil each year. This dependence on foreign oil has made the United States vulnerable to foreign conflicts. In 1974, several Arab countries refused to sell oil to the U.S. over its support of Israel. In 1991, Iraq invaded oil-rich Kuwait and threatened Saudi Arabia, which has the largest oil reserves of any nation. The price of oil spiked to $40 a barrel. Oil dependence has also put pressure on America's trade deficit, which exceeded $400 billion in 2002.

Despite the growing dependence on foreign oil, the U.S. has been somewhat careful about exploring for domestic oil. For two decades, there has been a moratorium on oil drilling in the waters off California and Florida, and offshore drilling in other areas has been tightly controlled, except in the Gulf of Mexico. In 1992, Congress declared the Alaska's Arctic Wildlife Refuge off limits to oil exploration. Proposals to open the refuge to oil exploration were defeated by Congress in 2002.

In 1975, Congress enacted Corporate Average Fuel Economy (CAFE) standards to encourage better fuel efficiency in cars and light trucks. In the 1970s, the average fuel efficiency was as low as 13.4 miles per gallon (mpg). In response to the CAFE standards and higher gasoline prices, vehicle manufacturers brought the average fuel efficiency up to 22.1 mpg in 1988. However, by 2002, the average fuel efficiency had slipped to 20.4 mpg (U.S. Environmental Protection Agency (EPA) 2003). Automobile manufacturers have largely resisted the CAFE standards, even though better gas mileage would reduce both air pollution and dependence on foreign oil.

Raising gasoline taxes would be one way to encourage the conservation of fossil fuel. However, federal, state, and local gasoline taxes are designed to raise revenue for road construction and maintenance, not to discourage oil consumption or to reflect the costs that cars and trucks impose on air and water quality, or the cost of disposing of aged vehicles. In 2000, federal gas taxes were $0.184 a gallon, and state taxes ranged from $0.542 a gallon in Hawaii to $0.264 a gallon in Alaska (Pachetti 2000, 36). These tax levels are well below gasoline taxes in Europe, which, for instance, top $3 a gallon in Great Britain.

Natural Gas

Natural gas supplied about 23% of America's energy needs in 1999, and slightly more than half of all U.S. homes were heated with natural gas. Natural gas is the cleanest burning of the hydrocarbons because it contains no sulfur and emits only low levels of carbon dioxide and hardly any particulate matter. Natural gas is now the fuel of choice, replacing coal, for new electrical-generating plants. Several new electrical plants are being built using double-cycle gas turbines with double the efficiency of coal-fired plants and one-quarter of the carbon emissions (Hawken *et al.* 1999, 248). Although America's oil reserves may be severely depleted within a few decades, U.S. natural gas reserves could last through much of the 21st century and even beyond (Easterbrook 1996, 346).

Nuclear Power

America's 104 nuclear power plants generated slightly more than one-fifth of the nation's electricity in 2001 (U.S. Bureau of the Census 2003, 575), but no new nuclear plants have been started since 1978. Nuclear power plants cost hundreds of millions, if not billions, of dollars to build and they have operating lives of about 50 years, after which they must be "decommissioned" and monitored for radiation leaks far into the future. Still, the main shortcoming of nuclear power is disposing of the radioactive waste. The plutonium that fuels nuclear plants is one of the most hazardous substances on earth. Moreover, it has an active

Oil wells and natural gas wells are potential sources of groundwater contamination. For instance, in Texas in 1997, there were 77 reported cases of groundwater pollution from oil and gas wells (Yardley 2000, A10). Oil companies are supposed to seal abandoned wells with cement, but some failed companies have not done so. Other companies have been allowed to pay $100 a year instead of plugging idle wells. As of 2000, there were approximately 25,000 abandoned oil wells, another 15,000 idled wells, and thousands of active wells—some of which could be leaking into underground aquifers (*ibid.*, A1). Meanwhile,

with its arid climate and a growing population, water in Texas is becoming increasingly scarce.

In Wyoming's Powder River Basin, the discovery of methane gas deposits has led to the practice of flooding millions of gallons of water down into coal to flush out the methane. Energy companies in 2000 were pumping out about 21 million gallons of water a day from aquifers for this purpose. The used water is held in reservoirs and ponds, diverted into streams, or simply dumped on the ground. However, the actual water quality impacts on surface waters and underground aquifers have not yet been determined. As of 2000, Wyoming had about 5,000 methane wells, with another 6,000 permitted. Wyoming's production of methane jumped from about 5 billion cubic feet in 1995 to more than 50 billion cubic feet in 1999 (Janofsky 2000, A1, A7).

"half-life" of thousands of years. As yet, there is no safe means of disposing of radioactive waste. Disposal costs have not been factored into the price of electricity from nuclear power plants; hence, consumers are not paying the true cost of nuclear-generated electricity.

The federal Nuclear Regulatory Agency issues licenses for the operation of nuclear power plants. The agency requires operators of nuclear power plants to draft emergency evacuation plans in case of a nuclear accident. These plans must then be approved by the Federal Emergency Management Agency.

Hydroelectric Dams

There are thousands of hydroelectric dams in the United States, ranging from small, "low-head" dams to the huge dams on the Columbia and Colorado Rivers. Hydroelectric dams generate about 5% of the nation's energy and have often been touted as a clean source of inexpensive electricity. However, these dams, many of which were built in the 1920s and 1930s, have greatly reduced fish runs and flooded millions of acres. In addition,

they are silting up. A number of older, smaller dams are being dismantled, such as two dams in California and Oregon in 1998, and the Edwards Dam in Augusta, Maine, in 1999 (Sheerman 1999, F1). The Pacific and Mountain states have most of the nation's untapped potential for new hydroelectric dams (U.S. Bureau of the Census 2001, 583), but new hydroelectric dams would be costly to build and would be sure to attract opposition from environmental groups.

Electricity

Generating electricity is a $220 billion per year industry in the United States (U.S. Bureau of the Census 2003, 568). In 2000, the leading uses of electricity were residential (35%), industrial (31%), commercial (30%), and other uses (4%) (*ibid.*, 573). The leading sources for electricity are coal, nuclear power, natural gas, and hydroelectric dams. About two-thirds of the nation's electricity comes from burning coal, natural gas, and oil. In 1999, electrical plants in general, and coal-fired plants in particular, produced 28% of the nation's nitrogen oxide emissions, 67% of the sulfur dioxide, 36% of the carbon dioxide, and 33% of the mercury emissions (Dunn and Flavin 2000, 151).

The nation's electrical grid has been described as aging. One reason is that the deregulation of utility companies has made them cautious about making new investments. Another is that the construction of new power plants takes longer for approvals and overcoming local opposition. Meanwhile, energy demands continue to grow. Severe brownouts in Silicon Valley in summer 2000 provided tangible proof of computer thirst for electricity. In the 1990s, the difference between electrical-generation capacity and peak load slipped from 20% to just over 10% (U.S. Bureau of the Census 2001, 579). With global warming a real likelihood and the nation's population growing by 3 million a year, the demand for air conditioning will continue to grow, creating pressure for additional generating plants.

There may be a need for as many as 1,000 new power plants between 2000 and 2020. It is important to note that the average size of new electrical-utility generating plants has decreased dramatically from 600 megawatts in the 1980s to just 21 megawatts in 1998 (Dunn and Flavin 2000, 144). Smaller plants are less obtrusive, but there are likely to be more of them in the future. Still, the location of new power plants, power lines, and even underground natural gas pipelines can be contentious issues in some communities.

Energy efficiency and conservation can decrease the need for new power plants as well as hold down electrical rates and benefit household budgets (see Figure 17-1). Greater residential energy efficiency can come through improved design and technology; buildings with super insulated windows, walls, and ceilings require less heating and cooling, and newer appliances use less energy. Residential energy conservation can be achieved through keeping the thermostat at no more than 68 degrees Fahrenheit in the winter and air conditioners at no less than 74 degrees Fahrenheit in the summer.

Electric utilities can invest in residential conservation in several ways, including home energy audits and weatherizing, low-flow showerheads (less water needs to be heated), and rebates for new appliances and air conditioners. The "payback" of these investments is generally much quicker than for a new generating plant and avoids potential plant-siting battles with neighbors and public officials. Educating consumers to think about and practice energy conservation will continue to pay dividends far into the future.

Some electric utilities have promoted greater energy efficiency through "cogeneration," selling their steam heat created in producing electricity to

17-1 Promoting energy conservation awareness in Portland, Oregon.

Source: Katherine Daniels

commercial and residential users. For example, Cambridge Electric in Massachusetts has long sold its steam to Harvard University. The Key-Span company of Brooklyn, New York, is building cogeneration plants that will produce electricity from natural gas and will sell the heat by-product to hospitals, apartments, and the city jail complex (Silver 2000, 4).

Renewable Energy

Renewable energy—not counting hydroelectricity—accounted for slightly less than 5% of total energy output in America in 1999, but renewable sources produced 26% more power than in 1990. Renewable energy sources are much less damaging to the environment and are becoming more economically competitive with conventional sources. The U.S. DOE (2000, 28) expects the amount of energy from renewable sources to nearly double between 1998 and 2020.

Wind

Wind energy can be generated on a commercial basis by wind turbines that reach up to 250 feet high, have blades of more than 100 feet long, and are located on windy hilltops. Although wind energy produces no pollution, the siting of several turbines on a wind farm can be controversial because of the visual impacts on the landscape. In addition, wind turbines may be fatal to birds and they produce some noise. However, wind energy has substantial potential. North Dakota has an estimated capacity to generate 250 *gigawatts* from wind power; compare this to the Grand Coulee Dam, one of the nation's largest hydroelectric dams, which produces just over 6 gigawatts of electricity (Dashefsky 1993, 264). (A watt is a measure of electrical power equal to 1 joule per second. A kilowatt is 1,000 watts. A megawatt is 1,000 kilowatts or 1 million watts, and a gigawatt is 1,000 megawatts or 1 billion watts).

The 107-megawatt wind power plant near Lake Benton, Minnesota—one of the largest in the world—can provide electricity to 43,000 homes (*ibid.*, 23). By the end of 2001, wind generators were expected to produce enough electricity for 1.7 million U.S. homes (Jehl 2000b, 46). Several states allow small-scale power system owners to sell electricity generated by methane, sun, and wind to the grid at the retail price, but commercial utilities are also getting into the electricity from wind business.

A major issue with the development of wind energy is the siting of turbines. Typically, ridgelines and hilltops are ideal for turbines. Yet, there may be visual impacts on neighboring landowners, and the turbines produce noise when the blades are spinning. While states have regulations governing the siting of electrical power plants, local governments would be wise to establish standards for the siting of wind generators.

Solar Energy

Nationwide, an estimated 156,000 homes used solar energy in 2002 (Rocky Mountain Institute 2002). Solar energy can provide hot water, electricity, and even cooling for homes, businesses, and industry. Solar energy systems come in two forms: active and passive. Active systems can provide hot water or electricity. Solar hot water systems feature panels mounted on a roof. The panels contain water or another fluid to absorb heat from the sun. The heated water is then pumped to a heat exchanger, which transfers the heat from the water to the home hot water heater. Hot water systems are used to heat homes and thousands of home swimming pools.

Photovoltaic cells mounted on roof panels convert sunlight to electricity. The cost of photovoltaics has come down in recent years, making them attractive for individual home use. The creation of large active solar power plants remains to be seen.

Passive systems feature trombe walls and barrels filled with water that heat up to provide space heating and hot water. Also, a solarium is a room that has a south to southeast exposure to capture sunshine; when the solarium heats up, the heat can be blown by fan to other parts of the house.

Solar energy use varies by time of year (hours of daylight) and geographic location. Solar energy has particular application in the southern and southwestern states where daylight hours are longer on average and there are more sunny days than in the northern states. Access to sunlight in the design of new buildings, and the retrofitting of older buildings and construction on neighboring lots to maintain solar access, are all important considerations for promoting solar energy. Local governments have enacted solar access ordinances so that new construction or alterations to existing buildings do not reduce the potential to use solar energy on neighboring properties.

Geothermal Energy

Geothermal energy is the tapping of the earth's heat primarily for turning turbines to make electricity. Deep geothermal sources are found only in a relatively few places—primarily in California and other western states where hot springs and volcanic activity are fairly common. By the late 1990s, geothermal sources generated about 6% of California's electricity. Also growing in popularity are heat pumps that draw on shallow geothermal sources. Contamination of groundwater is possible because some heat pumps use antifreeze. Geothermal heat may also be passive. For instance, "berm houses" are built partially underground to take advantage of the earth's relatively stable temperature. Typically, an earth berm is constructed outside the north-facing wall. Berm houses can easily be built to combine passive solar heating, with a southeast exposure and trombe walls, or active solar photovoltaic cells on the roof.

Biomass Energy

Biomass is energy from plant and animal products and includes: the burning of wood chips; ethanol from corn; and methane gas from animal manure, garbage, and composting wood. The burning of wood chips to generate electricity is a way to use harvest slash and lumber pieces that would otherwise end up abandoned or in landfills. However, the burning of wood chips raises air pollution concerns. Ethanol from corn has been widely used in midwestern Corn Belt states to power cars, usually as a mix with ordinary gasoline. A potential problem with ethanol is a harmful effect on the engine's carburetor that mixes air and fuel. Methane is naturally produced by decomposing organic matter. On livestock farms, animal manure digesters can capture methane gas to generate electricity. For example, Mason-Dixon Farms near Gettysburg, Pennsylvania, produces virtually all of the electricity used on the 2,000-head dairy farm. Decomposing garbage at landfills produces methane, which is increasingly sold to nearby users for generating electricity. Although methane is a greenhouse gas with more than 20 times the concentration of carbon dioxide, harnessing it as an energy source, rather than letting it escape into the atmosphere, makes sense (see Chapter 6).

Hydrogen Fuel Cells

Hydrogen fuel cells, touted as a coming technology to power cars, can also be used to generate heat and electricity for homes and commercial buildings. Hydrogen fuel, derived from natural gas, is passed through a membrane to produce electricity and generates heat and water as by-products. The only long-term drawback to hydrogen fuel cells is the use of natural gas as a feedstock.

FEDERAL ENERGY PLANNING

There are four federal agencies that deal directly with energy issues:

1. the DOE;
2. the EPA;
3. the Bureau of Land Management (BLM) within the Department of the Interior; and

4. the U.S. Forest Service within the Department of Agriculture.

The DOE has a wide array of programs that cover fossil fuel development, the promotion of alternative energy sources, and energy conservation. The EPA sets standards for energy efficiency of electrical appliances and computers. Also, the EPA sets fuel efficiency standards in mpg for motor vehicle fleets. Private energy companies are allowed to mine coal and uranium, and drill for oil and gas in parts of national forests and on some western lands managed by the BLM and the U.S. Forest Service.

The DOE was created in 1977 in response to oil supply shortages and the surge in oil prices that sparked America's first energy crisis. The department has struggled to forge a coherent, long-term energy planning strategy. Specific objectives of the DOE feature:

- reducing America's dependence on imported oil;
- promoting energy efficiency in homes and buildings;
- developing technologies that increase the production of domestic oil and natural gas;
- developing clean coal technology;
- developing nuclear fusion and safe disposal of nuclear waste;
- improving vehicle fuel efficiency and the use of alternative clean fuels; and
- developing alternative energy sources (U.S. DOE 2000).

This list of objectives appears somewhat contradictory, and setting energy priorities continues to be a challenge for the federal government. Significantly, energy conservation is not specifically mentioned. Rather, the DOE prefers to focus on greater energy production and energy efficiency. In large part, the federal government relies upon the private sector to produce coal, oil, natural gas, and electricity.

The Federal Energy Regulatory Commission (FERC) within the DOE regulates the transmission and sale of natural gas, oil, and electricity in interstate commerce. FERC also licenses and inspects private, municipal, and state hydroelectric projects and power plants. FERC's reviews of relicensing applications are likely to meet closer public scrutiny in the coming years as there is growing interest in taking down old dams that generate little hydroelectric power yet block significant fish runs. FERC also serves as the lead agency within the DOE for environmental matters involving the National Environmental Policy Act (NEPA).

The DOE also has direct involvement in energy operations. It oversees the Bonneville Power Authority, which operates the series of hydroelectric dams on the Columbia River system in the Pacific Northwest. The DOE manages the multi-million-barrel Strategic Petroleum Reserve. In 2000, President Clinton ordered 30 million barrels to be released from the reserve to help lower high oil prices and to offset potential shortages of heating oil in the northeast.

Since 1994, the DOE's Rebuild America program has promoted greater energy efficiency in the construction and retrofitting of commercial, institutional, and multifamily residential buildings. The DOE has a network of business, technical, and financial experts to work with communities in developing action plans that spell out energy choices and objectives. For instance, in 1999, Caldwell, Idaho, drafted a five-year energy and resource use action plan. The plan sought to identify and implement methods for controlling utility costs, conducting energy audits in city buildings, making investments in buildings to achieve greater energy efficiency, and forging partnerships with service and business organizations to promote energy efficiency in privately owned buildings. Finally, the plan included an annual report on the progress of the city's efforts.

STATE ENERGY PLANNING

In the wake of the energy crises of the 1970s, nearly every state created a state energy office.

The purpose of the offices has been to promote energy efficiency and conservation programs and to help local governments develop new energy sources. State energy offices can work with local governments, institutions, businesses, and individuals on energy audits to identify energy loss and recommend investments in energy efficiency, building design and weatherization assistance, low-interest loans for energy-saving projects, and tax credits for energy-saving projects and the installation of renewable energy sources.

Weatherization to keep out cold air in the winter and hot air in the summer is important for reducing energy use and expenses. A home energy audit can show where energy is leaking and how investments in weatherization can improve efficiency. The Oregon Office of Energy offers a free home energy audit and provides low-interest loans at 6.5% for up to $5,000 or rebates of up to $400 covering 25% of the cost of weatherization projects, such as weather stripping, insulation, clock thermostats, and energy-efficient fuel burners (Oregon DOE 2001a).

Oregon offers income tax credits of $50 to $200 for homeowners who make investments in energy-saving equipment, such as premium efficiency appliances (dishwashers, clothes washers, refrigerators, and water heaters). The state will grant a tax credit of up to $1,500 for the installation of a geothermal heat pump or a solar hot water heating system, solar space heating system, or solar photovoltaic cells that generate at least 10% of the home's energy use (Oregon DOE 2001b). Also, the state offers a tax credit of up to $750 for the purchase of an alternative fuel vehicle or the conversion of a conventional vehicle to alternative fuels. Business energy tax credits of 35% of eligible costs are available for a variety of energy-saving investments. So far, Oregon businesses have filed for more than 5,000 energy tax credits and made investments that have saved about $100 million a year (Oregon DOE 2001c). States can also require electric utilities to produce a certain percentage of their electricity from renewable energy sources. Texas, California, and Washington, for instance, have done this.

An important state energy planning function—usually under the authority of the state environmental agency or public utilities commission—is the review for siting new power plants. In 1975, the Oregon legislature created a seven-member Energy Facility Siting Council to ensure that large energy facilities are located, built, and operated so that public health and safety, and the environment are protected. Siting issues include noise, wetlands, water pollution, water rights, soil erosion, drainage, fish and wildlife habitats, aesthetic and scenic impacts, historic resources, recreation impacts, minimizing solid waste, and compliance with the local comprehensive plan and land use ordinances. If the council approves the construction of a new facility, it issues a permit that is binding on the state and local governments, and requires them to issue any necessary permits for construction and operation of the facility. After the facility is completed, the council monitors its operation. In 1997, the Oregon legislature gave the council authority to set carbon dioxide emission standards for new energy facilities.

Energy shortages can occur from natural disasters or from the cut-off of supplies from abroad. Since 1978, the California Energy Commission has issued emergency energy standards that must be incorporated into the design of new buildings and alterations to existing buildings in order to obtain a building permit (California Energy Commission 2002). The commission also works with local governments to draft energy shortage response plans to assess and respond to energy emergencies. A community appoints an emergency energy committee with members from local government and the private sector to assess energy needs and vulnerabilities. The committee drafts a plan for how to respond to energy emergencies: information gathering; analysis; lines of authority; coordination with local, state, and federal agencies; and emergency sources of power and fuel.

SIDEBAR 17-2

Promoting "Green" Buildings

Buildings use one-third of all energy consumed in America, and two-thirds of the nation's electricity (Hawken *et al.* 1999, 85). In May 2000, the New York legislature enacted a bill that offered $25 million in tax credits against state income taxes for building owners and developers who use energy- and water-saving technologies, install ozone-friendly air conditioning, and create spaces with clean air and natural lighting. A tax credit of 5% is available for new construction or renovations that meet energy, indoor air quality, water-use, and waste-disposal standards, while a 10% credit applies to the cost of installing new, ozone-friendly air conditioning. Additional credits may be claimed for the installation of fuel cells and solar photovoltaic panels, which produce electricity without pollution (Holusha 2002, Section 11, 1).

The New York program embodies the concept of payback (i.e., investments that retrofit buildings for energy conservation and greater energy efficiency will pay for themselves in energy savings within a certain period of time and then produce a net financial gain). It is a clear example of spending money to save money and to conserve natural resources in the long run.

LOCAL ENERGY PLANNING

Local energy planning should be part of the comprehensive planning process. Energy planning is important for minimizing environmental impacts as well as maintaining community health and safety and a vibrant economy. Because most communities rely on energy imports for much of their energy needs, local energy conservation can be an effective way to keep more money in the community and promote greater energy security. Since the 1980s, towns in Vermont have appointed a local energy coordinator who is responsible for developing a town energy plan and conducting the town energy audit to identify where energy savings can be made. Portland, Oregon, appointed an energy commission to work with the Portland Energy Office in implementing and updating the city's energy policy. Many communities have municipally owned utilities. These utilities can set an example for energy consumers by working for greater energy efficiency along with reduced environmental impacts. Seattle City Light has issued an environmental policy statement to monitor and improve its environmental stewardship. The statement commits the utility to "promote and support the efficient use of material and resources including water and electricity in all phases of a{n energy generating} facility's life" and "communicate this policy and environmental performance to employees, citizen-owners, and the public" (City of Seattle 2002).

Inventory

The Natural Resource Inventory section of the comprehensive plan should identify the types of energy used in the community, both conventional and renewable. Sources of electricity and the amount used, and the amount of oil and natural gas used, will be the main data. Most information should be available from the state energy office and local utilities.

Analysis

The analysis of energy sources and use will indicate imported and locally generated energy supplies, demands for energy created by land use patterns and transportation networks, and potential for energy conservation, greater efficiency, and renewable energy sources. A Metropolitan Planning Organization or the state department of transportation may be able to provide information on vehicle miles traveled in cars and trucks. Climate-related energy needs for heating and air conditioning

The Building Code and Energy Conservation

A building code is a set of standards for the design and construction of new buildings and alterations to existing buildings. A building code is primarily intended to ensure the safety of buildings, but it can also be used to promote energy conservation. For instance, a building code requirement for specific insulation levels (R-factors) in the walls and ceilings of new buildings is a good way to reduce heating and cooling needs. Double and triple glaze windows can cut heat loss. These energy-saving features are particularly important because the average house size has increased, generally requiring more heating and cooling. Also, many commercial buildings are constructed with windows that do not open. This can result in greater air conditioning and lighting needs. Retrofits to improve energy efficiency can pay back the cost, often within a few years, and then go on to generate savings in future years. Private companies, state energy offices, and the cooperative extension service can perform energy audits on older public and private buildings to identify investments that would reduce energy loss.

Local governments do not draft entire building codes from scratch, but rather adopt a standard form of code, and then adapt it to suit local needs. Most midwestern and northeastern states use *The Code of the Building Officials Conference of America*. Western states follow *The Uniform Building Code*. Most southern states use *The Southern Standard Building Code* (see Sidebar 12-3 in Chapter 12). Communities in some states may be required to follow the state's building code.

A local government generally will not issue an occupancy permit unless the property owner has complied with the building code. Before a new building can be used, the local government will issue a certificate of occupancy indicating compliance with the conditions of the building permit. A building inspector is responsible for inspecting all new buildings to ensure compliance with the building code.

should be noted, along with the capacity for energy suppliers to meet anticipated future demands. New energy-generation facilities or natural gas pipelines may be needed, and an evaluation of the desired types of energy sources should be made.

Goals and Objectives

The community's energy goals and objectives should focus on greater energy conservation, improved efficiency, energy production from alternative sources, and land use patterns that allow for a variety of transportation modes, especially bicycle and pedestrian access and mass transit (Table 17-1). Some communities will want to address the construction and location of new coal, oil, natural gas, or nuclear energy facilities, while other communities may want to keep out such new facilities. Energy goals and objectives should be included in the Natural Resources, Economic Base, Community Facilities, Land Use, and Transportation sections of the comprehensive plan.

Action Strategy

The Action Strategy should present techniques and programs for achieving the energy goals and objectives as well as a timetable. Energy conservation benchmarks should be identified and progress toward those benchmarks evaluated in an annual report on the environment. Specific recommendations might include:

- revising the local building code to require energy-saving materials and designs;
- revising the zoning ordinance to encourage compact developments to promote pedestrian and bicycle transportation as well as mass transit and shorter car trips;

Table 17-1
Sample Energy Goals and Objectives in the Comprehensive Plan

Natural Resources	
Goal	To promote energy conservation, efficiency, and the use of renewable energy sources.
Objective	Require the use of energy conservation in the construction, design, and location of new development and redevelopment projects.
Economic Base	
Objective	Promote energy conservation to keep more money in the community where it can be reinvested.
Community Facilities	
Objective	Promote energy conservation in all public buildings. Perform energy audits of all public buildings to identify energy loss and potential energy savings.
Land Use	
Objective	Promote compact, mixed-use development as a way to achieve energy conservation.
Transportation	
Objective	Promote energy conservation through multimodal transportation systems, including mass transit, bicycle paths, and pedestrian access.

- adopting a solar access ordinance; and
- exploring funding for the development or expansion of mass transit.

Zoning Ordinance

The local zoning ordinance can greatly influence energy use. Local zoning can promote compact development by allowing higher density development, small lot sizes, and a mix of commercial and residential uses in areas near schools and mass-transit stations. This will enable mass transit and bicycle and pedestrian traffic to compete as alternatives to the automobile.

Zoning can also allow for the use of a variety of renewable energy sources. A solar access ordinance can prohibit new buildings and alterations to existing buildings from interfering with the access to the sun of solar-heating devices on neighboring buildings. The ordinance may impose restrictions on the height, bulk, and siting of new buildings, and alterations to protect the exposure of existing buildings to the sun. Similarly, the ordinance may allow for different siting, such as a zero lot line (no building setbacks from a property line), to enable new buildings to be located to best capture the sun's rays. The ordinance should take into consideration a building's exposure during the winter months when the sun's rays are at a low angle. State-enabling legislation may be necessary in some states before cities and towns can enact such ordinances.

If a large energy facility is desired in the community, the future land use map of the comprehensive plan can identify appropriate sites. These sites could be included in zones where electrical-generating facilities would be allowed as a conditional use. A conditional use requires a thorough review and a decision by the elected governing body. The conditional use process is the correct way to scrutinize a proposed project with the potential to affect an entire community. The conditional use review process at the local level can help to focus reviews under a State Environmental Policy Act and any federal reviews under NEPA or by FERC.

If a community does not want a large energy facility, the zoning ordinance should not list such facilities as outright permitted uses, special exceptions, or conditional uses in any zone.

Table 17-2
A Checklist of Energy Issues for a Development Review

1.	What kind of energy will the proposed development use for heating and cooling?
2.	How has the proposed development been designed to promote energy efficiency and conservation?
3.	Does the proposed development involve alternative energy sources?
4.	Does the proposed development meet any local energy-related ordinances or standards?
5.	Has the proposed development incorporated bicycle and pedestrian paths?
6.	Is the proposed development accessible by mass transit?
7.	Has the developer obtained any necessary state or federal permits?

Subdivision Regulations

Subdivision regulations can be used to encourage developers to incorporate bicycle and pedestrian paths in their subdivision plans. Subdivision regulations can require vegetative buffers around single-family houses as a way to provide shade in summer and a windbreak in the winter. Zoning and subdivision regulations can permit and provide standards for on-site electrical generation through small, natural gas turbines; methane generation (from manure on farms); wind turbines; and even geothermal sources. For example, wind systems can be allowed in more rural areas with setbacks at least as long as the wind turbine tower, so that if the tower falls, it will not damage neighboring properties.

Capital Improvements Program

The community's capital improvements program (CIP) can include transportation projects that incorporate energy conservation in a variety of ways. New highway construction or road-widening projects can designate High Occupancy Vehicle lanes to encourage carpooling. Traffic-calming devices, such as narrower streets and tapered intersections, slow cars down; not only do cars use less energy at a constant lower speed, but narrow streets have proven to be safer as well. In addition, a community could use its CIP and zoning to help create transit-oriented development built around mass transit bus or rail service. The CIP will help a community to organize its finances as it explores funding sources for expanding mass transit.

Through the CIP, the community can construct public buildings that incorporate energy-efficient design. Such buildings send a message to the public that the local government is doing its part for energy efficiency.

What to Look for in a Development Review

A proposed development should be evaluated according to the current comprehensive plan, zoning ordinance, subdivision and land development ordinance, building codes, and other applicable local laws (see Table 17-2). For instance, paths that connect residential developments to schools, parks, and stores can encourage walking and bicycling. Duplexes and townhouses that share a common wall typically use less heat than single-family detached houses. Adding space for a bus stop or a park-and-ride is appropriate for large developments. The planner should make sure that new buildings or redevelopment does not violate any solar access ordinances. As a result, developments may often be made more environmentally friendly at relatively little cost. Energy-efficient design at the outset can promote energy conservation and can prevent costly building retrofits later.

18

Planning for a Sustainable Built Environment

We stand for the restoration of existing urban centers and towns within coherent metropolitan regions, the reconfiguration of sprawling suburbs into communities of real neighborhoods and diverse districts, the conservation of natural environments, and the preservation of our built legacy.

CHARTER OF THE NEW URBANISM

18-1 Downtown Portland, Oregon. Note the light-rail line, bicycle, cars, and pedestrians sharing space. Shade trees and street furniture add to the attractive surroundings.

Source: Katherine Daniels

There is an old debate about whether a person's genes or surroundings are more important in forming character and personality. While manipulating genes is newly upon us, humans have been creating cities and villages for thousands of years. When people build settlements, they alter the natural environment. How the built environment interacts with the natural environment gives a community or region its visual identity and greatly affects public health. Attractive buildings, a mix of different land uses, walkability, and access to greenspace can contribute much to a community's quality of life. A healthy built environment minimizes pollution and waste. Enduring buildings have cultural, aesthetic, historical, and economic value. They make a community recognizable and give it uniqueness and style. Well-designed streetscapes draw residents and visitors and weave important buildings and public gathering places into a community fabric (see Figure 18-1). Above all, planning for the built environment is about forming and maintaining healthy, attractive neighborhoods and communities for all Americans.

There are two kinds of planning for the built environment: remedial planning and anticipatory planning; or, more simply, developing and redeveloping urban areas and new construction on greenfield sites. This chapter focuses on the redevelopment of cities and older suburbs, infill development, and rehabilitating existing buildings to create sustainable and desirable cities and inner suburbs in which to live and work. Otherwise, people will continue to move to the outer suburbs, pushing development further into working landscapes and environmentally sensitive areas. In short, the revitalization of America's cities and older suburbs is necessary to improve the nation's built environment, to accommodate the growing numbers of Americans, and to provide an alternative to environmentally damaging sprawl.

In 1950, many cities in the eastern half of the United States reached their peak population. Since then, some cities (e.g., Baltimore, Cleveland, and Detroit) have lost more than 30% of their population, a setback that may be difficult, if not impossible, to overcome (Rusk 1993). In the 1950s, residential sprawl erupted in the form of large suburban subdivisions of tract housing. Federally funded urban renewal projects attempted to boost downtown retail centers and replace substandard housing, but many urban renewal projects were poorly designed. High-rise public housing often concentrated minorities and poverty, and lacked access to greenspace. In some cities, slums were cleared only to lie vacant for years or become parking lots. New commercial blocks lacked the grandeur of the buildings they replaced. Freeways and interstate highways bored through neighborhoods. All of these actions led to an exodus of people and businesses to the suburbs.

Then, in the 1960s and 1970s, suburban shopping centers arrived, so residents of the expanding suburbs would not have to travel to the central city to shop. Beginning in the 1980s, edge cities arose on the periphery of metro regions. Edge cities are distinctive because they have more jobs

than residents, at least 600,000 square feet of retail space, and at least 5 million square feet of leasable office space (Garreau 1991). Edge cities evolved through a combination of good highway access, cheap land, and the construction of office parks and large regional shopping malls. In turn, edge cities enabled workers to live even farther out in the exurbs. By 1990, more Americans lived in suburbs than in central cities; metropolitan counties housed four out of every five Americans and covered nearly 20% of the land area of the lower 48 states (U.S. Bureau of the Census 1997).

Figure 18-2 shows that in America's metropolitan areas from 1990 to 1999, population growth rates in the suburbs substantially exceeded the growth rates in the central cities. In the northeast, central cities lost population while suburbs added more people. Clearly, redevelopment of cities has been lagging behind the development of greenfield sites. In fact, the National Resources Inventory, conducted by the Natural Resources Conservation Service (NRCS), reported that the

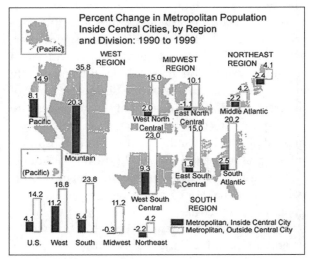

18-2 Percentage change in metropolitan population, central city and surroundings, 1990–1999.

Source: U.S. Bureau of the Census

total amount of developed land in America increased from 5% to 7% from 1992 to 1997, indicating a real estate development boom in keeping with the nation's strong economy over that time period (NRCS 2001).

The 2000 census revealed that central cities showed modest growth between 1990 and 2000. For many cities, this was a turnaround from decades of population loss to the suburbs. Contributing factors to the turnaround include a strong economy in the 1990s, a sharp decline in crime, federal tax incentives and infrastructure programs, and new private commercial and residential investment, which has improved the built environment as well as job and housing opportunities.

CHALLENGES TO CREATING A SUSTAINABLE BUILT ENVIRONMENT

Making Cities, Suburbs, and Villages into Livable Communities

How to Make Urban Redevelopment Competitive with Developments on Greenfield Sites

The overall challenge that cities face is how to make urban commercial and residential development competitive with developments on suburban greenfield sites. Developers often say that they build what the market wants. In fact, developers also build what local government ordinances allow and the federal tax code encourages. Most developers believe that it is cheaper to build on a greenfield site in the outer suburbs than to redevelop property in a city or inner suburb.

There are several reasons for this. First, land in the outer suburbs is generally cheaper, and it is easier to assemble large tracts for residential subdivisions and commercial projects. Second, there are usually fewer land use restrictions in the outer suburbs, and the approval process is quicker and more predictable. Third, the outer suburbs often have better highway access and are more attractive to prospective residents and businesses. Fourth, property taxes in the outer sub-

urbs are often lower than in a city or older suburb. Fifth, greenfield sites, especially if they are "shovel-ready," are usually more attractive to industrial companies than are old industrial sites—especially if those sites may have undetermined hazardous waste problems. The campus-style industrial park with new buildings set amid green lawns has become a standard feature of the American landscape.

Revitalizing Stagnant or Declining Cities and Older Suburbs

In most American cities, about 20% of the land is undeveloped. The figure is probably higher in most suburbs. In other words, in the majority of cities and suburbs, there is space to accommodate substantial population growth and new commercial activity through infill development. The redevelopment of older and vacant buildings, blighted areas, and brownfield sites can also attract new residents and private investment and broaden the tax base. However, to succeed, infill and redevelopment must take advantage of good design, mass transit, greenspaces, and a pedestrian orientation.

Mixed-Use Developments

Reform of local zoning and subdivision ordinances to allow, encourage, and even require compact, mixed-use developments within and adjacent to existing cities and suburbs is long overdue. Developers who want to employ good designs are often discouraged by the time and expense involved in obtaining variances and waivers from the zoning and subdivision regulations. If the design and location of new developments are to promote vibrant, livable communities, local ordinances must lead the way.

Particularly in the suburbs, rigid zoning has separated commercial and residential areas so that a car has become a necessity to get to work, a store, or a park. Residential areas are still often laid out in monotonous "cookie-cutter" lots of uniform lot sizes and dimensions. The houses look pretty much the same as well. To try to add variety to the acres of tract homes, developers have put in wide, curvilinear streets and cul-de-sacs, pejoratively known in planning lingo as "loops and lollipops." Amid the sea of houses, however, there is little identifiable or attractive public space. Developers often do not install sidewalks to save on costs and to achieve a sort of "faux rural" visual effect. Crosswalks and bicycle lanes are also avoided, which puts pedestrians, cyclists, roller bladers, and joggers at greater risk of collision with cars. An acute example of the separation of land uses in the suburbs is the spread of gated residential communities (Kay 1997, 31). Gated communities have two main negative effects:

1. they separate people from each other through economic and physical segregation; and

2. they make smooth transportation difficult by fragmenting the land base and road networks.

More Compact Development

Planners face two challenges in promoting more compact development: how to redevelop the central cities to make them more desirable places to live, and how to "densify" residential suburbs and integrate businesses into them. Redevelopment and infill development must contribute to an organized, efficient pattern. Mixed-use developments, distinct districts and neighborhoods, edges, nodes, landmarks, paths, and narrow streets with short blocks give a city or suburb identity and encourage pedestrian traffic.

Development for which adequate infrastructure is not provided places a strain on the community's public utilities, services, and transportation network. For instance, redevelopment should be directed to areas with access to mass transit. In the suburbs, densification can be achieved by zoning for multifamily housing—still a rarity in many suburbs—and a mix of residential and commercial uses.

Greenspaces

Nature does have a place in the city. Urban redevelopment in both residential and commercial areas must incorporate greenspaces for aesthetics, recreation opportunities, and stormwater control. Urban riparian greenways can provide recreation areas and wildlife habitat as well as intercept stormwater runoff. Greenspaces and parks help new developments fit into a neighborhood. The National Recreation and Park Association recommends that urban areas provide 5 acres of open greenspace for every 1,000 residents. In a city of 100,000, that works out to 500 acres of parkland, tot lots, and greenways. Greenspace provides important social, recreational, and environmental benefits that are especially valuable because of their relative scarcity in urban settings. Greenspace can be a required feature of redevelopment plans. Options include trails, community gardens, pocket parks, and tree plantings—all of which take up a small amount of land—as well as any sensitive environmental lands, such as steep slopes, floodplains, and wetlands, which should not be developed.

One side effect of promoting more compact development and infill development is likely to be an increase in impervious surfaces (Arnold and Gibbons 1996, 243-258). More pavement and buildings increase stormwater runoff and flooding. Thus, greenspaces are important for intercepting runoff as well as providing access to nature, recreation, and recycling carbon dioxide and oxygen. For example, in the early 1990s, voters within the growth boundary of Portland, Oregon, approved $135 million for the purchase of parkland and open space. Planting and maintaining trees are especially important. Trees add value and beauty to residential areas as well as serve to filter air pollution, intercept stormwater runoff, and reduce the urban heat island effect. An urban forestry program can help maintain and increase tree cover (see Chapter 14).

Parking

Parking is always a challenge to the visual character and function of downtowns areas. Most communities have parking spaces that are scattered, inconvenient, and visually unappealing. Parking lots on corner properties especially detract from the streetscape. Often, parking space requirements for new developments and renovations are expensive to meet and can hinder the construction of affordable housing and transit-oriented developments as well as the rehabilitation of historic buildings. In the suburbs, outdated zoning laws often require parking lots to accommodate the Christmas shopping rush, with twice as much parking area as needed on a typical day. A well-crafted parking plan can combine access to businesses and residences with the visual screening of trees, other vegetation, and buildings to reduce stormwater runoff, provide shade, and make parking areas fit in with the appearance of a city or village downtown. Any new surface parking lots should be small and located behind buildings whenever possible, and on-street parking should count toward parking requirements. Unattractive existing surface parking can be replaced with above- or below-ground parking. New surface parking in larger cities should be discouraged, and a maximum number of parking spaces set. Portland, Oregon, did this and brought increased ridership to its light-rail and bus systems. Portland is also one of America's most walkable cities. Eugene, Oregon; Cambridge, Massachusetts; and Gainesville, Florida, have also imposed limits on the number of parking spaces (Millard-Ball 2002, 16).

Affordable Housing

A challenge for urban redevelopment and suburban infill is to provide attractive affordable housing amid a quality environment. Traditionally, low-income people have been more likely to live near hazardous sites and in poorly maintained buildings. New inhabitants and new investment in run-down properties can result in gentrification. On the one hand, the newcomers and their money give a boost to the city; on the other, lower income renters and residents are often forced out. Montgomery County, Maryland, has enacted an inclusionary housing ordinance that requires developers who build a project with more than 50 units to make 15% of them available for low- and moderate-income people. The county has also actively purchased and managed low- and moderate-income housing, creating more than 35,000 affordable housing units in 25 years in the nation's sixth wealthiest county (Rusk 1999). Montgomery County has shown that a mix of affordable, small-scale, multifamily housing and single-family homes can be attractive.

Sensitivity to Surroundings

Redeveloped housing and residential infill development should be sensitive to the character of the surrounding community. Development that is out of scale or character with adjacent buildings create visual chaos. A problem that has arisen in San Francisco and other cities is the construction of "monster homes" that disrupt the visual scale of neighborhoods with more modest two- and three-story homes as well as drive up land values and property taxes. A similar problem occurs with "teardowns"—older homes that are demolished to make way for mansions of 4,000 square feet or more. Lincoln, Massachusetts (a Boston suburb) even enacted a "Large Impact Home ByLaw" that requires site plan approval for large homes when the floor area of the proposed house and outbuildings exceeds 4,000 square feet, or 8% of the lot (whichever is greater), or when the total floor area of the house is greater than 6,500 square feet (Szold 1999, 8-9).

Tastes and Preferences and Financial Incentives

There are both strong financial incentives and personal preferences that will continue to push development outward into the hinterlands. Personal preferences include desires for a more rural lifestyle, access to a cleaner environment, better schools, and avoiding crime and congestion. Financial incentives include lower property taxes in the exurbs compared to the inner city or suburbs, and the federal mortgage interest deduction from taxable income, which encourages people to buy a big house and build up equity over time. Moreover, in 1998, Congress exempted the first $250,000 on the sale of a person's primary residence from federal capital gains taxes (a $500,0000 exemption for a married couple). This financial incentive encourages people to buy a house in growing exurban areas where the appreciation potential is high, and not in an urban area where real estate values are stagnant.

The Importance of Good Urban Design

Several polls have shown that Americans dislike two things: density and sprawl. Density suggests congestion and the threat of crime. Individuals seem to dislike someone else's sprawl, but not their own. What people really dislike is poor design. Anonymous high-rise apartments are unattractive. McMansions on 5-acre lots that are sited as if they were randomly dropped from the sky do not enhance rural or suburban character. Strip malls along arterial roads disrupt the visual landscape and pull commercial activity away from traditional downtowns. Compact, dense developments can be aesthetically pleasing and efficiently tied to a variety of transportation choices and public open spaces. Even the National Association of Home Builders (NAHB) calls for "removing barriers to allow innovative land use planning techniques . . . in building higher density and mixed-use developments in suburban and inner city neighborhoods" (NAHB 2001).

A community's image is critical to its economic vitality. A community whose built environment conveys a sense of place and identity is a community worth caring about. In short, good design is good for business as well as for environmental quality and overall local quality of life. For instance, formulaic, Anywhere USA franchise architecture can be changed if the local government requires it to fit with the regional vernacular architecture.

Planner-designer Kevin Lynch described what have become widely accepted as the five main design elements of the built environment. How these elements blend together shapes the form, appearance, and functioning of a city, town, or village.

1. A *district* is an identifiable area that stands out based on its location, type of buildings, and function. San Francisco, for instance, has a financial district, Chinatown, and the Fisherman's Wharf tourist area. Smaller cities have a central business district featuring commercial and government buildings, churches, and cultural sites within walking distance of each other.

2. *Paths* give organization and shape to a district as well as provide connections between districts, and between the city and the outside world. Paths include streets, highways, sidewalks, linear parks (e.g., San Antonio's famous Riverwalk), subways, rivers, and railroad lines. Paths as transportation systems form the skeleton of the built environment. People see and interact with the built environment while moving through it on paths. Paths also determine the pace of activity. A pedestrian-oriented district has a much different and slower feel to it than a highway commercial strip.

3. *Nodes* are public spaces that provide important gathering places for social interaction and recreation, and a break from buildings. A node may be a public park (e.g., Central Park in New York City), an urban plaza, a town square at the center of the central business district (e.g., Pioneer Courthouse Square in Portland, Oregon), or a village green. A node is often where major paths intersect. Thus, a node may serve as a clearly defined core of a district.

4. *Landmarks* are prominent buildings, statutes, or monuments that are easy to find and enhance the sense of place of a node or district. Landmarks are often located within a node. In county seats, the county courthouse typically sits in the middle of the town square. Landmarks should be easily visible to enable them to stand out.

5. *Edges* emphasize the boundaries of a district, city, town, or village that keep it distinct. A river, major highway, or park may create a clearly defined edge. One of the unattractive features of many suburbs is their utter lack of edges; when driving through them, you cannot tell where one suburb ends and another begins. In a village, the most important edge is between the built environment and the surrounding countryside. It is visually appealing to be able to stand within the village and see out to the countryside. It is equally appealing to look from the countryside to the village and see a compact settlement with a distinct edge. This gives the village a sense of balance and harmony with the surrounding natural areas and working landscape.

These five design elements, together with the mix of land uses in each district, give the built environment its patterns, character, and charm. Districts are shaped by paths and nodes, set apart from other districts by edges, and dotted with landmarks. If the five design elements do not blend together, the result is an absence of clearly recognizable places and confusion over how the pieces of a community fit together. An absence of edges means no clear breaks, paths become snarled with traffic, nodes are avoided, landmarks are disregarded, and districts lose identity. Overall, the built environment loses both its functional purpose and its beauty.

Regulating Aesthetics

Regulating aesthetics is not easy. What is pleasing to one person may be repugnant to another. Local

SIDEBAR 18-1

The Americans with Disabilities Act

The Americans with Disabilities Act (ADA) was passed by Congress in 1990 to make sure that disabled people have equal access to public and private housing, stores, office buildings, transportation, and recreational facilities. The ADA does not grandfather buildings constructed before 1990. Instead, both existing and new buildings have had to be fitted with ramps and elevators, along with convenient parking spaces, sidewalks with curb cuts, and parking structures in order to comply with the provisions of the ADA (Szold 2002).

Planners should keep in mind the requirements of the ADA when reviewing site plans for new development and renovations to existing structures. The ADA can present special challenges for renovating historic buildings. Typically, ramps and elevators must be added, which can detract from the historic character of the building. Elevator requirements can make the renovation of second and third stories into office space and apartments very expensive.

opposition to a proposed development often focuses on the appearance of the development. Common complaints include that it is out of scale with the neighborhood, it has a different design compared with the surrounding buildings, or not enough open space would be retained.

The State of Vermont has an aesthetics criterion (8) in Act 250, the state land use and development law governing developments of regional impact. A ruling must be made whether the proposed project will "have an undue adverse effect on the scenic or natural beauty of the area, aesthetics, historic sites or rare and irreplaceable natural areas." For example, has the project been designed to minimize visual impact both on the site and on the surrounding area? Has vegetation been used to screen the project? What will be the impact of signage and lighting?

A common problem is that building codes often work against the restoration of older urban buildings that could be put to a commercial use, or a mix of commercial and residential uses. In 1997, the New Jersey legislature passed a Rehabilitation Subcode for the renovation of older buildings that combines maintaining historic features with certain safety requirements. According to Richard Moe of the National Trust for Historic Preservation, "Within a year of its adoption, rehab of older buildings jumped by 60% in Newark and 80% in Jersey City" (*Preservation* 2000, 6).

Many communities have appointed an architectural, historic, or design review board to:

- recommend standards and design control districts to guide the appearance of new development as well as major alterations to existing buildings; and
- advise the planning commission and local elected officials on the aesthetics and design of proposed developments.

The design standards may be incorporated as part of the zoning ordinance or allowed to stand alone as a design review ordinance. The standards may require the use of similar architectural styles existing within a district, including a certain pitch of roof, buildings of a maximum height, and certain construction materials. Architectural and historic review boards are more often found in cities rather than in suburbs, but design review boards are common in well-to-do suburbs and villages.

Architectural and historic review should be based on an inventory of federal, state, and local historically and architecturally significant structures and sites. Review standards should address proposed demolitions, removals, or major exterior alterations. Historic districts or site-by-site review can include design standards for new development adjacent to or near historic structures. Ideally, both the design review standards and the recommendations of the design review board should be based on a visual plan that identifies areas and buildings with historic or architectural significance. Also, the visual plan can cite places where elimination of blight or eyesores is a priority. Especially effective is a visual guide booklet together with the design standards to show prospective developers what the community wants. The booklet should include photographs or drawings of buildings that illustrate desirable design concepts as well as sketches of preferred lot layouts, access parking, and landscaping. Drawings can also be included in the zoning ordinance and subdivision and land development regulations to illustrate design concepts. Software packages are available that allow architects, developers, planners, local officials, and the public to visualize how a proposed development would look if it were built. These tools can help in the design or modification of a project to address public or local government concerns.

Downtowns

Many older cities and inner-ring suburbs have recognized the need to create or recreate traditional downtowns. In 1999, about 6,000 cities were actively renovating their downtowns or had recently completed downtown projects (Savoye 1999, 4); between 30 to 40 inner suburbs were designing new downtowns. In addition, roughly one in three new shopping malls were being located in city centers, rather than out on the highway strip. One of the potential advantages that cities have is that they are convenient places to live. Both empty nesters and younger people without children live in downtowns to enjoy the cultural attractions and pedestrian orientation. Downtowns can provide identity, a sense of place, and a feeling of community. They can draw residents and visitors alike. Despite the pricing advantage of big-box retailers and the acres of free parking at suburban shopping malls, downtowns can take advantage of distinctive historic architecture and social interaction in public gathering places.

Downtowns can also offer a mix of specialty shops, restaurants, and public events.

Big vs. Small Downtown Projects

Proponents of big projects can point to New York City's revitalization of Times Square in the 1990s with the help of a large investment by the Disney Company and generous financial incentives. As a general rule, however, several small, incremental redevelopment projects are preferable to one or two large projects. Small projects also involve buildings that have a human scale. Height limitations of between six to 10 stories in cities and three to five stories in smaller cities and towns can provide ample commercial, office, and residential spaces without making people feel like ants. Small projects can add up to significant, positive benefits in a neighborhood or district through a process of

gradual change that is less likely to disrupt the community appearance or infrastructure. A series of small projects can build on successes, adding layer upon layer of social and economic improvement to a neighborhood or community (see Figure 18-3). San Francisco's South of Market area, Cincinnati's loft district, and Denver's Lower Downtown have been redeveloped with transit, pedestrian access, apartments, and entertainment districts. The greater number of residents creates a market for a variety of new businesses.

In their book *Cities Back from the Edge*, Roberta Gratz and Norman Mintz describe how, in the Lower Manhattan district of Soho, the right design features came together to create a dynamic neighborhood (Gratz and Mintz 1998). Older manufacturing buildings were first turned into artists' studios and then to residential loft space. Small

18-3   The Church Street pedestrian mall has been a big success in Burlington, Vermont, which is often cited as one of the most livable small cities in the United States.

Source: Katherine Daniels

SIDEBAR 18-2

A Note on Land-Value Taxation

The property tax, which generates most of a city's tax revenues, is made up of two parts: the tax on land and the tax on buildings. Most cities apply the same property tax rate to land and buildings. This practice creates a disincentive to invest in buildings. Thus, business owners may decide to defer storefront improvements for fear of increasing their property tax burden; landlords may avoid improvements to rental units; and homeowners may defer maintenance. Moreover, owners of land with infill or redevelopment potential may decide to leave the land undeveloped.

Land-value taxation involves placing a higher tax rate on land than buildings. The heavier tax burden on land compels owners of open and underused land either to construct buildings or else sell the property to someone who will. Thus, the land-value tax encourages the construction of buildings on open, private land as well as improvements to existing buildings.

Since the 1970s, Pittsburgh, Pennsylvania, has used a land-value tax system with 70% of the tax rate on land and 30% on buildings. The land-value tax has spurred new development and helped to facilitate the city's transformation from a city famous for steel mills to a city known for its medical and high-tech industries and neotraditional neighborhood design.

businesses—especially bakeries, bookstores, and restaurants—soon followed. The result was a lively, mixed-use, pedestrian-oriented area, created almost entirely through private investment. Like Jane Jacobs before them, Gratz and Mintz argue for small blocks and public spaces to promote pedestrian activity (Jacobs 1961). Jacobs recognized that the key to safety was large numbers of people walking on the sidewalks.

Downtowns derive part of their character from the "street furniture." This furniture includes signs, lighting, trees, plantings, benches, and bike racks. These details are often afterthoughts in the urban design process, but they can have a noticeable impact on the appearance of a community and can reenforce the sense of pedestrian scale.

Suburban Redesign

In the suburbs, there are several design changes that would promote a greater sense of community while improving environmental quality (Adler 1995, 40-45; Calthorpe and Fulton 2001, 195-241) (see Table 18-1). Smaller house lots would mean less total space devoted to development (see Figure 18-

4). The creation of town centers would give a focal point to communities where mixed-use commercial and residential developments (and multifamily housing) could be built, and people would be able to walk to stores rather than drive. Mass-transit options also become possible. Parking lot sizes could be reduced, trees planted, and landscaping required to absorb stormwater runoff. In residential neighborhoods, streets could be narrower to promote traffic calming, and cul-de-sacs could be eliminated to allow for smoother traffic flow.

Nuisances, Noise Pollution, and Light Pollution

Nuisance ordinances are special laws enacted by local governing bodies to protect the health, safety, and welfare of community residents. A nuisance is a use of land or behavior that harms or bothers adjacent property owners or the general public. Nuisance ordinances typically regulate noise, odors, lights, junkyards, structures, or yard maintenance. Common nuisance problems include barking dogs; odors from pesticide sprays; manure; factory emissions; floodlights from resi-

Table 18-1
Typical and Recommended Residential Design in Suburbs

Typical Suburban Design	Recommended Suburban Design
Wide streets	Narrow streets
No sidewalks	Sidewalks
Parking in front of houses or on street	Parking in alleys and garages behind houses
Few street trees	Plenty of street trees
Cul-de-sacs and curvy streets	Thru-streets and rectilinear street grid
Long setbacks for buildings	Short setbacks for buildings
Only single-family houses in a neighborhood	Mix of housing types in neighborhood
Separation of houses and commercial areas	Mix of residential and commercial uses
Large house lots	Small house lots
Wasted private yard space	Public parks and tot lots
No town center	Town center

dential, commercial, and public properties; junk and debris accumulating in a yard; or a lawn allowed to grow overly high in grass and weeds.

A nuisance ordinance is a way to resolve land use conflicts and activities that could otherwise lead to legal challenges or physical confrontations. Local police are responsible for responding to nuisance complaints. Often, the aggrieved person

18-4 Suburban "snout houses" emphasize housing cars rather than people.

Source: Katherine Daniels

must attempt to resolve the problem before calling the police. Violators of a nuisance ordinance may be punished by a fine, a prison sentence, or both.

Noise Pollution

Peace and quiet are common property resources. No one owns peace and quiet, and everyone can enjoy peace and quiet without detracting from another's enjoyment. However, noise is a fact of modern life and interrupts the common peace and quiet. Noise can be considered a nuisance when it is loud enough to cause discomfort or harm. Noise pollution has not received nearly as much attention as polluted air and water, but noise is often the most pervasive form of pollution in large cities, in industrial suburbs, close to airports and freeways, and even in some rural areas. Noise pollution is also frequently mentioned by neighbors who are concerned about nearby proposed developments. The impacts of noise pollution include sleeplessness and lost work ability, frayed nerves, and hearing loss. Common sources of loud noise emanate from airports, highways, rail lines, and industrial areas. At a neighborhood level, loud noise may be generated by car horns and safety devices, police, fire, and ambulance sirens, lawn mowers, leaf blowers, snow blowers, stereos and televisions, dogs, and farm machinery.

Noise is measured in decibels (dB) on a logarithmic scale from 0 to 194. An increase of about 6 dB produces double the volume, and sound-induced pain occurs at 140 dB (the noise of a jet airplane taking off). A number of communities have identified areas near airports with a 65 dB or greater impact. In 1999, Arapahoe County, Colorado, placed a two-year moratorium on development near airports until a $400,000 noise study could be completed (*The Denver Post* 1999, B-10). Highway traffic typically produces a normal dB reading of 70, and snowmobiles are about 100 dB.

Noise pollution may be controlled by physical barriers or local noise ordinances. Many states have erected sound walls to deaden noise along major highways; the walls can cut noise levels in half. Other structural measures to reduce noise include earth berms, trees, or sound insulation within houses and commercial buildings. Many cities and suburbs have enacted local noise ordinances, which are a type of nuisance ordinance, so that one person's actions do not reduce neighbors' enjoyment of their property or reduce neighboring property values. Noise ordinances usually impose hours during which certain outdoor equipment cannot be operated. Some ordinances prohibit any noise above a certain dB level (e.g., 70 dB) during certain hours; these communities use a hand-held device to measure noise levels. Other communities prohibit loud continuous or repetitive noise, such as a barking dog, and will rely on a tape recording or a police officer's report. In many cases, noise ordinances may be difficult to enforce, especially involving noise from mobile sources.

West Dundee, Illinois (a suburban community northwest of Chicago), is typical of communities with noise ordinances. In 1999, West Dundee enacted an ordinance stating that musical and electronic equipment cannot produce any noise heard more than 50 feet away between 11 PM and 7 AM. Construction and commercial maintenance activities are limited to 7 AM to 8:30 PM Monday through Saturday and 8:30 AM to 8:30 PM on Sunday. Snow removal and street sweeping are exempt. Fines may be levied from $25 to $500 (Quirsfeld 1999, 7A).

Lighting

Lighting is an essential safety feature for pedestrians, bicyclists, and motorists. It is also helpful in deterring crime. Efficient, well-designed lighting can save energy and improve the attractiveness of streetscapes and the livability of neighborhoods.

Light pollution is a built environment problem that is often overlooked. Light pollution comes in three main forms: sky glow, light "trespassing," and glare. Night skies in cities are as much as 25 to 50 times brighter than the natural night sky; suburban skies are typically five to 10 times brighter. Many outdoor lights are poorly sited or shielded and are too bright. Floodlights in residential areas are becoming increasingly common, casting bright light into neighboring yards. Glare from light shining in one's eyes is uncomfortable and especially dangerous for motorists who may be temporarily blinded. As much as half of all light fails to illuminate as desired. This waste of light is also a waste of energy.

Communities can use zoning regulations, performance standards, a nuisance ordinance, or a building code to help improve the lighting design of new developments and major renovations. Energy-efficient, low- or high-pressure sodium lights can be required; other lights, such as searchlights or mercury vapor lights, can be prohibited. Lights should be required to be shielded so that light is properly directed and does not result in spillovers to neighboring properties. Pole height for parking lots and roadways can be specified to limit light trespass and glare, such as no more the 16 feet. Hours of lighting in commercial areas can be regulated, such as not between 11 PM and sunrise.

SIDEBAR 18-3

The Ahwahnee Principles for Development Design

Community Principles

a. All planning should be in the form of complete and integrated communities containing housing, shops, workplaces, schools, parks, and civic facilities essential to the daily life of the residents.

b. Community size should be designed so that housing, jobs, daily needs, and other activities are within easy walking distance of each other.

c. As many activities as possible should be located within easy walking distance of transit stops.

d. A community should contain a diversity of housing types to enable citizens from a wide range of economic levels and age groups to live within its boundaries.

e. The location and character of the community should be consistent with a larger transit network.

f. The community should have a center focus that combines commercial, civic, cultural and recreational uses.

g. The community should contain an ample supply of specialized open space in the form of squares, greens, and parks whose frequent use is encouraged through placement and design.

h. Each community or cluster of communities should have a well-defined edge, such as agri-cultural greenbelts or wildlife corridors, permanently protected from development.

i. Streets, pedestrian paths, and bike paths should contribute to a system of fully connected, interesting routes to all destinations. Their design should encourage pedestrian and bicycle use by being small and spatially defined by buildings, trees and lighting, and by discouraging high-speed traffic.

j. The community design should help conserve resources and minimize waste.

Regional Principles and Implementation Principles

a. The regional land-use planning structure should be integrated within a larger transportation network built around transit rather than freeways.

b. Regions should be bounded by and provide a continuous system of greenbelt/wildlife corridors to be determined by natural conditions.

c. Rather than allowing developer-initiated, piece-meal development, local governments should take charge of the planning process. General plans should designate where new growth, infill or redevelopment will be allowed to occur.

d. Plans should be developed through an open process and participants in the process should be provided visual models of all planning proposals.

Source: Corbett, Judith. "The Awahnee Principles: Toward More Liveable Communities," Local Government Commission, Sacramento, CA. www.lgc.org/clc/ahwnprin.html, 1997, p. 1.

New Urbanism and Traditional Neighborhood Design

In 1993, a group of architects formed the Congress for the New Urbanism, based on a set of guidelines known as the Ahwahnee Principles. The model for the New Urbanism is the traditional village, which features:

- a mix of commercial and residential space within walking distance;

- a human scale of buildings;
- a manageable pace;
- a clear edge between built-up areas and the countryside or open space;
- density, with houses close together; and
- parks, sidewalks, and squares for public places.

New Urbanist projects are known as traditional neighborhood developments (TNDs); as of 2000, there were about 200 TNDs around the United

States (Goldberger 2000, 128). TNDs come in three types: the free-standing village, suburban neighborhoods, and urban redevelopment. Seaside, Florida, designed by husband and wife architects Andres Duany and Elizabeth Plater-Zyberk, is perhaps the best example of a free-standing village. Seaside incorporates human-scale houses and buildings with narrow streets, sidewalks, front porches, and a town square. Orenco Station (outside of Portland, Oregon) is a transit-oriented village with a mix of commercial and residential uses, tied to the Portland metro area through a station on the west side light-rail line (see Chapter 5). Kentlands, another Duany and Plater-Zyberk design in suburban Maryland (outside of Washington, D.C.), successfully combines neo-Georgian architecture with zero lot lines and front porches in an aesthetically pleasing and financially profitable development. UDA Architects in Pittsburgh have designed and built several projects mixing housing and commercial space in a pedestrian-friendly setting. Riverside, designed by DPZ, is a mixed-use development of townhouses and apartments in the City of Atlanta, not in its sprawling suburbs.

In explaining the virtues of TNDs, Duany, Plater-Zyberk, and co-author Jeff Speck write, "Not only is a society healthier when its diverse members are in daily contact with one another, it is also more convenient. Imagine being able to grow old in a neighborhood that can accommodate your changing housing needs while also providing a home for your children and grandchildren" (quoted in Goldberger 2000, 131).

FEDERAL EFFORTS IN URBAN REDEVELOPMENT

The federal urban renewal programs of the 1950s and 1960s are widely recognized to have caused more harm than good for America's cities (Jackson 1985, Chapter 12). With impetus and funding from the federal government, thousands of older buildings—many with historic and architectural value—were demolished to make room for high-

rise public housing, apartments, parking garages, freeways, and commercial space. Low-income people were "warehoused," many middle- and upper-income people fled to the suburbs, businesses and jobs soon joined the exodus, and city tax bases shrank. In some communities, land cleared through urban renewal sat vacant for several years. However, even when redevelopment did occur, the scale of the buildings and architectural styles often did not mesh well with the surroundings.

The U.S. Department of Housing and Urban Development (HUD) has belatedly admitted that urban renewal "created 'no man's land' open space and buffers, permitted freeways and major roads to dissect neighborhoods and isolate communities, failed to coordinate transit investments with new housing and jobs, dispersed civic facilities and destroyed community focus, displaced small businesses, and damaged natural systems" (Calthorpe and Fulton 2001, 246). Moreover, urban renewal represented planning as "something done to people," rather than a rational, comprehensive, and participatory approach to problem solving.

Affordable housing, the upgrading or replacing of aging infrastructure, and brownfield redevelopment are major needs for revitalizing cities and older suburbs. HUD offers several programs to address these needs:

- Community Development Block Grant (CDBG) funds to state and local governments can be used to renovate buildings and provide new infrastructure in low- and moderate-income neighborhoods. CDBG Section 108 loan funds can be used to leverage private and public funds for community rehabilitation projects.

- HUD's Brownfields Economic Development Initiative makes grants to local governments that have acquired Section 108 loan guarantees to finance the redevelopment of brownfield sites. Grants by HUD and the U.S. Environmental Protection Agency (EPA), along with the reform of liability for cleaning up brownfields, have resulted in more than $1 billion in new private investment since the mid-1990s.

- The Empowerment Zone/Enterprise Community program offers grants and tax incentives to urban and rural communities to promote revitalization efforts, combining job development with new construction and renovation. This program has involved more than $3 billion in federal investment (Freilich 1999, 307).

- The Hope VI program provides funds to cities for the construction of public housing in the form of low-rise apartments (usually of no more than four stories) dispersed throughout a community. In this way, poverty can be deconcentrated and the buildings fit better visually with their surroundings. From 1993 to 1999, HUD made $3.75 billion in grants to 119 public housing authorities, which planned to demolish more than 82,000 old dwelling units and construct 51,000 new units (Hornstein 2000, 16).

- Section 8 rent subsidies are available for low-income housing.

In the early 1990s, HUD combined its programs into a single Consolidated Plan approach to encourage strategic, holistic community planning based upon a community vision. The Consolidated Plan approach has been adopted by several cities to acquire funding for housing, infrastructure, transportation, and economic development projects (Calthorpe and Fulton 2001, 246-253).

Other federal agencies operate a variety of programs designed to upgrade or replace vital infrastructure, such as transportation funding for roads and mass transit (see Chapter 16), tax credits for rehabilitating historic structures for commercial uses (see "Historic Preservation," below), and federal grants for water and wastewater systems (see Chapters 3 and 4). Yet, large amounts of federal funds are not enough to meet all of the needs in urban areas. On the one hand, for decades, federal tax incentives and subsidies have favored development in the suburbs and have drawn private investment away from central cities; on the other, private investment is essential for the economic stability, revitalization, and growth of downtowns, inner cities, and older suburbs as well as the quality of the built environment.

David Rusk lists three solutions: regional land use planning, regional tax-base sharing, and regional fair-share housing. Only by deconcentrating poverty, he believes, can cities and older suburbs achieve the diversity of people that make a sustainable community (Rusk 1999). Moreover, Rusk feels that the focus of government, business, and taxpayers must be on the regional built environment, in order to revive inner cities and older suburbs and slow the spread of suburban sprawl.

In the 1990s, some federal tax incentives were introduced to lure private investment back into cities. For instance, the Internal Revenue Service and state agencies administer the Low-Income Housing Tax Credit program, which offers tax credits to private developers of rental housing for low-income people. Another important ingredient has been the federal Community Reinvestment Act (CRA) of 1987, which requires lending institutions to make loans in a community based on a minimum percentage of deposits from that community. The CRA thus keeps money circulating within a community and helps the community or neighborhood reinvest in itself. Federal mortgage companies could offer lower interest rates to homeowners who purchase a house or apartment within the city limits. Finally, there are thousands of nonprofit organizations—Community Development Corporations, church-affiliated groups, economic development corporations, and neighborhood groups—that have worked with all levels of government and used federal grants and loans to revive parts of inner cities.

Brownfield Redevelopment

Clean-up and redevelopment of old industrial sites that may contain low-level hazardous waste are often crucial to turning around former industrial districts. The federal and state brownfield programs can help communities clean up these sites and turn them into housing, commercial areas, industrial uses, and public parks. Brownfield projects can be small (as in the case of abandoned gas stations or dry cleaning shops) or large (such as a defunct steel mill or factory), but much more work on rehabilitating the nation's 500,000 brownfield sites needs to be done (see Chapter 7).

Historic Preservation

Historic preservation and the adaptive reuse of older buildings are key elements of most urban redevelopment projects. Historic preservation is much more than just maintaining historic sites and museums. Historic preservation also features the adaptive reuse of older buildings and maintaining the architectural integrity of historic districts. Refurbished buildings can be used for retail space, restaurants, museums, offices, studios, and downtown housing. Often uses can be mixed. A retail business can occupy the ground floor, while the upper floors are used for apartments or offices. In many cases, the rehabilitation of historic buildings involves brownfield remediation, especially when industrial buildings are being renovated for commercial and residential uses and when asbestos is found in older commercial buildings.

Historic preservation protects a community's cultural and architectural heritage. Historic buildings often attract tourists, and form the centerpiece of the Main Street programs that have proven successful in more than 1,500 communities with populations of 5,000 to 50,000 people. In the 20 years since the Main Street Center of the National Trust for Historic Preservation began in 1980, Main Street communities have rehabilitated some 62,000 buildings, created 51,000 new businesses and 193,000 new jobs, and attracted $13 billion in downtown reinvestment (Moe 2001a, 6). Moreover, the rehabilitation of historic buildings often acts as a catalyst for other downtown development projects.

Historic preservation projects typically involve federal standards and investment tax credits, the state historic preservation office, local ordinances and building codes, and private investors. The National Historic Preservation Law of 1966 created the National Register of Historic Places, which by 2000 contained nearly 1 million records on historic buildings, sites, and districts. The total number of properties listed on the National Register of Historic Places has steadily increased from 873 in 1967 to more than 66,000 in 1996 (Council on Environmental Quality 1996, 262). Owners of properties listed on the National Register or located in one of the more than 11,000 districts certified as historic by the National Park Service are eligible for income tax credits to help defray the cost of refurbishing the buildings for commercial purposes. In addition, communities with official historic districts and buildings on the National Register can have a say in federal projects such as road widenings. Congress enacted the income tax credits for the rehabilitation of historic properties for commercial uses in 1976. Under the law, an investor could deduct up to 25% of the cost of rehabbing. Ten years later, Congress reduced the attractiveness of the tax credits, making them equal to 20% of the rehab investment of an income-producing property with a maximum credit of $9,000 per year, and no more than the net income from the property. A lesser tax credit of 10% of rehabilitation costs is available to owners of income-producing properties built before 1936 that are not on the National Register.

Since 1976, nearly 28,000 historic properties have been renovated with $20 billion in investment (Brown 2000, 13). In 1999 alone, historic preservation tax credits stimulated $2.3 billion worth of investment in historic structures and created thousands of jobs. However, even this level of investment is below the 1986 record of $2.5 billion, just before the reduction in historic tax credits took effect. Clearly, one of the most effective means of encouraging more investment in downtowns and older suburbs would be to increase the federal historic preservation tax credits. According to West Virginia developer Brooks McCabe, "The majority of these projects would not occur without tax credits" (*ibid.*).

Each state has a state historic preservation office to provide information on National Register nominations, the creation of historic districts, state and local tax incentives, and federal historic preservation tax credits. States have promoted historic preservation in several creative ways. Most states have compiled a State Register of Historic Places for structures and sites that may not meet the National Register Standards, but are worthy of special protection. Wisconsin requires a city with properties on the State or National Register to adopt an historic preservation ordinance (Beaumont 1996). Idaho requires tax assessors to consider any historic limitations in assessing real estate for property tax purposes. Sixteen states offer state historic tax credits to supplement the federal tax credits; and some states allow income tax credits for rehabbing historic private homes (*ibid.*). For instance, in 1998, North Carolina enacted a 20% income tax credit for the rehabbing of historic buildings. In 2000, North Carolina developers spent $45 million on renovating historic properties compared to just $6 million in 1997 (Moe 2001b).

Twenty-two states allow the use of transfer of development rights to protect historic properties. The most famous example of this happened in New York City when Grand Central Station was saved from demolition and the air rights above the station were transferred to another site. At this site, a building was then built higher than the zoning would normally allow. Several states have enacted "106" laws, which require a state review of state projects that would affect historic sites and discuss how proposed developments might be altered to minimize impacts (Beaumont 1996).

At the local level, several communities have entered into façade easements with commercial building owners. The owners agree to fix up their building fronts and, in return, the local government does not increase their assessed property value. Some communities have also worked with the private sector to raise low-interest loan funds for the renovation of storefronts.

STATE EFFORTS TO REVITALIZE CITIES

Adequate public infrastructure, good design, and private investment are all essential in making cities attractive places to live and work. Public spending and infrastructure investment can be redirected away from growing suburbs to revitalize cities and older suburbs. Efforts to revitalize cities are an important ingredient in the Smart Growth movement that has become popular since the late 1990s. Different states, cities, and communities define Smart Growth differently (see Table 18-2), but the common themes are less sprawl, greater efficiency of public services through targeting state infrastructure investment to existing communities, incentives for the private sector to invest in urban areas, improved development design, and a balance between economic growth and environmental quality.

In 1997, Maryland Governor Parris Glendening won legislative approval for his Smart Growth program—a set of planning initiatives and financial incentives to curb sprawl, promote more compact development, and focus state infrastructure spending in existing settlements. The legislation first called for city and county governments to identify Priority Funding Areas where state funds for schools, housing, and sewer and water facilities would be directed. The Priority Funding Areas must be existing settlements or adjacent lands designated for development. Priority Funding Areas must have at least 3.5 residential units per acre;

between 1997 and 2001, 99% of sewer and water connections were located in Priority Funding Areas (Nishida 2001). A large majority of state school construction funding is now going to build and renovate schools within Priority Funding Areas rather than build schools in the growing outer suburbs.

Next, the legislation featured a "Live Near Your Work" program that offers up to $3,000 for people who buy homes near their work. This program is an attempt to reduce traffic congestion by promoting transit, bicycle, and pedestrian modes of transport as well as encourage reinvestment in cities and villages. A job creation tax incentive program was enacted to grant state tax credits to employers who create 25 or more new jobs in Priority Fund-

ing Areas. A Brownfields Redevelopment Program was created to provide financial incentives and reduced liability for developers to clean up and develop brownfield sites in cities. As of 2001, some 70 brownfield projects were under way on 1,500 acres (*ibid.*). The Rural Legacy Program, the fifth component of Smart Growth, established and funded a competitive state grants program for counties and land trusts to purchase conservation easements on large, contiguous areas of farmlands, forests, and environmentally sensitive lands. Rural Legacy received an initial $100 million in funding over five years, and has a long-term goal to preserve 250,000 acres and thus help to limit sprawl.

Table 18-2
Vermont Forum on Sprawl Smart Growth Principles

1.	Plan development so as to maintain the historic settlement pattern of compact village and urban centers separated by rural countryside.
2.	Promote the health and quality of Vermont communities through economic and residential growth that is targeted to compact, mixed-use centers, including resort centers, at a scale convenient and accessible for pedestrians and appropriate for the community and region.
3.	Enable choice in the mode of transportation available and ensure that transportation options are integrated and consistent with land use objectives.
4.	Protect and preserve environmental quality and important natural resources and historic features of Vermont, including natural areas, water resources, air quality, scenic resources, and historic sites and districts.
5.	Provide the public with access to formal and informal open spaces, including parks, playgrounds, public greens, water bodies, forests, and mountains.
6.	Encourage and strengthen agricultural and forest enterprises and minimize conflicts of development with these businesses.
7.	Provide for housing that meets the needs of a diversity of social and income groups in each Vermont community, but especially in communities that are most rapidly growing.
8.	Support a diversity of viable business enterprises in downtowns and villages, including locally owned businesses, and a diversity of agricultural and forestry enterprises in the countryside.
9.	Balance growth with the availability of economic and efficient public utilities and services and through the investment of public funds consistent with these principles.
10.	Accomplish goals and strategies for smart growth through coalitions with stakeholders and the engagement of the public.

Source: Vermont Forum on Sprawl (2001), used by permission.

In 1998, Governor Glendening added an executive order requiring that state buildings and state workers remain in downtowns. The State of Maryland drafted a model infill development code and a uniform building code for communities to use in promoting development within Priority Funding Areas. In 2001, the Maryland legislature created a state Office of Smart Growth to promote growth management efforts within state agencies, local governments, and among developers.

Good design, public investment, and private development are all needed to create durable, attractive, and successful urban environments that provide a viable alternative to sprawl and save taxpayer dollars. For instance, in 2000, then-New Jersey Governor Christine Whitman canceled a new state office building in the suburbs, even though $3 million had already been spent on the project, and directed 900 state employees to continue to work in Trenton, the state capital. "Keeping jobs in our cities is our first priority," said Governor Whitman. "That's smart growth" (*The New York Times* 2000, B8). A 1992 Rutgers University study compared the costs of developing New Jersey from 1990 to 2010 according to current land use trends or a more compact form of growth called for in the New Jersey State Plan. The study estimated that the more compact pattern would develop 30,000 fewer acres of farmland, and save taxpayers $1.3 billion on infrastructure costs and $400 million in annual operating costs over 20 years (Burchell 1992).

LOCAL PLANNING FOR THE BUILT ENVIRONMENT

The purpose of a comprehensive plan is not to freeze a community's built environment at a certain point in time or in a certain style. Rather, the comprehensive plan expresses a vision and direction for the future growth and redevelopment of the community. The planning process offers many opportunities for urban areas to improve environmental quality, design, infrastructure, and the overall quality of life. Site-sensitive infill development, together with adaptive reuse of abandoned or underutilized buildings, can minimize the need for greenfield development as well as boost the city's economic well-being and number of residents.

The comprehensive planning process should also suggest how a local government can work with state and federal agencies and the private sector to promote the redevelopment of cities. For instance, across America, thousands of nonprofit organizations—Community Development Corporations, church-affiliated groups, economic development corporations, and neighborhood groups—have worked with all levels of government to revive parts of inner cities.

Inventory

The comprehensive plan should include an inventory and mapping of the industrial, commercial, residential, and public uses that make up the current land uses of the built environment. Geographic Information System (GIS) mapping is helpful, with color coding for different uses. The comprehensive plan should also include a visual survey to identify important landmarks, streetscapes, and neighborhoods or districts. Communities should inventory their historic and architecturally significant buildings and sites, just as they inventory their natural resources. Available open land for infill development and brownfields with potential for reuse should be identified and described. Some cities, such as Albany, New York, have conducted a survey of vacant buildings and created a GIS database. Areas of substandard housing and high-rise public housing projects should also be noted. An inventory of infrastructure—roads, schools, parks, and transit—can be useful as an indicator of redevelopment or infill potential in an area. Any areas with deteriorating infrastructure should be described.

Table 18-3
Sample Built Environment Goals and Objectives in the Comprehensive Plan

Land Use	
Goal	To redevelop blighted areas and brownfields, to promote the adaptive reuse of historic structures, and to promote and maintain distinctive districts and neighborhoods.
Objective	Pursue state and federal funding for brownfield redevelopment.
Objective	Adopt a building code and a design review ordinance to promote good design in the construction of new buildings and the renovation of older buildings.
Housing	
Goal	To provide an array of housing opportunities for all income levels through the redevelopment of substandard public and private housing and the promotion of mixed-use projects that combine residential and commercial uses.
Objective	Pursue state and federal loans and grants for the construction of public and private housing.
Economic Base	
Objective	Expand the community's property tax base and employment base by attracting new businesses through adaptive reuse of abandoned and underutilized buildings, and the redevelopment of brownfield sites.
Objective	Protect historic buildings that can be rehabilitated and can serve as the basis of a tourist industry or a downtown revitalization program.
Community Facilities	
Objective	Provide good quality roads, mass transit, utilities, parks, and schools in areas slated for redevelopment.
Objective	Improve streetscapes through tree plantings, street furniture, and sidewalks.
Natural Resources	
Objective	Avoid the development or redevelopment of environmentally sensitive areas.
Objective	Incorporate stormwater management practices in redevelopment and infill development projects.

Analysis

The comprehensive plan should present an analysis of ways in which the community can enhance the built environment. Areas with substandard housing units, vacant buildings, and brownfields should be evaluated for potential redevelopment, keeping in mind infrastructure availability and needs. The analysis should determine the potential for older and historic buildings for adaptive reuse. Areas available for infill development with residential, commercial, industrial, and public uses should be evaluated according to existing and needed proposed infrastructure improvements. Needs for parks, greenways, and trails that blend with the built environment should also be determined.

Goals and Objectives

Goals and objectives for the built environment should be presented in the Land Use, Housing, Economic Base, Community Facilities, Natural Resources, and Transportation sections of the comprehensive plan (see Table 18-3). These goals and objectives give direction to public officials, developers, property owners, and the community at large about what types of built environments are desired and where they should be located.

General goals should be to redevelop blighted areas, protect historic buildings, enhance streetscapes, and improve infrastructure.

Action Strategy

The Action Strategy should present techniques and programs for achieving the built environment goals and objectives of the comprehensive plan as well as a timetable. The future land use map and zoning map should identify future land uses and zone changes based on the analysis and evaluation of future needs. Benchmarks should be identified and progress toward those benchmarks evaluated in an annual report on the environment. Specific recommendations might include the following:

- Explore the creation of one or more historic districts to make property owners eligible for expanded federal tax credits for rehabilitating historic buildings.
- Appoint a design review board or architecture and historic review board, and draft a design review ordinance.
- Create a GIS inventory of existing brownfield sites.
- Apply for federal and state funding to assess the condition of brownfield sites for cleanup and potential redevelopment.
- Adopt mixed-use zoning to encourage projects that blend residential and commercial uses.
- Require greenspace, tree planting, and landscaping in redevelopment projects to provide recreation opportunities and absorb stormwater runoff.
- Promote the use of traffic-calming devices in residential neighborhoods to protect pedestrians and bicyclists.

Zoning Ordinance

Zoning ordinances have a direct influence on the appearance and functioning of infill development and redevelopment. An ordinance that allows mixed-use development can encourage greater density, more pedestrian traffic, and transit use. The zoning ordinance can promote the redevelopment of blighted areas and brownfield sites by allowing for a wide array of uses. Local zoning that encourages the rehabilitation of older buildings can give an enormous boost to urban revitalization.

Federal and state tax credit programs do not prevent the demolition, removal, or defacement of historic structures. This is where local governments must step in to adopt demolition ordinances that require a review and specific permits before the destruction of a building is allowed in a historic district or on the National Register. State-enabling legislation for the creation of historic districts is a first step in setting up historic ordinance guidelines. Zoning standards can be adopted for the review of proposed demolitions, removals, or major façade alterations. The standards may apply to buildings on the National Register, in a designated historic district, or to locally recognized historic buildings. Zoning standards may further require that new development adjacent to historic structures be compatible with the architectural character of the neighborhood. The demand for demolition permits for historic structures can be discouraged by allowing floor-to-area rations for new development to be no more than 80% to 90% of the existing floor area ratio of the building currently on site.

Adaptive reuse and conversions should be specific permitted uses and easier to obtain than permits for new development. Commercial and mixed-use zoning should allow apartments above shops and a mix of offices and apartments. Commercial zoning in recent decades has often resulted in strip development along highways and the introduction of big-box retail stores on the outskirts of cities, towns, and villages. Communities can limit the number of "curb cuts" (driveways) per mile and can require deep setbacks from roads to create some greenspace and make commercial developments less obtrusive. A sign ordinance limiting the size and height of signs, and hence reducing visual clutter, is another a good idea. Communities can also draft zoning provisions that restrict the square footage of commercial buildings. For instance, Skaneateles, New York, limits the size of new commercial buildings to a maximum of 45,000 square feet. Newport, Rhode Island, enacted a zoning ordinance that allows the city to limit the number of similar types of businesses. The city reasoned that it did not want to see new businesses taking customers from established ones.

Heavy industrial sites should be located away from residential and commercial areas. It is important to zone land for industrial use where the necessary large tracts and sewer, water, electricity, highway, and, ideally, mass-transit facilities exist. Many communities have zoned extensive areas for industrial uses that lack suitable infrastructure, and industry generally will not spend the money to install sewer and water lines or upgrade roads. Industrial sites that have remained undeveloped need to be analyzed for other uses and even rezoned to commercial, residential, or public uses.

Performance Zoning

A city or suburb can use performance zoning standards to maintain the overall quality of the environment as development occurs. The idea is to regulate the impacts of development rather than developments themselves. Performance standards typically refer to the retention of trees and forests, the protection of views, and a minimum of ground disturbance in the development construction process. However, standards also relate to the operation of completed projects for activities that could spill over onto nearby properties. Such activities include dust, fumes, odors, vibrations, light, heat, and glare.

Subdivision Regulations

Subdivision regulations can be helpful in encouraging good urban design and facilitating urban development. Subdivision standards should include flexible parking and access for infill and redevel-

opment projects. Mandatory dedication of parkland can apply to commercial as well as residential development and should promote the creation of pocket parks, community gardens, and bicycle and walking paths. Landscaping requirements can call for the planting of vegetation along sidewalks and encourage the creation of roof-top gardens. Standards for narrow roads can promote traffic calming, and a requirement for interconnected roads maintains traffic flow. Also, it is a good idea to require the burying of electricity and telephone utility lines for new developments. This minimizes a cluttered appearance, enables solar access, and allows space for trees to grow.

Illustrations of desirable design and siting in the community's land development and subdivision regulations can help developers and landowners understand what the community desires in development layout, the siting of buildings, building and landscaping design, and the provision of infrastructure, such as sewer, water, and roads.

Capital Improvements Program

Capital improvements drive the built environment. Adequate roads, mass transit, central sewer and water, public greenspace, police and fire stations, and schools are all critical to the safe and efficient functioning of a neighborhood, district, or city. The capital improvements program (CIP) must be coordinated with the zoning ordinance. This is especially important for the construction of new infrastructure to support infill development and the redevelopment of blighted areas and brownfields. New or widened roads should be sized to accommodate bike lanes or light-rail corridors where appropriate. Old sewer and water lines should be replaced whenever leakage or infiltration is discovered, if not before.

State and federal grants for infrastructure are an important source of financing. At the local level, bonding is a common way to pay for large urban sewer, water, and street projects. These are long-term investments for which long-term

Table 18-4
A Checklist of Built Environment Issues in a Development Review

1.	What are the size, location, and land uses of the proposed development?
2.	Is the proposed development allowed in the particular zone?
3.	Does the proposed development meet the setback, height, and bulk coverage requirements?
4.	What are the land uses on the adjacent properties?
5.	How will sewer and water service be provided?
6.	What will be the impact on traffic and parking?
7.	Does the proposed development involve demolition of one or more existing buildings? Are any historic structures involved?
8.	What will the proposed development look like? Has there been a design review by the local design review board?
9.	Has the developer obtained any necessary state or federal permits?

financing is appropriate. Cities can influence the location of development through impact fees. For instance, the City of Lancaster, California, charges developers impact fees based on the distance from the city center: the farther away from the center, the higher the fees. Tax-increment financing has been a popular technique to upgrade a city district or downtown. Tax-increment financing involves the sale of bonds to raise revenue to make physical improvements to a district or downtown, such as new street furniture, sidewalks, and streetlights. The property owners in a district are assessed higher property taxes because the improvements will raise property values. The additional property taxes (or the increment in property taxes) are earmarked for paying off the bonds. In addition, communities can use property tax abatements, covering business relocation costs, and tax credits for the creation of new jobs to attract new private investment and redevelopment into downtowns.

What to Look for in a Development Review

A proposed development should be evaluated according to the comprehensive plan, zoning ordi-

nance, subdivision and land development regulations, CIP, and other relevant ordinances. Size, location, proposed uses, and design are the four main considerations in a development review involving the built environment (see Table 18-4). New and redeveloped buildings should fit in with existing and planned transportation networks, sewer and water facilities, and the surrounding neighborhood. The proposed use of a site should have a design compatible with nearby land uses, and the light, noise, and traffic it will likely generate should be consistent with the existing uses in the vicinity.

CASE STUDY

Revitalizing America's cities is a tall order. The following case study describes how Chattanooga, Tennessee, reinvented itself to become an economically and environmentally sustainable urban destination. Not every city will do as well as Chattanooga, but with time, imagination, private investment, local leadership, and the goal of a sustainable built environment, American cities can be good places to live, work, and visit.

CASE STUDY 18-1
**Chattanooga, Tennessee:
From Worst to First**

In the 1990s, nearly every city in America that was serious about revitalization sent a delegation to visit Chattanooga, Tennessee, population 155,000. The city had become famous as a model of the successful turnaround of a gritty, industrial urban area to an attractive, vital metropolis. After the Civil War, Chattanooga became a major industrial center. The creation of the Tennessee Valley Authority in the 1930s and the availability of cheap hydroelectric power strengthened Chattanooga's industrial sector. However, industry waned in the 1950s and 1960s, and by 1969, according to the EPA, Chattanooga had become the dirtiest city in America. The smog was so heavy that people often had to drive with their headlights on in the middle of the day. Today, Chattanooga is famous for its cleanliness, sustainable development, and environmental design. What happened?

Chattanooga's efforts have featured active cooperation between the public and private sectors, an emphasis on good urban design, and comprehensive planning. In 1981, the nonprofit Riverfront/Downtown Planning and Design Center was created to help revitalize the appearance of downtown and provide guidance on good design. In 1984, the nonprofit organization Chattanooga Venture was formed to revive the downtown, build affordable housing, and clean up the environment. Chattanooga Venture, together with the city government, launched a Community Visioning and Vision 2000 initiative to set goals and objectives for action. The city sponsored charettes—day-long intensive participation exercises focused on potential designs of particular sites and neighborhoods. From the charettes, a consensus of 40 goals and 223 proposed programs and projects evolved, which were incorporated into the city's comprehensive plan and zoning regulations.

Revitalizing the downtown along the Tennessee River was the cornerstone of the city's effort. Chattanooga received $45 million in private donations to construct its renowned Tennessee Aquarium, completed in 1992. More than 1 million visitors come to the aquarium each year. The South Business District today includes an eco-industrial zone for zero-emissions manufacturing together with a range of housing types, a stadium, an expanded trade center, and Riverwalk—a network of greenways with walking trails and bike paths along the river. The city developed a free shuttle of electric buses in the downtown, reducing auto use and air pollution, while encouraging pedestrian traffic. Three parking garages along the shuttle route make it convenient to gain access to the shuttle. Hundreds of thousands of people ride the shuttle buses each year.

Chattanooga moved to reduce substandard housing by developing, financing, renovating, and managing housing for low- to moderate-income residents. The nonprofit Chattanooga Neighborhood Enterprise (CNE) was founded to promote affordable housing by providing low-interest loans for purchasing and rehabilitating housing and building new housing. By 1995, the CNE was "the largest single producer of affordable housing in the country, due in part to their ability to leverage public funding from private dollars" (Beatley and Manning 1997, 191). The CNE produced 300 new, low-income rental units; helped 1,000 first-time home buyers; and offered loans for home repairs to 1,300 low-income families.

Chattanooga is working to expand its system of greenways that will run along riverbanks, ridgelines, and abandoned railroad corridors to link neighborhoods, parks, and the downtown. So far, about 15 miles of the projected 75-mile system have been completed. The greenway will protect natural and cultural resources, help to control air and water pollution, and provide recreational opportunities and bicycle and pedestrian transportation routes.

The private and public investment in the city has expanded the property tax base, enabling the city to sell $125 million in bonds in the late 1990s to finance the construction of a convention center and an international trade center. Finally, the city is working with the federal government to reclaim a 6,300-acre abandoned dynamite plant from a brownfield into parkland and commercial space (Kinsey 2001).

In 1998, the State of Tennessee passed a law requiring all counties and cities to draft urban growth boundaries by July 2001. This planning effort will surely solidify Chattanooga's position as the center of its metropolitan region, unlike many cities that have lost their vitality to the suburbs.

19

Planning for the Built Environment: Greenfield Development and Site Design

The rural environment is changing into sprawling subdivisions and strip development along the County's major roadways. Further, uncontrolled growth is erasing the boundaries between small community centers and rural areas.

IMAGINE RICHLAND 2020,
RICHLAND COUNTY, SOUTH CAROLINA

Sprawl is America's most lethal disease.

ROBERT FREILICH, NOTED LAND
USE ATTORNEY (FREILICH 1999, XVII)

Most of America's built environment has been created since World War II, but changes to the American landscape since 1980 have been both remarkable and alarming. From 1982 to 1997, the amount of developed land in the United States increased by 34%, from 63 million acres to 98 million acres. In the process, 16 million acres of farmland and 6 million acres of forestland were converted to urban and suburban development (Natural Resources Conservation Service (NRCS) 2001). In the 1990s, more than four out of every five new homes were built in the suburbs (Hirschorn 2000, 10). According to Stuart Meck of the American Planning Association, between 1994 and 1997, a total of 5.23 million single-family homes were built on 9.73 million acres. Moreover, one-third of the new homes were on lots of more than 1 acre and consumed 91% of the land used for new house lots. If these new homes had been built on lots of a half-acre or less, 2 million acres a year could have been conserved (Meck 2000).

According to the Natural Resources Inventory, only about 7% of America's land base has been transformed into urban-type uses (NRCS 2001). Of the remaining 93%, nearly one-third (more than 600 million acres) is federally owned, and much of the privately held land is in places that are cold, steep, rocky, remote, or lacking water. Because the amount of attractive, privately owned land for settlement is limited, the loss of open space, farmland, woodland, and natural areas are concerns in communities across the United States (see Figure 19-1).

The patterns of development that are consuming so much open land involve three forms of sprawl:

1. *Urban sprawl* describes cities that expand in a disorderly fashion through annexation or cities with large boundaries that fill up with poorly coordinated development. Cities in the West, South, and Midwest have been fairly aggressive in their use of annexation powers to add to their land area. Often, there is little advance planning for what to do with the new city land, other than to extend sewer and water lines through it. As new land within the city limits becomes

developed, it is often not well coordinated with the existing road network, mass-transit systems, or park system. The resulting development has a haphazard appearance and does not function smoothly.

2. *Suburban sprawl* defines suburbs with one-quarter-acre to 2-acre lots that proliferate through the extension of sewer and water lines into the countryside. Often, this pattern of development leapfrogs beyond existing settlements and isolates parcels of farmland, forestland, and open space. Much new suburban development promotes the fragmentation of natural areas and working landscapes and the separation of land uses, especially residential and commercial spaces, through a combination of zoning and highways. Huge shopping malls, commercial strips, office parks, and large residential subdivisions dominate the landscape. Open space is an afterthought.

3. *Rural sprawl* includes single-family homes and commercial strip development on large lots of anywhere from 1 to 10 acres scattered

19-1 Houses encroaching on a farm in the competition for space.

Source: Lancaster County, Pennsylvania, Agricultural Preserve Board

like buckshot along country roads and arterials. This type of development is made possible by on-site septic systems and private wells. Rural sprawl is most often associated with the rural-urban fringe, where farmland and forests are giving way to suburban residential and commercial development. Typically, expanding cities and suburbs eventually overtake the existing rural sprawl, and new rural sprawl sprouts farther out in the countryside. However, as urban policy expert David Rusk has noted, cities and suburbs are expanding less rapidly than the rural sprawl (Rusk 1999). For instance, from 1990 to 1999, the population density of 225 of the nation's 271 metropolitan areas decreased, meaning that more people were settling in those parts of metropolitan regions with fewer than 1,000 people per square mile (El Nasser 2001, 1A).

THE CHALLENGE OF SPRAWL

Much, if not most, of America's development in the next several decades will likely occur on greenfield sites. Communities face four main challenges in accommodating greenfield development:

1. where to put it;
2. how to arrange it;
3. what it looks like; and
4. how it impacts the natural environment and working landscapes.

The nemesis of these challenges is sprawling development that knows no limits, is scattered across the landscape, looks ugly, and destroys natural areas, forests, and farmland.

Government Programs That Encourage Sprawl

America's sprawling growth is not so much a matter of personal tastes or "the market." Rather, it is the result of poor local government planning combined with state and federal tax incentives and spending programs that encourage the develop-

Table 19-1
The Six Metropolitan Areas
Most Likely to Sprawl (2000–2025)

1.	Phoenix–Mesa, Arizona
2.	Miami–Fort Lauderdale, Florida
3.	Las Vegas, Nevada
4.	Los Angeles–Riverside–Orange County, California
5.	Denver–Boulder–Greeley, Colorado
6.	Orlando, Florida

Source: Burchell (2000)

ment of open land—often called greenfields—rather than the redevelopment of existing built environments. Despite efforts to revitalize the nation's cities and inner suburbs, greenfield development will most likely absorb most of the new population growth and development over the next 50 years. This means more conversion of farmlands, forestlands, and environmentally sensitive areas to residential, commercial, and industrial uses.

Take, for instance, the Intermountain West, which was the fastest growing region of the United States in the 1990s (U.S. Bureau of the Census 2002). This region, along with California and Florida, is expected to experience considerable sprawl between 2000 and 2025 (see Table 19-1). Environmental planning and land use controls have struggled to keep pace in this politically conservative region. Arizona and Colorado voters rejected statewide growth controls in 2000. Yet, Arizona has experienced numerous so-called "wildcat subdivisions" in which developers legally create and sell new building lots without paved roads, curbs and gutters, or sewer lines and storm drains (Davis 2000). Colorado's sprawling Front Range growth corridor extends over 150 miles from Colorado Springs north to Fort Collins.

Environmental Harm from Sprawl

Sprawling greenfield development can have several serious consequences. First, open space is fragmented into smaller ownerships and by new roads, which may reduce the critical mass of farmlands, ranchlands, or forestlands needed to sustain these economic activities. Also, a critical mass of wildlife habitat needed to maintain healthy wildlife populations may be lost. The loss of open space also means the loss of natural areas and their environmental benefits, such as groundwater recharge and filtration. Second, sprawl has transportation, air quality, and energy impacts. Sprawling developments are almost exclusively dependent on cars for mobility and trucks for freight, increasing dependence on imported oil and generating air pollution. In addition, mass transit is rarely an option because of the scattered development, which also discourages the provision of pedestrian and bicycle paths. Third, sprawl has water quality impacts. New road construction and commercial and residential development create more impervious surfaces that increase stormwater runoff, water pollution, and downstream flooding. The application of fertilizers and herbicides on suburban lawns produces nutrient and chemical runoff into rivers, streams, and lakes. Rural sprawl relies heavily upon on-site septic systems and wells that were never intended for widespread use. Poorly sited and maintained septic systems and leach fields too close to wells will continue to cause groundwater pollution and bring calls for extensions of sewer and water lines out into the countryside. When extensions occur, additional development follows.

Financial and Social Impacts of Sprawl

Sprawl has financial and social impacts. The construction of new infrastructure—sewer and water facilities and schools—in the expanding suburbs is not only expensive but has taken money away from inner cities and older suburbs, where many schools and other infrastructure are in need of repair. In short, Americans have been abandoning the older built environment to create a new built environment on greenfield sites. In some places, such as metropolitan Chicago, this has happened with little increase in population. Between 1970 and 1990, greater Chicago grew to cover 46% more land area while the population increased by only 4% (Peirce 1993, 28). Sprawl also causes social isolation through the use of cul-de-sacs and large-lot zoning as well as through long commutes to work and shopping.

The Need for Housing

America's sprawling pattern of development is not economically or environmentally sustainable. Yet, the National Association of Home Builders (NAHB) has argued that the U.S. needs to construct between 1.3 and 1.5 million new housing units annually during the next decade (2000-2010) simply to accommodate an anticipated 30 million increase in the nation's population (NAHB 1999a). In fact, housing starts in the United States stood at 1.67 million units in 1999 and 1.59 million in 2000 (NAHB 2001a). However, the average size of a single-family house in 2000 was 2,266 square feet, up from an average of 1,500 square feet in 1970. Moreover, 18% of the new homes built in 2000 exceeded 3,000 square feet (Lang and Danielsen 2002, 24). Large houses require more energy to heat and cool than small houses, cover more area with impervious surface, and tend to be built on large lots, consuming more space.

The number of multifamily housing starts fell from 631,000 a year in 1985 to 332,000 in 2000, underscoring the dominance of single-family homes (NAHB 2001b). The NAHB sees the trend of suburban growth continuing: "Equally important, the vast majority of consumers overwhelmingly prefer a single-family home in a suburban neighborhood. The suburbs are growing because that's where most Americans want to live" (*ibid.*).

Building Compact Developments

Sprawl is not inevitable. It can be limited and discouraged, but it will take considerable reform in local planning and state and federal programs. The challenge for local governments and the development community is how to design developments that are fairly dense, contain the amenities and security that will attract residents and businesses, and connect via paths and trails to shopping, jobs, schools, and playgrounds. Compact development can reduce land consumption, maintain farm and forest operations, reduce the fragmentation of open space and environmentally sensitive areas, and conserve energy. Compact development can be more efficiently served by public transportation networks and central sewer and water systems. Other facilities, such as schools, libraries, and community centers, can better serve their target populations when they are centrally located in compact communities. Moreover, because less land and infrastructure are needed to serve the same number of people, compact development creates opportunities to reduce the cost of housing. As discussed in Chapter 18, the redevelopment of blighted urban neighborhoods and inner suburbs into attractive, efficient, and livable places is essential to slowing sprawl and promoting compact development. Some greenfield development will certainly continue, but it can be accommodated on less land than 2- to 5-acre house lots.

Professor Robert Burchell has estimated that between 2000 and 2025, Americans will build 25 million new housing units. He then compared the likely savings from accommodating these new dwellings in a compact form as opposed to a sprawling pattern (see Table 19-2). Burchell's concept of compact form embodies modestly higher density, mixed-use development, redevelopment of cities and inner suburbs, transit-oriented development (TOD), traffic-calming, open space protection, and park and recreation areas (Burchell 2000, 12). Overall estimated savings through more com-

Table 19-2
Savings Through Compact Development vs. Sprawl for 25 Million Dwelling Units (2000–2025)

Savings–Areas	Savings–Units	Savings (in billions)
Land	3.1 million acres	$15.50
Local Roads	91,000 lane miles	$33.13
State Roads	3,000 lane miles	$2.66
Water Laterals	2.25 million water laterals	$4.64
Sewer Laterals	2.42 million sewer laterals	$4.19
Housing Costs	$5,792 per dwelling unit	$144.80
Nonresidential Costs	$861.25 per 1,000 sq. ft.	$21.53
Fiscal Impacts	$964.02 per dwelling unit	$24.10
Total: $250 billion or $10,000 per dwelling unit		

Source: Burchell (2000)

pact development were $10,000 per housing unit, a significant amount that could help make housing more affordable.

Avoiding the Suburban "Pod" Style

The standard suburban residential "pod" of single-family homes covers 40 to 100 acres, laid out with curving interior streets and cul-de-sacs (also known as "loops and lollipops"), which feed into one or two collector streets that empty onto a major arterial highway (see Figure 19-2). While the pod is safe from thru-traffic, police, firefighters, ambulance drivers, and delivery personnel have a difficult time finding the right address. Add in the lack of sidewalks to discourage pedestrian traffic and the lack of public playgrounds, and it's small wonder that obesity is on the rise in the suburbs (Centers for Disease Control 2001). The pods tend to look all the same; they are visually dull, with large garages dominating the homes.

FEDERAL PROGRAMS TO MANAGE GREENFIELD DEVELOPMENT

Federal spending, taxation, and regulatory programs have encouraged rather than discouraged the development of greenfields. Federal subsidies for highways and sewer and water lines have opened up huge areas to suburban expansion. Federal gasoline taxes have not been sufficiently high to discourage sprawling, automobile-dependent development. Federal transportation policy and funding has long emphasized road construction and maintenance over mass-transit systems.

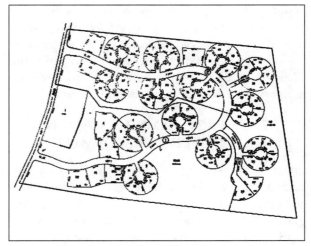

19-2 Typical suburban residential "pod" layout.
Source: Dutchess County, New York

Homeownership has been a cornerstone of the America Dream. The federal mortgage interest deduction, which allows a homeowner to deduct the cost of mortgage interest from taxable income, is a subsidy worth tens of billions of dollars each year (Daniels 1999). In addition, homeowners may deduct local property taxes from federal taxable income. In 1998, Congress enacted legislation to allow a homeowner who sells a primary residence to exempt up to $250,000 in capital gains from federal taxes. If a couple sells the house, the exemption is up to $500,000 in capital gains. For years, the suburbs have been growing faster than the inner cities. Given that the appreciate potential of residential real estate is higher in the outer, growing suburbs than in cities and older suburbs, these federal tax incentives are in effect subsidizing sprawl. At the same time, federal tax laws that allow developers to rapidly depreciate new commercial buildings are encouraging commercial development in outer suburbs.

Finally, federal regulations have not been geared toward slowing sprawl. The National Environmental Policy Act (NEPA) could have curtailed many federal projects because they would induce environmentally harmful sprawl. However, even though most NEPA reviews involve Federal Highway Administration projects, these projects have rarely been stopped. While transportation planning has changed under the Intermodal Surface Transportation Efficiency Act and the Clean Air Act, sprawl and air quality remain major problems in many metropolitan areas.

STATE PROGRAMS TO MANAGE GREENFIELD DEVELOPMENT

The principles of open space conservation and compact development have been embodied in state legislation across the nation, including Oregon's 1973 Land Use Act, Florida's 1985 Growth Management Act, Washington State's Growth Management Act of 1991, the New Jersey State Plan of 1994, Maryland's Smart Growth Legisla-

tion of 1997, and Tennessee's 1998 Land Use Act. Oregon's program requires cities and counties to jointly adopt urban growth boundaries as a way to limit infrastructure extensions and concentrate development in and adjacent to existing settlements. Florida requires that local governments practice "concurrency"—not allowing new development until the necessary infrastructure is in place. Washington followed Oregon's lead in requiring growth boundaries around major cities, and New Jersey instituted a "tier" system with state infrastructure targeted to existing settlements and adjacent expansion areas, not in the countryside. The State of Maryland directs state infrastructure dollars to Priority Funding Areas and offers an array of financial incentives to promote compact growth. Tennessee requires cities and counties to adopt comprehensive plans and 20-year growth boundaries, patterned after Oregon's program.

Delaware may well be the next state to undertake state-level planning to encourage or mandate more compact development. In 1999, the Governor of Delaware's Cabinet Committee on State Planning Issues reported that unless future development occurs at a density of greater than one dwelling per acre, there will not be enough land available in one of the state's three counties—New Castle County—to accommodate the projected increase of 55,000 more residents by the year 2020 (see Table 19-3).

Developments of Regional Impact

Permit systems to review developments of regional impact (DRIs) are critical for evaluating the potential impacts of large developments on the environment, development patterns, capital facilities, and traffic in more than one municipality or county. Yet, historically, municipalities or counties have each conducted their own reviews without consideration of the impacts on neighboring communities. Vermont has pioneered the DRI process through Act 250, passed in 1970. Under Act

Table 19-3
Available Acreage vs. Needed Acreage in Delaware (1997–2020)

County	Ratio of Available Acres to Needed Acres			
	At 1 dwelling unit per acre	At 3 dwelling units per acre	At 5 dwelling units per acre	At 7 dwelling units per acre
Kent	2.66	7.97	13.29	18.60
New Castle	0.91	2.73	4.55	6.37
Sussex	3.00	8.99	14.98	20.98
All of Delaware	1.78	5.34	8.90	12.47

Note: The figures do not include the potential for urban or suburban redevelopment.

Source: Delaware Office of State Planning Coordination (1999)

250, a proposed development above a certain size is reviewed for its potential effects on air and water quality, sewage disposal, agricultural soils, wildlife, traffic, and government services. Vermont established a state environmental board and 10 district environmental commissions with members appointed by the governor and supported by professional staff to respond to applications by developers. Although nearly all development applications have been approved, most have specific conditions attached. The general consensus is that the Act 250 process has improved the quality of development by discouraging bad proposals and compelling approved projects to meet state standards. Florida has required the review of DRIs since 1972. A total of 28 states and the Cape Cod Regional Commission in Massachusetts now provide for at least some review of DRIs.

Defining what size development constitutes a DRI is crucial. In Vermont, a DRI is 10 or more lots, 10 or more dwelling units, or commercial development of more than 10 acres (more than 1 acre if there is no local comprehensive plan). In Florida, a DRI is more than 2,500 dwelling units. As a result, Florida communities have greater say over development decisions than in Vermont. Generally, shopping malls, airports, sports arenas, large factories, and large residential subdivisions constitute DRIs. In order to regulate DRIs, state legislation is needed, and a regional permitting

system must be established. An important part of the process is the use of developer agreements to ensure that, once a DRI is approved, the developer does not build or operate the project in a detrimental fashion.

State Environmental Policy Acts

State Environmental Policy Acts (SEPAs) are found in 22 states and the District of Columbia. SEPAs require a review of proposed state actions and often local government actions, and sometimes private development, to determine potential impacts on the environment. SEPAs are modeled after NEPA of 1970, which requires a review of major federal actions before they can proceed. A SEPA can address environmental issues specific to a proposed development that the comprehensive plan and zoning and subdivision regulations often do not. For instance, a SEPA can require:

- an assessment of significant environmental impacts;
- an assessment of the cumulative impacts of development projects;
- an analysis of alternatives to the proposed development project; and
- mitigation and modification of projects.

SEPA reviews are usually required for fairly large proposed developments. Whereas DRIs normally involve a regional-level review, SEPA projects may receive only local-level reviews.

Noted Washington University law professor Daniel Mandelker argues that a SEPA can be more important than a comprehensive plan and zoning ordinance in protecting the environment (Mandelker 2000). However, SEPAs have the serious drawback of being a reactive rather than proactive tool, and seldom result in the denial of a project. SEPAs are therefore most effective as an addition to comprehensive planning and zoning and subdivision review.

REGIONAL AND LOCAL MANAGEMENT OF GREENFIELD DEVELOPMENT

As populations grow and the need for land increases, the challenge is how to direct the location of new development, influence its timing, and shape its character to minimize impacts on the natural environment and working landscapes. Different lands vary in their development capabilities and constraints. It is primarily up to cities, townships, and counties to determine these capabilities and constraints to guide growth through comprehensive plans, zoning and subdivision regulations, and capital improvements programs (CIPs).

The McHarg Layers Approach

In his classic book *Design With Nature* (1971), Ian McHarg emphasized the need to understand the physical carrying capacity of both a region and particular tracts of land in planning for development. He devised a method for determining how much development a region or tract can support and how to find the best locations for development. First, McHarg recommended the compilation of a regional Natural Resources Inventory, especially for a watershed or subbasin area (see Chapter 1). This inventory should include the following features:

- soils, including high-quality agricultural and forestry soils;
- vegetation;

> ### SIDEBAR 19-1
> ## Los Angeles: Can the Environment Keep Pace?
>
> The Los Angeles region has long been a poster child for the worst aspects of sprawl: clogged freeways, smog, dependence on imported water, swarms of tract homes, and relentless outward growth. Between 1970 and 1990, the population of greater Los Angeles grew by 45% and its developed area by 300% (Davis 1999, 86). From 2000 to 2025, the Los Angeles region is expected to increase by *6 million* people. At that rate, the region will need to add about 25,000 housing units a year (Purdum 2000, A1). Urban infill and downtown redevelopment will not provide much new housing. Suburban sprawl appears to be the only housing solution, which will involve more roads, more cars, and more congestion. At the same time, such enormous population growth will place huge demands on water supplies, sewage and waste disposal, and open space opportunities. The real question is: When will the environment become a binding constraint to the growth of greater Los Angeles?

- slope;
- drainage;
- water bodies, wetlands, and aquifers;
- wildlife habitat and wildlife;
- geological features, especially outcroppings, potential landslide areas, and shallow depth to bedrock; and
- viewsheds.

McHarg recommended that these inventory "layers" be placed one on top of the other to help identify areas that could support intensive, limited, or no development. In the early 1960s, McHarg and Dr. David Wallace were hired by a group of citizens to draft a land use plan for the valleys region of Baltimore County, Maryland—an area of rolling piedmont northwest of the City of Baltimore. The Plan for the Valleys emphasized the carrying capacity of the region. First, Wallace estimated the likely impacts if current trends in private development, in public highways, and sewers were to continue. Next, an analysis of housing demand by type, price, and location was conducted. Wallace then identified both graphically and in financial terms the pattern of growth that would likely occur without any new plans or land use controls. Next, McHarg produced what he considered the optimum development pattern given the physical constraints of the area. He recommended that most development be kept off the valley floors, where the best farming soils were, and away from streams and floodplains. The unforested plateaus were identified as the most suitable sites for development, but even here McHarg recommended low-density residential uses and no commercial or industrial development (McHarg 1971, 79-93).

Today, thousands of acres of the valleys are zoned at a density of one dwelling per 50 acres. Much of the valleys region lies outside the county's rural-urban demarcation line, which is in effect a growth boundary beyond which sewer service has not been extended. In addition, Baltimore County has preserved more than 40,000 acres of land in the valleys region through the purchase and donation of development rights.

Although McHarg pioneered the layers technique over large areas of land, the same approach can now be applied to smaller areas and individual tracts of land. Today, layered resource mapping and analysis can be done conveniently with a computerized Geographic Information System (GIS). The layers approach is useful in identifying land suitable for development and land with constraints as part of the comprehensive planning process. The layers approach is also helpful for reviewing development proposals on greenfield sites. A planner can identify the parts of a site that are not appropriate for development, such as slopes over 15%, areas with wet soils, or a shallow depth to bedrock.

Urban Growth Boundaries

Urban and village growth boundaries have been gaining in popularity as a way to accommodate growth in a more compact pattern that conserves open space. A growth boundary is a line drawn on a zoning map that indicates the limits to planned growth within a specific period of time (see Chapter 13). A growth boundary typically requires an agreement between a city and the surrounding county or towns that identifies an area where growth will be encouraged and accommodated, usually over the next 10 to 20 years (see Daniels and Bowers 1997, 284-288). The boundary is drawn based on population projections for the urban area and the land use needs for that projected population. The city and county or towns should agree that urban services—public *and private* sewer and water lines, schools, and major new roads—will not be extended outside of the growth boundary.

Growth boundaries can be an effective tool to spur growth in and adjacent to existing settlements and to curb sprawl. As planner-architect Jonathan Barnett explains:

> "Restricting growth at the urban fringe and making improvements in bypassed parts of the older city are interdependent policies. Growth restraints at the fringe make bypassed areas a more significant alternative, but only if a decisive effort makes new investment possible" (Barnett 1995, 160).

Although state-enabling legislation may not be needed in order to create growth boundaries, such legislation is certainly helpful. The State of Oregon required the state's 236 cities and 36 counties to agree on growth boundaries as part of the 1973 state land use act (see Figure 13-3). Yet, despite the absence of specific state-enabling legislation, Lexington, Kentucky, and surrounding Fayette County have had a growth boundary since the 1950s. In Lancaster County, Pennsylvania, in the 1990s, 22 urban and village growth boundaries were created through a voluntary process with incentives from the county government. In the late 1990s, voters and city councils in the San Francisco Bay Area approved the creation of more than half a dozen growth boundaries (Daniels 1999, 257). A recent survey of growth boundaries found more than 80 of them in use nationwide (Burby *et al.* 2001, 475-490).

The purposes of growth boundaries are:

- to create a more compact form of development that is less expensive to service than a sprawl pattern;
- to minimize sprawl, and so protect farmlands, forestlands, and sensitive environmental areas;
- to promote reinvestment and revitalization in urban areas; and
- to provide greater certainty to developers about where development is desired.

It is important to note that developers in Lancaster County, Pennsylvania, and greater Portland, Oregon, support the growth boundary concept because it provides them with greater certainty, reducing approval times and minimizing the need for rezonings. Nonetheless, the NAHB has criticized Portland's growth boundary for raising land and housing prices:

> "The so-called 'Wall of Portland' is having severe but predictable consequences as the supply of developable land runs low. Once known as one of the nation's most affordable housing markets, Portland is now the fourth least affordable metro area according to NAHB's second quarter 1998 Housing Opportunity Index" (NAHB 2002).

However, economist-planner Gerrit Knaap compared Portland's land and housing prices to other cities in the western United States without growth boundaries and concluded, "Clearly land and housing price levels in Portland are not out of line with those in other Western metropolitan areas" (Knaap 2000). In 1999, even with its growth boundaries, Lancaster County, Pennsylvania, was rated the most affordable housing market in the state (Building Industry Association of Lancaster County 2002).

Growth boundaries should be reviewed periodically to ensure that they contain a reasonable amount of land in a variety of zoning districts to meet projected future needs within a given time frame. The boundaries can be expanded, but only after a careful review with the agreement of all jurisdictions involved. Thus, growth boundaries can be a good way to avoid annexation battles between cities and counties. Review and expansion are often necessary to avoid land availability constraints that might increase housing costs within the boundaries. Yet, growth boundaries that are overly large can result in a pattern of "contained sprawl" rather than a set of connected, livable communities. Communities can address this potential problem by phasing growth through a concurrency policy that requires the public services to be in place before development can proceed within undeveloped portions of the boundaries.

Growth boundaries are only effective if restrictive zoning, such as one house per 20 acres or more, is used in the countryside. The success of the growth-boundary strategy is crucial if working landscapes of farm and forestlands and environmentally sensitive areas are to be conserved and urban areas revitalized. Development within the boundaries must be convenient, attractive, and affordable; otherwise, people will choose to live in the countryside and continue to contribute to sprawl.

Build-out Analysis

Many rural and urban fringe communities are "zoned for sprawl" at minimum lot sizes of 1 or 2 acres throughout the countryside. Perhaps the single greatest difficulty in enacting effective zoning is the lack of political will to adopt zoning that increases density in planned growth areas to better accommodate development and reduces densities in planned protection areas to discourage development. An important first step in evaluating a community's zoning is to open the eyes of local residents to the potential transformation of the countryside under existing regulations.

A build-out analysis can be conducted to estimate how much new development could occur and where it could occur under the current zoning. Most rural-suburban fringe areas allow much more development than the communities want or could reasonably absorb. "Overzoning" makes a community vulnerable to rapid change, increasing traffic congestion, and new and expensive public service demands, such as new schools, to meet rapidly growing enrollments. Overzoning can be avoided by tying the amount of land planned for growth and development to future growth projections, typically for 20 years into the future. Also, most population growth needs to be directed into and adjacent to existing settlements.

The State of Massachusetts will do a GIS-based build-out scenario, using the local zoning, for any community in the state. The GIS analysis can identify impacts on sensitive environmental features and transportation systems. The build-out scenario can help determine whether there is too much land zoned for some purposes and not enough for others when compared to the population projections. The build-out scenario will be helpful in drafting the future land use map on which the zoning map is based.

Some communities that conduct build-out analyses include an estimate of the probable increase in demand for community services (e.g., police, fire protection, parks, and roads) and the necessary tax increases to meet those demands. A build-out analysis can be an effective wake-up call to a community that is growing faster than it desires. Unfortunately, if a community waits too long to reevaluate its zoning, property values may rise to the point at which it is politically difficult to downzone. While zoning is an emotionally charged and politically sensitive issue, places that have zoning that restricts development to less than one dwelling per 20 acres are some of the most desirable places to live in the United States (Daniels and Bowers 1997, Chapter 13).

Cost of Community Services

Most communities and counties have long labored under the assumption that growth is good without examining the public service costs of different development projects. Local elected officials often support large-lot residential development because they think these lots generate more in property taxes than they demand in services, and that they can support on-site septic systems and wells that obviate the need to build or extend expensive public sewer and water systems. However, if these on-site systems fail, extensions of public sewer and water will be needed. These extensions can be expensive to the public as well as promote more sprawl.

In the 1990s, the American Farmland Trust performed several cost of community services studies comparing the property tax revenues generated by different land uses and the public service costs for those uses. In every study, residential development demanded more in services than it produced in tax revenues, while commercial and industrial land generated more tax revenues than they used in services. Farmland, forestland, and open space also cost far less in services required than they generated in property taxes (*ibid.*, 55-56). Reliance on the property tax as the main source of revenue for local governments has created an incentive to develop land for commercial, industrial, and "high-end" residential uses. Local officials often overlook the net fiscal benefits of farmland, forestland, and open space. Communities can do their own cost of community services studies:

- to understand the difference in tax contributions and public service costs for different land uses; and
- to project the fiscal impact of future residential or commercial development based on a build-out scenario of the community's zoning map.

Adequate Public Facilities Ordinance

An adequate public facilities ordinance permits new construction only when water, sewer, schools, and transportation are in place and available to provide adequate service. The ordinance avoids the problem of wildcat subdivisions where developers create and sell lots without adequate services, and it avoids premature extensions of services that often cause sprawl. As a result, new developments are more likely to be compact and adjacent to existing settlements, schools are less likely to become overcrowded, and public sewer and water systems are likely to serve a higher proportion of the population. Adequate public facilities ordinances help ensure that the pace of development in a community will be manageable for taxpayers and the environment.

On-Site Septic System Ordinance

An on-site septic system ordinance requires testing for the suitability of soils prior to installation and the proper maintenance of septic systems, including regular pumping out (see Chapter 3). Limiting factors for septic systems include slopes of more than 15%, shallow depth to bedrock, soils with high clay content, high water tables, and floodplains. Mound systems are often used when the soil does not percolate because of heavy, semi-impervious clay or shallow depth to bedrock. However, mound systems are inferior to standard systems and should be avoided (New Castle County Council 1997, 10). A rule of thumb is a minimum lot of 2 acres if an on-site septic system will be used, because at some future time, there will probably be a need to move the system and provide another leach field. Sewage effluent from septic tanks should be pumped out at least every three years for the system to work effectively. Properly maintained septic systems avoid the need to extend sprawl-inducing sewer and water lines. When capital improvements respond to failing septic systems, this illustrates the reverse of good planning. The CIP should influence the loca-

tion, timing, and character of development, rather than poorly sited and serviced, scattered development driving the location and timing of capital improvements.

Sunsetting Regulations

Sunsetting regulations place time limits on the start and completion of recorded subdivision and land development plans. Unbuilt plans more than five years old should be canceled or required to go through the approval process again to ensure consistency with current zoning and subdivision regulations, infrastructure capacity, and building codes. Sunsetting provisions help ensure that growth and development remain consistent with the comprehensive plan and implementing ordinances.

Around the nation, there are many examples of antiquated paper subdivisions that were filed dozens of years ago on land that today would fail to meet numerous zoning and subdivision requirements, such as lot size, water supply, and road access. In many cases, these subdivisions are unbuildable, but there are few legal ways to retire the subdivision plans. Where lots within an antiquated subdivision are still largely held by one or a few landowners, communities may require that all contiguous lots in a single ownership as of the date of the zoning ordinance be considered one lot. This can minimize the number of grandfathered substandard lots of record.

Inclusionary Housing Ordinance

An inclusionary zoning ordinance for affordable housing is a good way to ensure the availability of affordable housing for low- and moderate-income people. Sometimes environmental planning is used as a cover for exclusionary housing practices. A suburb with zoning that allows only single-family houses on large lots and has no land zoned for multifamily housing is one such example. In such cases, affordable housing is frequently mentioned as a casualty of growth management and environmental planning. However, legitimate and effective environmental planning promotes compact development in areas intended for growth and restricted development in working landscapes and environmentally sensitive areas. Compact development is more likely to put new dwelling units within the reach of low- and moderate-income people because the land costs and infrastructure costs per dwelling unit are lower.

Montgomery County, Maryland (a county of 900,000 just northwest of Washington, D.C.), has gained national prominence both for its farmland preservation program, which has preserved more than 50,000 acres, and its affordable housing programs, which have provided thousands of affordable housing units (Rusk 1999). Similarly, the Vermont Housing and Conservation Board has funneled state money into the preservation of more than 80,000 acres of farmland and the construction and renovation of thousands of affordable housing units (Libby and Bradley 2000). The Vermont Forum on Sprawl includes as one of its smart growth principles: "Provide for housing that meets the needs of a diversity of social and income groups in each community but especially in communities that are most rapidly-growing" (Vermont Forum on Sprawl 1999). Several community land trusts are emerging with the goal of creating permanently affordable housing, while increasing home ownership (Abromowitz 2000).

Limiting Building Potential

A community can legally limit the number of building permits issued each year, as long as that number is linked to the community's ability to provide services. Several communities do this to keep the demand for public services in line with public finances, and to keep the character of the community from rapidly changing. Since 1975, the City of Petaluma, California, has restricted the number of building permits it issues to 400 a year (see *Construction Industry Association of Sonoma County v. City of Petaluma*, 375 F. Supp. 574, 6ERC 1453 (N.D. Cal. 1974)). The suburban Town of Williston, Vermont, has a limit of 80 residential building permits a year, while the rural Town of Fairfield, Vermont, has a limit of just eight residential building permits a year (Vermont Forum on Sprawl 2001).

Moratorium

A moratorium is a temporary ban on new residential and/or commercial construction or new public services in a community. Elected officials sometimes enact a moratorium as a last resort when rapid private development and population growth result in haphazard land use patterns and have outpaced the community's ability to provide necessary public services. Typically, a community's sewage treatment plant has reached capacity and can accept no more new sewer hook-ups. A moratorium may also be enacted when water supplies are insufficient or schools are overcrowded. Some communities have adopted a moratorium when revising the comprehensive plan or zoning ordinance.

The use of a moratorium often means that a community has done an inadequate job of comprehensive planning, zoning, subdivision review, or capital improvements planning for growth and development. A moratorium should exist for a limited period, such as six to 12 months, and local officials should clearly state the purpose of the moratorium, such as "to give the community time to complete or update the comprehensive plan and zoning ordinance" or "to make needed infrastructure improvements." For example, Forsyth County, Georgia—a booming suburb north of Atlanta—put a moratorium on new residential and commercial development from April 1999 to April 2000, in order to install needed sewer and water service (Ehrenhalt 1999, 26). Moratoriums also often apply to specific zones or areas of a community, rather than to the entire community. By contrast, an outright ban on all new development for the foreseeable future could lead to legal action against the community.

The U.S. Supreme Court ruled that a moratorium did not automatically constitute a "taking" of private property in the 2002 case *Tahoe-Sierra Preservation Council v. Tahoe Regional Planning Agency*, No. 00-1167 (Lucero and Soule 2002, 4-7). The Tahoe Regional Planning Agency had imposed a moratorium on development for 32 months from 1981 to 1984 while it drafted a new comprehensive plan for the region around Lake Tahoe between California and Nevada.

Planned-Unit Developments and Master Planning

One technique used to alleviate hodgepodge development patterns is the planned-unit development (PUD). PUDs first appeared in 1963 as a way for developers to mix commercial and residential uses through flexible site design standards while going through a single approval process. A PUD zone works much like a floating zone. It is not shown on the zoning map, but it is listed and described in the text of the zoning ordinance. PUDs are typically permitted in higher density residential or commercial zones where public sewer and water are available.

PUD proposals with hundreds or thousands of housing units and acres of commercial space are known as master planned communities. These developments are built in phases over several years. An advantage of master planned communities is that they can provide a single integrated and coordinated development, featuring an interconnected road network, sewer and water service, parks, school sites, and a mix of residential and commercial land uses. Master planned communities often fit better into both the local setting and regional land use patterns than several scattered residential subdivisions and strip malls.

A large master planned community could be considered a "new town." The New Town movement began in England in the late 1890s as a way to provide affordable, attractive, and mixed-use communities with a limit of 30,000 people. Ebe-neezer Howard in his book *Garden Cities of Tomorrow* envisioned a network of new towns connected by railroad with large areas of greenspace between them. This design has clear environmental advantages over haphazard sprawl throughout the countryside. The community of Greenbelt, Maryland, now a suburb of Washington, D.C., was one such new town built in the U.S. in the 1930s.

The disadvantage of master planned communities is that they are huge projects with potentially large impacts on sewage disposal, water supply, local schools, highway traffic, and natural areas. The cumulative effects of a master planned community can sometimes overwhelm a community, particularly where environmental changes and infrastructure needs were not anticipated. Proposals for master planned communities should be required to include traffic impact studies, cost of public services projections, and environmental impact assessments. Requirements for impact fees and parkland dedication should be in place before communities entertain the review of large PUDs or master planned communities.

Site Design Standards

Many planners associate environmental planning with site planning: organizing the development of a tract of land to minimize stormwater runoff, avoid steep slopes and wetlands, and blend in with the natural surroundings. Where planning differs notably from landscape architecture is in how the development of one site fits in with the neighboring properties, the available public services, and the whole community or region. Planning is supposed to be comprehensive and not specific to one site. The character of a particular residential subdivision or commercial development comes from the siting, scale, design, and density of buildings as well as landscaping of grounds. The purpose of environmental design is to site buildings and infrastructure in ways that have a minimal impact on air quality, soils, wildlife, and water supplies, while creating developments that are safe, functional, and aesthetically pleasing.

Density joined with pleasing design is key to accommodating population growth and development. For instance, residential zoning of four dwellings per acre uses up only one-fourth as much land to accommodate the same number of people as do four dwellings each on its own acre lot. Local governments can require developers to dedicate parkland or pay fees in lieu of parkland based on each new dwelling unit or on so many square feet of new residential space (see Chapter 8).

There are several design principles that can be effectively applied to guide state and local regulations and spending programs to make greenfield development compact, attractive, and environmentally sound. Edges separate the built environment from working landscapes and the natural environment. Edges occur naturally in the form of streams, rivers, lakes, hills, ridges, and woods, or as man-made roads and fences. Houses and commercial strips scattered through the countryside give a cluttered appearance, break up wildlife corridors and farm and forestlands, and waste space. Compact development at the edge of existing suburbs and villages can help to maintain edges.

Human-scale developments can blend in with the natural environment. A major problem with sprawl is the size of the developments that are placed on greenfields. Big-box chain stores and enormous regional shopping malls are two such examples. They consume large amounts of land, generate thousands of car trips a day, and are rarely tied to effective mass transit (Beaumont 1994; Walters 2000, 48-51). If urban revitalization is to occur, large retail outlets in the suburbs and exurbs should be discouraged.

The protection of water quality and supplies is essential for sustainable development. Trees, streambank buffers, and stormwater management practices are the most cost-effective ways to intercept nonpoint source runoff and keep it from entering waterways. The construction of new on-site wells and septic systems should be minimized to limit potential groundwater pollution. Water from on-site wells should be regularly tested for quality. Wellhead protection ordinances should be adopted to safeguard public groundwater supplies from threats of contamination.

New development on greenfields should avoid natural hazards. Buildings should not be placed on steep slopes, in floodplains, on wetlands or hydric soils, or on soils with shallow depth to bedrock. New development should be sensitive to its surroundings and maintain viewsheds. Scenic views provide enjoyment and help people feel they are part of the landscape. Landscaping and design standards can assure that new development blends in with the natural surroundings and does not obstruct views. A ridgeline ordinance can keep development off ridgelines and thus maintain scenic views.

Greenfield development should respect historic and cultural landscapes. These special landscapes should be protected. Development on adjacent lands should be required to meet design, setback, and screening requirements so that new development does not conflict with or detract from historic or cultural landscapes. Greenfield development should avoid identified core habitat areas and migration corridors, wetlands, and working landscapes. Farmland is often the easiest land to develop because of its level, deep, and well-drained soils. Many people like to have a home in the woods because of the privacy, but the conversion of farm and forestlands to residential sites can lead to a decline in the local farming and forestry industries. A zoning ordinance can require that residential development be sited on lots of no more than 2 acres and on lower productivity soils. For instance, the use of a 2-acre maximum lot size for nonfarm development is common in the agricultural zoning ordinances of townships in Lancaster County, Pennsylvania (Daniels and Bowers 1997, 263-269).

SIDEBAR 19-2

Density Choices, Comprehensive Planning, and Zoning

Chester County, Pennsylvania, is located 15 miles west of Philadelphia—the nation's fifth largest city. The county covers 486,000 acres and is home to 430,000 residents. There are 15 villages, one small city, and a rolling countryside that supports a $342 million a year agricultural industry. However, from 1970 to 1995, Chester County experienced more development than it had in the previous 300 years. Between 1982 and 1997, more than 44,000 acres of farmland were converted to development.

Chester County's comprehensive plan, *Landscapes* (1996), received the 1998 Outstanding Planning Award from the American Planning Association. The plan cited sprawl as the major threat and estimated that if current trends continued, from 2000 to 2020, another 74,000 acres would be developed at an average county-wide density of one dwelling per acre. *Landscapes* described three alternative growth scenarios to continued sprawl: local development centers, community service centers, and regional centers and corridors. The local development centers approach would target most residential growth in each of the county's 57 townships and 15 villages to at least one local center. New residential development would average three-quarters of an acre per dwelling unit, although a wide range of lot sizes would exist (Chester County, Pennsylvania 1996, 108). The community service centers strategy would direct new development to community centers within each school district where public sewer and water systems would be available. New residential development would average half an acre per dwelling. The regional centers and corridors scenario would direct growth to regional centers with access to mass transit and public sewer and water. Residential growth would average half an acre per dwelling.

Landscapes is only advisory, however. The local governments are not required to follow it, yet most local governments have agreed to the concept of the centers approach. With the large majority of the countryside in Chester County currently zoned for 2-acre lots, sprawl is likely to remain a serious problem. It is interesting to compare Chester County's proposed future development densities and projected acreage needed for development to the plans of its neighbor to the west, Lancaster County. There, the cities and villages have gone a step further by adopting urban growth boundaries to promote more compact development and limit sprawl. Also, most of Lancaster County's countryside is zoned for agriculture at an average density of one dwelling per 25 acres.

To achieve denser, mixed-use development, local governments will have to revise their comprehensive plans and zoning and subdivision ordinances. They will also have to work more closely with developers. In turn, developers must convince both lenders and local governments that more compact developments will be financially and fiscally successful.

One such mixed-use development has been proposed in Chesterfield Township in Burlington County, New Jersey. The township adopted a transfer of development rights (TDR) ordinance to move development potential away from 7,500 acres of farmland. A developer then proposed to create a neotraditional village with 1,220 houses and commercial space on 575 acres in the township's designated receiving area for TDRs where growth is desired. The township would thus be able to accommodate growth in a compact fashion and preserve its farmland at the same time (Craft 2001).

Dense, mixed-use design can be employed in urban redevelopment, TOD in cities and suburbs, and for the creation of entire new villages, such as Orenco Station (see Case Study 5-2). Dense developments enable a regional strategy of promoting centers and connecting them with transportation corridors while retaining more open space. Just as wildlife habitats must have large, unfragmented core areas and corridors for migration and travel to other core areas, cities and suburbs can act as core areas for human habitation and commerce, with highways and transit corridors linking core areas.

Cluster Development

A zoning technique that has received considerable attention is cluster zoning, also known as open space or conservation zoning. Cluster zoning allows the placement of building lots on a portion of a parcel and requires that a certain percentage of the parcel be retained as open space. The open space can be put under the control of a homeowners' association made up of the people who live in the houses built on the main parcel, or the open space can be placed under a conservation easement held by a local land trust or a local government. Open space or cluster zoning is essentially a suburban style of zoning that is designed to allow the same number of lots as in the previous zone but sited to protect some open space and natural features (see Figures 19-3 and 19-4). For example, a cluster zoning ordinance might allow or require a subdivision involving the creation of five or more lots to set aside 40% of the land area as permanent open space. However, often the underlying zoning density is quite high, such as one or two dwelling units per acre, resulting in a suburban-type density in a rural area.

A variation of the open space zone, known as residential conservation zoning, has been described as a golf course development without the golf course. Houses are placed to retain sensitive natural features, such as wetlands and steep slopes. Typically, these developments are for upscale buyers. These developments might also be described as "gated communities without the gates." The private greenspace of the conserva-

19-3 Residential strip development and cluster residential development.

Source: Dutchess County Department of Planning, New York

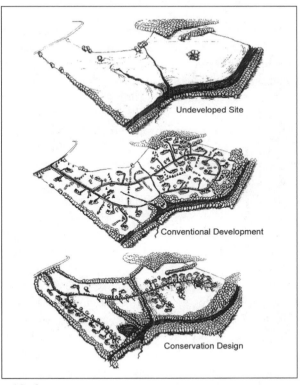

19-4 Residential pod reconfigured to retain open space.

Source: University of Connecticut, Cooperative Extension Service, Nonpoint Pollution Education for Municipal Officials #9

tion subdivision is for members only and not open to the public.

The danger with open space zoning is its potential overuse, resulting in clustered, automobile-dependent sprawl. Concentrated development in rural areas can also contribute to groundwater overdraft, septic system failure, and groundwater contamination. Open space zoning works best in areas that are adjacent to villages and small cities, where public sewer and water are available to service the lots that are clustered close together.

An important issue in cluster zoning standards is whether unbuildable lands are "netted out" before determining the number of dwellings permitted on a tract of land. Netting out results in fewer permitted dwellings, particularly in areas with extensive unbuildable lands. For instance, if 3 of 10 acres in an area with 1-acre zoning were unbuildable, only seven units could be built on the 10 acres. Yet, some communities with cluster zoning do not net out unbuildable lands, resulting in a higher density on buildable portions of a tract than under conventional zoning. A further factor is that some communities grant a bonus of extra dwelling units to encourage cluster subdivisions. The purpose of a cluster should be to fit in with the surroundings, not simply put more people in the countryside.

It is possible to rate situations where a cluster approach is appropriate (see Table 19-4). Potential clusters can be evaluated according to proposed location, density allowed, and amount of open space retained. A location near existing development is preferable to siting in a remote area amid working landscapes or natural areas. The higher the density and the larger the number of units allowed, the closer to existing development and infrastructure the cluster should be.

Cluster ordinances should specify the retention of at least 50% of a site as open space. The disposition and use of this open space are important issues. Open space lands may be dedicated to a local government, but the local government must

---

SIDEBAR 19-3

A Note on Golf Courses

Golf has become one of America's most popular pastimes. In 2001, there were more than 26 million golfers and 16,700 golf courses covering 3.5 million acres (Morgan 2001, 40). Nearly three-quarters of the nation's golf courses are open to the public. Golf course developments that combine 18 holes and residences are fairly common, but, surprisingly, relatively few people who buy homes next to a golf course actually play golf. Many people see golf courses as providing needed open space, especially in suburban areas. Yet, the question arises: Are golf courses sustainable development? They consume large amounts of water, pesticides, herbicides, and fertilizers to keep fairways and greens looking their best. Moreover, golf course developments displace working landscapes and can help to foster suburban sprawl.

---

decide whether to accept these lands. Public open space is generally preferable to private open space in affording greater access to recreation and contact with nature. Clustered open-space standards should be consistent with local requirements for the dedication of public parkland to serve new residents, particularly where there is potential to create interconnected trail networks for public use. Open space may be placed under a conservation easement and transferred to a conservation organization or land trust, but the easement does not necessarily have to allow public access. If the open space area is large enough, it might be sold or leased to a local farmer. Another alternative is that a homeowners' association might hold the open land in common for the benefit of the homeowners in the cluster development.

Clustering generally increases the number of people moving to the countryside and can intensify conflicts between newcomers and owners of the working landscape. The cluster concept arose

Table 19-4
A Comparison of Cluster Development Approaches

	Location	Density	Open Space Percentage	Open Space Function
1.	Adjacent to Existing Development with Access to Central Sewer and Water	4 to 10 units per acre	50% to 60%	Public park and trails
2.	One to Five Miles from Central Sewer and Water	One unit per 5 acres, after unbuildable land is netted out	50% to 70%	Working landscape, natural area, open space buffer, or park
3.	Remote: Over 5 Miles from Central Sewer and Water	One unit per 10 acres, after unbuildable land is netted out	50% to 80%	Working landscape, natural area, open space buffer, or park

in Massachusetts, which is not a major farming or forestry area; the state attorney general would not allow stricter rural zoning than a 2-acre minimum lot size per dwelling (Daniels 1997). The California Farm Bureau has come out against cluster development in farming areas as "ill-conceived land use planning at its worst." According to Farm Bureau attorney David Guy, "Mixing housing and agriculture just doesn't work" (California Farm Bureau 1998). Any farmland that remains after a cluster development built is most likely to be used for low-value crops, such as hay, because animal agriculture with its manure smells is not very compatible with nonfarm neighbors.

Cluster advocate Randall Arendt warns that clustering is primarily a technique to retain some rural character and open space, rather than a working landscape:

> "[cluster zoning] is definitely a second best technique if not third best. If you want suburbia, have a suburban zoning density. If you want to remain agricultural, have an ag zoning density, which would begin at one [dwelling] per 25 acres. Communities where open space zoning is appropriate are those with one [dwelling] per 3 acres. [But they] should realize they will not remain rural" (*Farmland Preservation Report* 1995).

Clustering in the countryside should limit the number of units through:

- a fairly low base density, such as one dwelling per 10 acres, as is done in Larimer County, Colorado;
- netting out the unbuildable land when computing the number of units allowed (also done in Larimer's Open Space zone), and
- placing a maximum lot size on the permitted building lots (Larimer uses a 2-acre lot size with on-site septic systems) (Larimer County 1999, 4-9).

To illustrate, consider a 100-acre tract located more than 5 miles from central sewer and water. The base density is one dwelling unit per 10 acres, which would allow 10 units. After netting out 20 acres of unbuildable land—such as steep slopes, floodplains, and wetlands—80 buildable acres remain, on which eight units would be allowed. Sixty percent of the original tract, in this case 60 acres, must remain as open space. These 60 acres would include the unbuildable lands as well as other land left as open space. The eight dwelling units must then be clustered on the remaining 40 acres. One way to do this is to limit each house lot to a maximum of 5 acres or, where adequate groundwater is available and the soils are suitable for on-site sewage disposal, smaller lots are appropriate.

A further refinement of clustering in the countryside would be to set a maximum limit on the number of dwelling units allowed to be created from a parcel of more than 100 acres. This would help keep larger parcels with value for farming, forestry, and natural areas from being fragmented, and might involve preserving the remainder of these parcels through public purchase of development rights programs or private land trust acquisition of conservation easements. The restriction on the total number of building lots means there would be fewer lots encroaching on farming and forestry operations and natural areas. Also, the restriction prevents a large concentration of dozens of dwellings served by on-site septic systems and wells that could overdraw or contaminate groundwater supplies.

Cluster development ordinances should provide incentives for the creation of public rather than private open space. This can include density bonuses or reductions in open space requirements. Clustered open space requirements should be consistent with any local requirement for the dedication of public parkland to serve the new residents, particularly where there is potential to create interconnected trail networks for public use.

Should clustering be mandatory? In locations where there is access to public sewer and water, mandatory clustering can make sense. Although the compact design of clusters can provide cost savings to the developer, a density bonus of one or two dwellings per acre is often needed as an incentive to encourage clustering and the retention of open space. Clusters in rural areas without access to public sewer and water should be limited in size, reflecting the carrying capacity of the environment and potential impacts on adjacent land uses to avoid scattered "pods" of homes that amount to clustered sprawl.

Impact Fees

During the great suburban boom from the late 1940s to 1970, local governments usually picked up the costs of providing roads, schools, and sewer and water facilities that benefited private development. Because developers largely avoided these costs, their profits increased. Starting in the 1960s, new home buyers were typically charged a special assessment (an addition to the property tax) for new sewer and water lines. In the 1980s, impact fees and fees in lieu of land dedication became popular as ways to compel developers to contribute toward the cost of providing new roads, parks, and school lands that new residents will use. Since 1993, Lancaster, California, has used impact fees to discourage sprawl by charging developers higher fees the further they build from the city core. A house built 6 miles from the city core would pay about twice the impact fees (about $10,000) compared to a house built within or adjacent to the core. The link between higher impact fees and distance reflects the higher cost of providing urban services to sprawling development, and places the financial burden on the developers and new residents (Snyder and Bird 2001). However, a shortcoming of impact fees is that the money raised can only be spent on building new infrastructure, not repairing worn infrastructure.

Public Participation in Greenfield Development

Keeping an Eye on Development Proposals

The land use planning process is a political process, involving public participation, not decisions made between local governments and developers behind closed doors. State "Sunshine Laws" are meant to ensure that government decisions are made in the light of public scrutiny. There are two main types of citizens' groups that monitor land use planning decisions. Neighbors and concerned citizens sometimes form ad-hoc groups to oppose a certain development proposal. These groups are often referred to as "Not In My Back Yard" people. Developers have become wary of these groups and have sometimes initiated Strategic Lawsuits Against Public Participation. These lawsuits are aimed at deterring ad-hoc groups from lobbying local officials to deny their building projects or from filing lawsuits to delay projects. Ad-hoc groups typically disband after a development issue has been finally settled, but some have evolved into standing organizations to monitor and participate in community land use decisions.

Since the 1970s, private, nonprofit, land use watchdog groups with paid staff have become popular throughout the United States. These groups may have a local, regional, or statewide focus in their activities. In the early 1990s, a group of businesspeople and neighbors formed Citizens Against Urban Sprawl Everywhere (CAUSE) in Durham, North Carolina, to oppose the glut of rezoning requests that threatened to bring overdevelopment. CAUSE members scrutinize planning and zoning issues and development proposals. They also monitor construction sites for stormwater runoff. They have filed suit to stop a proposed 1.3 million-square-foot mall that they feel would bring traffic congestion and major changes to the community.

The Greenbelt Alliance, based in San Francisco, has not only monitored development trends in the Bay Area since the early 1980s, but has also played a pivotal role in promoting the protection of greenspace and the adoption of urban growth boundaries by several communities.

The granddaddy of land use watchdog organizations is 1000 Friends of Oregon, started in 1975. 1000 Friends has been instrumental in shaping the legal decisions implementing Oregon's pioneering 1973 State Land Use Act, particularly in enforcing strict farm and forestland protection and promoting development inside urban growth boundaries. The 1000 Friends model has been copied in several states, including Florida, Hawaii, Iowa, Maryland, Minnesota, New Mexico, Pennsylvania, Washington, and Wisconsin.

Planning for Locally Unwanted Land Uses

Greenfield sites in general and rural areas in particular are often targeted for developments that most people would not choose to live near. These devel-opments typically cover several acres and produce noise, odors, bright lights, air and water pollution, and traffic that spill over onto neighboring properties and sometimes throughout the community as well. These developments include landfills, hazardous waste processing facilities, power plants, mining operations, airports, prisons, and confined animal feeding operations. Proposals for these developments are frequently met with a storm of protest from concerned citizens and neighbors. Court battles over these proposals are common.

Some of the decisions about the location of Locally Unwanted Land Uses (LULUs) require federal approval, such as the siting of new airports or the expansion of existing airports. For other uses, the state does the primary review, as in the case of the siting of new power plants. Local governments have a voice in federal and state decisions, and the opposition of local elected officials usually can kill a proposed project. Notable exceptions are the federal preemption of local ordinances that ban cellular phone towers and, in some states, the state preemption of local zoning provisions to control or ban mining or intensive livestock operations. Frequently, local officials favor even controversial projects for the jobs and property tax revenue they would bring to communities, despite some local public opposition.

Local governments can use the zoning process to respond to LULU proposals in ways that are legally sound and carefully considered. The zoning ordinance can specify land uses that are permitted in each zoning district and prohibit all other uses. The adoption of local health or nuisance ordinances regulating air and water quality can provide a way around the state preemption of local zoning against confined livestock operations or mining. Another approach is to allow certain intensive uses only through the conditional use permit process, or requiring a local environmental impact statement (see Appendix). Using these approaches, elected officials could attach specific siting, operating, and design conditions to an approval.

Environmental Dispute Resolution

Disagreements over proposals for new development are very common. From a developer's perspective, delays in project approval, additional planning studies, and court battles drive up costs and reduce profits. From a legal standpoint, the developer is entitled to due process: an approval or denial from the local government within a reasonable time frame, and a review of the development proposal based on clear and objective standards. Often, local zoning and subdivision regulations are poorly drafted. They either allow little leeway for negotiation, or have inadequately defined review standards that seem to permit almost any type of development anywhere. To concerned citizens, the proposed project may have objectionable features, such as out of scale, increased traffic, loss of open space, and aesthetics. If citizens are unable to convince local elected officials to deny or modify the development proposal, or if local officials feel that their regulations do not permit them to deny or modify a proposed project, a lawsuit is often the last resort.

Legal battles over land use and the environment have a number of drawbacks. They are expensive and time consuming, cause long-standing bad feelings, and the outcomes are uncertain. Moreover, many lawyers and judges are not well versed in land use law. All interested parties may gain if a dispute over development can be settled through negotiation. The savings in time and money, and the generation of good will, can be substantial (Fisher *et al.* 1991). The key elements of negotiation are:

- Negotiate based on your larger interests, not specific positions; that is, what outcomes do you want to see. Set personalities aside.
- Understand the interests of other groups and individuals involved.
- Identify common interests.
- Determine your willingness to compromise and bargain.

- Consider bringing in an outside mediator to help negotiate the dispute.
- Make sure you involve all interested parties in the negotiations.
- Set out the facts.
- Set out options.
- Identify and clearly spell out areas of agreement and disagreement.
- Arrive at a written agreement and implement it.
- Monitor the implementation of the agreement; renegotiate as needed.

Negotiation does not always work. This is often the case when one or both parties adamantly stick to an entrenched position. All-or-nothing positions will usually lead to a long struggle in the courts.

LOCAL PLANNING FOR GREENFIELD DEVELOPMENT

Comprehensive planning by cities, towns, and counties sets the stage for future development and environmental protection. The township form of government, planning, zoning control, dominant in the Northeast and in parts of the Midwest, tends to promote overzoning and overdevelopment as each municipality vies against the other for property tax base; that is, fragmented legal control of development leads to fragmented planning and zoning. By contrast, the county and city form of government, planning and zoning, found in the West and the South, potentially allows for greater control; yet, in those places, the ability of cities to expand through the annexation of county land, and the lower property taxes on county land, have been strong inducements to sprawl.

Communities and counties can allow for some greenfield development while promoting compact growth patterns in their comprehensive plans, zoning and subdivision regulations, and CIPs. For example, Jefferson County, Kansas, set goals to:

"Designate growth areas around cities with enough buildable land to support development over the next 20 years. Indicate where public sewer, water, and other services are to be located ... Urban subdivisions should be expedited and given bonus densities to encourage growth in designated areas. Impact fees should be set to help direct development towards the towns, with lower fees near the towns" (Jefferson County 2000).

Adams County, Pennsylvania's 1991 comprehensive plan includes a Growth Management Plan and Land Use Plan with recommended growth areas that center around existing boroughs, unincorporated villages, highway interchanges, and other settings where development can be accommodated. The identification of these areas is intended to promote compact growth patterns and discourage nonagricultural development in the county's farming areas.

Inventory

As part of a Natural Resources Inventory and land suitability analysis, communities should identify and map lands that can support development, based on soils, constraints, and access to transportation networks, public services, and existing developed areas. The carrying capacity of specific sites will influence the potential density of development. Maps should incorporate the McHarg layers approach in a GIS database.

Analysis

The comprehensive plan should include an analysis of areas needed for residential, commercial, industrial, and public uses based on population projections and land suitability. These areas should be designated on the future land use map together with proposed infrastructure improvements. A community may want to conduct a build-out analysis of existing zoning, and even a study on the cost of community services. These methods can help the public understand the potential amount of development on greenfield sites and public service costs under the existing zoning.

Goals and Objectives

Goals for the community's open lands should be drafted in the Land Use section of the comprehensive plan (see Table 19-5). The goals should seek to

Table 19-5
Sample Greenfield Development Goals and Objectives in the Comprehensive Plan

Land Use		
Goal	To designate enough, but not more than enough, land to meet projected future development needs for the next 20 years.	
Goal	To promote compact development within and immediately adjacent to existing settlements compatible with the carrying capacity of the land.	
Objective	Promote good design in the development of greenfield sites.	
Objective	Provide an array of housing opportunities for all income levels by providing buildable land for all dwelling types, and the promotion of mixed-use projects that combine residential and commercial uses.	
Community Facilities		
Objective	Ensure that adequate community facilities, including good quality roads, mass transit, utilities, parks, and schools, are provided in areas slated for greenfield development.	
Natural Resources		
Objective	Avoid developments on working landscapes and in environmentally sensitive areas.	

allow for the development of some greenfield sites but with an eye to conserving as much open land as possible. Objectives to help achieve these goals should be listed in the Community Facilities and Transportation sections to coordinate infrastructure investment with planned development areas, and in the Natural Resources section to keep development away from productive farm and forestlands as much as possible.

Action Strategy

The Action Strategy should present techniques and programs for achieving the greenfield goals and objectives as well as a timetable. Benchmarks for the retention of farmland, forestland, and open space are most often expressed as an acceptable number of acres lost or the rate of acres lost to greenfield development. Progress toward slowing the rate of conversion of these lands to greenfield development should be evaluated in an annual report on the environment. Specific recommendations might include the following:

- Enter into intermunicipal agreements to formalize timing of infrastructure expansion and annexation. Consider creating urban and village growth boundaries to limit sprawl into greenfields.
- Appoint a design review board and draft a design review ordinance to apply to new development on greenfield sites.
- Conduct a GIS-based, build-out analysis of existing greenfield sites based on current zoning.
- Adopt mixed-use zoning to encourage projects that blend residential and commercial uses.
- Require greenspace, tree planting, and landscaping in development projects to provide recreation opportunities and absorb stormwater runoff.
- Adopt an adequate public facilities ordinance to ensure concurrency in the provision of needed infrastructure.

Zoning Ordinance

Zoning is fundamental to promoting compact, mixed-use developments and protecting open lands. Zoning must be tied to the population projections and land suitability and capability identified in the comprehensive plan in order to avoid or correct overzoning that can promote sprawl. In other words, a community needs only to zone as much land for development as it has projected to need over the next 20 years.

Perhaps the thorniest issue with which politicians and planners have wrestled since the 1970s is how much residential development to allow in the countryside. Given that it is impossible to keep people from moving to the countryside altogether, are there ways to provide living space that also conserves working landscape and natural areas? Agricultural zoning has worked well in several counties with strong agricultural industries or where county residents have supported a slow-growth strategy. In these places, large minimum lot sizes—usually 40 acres or more—have discouraged buyers seeking building lots for house sites. In less prominent farming areas, it is common to find so-called agricultural zoning with 2-, 5-, or 10-acre minimum lot sizes. The minimum lot size in an agricultural zone should reflect the smallest viable commercial farm size for that jurisdiction. Minimum lot sizes of 10 acres or less are forms of rural residential zoning that do not encourage agriculture but allow the fragmentation of the working landscape into parcels that are "too big to mow and too small to plow."

Rural residential zoning can provide areas to accommodate people who want to live in the countryside, but should be located in places that will not conflict with commercial farming and forestry operations. For more than 20 years, Oregon counties have used rural residential zoning at carefully selected locations. The zones typically have a 3- to 5-acre minimum lot size. This is usually enough acreage to support an on-site septic system and a well. Ideally, rural residential zones should be separated from active farm and forestlands by roads, streams, and hills.

A limited use of clustering of homes in rural residential zones may be appropriate to protect natural features and to avoid sensitive areas, such as steep slopes and wetlands, but the widespread use of clustering should be avoided.

The zoning map can designate "tiers" of land that will be provided with higher levels of public services as they become ready for development. Some outer tiers will be designated rural with very limited services. The tiers help to phase development in an orderly fashion. The zoning ordinance can promote the use of neotraditional zoning in areas close to existing villages and cities to permit the extension of traditional compact development patterns.

Subdivision Regulations

Subdivision and land development regulations are important for requiring adequate infrastructure for greenfield development. Much greenfield development relies upon the use of on-site septic systems and wells. The subdivision ordinance can require that these systems be properly located and maintained to avoid groundwater contamination problems. The subdivision ordinance should require that adequate water supplies be proven before development can occur. New residential subdivisions and commercial and industrial development within a half mile of public sewer and water should be required to connect with it.

Regulations that include the mandatory dedication of parkland and open space, clustering, and stormwater management are all helpful in maintaining as much open space as possible while allowing greenfield development. Also, it is a good idea to require the burying of electricity and telephone utility lines for new developments. This minimizes a cluttered appearance, enables solar access, and allows space for trees to grow.

Capital Improvements Program

Capital improvements provide the skeleton for the development of greenfield sites. Communities must take the lead in closely coordinating with sewer and water authorities and school districts to ensure consistency in planned growth areas. Capital improvements should avoid promoting leapfrog patterns of development through sewer and water extensions or the siting of schools. As much as possible, infrastructure should promote compact development that is adjacent to existing settlements. Adequate public facilities ordinances can require that infrastructure be installed before development can occur. The capital improvements program (CIP) then spells out what infrastructure will be extended where and when. The Town of Ramapo, New York, won a major court case that upheld the town's plans to make new public services available when the town felt it could afford them (*Golden v Planning Board of Town of Ramapo*, 30 N.Y. S. 2d 138, 285 N.E. 2d 291 (1972)). This was the start of "phased growth." Communities should also consider adopting impact fees to ensure that new public service costs associated with new development are paid for by the developers.

What to Look for in a Development Review

When a planning commission looks at a development project, it should evaluate the project for consistency with the comprehensive plan, zoning ordinance, subdivision and land development regulations, CIP, and any other applicable local laws. The review of development proposals on greenfield sites should focus on the proposed uses, the provision of necessary services, and the potential to promote additional development in the area (see Table 19-6). Leapfrog development and potential conflicts with owners of farm, forestry, and mining operations should be mitigated or avoided.

Table 19-6
A Checklist of Greenfield Development Issues in a Development Review

1.	What are the size, location, and land uses of the proposed development?
2.	Is the proposed development allowed in the particular zone?
3.	Does the proposed development meet the setback, height, and bulk coverage requirements?
4.	What are the land uses on the adjacent properties?
5.	How will sewage disposal and water service be provided: on site or through a public central service, or some combination, such as public water and on-site septic systems, or private wells and a community on-lot septic system?
6.	How much open space will be retained? How will that open space be used? Who will manage it?
7.	What is the road and street layout of the site? Do new roads and streets meet the necessary design standards?
8.	What is the water drainage of the site, and how has stormwater runoff been addressed?
9.	What is the current use of the site? How will vegetative cover, wildlife habitat, and productive farm and forestlands be affected?
10.	What development limitations exist, such as steep slopes and wetlands?
11.	Does the development lend itself to mass-transit service, or will it be automobile-dependent?
12.	What will the impact of the development be on local government services and schools?
13.	Has the developer obtained any necessary state or federal permits?

CASE STUDIES

The following case studies of greenfield development raise questions of whether the sites are of an appropriate size and in the right location. A common shortcoming of greenfield development is often a focus on site design for a specific parcel of land, without an understanding of how that development would fit into a regional network of land use, transportation, and water supplies. Planners must be careful to ensure that these developments have adequate public facilities and minimize impacts on the environment.

CASE STUDY 19-1
Newhall Ranch, Los
Angeles County, California

The Newhall Ranch, located on the north central edge of Los Angeles County, would be the single largest housing development ever approved in that county. The Newhall Land and Farming Company has proposed building 21,615 housing units with about 1,000 acres of commercial and industrial space on the 11,963-acre site (*The Planning Report* 1998). Roughly 10% of the housing units will be designated for low-income housing. The Newhall Ranch will take 20 years to complete and is expected to have 70,000 residents (Purdum 2000, 1).

To reduce environmental impacts, the Newhall Land and Farming Company has offered to set aside nearly 6,000 acres—about half of the entire site—as open space. About 4,000 acres of this land is hilly and mountainous, and would be managed by the Center for Natural Lands Management, a private land trust. Another 1,000 acres straddle the banks of several miles of the Santa Clara River, which is subject to flooding, and contains several endangered species. Newhall has proposed placing these riparian areas under the control of the center as well (*The Planning Report* 1998). About

1,000 acres would be kept as open space close to the built-up areas.

Servicing the site will require a large investment in infrastructure. "We expect to be able to supply the project without using groundwater," said Newhall Chairman and Chief Executive Officer Thomas L. Lee (*ibid.*), but adequate surface water availability is not a sure thing in this dry Mediterranean climate. The eastern part of the Newhall development will be within a mile of the Interstate 5 interchange with State Highway 126. When the Newhall project is completed, highway planners predict that Highway 126 will experience a whopping 360,000 trips a day. Newhall expects to pay millions of dollars in highway improvements, perhaps including the widening of Highway 126. These road improvements, in turn, could open up other land in the vicinity to development. Already, some 40,000 housing units have been approved but not yet built in the Santa Clarita Valley near the Newhall Ranch (Purdum 2000, 32).

Newhall Ranch must resolve a legal challenge before construction can begin. A local group, the Santa Clarita Organization for Planning and Environment, joined with several other environmental groups, neighboring Ventura County, and the California Attorney General's Office to file a suit claiming that Los Angeles County did not perform an adequate assessment of the environmental impacts of the Newhall Ranch under the California Environmental Quality Review Act (*ibid.*). In June 2000, a superior court judge ordered a halt to the construction of Newhall Ranch. He expressed a concern that there might not be enough water available for the estimated 60,000 people who would live there (Garrett and Bowles 2000, 1).

CASE STUDY 19-2
Prairie Crossing, Illinois

Prairie Crossing is a planned community taking shape on a 667-acre site 40 miles northwest of Chicago. Eighty percent of the site has been retained as open space and farmland, and 337 homes are clustered on 132 acres. The historic barn, schoolhouse, and farmhouse have also been retained. One benefit of clustering the homes has been a reduction in impervious surface, as fewer roads and sidewalks are needed, and hence there is less stormwater runoff than in a conventional subdivision. Moreover, the stormwater is filtered through swales and across reconstructed prairies into wetlands along a 22-acre lake. The stormwater is thus cleaner and a higher amount of water returns to groundwater than with a piped storm sewer system (Prairie Crossing 2002). Prairie Crossing has miles of trails that residents can use and is adjacent to the 2,500-acre Liberty Prairie Reserve.

Despite the sensitive site design, however, Prairie Crossing also shows the difficulty of placing such a development within a regional context. The development is an hour drive south of Milwaukee and an hour drive north of Chicago. There is no commercial development within walking distance, though a nearby railroad station connects to downtown Chicago and O'Hare airport. A second train station with connections to Milwaukee is under construction. Finally, the Prairie Crossing development suggests that good design is expensive. The cost of homes in Prairie Crossing ranges from $269,900 to $427,900.

CASE STUDY 19-3
Tracking Greenfield and Urban Development in Lancaster County, Pennsylvania

Lancaster County is tracking the development of greenfield growth and urban development through a GIS database. Lancaster County, which is in the path of the westward-expanding Philadelphia suburbs, had 470,000 residents in 2000 and is expected to have a population of 600,000 by the year 2020. Lancaster County is famous for its Amish population and strong farming economy. In the early 1990s, the county embarked on a growth management program to direct most new development inside urban and village growth boundaries.

One of the strengths of the Lancaster County plan is its commitment to monitoring and analysis of how its urban and village growth boundaries are performing. In 1995, the county planning commission initiated a benchmarking program based on the county comprehensive plan. Each county department and leading nonprofit organizations in the community were asked to set quantifiable goals for the following year. Each year, progress toward those goals is noted in an annual report. In 1997, the county began to keep track of growth and development through a GIS system. Each subdivision and building approval is logged into the system and its location noted (Figure 19-5).

The county planning commission's goal is to accommodate 80% of new development inside the growth boundaries at an average density of 5.5 units per acre. In 1999, the growth tracking report showed that between 1994 and 1997, about three-fourths of new housing units were built inside the county's growth boundaries, but 61% of the land developed had occurred outside of the boundaries (Daniels 2000, 14-17). Densities for new development inside the boundaries are running between 2.5 and 3 units per acre. If this trend continues, the area inside the growth boundaries will fill up faster than anticipated and become merely contained sprawl. Also, the demand to expand the boundaries out into farming areas will be intense and premature. In this case, the selected goals and benchmarks were not met, suggesting that additional incentives may be needed to encourage more dense development inside the growth boundaries.

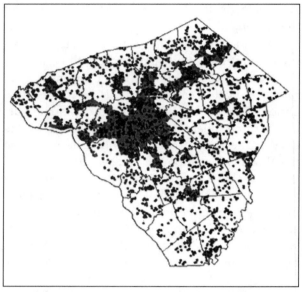

19-5 Tracking of new development in Lancaster County, Pennsylvania, 1993–1996.

Source: Lancaster County GIS Department, Lancaster, Pennsylvania

Environmental Planning Challenges at Home and Abroad

20

Positive Trends and Urgent Needs for Sustainable Environmental Planning

Just as we must carefully plan for and invest our capital in infrastructure—our roads, our bridges, and water lines—we must also invest in our environment, our green infrastructure—our forests, our wetlands, our streams and rivers.

PARRIS GLENDENING, FORMER GOVERNOR
OF MARYLAND (GLENDENING 1999, A12)

Solutions are almost never permanent, so plan to keep on planning.

CHRIS BRIGHT, WORLDWATCH
INSTITUTE (BRIGHT 2000, 38)

Each of the chapters presented so far indicates important new trends that are emerging in environmental planning. These trends build upon national legislation, state and local planning efforts, innovations by companies, and greater involvement by nonprofit organizations and concerned citizens. It is difficult to pick up a major daily newspaper today and not find at least one article on the environment. The public has become much more aware of environmental quality, threats, and decisions, and the media has responded to the public's interest.

Environmental planning is still a young field of practice. Yet, environmental planners at all levels of government and in the private sector continue to search for broad, holistic approaches to solve interrelated environmental problems, such as transportation, air pollution, and sprawl. New ideas in environmental planning will take shape over time; environmental planning, like the environment itself, is constantly evolving.

POSITIVE ENVIRONMENTAL TRENDS

Recall the environmental crises mentioned in the Introduction:

- decline in the quality of the built environment in many inner cities and older suburbs;
- loss of agricultural land, forestlands, wildlife habitats, and open space to sprawling development;
- overconsumption of energy brought about by sprawling development that relies heavily on motor vehicles;
- lack of infrastructure investment as sprawling development moves farther away from the urban core;
- degradation of the air and water quality;
- lack of energy conservation and the need to develop renewable energy sources;
- need to recycle, reuse, and reduce consumption along with safe disposal of solid waste and hazardous waste;

- reduction of the production of toxic chemicals; and
- provision for long-term adequate supplies of clean water as populations continue to grow.

There have been positive responses to most of these environmental crises, and the trends are encouraging, but other improvements and changes are needed if communities and regions are to enjoy truly sustainable environments over the long run. Business and industry will need to continue to reduce pollution and the use of toxic substances as well as increase recycling efforts. Individuals and families will need to change their lifestyles toward living in more compact settlements, using mass transit, reducing energy and resource consumption, and increasing recycling. Reform of government land use, taxation, and spending programs to promote attractive compact development, mass transit, and good stewardship of rural lands will take time. Still, the potential for reform is an essential feature of the democratic political process on which environmental planning ultimately depends. Local planners can play an important role in shaping public debate and educating the community about environmental trends, progress, and needs. Above all, greater cooperation from landowners, politicians, developers, lenders, and the general public will be needed to forge healthy sustainable communities and regions.

TREND 1
Greater Local Responsibility, Planning Effort, and Implementation

Perhaps the single most encouraging trend is that communities and regions are taking steps to assess and protect their environments. In the early 1970s, federal and state laws and regulations were usually needed to compel action by local governments. Now, many communities are enacting their own programs to protect the environment. For instance, watershed groups are springing up throughout the country to safeguard local and regional water quality. They are recognizing that a quality environment is necessary for a sustainable economy as well as public health.

Baltimore County, Maryland, officials responded to public concerns about sprawl in the mid-1990s by downzoning 10,000 acres of rural land zoned at one dwelling per 5 acres (Resource Conservation) to one dwelling per 50 acres (Agricultural) in order to reduce development potential in the countryside. In 1998, Ventura County, California, voters approved a ballot measure that subjects any rezoning proposal in the agricultural zone to a voter referendum for the next 20 years. In New Jersey, thanks to state-enabling legislation and grants, 17 counties and 118 municipalities have drafted open space plans and established open space trust funds to buy land and development rights (The Trust for Public Land 2000, 7).

Public participation in the environmental planning process is on the rise. As author Mark Dowie noted:

> "It has become virtually impossible to build a dam, open a landfill, fire up an incinerator, drill a deep injection well, or store nuclear waste without an immediate, well-organized response from surrounding communities, backed by solid understanding of all relevant laws and regulations" (Dowie 1995, 220).

A greater awareness of environmental quality and threats has also led to more activism by citizens' groups. Often, these groups are labeled "Not in My Back Yard" people because of their opposition to nearby proposed developments—everything from shopping malls, to residential subdivisions, to industrial plants. However, the citizens who form these groups are exercising their right to participate in the environmental planning process.

A variety of tools (e.g., Geographic Information Systems (GISs), remote sensing, and a host of Internet sites) are providing planners, developers, local officials, and the public with a wealth of information and analysis about local and regional environments. As a result, they can better identify where development should go and where environmental constraints, unique landscapes, or productive natural resources make development undesirable or physically difficult and financially expensive. All of this information is fundamental to drafting effective comprehensive plans, zoning and subdivision regulations, and capital improvements programs. Information systems are also helpful in tracking development, setting benchmarks for environmental preservation and improvement, and monitoring progress toward those benchmarks.

TREND 2
Investing in Green Infrastructure

Planning in America has traditionally meant "planning for development." However, it has dawned on residents in hundreds of communities and regions that it is also necessary to plan for the preservation of land and the sustainability of the air, water, and natural environment, which provide healthy places to live and work. The environment is a good investment. In the New Information Economy, businesses and individuals are more footloose than ever. Communities and regions are recognizing that environmental quality contributes significantly to overall quality of life, which in turn is a valuable economic asset that can attract new businesses and encourage local businesses and workers to stay where they are.

Dozens of states, counties, and communities across America are buying open space and conservation easements to private land to channel development away from important resource lands and natural areas. These state and local governments run the gamut of political persuasions, proof that environmental protection is a bipartisan issue. Private, nonprofit organizations are also preserving large amounts of land both by themselves and in partnerships with all levels of government. Taxpayers have generally shown a willingness to pay to keep land open. For instance, in 2000, California voters passed the $2.1 billion Neighborhood

Parks, Clean Water, Clean Air and Coastal Protection Bond Act. The money will provide funds to:
- protect land around lakes, rivers, streams, and the coast to improve water quality and ensure clean drinking water;
- protect forests and plant trees to improve air quality;
- preserve open space and farmland threatened by unplanned development; and
- protect wildlife habitats, and repair and improve the safety of state and neighborhood parks (*Farmland Preservation Report* 2000, 1).

Between 1998 and 2002, voters across America approved more than 500 ballot measures involving over $20 billion in land preservation and smart growth projects (Land Trust Alliance 2002). Yet, despite increased land preservation efforts, many parts of the United States are in a race against time to protect important lands from development. Given current rates of population growth, development, and land protection, the race in many communities will be largely won or lost within the next 20 years.

TREND 3
Taking the Long-Term View

Planning for major expenditures and change—whether by a business, a government, or an individual—requires a long-term view. The public and elected officials must learn to accept the fact that quick solutions to environmental problems are rare. One of the shortcomings of the usual comprehensive planning process is that it has a time horizon of only 10 to 20 years. Effective planning for watersheds, wellhead protection and water supplies, mitigating natural hazards, retention of farm and forestlands, and protection of wildlife habitats and wilderness areas all require a time horizon of longer than 20 years. Similarly, the clean-up of polluted waters and brownfield sites, and the accommodation of thousands of new residents within cities or on greenfield sites, do not happen overnight. Twenty years is not enough time to forge a truly long-range vision for a sustainable community or region.

Communities and regions are beginning to recognize the need for longer term planning. For instance, the regional government in Portland, Oregon—Metro—adopted its 2040 plan in 1995, a 45-year time horizon. Maryland's Smart Growth program is aimed at accommodating growth and development over the long run, while improving the water quality of the Chesapeake Bay. Businesses are beginning to take a long-term view by adding environmental compliance departments to avoid running afoul of environmental laws and regulations. In addition, many companies have altered their products and manufacturing processes to simultaneously reduce pollution and save money. Individual Americans have demonstrated greater conservation of water resources and increased recycling efforts. Many consumers now go out of their way to purchase certified wood products and locally grown foods.

Some people argue that there is a trade-off between environmental quality and economic growth, depicted simply as "jobs vs. the environment," or sacrificing long-term environmental quality for short economic gain. The Institute for Southern Studies has tracked the economic performance and environmental quality of all 50 states using 20 economic and 20 environmental indicators. The institute's report, *Gold and Green 2000*, found that seven states ranked among the top 15 for both economic and environmental health; by contrast, 10 states were among the bottom 15 on both lists (Institute for Southern Studies 2001).

Since 1970, Americans have spent more money on environmental protection and clean-up than any other country in the world. Yet, studies have estimated that the benefits of environmental regulations have exceeded the costs (Goodstein 1999). A 1996 study by the American Enterprise Institute estimated that the costs of environmental regulations were about $200 billion a year and the benefits exceeded $250 billion (Hahn 1996). A 1997 study by the U.S. Office of Management and Budget (USOMB) estimated the additional amount of benefits over costs of environmental regulations at $18 billion a year (USOMB 1997).

TREND 4
Changes in Transportation Modes Will Mean Changes in Land Use Patterns and Pollution

Both the Intermodal Surface Transportation Efficiency Act (ISTEA), passed in 1991, and the Transportation Equity Act for the 21st Century (TEA-21), passed in 1997, emphasize multimodal transportation. Yet, both laws pumped the majority of authorized funding—tens of billions of dollars—into new highway construction and road repairs. New highways will mainly serve to extend suburban development farther out into the countryside and promote sprawling land use patterns. Even so, the hottest transportation trend to emerge at the end of the 20th century is the development of light-rail systems for large- and medium-size metropolitan areas.

Many metro areas are facing substantial population increases over the next few decades along with the threat of increasing traffic congestion and reduced air quality. Greater Portland, Oregon, showed that light rail could be successful in promoting a compact development pattern of centers and corridors, revitalizing the downtown, reducing automobile dependence, and alleviating air pollution. Several other metropolitan regions are following Portland's lead. For instance, San Diego County is betting heavily on a pattern of transit corridors to accommodate the additional 1 million residents that are expected between 2000 and 2020. Intermodal transportation systems are emerging as well—from the joining of bicycles and buses in Austin, Texas, to driving to and from a "park-and-ride" transit station, to walking to a bus stop.

TREND 5

A Greater State Role in Environmental Planning, Regulation, and Spending Programs

In the 1970s and 1980s, the federal government used a "command and control" approach to regulate pollution. The trend in the 1990s and early 2000s has been to turn over more regulatory authority from the federal government to the states. In addition, a variety of programs for environmental protection, besides enforcing federal laws, has emerged at the state level. On several environmental planning issues, the states are ahead of the federal government. California's air quality and motor vehicle standards are more stringent than the federal standards. Pennsylvania has created a brownfield clean-up and liability protection program that has so far produced more impressive results than the combined efforts of the U.S. Environmental Protection Agency (EPA) and the U.S. Department of Housing and Urban Development.

By 2001, Maryland's farmland preservation program had spent six times as much money in one state as Congress had spent to save farmland nationwide. The state's Smart Growth legislation directs state infrastructure spending toward existing communities, provides incentives for private investment in existing communities, and purchases conservation easements on private rural lands. Oregon has led the way in curbing sprawl by requiring local governments to adopt urban growth boundaries and strict agricultural and timberland zoning. Vermont's ban on spreading animal manure in the winter exceeds national best management practices to protect water quality. In 2002, California passed standards for carbon dioxide emissions from cars, even though such standards do not yet exist at the federal level.

TREND 6

Private, Nonprofit Organizations Are Influencing Local, Regional, and National Environmental Programs

Private, nonprofit organizations—both big and small—are having a significant impact on environmental regulations, the preservation of land and water resources, and major development proposals. National organizations, such as the Natural Resources Defense Council (NRDC), Environmental Defense, and the Sierra Club Legal Defense Fund, have been involved in important lawsuits that have shaped how the EPA enforces environmental laws and how private companies operate. For instance, the NRDC successfully sued the EPA to require states to undertake the clean-up of impaired waters through the Total Maximum Daily Load (TMDL) process under the 1972 Clean Water Act. National organizations also actively lobby Congress and even participate in drafting environmental legislation. The 1990 Amendments to the Clean Air Act were written in part by representatives from the NRDC, Environmental Defense, the Sierra Club, the National Wildlife Federation, and the National Audubon Society (Dowie 1995, 87).

Local and regional land trusts have preserved millions of acres through land acquisition and the purchase and donation of conservation easements. Most of the nation's more than 1,200 land trusts are small but visible in their communities. Their numbers have about doubled since 1980. Private, nonprofit watershed associations are protecting water quality and undertaking clean-up efforts. Regional transportation groups are important lobbyists and promoters of mass transit. Nonprofit organizations are using information and analysis techniques, such as GIS, to identify and rate important natural resources for internal planning purposes. The Nature Conservancy has launched a "Last Great Places" campaign based on its evaluation of remaining intact ecosystems that can still

Table 20-1
Leading Environmental Planning Challenges in America

Issue	Challenge
Population Growth	• 400 million Americans by 2050 • Spread of metropolitan areas
Water	• Adequate long-term supplies • Maintaining and improving water quality
Air	• Maintaining and improving air quality
Energy	• Depletion of fossil fuels • Development of alternative, cleaner energy sources • Increased energy conservation and greater energy efficiency
Transportation	• Optimal mix of mass transit, individual transit, and freight hauling
Solid Waste	• Increased recycling, reuse, and recovery of materials • Siting and operation of landfills
Toxics	• Reduction in production of toxic substances • Safe disposal and recycling • Clean-up of hazardous waste sites • Brownfield redevelopment
Wilderness	• Maintaining large contiguous blocks of land for ecosystems • Increasing the amount of protected wilderness areas
Wildlife	• Protecting rare and endangered species • Maintaining biodiversity, habitats, and ecosystems
Wetlands	• Attaining no net loss of wetlands
Coastal Resources	• Protecting beaches, dunes, and estuaries • Protecting fisheries and recreation areas
Natural Hazards	• Discouraging development in areas with physical constraints and high risk of natural disasters
Agriculture	• Reduction of chemical and nutrient pollution and soil erosion • Slowing the conversion of farm and ranchlands
Forestry	• Reduction of chemical pollution and soil erosion • Multiple-use, sustained yield of national forests • Slowing the conversion of private forestlands
Mining	• Reduction of pollution from mines, such as acid mine drainage
Built Environment	• Revitalizing cities and older suburbs • Historic preservation and adaptive reuse of buildings
Greenfield Development	• Minimizing sprawl • Promoting environmentally sensitive design

be adequately protected. This kind of strategic planning by nonprofits can also result in better public sector planning by compelling governments to think about where development should or should not be located.

ENVIRONMENTAL PLANNING NEEDS AND CHALLENGES

There are several actions governments, businesses, and individuals could take that would improve environmental quality, the conservation of natural resources, and the environmental planning process. Even with the progress Americans have made in cleaning up and protecting the environment since 1970, much work and sustainable environmental planning remains to be done (see Table 20-1).

Needed environmental actions include those that can be taken by local and regional governments, actions that require state and federal legislation, and international agreements. In most cases, needed actions can be taken without significant disruption to the local, regional, or national economy. The danger of not addressing these needs now is that the problems described will only get worse, resulting in higher costs, more draconian environmental clean-up standards, and more restrictive land use planning programs.

Local and Regional Environmental Planning Needs

NEED 1
Limits on Population Growth or Communities and Regions

The 2000 census reported that there were 281.4 million Americans, an increase of 32.7 million or 13.2% over the 1990 census (U.S. Bureau of the Census 2001) (see Figure 20-1). Moreover, the U.S. Bureau of the Census has estimated that there could be as many as 400 million Americans by 2050, and 570 million by 2100 (U.S. Bureau of the Census 2000). The United States has one of the highest rates of population growth among the industrialized nations at slightly more than 1% a year. This translates into about 3 million additional Americans each year.

Unless new technologies are developed and public policies adopted to increase water conservation, alternative energy sources, substitutes for nonrenewable resources, recycling, waste disposal, and food production, continued population growth will pose serious threats to public health, the natural environment, and working landscapes. Unless the increasing populations can be accommodated mainly in compact cities, villages, and suburbs, they will consume much more open space, productive farm and forestlands, environmental resources, and wildlife habitats. How will greater Los Angeles accommodate an anticipated 6 million additional residents between 2000 and 2025? How will Arizona or greater Las Vegas accommodate their rapid rates of population growth? Where will the water come from?

It is becoming increasingly obvious that population levels and development in some parts of the United States are exceeding local and regional carrying capacities. Some metro regions are approaching physical limits to growth in available water and land area. It is fair to say that there is an ultimate "ideal" population level for each metro area based on sustainable environmental protection. Yet, the 14th Amendment guarantees the right of free travel for all Americans. This means that anyone can choose to live anywhere they want to, if they can afford it; however, rights must be balanced with responsibilities. Simply put, does the right to free travel give us the right to exceed carrying capacity? The 10th Amendment allows the use of government "police power" to protect public health, safety, and welfare. If a community makes a cogent argument to limit growth based on studies and goals in its comprehensive plan, it could stand up to a legal challenge. Communities should not make population projections as if population growth is fated to happen. Rather, projec-

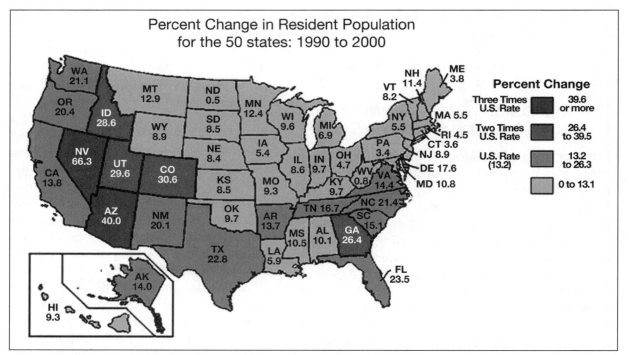

20-1 Percentage growth of U.S. population by states, 1990–2000.

Source: U.S. Bureau of the Census

tions should be conscious, desired, and supportable future estimates. Settlement policy may be needed to impose population caps in certain cities and communities, and limits on the number of new building permits issued in others. Still, a change in the legal interpretation of the right of free travel may be needed in order to enable communities and regions to truly control their populations and environmental destinies.

NEED 2
Better Regional Planning to Curb Sprawl, Planning for Adequate Public Facilities, and Creation of Regional Governments

Many land use and environmental problems are regional in scope. Yet, America's local governments are noted for their often parochial approach to planning, featuring the competitive pursuit of development to expand the local property tax base. Communities have long argued to keep "local control." Yet, too often, this is an excuse to continue a "do nothing" approach to land use planning and environmental protection. A plethora of "quasi-governments" in the form of sewer and water authorities, industrial development authorities, and school districts undertake their own planning and development processes, which may not concur with local or county land use plans, and which have contributed significantly to sprawl. The development decisions of local municipalities, authorities, and special districts in one community not only can conflict with each other but can easily create impacts that spill over into neighboring communities. A governmental process is needed to review, approve, modify, or disapprove such developments of regional impact.

Many communities have major infrastructure gaps, such as needs for new roads, schools, and sewer and water facilities. A community can use an adequate public facilities ordinance as a way to require developers to have the necessary infrastructure in place before building commences. This concept, called concurrency, is a way to guard the public purse by making developers pay the true cost of their developments, and a way to ensure that development does not happen too rapidly and outpace the capacity of public facilities. Adequate public facilities ordinances put concurrency into practice by creating procedures, standards, and enforcement measures to ensure that construction does not happen in places where services would fall below accepted standards. Such ordinances can help to promote orderly development and fiscal responsibility while avoiding overreliance on on-site septic systems and wells. Urban and village growth boundaries help to implement concurrency and adequate public facilities ordinances by setting a physical limit to the extension of sewer and water facilities. In short, concurrency, adequate public facilities ordinances, and growth boundaries can work together to influence the timing and sequencing of growth to promote developments that are less expensive to service, more compact, and consume less open space.

Regional planning commissions have existed in most parts of the United States since the mid-1960s. The function of regional planning commissions is to provide technical planning assistance to local governments and to help local governments obtain grants. Regional planning commissions often draft regional comprehensive plans, but these plans are usually advisory and place no legal obligations on local governments. A regional planning commission could become a true force for planning under a regional government with control over planning, zoning, subdivision, and capital improvements for an entire region. The Metropolitan Planning Organizations required under ISTEA and the TEA-21 could serve as models for regional planning commissions, which could draft plans for metro areas that are consistent with state goals and guidelines to control sprawl.

It may be tempting to advocate the creation of a regional planning authority to have countervailing power over utility authorities and special districts, but authorities are not democratic entities, and planning is a democratic process. Instead, special districts and authorities and the land use planning activities of local governments should ideally be combined into a single, democratically elected regional government. A state legislature can grant a regional government powers for planning, zoning, transportation, solid waste, and sewer and water service. For example, Metro of greater Portland, Oregon, encompasses parts of three counties and 24 municipalities. It is the nation's only elected regional government and has authority over transit, sewer service, and general land use planning. The missing link in the case of Metro is control over the school districts, and specifically the consolidation of school districts within its boundary. Regionalization of school districts would reduce school funding disparities among communities.

Compare Metro's single regional government approach with the Pioneer Valley of central Massachusetts, made up of 43 communities and more than 600,000 people. Twenty-two of those communities had no comprehensive plan as of 1997. Of the 21 with comprehensive plans, only four had been updated since 1990. In the meantime, many towns have seen significant population growth with few strategies to combat sprawl. For instance, the population of the Town of Belchertown more than doubled from 5,800 to 12,900 residents between 1970 and 2000. There is no county government, and regional planning commissions have little power. Land use planning and zoning control is fragmented among the municipalities, and the result is a sprawling pattern of "substantial growth in outlying communities" (Pioneer Valley Planning Commission 2002).

NEED 3

Reform or Elimination of the Property Tax to Fund Education and Local Government

At first blush, the reform of the property tax does not appear to be an environmental issue. On closer examination, however, it becomes clear that local dependence on the property tax is undermining community efforts to promote intelligent land use and protection of the environment. The reliance on the property tax causes local communities to emphasize short-term economic gain over long-term environmental quality. The 1990 Governor's Commission on Vermont's Future summarized the problem as follows:

> "Most towns, confronted with rising costs of services, compete for development to increase their tax base. This competition conflicts with the planning process. Towns are forced to waive zoning requirements, make improper siting decisions, and, in general, pursue short-term objectives at the expense of long-term goals" (Ad Hoc Associates 1990).

The property tax places local jurisdictions in competition with each other to attract commercial and industrial development and expensive houses on large lots, which generate more in property taxes than they demand in public services. This competition produces confusing, inefficient land use patterns, overdevelopment, and the loss of open space. As development increases, property taxes rise, especially to pay for educating more children. The higher property taxes can compel landowners to sell land for development, thus reducing the stock of open space, natural areas, and productive farm and forestlands.

Funding education from a progressive, statewide income tax makes far more sense than the local property tax. A fee-for-service approach for other government services would place the cost burden on those who use them, such as garbage collection, sewer, and water supply. A local income tax, such as a flat percentage of wage earnings, could cover other government services, such as police and fire protection. Such measures could significantly reduce the pressures on local governments to approve inappropriate development and would go a long way toward protecting the environment.

NEED 4

Environmental Mediation

Mediation is the attempt to resolve disputes through negotiation rather than through lawsuits, government regulation, or legislation. Mediation involves the use of a third party to reach a consensus and a settlement between two or more opposing factions. Mediation may be attractive because:

- a mutually satisfactory result may be less expensive and quicker to reach than through the courts, government bureaucracy, or a legislature; and
- public opinion is likely to favor parties who reach voluntary settlements as opposed to those who struggle through the legal or political process.

Mediation depends on the willingness of contending parties to negotiate. If one party refuses to talk to the other, a stalemate will prevail. It is often difficult to leave personalities out of the negotiation process, but successful negotiation usually occurs when parties can bargain in good faith based on their overall interests rather than particular positions. Reaching an agreement is only one step in the mediation process. The contending parties must also carry out their obligations under the agreement. Some sort of monitoring, evaluation, and enforcement mechanism must be in place to assure the parties that the agreement is being upheld.

Environmental mediation is fairly common in the resolution of land use disputes. The location, type, size, and configuration of development are often issues of debate between developers and neighborhood groups, environmental groups, or even local governments. Policy conflicts between public agencies have also been mediated over

SIDEBAR 20-1

The Supplemental Environmental Project Policy of the Environmental Protection Agency

For many years, the U.S. Environmental Protection Agency (EPA) and several states have offered individuals and businesses an alternative to paying a significant fine for violating the Clean Air Act, the Clean Water Act, the Superfund Law, the Resource Conservation and Recovery Act, or the Toxic Substances Control Act. This alternative comes under the EPA's Supplemental Environmental Project (SEP) policy. A SEP is an environmentally beneficial project that a violator voluntarily agrees to perform as part of the settlement of an enforcement action. In return, the EPA agrees to reduce the monetary fine that would otherwise apply. For instance, as part of an agreement to clean up a Superfund site in the Rocky Mountains, the violator donated $750,000 to a county open space authority to purchase 30 acres of ranchland adjacent to existing protected open space and a 15-acre pond (U.S. EPA 2000).

land use, natural resources and public lands, and the siting of power plants (Bingham 1986, 32-33). Some states have even written mediation into law for resolving environmental disputes, particularly in the siting of hazardous waste facilities.

A number of environmental disputes may not lend themselves to mediation, however. Locally Unwanted Land Uses (LULUs) are a frequent example of "all or nothing" situations. Either a power plant is built or it isn't; you don't end up with half a power plant. The location of LULUs is often decided by the courts or state regulators. Lawsuits are both expensive and often leave bad feelings, whatever the outcome.

While compromise is the currency of politics, ecology is a natural science, not a political science.

That, in a nutshell, is the challenge in reaching mutually acceptable, workable, and sustainable solutions to environmental problems.

NEED 5

The Replacement of Aging Infrastructure and Planning for New Infrastructure

According to some experts, the United States may be up to $4 trillion behind in needed infrastructure construction and improvements (Burchell *et al.* 1998). In particular, spending for water and sewer infrastructure will become increasingly important. The EPA has estimated that governments spent $1 trillion on water and wastewater facilities between 1956 and 1992. However, the EPA has predicted that another $1 trillion will be needed for additional facilities between 1993 and 2009, and a further $1 trillion between 2010 and 2020 (U.S. General Accounting Office (GAO) 2000, 115-116). In fiscal 2000, federal spending on water and wastewater systems was just $4.3 billion, and state and local governments added about $14.1 billion. If this level of funding continues, there will be a shortfall of $80 billion in water and wastewater treatment projects each year to 2020. In other words, we are investing about 20% of what we should be in these treatment processes.

Especially in many smaller communities, federal grants and technical assistance will be needed to make the necessary environmental improvements, in particular for public supplies of clean water. Adequate public facilities ordinances can help stimulate private investment in utilities by requiring that sewer and water lines be in place before development can begin. A surcharge on sewer and water extensions can be levied to make new users pay the (higher) marginal cost, rather than the (lower) average cost, of extending those services. Zoning to permit densities higher than two dwelling units per acre is necessary to make the provision of public sewer and water cost effective. Growth boundaries can limit the extension of sewer and water lines into the countryside. Also, zoning at very low densities (one dwelling per 20 acres or more) can be used to discourage a proliferation of on-lot septic systems and wells that can lead to groundwater contamination and force the costly extension of sewer and water lines into areas not planned for growth.

NEED 6

Linking Local Land Use Plans with
Multimodal Transportation Planning

Transportation systems are the skeleton of the community or region. Yet, America's heavy reliance on motor vehicles has created major traffic congestion, sprawl, and air pollution problems. New road construction, bypasses, and road widenings alone will not solve these problems. Multimodal and intermodal transportation systems must be developed and improved to provide more transport alternatives and better movement. These transportation systems must coordinate land use and transportation. Transit-oriented development in tandem with rail and bus transit corridors holds considerable promise for accommodating growing population numbers and transportation needs, promoting more pedestrian-friendly environments, and reducing sprawl through more compact and mixed-use development. Greater emphasis on pedestrian walkways, bike paths, and trails that interconnect the places people live to where they work, shop, and play provides further transport alternatives. Finally, mixed-use zoning, neotraditional neighborhood zoning, and effective zoning of working landscapes reduce the need to travel great distances by encouraging a variety of uses close together and by directing growth into and adjacent to existing communities.

NEED 7

Better Monitoring and Enforcement
of Land Use Plans, Zoning, Land Use
Changes, and Environmental Quality

Taking stock of the local or regional environment is not a once-and-done exercise. Local governments need to understand how their environmental planning efforts are performing. Keeping track of land use changes, development, and air and water quality provides essential information for decision makers to use in making changes to comprehensive plans and programs. The achievement of long-term planning goals and objectives depends upon the tracking of day-to-day decisions about development and preservation. GISs have the capacity to store and analyze data on land use and environmental features. Building permits, subdivision approvals, zoning changes, and air and water quality can all be tracked on a GIS to show what kind of development is happening where and the related environmental impacts. Monitoring can provide useful information about the progress of planning, but often enforcement is required to correct shortcomings. Violations of air and water discharge permits, zoning permits, and developer agreements must be addressed swiftly and fairly. Finally, communities can use action plans with measurable benchmarks, and report progress toward those benchmarks in an annual report.

NEED 8

Planning for Natural Hazards and Disasters

A combination of growing populations and the likelihood of more severe weather caused by global warming will require local governments to better anticipate and respond to natural disasters. For instance, as more Americans choose to live farther away from established settlements, they are building houses and businesses in the woods and near wilderness areas. An estimated 43 million Americans now live in places that are vulnerable to wildfires, especially in western states. Local governments need to employ zoning, conservation easements, and land acquisition to keep development away from natural hazards such as steep slopes, floodplains, coastal areas, and fault lines. Local building codes need to be strict, especially in areas subject to hurricanes, and the retro-

Table 20-2
The Predicted Ten Fastest
Growing States (1995–2025)

State	Projected Change in Population
California	56%
New Mexico	55%
Hawaii	53%
Arizona	52%
Nevada	51%
Idaho	50%
Utah	48%
Alaska	47%
Florida	46%
Texas	45%

Source: U.S. Bureau of the Census (2002)

fit of public buildings undertaken to minimize damage from hurricanes and earthquakes.

State and Federal Environmental Planning Needs

NEED 1
A National Population Policy

A national population policy would help the United States better control population growth and provide direction for state and local governments in balancing population growth and carrying capacity. Many of the environmental problems discussed in this book can be attributed to population growth and the high material living standard of that population. Because Americans are not likely to change their lifestyles dramatically, limiting population growth will be necessary to minimize environmental impacts (see Table 20-2). A limit of two child dependents that can be claimed as federal income tax deductions would be a start. While limiting the number of child dependents

may seem like a small disincentive toward having more than two children, it sends a message.

Immigration is a controversial subject. America has long been the land of opportunity. Many of the best and brightest from around the world come to study and work here, but many poor people looking for a better life come to America as well. For instance, American agriculture would be strapped without immigrant migrant laborers. Legal immigration into the United States reached nearly 1 million a year in the 1990s and accounted for one-third of the nation's population growth for the decade. Illegal immigration is estimated at about 300,000 a year. A limit on legal immigration is probably warranted somewhere in the range of 250,000 to 500,000 people a year. Illegal immigration is, of course, a more complicated problem. In 2000, there were an estimated 5 million illegal immigrants in the United States. The key to reducing illegal immigration is improved standards of living in developing countries.

NEED 2
The Rehabilitation and Revitalization of Urban Areas and Older Suburbs

To curb sprawl, cities and inner suburbs must become attractive alternatives to the outer suburbs and countryside. Brownfield clean-up, mass transit, incentives for private investment, better urban schools, and good design with greenspace will be needed. The U.S. Conference of Mayors named brownfield clean-up and redevelopment its number one priority in 1994. Recycling brownfields would create housing, commercial and industrial space, employment, and tax base. In addition, brownfield remediation would clean up hazardous waste and reduce the potential for groundwater contamination. Pennsylvania has created a model brownfield clean-up program.

Federal and state tax incentives can go far toward encouraging private investment in central cities and inner suburbs. Maryland offers tax credits for employers who create 25 or more jobs in

Priority Funding Areas, mainly in cities and older suburbs. A land value tax—a property tax that taxes land at a higher rate than buildings—would encourage redevelopment and infill development on vacant urban land. Federal empowerment zones and state enterprise zones can target urban areas for job creation and property tax abatement. Restoring the federal historic preservation tax credit to its 1976 level would help spur the rehabilitation of buildings in older downtowns. Tax credits for new housing in central cities and older suburbs would help attract new residents. Federal transportation funds need to be reallocated away from new road construction toward the construction and expansion of mass-transit systems. Finally, state and federal infrastructure dollars are needed to upgrade recreation areas and schools. Urban parks and greenways need to be developed. Equally, if not more important, urban and inner suburban schools require significant state and federal investment. One of the most often cited reasons for city dwellers moving to the outer suburbs is the decline of the quality of urban schools (Orfield 1997).

NEED 3

Increased Energy Conservation and Efficiency, Alternative Energy Sources, and the Clean-up of Coal-Fired Power Plants

America's dependency on foreign oil is not sustainable in the long run. Driving less and the development and expansion of mass-transit systems can help conserve the use of oil as well as reduce pollution. Energy conservation—using less energy—is a proven means to reduce the use of fossil fuels, save money, and improve environmental quality. Greater energy efficiency also reduces energy consumption. Governments can lead the way by purchasing energy-efficient products and by setting energy-efficiency standards for appliances and in building construction. Federal energy-efficiency standards along with financial incentives can compel industry to produce more

energy-efficient appliances, motors, and cars. Federal and state financial incentives can encourage consumers to buy energy-efficient products. State building codes can require greater energy efficiency in the construction and renovation of homes and buildings. Financial incentives can promote more weatherization and insulation to conserve energy. Greater fuel efficiency in motor vehicles would reduce dependence on foreign oil as well as reduce air pollution. This could be achieved in part by raising the federal fuel economy standards for cars, pick-ups, minivans, and sport utility vehicles.

One way to discourage sprawl and improve air quality is to make use of the automobile more expensive. This could be achieved through raising state and federal gasoline taxes. However, the revenues from gasoline taxes should at least in part be spent on developing and improving mass-transit systems and bicycle and pedestrian paths. The increased tax would more closely reflect the true cost of gasoline in terms of the health and environmental effects of smog and acid rain.

Alternative, renewable energy sources that produce little pollution should be encouraged. Solar, wind, and geothermal power hold considerable potential. New energy technologies should be fostered through government research grants and investment tax credits, especially nonpolluting fuel cells for cars and buildings. Some states have begun to require that a minimum percentage of energy produced comes from alternative, renewable energy sources.

The electrical utility industry was granted certain exemptions from the Clean Air Act that have enabled older, higher polluting, coal-fired plants to continue to operate, even though they are major sources of acid deposition and greenhouse gases. It is time for this exemption to end. While pollution trading credits have helped reduce sulfur dioxide emissions, nitrogen oxide and mercury pollution remain serious problems. The electric utilities should be granted no more than a few additional years to fully comply with Clean Air standards and then face stiff, daily fines until their plants meet those standards.

NEED 4
Make Businesses Pay the True Cost of Their Operations and Individuals Pay the True Cost of Their Lifestyles

The costs borne by the environment in the production of goods and services have generally not been included in the price of those goods and services. Businesses need to charge prices based on the true cost of producing goods and services, and consumers need to understand why prices are higher. Businesses have received enormous federal subsidies for harvesting timber in national forests, for mining on federal lands, and for irrigating crops and watering livestock in the western states. This has resulted in clear cutting in national forests, the literal giveaway of the nation's mineral wealth, and the production of water-dependent crops in deserts. It is time to level the playing field and require that federal timber, minerals, and water be sold at market rates that reflect the true unsubsidized production and environmental costs of harvesting those resources. This will compel farmers and ranchers to conserve on water use, require mining companies to contribute substantial royalties to the national treasury, and guide timber companies to harvest only trees that will make profitable products.

The federal mortgage interest deduction has encouraged low-density sprawl. People buy as much house as possible to maximize the deduction. Average home sizes are increasing even as average household size is declining. The construction of large houses on lots larger than 1 acre is rapidly consuming open space, resource lands, and wildlife habitats. The mortgage interest deduction should be limited to only one private residence and capped at $20,000 a year. This would mean that people who want to pay more than about $300,000 for a house would receive only a partial mortgage interest deduction. A cap on the mortgage interest deduction would also tend to encourage housing on smaller lots, including more multifamily and townhouse construction. The result would be more compact development.

NEED 5
Greater State and Federal Funding for the Preservation of Working Landscapes and Open Space

Local voters have shown a willingness to tax themselves to raise revenues to buy land for the public domain and to buy development rights to preserve privately held land, but the funding for these programs should be augmented through state and federal sources. Funding levels for four federal programs, in particular, should be expanded:

1. the Farmland Preservation Program (a total of just over $1 billion authorized as of 2002);
2. the Forest Legacy Program (less than $100 million spent as of 2000);
3. the Wetlands Reserve Program (slightly under $200 million spent as of 2000); and
4. the Land and Water Conservation Fund (authorized at $900 million a year, but typically funded at about $200 million a year).

Compare these levels of funding to the $400 *billion* spent on transportation—mainly roads—in the 1990s through the ISTEA and TEA-21 programs.

Federal funding for farmland preservation pales in comparison to the federal farm subsidies that topped $20 billion in 2001 alone. Federal farm subsidies under the 2002 Farm Bill will average $18 billion a year over 10 years. Yet, subsidies are simple payouts, and the federal government gets nothing in return. Farmers can pocket the subsidies and turn around and sell their land for development the following year. The preservation of farmland, especially in metropolitan areas, is a good long-term investment both for maintaining agricultural output in these areas under development pressure and for managing growth.

The Forest Legacy Program has already resulted in the preservation of large tracts of active timberlands, environmentally sensitive areas, and wildlife habitat. Private forestlands are coming under significant development pressure for second homes and rural residences. Because an increasing amount of the nation's timber production is coming from private timberlands, protection of private timberlands is important for the long-term production of wood products. At the same time, these lands provide species diversity, water sources, and recreation opportunities.

In the past, farmers have been responsible for the loss of millions of acres of wetlands. The Wetlands Reserve Program has helped reduce the rate of conversion of wetlands in agricultural areas. If the United States is to achieve the goal of no net loss of wetlands, this program will need more funding. With the 2001 U.S. Supreme Court ruling against federal authority over isolated wetlands, the Wetlands Reserve Program will be relied upon to provide farmers with a financial incentive not to dredge and fill these wetlands.

The Land and Water Conservation Fund plays an important role in preserving wilderness areas, wildlife refuges, and greenways. The economic value of these lands should not be underestimated. Hunters, fishermen, and bird watchers contribute billions of dollars each year to local, mostly rural economies. Full funding of the Land and Water Conservation Fund at $900 million a year is a good investment in long-term ecological protection and biodiversity.

NEED 6
Increased Recycling and Reuse of Products and Materials and a Reduction in Consumption

Americans are recycling only about one-quarter of their trash. A national returnable container bill would be a quick, uniform, and fair way to encourage more recycling. If states as large as New York and as small as Vermont can operate successful returnable container programs, any state in the nation can. Higher tipping fees at landfills would create an incentive for consumers to recycle or simply to consume less. Incentives and regulations for manufacturers to recover their products and recycle them into new products would help reduce the amount of garbage going into landfills.

Recycling and reducing consumption are especially important to conserve scarce natural resources and minimize the use of toxic substances. A disincentive in the form of a tax on the use of virgin materials and toxic substances would discourage the "throughput" of these materials and substances, and encourage the substitution of nontoxic, recycled, and reused materials. Government procurement programs that give preference to recycled products should be expanded to create needed markets that help make recycling products and materials more profitable.

NEED 7
Water Clean-up

More than one-third of America's waterways are considered "impaired." State, local, and federal governments will need to coordinate efforts with industry and individuals to improve the quality of these waterways. The EPA will need to monitor and enforce the TMDL process of the Clean Water Act to ensure that states make progress toward cleaning up impaired waterways. Businesses, governments, and individuals should be required to have discharge levels that do not exceed the assimilative capacity of the receiving waterway.

Much more needs to be done to reduce nonpoint pollution sources from lawns, urban stormwater runoff, forestry, construction sites, and farming and mining operations. Federal funding for streamside buffer strips, soil and water conservation plans, nutrient management plans, and wellhead protection plans should be increased, but these plans also need to be monitored and enforced, if necessary.

NEED 8
Enforcement of Environmental Laws

The federal government needs to set an example for state and local governments by enforcing environmental laws. Perhaps the most troubling practice has been the selective enforcement of the Clean Air Act. The EPA did withhold federal highway funding from greater Atlanta because the region failed to meet federal clean air standards. However, Los Angeles and Houston have had worse smog pollution than Atlanta, yet these cities have not lost federal highway funds.

The EPA has yet to fully enforce the TMDL process for states to implement in the clean-up of the nation's impaired waters. The TMDL process will be perhaps the major test of the EPA's enforcement powers and the agency's will to enforce environmental laws in the coming decade.

Meanwhile, primary responsibility for the implementation and enforcement of the nation's environmental laws has largely been turned over to the individual states. The level of monitoring and enforcement of environmental standards varies considerably from state to state. Instead, the EPA should require all states to meet national standards, especially for air and drinking water quality. The EPA is not a cabinet-level agency in the executive branch of the federal government. Attempts to elevate the EPA to that status have failed in Congress. Perhaps the solution is to make the EPA an independent government agency such as the Federal Reserve Board. That way, the EPA could render technical judgments and enforce laws and standards with a minimum of political interference.

NEED 9
Better Coordination of Federal, State, and Local Government Programs

The federal government has a host of laws, regulations, and taxation and spending programs that affect the environment. Unfortunately, these federal rules and programs are not well coordinated.

In addition, federal economic development and infrastructure programs often work against environmental protection. Even the National Environmental Policy Act review process, which was designed to minimize the environmental impacts of federal projects, has not limited sprawling development, spurred in part by federal highway and sewer and water programs. The shift in responsibility for much of the monitoring and enforcement of the Clear Air and Clean Water Acts from the federal government to the states needs improvement and consistency. Given that billions more dollars will have to be spent on water and sewage treatment plants and cleaning up waterways through the TMDL process, greater state accountability is paramount. The EPA will also need to ensure that state air quality improvement plans and transportation improvement plans are consistent and will make progress toward reaching air quality standards.

There is currently little direct coordination of federal programs with state and local environmental goals. A 2000 GAO study reported that the leading desire among communities concerned about sprawl was to require that federal road and highway funding be tied to local land use plans (US GAO 2000, 141). The second desire was for increased federal incentives for local governments to pursue "smart growth" and regional solutions to managing growth. Third, communities wanted to see federal infrastructure funds, particularly for sewer and water, targeted to existing cities or areas designated for growth by states. One-third of the communities concerned about sprawl strongly supported:

- expanded federal tax benefits for historic properties to include the renovation of residential properties;
- federal tax incentives for developers who build in areas designated for growth; and
- more federal tax incentives for developers who rebuild on brownfields (*ibid.*, 142).

All of these concerns reflect a desire for federal planning and funding programs to support sound local and regional planning policies.

A 1999 study by the American Planning Association (APA) reported that about half of all states were still using planning-enabling legislation based on the federal model of the 1920s (APA 1999, 1). In addition, most states do not require local governments to draft comprehensive plans or adopt the zoning and subdivision ordinances that would put plans into action. Modernizing state statutes to require local planning and regulation to enable local governments to use an array of land use controls is fundamental to sustainable environmental planning. Often, a strong state role is needed to protect critical natural resources of statewide importance and to offer funding for local governments to undertake planning and land preservation. For instance, Florida can designate and protect up to 5% of the state as critical areas, and Washington has made more than $3 million in planning grants to local governments to combine land use planning and environmental protection (Johnson 1999, 79).

NEED 10
Environmental Education, Data Collection and Analysis, and Scientific Research

A common need at the local, regional, state, and national levels is environmental education. Many American children are growing up environmentally illiterate. They know little about air and water quality or the wildlife found in their communities. Americans need to understand the enormous value of ecosystem services. The basis of a successfully functioning democracy is an informed public. The more aware Americans are about the environment and how the choices they make individually and collectively affect the environment, the more likely they are to support government officials and business accountability, and the better planning decisions are likely to be. Environmental education should be presented in elementary and secondary schools. Environmental studies programs offered at many colleges and universities should be expanded. Local governments can use their web sites to post information on the local environment.

Collecting data on environmental quality at the local and regional levels is important for land use planning and day-to-day land use decisions by local and regional governments. The proliferation and refinement of GISs are already proving extremely helpful. At the same time, more and better research at the state and national levels needs to be done on various effects on the environment, such as the effects of certain chemicals. Good science that produces reliable information is necessary to enable planners, politicians, businesspeople, citizens' groups, and voters to make informed choices.

NEED 11
A National Vision of Environmental Quality and Natural Resource Conservation

A vision statement is a summary of purpose, direction, and goals for which to strive. In the 1990s, many businesses and nonprofit groups drafted mission statements to better explain the purpose of their organizations and what they were trying to accomplish. The purpose of government is to protect the public health, safety, and welfare. Good environmental quality is essential for public health and safety. Conservation of natural resources is essential for sustainable economic growth over time. Yet, the federal government has not expressed a clear statement of sustainable environmental quality and natural resource use for the nation. Environmental policies and resource use are interrelated. For example, transportation policies and programs have consequences for energy use and air quality. These connections should be clearly spelled out in a general vision statement.

It is time for the federal government to hold an Environmental Summit of the key departments, representatives of state and local government, businesses both large and small, environmentalists, and consumer groups. The goal of the summit should be to hammer out a consensus vision for the nation's environmental quality and resource use in the built environment, working landscapes, and natural areas over the next 20 to 50 years. The vision statement should guide federal policy and spending, taxation, and regulatory programs that in turn influence business practices and consumer behavior. The summit should also produce detailed recommendations for federal action as well as actions by businesses and consumers. These recommendations could serve as the basis for a national environmental action plan.

INTERNATIONAL ENVIRONMENTAL PLANNING NEEDS

"We have to stabilize the population of this planet. Quite simply, there is a limit to the pressures our global environment can stand."

KOFI ANNAN, UNITED NATIONS
SECRETARY GENERAL (HART 1999, B3)

Human population growth, economic growth, new technologies, and use of natural resources have produced enormous global environmental changes. The United States is part of a global ecosystem and a global economy. Americans make up about 5% of the earth's population and account for about 25% of the natural resources consumed worldwide each year. Other countries look to America for political and economic leadership. America must assume a leadership role to address the international challenges of global warming, depletion of agricultural soils and timber resources, the increasing demands on water supplies and nonrenewable resources, and the loss of wildlife species and biodiversity.

In 1992, nearly all of the world's nations met in Rio de Janeiro at the United Nations Conference on Environment and Development. Better known as the Earth Summit, this meeting produced a monumental agreement to work toward ecologically sustainable development for the good of the planet. However, 10 years later, the United States still did not have a national strategy for achieving sustainable development or any clear benchmarks for assessing progress toward these goals (Dernbach 2002). In fact, America's environmental quality appears to have declined slightly since the Earth Summit (*ibid.*, p. 3). In areas such as land preservation and protection of drinking water supplies, states, local governments, and nonprofit organizations have taken the lead in protecting the environment. The federal government must assert a leadership role to reshape the nation's economy and lifestyles toward achieving a sustainable environment both for the long-term benefit of Americans and other global residents. At the same time, America must work with other nations toward ensuring a sustainable global environment. America's foreign aid should be targeted toward international improvements in drinking water supplies, sewage treatment and sanitation, pollution abatement, alternative energy sources, family planning, and adequate housing. If international environmental planning fails, the following situations could easily happen:

- The next Middle East war could be fought over water supplies rather than religious beliefs.
- Increased illegal immigration to the United States could occur because people want to escape the squalor caused by overpopulation in developing countries.
- Global warming could result in severe droughts in major farming areas, bring more devastating storms to coastal communities, force species migration, and melt enough of the polar icecaps to raise ocean levels and flood coastal cities.
- The collapse of important fisheries and the accelerated extinction of rare and endangered plant and animal species could occur.

The stakes are high. If industrial development and population continue unabated, these environmental problems could affect life on earth for generations to come. Vigorous international environmental planning and cooperation are ultimately essential to sustaining life on earth.

NEED 1
A Global Population Stabilization Policy

In the 30 years from 1972 to 2002, the earth's population grew by 2.2 billion people to more than 6 billion (United Nations Environmental Program (UNEP) 2002). Each day, the earth adds a net of more than 200,000 people. This adds up to an annual increase of nearly 80 million people, more than the combined populations of California, New York, and Texas. Water shortages, poor air and water quality, depletion of agricultural and forestlands, and the loss of wildlife habitats are severe problems in many developing countries. A 2001 study by the United Nations Population Division estimated that the world's population would reach 9.3 billion by 2050, with almost nine out of 10 people living in a developing country (Lee 2001, A1). Sustainable economic development and environmental quality will not be possible unless population growth is brought under control. The most expedient route to this goal has been shown to be through education and improved health standards.

NEED 2
Action on Reducing the Emission of Greenhouse Gases

The United States is the leading producer of greenhouse gases that contribute to global warming. Worldwide levels of carbon dioxide—the leading greenhouse gas—have risen by roughly 25% over the last 100 years (Easterbrook 1996, 22). The decade of the 1990s was the warmest in America since temperatures were first regularly recorded in the 1880s. Severe droughts have been occurring in some parts of the world, along with more violent storms. The discovery of open water at the North Pole during the summer of 2000 raised awareness that global warming is real. The polar icecaps are shrinking. If oceans rise, major coastal cities could be flooded. Although nearly every nation except the United States signed the Kyoto Accord of 1997 to reduce the emission of greenhouse gases, actual progress has been slow. Reducing carbon dioxide levels in the atmosphere will take centuries because carbon dioxide is only gradually absorbed by the oceans, trees, and plants (McNeil 2000, 115).

One of the fundamental ways to combat greenhouse gases is the development of energy sources other than fossil fuels. Yet, many developing nations are relying heavily on fossil fuels to drive their growing economies. China, for instance, has 1.5 billion people, a growing economy, and large coal reserves. If China uses coal to generate electricity, if more Chinese buy gasoline-powered cars, and if more forests are cut for fuel and timber, China's contribution to greenhouse gases will greatly increase.

Better farming methods that employ no-till planting can help reduce the release of carbon into the atmosphere. The conservation of forestlands reduces carbon dioxide in the air by absorbing it. According to recent estimates, Latin America has lost almost one-third of its forests, Africa about half, and Indonesia about one-third (*ibid.*, 236). Developing and developed nations should implement tradable carbon sequestration credits for planting trees and retaining existing trees.

NEED 3
Protection of Rare and Endangered Species

Rare and endangered plant and animal species are disappearing at a rate faster than at any time since the extinction of the dinosaurs 65 million years ago. A 2002 United Nations report estimated that about one-quarter of all mammals and 12% of the earth's birds are threatened (UNEP 2002). Wildlife habitats are being destroyed by human population growth and development, slash-and-burn agriculture, and the logging off of more than 30 million acres of tropical forests each year (McNeil 2000, 185). In addition, international travel and trade is increasing the spread of invasive exotic plants, animals, and diseases that threaten native species.

The loss of plant and animal species disrupts the food chain, and can damage the health and functioning of entire ecosystems. Plant and animal species arguably also have an intrinsic right to exist. In addition, they provide humans with beauty, entertainment, education, and commercially beneficial products. The practical uses of many plant species, particularly in tropical rainforests, have only just begun to be explored. There may be many as yet undiscovered plant and animal species useful to human health. Debt-for-nature protection swaps, in which a country's international debts are canceled in return for long-term protection of large land areas, are likely to become more popular to protect sensitive environments and valuable wildlife habitat.

NEED 4
International Fisheries Protection

Several nations without large amounts of arable land have historically depended on the seas for food. At the beginning of the 21st century, about 1 billion people obtained most of their animal protein from fish (*ibid.*, 246). Today's fish-harvesting technology features huge trawlers with nets that stretch up to 30 miles. The "bycatch" of marine species that are killed in fishing and tossed back into the sea has been estimated at 20 million tons a year (Hawken *et al.* 1999, 149). As a result, the world's fisheries are in danger of collapse in many places. The Food and Agriculture Organization of the United Nations has estimated that 11 of the world's 15 primary fishing grounds and 70% of major food fish species are overexploited (French 2000, 187). Coastal areas and coral reefs are especially important breeding and feeding grounds for fish. According to the International Coral Reef Information Network, more than one-quarter of

the world's coral reefs have been destroyed and a total of 60% could be lost over the next 30 years (International Coral Reef Information Network 2002). Coastal development, pollution, the use of dynamite, and global warming pose serious threats to coral reefs.

International monitoring of fisheries and international agreements must be forged to protect endangered fisheries and allow them to recover. The more than 100 "no take" reserves worldwide are showing positive results in rejuvenating the number, size, and species of fish as well as increasing fish stock in nearby fishing grounds (*The Economist* 2001, 83).

NEED 5
Sustainable Urban Environments

Sometime within the first two decades of the 21st century, urban dwellers will account for more than half of the world's population. Especially in developing nations, people are flocking from the countryside to the cities as the working landscape becomes more mechanized and the better paying jobs are found in urban areas. Access to clean drinking water, decent housing, sewage treatment, efficient transit, good quality air, greenspaces for recreation, and solid waste disposal are fundamental needs for sustainable cities. To achieve improvements in all of these areas, governments around the world will have to devote more money to environmental protection, not just in the cities themselves but in the surrounding areas. These outlying areas provide much of the natural resources for cities as well as absorb substantial amounts of urban waste. More careful planning will be needed along with political will and grants from wealthier nations to poorer nations.

A FINAL NOTE ON SUSTAINABLE ENVIRONMENTAL PLANNING

Sustainable environments depend on continuous efforts to improve and maintain environmental quality. These efforts include reducing pollution and waste, repairing environmental damage, conserving natural and working landscapes, and creating and fostering livable built environments. Environmental progress will require cooperation between business and government; careful planning at the local and regional levels; enforceable environmental quality and land-protection standards; the active participation of nonprofit groups; and financial support from federal, state, and local governments. In addition, individual choices and lifestyles that reduce consumption and waste will be necessary.

Those distrustful or openly opposed to government planning as social engineering should recognize that the issue is not whether there will be any planning, but what kind of planning will prevail. Laissez-faire was the dominant form of social engineering in the 19th century, and produced the dark, Satanic mills of the industrial revolution; widespread air and water pollution; and rapacious exploitation of agricultural, timber, and mineral resources. No one seriously suggests that we return to those days.

The federal government can play a pivotal role in creating and enforcing general environmental standards to protect public health and safety, arbitrating environmental disputes between regions, spending money to encourage smart growth, and offering financial incentives for more environmentally friendly business and consumer practices. Accurate pricing of natural resources and imposing pollution and development costs on those who create them are paramount for the market to produce socially desirable outcomes. State governments can play a key role in more effectively administering many federal environmental programs as well as setting regulations, tax incentives, and government spending programs to shape local and regional sustainable development.

Sustainable communities and regions will be those that can manage both current planning and long-range planning to balance economic growth, environmental protection, and social harmony. This is a fragile balance, and the emphasis must be on environmental quality if sustainability is to be achieved in the long run. The balance requires cooperation among five main interests:

1. landowners;
2. the development community;
3. lending institutions;
4. elected officials; and
5. the general public.

Landowners must be committed to the stewardship of their land and its productive and environmentally sound use. Developers must be committed to building well-designed projects in the right locations, according to adopted planning standards. Lending institutions must finance well-designed and properly located commercial and residential developments, especially developments that have a mix of uses. Elected officials must have the political will to support the comprehensive planning process, implement ordinances, and make strategic investments in both traditional infrastructure and "green" infrastructure. Finally, the public must participate in the planning process and be committed to electing officials who support sustainable growth and environmental protection. This scenario of balance, cooperation, and commitment demands constant planning, evaluation, and revision. The future of America's communities and regions, and the people who live there today and in the future, depends upon making planning work.

**Sample Environmental Impact Assessment Report
within the Local Subdivision and Land Development Regulations**

Section 1.1 Environmental Impact Assessment Report

A. In order for a more effective evaluation of subdivision and land development proposals, the applicant shall be required to disclose the environmental consequences of such proposals through the submission of an Environmental Impact Assessment (EIA) report.

  (1) An EIA report shall be submitted with the Preliminary Plan for:

   (a) any proposed land development or subdivision of land which consists of ten (10) or more dwelling units;

   (b) any nonresidential land development in excess of one (1) acre of land that is disturbed, including land that is cleared, paved, improved or otherwise substantially changed from its natural state;

   (c) any proposed subdivision or land development, or any portion thereof, located in the Conservation Zoning District or Steep Slope Zoning District as set forth in the (Municipal or County) Zoning Ordinance; and

   (d) any proposed subdivision or land development, or any portion thereof, containing areas designated as floodplain or flood prone as set forth in the (Municipal or County) Zoning Ordinance.

  (2) An EIA report shall accompany and form a part of the Final Plan for any of the above proposed subdivisions or land development plans.

B. The study shall be prepared by a qualified consultant who shall be mutually agreed upon by the developer and the (Municipality or County). The consultant shall have sufficient documented prior environmental study experience to perform the study and render opinions and recommendations. The cost to prepare the study will be borne entirely by the developer.

C. Five (5) copies of the EIA report shall be submitted in accordance with the format and content specified below. The EIA report shall contain text, tables, maps and analyses, which document the probable impacts resulting from the proposed subdivision or land development plan. Within the EIA report, specific emphasis shall be directed toward the effects of the proposed project on and relationship to the applicable site, neighborhood, and municipal- or county-wide resources, conditions, or characteristics. At a minimum, the EIA report shall include the following:

  (1) A map identifying the site location and area. The map shall be drawn at a scale of not more than 200 feet to the inch. The location map shall depict all streets and roads, adjoining properties, zoning district boundaries and municipal boundaries within two thousand (2000) feet of any part of the tract. In the case of a development of a section of the entire tract, the location map shall show the relationship of the section to the entire tract.

  (2) An identification of the site character and appearance through the presentation of black-and-white photographs or copies thereof. Such photographs shall show the appearance of the site from the ground. Photographs shall be properly identified and shall be keyed to a map of the site.

  (3) A site development plan, including notes describing the number and type of lots or units, the square footage or acreage of the tract, and a depiction of the features proposed, such as streets, driveways, parking

areas, buildings and other structures, and all impervious surfaces. The plan shall be drawn at a scale of not more than one hundred (100) feet to the inch and may be submitted as an attachment to the EIA report. The plan shall include all the information required for a Preliminary Plan.

(4) A statement indicating the proposed staging or phasing of the project and a map depicting the boundaries of each stage or phase of the project. Such boundaries shall be superimposed on a version of the site development plan.

(5) An identification of the natural physical resources of the tract, including geology, topography, soils, and hydrology. The identification of physical resources shall include a narrative description of the quality and quantity of each resource. In addition, these resources shall be mapped at a scale of not more than one hundred (100) feet to the inch as specified below.

(6) A map depicting the geological characteristics of the tract, including the location and boundaries of the rock formations and features such as faults and/or fractures.

(7) A map depicting the topographical characteristics of the tract, showing contours with at least two (2)-foot intervals; slopes from 0% to 3%, 3% to 8%, 8% to 15%, 15% to 25%, and greater than 25%.

(8) A map depicting the soil characteristics of the tract, including all soil types and characteristics pertinent to the proposed subdivision or development, such as depth of bedrock, depth of water table, flood hazard potential, and limitations for septic tank filter fields.

(9) A map depicting the hydrological characteristics of the tract, including surface water resources, drainage, watersheds and floodplains, and groundwater resources. Surface water resources include streams, rivers, creeks, runs, ponds, lakes, springs, wetlands, and any man-made impoundments. Groundwater resources include aquifers and aquifer recharge areas.

(10) An identification of the biological resources of the tract, including vegetation and wildlife. These resources shall be described in a narrative and depicted on the following maps at a scale of not more than one hundred (100) feet to the inch. A map of the vegetation characteristics of the tract, including the locations and boundaries of wooded areas and the vegetation species types and sizes. In addition, all trees 12 inches in caliper or greater shall be accurately located on the map either as free-standing trees or tree masses.

(11) An identification of the land use conditions and characteristics associated with the tract, such as current and past use, land cover, and encumbrances; and the relationship of these to adjacent tracts. In addition to a narrative description of land use conditions and characteristics, the following maps shall be drawn at a scale of not more than one hundred (100) feet to the inch. A map shall depict the land cover characteristics of the tract, including paved or other impervious surfaces, wooded areas, cultivated areas, pastures, old fields, lawns, and landscaped areas.

(12) An identification of the historic resources associated with the tract, such as areas, structures and/or routes and trails that are significant, especially those included on the National Register of Historic Places, the State Inventory of Historic Places, the Historic American Building Survey, and the comprehensive plan.

(13) An identification of the visual resources associated with the tract, such as areas that have a particular amenity value and areas that offer interesting views. In addition to a narrative description of the visual resources, a map shall be drawn at a scale

of not more than one hundred (100) feet to the inch depicting the visual resources.

(14) An identification of characteristics and conditions associated with existing, construction- related, and future air and water quality, noise levels, vibration, toxic materials, electrical interference, odor, glare and heat, fire and explosion, smoke, dust, fumes, vapors and gases, and radioactive materials.

(15) The implications of the proposed subdivision and land development in terms of the type of beneficial or adverse effects that may result from it, and the short- or long-term duration of these effects.

(16) Alternatives to the proposed subdivision or land development. The applicant shall submit exhibits or diagrams depicting the types of alternatives described in narrative form. The applicant shall comment on how alternatives would avoid or reduce potential adverse impacts or produce beneficial effects. These alternatives shall include revised location, redesign, layout, or siting of buildings and roads; alternate methods for sewage disposal and water supply; and reduction in the size of proposed structures or number of structures.

(17) Probable adverse impacts that cannot be avoided.

(18) Measures to mitigate adverse effects. The applicant shall submit exhibits or diagrams depicting the type of remedial, protective, and mitigative measures described in a narrative. These mitigation measures pertain to existing procedures and standards currently required by the state, county, or municipality for actions such as sedimentation and erosion control, stormwater runoff control, wetlands, water quality control, and air quality control. Mitigation measures that pertain to impacts may be unique to a subdivision or land development, such as revegetation, screening, fencing, emissions control, traffic control, noise control, relocation of people or businesses, and land acquisition.

(19) Any irreversible environmental changes that would occur from the proposed subdivision or land development should it be implemented. The use of nonrenewable resources during the initial and continued phases of the subdivision or land development shall be discussed. The quantity of loss of environmental resources and the qualitative effects shall be indicated.

(20) In making their evaluation, the Planning Commission or Elected Officials may request any additional information they deem necessary to adequately assess potential environmental impacts.

Glossary

Acid deposition: Rain, snow, or fog that has a high content of nitric acid from nitrogen oxides or sulfuric acid from sulfur dioxide. Can destroy trees, kill fish in lakes, and erode buildings. Acid rain is a popular term for acid deposition.

Acid mine drainage: Runoff and seepage from mines that enter surface and groundwater. Occurs in places where rock and soil contain high levels of iron sulfides (pyrites) that break down into water-soluble sulfuric acid. This acid contaminates drinking wells, kills fish in streams, and pollutes soils so that vegetative growth is stunted.

Acid rain: A popular term for acid deposition.

Action Strategy: A set of land use controls, infrastructure spending, tax programs, and other regulations and incentives that will put the comprehensive plan and Environmental Action Plan into practice.

Adequate Public Facilities Ordinance: A local government law that requires public facilities (sewer, water, roads, schools, etc.) to be in place before development is allowed to occur (see *Concurrency*).

Aesthetics: The appearance of buildings and landscapes; beauty.

Aggregate resources: Crushed stone, gravel, and sand used to make roads, bricks, concrete, glass, lime for soil treatments, and many other products.

Agricultural district: A joint state and local program that offers farmers certain protections without using land use restrictions such as zoning. Farmers voluntarily enroll a certain minimum amount of land, and receive benefits that may include preferential property tax assessment, exemption from local nuisance laws that would restrict normal farming practices, and greater protection from eminent domain actions by governments, among others.

Airshed: A local or regional air supply.

Air quality: The level of pollutants in the air in a community or region (see *Clean Air Act; National Ambient Air Quality Standards*).

Appropriation doctrine: A water law principle that applies in the drier western states to allocate water use. The guiding principle is "first in time, first in right." Whoever files a claim first gets first rights to use the water. However, if a water user ceases to draw water or reduces the amount used, the user may lose future rights to the water.

Aquifer: An underground body of water that is large enough for drinking water supplies, irrigation, etc.

Army Corps of Engineers: A federal agency that has built more than 250 dams for flood control, water transport, and hydroelectricity, and is responsible for administering (with the U.S. Environmental Protection Agency) the wetlands permit program under Section 404 of the Clean Water Act.

Biodiversity: The variety of plant and animal species within an ecosystem or geographic area.

Biological oxygen demand or biochemical oxygen demand (BOD): A measure of the amount of oxygen needed by bacteria and other microorganisms to break down organic material in a body of water, at a certain temperature, and over a certain period of time. The more organic matter in the water, the higher the BOD.

Bioregion: A distinct collection of plant and animal ecosystems in a geographic area that functions in certain ways and has particular needs for survival. Temperature and precipitation primarily determine most bioregions, with elevation, soils, watersheds, and microclimates as contributing factors.

Brownfields: Contaminated former industrial sites that have the potential for reuse after remediation. The level of clean-up required and cost involved varies from site to site.

Build-out analysis or scenario: The estimation of the amount, location, and type of development that could occur if an area were fully developed according to the existing zoning ordinance.

Built environment: Consists of cities, suburbs, villages, buildings, and infrastructure (sewer and water, pipelines, and transportation networks).

Built Environment Inventory: An inventory of the location, number, age, and condition of the housing stock, commercial and industrial buildings, and public buildings. The inventory should also include the location and condition of the public infrastructure.

Bureau of Land Management (BLM): A federal agency that manages more than 260 million acres of federal land in the western states and Alaska.

Bureau of Reclamation: A federal agency created in 1902 to develop water projects in 17 western states and Hawaii. The bureau built the enormous Hoover Dam on the Colorado River, a series of major dams on the Columbia River, and the Central Valley Project in California.

California Coastal Commission (CCC): A state agency that regulates development along California's 1,100 miles of Pacific coast, promotes public access to the coast, and protects sensitive coastal and marine resources.

Cap and trade: A market mechanism in which the federal government sets a national limit on pollution emissions and allocates pollution allowances among polluters. Polluters who exceed their annual allowance must buy "pollution credits" from polluters who emit less than their allowance. Polluters have an incentive to reduce emissions both to save money and to earn it through trading credits.

Capital improvements program (CIP): A schedule of what public infrastructure the community will build or repair, where and when, and how the infrastructure will be paid for.

Carbon cycle: Involves the process of photosynthesis, in which energy from the sun converts carbon and water in plants into sugar molecules, which plants absorb as food. Plants take in carbon dioxide and emit oxygen, and release carbon into the atmosphere, soil, and water when they die, decay, or are burned.

Carbon sequestration: The storing of carbon in trees and fields. Usually refers to paying landowners not to cut timber or plow fields.

Carrying capacity: The physical ability of natural resources to support a given population and level of development before serious negative impacts on the natural environment occur.

Clean Air Act (1972): Allows the Environmental Protection Agency to set national emission and ambient air quality standards. The 1990 Amendments instituted pollution credits trading and linked transportation planning with air quality planning.

Clean Water Act (1970): Created America's primary legislation for surface water quality standards, protection, and pollution clean-up.

Cluster development: A form of development that involves the concentration of development on part of a tract of land and the retention of a certain amount of open space.

Coastal zone: The zone, defined under the 1972 Coastal Zone Management Act, extending 3 miles into the water from the mean high water mark, is the same for all states. Each state sets the inland extent of the coastal zone.

Coastal Zone Management Act (CZMA) (1972): Provided federal funds to coastal states to undertake voluntary planning to protect coastal resources.

Combined sewer overflow: A common problem in cities with sewer systems that do not have separate sanitary and storm sewers. Heavy rainfall can cause sewer systems to overflow, releasing raw sewage into waterways and posing health threats.

Common property resource: A natural resource, such as a fisheries, that does not have a clear distribution of property rights (who owns the fish in the ocean?). The resource tends to be overexploited (tragedy of the commons), because each person has an incentive to harvest as much (fish) as possible.

Comprehensive Environmental Response, Compensation, and Liability Act (CERCLA) (1980): Created the Superfund for cleaning up major hazardous waste sites and imposed liability on polluters to pay for the clean-up.

Comprehensive plan: A community's blueprint for future growth, identifying where development should and should not occur, and the level of services that will be needed to support development. Legal basis for the zoning and subdivision regulations.

Concurrency: A policy that calls for infrastructure to be in place before private construction can begin.

Confined animal feeding operation (CAFO): A farm livestock operation (cattle, hogs, poultry) that has 1,000 or more animal units, with a unit equal to 1,000 pounds. These large complexes can produce huge amounts of manure.

Conservation easement: A restriction on the use of land that is voluntarily sold or donated by a landowner to a private land trust or a government agency (see *Development rights*).

Constructed wetlands: Human-made wetlands for wastewater treatment or for providing the many functions of natural wetlands.

Contingent valuation: A survey method that asks taxpayers how much they would be willing to pay for an environmental benefit, such as a park, for which there is no private market. Economists try to estimate the "public" price taxpayers would be willing to pay.

Cornucopians: People who believe that the earth has an abundance of resources and that market forces will result in the efficient allocation and use of those resources.

Corporate Average Fuel Economy (CAFE) standards: Federal motor vehicle fuel efficiency standards; in 2002, they were 27.5 miles per gallon for cars and 20.5 miles per gallon for trucks, minivans, and sport utility vehicles.

Cost-benefit analysis: The use of discounted cash flow analysis to estimate the financial costs and benefits of a proposed large development project or government program. A guide to decision making, which does not provide conclusive evidence of all costs or benefits because it is often difficult to put a dollar value on nonmarket environmental costs and benefits.

Critical areas: Natural areas of statewide concern, such as wildlife habitats, wetlands, and coastal areas.

Critical mass: The minimum amount, usually of land, needed to support and sustain certain activities, such as wildlife habitat and farming.

Cumulative impact: The total effects of several developments over time on environmental quality, traffic, aesthetics, etc.

Current Trends Analysis: An evaluation of the environmental strengths, weaknesses, opportunities, and threats to the community or region as identified in the Natural Resources Inventory and the Built Environment Inventory.

Deep ecology: The belief that nature is sacred above and beyond human needs and that the sustainability of the natural environment is paramount. Humans present threats to that sustainability and must learn to make their needs subservient to the needs of nature.

Density: The number of dwelling units or amount of commercial or industrial development on a parcel of land, usually per acre.

Design review: A process to guide the appearance of proposed new development, conducted by a planning commission or a design review board.

Development of regional impact (DRI): A large residential, commercial, industrial, or institutional development project that can affect the environment, development patterns, capital facilities, and traffic in more than one municipality or county.

Development rights: A landowner's right to develop his or her property. This right may be voluntarily sold or donated to a governmental agency or a private land trust (see *Conservation easement*).

Ecology: The science of how plants, animals, air, water, soil, and climate interact in a specific environment (e.g., forest ecology, coastal ecology, and prairie ecology).

Ecosystem: The diversity of plant and animal species in a geographic area and how they interact.

Ecotone: Where two ecosystems overlap in an area of transition from one biological community to another.

Edge effects: The impacts on one ecosystem from being in close contact with another ecosystem; usually the impact on natural areas from close proximity to built environments.

Endangered Species Act (ESA) (1973): Administered by the U.S. Fish and Wildlife Service to identify and protect rare plant and animal species threatened with extinction.

Environment: Natural places and processes, working landscapes, and human settlements; one's immediate surroundings.

Environmental Action Plan: A plan that may stand alone or be incorporated into the traditional comprehensive plan, and that includes an inventory, an analysis, goals and objectives, and an Action Strategy to maintain and improve a community or region's environment.

Environmental economics: The study of how scarce natural resources are allocated among competing uses, and how human production and consumption choices affect the environment.

Environmental impact assessment (EIA): A study of the potential effects a proposed development or government program would have on the environment.

Environmental impact statement (EIS): A development review document required of federal projects under the National Environmental Policy Act to assess potential environmental impacts.

Environmental justice: The right of all people to enjoy a safe, clean, and healthy environment. The practice of fairness across income, ethnic, and racial groups in the siting of large, unwanted land uses, such as power plants and landfills.

Environmental mediation: The attempt to resolve disputes about the environment through third-party negotiation rather than through lawsuits, government regulation, or legislation.

Environmental Needs Assessment Survey: A survey of community residents on environmental conditions and needed improvements.

Environmental planning: A technical, political, and legal process in which a community or region makes choices through a comprehensive plan, growth management regulations, and financial incentives to protect and improve the condition of the natural environment, working landscape, and the built environment.

[U.S.] Environmental Protection Agency (EPA): A federal agency created in 1970 to administer a variety of environmental laws, such as the Clean Air Act and Clean Water Act, and to conduct scientific research.

Environmental quality: The condition of the natural environment (especially air, water, and land quality), the health of the working landscape, and the aesthetics and functioning of the built environment.

Estuary: Where salt water and fresh water meet, including salt marshes and tidal wetlands. Estuaries provide the main spawning grounds for most commercial varieties of fish and shellfish.

Eutrophication: The aging process of a body of water. Occurs when excessive phosphorous and nitrogen are released into a body of water. These nutrients cause algae blooms, which use up oxygen in the water and block sunlight to underwater vegetation needed for fish and other aquatic life.

Fair share: The amount of low-income housing, elderly housing, or other type of development that a community must by law or practice accept and accommodate; often referred to as "regional fair share."

Farmland preservation: The purchase of development rights or a conservation easement from a farmer so that the land can be used only for farming purposes or as open space.

Federal Emergency Management Agency (FEMA): A federal agency responsible for reducing threats to property and life from natural hazards and for managing federal responses to disasters and emergencies.

Federal Insecticide, Fungicide, and Rodenticide Act (FIFRA) (1972): Requires manufacturers of certain chemicals to register them with the Environmental Protection Agency before they are distributed. The chemicals must also be labeled, stored, handled, and applied according to certain standards.

Fiscal impact study: An estimate of the likely net public costs to a community associated with a proposed private development project or the ultimate build-out of the community. The study typically looks at the demands for new infrastructure compared to the property taxes and sales taxes that the proposed development or build-out would generate.

Floodplain: Land that is subject to periodic flooding, made up of the floodway and flood fringe, as identified by the Federal Emergency Management Agency. Typically identified by the extent of the largest flood likely to occur in a 100-year period.

Forest Legacy Program: A 1990 act giving the U.S. Forest Service the authority and funding to purchase permanent conservation easements on forestlands, purchase forestlands, or make grants to states to purchase easements and forestlands.

Fragmentation: The division of land into parcels too small to support extensive farming or forestry, or to serve effectively as wildlife habitat.

Gap analysis: A regional assessment of the conservation status of native plant and vertebrate species; features the documenting of gaps in biodiversity in vertebrates and vegetative land cover types.

Geographic Information System (GIS): A computerized method of storing and analyzing information, which is processed in layers and often displayed as maps.

Global warming: An increase in the temperature of the earth's atmosphere, caused mainly by increasing levels of carbon dioxide from the burning of fossil fuels.

Green accounting: Including changes in environmental quality in measures of human or community well-being.

Green infrastructure: The natural areas (woods, wetlands, floodplains, and open space), farm and timberlands, and parks in a community or region.

Greenfields: Open space on which there is no development, including working landscapes and the natural environment.

Greenfields development: New commercial, residential, or industrial projects on open land that has never been built on before.

Greenhouse gases: The leading greenhouse gases are carbon dioxide and methane, which build up in the earth's atmosphere like hot air within a greenhouse and add to global warming. Most carbon dioxide is created through the burning of fossil fuels. Methane is a natural gas.

Greenways: Linear open space that may serve a variety of environmental and recreational functions along rivers, lakes, and roads. Can also provide wildlife habitat and include walking, hiking, and biking trails.

Habitat conservation plan (HCP): A negotiated plan under the Endangered Species Act in which the federal government, landowners, and other participants determine where habitats for rare and endangered species will be protected and where land will be made available for development.

Hazard mitigation: Actions and techniques to minimize potential damage to existing buildings and injury to humans from floods and other natural disasters.

Hazardous waste: Chemical, biological, or radioactive residuals that pose serious threats to human health.

Haz-mat (short for "hazardous materials"): The federal procedures under the Emergency Planning and Community Right-to-Know Act of 1986 for planning and implementing the containment of hazardous waste spills as well as action plans to remediate areas in which hazardous releases occur.

Historic preservation: The redevelopment, rehabilitation, or designation of architecturally or historically important buildings over 50 years old.

Hydrologic cycle: Also known as the water cycle, this is the movement of water from the atmosphere through precipitation to the land's surface, where it either runs off into streams and the ocean, recharges underground aquifers, evaporates, or is taken up by plants and released back into the atmosphere by evapotranspiration.

Impaired waterway: A body of water that does not meet federal water quality standards for drinkable or swimmable water.

Impervious surface: A material through which water cannot pass, such as asphalt, brick, stone, or concrete in streets, buildings, parking lots, and sidewalks.

Inclusionary zoning ordinance: A local law that requires developers to provide a certain percentage of new units for affordable housing for low- and moderate-income people.

Industrial forest: Forests in large, contiguous blocks that are owned and managed by timber companies with access to lumber and paper mills.

Infrastructure: The support networks of the built environment, such as sewer and water facilities, roads and streets, schools, and parks.

Intergenerational equity: Fairness in the use and consumption of natural resources across generations (see *Sustainable development*).

Intermodal Surface Transportation Efficiency Act (ISTEA) (1991): Established regional transportation planning through Metropolitan Planning Organizations. Provided $155 billion in transportation funding.

Intermodal transportation: The linking of different transportation networks (e.g., buses and light rail, bicycles and buses, airports and light rail, boats and buses, or cars and trains) so that people and goods move more smoothly.

Land and Water Conservation Fund: Established by Congress in 1965, the fund uses royalties from offshore oil and gas leases in the continental shelf to add land to the national parks, national forests, and the National Wildlife Refuge System as well as state and local conservation projects.

Land and Water Suitability Analysis: An evaluation of the capacity and constraints of different soils and water supplies to support different types of development. Suitability is usually depicted on a set of maps.

Land Evaluation and Site Assessment (LESA) system: A numerical method to rate the suitability of land for farming based on the productivity of the land and the surrounding economic, social, and geographic features that measure development pressures and indicate farm viability.

Landfill: A solid waste disposal site where waste is buried.

Land trust: A private, nonprofit land conservation organization that has received a 501c(3) designation from the Internal Revenue Service and may accept donations of land, cash, and conservation easements, and may purchase conservation easements and land.

Land use: The type of activity occurring on a parcel of land. Land uses include residential, commercial, industrial, institutional, public, agriculture, conservation, forestry, and mineral extraction.

Landscape ecology: The study of how multiple ecosystems fit together into a mosaic of a regional landscape.

Layers approach: A method of evaluating the development potential of a site or a region, pioneered by planner Ian McHarg. Layers of information include geology, soils, water, vegetation, and wildlife habitat, among others. Ideal for use in Geographic Information Systems.

Level of service study: A measure of the time a vehicle must wait to move through an intersection or travel along a road.

Locally Unwanted Land Use (LULU): A large, unwanted land use to which area residents are opposed.

Market failure: A situation that occurs when market prices and public values differ, resulting in the inefficient allocation and use of resources.

Mass transit: Transportation systems that can move large numbers of people, such as light rail, bus, subway, and ferries.

Master planned community: A mixed-use, planned-unit development proposal with hundreds or thousands of housing units and commercial space that is built in phases over several years.

McMansion: A new house of 3,000 or more square feet in the outer suburbs set on anywhere from 1 to 10 acres of land.

Metropolitan area: A county with a central city of at least 50,000 and adjacent counties that are economically tied into a region.

Metropolitan Planning Organization (MPO): A public body required under the Intermodal Surface Transportation Efficiency Act for drafting regional transportation plans.

Mining Law (1872): Applies to hard-rock minerals such as copper, gold, molybdenum, or silver. Allows individuals and companies to buy mining claims on federal land for $2.50 to $5 an acre without any obligation to pay royalties to the government for the minerals extracted.

Mitigation bank: A process set up by a government agency; a land trust; or other private, nonprofit organization to preserve land or wetlands through the sale of mitigation credits to developers.

Mixed-use development: The blending or allowing of two or more land uses in a single development or zone, such as residential and commercial uses.

Moratorium: A temporary local government ban on new (usually residential) construction that may be enacted when rapid development and population growth have outpaced either the community's ability to provide the necessary public services or the community's planning and zoning.

Multiple use-sustained yield: The guiding principles that the U.S. Forest Service is supposed to follow in managing the 155 national forests. Includes timber harvesting, watershed management, recreation, grazing, wildlife habitat, and wilderness areas. Sustained yield means maintaining long-term productivity levels.

National Ambient Air Quality Standards (NAAQS): Federal air quality standards created under the Clean Air Act.

National Environmental Policy Act (NEPA) (1970): Federal act that created a process to screen all proposed federal projects, funding, permits, and actions for potential environmental effects. May require an environmental impact statement.

National Flood Insurance Program (NFIP): Federal flood insurance available to home and business owners in communities that have adopted and enforced a floodplain management ordinance to reduce risks to new construction in Special Flood Hazard Areas.

National Oceanic and Atmospheric Administration (NOAA): Federal agency that manages the Coastal Zone Management Act, the Marine Protection Act, and the Estuarine Research Reserve System.

National Park Service: Federal agency created in 1916 to manage the national park system, national monuments, and national recreation areas.

National Pollutant Discharge Elimination System (NPDES): Created under the Clean Water Act. Requires operators of point water pollution sources to obtain a permit from the U.S. Environmental Protection Agency regarding acceptable pollution discharge levels.

National Register of Historic Places: A list of historic places that have been approved by the U.S. Department of the Interior and are eligible for special rehabilitation tax credits.

Natural environment: Consists of wildlife habitats, wetlands, undeveloped coastal and riparian areas, floodplains, and wilderness.

Natural hazards: Naturally occurring threats to property and life, such as floods, earthquakes, wildfires, hurricanes, and landslides.

Natural Resources Inventory: A factual database of a community's air, water, soils, geologic formations, farmlands, forestlands, minerals, wetlands, and plant and animal species and habitats.

Natural Resources Conservation Service (NRCS): A federal agency within the U.S. Department of Agriculture that is responsible for soil conservation and farmland preservation programs.

New Urbanism: A set of neotraditional design and development principles featuring human scale, walkability, mass transit, greenspace, attractive buildings, and neighborhoods.

Netting out: Subtracting unbuildable land in determining the number of lots that can be created or units built on a parcel.

NIMBY (Not In My Back Yard): A person who is opposed to proposed new development near where he or she lives.

Nonindustrial forest: Private forestlands, usually in parcels of less than 50 acres, owned by rural residents, people with second homes, farmers, and others. Some nonindustrial forests are occasionally logged or cut for firewood, but most are not managed for timber production.

Nonpoint source pollution: A source of water pollution that is not fixed in location, but is dispersed, such as stormwater runoff from a farm field or city street.

Nonrenewable resource: A natural resource that cannot be regenerated within a time horizon that is useful to humans (e.g., oil, minerals, old-growth forests, and water trapped in deep aquifers).

Nuisance ordinance: A local law enacted to prohibit certain activities, such as loud noise and junkyards, that reduce the value of neighboring property or the neighbor's enjoyment of it.

Offset: A way to maintain or improve air or water quality by reducing a specific source of pollution to allow the development of a project that would generate the same or less pollution.

Off-site mitigation: The replacement or protection of a resource in one place, while allowing development (destruction) in another place, such as for wetlands.

Old-growth forest: A climax ecosystem featuring mature trees that grew naturally on forestland that has never been harvested.

On-site septic system ordinance: A local law used to regulate the siting, maintenance, and clean-out of on-site septic systems to help ensure that they function properly and do not pollute groundwater.

Overlay zone: Used to protect sensitive resources, such as floodplains and areas with steep slopes. Applied on top of a base zone. Imposes a second set of development review standards.

Ozone: A poisonous form of oxygen created by nitrogen oxide and volatile organic compounds that reacts with sunlight to produce photochemical smog. In the lower atmosphere, ozone is a form of air pollution. In the upper atmosphere, ozone blocks ultraviolet rays that can cause a variety of cancers.

Particulates: Pollution from microscopic dust, soot, smoke, and exhaust that combines with water droplets in the air. The primary cause of haze and air pollution; can cause nose and throat irritation, respiratory ailments, and premature death.

Planned-unit development (PUD): A large development that often combines residential, commercial, and even institutional uses.

Point source pollution: A source of water pollution that is fixed in location, such as a pipe from a factory that discharges into a waterway.

Preferential assessment: Basing the value of real estate for property tax purposes on its current use, rather than its "highest and best" use. Often applied to farm and forestland.

Primary water treatment: The removal of solids and some nutrients from water for drinking purposes; no longer considered adequate under the Clean Water Act.

Prime farmland: Land that is the easiest to farm and the most productive for a given level of inputs. Usually rated Class I or II.

Proactive planning: Comprehensive plans and land use ordinances that anticipate change and shape it by identifying where different kinds of development should or should not be located. The opposite of *reactive planning*.

Public good: A publicly owned resource, such as a park, from which no one can be excluded.

Public trust doctrine: A legal principle in which the private use of resources must take into consideration public entitlement to the benefit of natural systems. Often applied in water and public land access situations.

Public water system: A public utility that is responsible for providing an adequate supply of potable water to meet present and projected future needs in the communities it serves. These public utilities are regulated by the U.S. Environmental Protection Agency as well as the states.

Purchase of development rights (PDR): A voluntary transaction in which a landowner receives a cash payment in return for signing a contract, called a deed of easement, that restricts the use of the land to farming or open space (see *Conservation easement*).

Quality of life: A general description of how much people enjoy living in a community or region. A high quality of life connotes social, economic, and environmental well-being.

Reactive planning: Local responses to development proposals in the absence of clear standards for what kind of development is desired and where.

Recycling: The transformation of waste into useful materials and products, such as used paper into new paper or the refurbishing of an older building for a new purpose.

Renewable energy: Energy sources (e.g., wind, solar power, biomass, and hydropower) that can be regenerated and that are much less polluting than nuclear power or fossil fuels.

Renewable resource: A natural resource that is able to regenerate, either by itself or with human help, over a short to moderate time horizon (e.g., fish, food crops, and trees).

Regional Transportation Plan (RTP): A 20-year plan drafted by a Metropolitan Planning Organization that must be consistent with both the state transportation improvement plan and state air quality improvement plan.

Resource Conservation and Recovery Act (RCRA) (1976): Empowered the U.S. Environmental Protection Agency to set minimum national standards for states to follow in permitting new, existing, or expansions of public or privately owned and operated municipal solid waste landfills.

Retention pond: A stormwater management technique to reduce runoff by collecting stormwater in a pond and allowing it to evaporate.

Right-to-farm law: A state or local law that says a farmer cannot be found to create a nuisance if following standard farming practices. However, a right-to-farm law does not make farmers exempt from state and federal pollution and safety laws.

Riparian doctrine: Water law principle found in the eastern states that allows a landowner adjacent to a river or stream to withdraw and use the water. Water rights pass with the property to subsequent landowners.

River basin: A geographic area that includes the watershed for a major river.

Rural residential zone: A zoning district in which residential uses on large lots are preferred, such as 3-acre minimum lot sizes.

Safe Drinking Water Act (SDWA) (1974): Set national standards for drinking water supplies. Amended in 1996 to require treatment of all surface water supplies and source water protection.

Secondary water treatment: Advanced chemical and biological treatments used to break down organic matter and remove chemicals such as nitrogen and phosphorus from the water. Required by the Clean Water Act.

Section 404 permits: Section 404 of the Clean Water Act Amendments of 1972 and 1977 established a permit process for the review of projects that would involve the dredging or filling of wetlands. The permit process is administered by the U.S. Army Corps of Engineers and the U.S. Environmental Protection Agency.

Site plan: A map and a description of a parcel proposed for development or subdivision that typically identifies the proposed land use, the location and size of buildings, drainage patterns, roads and streets, planned sewer and water facilities, and neighboring land uses.

Smart growth: A set of planning design principles, regulations, and financial incentives intended to combat sprawl by promoting more compact development and preserving farmlands, forestlands, and natural areas.

Soil survey: A county soil survey complied by the U.S. Natural Resources Conservation Service that describes and maps local soils, their productivity for farming and forestry, and limitations for development, such as wetness and slope.

Solid waste: Trash and garbage that must be disposed of in a landfill or else incinerated, if not recycled.

Sprawl: A haphazard development pattern of dispersed, leap-frog, and strip growth in suburbs and rural areas and along highways.

State Environmental Quality Review Acts (SEPAs): These acts, found in more than 20 states, require state agencies to perform reviews of state projects or approvals that would affect the environment. Modeled to some degree after the National Environmental Policy Act.

State Improvement Plan (SIP): A state air quality improvement plan required under the federal Clean Air Act.

State Pollution Discharge Elimination System (SPDES or Speedies): State-issued permits for operators of point source water pollution, under the Clean Water Act.

Steep slope: Usually land having a slope of 15% or more.

Stewardship: The wise use and management of land and natural resources so that adequate resources are available for future generations (see *Sustainability*).

Stormwater runoff: Rainwater that is not absorbed where it falls, but rather flows off site to streams and other surface water bodies. May carry a variety of pollutants from farm fields, suburban lawns, or urban streets.

Subdivision: The creation of new lots or tracts from a parent parcel of land, usually a residential development in which several lots have been created.

Subdivision and land development ordinance: Regulations that govern the proper creation and layout of lots, necessary roads, sewage disposal, drinking water supplies, and stormwater drainage as well as the retention of open space and vegetation.

Superfund: A federal fund established under the Comprehensive Environmental Response, Compensation, and Liability Act to help pay for the clean-up of highly toxic hazardous waste sites.

Superfund site: A highly toxic hazardous waste site identified by the U.S. Environmental Protection Agency under the Comprehensive Environmental Response, Compensation, and Liability Act as being in need of clean-up.

Sustainability: Durability; a manageable condition over the long run.

Sustainable development: As defined by the Bruntland Report, "development that meets the needs of the present without compromising the ability of future generations to meet their own needs."

Taking: Where a government has physically taken possession of or eliminated all reasonable economic value of a private property without paying "just compensation," according to the 5th Amendment to the U.S. Constitution.

Transportation Equity Act for the 21st Century (TEA-21) (1997): An act that provided more than $200 billion in federal transportation funding.

Tertiary water treatment: Treatment that removes virtually all contaminants. Required under the Clean Water Act in some high-quality watersheds.

Threshold effect: The amount of pollution an ecosystem can absorb before it "crashes" and can no longer support life.

Total Maximum Daily Load (TMDL): Section 303(d) of the Clean Water Act requires states to draft and implement TMDL plans to clean up "impaired" waterways by setting limits on the amount of pollutants that may be discharged into a waterway.

Toxics: Hazardous substances that can cause severe harm or death in relatively small amounts.

Traffic calming: The use of physical devices, such as speed bumps, planters, rumple strips, and barriers, to control speed or reroute traffic off local streets.

Traffic impact study: A study used as the basis for deciding needed traffic improvements, such as traffic lights and turn lanes, and exactions from developers to make traffic improvements as part of the subdivision and land development process.

Transfer of development rights (TDR): A way to preserve open space, farmland, or historic sites by moving development potential from one parcel of land to another. A local government creates a market in TDRs by creating a sending area and a receiving area for development credits. Landowners in the sending area sell credits to developers who want to develop at higher densities in the receiving area.

Transit corridor: An area for development along a bus route or light-rail line.

Transit-oriented development (TOD): Compact, high-density development "nodes" at intervals along rail or bus lines, with transit stations serving as the centers.

Transportation Improvement Plan (TIP): A three-year plan, which is essentially an update of the Regional

Transportation Plan, required under the Intermodal Surface Transportation Efficiency Act.

Turbidity: A measure of the suspended solids in water that affect water clarity.

Urban growth boundary: An area around a city within which there is enough buildable land to accommodate development for the next 20 years and beyond which urban services are not extended.

U.S. Fish and Wildlife Service (FWS): A federal agency responsible for administering the Endangered Species Act and the National Wildlife Refuge system.

U.S. Forest Service (USFS): A federal agency created in 1904 to manage the National Forest System.

U.S. Geological Survey (USGS): A federal agency that conducts studies of biological, geological, and water resources. Known for creating topographic or "quad" maps.

Utilitarians: People who believe that natural resources should be used and wisely managed for the benefit of humans. Utilitarians do not advocate the creation or designation of wilderness areas.

Vehicle miles traveled (VMT): The total number of miles traveled by cars and trucks in a day, week, month, or year in a given geographic area.

Vegetated swales: A stormwater retention technique featuring grassed ditches to absorb stormwater runoff.

Volatile organic compounds (VOCs): Hydrogen compounds that are released from internal combustion engines, factories, paints, solvents, glues, fireplaces, and wood stoves. Include such toxic chemicals as benzene, ethylene, formaldehyde, toluene, methyl chloride, and methyl chloroform. Can cause cancer and a variety of serious ailments.

Water supply plan: A plan developed by a community or county to ensure that existing community water systems within its boundaries are prepared and able to meet anticipated future water demands.

Watershed: The land area that drains into the surface water system of a geographic region, including streams, rivers, lakes, estuaries, and bays.

Wellhead protection: Efforts to keep potentially contaminating land uses and activities away from wells that provide public drinking water.

Wetland: An area of land that has a certain plant community, standing water of 18 inches or more at least one week during the growing season, and hydric soils and a high water table of less than half a foot for at least one week of the growing season. Includes bogs, swamps, ponds, and prairie potholes.

Wild and Scenic Rivers System: Created by Congress in 1968 and managed by the Secretary of the Interior. Designated rivers cover almost 11,000 miles in 36 states and may not be dammed or diverted. Commercial and industrial uses of the riverbanks are prohibited, and any other development must meet federal standards.

Wilderness Act (1964): Allows Congress to designate parts of national forests as wilderness areas, which must be managed for "the preservation of their wilderness character."

Wildlife corridor: An area of land along which wildlife migrate or travel for feeding and to reach spawning and nesting grounds. Corridors are used to link "core" wildlife areas.

Working landscape: Consists of farms, ranchlands, timberlands, and mines.

Zoning: Designation of permitted and conditional land uses, densities, lot size, lot coverage, building setbacks, and height limits of proposed development.

Zoning ordinance: Consists of two parts: a text describing the rules for each zoning district (Residential, R-1 Single Family; R-2 Multifamily; Commercial C-1; Manufacturing M-1, etc.) and a map showing the location and boundaries of the zoning districts.

Contacts

General Land Use Planning

American Planning Association
    122 S. Michigan Avenue, Suite 1600
    Chicago, IL 60603
    (312) 431-9100
    www.planning.org

    A collection of current articles and reports on
    planning issues is available on line and updated
    daily at www.Planetizen.com

CHAPTER 1: TAKING STOCK OF THE LOCAL ENVIRONMENT AND CREATING AN ENVIRONMENTAL ACTION PLAN

Columbus Health Department
    181 Washington Blvd.
    Columbus, OH 43215
    (614) 645-6189
    www.cmhhealth.org

Jacksonville Quality Indicators Project
    c/o Jacksonville Community Council, Inc.
    2434 Atlantic Blvd., Suite 100
    Jacksonville, FL 32207
    (904) 396-3052

Sustainable Seattle
    c/o Kara Palmer, Program Director
    Metrocenter YMCA
    909 Fourth Ave.
    Seattle, WA 98104
    (206) 382-5013, ext. 5072
    e-mail: sustsea@halcyon.com
    www.scn.org/sustainable/susthome.html

Urban Quality Indicators newsletter
    $21.75 first year; $29 a year thereafter
    1756 Plymouth Rd., #239
    Ann Arbor, MI 48105
    (734) 996-8610

CHAPTER 2: THE LEGAL, ECONOMIC, ETHICAL, AND ECOLOGICAL FOUNDATIONS OF ENVIRONMENTAL PLANNING

Ecology

National Center for Ecological Analysis and Synthesis
    www.nceas.ucsb.edu

National Information Center for Ecology
    www.nas.com/~greenhouse

Environmental Economics

H. John Heinz, III Center for Science, Economics,
    and the Environment
    1001 Pennsylvania Ave., NW, Suite 375 South
    Washington, DC 20004
    (202) 737-6307
    www.heinzctr.org

Resources for the Future
    1616 P St., NW
    Washington, DC 20036
    (202) 939-3460
    www.rff.org

Environmental Ethics

Center for Environmental Philosophy
    www.cep.unt.edu

Environmental Law

Conservation Law Foundation
    62 Summer St.
    Boston, MA 02110-1016
    (617) 350-0990
    www.clf.org

Council on Environmental Quality
    722 Jackson Place, NW
    Washington, DC 20503
    (202) 456-6224
    (202) 456-2710 fax
    www.whitehouse.gov/ceq

Environmental Law Institute
    1616 P St., NW, Suite 200
    Washington, DC 20036
    (202) 939-3800
    www.eli.org

Library of Congress
Thomas Legislative Information on the Internet
thomas.loc.gov

Pace Virtual Environmental Law Library
Pace University School of Law
White Plains, NY
www.law.pace.edu/env/vell6.html

Sierra Legal Defense Fund
www.sierralegal.org

CHAPTER 3: PLANNING FOR SUSTAINABLE WATER SUPPLY

American Water Works Association
6666 West Quincy Ave.
Denver, CO 80235
(303) 794-7711
www.awwa.org

EPA Office of Water
www.epa.gov/ow

National Rural Water Association
www.nrwa.org

CHAPTER 4: PLANNING FOR SUSTAINABLE WATER QUALITY

Water Quality

Center for Watershed Protection
8391 Main St.
Ellicott City, MD 21043-4605
(410) 461-8323
(410) 461-8324 fax
e-mail: center@cwp.org
www.cwp.org

Watershed Alliances Web Sites

Alliance for the Chesapeake Bay (www.acb-online.org)
Kentucky Waterways Alliance
(http://members.iglou.com/kwanews)
Mississippi Basin Alliance (www.mrba.org)
Rio Grande Alliance (www.riogrande.org)
Upper White River Watershed Alliance–Indiana
(www.whiteriveralliance.org)
Upper Gila Watershed Alliance–New Mexico
(www.ugwa.org)
Loramie Valley Alliance–Ohio
(www.loramievalleyalliance.org)

Environmental Working Group
http://www.ewg.org

Click on *Where You Live* by state and county to find public and private water systems that have violated federal water quality standards.

National Environmental Advocacy Organizations include:
Environmental Defense
257 Park Ave. South
New York, NY 10010
(800) 684-3322
www.edf.org

Natural Resources Defense Council
40 West 20th St.
New York, NY 10011
(212) 727-2700
(212) 727-1773 fax
www.nrdc.org

U.S.Environmental Protection Agency (www.epa.gov)

EPA Office of Ground Water and Drinking Water
(www.epa.gov/OGWDW)

EPA Office of Underground Storage Tanks
(www.epa.gov/OUST)

EPA Office of Wastewater Management
(202) 260-5816
www.epa.gov/owm/sw

The EPA and the Urban Land Institute have set up a Smart Growth Network
http://www.smartgrowth.org

CHAPTER 5: PLANNING FOR SUSTAINABLE AIR QUALITY

Acid rain
www.epa.gov/acidrain

Acid rain hotline
(202) 564-9620

air quality data
www.epa.gov/airsdata

Real-time air quality Maps and Forecasts
www.epa.gov/airnow

Stratospheric ozone hotline
(800) 296-1996

CHAPTER 6: PLANNING FOR
SOLID WASTE AND RECYCLING

Recycling

The National Recycling Coalition
www.nrc-recycle.org

Solid Waste

EPA Office of Solid Waste and Emergency Response
www.epa.gov/epaowser

EPA Solid Waste Assistance Program
(800) 677-9424

Solid Waste Assistance Program
P.O. Box 7219
Silver Spring, MD 20910

CHAPTER 7: PLANNING FOR TOXIC
SUBSTANCES AND TOXIC WASTE

Brownfields

www.usmayors.org/uscm/brownfields
www.epa.gov/brownfields
www.hud.gov/bfields.html
www.dep.state.pa.us

Department of Housing and Urban Development
http://iis-mapping3.hud.gov/maplib
A web page with the location of Superfund sites

Toxic Substances and Toxic Waste

RCRA hotline
(800) 424-9346

The U.S. Environmental Protection Agency has
compiled a CD-ROM of Risk-Screening
Environmental Indicators with national data on
toxic chemical emissions from the Toxic Release
Inventory.

Citizens' Clearing House for Hazardous Wastes
www.epa.gov/opptintr/env_ind/index.html

CHAPTER 8: PROTECTING THE
NATION'S LANDSCAPE TREASURES

American Heritage Rivers Program
(888) 407-4837
www.epa.gov/rivers/services

Land Trusts

The Land Trust Alliance
1331 H St., NW, Suite 400
Washington, DC 20005-4711
(202) 638-4725
(202) 638-4730 fax
www.lta.org

The Land Trust Alliance sponsors an annual Land
Trust Rally, which features a wide range of
presentations on land trust operations, land
protection, and land stewardship topics. Highly
recommended. The Land Trust Alliance also
publishes books on land conservation, including the
National Directory of Conservation Land Trusts.

National Heritage Areas

National Heritage Areas
National Park Service
(202) 565-1179

*National Organizations That Protect
Land for Natural Areas or for Public Use*

American Rivers
1025 Vermont Ave., NW, Suite 720
Washington, DC 20005
(877) 347-7550
www.americanrivers.org

The Conservation Fund
1800 North Kent St., Suite 1120
Arlington, VA 22209
(703) 525-6300
www.conservationfund.org

Sierra Club
85 Second St., Second Floor
San Francisco, CA 94105-3441
(415) 977-5500
(415) 977-5799 fax
www.sierraclub.org

The Trust for Public Land
116 New Montgomery St., 4th Floor
San Francisco, CA 94105
(415) 495-4014
(415) 495-4103 fax
www.tpl.org

The Wilderness Society
1615 M St., NW
Washington, DC 20036
(800) 843-9453
www.wilderness.org

State and Local Land Trusts

Montana Land Reliance
324 Fuller Ave.
P.O. Box 355
Helena, MT 59624-0355
(406) 433-7027
www.mtlandreliance.org

Peninsula Open Space Trust
3000 Sand Hill Rd., Bldg. 4, Suite 135
Menlo Park, CA 94025
(650) 854-7696
www.openspacetrust.org

Vermont Land Trust
8 Bailey Ave.
Montpelier, VT 05602
(802) 223-5234
www.vlt.org

Urban Parks and Recreation Recovery Program

National Park Service
National Center for Recreation and Conservation
Room 3624
1849 C Street, N.W.
Washington, DC 20240
(202) 565-1200

CHAPTER 9: PLANNING FOR WILDLIFE HABITAT

U.S. Geological Survey
Biological Resources Division
biology.usgs.gov

National Wildlife Organizations

American Fisheries Society
5410 Grosvenor Ln.

Bethesda, MD 20814
(301) 897-8616
www.fisheries.org

The Izaak Walton League
707 Conservation Ln.
Gaithersburg, MD 20878
(800) 453-5463
www.iwla.org

National Audubon Society
700 Broadway
New York, NY 10003
(212) 979-3000
(212) 979-3188 fax
www.audubon.org

National Wildlife Federation
8925 Leesburg Pike
Vienna, VA 22184
(703) 790-4000
www.nwf.org

The Nature Conservancy
1815 North Lynn
Arlington, VA 22209
www.tnc.org

Rocky Mountain Elk Foundation
2291 W. Broadway
P.O. Box 8249
Missoula, MT 59809
(800) 225-5355
www.rmef.org

Trout Unlimited
1500 Wilson Blvd., # 310
Arlington, VA 22209-2404
www.tu.org

The Wildlands Project
1955 W. Grant Rd. #145
Tucson, AZ 85745
(520) 884-0875
www.twp.org

CHAPTER 10: PLANNING AND MANAGING WETLANDS

Center for Natural Lands Management
425 E. Alvarado St., Suite H
Fallbrook, CA 92028-2960

Ducks Unlimited, Inc.
One Waterfowl Way
Memphis, TN 38120
(800) 453-8257
www.ducks.org

U.S. Environmental Protection Agency

Wetlands Information Hotline
(800) 832-7828

Wetlands Information Hotline
SC & A, Inc.
1355 Beverly Rd., Suite 250
McLean, VA 22101

Wetlands Division
www.epa.gov/owow/wetlands

The Wetlands Regulation Center
Environmental Technical Services Company
834 Castle Ridge Rd.
Austin, TX 78746-5152
www.wetlands.com

CHAPTER 11: COASTAL ZONE MANAGEMENT

The Big Sur Land Trust
P.O. Box 221864
Carmel, CA 93922
(831) 625-5523
(831) 625-0716 fax
www.bigsurlandtrust.org

California Coastal Commission
45 Fremont St., Suite 2000
San Francisco, CA 94105-2219
(415) 904-5200

California Coastal Conservancy
1330 Broadway, 11th Floor
Oakland, CA 94612
(510) 286-1015
(510) 286-0470 fax
www.coastalconservancy.ca.gov

National Oceanic and Atmospheric Administration
Coastal Services Center
2234 South Hobson Ave.
Charleston, SC 29405-2413

(843) 740-1200
(843) 740-1224 fax

National Oceanic and Atmospheric Administration
Office of Ocean and Resource Management
Coastal Programs Division
1305 East-West Highway
Silver Spring, MD 20910

CHAPTER 12: PLANNING FOR NATURAL HAZARDS AND NATURAL DISASTERS

Federal Emergency Management Agency
www.fema.gov

Natural Hazards Center
www.Colorado.EDU/hazards

Coastal Erosion

H. John Heinz, III Center for Science, Economics and Environment
www.heinzcenter.org

Earthquakes

National Earthquake Information Center
U.S. Geological Survey, Federal Center
P.O. Box 25046
Denver, CO 80255
(303) 273-8500
www.neic.cr.usgs.gov

National Institute of Building Sciences
Multihazard Mitigation Council
1090 Vermont Ave., NW, Suite 700
Washington, DC 20005-4905
(202) 289-7800

Landslides

National Landslide Information Center
U.S. Geological Survey, Federal Center
P.O. Box 25046
Denver, CO 80255
(800) 654-4966
www.landslides.usgs.gov

CHAPTER 13: PLANNING FOR SUSTAINABLE WORKING LANDSCAPES: FARMLAND AND RANCHLAND

Conservation Practices

Natural Resources Conservation Service
    National Handbook of Conservation Practices, 1996
    www.ncg.nrcs.usda.gov/nhcp_2html

Farmland Protection

Agricultural Preserve Board of Lancaster County
    50 North Duke St.
    P.O. Box 83480
    Lancaster, PA 17608-3480
    (717) 299-8355
    www.co.lancaster.pa.us

American Farmland Trust
    1920 N St., NW, Suite 400
    Washington, DC 20036
    (202) 659-5170
    www.farmland.org

    The American Farmland Trust also has field offices in California, Colorado, Massachusetts, Michigan, New York, North Carolina, Ohio, Texas, Washington, and Wisconsin.

Farmland Preservation Report
    900 LaGrange Rd.
    Street, MD 21154
    (410) 692-2708

Marin Agricultural Land Trust
    P.O. Box 809
    Point Reyes Station, CA 94956
    (415) 663-1158

Vermont Land Trust
    8 Bailey Ave.
    Montpelier, VT 05602
    (802) 223-5234
    (802) 223-4223 fax
    www.vlt.org

Transfer of Development Rights

Farmland Information Library

    A bibliography and abstracts of farmland protection topics, state statutes relating to farmland protection,

and news and upcoming events.
    www.farmlandinfo.org

Montgomery County Ag Services
    18410 Muncaster Rd.
    Derwent, MD 20855

CHAPTER 14: PLANNING FOR SUSTAINABLE WORKING LANDSCAPES: FORESTRY

American Forests
    www.americanforests.org

U.S. Forest Service
    210 14th St., SW
    Auditors Building
    Washington, DC 20250
    (202) 205-0957
    (202) 205-0885 fax
    www.fs.fed.us

Carbon Sequestration in Forests and Global Warming

Pew Center on Global Climate Change
    2101 Wilson Blvd., Suite 550
    Arlington, VA 22201
    (703) 516-4146
    www.pewclimate.org

Federal Forest Legacy Program

U.S. Forest Service Cooperative Forestry
    Ted Beauvais
    201 14th St., SW
    Washington, DC 20024

Land Trusts and Forestland Preservation

New Hampshire Society for the Protection of New Hampshire Forests
    54 Portsmouth St.
    Concord, NH 03301-5400
    (603) 224-9945
    www.spnf.org

The Pacific Forest Trust
    P.O. Box 879
    Boonville, CA 95415
    (707) 895-2090
    (707) 895-2138 fax
    e-mail: pft@pacificforest.org
    www.pacificforest.org

Ask for the publication "Working in the Woods: Using Easements to Guide Forest Management."

Sustainable Forest and Wood Certification Programs

The Certified Forest Products Council
www.certifiedproducts.org

The Forest Stewardship Council
www.fscoax.org

Scientific Certification Systems
www.scs1.com

SmartWood
Goodwin-Baker Building
61 Millet St.
Richmond, VT 05477
(802) 434-5491
www.smartwood.org

CHAPTER 15: PLANNING FOR MINING

Mineral and Aggregate Mining

The National Stone Association
www.aggregates.org

Pennsylvania Department of Environmental Protection
www.dep.state.pa.us

U.S. Geological Survey Information Services
P.O. Box 25286
Denver Federal Center
Denver, CO 80225

CHAPTER 16: TRANSPORTATION PLANNING AND THE ENVIRONMENT

Light Rail

Rail Volution
www.railvolution.com

Rails-to-Trails Projects

The Rails-to-Trails Conservancy
1100 17th St., NW, 10th Floor
Washington, DC 20036
(202) 466-3742 fax
www.railtrails.org

Road Networks

Geographic Data Technology
11 Lafayette St.
Lebanon, NH 03766

(800) 331-7881
www.geographic.com

Transportation Issues

Surface Transportation Policy Project
1400 16th St., NW, Suite 300
Washington, DC 20036
(202) 466-2636
www.transact.org/stpp.htm

Transportation and Community System Pilot Program
tcsp-fhwa.volpe.dot.gov

CHAPTER 17: PLANNING FOR ENERGY

Energy Issues

Oregon Office of Energy
www.energy.state.or.us

U.S. Department of Energy
1000 Independence Ave., SW
Washington, D.C. 20585
(800) 342-5363
(202) 586-4403 fax
www.energy.gov

CHAPTER 18: PLANNING FOR A SUSTAINABLE BUILT ENVIRONMENT

Community Design Issues

American Planning Association's Smart Growth Program
Stuart Meck
American Planning Association
122 S. Michigan Ave., Suite 1600
Chicago, IL 60603
(312) 431-9100
(312) 431-9985 fax
www.planning.org

The Center for Livable Communities
1414 K St., Suite 250
Sacramento, CA 95814
(916) 448-1198
www.lgc.org

A nonprofit organization that assists local governments in California and other states. Programs are aimed at expanding transportation alternatives, reducing infrastructure costs, creating more affordable housing, conserving farmland and natural resources, and restoring economic and social vitality. The center publishes *Livable Places Update,* a monthly newsletter.

The Congress for the New Urbanism
The Hearst Building
5 Third St., Suite 725
San Francisco, CA 94103-3296
(415) 495-2255
(415) 495-1731 fax
www.cnu.org

National Association of Home Builders
Smart Growth
(202) 822-0200
www.nahb.com

The National Livability Resource Center
Federal government's Livable Communities
Program
www.livablecommunities.gov/tools and resources

New Urban News
P.O. Box 6515
Ithaca, NY 14851
(607) 275-3087
www.newurbannews.com

The Planning Commissioners Journal
Sprawl Resource Guide
www.plannersweb.com

Subscription ($45 for 1-year subscription)
P.O. Box 4295
Burlington, VT 05406
(802) 864-9083
(802) 862-1882 fax

Scenic America
801 Pennsylvania Ave., SE, Suite 300
Washington, DC 20003
(202) 543-6200
www.scenic.org

The University of Louisville
Sustainable Urban Neighborhoods program
www.louisville.edu/org/sun

Design of "Green" Buildings

The U.S. Green Building Council
www.usgbc.org

Development Issues and Innovations

Center for Neighborhood Technology
www.cnt.org

The National Neighborhood Coalition
www.neighborhoodcoalition.org

The Project for Public Spaces
www.pps.org

Sustainable Communities Network
(202) 387-3378
www.sustainable.org

The Urban Land Institute
1025 Thomas Jefferson St., NW
Suite 500 West
Washington, DC 20007
(800) 321-5011
www.uli.org

Historic Preservation and Redevelopment

The National Trust for Historic Preservation
1785 Massachusetts Ave., NW
Washington, DC 20036
(202) 588-6000
www.nationaltrust.org

Noise Pollution

The Noise Pollution Clearinghouse
P.O. Box 1137
Montpelier, VT 05601-1137
(888) 200-8332
www.nonoise.org

CHAPTER 19: PLANNING FOR THE BUILT ENVIRONMENT: GREENFIELD DEVELOPMENT AND SITE DESIGN

Urban Growth Boundaries and Greenbelts

Center of Excellence for Sustainable Development
U.S. Department of Energy
Office of Energy Efficiency and Renewable Energy
Denver Regional Support Office
1617 Cole Blvd.
Golden, CO 80401
(800) 363-3732
www.sustainable.doe.gov

Greenbelt Alliance
530 Bush St., Suite 303

San Francisco, CA 94108
(415) 398-3730
www.greenbelt.org

National Association of Home Builders
(202) 822-0200
www.nahb.com

Prairie Crossing Information Office
1493 Patawatomi Rd.
Grayslake, IL 60030
(847) 548-5400
www.prairiecrossing.com

The Smart Growth Network
www.smartgrowth.org

Sprawlwatch
www.sprawlwatch.org

Vermont Forum on Sprawl
110 Main St.
Burlington, VT 05401
(802) 864-6310
(802) 862-4487 fax
www.vtsprawl.org

CHAPTER 20: POSITIVE TRENDS AND URGENT NEEDS FOR SUSTAINABLE ENVIRONMENTAL PLANNING

Institute for Southern Studies
www.southernstudies.org

Renewable Resources Institute
www.rri.org

Resource Management Institute
www.rmi.org

Bibliography

INTRODUCTION

American Planning Association. "Planning for Sustainability," April 16, 2000. www.planning.org/policyguides/sustainability.htm

American Society of Civil Engineers. *The 2001 Report Card for America's Infrastructure*. Washington, DC: ASCE, 2001.

Beatley, Timothy. "Planning and Sustainability: The Elements of a New (Improved?) Paradigm," *Journal of Planning Literature* 9:4, 1995.

Berke, Philip and Maria Conroy. "Are We Planning for Sustainable Development?: An Evaluation of 30 Comprehensive Plans," *Journal of the American Planning Association* 66:1, 2000.

Commoner, Barry. *The Closing Circle: Nature, Man, and Technology*. New York: Random House, 1971.

Dernbach, John. "Synthesis," in Dernbach, ed., *Stumbling Toward Sustainability*. Washington, DC: Environmental Law Institute, 2002.

Greider, William. *One World Ready or Not: The Manic Logic of Global Capitalism*. New York: Touchstone, 1998.

Lee, Kai N. *Compass and Gyroscope: Integrating Science and Politics for the Environment*. Washington, DC: Island Press, 1993.

Meadows, D.H., D.L. Meadows, J. Randers, and W.W. Behrens. *The Limits to Growth: A Report for the Club of Rome's Project on the Predicament of Mankind*. New York: Universe Books, 1972.

Sustainable Seattle. *Sustainable Seattle Indicators of Sustainable Community: A Report to Citizens on Long Term Trends in Their Community*. Seattle, WA: Sustainable Seattle, 1993.

U.S. Department of Energy, Energy Information Administration. *Annual Energy Review 2000*. Washington, DC: USDOE, 2001.

U.S. Environmental Protection Agency. *Climate Action Report 2002*. Washington, DC: USEPA, 2002.

The World Commission on Environment and Development. *Our Common Future* (The Bruntland Report). Oxford, UK: Oxford University Press, 1987.

CHAPTER 1: TAKING STOCK OF THE LOCAL ENVIRONMENT AND CREATING AN ENVIRONMENTAL ACTION PLAN

Carson, Rachel. *Silent Spring*. Boston: Houghton Mifflin, 1962.

Center for Energy and Environment, Minnesotans for an Energy-Efficient Economy, and 1000 Friends of Minnesota. *Two Roads Diverge: Analyzing Growth Scenarios for the Twin Cities Region*. St. Paul, MN: Minnesota Legislative Commission on Minnesota Resources, 1999.

City of Albuquerque, New Mexico, May 14, 2001. www.cabq.gov/profress/sir/summsry.htm

City of San Francisco. *Sustainability Plan*, 1997.

Columbus Health Department. *Environmental Snapshot, 2001*. Columbus, OH: CHD, 2001.

——. *Environmental Snapshot, 1998*. Columbus, OH: CHD, 1998.

Daniels, Thomas L., John W. Keller, and Mark B. Lapping. *The Small Town Planning Handbook*. 2d ed. Chicago: American Planning Association, 1995.

Dowie, Mark. *Losing Ground: American Environmentalism at the Close of the Twentieth Century*. Cambridge, MA: MIT Press, 1995.

Freilich, Robert H. and Michael M. Schultz. *Model Subdivision Regulations*. Chicago: American Planning Association, 1995.

Hawken, Paul, Amory Lovins, and L. Hunter Lovins. *Natural Capitalism: Creating the Next Industrial Revolution*. Boston: Little Brown and Company, 1999.

Humstone, Elizabeth, Julie Campoli, and Alex McLean. *Above and Beyond: Visualizing Change in Small Towns and Rural Areas*. Chicago: American Planning Association, 2001.

Lancaster County Planning Commission. *Growth Tracking Report*. Lancaster, PA: LCPC, 1999.

Marsden, Virginia W. "Urban Sustainability Reporting," *Journal of the American Planning Association* 62:2, Spring 1996.

Minneapolis-St. Paul Metropolitan Council. *State of the Region (1999)*. St. Paul, MN: Metropolitan Council, 1999.

Moudon, Anne Vernez and Michael Hubner, eds. *Monitoring Land Supply with Geographic Information Systems*. New York: John Wiley & Sons, 2000.

Stokes, Samuel N., A. Elizabeth Watson, and Shelley Mastran. *Saving America's Countryside: A Guide to Rural Conservation.* 2d ed. Baltimore: Johns Hopkins University Press, 1997.

Sustainable Seattle. *Indicators of Sustainable Community, 1998.* Seattle, WA: Sustainable Seattle, 1998. www.scn.org/sustainable/Indicators/indicators98/vehicle98and/water98

Toner, William. "Environmental Land Use Planning," in So et al., eds., *The Practice of Local Government Planning.* Washington, DC: International City Managers' Association, 1988.

U.S. Department of Commerce, U.S. Bureau of the Census in *The World Almanac and Book of Facts, 1999.* Mahwah, NJ: Primedia, 1998.

CHAPTER 2: THE LEGAL, ECONOMIC, ETHICAL, AND ECOLOGICAL FOUNDATIONS OF ENVIRONMENTAL PLANNING

American Planning Association. "Planning for Sustainability," April 16, 2000. www.planning.org/policyguides/sustainability.htm

Anderson, Frederick R. *NEPA in the Courts: A Legal Analysis of the National Environmental Policy Act.* Baltimore: Resources for the Future/Johns Hopkins University Press, 1973.

Barnett, Harold J. and Chandler Morse. *Scarcity and Growth: The Economics of Natural Resource Availability.* Baltimore: Johns Hopkins University Press for Resources for the Future, 1963.

Bass, Ronald E. and Albert I. Herson. *Mastering NEPA: A Step-by-Step Approach.* Point Arena, CA: Solano Press Books, 1993.

Bator, Francis. "The Anatomy of Market Failure," *Quarterly Journal of Economics* 72:351-379, 1958.

Burchell, Robert W. *Fiscal Impact Handbook: Estimating Costs and Revenues of Land Development.* New Brunswick, NJ: Rutgers University Press, 1978.

Burchell, Robert W. *et al.* (9 co-authors). *The Costs of Sprawl Revisited.* Transit Cooperative Research Program Report 39. Washington, DC: Transportation Research Board, National Research Council, 1998.

Callies, David L., Robert H. Freilich, and Thomas E. Roberts. *Cases and Materials on Land Use.* 3d ed. St. Paul, MN: The West Group, 1999.

Carson, Rachel. *Silent Spring.* Boston: Houghton Mifflin, 1962.

Carter, Virgil and Tom Dale. *Topsoil and Civilization.* Norman, OK: University of Oklahoma Press, 1955.

Clark, Colin. "The Economics of Overexploitation," *Science* 181, 1974.

Commoner, Barry. *The Closing Circle: Nature, Man, and Technology.* New York: Random House, 1971.

Council on Environmental Quality. *Annual Report, 1996.* Washington, DC: U.S. Government Printing Office, 1996.

Cronon, William. *Uncommon Ground: Rethinking the Human Place in Nature.* New York: W.W. Norton, 1996.

———. *Changes in the Land: Indians, Colonists, and the Ecology of New England.* New York: Hill and Wang, 1983.

Daly, Herman. *Toward a Steady-State Economy.* San Francisco: W.H. Freeman, 1973.

Daly, Herman and K. H. Townsend. *Valuing the Earth: Economics, Ecology, Ethics.* Cambridge, MA: MIT Press, 1992.

Dowie, Mark. *Losing Ground: American Environmentalism at the Close of the Twentieth Century.* Cambridge, MA: MIT Press, 1995.

Easterbrook, Gregg. *A Moment on the Earth.* New York: Penguin Books, 1996.

Eisenberg, Evan. *The Ecology of Eden.* New York: Vintage Books, 1999.

Fisher, Anthony. *Resource and Environmental Economics.* New York: Cambridge University Press, 1981.

Freeman, Myrick, III. *The Benefits of Environmental Improvement.* Baltimore: Johns Hopkins University Press for Resources for the Future, 1979.

Freilich, Robert H. *From Sprawl to Smart Growth: Successful Legal, Planning, and Environmental Systems.* Chicago: American Bar Association, Section of State and Local Government Law, 1999.

Freilich, Robert H. and Jason M. Divelbiss. "The Public Interest Is Vindicated: City of Monterey v. Del Monte Dunes," in Salkin and Freilich, eds., *Hot Topics in Land Use Law: From the Comprehensive Plan to Del Monte Dunes.* Chicago: American Bar Association, Section of State and Local Government Law, 2000.

Gill, Vernon and Tom Carter. *Topsoil and Civilization.* Norman, OK: University of Oklahoma Press, 1955.

Hardin, Garrett. "Tragedy of the Commons," *Science* 162, 1968.

Hawken, Paul. *The Ecology of Commerce.* New York: HarperBusiness, 1993.

Hawken, Paul, Amory Lovins, and L. Hunter Lovins. *Natural Capitalism: Creating the Next Industrial Revolution.* Boston: Little Brown and Company, 1999.

High Country News, May 30, 1994.

Howe, Charles W. *Natural Resource Economics: Issues, Analysis, and Policy.* New York: John Wiley & Sons, 1979.

Kuttner, Robert. *Everything for Sale: The Virtues and Limits of Markets.* New York: Alfred A. Knopf, 1996.

Leopold, Aldo. *A Sand County Almanac.* New York: Balantine Books, 1970.

Lindsey, Greg and Gerrit Knaap. "Willingness to Pay for Urban Greenway Projects," *Journal of the American Planning Association* 65: 3, 1999.

Lovelock, James E. *Gaia: A New Look at Life on Earth.* New York: Oxford University Press, 1979.

MacDonnell, Lawrence J. and Sarah F. Bates, eds. *Natural Resources Policy and Law.* Washington, DC: Island Press, 1993.

Malthus, Thomas Robert. *An Essay on the Principle of Population (1798).* Reprinted. New York: Oxford University Press, 1994.

Mandelker, Daniel R. "Melding State Environmental Policy Acts with Land-Use Planning and Regulations," *Land Use Law,* March 1997.

Marsh, George Perkins (D. Lowenthal, ed.). *Man and Nature, or Physical Geography as Modified by Human Nature (1864).* Reprinted. Cambridge, MA: Harvard University Press, 1965.

Marx, Leo. *The Machine in the Garden: Technology and the Pastoral Ideal in America.* New York: Oxford University Press, 1967.

McAllister, Donald. *Evaluation in Environmental Planning: Assessing Environmental, Social, Economic, and Political Trade-offs.* Cambridge, MA; MIT Press, 1982.

McNeil, J.R. *Something New Under the Sun: An Environmental History of the Twentieth Century World.* New York: W.W. Norton & Company, 2000.

McPhee, John A. *The Control of Nature.* New York: Farrar, Straus and Giroux, 1989.

Meadows, Donella H., Dennis L. Meadows, Jorgen Randers, and W.W. Behrens. *The Limits to Growth.* New York: Universe Books, 1972.

Nash, Roderick F. *The Rights of Nature: A History of Environmental Ethics.* Madison, WI: University of Wisconsin Press, 1989.

Natural Resources Conservation Service. Program Status–Wetlands Reserve Program, February 27, 2001.

Odum, Eugene P. *Ecology: A Bridge Between Science and Society.* Sunderland, MA: Sinaur Associates, 1997.

Phillips, Claudia Goetz and John Randolph. "The Relationship of Ecosystem Management to NEPA and Its Goals," *Environmental Management* 26:1, 2000.

Planning, "Court Finds Wetlands Rule Doesn't Violate Rights," 65:11, November 1999.

Portney, Paul R. and Robert H. Stavins. *Public Policies for Environmental Protection.* 2d ed. Washington, DC: Resources for the Future, 2000.

Reisner, Marc. *Cadillac Desert: The American West and Its Disappearing Water.* New York: Penguin Books, 1986.

Rolston, H. *Environmental Ethics: Duties to and Values in the Natural World.* Philadelphia: Temple University Press, 1987.

Sargent, Frederick. O., Paul Lusk, Jose A. Rivera, and Maria Varela. *Rural Environmental Planning for Sustainable Communities.* Washington, DC: Island Press, 1991.

Schneider, Devon M., David R. Godschalk, and Norman Axler. *The Carrying Capacity Concept as a Planning Tool.* Chicago: American Planning Association, 1978.

Schumacher, E.F. *Small Is Beautiful: Economics as if People Mattered.* New York: Harper and Row, 1977.

Simon, Julian L. *The Ultimate Resource.* Princeton, NJ: Princeton University Press, 1981.

Smith, R.L. *Elements of Ecology.* 3d ed. New York: Harper and Row, 1992.

Smith, V. Kerry, ed. *Scarcity and Growth Reconsidered.* Baltimore: Johns Hopkins University Press, 1979.

Stone, Christopher. "Should Trees Have Standing?" in Cahn and O'Brien, eds., *Thinking About the Environment: Readings on Politics, Property and the Physical World.* Armonk, NY: M.E. Sharpe, 1996.

Strong, Ann Louise, Daniel R. Mandelker, and Eric Damian Kelly. "Property Rights and Takings," *Journal of the American Planning Association* 62:1, Winter 1996.

U.S. Department of Agriculture. *National Resources Inventory, 1997.* Washington, DC: U.S. Government Printing Office, 2001.

U.S. Environmental Protection Agency. *The Benefits and Costs of the Clean Air Act Amendments of 1990.* Washington, DC: USEPA, November 1999.

——. *The Benefits and Costs of the Clean Air Act.* Washington, DC: USEPA, 1997.

Wiebe, Keith, Abebayehu Tegene, and Betsy Kuhn. *Partial Interests in Land: Policy Tools for Resource Use and Conservation.* Washington, DC: U.S. Department of Agriculture, Economic Research Service Report No. 744, 1996.

The World Commission on Environment and Development. *Our Common Future.* Oxford, UK: Oxford University Press, 1996.

——. *Our Common Future* (The Bruntland Report). Oxford, UK: Oxford University Press, 1987.

CHAPTER 3: PLANNING FOR SUSTAINABLE WATER SUPPLY

Adams County, Pennsylvania. *Water Supply and Wellhead Protection Plan.* Gettysburg, PA: Adams County Planning Department, 2001.

American Planning Association. "Planning for Sustainability," April 16, 2000. www.planning.org/policyguides/sustainability.htm

Beach, Dana. *Coastal Sprawl: The Effects of Urban Design on Aquatic Ecosystems in the United States.* Arlington, VA: Pew Oceans Commission, 2002.

Belsie, Laurent. "Americans Losing the Drive to Conserve," *The Christian Science Monitor,* August 30, 1999.

Council on Environmental Quality. *Annual Report, 1996.* Washington, DC: U.S. Government Printing Office, 1996.

Crook, James, David K. Ammerman, and Daniel Okun. *Guidelines for Water Reuse.* Washington, DC: U.S. Environmental Protection Agency/Camp Dress & McKee, 1992.

The Denver Post, April 2000. www.denverpost.com/ The Colorado: River of No Return

Easterbrook, Gregg. *A Moment on the Earth.* New York: Penguin Books, 1996.

Egan, Timothy. "Las Vegas Bet on Growth But Doesn't Love Pay Off," *The New York Times,* January 26, 2001.

Firestone, David. "Booming Atlanta Saps Water as Drought Wilts Georgia," *The New York Times,* June 15, 2000.

Florida Department of Environmental Protection. "Florida's Reuse Projects," July 10, 2001. www.dep.state.fl.us/water/wf/dom/reuse/projects.htm

Getches, David H. "Water Resources: A Wider World," in MacDonnell and Bates, eds., *Natural Resources Policy and Law.* Washington, DC: Island Press, 1993.

Greene, Susan. "The Colorado: River of No Return," *The Denver Post,* September 24, 2000.

Homsy, George. "Liquid Gold," *Planning* 63:5, 1997.

Jaffe, Martin and Frank DiNovo. *Local Groundwater Protection.* Chicago: American Planning Association, 1987.

Jehl, Douglas. "A New Frontier in Water Emerges in the East," *The New York Times,* March 3, 2003.

——. "Tampa Bay Looks to the Sea to Quench Its Thirst," *The New York Times,* March 12, 2000.

Lowy, Joan. "Water, Hope, Money All Dry Up." Scripps Howard News Service, printed in *Times Union* (Albany, NY), July 16, 2000.

Meeks, Phillip. "How Does Your Garden Grow?" *Planning* 68:5, May 2002.

Metropolitan Council. "Natural Environment Trends." *State of the Region.* St. Paul, MN: Metropolitan Council, 1999.

Metropolitan Water District of Southern California, May 10, 2001. www.mwd.dst.ca.us/index.htm

National Research Council. *Watershed Management for Potable Water: Assessing the New York City Strategy.* Washington, DC: National Academy Press, 2000.

——. *In Our Own Backyard: Principles for Effective Improvement of the Nation's Infrastructure.* Washington, DC: National Academy Press, 1993.

Natural Resources Defense Council. *The Amicus Journal,* Summer 2001.

The New York Times. "Florida Drinking Water From the Sea," March 27, 2003.

——. "Politics and the Watershed," April 8, 1999.

Owen, Oliver S., David D. Chiras, and John P. Reganold. *Natural Resource Conservation.* 7th ed. Upper Saddle River, NJ: Prentice-Hall, 1998.

Page, G. William, ed. *Planning for Groundwater Protection.* New York: Academic Press, 1987.

Perry, Tony. "What Now for Water Agency?" *Los Angeles Times,* January 2, 2003.

Postel, Sandra. "Redesigning Irrigated Agriculture," in Worldwatch Institute, *State of the World 2000*. New York: W.W. Norton, 2000.

Reisner, Marc. *Cadillac Desert: The American West and Its Disappearing Water*. New York: Penguin Books, 1987.

Renwick, Mary E. and Richard D. Green. "Do Residential Water Demand Side Management Policies Measure Up? An Analysis of Eight California Water Agencies," *Journal of Environmental Economics and Management* 40, 2000.

Revkin, Andrew C. "Sewage Work Lags at Source of Tap Water," *The New York Times*, April 19, 2000.

——. "Billion-Dollar Plan to Clean the City's Water at Its Source." *The New York Times*, August 31, 1997.

Sanchez, Rene. "New Calif. Water Law Seeks to Curb Runaway Sprawl," *The Washington Post*, December 23, 2001.

Sax, Joseph L. "Bringing an Ecological Perspective to Natural Resources Law: Fulfilling the Promise of the Public Trust," in MacDonnell and Bates, eds., *Natural Resources Policy and Law*. Washington, DC: Island Press, 1993.

Shigley, Paul and John Krist. "Drip Drip Drip," *Planning* 68:5, May 2002.

Stevens, William K. "Persistent and Severe, Drought Strikes Again," *The New York Times*, April 25, 2000.

Tarlock, Dan A. "Water Supply as New Growth Management Tool," *Land Use Law*, November 1998.

Texas Water Development Board. *Water for Texas-2002*. Austin, TX: TWDB, 2002.

Trust for Public Land. *Protecting the Source: Land Conservation and the Future of America's Drinking Water*. San Francisco: TPL, 1997.

U.S. Bureau of the Census. *Population Projections: States, 1995-2025*. Washington, DC: U.S. Government Printing Office, 1997.

U.S. Environmental Protection Agency. Office of Water. "Using the State Revolving Fund Set-Aside Funds for Source Water Protection." Washington, DC: USEPA, March 2000a.

——. "Public Water System Supervision Program," April 26, 2000b. www.epa.gov

——. *Public Water Supply Supervision Program Water Supply Guidance Manual*. EPA 816-R-00-003. Washington, DC: USEPA, January 2000c.

——. "Today's Challenges," *Liquid Assets 2000: America's Water Resources at a Turning Point*. Washington, DC: USEPA, 2000d.

——. Office of Ground Water and Drinking Water, August 2000e. www.epa.gov

——. *State Source Water Assessment Programs*. Washington, DC: USEPA, December 1999.

——. Office of Water. *Drinking Water Infrastructure Needs Survey: First Report to Congress*. EPA 812-R-97-001. Washington, DC: USEPA, January 1997a.

——. *State Method for Delineating Source Water Protection Areas for Surface Water Supplied Sources of Drinking Water*. Washington, DC: USEPA, 1997b.

——. *Liquid Assets*. Washington, DC: USEPA, Executive Summary, 1996.

——. *State Ground Water Protection Program Guidance*. Washington, DC: USEPA, December 1992.

U.S. Geological Survey. "Estimated Use of Water in the United States in 1995," water.usgs.gov/watuse/pdf1995/html, October 10, 2002.

Ward, Jenna. "Water for the Desert Miracle," in David Littlejohn, ed., *The Real Las Vegas: Life Beyond the Strip*. New York: Oxford University Press, 1999.

Whitten, Jon. "The Basics of Groundwater Protection," *Planning* 58:6, June 1992.

Whitten, Jon and Scott Horsley. *A Guide to Wellhead Protection*. Chicago: American Planning Association, Planning Advisory Service Report No. 457/458, 1995.

Yardley, Jim. "For Texas Now, Water and Not Oil is Liquid Gold," *The New York Times*, April 16, 2001.

CHAPTER 4: PLANNING FOR SUSTAINABLE WATER QUALITY

Beach, Dana. *Coastal Sprawl: The Effects of Urban Design on Aquatic Ecosystems in the United States*. Arlington, VA: Pew Oceans Commission, 2002.

Boise City Planning and Development Services. *Hammer & Nail News* 6:1, Winter 2000.

Chesapeake Bay Foundation. "CBF Fact Sheet." Annapolis, MD: CBF, June 14, 2000. www.cbf.org/resources/facts/sprawl

Coequyt, John and Richard Wiles. *Prime Suspects: The Law Breaking Polluters America Fails to Inspect*. Washington, DC: Environmental Working Group, 2000.

Council on Environmental Quality. *Annual Report, 1996*. Washington, DC: U.S. Government Printing Office, 1996.

Daniels, Tom. *When City and Country Collide: Managing Growth in the Metropolitan Fringe.* Washington, DC: Island Press, 1999.

Easterbrook, Greg. "Here Comes the Sun," *The New Yorker,* April 10, 1995.

Environmental Working Group. *Clean Water Report Card.* Washington, DC: EWG, 2000.

Finucan, Karen. "New Jersey," in *Planning Communities for the 21st Century.* Chicago: American Planning Association, 1999.

Homsy, George. "Liquid Gold," *Planning* 63:5, 1997.

Horton, Tom and William Eichbaum. *Turning the Tide: Saving the Chesapeake Bay.* Washington, DC: Chesapeake Bay Foundation and Island Press, 1991.

Jeer, Sanjay. *Nonpoint Source Pollution.* Planning Advisory Service Report No. 476. Chicago: American Planning Association, 1997.

Johnson, Denny. "Oregon," in *Planning Communities for the 21st Century.* Chicago: American Planning Association, 1999.

Marsh, William M. *Landscape Planning: Environmental Applications.* 3d ed. New York: John Wiley & Sons, 1998.

Maryland Department of Agriculture. Maryland Agricultural Cost Share Program, August 15, 2001. www.mda.state.md.us

Maryland Department of Natural Resources. *Maryland's Clean Water Action Plan.* Annapolis, MD: MDNR, 1998.

Maryland's Tributary Teams. *Picture Maryland: Where Do We Grow From Here?* Annapolis, MD: Maryland Department of Natural Resources, 2000.

Meridian Institute. *Final Report of the National Watershed Forum, June 27–July 1, 2001.* Arlington, VA: Meridian Institute, 2001.

National Research Council, Committee to Assess the Scientific Basis of the Total Maximum Daily Load Approach to Water Pollution Reduction, Water Science and Technology Board. *Assessing the TMDL Approach to Water Quality Management.* Washington, DC: National Academy Press, 2001.

National Wildlife Federation. *Pollution Paralysis II: Code Red for Watersheds.* Washington, DC: NWF, 2000.

Natural Resources Defense Council. *Land Use Controls in the United States.* New York: The Dial Press, 1977.

New York Department of Environmental Conservation. Unified Watershed Assessment, July 31, 2002.

www.dec.state.ny.us/website/dow/uwa/uwarpt98.htm

Owen, Oliver S., Daniel D. Chiras, and John P. Reganold. *Natural Resource Conservation.* 7th ed. Upper Saddle River, NJ: Prentice-Hall, 1998.

Pear, Robert. "Shift of Power from Washington Is Seen Under Bush," *The New York Times,* January 7, 2001.

Rubin, A.R., S. Hogye, and J. Hudson. "Development of EPA Guidelines for Management of Onsite/Decentralized Wastewater Systems." 2000 National Organization of Water Resources Administrators Proceedings. Washington, DC: NOWRA, 2000.

Society for the Protection of New Hampshire Forests, May 12, 2001. www.spnhf.org

Swope, Christopher. "Water Merchant," *Governing,* June 2000.

Times Union (Albany, NY). "E. Coli Outbreak Still Unsolved," April 1, 2000a.

——. "Fair Makes Changes to Meet New Water Rules," July 31, 2000b.

Toner, William. "Environmental Land Use Planning," in So *et al.,* eds., *The Practice of Local Government Planning.* Washington, DC: International City Managers' Association, 1988.

Tri-County Regional Planning Commission. *Model Groundwater Recharge Area Preservation Ordinance (Draft).* Lansing, MI: Tri-County Regional Planning Commission, 1983.

USA Today. "EPA to Propose New Rules for Safeguarding Water Supplies," April 17, 2000.

U.S. Bureau of the Census. *Statistical Abstract of the United States, 1999.* Washington, DC: U.S. Government Printing Office, 2000.

U.S. Environmental Protection Agency. Office of Water. *A Review of Statewide Watershed Management Approaches.* Washington, DC: USEPA, 2002.

——. *Report to Congress: Implementation and Enforcement of the Combined Sewer Overflow Control Policy.* Washington, DC: USEPA, 2001.

——. *Liquid Assets 2000: America's Water Resources at a Turning Point.* Washington, DC: USEPA, 2000a.

——. Office of Water. *Water Quality Conditions in the United States: A Profile from the 1998 National Water Quality Inventory Report to Congress.* Washington, DC: USEPA, June 2000b.

———. Office of Water. "Storm Water Phase II Final Rule," EPA 833-F-00-001. Washington, DC: USEPA, January 2000c.

———. Office of Water. *The Quality of Our Nation's Waters: A Summary of the National Water Quality Inventory: 1998 Report to Congress.* EPA 841-S-00-001. Washington, DC: USEPA, June 2000d.

———. *Report to Congress on a Compliance Plan for the Underground Storage Tank Program.* EPA-510-R-00-001. Washington, DC: USEPA, June 2000e.

———. *National Water Quality Inventory: 1998 Report to Congress.* Washington, DC: USEPA, 2000f.

———. *National Listing of Fish and Wildlife Consumption Advisories,* EPA-823-F-99-005. Washington, DC: USEPA, July 1999.

———. *National Water Quality Inventory: 1996 Report to Congress,* EPA-841-F-97-003. Washington, DC: USEPA, April 1998a.

———. Centers for Disease Control Workshop on Waterborne Disease Occurrence Studies–Summary Report, March 12-13, 1997. Washington, DC: USEPA, August 1998b.

———. "Economics of Riparian Forest Buffers," EPA 903-F-98-003. Washington: DC: USEPA, May 1998c.

———. *Report to Congress on Use of Decentralized Wastewater Treatment Systems.* Washington, DC: USEPA, 1997.

U.S. General Accounting Office. *Community Development: Local Growth Issues—Federal Opportunities and Challenges,* GAO/RCED-00-178. Washington, DC: USGAO, 2000a.

———. *Environmental Protection: More Consistency Needed Among EPA Regions in Approach to Enforcement.* Washington, DC: USGAO, June 2000b.

Whitaker, Barbara. "Los Angeles Admits Fault in Sewer Spills Cited in Suit," *The New York Times,* April 23, 2003.

Zielbauer, Paul. "States and Cities Flout Law on Underground Fuel Tanks," *The New York Times,* August 8, 2000.

CHAPTER 5: PLANNING FOR SUSTAINABLE AIR QUALITY

American Council on Intergovernmental Relations. *Clean Air Act Report.* Washington, DC: ACIR, 1996.

American Lung Association, May 12, 2001. www.lungusa.org

Archibold, Randal C. "Tentative Deal on Acid Rain Is Reached with Third Utility," *The New York Times,* December 22, 2000.

Arrandale, Tom. "Trading Off Summer Smog," *Governing,* June 2000.

Belsie, Laurent. "Americans Losing the Drive to Conserve," *The Christian Science Monitor,* August 30, 1999.

Bradsher, Keith. "Detroit Plays Catch-up in Race for Hybrid Car," *The New York Times,* January 1, 2000.

Calthorpe, Peter. *The Next American Metropolis: Ecology, Community, and the American Dream.* New York: Simon & Schuster, 1993.

Cappiello, Dina. "Alcove's Fish Worry Critics," *Times Union* (Albany, NY), November 26, 1999a.

———. "Pataki Mandates Emissions Cuts," *Times Union* (Albany, NY), October 15, 1999b.

City of Portland, Oregon. "Land Use, Transportation, Air Quality Connection." Portland, OR: City of Portland, 1994.

Coequyt, John and Richard Wiles. *Prime Suspects: The Law Breaking Polluters America Fails to Inspect.* Washington, DC: Environmental Working Group, 2000.

Council on Environmental Quality. *Annual Report, 1996.* Washington, DC: U.S. Government Printing Office, 1996.

Dao, James. "Acid Rain Law Found to Fail in Adirondacks," *The New York Times,* March 27, 2000.

DePalma, Anthony. "NAFTA's Powerful Little Secret," *The New York Times,* March 11, 2001.

Dowie, Mark. *Losing Ground: American Environmentalism at the Close of the Twentieth Century.* Cambridge, MA: MIT Press, 1995.

Dunn, Seth and Christopher Flavin. "Moving the Climate Change Agenda Forward," in L. Starke, ed., "Reducing Our Toxic Burden," in L. Starke, ed., for The Worldwatch Institute. *State of the World 2002.* New York: W.W. Norton & Company, 2002.

Easterbrook, Gregg. *A Moment on the Earth: The Coming Age of Environmental Optimism.* New York: Penguin Books, 1996.

The Economist, March 31, 2001a.

———, June 16, 2001b.

Eds. of *E: The Environmental Magazine.* "To Build a Fire," reprinted in *Environmental Defense Newsletter* 31:3, September 2000.

Ehrenhalt, Alan. "The Czar of Gridlock," *Governing,* May 1999.

Firestone, David. "Collapse of Atlanta Talks Keeps Road Builders Idle," *The New York Times,* January 4, 2001.

——. "Suburban Comforts Thwart Atlanta's Plans to Limit Sprawl," *The New York Times,* November 21, 1999.

Greider, William. "Carbongate," Natural Resources Defense Council, *The Amicus Journal,* Summer 2001.

Hakim, Danny. "Auto Emission Rules in California Are Forcing Changes," *The New York Times,* July 22, 2002.

Hawken, Paul, Amory Lovins, and L. Hunter Lovins. *Natural Capitalism: Creating the Next Industrial Revolution.* Boston: Little Brown and Company, 1999.

Little, Charles. *The Dying of the Trees.* New York: Penguin Books, 1997.

Lowy, Joan. "Guzzler Nation," Scripps Howard News Service, June 17, 2001.

Major, Michael J. "Containing Growth in the Pacific Northwest," *Urban Land,* March 1994.

McPhee, John. *The Control of Nature.* New York: Farrar, Straus, and Giroux, 1989.

Money advertisement: "Introducing the Honda FCX, the first zero-emission fuel-cell car on the road," February 2003.

Moore, Curtis A. *Smart Growth and the Clean Air Act.* Washington, DC: Northeast-Midwest Institute, 2001.

Natural Resources Defense Council, May 6, 2001. www.nrdc.org/brie/fbair.htm

——. *The Amicus Journal,* Spring 2000.

——. *Land Use Controls in the United States.* New York: The Dial Press, 1977.

1000 Friends of Oregon. *Making the Connections: A Summary of the LUTRAQ (Land Use Transportation Air Quality) Project, Volume 7: Integrating Land-Use and Transportation Planning for Livable Communities.* Portland, OR: 1000 Friends of Oregon, 1997.

Owen, Oliver S., Daniel D. Chiras, and John P. Reganold. *Natural Resource Conservation.* 7th ed. Upper Saddle River, NJ: Prentice-Hall, 1998.

Perez-Pena, Richard. "Plants in South to Cut Emissions That Produce Smog in Northeast," *The New York Times,* November 16, 2000.

——. "Pataki to Impose Strict New Limits on Auto Emissions," *The New York Times,* November 7, 1999.

Pollack, Andrew. "California Adopts Plan for Electric Cars," *The New York Times,* January 27, 2001.

Revkin, Andrew C. "U.S. Is Pressuring Industries to Cut Greenhouse Gases," *The New York Times,* January 20, 2003.

Saar, Robert A. "In the Backyard, a Potent Source of Pollution," *The New York Times,* January 4, 2000.

Schrank, David and Tim Lomax. *The 2001 Urban Mobility Report.* College Station, TX: Texas Transportation Institute, Texas A&M University, 2001.

Southern California Air Quality District, March 2000. www.aqmd.gov/matesiidf/matestoc.htm

Stein, Theo. " 'Clean Air' City is Closer," *The Denver Post,* August 31, 2001.

Stephenson, John B., Director Natural Resources and Environment, U.S. General Accounting Office. *Environmental Protection: The Federal Government Could Help Communities Better Plan for Transportation That Protects Air Quality.* Testimony Before the Committee on Environment and Public Works, U.S. Senate, July 30, 2002.

Stevens, William K. "Pollution Takes Toll on Clouds and Rain," *The New York Times,* March 14, 2000.

Stout, David, "7 Utilities Sued by U.S. on Charges of Polluting Air," *The New York Times,* November 4, 1999.

Times Union (Albany, NY), March 29, 2000.

U.S. Bureau of the Census. *Statistical Abstract of the United States: 2002.* Washington, DC: U.S. Government Printing Office, 2003.

——. *Statistical Abstract of the United States: 2000.* Washington, DC: U.S. Government Printing Office, 2001.

U.S. Energy Information Agency. *Oil, Natural Gas, Coal, Electricity Environment Profile.* Washington, DC: U.S. Department of Energy, 2001.

U.S. Environmental Protection Agency. Envirofacts, July, 31, 2002. www.epa.gov/enviro/html/topics.htm#Air

——, March 12, 2001a. www.epa.gov/iaq/radon/index.htm

——. *Latest Findings on National Air Quality: 2000 Status and Trends.* Washington, DC: USEPA, 2001b.

——. *Light-Duty Automotive Technology and Fuel Economy Trends Through 1999.* Washington, DC: U.S. Government Printing Office, 2000a.

——. Office of Air Quality Planning and Standards. *Latest Findings on National Air Quality: 1999 Status and*

Trends. EPA-454/F-00-002. Research Triangle Park, NC: USEPA, August 2000b.

——. *State and Local Government Pioneers: How State and Local Governments Are Implementing Environmentally Preferable Purchasing Practices.* Washington, DC: USEPA, 2000c.

——. Office of Air and Radiation. *Analysis of the Acid Deposition and Ozone Control Act (S. 172).* Washington, DC: USEPA, 2000d.

——. Press Release: "EPA Proposes New Standards to Protect Public Health from Radon in Drinking Water and Indoor Air." Washington, DC: USEPA, October 19, 1999a.

——. *The Benefits and Costs of the Clean Air Act Amendments of 1990.* Washington, DC: USEPA, 1999b.

——. Office of Air Quality Planning and Standards. "The Plain English Guide to the Clean Air Act," November 30, 1999c.

——. Press Release: "EPA Releases Most Recent Community Right-to-Know Data on Toxic Releases," May 13, 1999d.

——. *1997 Toxic Release Inventory Public Data Release Report.* Washington, DC: USEPA, 1999e.

——. *National Listing of Fish and Wildlife Consumption Advisories,* EPA-823-F-99-005. Washington, DC: USEPA, July 1999f.

Use Measures: Policy Options. Washington, DC: US Government Printing Office, September 1999g.

——. *State Air Pollution Implementation Plan Progress Report.* Washington, DC: USEPA, 1999h.

——. Office of Inspector General. *Consolidated Report on [Office of Compliance Assistance] OECA's Oversight of Regional and State Air Enforcement Programs.* Washington, DC: USEPA, September 1998.

——. *The Benefits and Costs of the Clean Air Act, 1970 to 1990.* Washington, DC: USEPA, 1997.

Wald, Matthew L. "Clean Air Battlefield," *The New York Times,* December 1, 2002.

——. "Plywood Pollution Case is Settled for $93.2 Million," *The New York Times,* July 21, 2000a.

——. "13 States to Unite to Cut Truck Emissions," *The New York Times,* November 21, 2000b.

——. "Citing Health Risk, E.P.E. Cuts Sulfur in Diesel Fuel," *The New York Times,* March 15, 2000c.

——. "Stricter Pollution Controls Set for Cars and Light Trucks," *The New York Times,* December 21, 1999.

Yardley, Jim. "Houston, Smarting Economically From Smog, Searches for Remedies," *The New York Times,* September 24, 2000.

——. "Bush Approach to Pollution: Preference for Self-Policing," *The New York Times,* November 9, 1999.

CHAPTER 6: PLANNING FOR SOLID WASTE AND RECYCLING

Abramovitz, Janet N. and Ashley T. Mattoon. "Recovering the Paper Landscape," in Worldwatch, *The State of the World 2000.* New York: W.W. Norton, 2000.

Ackerman, Frank. *Why Do We Recycle? Markets, Values, and Public Policy.* Washington, DC: Island Press, 1997.

Chertow, Marian. "Municipal Solid Waste," in Dernbach, ed., *Stumbling Toward Sustainability.* Washington, DC: Environmental Law Institute, 2002.

Clines, Francis X. "Cleanup Fights Hillbilly Stereotype," *The New York Times,* September 21, 2000.

Dernbach, John. "Synthesis," in Dernbach, ed., *Stumbling Toward Sustainability.* Washington, DC: Environmental Law Institute, 2002.

Easterbrook, Gregg. *A Moment on the Earth: The Coming Age of Environmental Optimism.* New York: Penguin Books, 1996.

Franklin Associates, Ltd. "Characterization of Municipal Solid Waste in the United States: 1996 Update." Report prepared for the U.S. Environmental Protection Agency, Municipal and Industrial Solid Waste Division, Office of Solid Waste, 1997.

Gardner, Gary and Payal Sampat. "Forging a Sustainable Materials Economy," in World Watch Institute, *State of the World 1999.* New York: W.W. Norton & Company, 1999.

Goldstein, Nora and Celeste Madtes. "The State of Garbage in America," *BioCycle,* December 2001.

Hawken, Paul. *The Ecology of Commerce: A Declaration of Sustainability.* New York: HarperBusiness, 1993.

Hawken, Paul, Amory Lovins, and L. Hunter Lovins. *Natural Capitalism: Creating the Next Industrial Revolution.* Boston: Little Brown and Company, 1999.

Hui, Gordon, Jr. *Pay-As-You-Throw Communities Continue to Grow.* Washington, DC: U.S. Environmental Protection Agency, May 1999.

Ince, Peter J. "Recycling of Wood and Paper Products in the United States." Madison, WI: U.S. Forest Service, Forest Products Laboratory, January 1996.

Institute for Local Self-Reliance. News Release, March 27, 2000. www.ilsr.org/recycling/w2kpr.htm

Lende, Heather. "A Royal Mess." *The Christian Science Monitor,* November 24, 1999.

Leroux, Kivi. "Solid Waste: Lettuce Recycle: Putting Food to Waste to Work," *American City & County,* October 1, 1999.

Lipton, Eric. "Efforts to Close Fresh Kills are Taking Unforeseen Tolls," *The New York Times,* February 21, 2000.

Merrill, Lynn, "Waste by Rail: Still on the Main Line?" *World Wastes,* November 1, 1999.

Miller, G.T., Jr. *Living in the Environment.* 10th ed. Belmont, CA: Wadsworth Publishing Company, 1998.

National Solid Wastes Management Association, Environmental Industries Association, *Municipal Solid Waste Disposal Trends: 1996 Update.* Washington, DC: EIA, 1996.

Times Union (Albany, NY), July 16, 2000.

Times Union (Albany, NY). "State's waste stream flows across border," October 27, 1999.

U.S. Bureau of the Census. *Statistical Abstract of the United States: 2002.* Washington, DC: U.S. Government Printing Office, 2003.

——. *Statistical Abstract of the United States: 2001.* Washington, DC: U.S. Government Printing Office, 2002.

——. *Statistical Abstract of the United States: 2000.* Washington, DC: U.S. Government Printing Office, 2001.

U.S. Environmental Protection Agency. "List of Municipal Solid Waste Landfills," May 15, 2002a. www.epa.gov/epaoswer/non-hw/muncpl/landfill.htm

——, May 18, 2002b. www.epa.gov/outreach/lmop/about.htm

——. *Characterization of Municipal Solid Waste: 1996 Update.* Washington, DC: USEPA, 2000a.

——. *Characterization of Municipal Solid Waste: 1996 Update 2.* Washington, DC: USEPA, 2000b.

——. *Making Solid Waste Decisions with Full Cost Accounting.* Washington, DC: USEPA, June 1996a.

——. *Turning a Liability into an Asset: A Landfill Gas-to-Energy Project Development Handbook.* Washington, DC: USEPA, September 1996b.

——. *Directory and Atlas of Solid Waste Disposal Facilities.* Washington, DC: USEPA, 1996c.

CHAPTER 7: PLANNING FOR TOXIC SUBSTANCES AND TOXIC WASTE

American Petroleum Institute. "Influence of the Oil Pollution Act of 1990," June 2, 1999. www.api.org/oilspills/opa.htm

Brower, Michael and Warren Leon. *The Consumer's Guide to Effective Environmental Choices: Practical Advice from the Union of Concerned Scientists.* New York: Three Rivers Press, 1999.

Carson, Rachel. *Silent Spring.* Boston: Houghton Mifflin, 1962.

Council on Environmental Quality. *Annual Report, 1996.* Washington, DC: U.S. Government Printing Office, 1996.

Davis, Todd S. *Brownfields: A Comprehensive Guide to Redeveloping Contaminated Property.* 2d ed. Chicago: American Bar Association, 2002.

Dernbach, John. "Synthesis," in Dernbach, ed., *Stumbling Toward Sustainability.* Washington, DC: Environmental Law Institute, 2002.

Dowie, Mark. *Losing Ground: American Environmentalism at the Close of the Twentieth Century.* Cambridge: MA: MIT Press, 1995.

Eisen, Joel B. "Brownfields Redevelopment," in Dernbach, ed., *Stumbling Toward Sustainability.* Washington, DC: Environmental Law Institute, 2002.

Epstein, Samuel S., Lester O. Brown, and Carl Pope. *Hazardous Waste in America.* San Francisco: Sierra Club Books, 1982.

Gibbs, Lois Marie. *Learning from Love Canal: A 20th Anniversary Retrospective,* May 10, 2001. arts.envirolink.org/arts_and_activism/LoisGibbs.htm

Harr, Jonathan. *A Civil Action.* New York: Vintage Books, 1996.

Hinnefeld, Steven. "State to Run PCB Cleanup Facility," *Herald-Times* (Bloomington, IN), August 1, 2001.

Janofsky, Michael. "Pact Signed to Clean Up Nuclear Sites," *The New York Times,* September 11, 1999.

Jehl, Douglas. "Plan to Dump Coal Ash Adds Salt to a Wound," *The New York Times,* April 14, 2000.

Johnson, Kirk. "E.P.A. to Proceed on Dredging Plan for Hudson PCB's," *The New York Times,* August 1, 2001.

Johnson, Mark. "Brownfields Are Looking Greener," *Planning* 68:6, June 2002.

McGinn, Anne Platt. "Reducing Our Toxic Burden," in L. Starke, ed., for The Worldwatch Institute. *State of the World 2002.* New York: W.W. Norton & Company, 2002.

Mineral Policy Center. *Golden Dreams, Poisoned Streams.* Washington, DC: MPC, 1997.

Mintz, Joel A. "Hazardous Waste and Superfund" in Dernbach, ed., *Stumbling Toward Sustainability.* Washington, DC: Environmental Law Institute, 2002.

The New York Times, "Money to Clean Up Polluted Sites is Authorized," January 12, 2002.

——. "Deal is Reached to Clean Up Polluted Mine in California," October 22, 2000.

——. "Developer is Convicted in Toxic-Debris Dumping," October 10, 1999a.

——, November 11, 1999b.

O'Meara, Molly. "Harnessing Information Technologies for the Environment," in Worldwatch, *The State of the World 2000.* New York: W.W. Norton, 2000.

Owen, Oliver S., David D. Chiras, and John P. Reganold. *Natural Resource Conservation.* 7th ed. Upper Saddle River, NJ: Prentice-Hall, 1998.

Page, G. William and H. Rabinowitz. "Potential for Redevelopment of Contaminated Brownfields Sites," *Economic Development Quarterly* 8:4, 1994.

Pankratz, Howard. "Grand Jury Could Change Much—Many Observers Uneasy." *The Denver Post,* July 2, 1997.

Pennsylvania Department of Environmental Protection. Pennsylvania's Land Recycling Program, May 10, 2003.
www.dep.state.pa.us/dep/deputate/airwaste/wm/landrecy/factsFS.htm

Platt, Rutherford H. *Land Use and Society: Geography, Law, and Public Policy.* Washington, DC: Island Press, 1996.

Probst, Katherine N. and David M. Konisky. *Superfund's Future: What Will It Cost?* Washington, DC: Resources for the Future, 2001.

Ryan, Karen-Lee. "Toxic Turnabouts," *Planning,* December 1998.

Salkin, Patricia. "The Smart Growth Agenda: A Snapshot of State Activity at the Turn of the Century," *Saint Louis University Public Law Review* 21:2, 2002.

Schuessler, Heidi. "All Used Up With Somewhere to Go," *The New York Times,* November 23, 2000.

U.S. Bureau of the Census. *Statistical Abstract of the United States 2002.* Washington, DC: U.S. Government Printing Office, 2003.

——. *Statistical Abstract of the United States 2000.* Washington, DC: U.S. Government Printing Office, 2001.

U.S. Conference of Mayors. *Recycling America's Land: A National Report on Brownfields Redevelopment,* Vol. 3, 1997.

U.S. Environmental Protection Agency. "Cleaning Up UST System Releases," January 13, 2003.
www.epa.gov/swerust1/cat/index.htm

——. "Whitman Announces Availability of Latest Toxic Release Inventory," May 23, 2002a.
www.epa.gov

——, May 4, 2002b. www.epa.gov

——, March 22, 2001. Brownfields Home Page:
www.epa.gov/swerosps/bf/index.htm

——. Office of Water. *Liquid Assets 2000: America's Water Resources at a Turning Point.* Washington, DC: USEPA, 2000.

——. *Making Solid Waste Decisions with Full Cost Accounting.* Washington, DC: USEPA, June 1996.

——. *Criteria for Solid Waste Disposal Facilities: A Guide for Owners/Operators.* Washington, DC: USEPA, 1993.

U.S. General Accounting Office. *Siting Hazardous Waste Landfills and Their Correlation with the Racial and Economic Status of Surrounding Communities.* Washington, DC: U.S. Government Printing Office, 1983.

Wald, Matthew L. "Nevada Site Urged for Nuclear Dump," *The New York Times,* January 11, 2002.

Zielbauer, Paul. "States and Cities Flout Law on Underground Fuel Tanks," *The New York Times,* August 8, 2000.

CHAPTER 8: PROTECTING THE NATION'S LANDSCAPE TREASURES

American Rivers, May 12, 2001.
www.americanrivers.org/whatwedo/default.htm

Beatley, Timothy. "Preserving Biodiversity: Challenges for Planners," *Journal of the American Planning Association* 66:1, Winter 2000.

Beatley, Timothy and Katherine Manning. *The Ecology of Place: Planning for Environment, Economy, and Community.* Washington, DC: Island Press, 1998.

Brennan, Margaret F., Donn A. Derr, and Mark J. Reggimenti. "Lessons Learned: An Examination of Transfer of Development Rights Programs." West Windsor, NJ: American Farmland Trust Conference, April 10, 2000.

Bryson, Bill. *A Walk in the Woods.* New York: Broadway Books, 1999.

Bureau of Land Management, August 10, 2002. www.blm.gov

The Conservation Fund, August 22, 2002. www.conservationfund.org/conservation.htm

Council on Environmental Quality. *Annual Report, 1996.* Washington, DC: U.S. Government Printing Office, 1996.

Daniels, Tom. *When City and Country Collide: Managing Growth in the Metropolitan Fringe.* Washington, DC: Island Press, 1999.

Daniels, Tom and Deborah Bowers. *Holding Our Ground: Protecting America's Farms and Farmlands.* Washington, DC: Island Press, 1997.

Duane, T.P. *Shaping the Sierra: Nature, Culture and Conflict in the Changing West.* Berkeley, CA: University of California Press, 1999.

Easterbrook, Gregg. *A Moment on the Earth: The Coming Age of Environmental Optimism.* New York: Penguin Books, 1996.

Egan, Timothy. "Alaska Changes View on Carter After 20 Years," *The New York Times,* August 25, 2000.

Endicott, Eve, ed. *Land Conservation through Public-Private Partnerships.* Washington, DC: Island Press, 1994.

Farmland Preservation Report. Street, MD: Bowers Publishing, May 2000.

Flink, Charles A. and Robert M. Seams. *Greenways: A Guide to Planning, Design, and Development.* Washington, DC: Island Press, 1993.

Florida Department of Environmental Protection. *Plan for a Statewide System of Greenways: Five Year Florida Greenways System Implementation.* Tallahassee, FL: FDEP, 1998.

Healy, Robert G. and John S. Rosenberg. *Land Use and the States.* 2d ed. Baltimore: Johns Hopkins University Press, 1979.

Holmes, Steven A. "Compromise Reached on Conservation Bill," *The New York Times,* September 30, 2000.

Howe, J., Edward McMahon, *et al. Balancing Nature and Commerce in Gateway Communities.* Washington, DC: Island Press, 1997.

Indy Greenways, April 20, 2001. www.indygreenways.org

Janofsky, Michael. "Environmental Groups' Ratings Rile Ski Industry," *The New York Times,* December 3, 2000.

——. "National Parks, Strained by Record Crowds, Face a Crisis," *The New York Times,* July 25, 1999.

Jehl, Douglas. "Roads Barred for One-Third of U.S. Forests," *The New York Times,* January 5, 2001.

Land Trust Alliance. December 20, 2002a. www.lta.org/policy/referenda2002.htm

——. March 15, 2002b. www.lta.org/policy/referenda2001.htm

Lerner, Steve and William Poole. "The Economic Benefits of Parks and Open Space," The Trust for Public Land, December 10, 1999. www.tpl.org/newsroom

Lucero, Lora and Jeff Soule. "A Win for Lake Tahoe," *Planning* 68:6, June 2002.

McDowell, Edwin. "Sierra Club Sues Hawaii on Tourism Promotion," *The New York Times,* Section 5, April 23, 2000.

Mid-Ohio Regional Planning Commission. *Greenways: A Plan for Franklin County (Ohio).* Columbus: MORPC, 1999.

Montana Land Reliance, August 22, 2002. www.mtlandreliance.org

National Park Service. Land and Water Conservation Fund, October 10, 2001. www.ncrc.nps.gov/programs/lwcf.htm

Natural Resources Defense Council. *The Amicus Journal,* Winter 2001.

The Nature Conservancy, July 15, 2002. www.tnc.org

Peninsula Open Space Trust, May 19, 2002. www.openspacetrust.org

Platt, Kalvin. "Going Green," *Planning* 66:8, August 2000.

Pruetz, Rick. *Saved by Development.* Burbank, CA: Arje Press, 1997.

Salkin, Patricia. "The Smart Growth Agenda: A Snapshot of State Activity at the Turn of the Century." *Saint Louis University Public Law Review* 21:2, 2002.

Seelye, Katherine Q. "Complex Deal Is First Step to Create New National Park," *The New York Times,* January 31, 2002.

Small, Stephen J. *Preserving Family Lands.* 2d ed. Boston: Landowner Planning Center, 1992.

Thomson, Rod. "Voters Approve Tax Hike," *Sarasota Herald Tribune,* March 9, 1999.

Trust for Public Land. *Doing Deals: A Guide to Buying Land for Conservation.* Washington, DC: Land Trust Alliance and TPL, 1995.

U.S. Bureau of the Census. *Statistical Abstract of the United States, 2002.* Washington, DC: U.S. Government Printing Office, 2003.

U.S. Department of the Interior, October 9, 2000. www.doi.gov/budget

U.S. Environmental Protection Agency. Office of Policy, Economics, and Innovation. *A Method to Quantify Environmental Indicators of Selected Leisure Activities in the United States.* Washington, DC: USEPA, 2000. *See* www.epa.gov/innovations/sectors/pdf/leisure.pdf

Vermont Land Trust. *Annual Report 2001.* Montpelier, VT: VLT, 2002.

The Wilderness Society, November 15, 1999. www.wilderness.org/newsroom/15 most/map.htm

Wright, Jack. *Montana Ghost Dance.* Austin, TX: University of Texas Press, 1998.

CHAPTER 9: PLANNING FOR WILDLIFE HABITAT

Balzar, John. "Extinction of Fish Species Possible, Experts Now Warn," *Los Angeles Times,* November 16, 2000.

Beatley, Timothy. "Preserving Biodiversity: Challenges for Planners," *Journal of the American Planning Association* 66:1, Winter 2000.

——. *Habitat Conservation Planning: Endangered Species and Urban Growth.* Austin, TX: University of Texas Press, 1994.

Center for Natural Lands Management. "Manchester Mitigation Bank," September 4, 2001. www.cnlm.org/manchmb.htm

Council on Environmental Quality. *Annual Report, 1996.* Washington, DC: U.S. Government Printing Office, 1996.

——. *1993 Annual Report on Environmental Quality.* Washington, DC: U.S. Government Printing Office, 1993.

Davis, Mike. *Ecology of Fear.* New York: Vintage Books, 1999.

Ducks Unlimited, May 28, 2002. www.ducks.org/news

Easterbrook, Gregg. *A Moment on the Earth: The Coming Age of Environmental Optimism.* New York: Penguin Books, 1996.

The Economist. "The Rio Grande: Not Big Enough Any More," August 19, 2000.

Forman, R.T.T. *Land Mosaics: The Ecology of Landscapes and Regions.* Cambridge, UK: Cambridge University Press, 1995.

The Great Outdoors Colorado Trust Fund. *Managing Development for People and Wildlife: A Handbook for Habitat Protection by Local Governments.* Denver, CO: Great Outdoors Colorado, 1997.

Interagency Ecosystem Management Task Force. *The Ecosystem Approach: Healthy Ecosystems and Sustainable Economies.* Springfield, VA: National Technical Information Services, 1995.

Jehl, Douglas. "Sacrifices to a Green Agenda," *The New York Times,* Section 4, June 24, 2001.

Karamanos, Panagiotis. "Voluntary Environmental Agreements: Evolution and Definition of a New Environmental Policy Approach," *Journal of Environmental Planning and Management* 44:1, 2001.

Lidicker, William Z., Jr. "Responses of Mammals to Habitat Edges: An Overview," *Landscape Ecology* 14, 1999.

McNeil, J.R. *Something New Under the Sun.* New York: W.W. Norton, 2000.

Musick, John A. *et al.* "Marine, Estuarine, and Diadromous Fish Stocks at Risk of Extinction in North America (Exclusive of Pacific Salmonids)," *Fisheries.* American Fisheries Society, November 2000.

National Academy of Sciences. *Science and the Endangered Species Act.* Washington, DC: National Academy of Sciences, 1995.

National Biological Information Infrastructure, January 15, 2003. www.nbii.gov

National Geographic Society, July 20, 2001. www.Millenium@NationalGeographic.com

National Wildlife Federation, February 21, 2001. www.nwf.org/endangered/species/a6bulwar.htm

——. "HCP Update," March 22, 1999. www.nwf.org

Natural Resources Conservation Service. *Farm Bill 2002: Wildlife Habitat Incentives Program.* Washington, DC: NRCS, May 2002.

——. *Wildlife Habitat Incentives Program, 1998 Program Accomplishments.* Washington, DC: U.S. Department of Agriculture, 1999.

Natural Resources Defense Council. *The Amicus Journal,* Summer 1997.

The Nature Conservancy. *50 Years of Saving Great Places* 51:1, January/February 2001.

Noss, Reed F., Edward T. LaRoe, III, and J. Michael Scott. *Endangered Ecosystems of the United States: A Preliminary Assessment of Loss and Degradation.* Denver, CO: U.S. Geological Survey, Biological Resources, 1995.

Odum, Eugene P. *Ecology: A Bridge Between Science and Society.* Sunderland, MA: Sinauer Associates, Inc., 1997.

Oregon Department of Land Conservation and Development. *Oregon's Statewide Planning Goals.* Salem, OR: ODLCD, 1985.

Owen, Oliver S., David D. Chiras, and John P. Reganold. *Natural Resource Conservation.* 7th ed. Upper Saddle River, NJ: Prentice-Hall, 1998.

Peck, Sheila. *Planning for Biodiversity: Issues and Examples.* Washington, DC: Island Press, 1998.

Rickets, T.H., E. Dinerstein, D.M. Olson, and C.J. Loucks, eds. *Terrestrial Ecosystems of North America: A Conservation Assessment.* Washington, DC: Island Press, 1999.

Rocky Mountain Elk Foundation, March 29, 2001. www.rmef.org

San Diego Association of Governments. "Region 2020." San Diego: SANDAG, March 2000.

Soule, M.E. "Land Use Planning and Wildlife Maintenance: Guidelines for Conserving Wildlife in Urban Landscapes," *Journal of the American Planning Association* 57:3, 1991.

Stein, Bruce A., Lynn S. Kutner, and Jonathan S. Adams. *Precious Heritage: The Status of Biodiversity in the U.S.* New York: Oxford University Press, 2000.

Sternold, James. "California Wine Region Torn by Debate Over Use of Land," *The New York Times,* April 3, 2000.

Stevens, William K. "U.S. Found to Be a Leader in Its Diversity of Wildlife," *The New York Times,* March 16, 2000.

Stout, David. "A Battle Over Beetles Takes on an Urgency," *The New York Times,* March 20, 2000.

Summit County, Colorado, Zoning Ordinance, adopted 1994.

Tarlock, A. Dan. "Biodiversity and Endangered Species," in Dernbach, ed., *Stumbling Toward Sustainability.* Washington, DC: Environmental Law Institute, 2002.

Trombulak, Steve and C. Frissell. "A Review of the Ecological Effects of Roads on Terrestrial and Aquatic Ecosystems," *Conservation Biology* 14, 2000.

U.S. Bureau of the Census. *Statistical Abstract of the United States, 2002.* Washington, DC: U.S. Government Printing Office, 2003.

———. *Statistical Abstract of the United States, 1999.* Washington, DC: U.S. Government Printing Office, 2000.

U.S. Department of Agriculture, Natural Resources Conservation Service. "Conservation Corridor Planning at the Landscape Level" in *National Biology Handbook,* Part 616.4. Washington, DC: USDA, 1999.

U.S. Environmental Protection Agency, Science Advisory Board. *Reducing Risk: Setting Priorities and Strategies for Environmental Protection.* Washington, DC: USEPA, 1991.

U.S. Fish and Wildlife Service, May 10, 2003a. http://ecos.fws.gov/servlet/TESSUs/map?status=listed

———. May 10, 2003b. http://ecos.fws.gov/tess/html/boxscore.htm

———. Habitat Protection Plans, May 22, 2002. ecos.fws.gov

———. Pacific Region. Press Release: "Emergency Protection Given to Santa Barbara County Population of California Tiger Salamander," January 19, 2000.

———. Press Release: "Nation Marks 25 Years of Endangered Species Protection," December 23, 1998.

U.S. Geological Survey. *Status and Trends of the Nation's Biological Resources.* Washington, DC: USGS, 1999.

U.S. Forest Service. *Ecological Subregions of the United States.* Washington, DC: USFS, 1993.

Vermont Natural Resources Council. Personal Communication, December 6, 2000.

The Wildlands Project, May 13, 2001. www.twp.org/aboutus/thevision/theproblem_content.htm

Wilson, E. O., ed. *Biodiversity.* Washington, DC: National Academy Press, 1988.

Wortman, Dave. "Can Cities and Salmon Coexist?" *Planning* 68:5, May 2002.

CHAPTER 10: PLANNING AND MANAGING WETLANDS

Beatley, Timothy. "Preserving Biodiversity: Challenges for Planners," *Journal of the American Planning Association* 66:1, Winter 2000.

Bridgham, Scott D., Carol A. Johnston, John Pastor, and Karen Undegraff. "Potential Feedbacks of Northern Wetlands on Climate Change." *BioScience* 45:4, 1995.

Council on Environmental Quality. *Annual Report, 1996,* Washington, DC: U.S. Government Printing Office, 1996.

Cowardin, Lewis M. *United States Fish and Wildlife Service Wetland Classification System.* Washington, DC: USFWS, 1979.

Dennison, Mark S. and James Berry. *Wetlands: A Guide to Science, Law, and Technology.* Park Ridge, NJ: Noyes Publications, 1993.

Ducks Unlimited, May 28, 2002. www.ducks.org/news

——. *Annual Report 2001.* Memphis, TN: Ducks Unlimited, 2001.

Easterbrook, Gregg. *A Moment on the Earth: The Coming Age of Environmental Optimism.* New York: Penguin Books, 1996.

Farm Service Agency, Status of Conservation Reserve Enhancement Program Applications, August 12, 2002. www.fsa.gov

Hunt, Randall. "Do Created Wetlands Replace the Wetlands That Are Destroyed?" Washington, DC: USGS, 1998.

Maltby, Edward. *Waterlogged Wealth: Why Waste the World's Wet Places.* Washington, DC: International Institute for Environment and Health, 1986.

Maryland Department of the Environment, March 6, 2002.
www.mde.state.md.us/wetlands/
lawsandprograms.htm

McCormick, Anita Louise. *Vanishing Wetlands.* San Diego: Lucent Books, Inc, 1995.

Moshiri, Gerald. *Constructed Wetlands for Water Quality Improvement.* New York: Lewis Publishers, CRC Press, 1993.

National Academy of Sciences. *Compensating for Wetland Losses Under the Clean Water Act.* Washington, DC: National Academy Press, 2001.

Natural Resources Conservation Service. Wetlands Reserve Status Report, May 26, 2001a.
www.nrcs.gov

——. *National Resources Inventory.* Washington, DC: NRCS, January 2001b.

——. *National Resources Inventory, 1997.* Highlights. Washington, DC: U.S. Government Printing Office, 1999.

The New York Times. "An Everglades Action Plan," July 13, 2000.

Perciasepe, Robert. Testimony of Robert Perciasepe of the EPA to the U.S. Senate, November 1, 1995.

Platt, Rutherford H. *Land Use and Society: Geography, Law, and Public Policy.* Washington, DC: Island Press, 1996.

Realty Times. "Wetlands Not Likely to Make Any Rain for Builders," February 14, 2000.

Schmitt, Eric. "Everglades Restoration Plan Passes House, With Final Approval Seen," *The New York Times,* October 20, 2000.

U.S. Army Corps of Engineers. "Regulatory Program Overview," June 14, 2001.
www.usace.army.mi/inet/functions/cw/cecwo/
reg/oceover.htm

U.S. Environmental Protection Agency. Office of Water. *Water Quality Conditions in the United States: A Profile from the 1998 National Water Quality Inventory Report to Congress.* Washington, DC: USEPA, June 2000.

U.S. Fish and Wildlife Service. Press Release: "U.S. Fish and Wildlife Service Awards $9.4 Million for Wetland Restoration Projects in 1999," October 2, 1998.

CHAPTER 11: COASTAL ZONE MANAGEMENT

Associated Press. "Clinton Creates Huge Underwater Nature Preserve in Hawaii," *The New York Times,* December 5, 2000.

Beach, Dana. *Coastal Sprawl: The Effects of Urban Design on Aquatic Ecosystems in the United States.* Arlington, VA: Pew Oceans Commission, 2002.

Beatley, Timothy, David J. Brower, and Anna K. Schwab. *An Introduction to Coastal Zone Management.* 2d ed. Washington, DC: Island Press, 2002.

——. *An Introduction to Coastal Zone Management.* Washington, DC: Island Press, 1994.

California Coastal Commission. *Strategic Plan, 1997.* San Francisco: CCC, 1997.

Chesapeake Bay Foundation. Press Release: "Another Mixed Year for the Bay's Health, Says CBF Report," September 20, 2000a.

——. Fact Sheet. "Growth, Sprawl and the Chesapeake Bay: Facts About Growth and Land Use," 2000b.

Clines, Francis X. "Governments Tighten Goals for Restoring Chesapeake," *The New York Times,* June 29, 2000.

Council on Environmental Quality. *Annual Report, 1996*. Washington, DC: U.S. Government Printing Office, 1996.

Godschalk, David R. "Implementing Coastal Zone Management: 1972-1990," *Coastal Management* 20, 1992.

Godschalk, David R., David J. Brower, and Timothy Beatley. *Catastrophic Coastal Storms: Hazard Mitigation and Development Management*. Durham, NC: Duke University Press, 1989.

Healy, Robert and John Rosenberg. *Land Use and the States*. 2d ed. Baltimore: Johns Hopkins University Press, 1979.

H. John Heinz Center for Science, Economics, and the Environment. *Evaluation of Erosion Hazards*. Washington, DC: Federal Emergency Management Agency, 2000.

Jehl, Douglas. "Federal Money is Following Rebuilt Beaches Out to Sea," *The New York Times*, July 1, 2001.

Lacey, Mark. "Clinton Offers Plan to Protect Nation's Shorelines," *The New York Times*, May 27, 2000.

Land Use Law and Zoning Digest, September 1999. *Bolsa Chica Land Trust v. Superior Court*, California Court of Appeal, 83 Cal. Rptr. 2d 850, April 1999.

McHarg, Ian. *Design With Nature*. New York: Doubleday, 1971.

National Academy of Sciences. *Clear Coastal Waters: Understanding the Effects of Nutrient Pollution*. Washington, DC: NAS, 2000.

National Wildlife Federation. *Pollution Paralysis II: Code Red for Watersheds*. Washington, DC: NWF, 2000.

The Nature Conservancy. "The Queen of Forests Keeps Her Crown," *Nature Conservancy Magazine*, Fall 2002.

Oregon Department of Land Conservation and Development. *Oregon's Statewide Planning Goals*. Salem, OR: ODLCD, 1985.

Platt, Rutherford H. *Land Use and Society: Geography, Law, and Public Policy*. Washington, DC: Island Press, 1996.

Restore America's Estuaries. *A National Strategy to Restore Coastal and Estuarine Habitat*. Arlington, VA: Restore America's Estuaries, 2002.

Svarney, Thomas E. and Patricia Barnes-Svarney. *The Handy Ocean Answer Book*. Canton, MI: Visible Ink Press, 2000.

U.S. Coast Guard. *Harmful Algal Blooms and Hypoxia*. Coast Guard Authorization Act of 1998, Title VI. PL 105-383, 1998.

U.S. Environmental Protection Agency. Office of Water. "About the National Estuary Program." Washington, DC: USEPA, July 31, 2002. www.epa.gov/owow/estuaries

——. Great Lakes Program Office, August 1, 2002b. www.epa.gov/glnpo/about.htm

——. Office of Water. "About Estuaries: Why Protect Estuaries?" Washington, DC: USEPA, July 31, 2001a. www.epa.gov/owow/estuaries/about1.htm

——. Office of Water. *Clean Water Action Plan: National Coastal Condition Report (Draft)*. Washington, DC: USEPA, 2001b.

——. "The Business of Clean Water," December 10, 2000a. ww.epa.gov/ow/liquidassets/business.htm

——. Office of Water. *Liquid Assets 2000: America's Water Resources at a Turning Point*. Washington, DC: USEPA, 2000b.

——. Office of Water. *Water Quality Conditions in the United States: A Profile from the 1998 National Water Quality Inventory Report to Congress*. Washington, DC: USEPA, June 2000c.

——. *National Water Quality Inventory, 1998*. Washington, DC: USEPA, 1998a.

——. *National Water Quality Inventory: 1996 Report to Congress*, EPA-841-F-97-003. Washington, DC: USEPA, April 1998b.

Whitaker, Barbara. "Beach Closings and Advisories Reach Record, Report Shows," *The New York Times*, August 9, 2001.

CHAPTER 12: PLANNING FOR NATURAL HAZARDS AND NATURAL DISASTERS

Burby, Raymond J., ed. *Cooperating with Nature: Confronting Natural Hazards with Land Use Planning for Sustainable Communities*. Washington, DC: Joseph Henry/National Academy Press, 1998.

Burby, Raymond J. *et al.* "Unleashing the Power of Planning to Create Disaster-Resistant Communities," *Journal of the American Planning Association* 65:3, Summer 1999.

Chang, Kenneth. "Agency Projects Economic Risks of Earthquakes Across U.S.," *The New York Times*, September 21, 2000.

City of Sanibel, Florida. *Sanibel Plan.* City of Sanibel, Florida, 1997.

Davis, Mike. *Ecology of Fear.* New York: Vintage Books, 1999.

The Economist. "Desiccation Row," June 29, 2002.

——. "God, Man, and the Fires," August 12, 2000.

Federal Emergency Management Agency, May 3, 2001. www.fema.gov/about

——. "Project Impact: Building Disaster Resistant Communities." Washington, DC: FEMA, February, 7, 2000a.

——. February 14, 2000b. www.fema.gov

——. Project Impact Slide Presentation, Washington, DC: FEMA, 1999a.

——. "Mandatory Purchase of Flood Insurance Guidelines," Washington, DC: FEMA, September 1999b.

——. Region VIII, Press Release: "Acquisition Means Flood Prone Area Will Not Be Developed, Area Will Become Park Land," April 13, 1999c.

——. *A Unified National Program for Floodplain Management.* Washington, DC: FEMA, 1994.

Firestone, David. "Lingering Hazards Cover Carolina's Sea of Trouble," *The New York Times,* September 22, 1999a.

——. "In Carolina, a Fight for Electricity and Water," *The New York Times,* September 23, 1999b.

Godschalk, David R., Timothy Beatley, Philip R. Berke, David J. Brower, and Edward J. Kaiser. *Natural Hazard Mitigation: Recasting Disaster Policy and Planning.* Washington, DC: Island Press, 1999.

Godschalk, David R., David J. Brower, and Timothy Beatley. *Catastrophic Coastal Storms: Hazard Mitigation and Development Management.* Durham, NC: Duke University Press, 1989.

Grunwald, Michael. "Disasters All, But Not As Natural As You Think," *The Washington Post,* May 6, 2001.

Hampson, Rick. "Where Nature is an Immovable Object," *USA Today,* July 28, 2000.

Healy, Robert G. and John S. Rosenberg. *Land Use and the States.* 2d ed., Chapter 4. Baltimore: Johns Hopkins University Press, 1979.

Heinz, H. John III. Center for Science, Economics and the Environment. *Evaluation of Erosion Hazards.* Washington, DC: Federal Emergency Management Agency, 2000.

Janofsky, Michael. "Parched U.S. Faces Worst Year for Fires Since Mid-80's," *The New York Times,* August 3, 2000.

Jehl, Douglas. "Mississippi Flooding is Reviving a Debate on Government Role," *The New York Times,* April 27, 2001.

——. "Population Shift in the West Raises Wildfire Concerns," *The New York Times,* May 30, 2000.

McFadden, Robert D. "Rare Avalanche Kills One on Adirondack Slope," *The New York Times,* February 21, 2000.

McNeil, J.R. *Something New Under the Sun.* New York: W.W. Norton, 2000.

Mileti, Dennis. *Designing Future Disasters: A Sustainable Approach for Hazards Research and Application in the United States.* Washington, DC: Joseph Henry/National Academy Press, 1999.

Milloy, Ross E. "Population Trends Heighten West's Fire Woes," *The New York Times,* August 10, 2000.

Morris, Marya. *Subdivision Design in Flood Hazard Areas.* Planning Advisory Service Report No. 473. Chicago: American Planning Association, 1997.

The New York Times. "Agencies Preparing Now to Fight Rural Wildfires," November 26, 2000.

North Carolina Department of Emergency Management, August 2, 2002. www.dem.dcc.state.nc.us/mitigation/dma_2000.htm

Olshansky, Robert. *Planning for Hillside Development.* Planning Advisory Service Report No. 466. Chicago: American Planning Association, 1996.

Planning. "Government Buys 1,700 More Homes Flooded by Hurricane Floyd," October 2000.

Platt, Rutherford. *Land Use and Society: Geography, Law, and Public Policy.* Washington, DC: Island Press, 1996.

Razzi, Elizabeth. "Washed Away," *Kiplinger's Personal Finance Magazine,* February 2000.

Steinberg, Michele and Raymond J. Burby. "Growing Safe," *Planning* 68:4, April 2002.

Ullmann, Owen. "Growth Pressure Keeps Building," *USA Today,* July 27, 2000.

USA Today. "How Your Dollars Let Others Live at the Beach," July 27, 2000.

U.S. Bureau of the Census. *Statistical Abstract of the United States, 2002.* Washington, DC: U.S. Government Printing Office, 2003.

U.S. Environmental Protection Agency, August 5, 2001. www.epa.gov/globlawarming/impacts/coastal/index.htm

U.S. General Accounting Office. *Federal Wildfire Activities.* Washington, DC: USGAO, 1999.

U.S. Geological Survey. "The National Landslide Hazards Program." landslides.usgs.gov, July 7, 2002.

——. "Seattle Area Natural Hazards." seattlehazards.usgs.gov, February 2000.

Wilkinson, Todd. "Prometheus Unbound," *The Nature Conservancy* 51: 3, 2001.

Wright, John B. *Montana Ghost Dance.* Austin, TX: University of Texas Press, 1998.

CHAPTER 13: PLANNING FOR SUSTAINABLE WORKING LANDSCAPES: FARMLAND AND RANCHLAND

American Farmland Trust. "Congress Commits $1 Billion to Farmland Protection Program," *American Farmland,* Spring 2002.

——. *Farming on the Edge.* Washington, DC: AFT, 1996.

——. *Alternatives for Future Urban Growth in California's Central Valley: The Bottom Line for Agriculture and Taxpayers.* Washington, DC: AFT, 1995.

Burby, Raymond J., Arthur C. Nelson, Dennis Parker, and John Handmer. "Urban Containment Policy and Exposure to Natural Hazards: Is There a Connection?" *Journal of Environmental Planning and Management* 44, 2001.

Coughlin, Robert E. and John C. Keene, eds. *National Agricultural Lands Study, The Protection of Farmland: A Reference Book for State and Local Governments.* Washington, DC: U.S. Government Printing Office, 1981.

Council on Environmental Quality. *Annual Report, 1996.* Washington, DC: U.S. Government Printing Office, 1996.

——. *1982 Annual Report.* Washington, DC: U.S. Government Printing Office, 1982.

Daniels, Thomas L. "The Purchase of Development Rights: Preserving Agricultural Land and Open Space," *Journal of the American Planning Association* 57: 4, 1991.

Daniels, Tom. "Critical Mass and Farmland Preservation." Paper presented at the American Farmland Trust National Conference, St. Charles, IL, November 12, 2001.

——. *When City and Country Collide: Managing Growth in the Metropolitan Fringe.* Washington, DC: Island Press, 1999.

——. "Where Does Cluster Development Fit in Farmland Preservation?" *Journal of the American Planning Association* 63:1, 1997.

Daniels, Tom and Deborah Bowers. *Holding Our Ground: Protecting America's Farms and Farmland.* Washington, DC: Island Press, 1997.

Eisenberg, Evan. *The Ecology of Eden,* New York: Vintage Books, 1999.

Farmland Preservation Report. Street, MD: Bowers Publishing, May 2002a.

——. April 2002b.

——. July-August 2002c.

——. June 2001.

Johnston, Robert A. and Mary E. Madison. "From Landmarks to Landscapes: A Review of Current Practices in the Transfer of Development Rights." *Journal of the American Planning Association* 63:3, 1997.

Lockeretz, William, ed. *Sustaining Agriculture Near Cities,* Ankeny, IA: Soil and Water Conservation Society, 1987.

Lugar, Dick. "The Farm Bill Charade," *The New York Times,* January 21, 2002.

Natural Resources Conservation Service. *National Resources Inventory, 1997* (Revised). Washington, DC: U.S. Department of Agriculture, 2001.

——. "NRCS This Week, October 13, 2000," October 20, 2000. www.nhq.nrcs.usda/CCS/ThisWeek/NWk10-13.htm

——. *National Resources Inventory, 1997.* Washington, DC: U.S. Department of Agriculture, 1999.

Pruetz, Rick. *Saved by Development: Preserving Environmental Areas, Farmland.* Burbank, CA: Arje Press, 1997.

Purdy, Jedediah. "The New Culture of Rural America," *The American Prospect* 11:3, December 20, 1999.

U.S. Bureau of the Census. *Statistical Abstract of the United States, 2002.* Washington, DC: U.S. Government Printing Office, 2003.

U.S. Department of Agriculture. *1997 Census of Agriculture.* Washington, DC: U.S. Government Printing Office, 1999a.

—— and U.S. Environmental Protection Agency. *Unified National Strategy for Animal Feeding Operations.* Washington, DC: USDA and USEPA, March 1999b.

——. Economic Research Service. *Urbanization of Rural Land in the United States.* Washington, DC: U.S. Government Printing Office, 1994.

——. Soil Conservation Service. *National Agricultural Land Evaluation and Site Assessment Handbook.* Washington, DC: USDA, 1983.

U.S. Environmental Protection Agency. "CAFO Final Rule," December 17, 2002. cfpub.epa.gov/npdes/afo/cafofinalrule.cfm

——. Office of Water Management. *State Compendium: Programs and Regulatory Activities Related to Animal Feeding Operations.* Washington, DC: USEPA, August 1999.

——. *Pesticide Industry Sales and Usage: 1994 and 1995 Market Estimates.* Washington, DC: USEPA, 1997.

U.S. General Accounting Office. *Community Development: Local Growth Issues—Federal Opportunities and Challenges,* GAO/RCED-00-178. Washington, DC: USGAO, September 2000.

CHAPTER 14: PLANNING FOR SUSTAINABLE WORKING LANDSCAPES: FORESTRY

Abramovitz, Janet N. and Ashley T. Mattoon. "Recovering the Paper Landscape" in Worldwatch, *The State of the World 2000.* New York: W.W. Norton, 2000.

Adams, Glenn. "Deal Preserves Huge Area in Maine," Associated Press in *Burlington Free Press* (Vermont), March 21, 2001.

Brinckman, Jonathan. "Oregon Supreme Court Allows Logging-Restriction Rule," *The Oregonian,* April 12, 1997.

Bryson, Bill. *A Walk in the Woods.* New York: Broadway Books, 1999.

Council on Environmental Quality. *Annual Report, 1996.* Washington, DC: U.S. Government Printing Office, 1996.

Cromwell, David A. "Strategies for Dealing with the Urban/Forest Interface: The Recent California Experience," in G.A. Bradley, ed., *Land Use and Forest Resources in a Changing Environment.* Seattle: University of Washington Press, 1984.

Daniels, Thomas L. "State and Local Efforts in Conserving Privately-Owned Working Landscapes." Washington, DC: National Governors' Association, 2001.

Egan, Timothy. "Alaska, No Longer So Frigid, Starts to Crack, Burn and Sag," *The New York Times,* June 16, 2002.

Fischman, Robert L. "Forestry," in Dernbach, ed., *Stumbling Toward Sustainability.* Washington, DC: Environmental Law Institute, 2002.

Greene, Stephen. "Preserving Open Space for the Ages," *The Chronicle of Philanthropy,* July 29, 1999.

Harris, David. *The Last Stand.* San Francisco: Sierra Club Books, 1997.

Janofsky, Michael. "Citing Poor Plan, U.S. Takes Blame in Los Alamos Fire," *The New York Times,* May 19, 2000.

Jehl, Douglas. "Logging's Shift South Brings Concern on Oversight," *The New York Times,* August 8, 2000.

Little, Charles. *The Dying of the Trees.* New York: Penguin Books, 1997.

Montaigne, Fen. "There Goes the Neighborhood," *Audubon,* March-April 2000.

Natural Resources Conservation Service. "National Resources Inventory." Washington, DC: NRCS, January 2001.

The New York Times. "Forest Chief Will Make Logging Decisions," June 8, 2001.

——. "The Redwoods Deal," March 4, 1999.

Nieves, Evelyn. "Lumber Company Approves U.S. Deal to Save Redwoods," *The New York Times,* March 3, 1999.

Oregon Department of Forestry. "Forest Practice Notes," No. 8. Salem, OR: ODF, December 1994.

O'Toole, Randall. "National Forest Timber Sales Receipts and Costs in 1995," *Different Drummer* 3:4, 1997.

——. *Reforming the Forest Service.* Washington, DC: Island Press, 1988.

Pacific Forest Trust. *Pacific Forests.* Boonville, CA: PFT, Spring 2000, Spring 2001.

——. Press Release: "Energy Company Buys Carbon Credits in Conserved California Redwood Forest," November 9, 2000.

——. *Annual Report, 1998.* Boonville, CA: PFT, 1999.

——. *Annual Report, 1997.* Boonville, CA: PFT, 1998.

Powell, Douglas *et al. Forest Resources of the United States 1992.* Fort Collins, CO: U.S. Forest Service Rocky Mountain Forest and Range Experiment Station, 1993.

Revkin, Andrew. "$76 Million Deal to Save Woods and Wetlands," *The New York Times,* December 10, 1998.

Revkin, Andrew C. "A Question of Green: Forests Versus Money." *The New York Times,* November 17, 1997.

Richardson, Jean. *Partnerships in Communities: Reweaving the Fabric of Rural America.* Washington, DC: Island Press, 2000.

Schlamadinger, Bernhard and Gregg Marland. *Land Use and Global Climate Change: Forests, Land Management, and the Kyoto Protocol.* Arlington, VA: Pew Center on Global Climate Change, 2000.

Smith, W. Brad, John Vissage, Raymond Sheffield, and David Darr. *Forest Statistics of the United States, 1997.* St. Paul, MN: U.S. Department of Agriculture Forest Service North Central Forest Experiment Station, 2001.

U.S. Bureau of the Census. *Statistical Abstract of the United States, 2002.* Washington, DC: U.S. Government Printing Office, 2003.

U.S. Department of Agriculture, U.S. Forest Service. *U.S. Forest Facts and Historical Trends.* Washington, DC: USDA, USFS, 2001.

———. *2000 Resources Planning Act Assessment of Forest and Range Lands.* Washington, DC: USDA, 2000a.

———. *Southern Resources Assessment (Draft).* Washington, DC: USFS, 2000b.

U.S. Environmental Protection Agency. "Economics of Riparian Forest Buffers," EPA 903-F-98-003. Washington, DC: USEPA, May 1998.

U.S. News and World Report. "A Pixel Worth 1,000 Words," July 19, 1999.

William, Phil and Victoria Bruce. "Atlanta an 'Urban Heat Island' with Higher Temperatures than Surrounding Area, According to New NASA-Sponsored Study," University of Georgia, March 19, 1999.

CHAPTER 15: PLANNING FOR MINING

Associated Press. "Coal Mining Deaths Rise for Third Year in a Row," *The New York Times,* January 4, 2001.

Brooke, James. "West Celebrates Mining's Past, But Not Its Future," *The New York Times,* October 4, 1998.

Bureau of Land Management. *Abandoned Mine Lands,* September 4, 2002.
www.blm.gov/aml/faqs/htm#top

———, June 2, 2001.
www.co.blm.gov/mines/default.htm

Council on Environmental Quality. *Annual Report, 1996.* Washington, DC: U.S. Government Printing Office, 1996.

Egan, Timothy. "Death of River Looms Over Bush Choice," *The New York Times,* January 7, 2001.

Goreham, Gary A., ed. *Encyclopedia of Rural America.* Santa Barbara, CA: ABC-CLIO, Inc., 1997.

MacDonnell, Lawrence J. "Mineral Law in the United States," in MacDonnell and Bates, eds., *Natural Resources Policy and Law: Trends and Directions.* Washington, DC: Island Press, 1993.

MacDonnell, Lawrence J. and Sarah Bates, eds., *Natural Resources Policy and Law: Trends and Directions.* Washington, DC: Island Press, 1993.

Pennsylvania Department of Environmental Protection. Reclaim PA, July 7, 1999. www.dep.state.pa.us

U.S. Bureau of the Census. *Statistical Abstract of the United States, 2002.* Washington, DC: U.S. Government Printing Office, 2003.

———. *Statistical Abstract of the United States, 2000.* Washington, DC: U.S. Department of Commerce, 2001.

U.S. General Accounting Office. *Federal Lands Management: Information on Efforts to Inventory Hard Rock Mines.* Washington, DC: USGAO, 1996.

U.S. Geological Survey. "U.S. Geological Survey Reports Increased U.S. Reliance on Imported Minerals." Press Release, Reston, VA: USGS, July 10, 2001.

Wernstedt, Kris. "Plans, Planners, and Aggregates Mining: Constructing an Understanding," *Journal of Planning Education and Research* 20:1, 2000.

Wright, John. *Montana Ghost Dance.* Austin, TX: Texas University Press, 1998.

CHAPTER 16: TRANSPORTATION PLANNING AND THE ENVIRONMENT

American Association of State Highway and Transportation Officials. *A Policy on Geometric Design of Highways and Streets.* Washington, DC: AASHTO, 2001.

Armas, Genero C. "Census: More Commuters Drive Alone," Associated Press, August 21, 2002.

Associated Press. "More Than 25% of Bridges in USA Rated 'Deficient' by Feds," *USA Today,* February 20, 2001.

Belsie, Laurent. "Americans Losing the Drive to Conserve," *The Christian Science Monitor,* August 30, 1999.

Bernick, Michael S. and Robert B. Cervero. *Transit Villages in the 21st Century*. New York: McGraw-Hill, 1996.

The Brookings Institution, March 12, 2001. www.brookings.edu/es/urban/ballotbox/Sanarea.htm

Cervero, Robert B. *The Transit Metropolis: A Global Inquiry*. Washington, DC: Island Press, 1998.

——. *Suburban Gridlock*. New Brunswick, NJ: Center for Urban Policy Research, Rutgers University, 1986.

Charlotte Area Transit System. *Corridor System Plan*. Charlotte, NC: CATS, 2002.

Charlotte, North Carolina, City of, May 15, 2001. www.ci.charlotte.nc.us/ciplannin

Cho, Aileen. "Roads Less Taken." *Engineering News Record* 240:2, January 12, 1998.

Council on Environmental Quality. *Annual Report, 1996*. Washington, DC: U.S. Government Printing Office, 1996.

Dallas Area Rapid Transit. *DART Annual Report 2002*, May 14, 2003. www.dart.org/newsroommain.asp?zeon=annualreport

Daniels, Tom. *When City and Country Collide*. Washington, DC: Island Press, 1999.

Dernbach, John. "Synthesis," in Dernbach, ed., *Stumbling Toward Sustainability*. Washington, DC: Environmental Law Institute, 2002.

Dittmar, Hank, Barbara McCann, and Gloria Ohland. *Realizing GRTA's Potential: Lessons from Around the Country*. Washington, DC: Surface Transportation Policy Project, 1999.

Downs, Anthony. "Some Realities About Sprawl and Urban Decline," *Housing Policy Debate* 10:4, 1999.

——. *Stuck in Traffic: Coping with Peak Hour Traffic Congestion*. Washington, DC: The Brookings Institute, 1992.

The Economist. "What the Internet Cannot Do," August 19, 2000.

Edwards, John D., Jr. *Transportation Planning Handbook*. 2d ed. Upper Saddle River, NJ: Prentice-Hall, 1999.

Ehrenhalt, Alan. "How Light Rail Went Bigtime in Portland," *The Sacramento Bee*, August 27, 2000.

Ewing, Reid. "Is Los Angeles Style Sprawl Desirable?" *Journal of the American Planning Association* 63:1, 1997.

Federal Transit Administration. *Building Livable Communities with Transit*. Washington, DC: U.S. Department of Transportation, 1999.

Ferguson, Erik. *Travel Demand Management and Public Policy*. Ashgate, UK: Ashgate, 2000.

Freilich, Robert H. *From Sprawl to Smart Growth: Successful Legal, Planning, and Environmental Systems*. Chicago: American Bar Association, Section of State and Local Government Law, 1999.

Fulton, William and Peter Calthorpe. *The Regional City*. Washington, DC: Island Press, 2001.

Garreau, Joel. *Edge City*. New York: Anchor Books, 1991.

Gephardt, Richard A. Earth Day Press Release, April 21, 1999.

Hafner, Katie. "Working at Home Today?" *The New York Times*, November 2, 2000.

Hawken, Paul, Amory Lovins, and L. Hunter Lovins. *Natural Capitalism: Creating the Next Industrial Revolution*. Boston: Little Brown and Company, 1999.

Hoyle, Cynthia L. *Traffic Calming*. Planning Advisory Service Report No. 456. Chicago: American Planning Association, 1995.

Kansas City, Missouri, City of. *Making Connections: Central Business Corridor Transit Plan*. Kansas City, MO, 2000.

Kay, Jane Holtz. *Asphalt Nation: How the Automobile Took Over America, and How We Can Take It Back*. New York: Crown Publishers, Inc., 1997.

Knack, Ruth Eckdish. "Drive Nicely," *Planning*, December 1998.

Kreyling, Christine. "Hug That Transit Station," *Planning*, January 2001.

——. "Getting the Runaround," *Planning*, November 2000.

Layton, Lyndsey. "Metro Sees $3.7 Billion Shortfall 2025," *The Washington Post*, August 18, 2001.

——. "Mass Transit Popularity Surges in U.S.," *The Washington Post*, April 30, 2000.

Lucy, William H., "Watch Out: It's Dangerous in Exurbia," *Planning*, November 2000.

Myerson, Deborah L. *Getting It Right in the Right-of-Way: Citizen Participation in Context-Sensitive Highway Design*. Washington, DC: Scenic America, 1998.

Natural Resources Defense Council. *The Amicus Journal*, Summer 2000.

Nelson, Dick. Personal communication, April 22, 1999.

Newman, Oscar. "Defensible Space: A New Physical Planning Tool for Urban Revitalization," *Journal of the American Planning Association* 61:2, 1995.

Newman, Peter and Jeffrey Kenworthy. *Sustainability and Cities: Overcoming Automobile Dependence.* Washington, DC: Island Press, 1999.

The New York Times. "Study Names 18 Worst Sites for Tie-ups on U.S. Roads," November 28, 1999.

North American Light Rail Industry, March 23, 2000. www.lightrail.com

Office of Technological Assessment. *The Technological Reshaping of Metropolitan America.* Washington, DC: U.S. Government Printing Office, 1995.

Orsbon, Ben. "Reauthorization of ISTEA," Small Town and Rural Planning Division of the American Planning Association newsletter, July 1997.

Planning. "Transit Use Still Growing, But So Are Traffic Delays," June 2001.

Pushkarev, B.S. and J. Zupan. *Public Transportation and Land-Use Policy.* Bloomington, IN: Indiana University Press, 1977.

Rein, Lisa. "Country Roads, Taking Forever," *The Washington Post,* May 21, 2000.

San Diego Association of Governments, "Region 2020." San Diego: SDAG, March 2000.

San Diego, City of. *Transit-Oriented Development Guidelines.* Prepared by Calthorpe Associates, 1992.

Shrank, David and Tim Lomax. *The 2001 Urban Mobility Report.* College Station, TX: Texas Transportation Institute, Texas A&M University, Short Report, 2001.

Singleton, Kite. Remarks at the Planning and Zoning for Community Land-Use Management Workshop, Charlotte, NC, March 27, 2000.

Stephenson, John B., Director Natural Resources and Environment, U.S. General Accounting Office. "Environmental Protection: The Federal Government Could Help Communities Better Plan for Transportation That Protects Air Quality." Testimony Before the Committee on Environment and Public Works, U.S. Senate, July 30, 2002.

Surface Transportation Policy Project. Press Release: "Transit Grows Faster than Driving for Fifth Year in a Row," April 17, 2002.

———. *Changing Direction: Federal Transportation Spending in the 1990s.* Washington, DC: STPP, 2000a.

———. *Mean Streets 2000.* Washington, DC: STPP, 2000b.

U.S. Bureau of the Census. *Statistical Abstract of the United States: 2002.* Washington, DC: U.S. Government Printing Office, 2003.

———. *Statistical Abstract of the United States: 2000.* Washington, DC: U.S. Government Printing Office, 2001.

U.S. Department of Energy. *Powering the New Economy: Accomplishments, Investments, Challenges.* DOE/PO-0062. Washington, DC: U.S. Government Printing Office, September 2000.

U.S. Department of Transportation, Federal Transit Administration. *Building Livable Communities with Transit.* Washington, DC: FTA, 1999.

———. *National Transportation Statistics.* Washington, DC: U.S. Department of Transportation, 1995.

U.S. Environmental Protection Agency, Office of Solid Waste and Emergency Response. *Superfund: 20 Years of Protecting Human and the Environment,* EPA 540-R-00-007. Washington, DC: USEPA, 2000.

U.S. General Accounting Office. *Community Development: Local Growth Issues—Federal Opportunities and Challenges,* GAO/RCED-00-178. Washington, DC: USGAO, September 2000.

Wald, Matthew L. "Despite More Cars, Miles Fall for the First Time in 20 Years," *The New York Times,* April 2, 2001.

White, S. Mark. *Using Adequate Public Facilities Ordinances for Traffic Management.* Planning Advisory Service Report No. 465. Chicago: American Planning Association, 1996.

White, S. Mark and Dawn Jourdan. "Neotraditional Development: A Legal Analysis," *Land Use Law,* August 1997.

Zero Population Growth. *The ZPG Reporter,* Spring 2000.

CHAPTER 17: PLANNING FOR ENERGY

Belsie, Laurent. "Americans Losing the Drive to Conserve," *The Christian Science Monitor,* August 30, 1999.

California Energy Commission, September 12, 2002. www.energy.gov/contingency/ contingencylocal.htm

City of Seattle. "Seattle City Light Environmental Policy Statement," September 12, 2002. www.city of seattle.net/light/ environment/ev4_eps.htm

Dashefsky, H. Steven. *Environmental Literacy.* New York: Random House, 1993.

Dunn, Seth and Christopher Flavin. "Sizing Up Micropower," in Worldwatch, *State of the World 2000.* New York: W.W. Norton, 2000.

Easterbrook, Gregg. *A Moment on the Earth: The Coming Age of Environmental Optimism.* New York: Penguin Books, 1996.

The Economist. June 29, 2002.

Edwards, Cliff. "High-Tech Companies Face Energy Shortage," Associated Press in *The Denver Post,* June 11, 2000.

Hawken, Paul, Amory Lovins, and L. Hunter Lovins. *Natural Capitalism: Creating the Next Industrial Revolution.* Boston: Little Brown and Company, 1999.

Holusha, John. "Commercial Property; Downtown, A Menu of Incentives," *The New York Times,* May 19, 2002.

Janofsky, Michael. "Methane Boom in Wyoming Proves to Be Mixed Blessing," *The New York Times,* April 8, 2000.

Jehl, Douglas. "Plan to Dump Coal Ash Adds Salt to a Wound," *The New York Times,* April 14, 2000a.

——. "Curse of the Wind Turns to Farmers' Blessing," *The New York Times,* November 26, 2000b.

Lawrence Livermore National Laboratory. Heat Island Group, May 22, 2001.
http://eetd.ibl.HeatIsland/CoolRoofs

Meck, Stuart. Remarks at the American Planning Association Conference, New York, NY, April 18, 2000.

Myerson, Allen R. "U.S. Splurging on Energy After Falling Off Its Diet," *The New York Times,* October 22, 1998.

Oregon Department of Energy. Weatherizing Your Home, March 29, 2001a.
www.energy.state.or.us/res/weather/weahome.htm

——. Oregon Residential Energy Tax Credit Program, March 29, 2001b.
www.energy.state.or.us/res/tax/taxcdt.htm

——. Oregon Business Energy Tax Credit Program, March 29, 2001c.
www.energy.state.or.us/bus/tax/taxcdt.htm

Pachetti, Nick. "Crude Economics," *The New York Times Magazine,* April 23, 2000.

Rocky Mountain Institute, May 14, 2002.
rmi.org/sitepages/art129.php

——. *Community Energy Workbook.* Snowmass, CO: Rocky Mountain Institute, 1995.

Rozhon, Tracie. "Be It Ever Less Humble: American Homes Get Bigger," *The New York Times,* Section 4, October 22, 1999.

Sheerman, Thomas J. "Undevelopment Blooming," Associated Press in *Times Union* (Albany, NY), October 31, 1999.

Silver, Elaine S. "In Search of Profit, Outside the Power Grid," *The New York Times,* Section 3, February 13, 2000.

U.S. Bureau of the Census. *Statistical Abstract of the United States, 2002.* Washington, DC: U.S. Government Printing Office, 2003.

——. *Statistical Abstract of the United States, 2000.* Washington, DC: U.S. Government Printing Office, 2001.

U.S. Department of Energy. *Powering the New Economy: Accomplishments, Investments, Challenges.* DOE/PO-0062. Washington, DC: U.S. Government Printing Office, September 2000.

U.S. Environmental Protection Agency. *Light-Duty Automotive Technology and Fuel Economy Trends: 1975 Through 2003.* Washington, DC: USEPA, May 2003.

Yardley, Jim. "In a Changed Texas, Ranchers Battle Oilmen," *The New York Times,* May 29, 2000.

Zipkin, Amy. "Homeowners' Revenge: Selling Power to the Utility," *The New York Times,* Section 3, November 12, 2000.

CHAPTER 18: PLANNING FOR A SUSTAINABLE BUILT ENVIRONMENT

Adler, Jerry. "Bye-Bye Suburban Dream," *Newsweek,* May 15, 1995.

Alexander, Christopher, Sara Ishikawa, and Murray Silverstein. *A Pattern Language: Towns, Building, Construction.* New York: Oxford University Press, 1977.

Anderson, Larz T. *Planning the Built Environment.* Chicago: American Planning Association, 2000.

Arnold, C.L. and C.J. Gibbons. "Impervious Surface Coverage: The Emergence of a Key Environmental Indicator," *Journal of the American Planning Association* 62:2, 1996.

Beatley, Timothy and Katherine Manning. *The Ecology of Place: Planning for Environment, Economy, and Community.* Washington, DC: Island Press, 1997.

Beaumont, Constance. *Smart States, Better Communities.* Washington, DC: National Trust for Historic Preservation, 1996.

Brown, Ben. "Taking Credits," *Preservation,* July/August 2000.

Burchell, Robert W. *Impact Assessment of the New Jersey Interim State Development and Redevelopment Plan.* New Brunswick, NJ: Rutgers Center for Urban Policy Research, 1992.

Calthorpe, Peter and William Fulton. *The Regional City: Planning for the End of Sprawl.* Washington, DC: Island Press, 2001.

Campbell, Scott. "Green Cities, Growing Cities, Just Cities?: Urban Planning and the Contradictions of Sustainable Development," *Journal of the American Planning Association* 62:3, Fall 1996.

Christoforidis, Alexander. "New Alternatives to the Suburb: Neo-traditional Developments," *Journal of Planning Literature* 8:4, May 1994.

Corbett, Judith. "The Awahnee Principles: Toward More Liveable Communities," Local Government Commission, Sacramento, CA, 1997. www.lgc.org/clc/ahwnprin.htm

Council on Environmental Quality. *Annual Report, 1996.* Washington, DC: U.S. Government Printing Office, 1996.

The Denver Post, November 17, 1999.

Duany, Andres and Elizabeth Plater-Zyberk. *Suburban Nation: The Rise of Sprawl and the Decline of the American Dream.* San Francisco: North Point Press, 2000.

Freilich, Robert. *From Sprawl to Smart Growth.* Chicago: American Bar Association, 1999.

Garreau, Joel. *Edge City: Life on the New Frontier.* New York: Doubleday, 1991.

Goldberger, Paul. "It Takes a Village," *The New Yorker,* March 27, 2000.

Gratz, Roberta and Norman Mintz. *Cities Back from the Edge.* New York: John Wiley & Sons, 1998.

Hawken, Paul. *The Ecology of Commerce.* New York: HarperCollins, 1993.

Hawken, Paul, Amory Lovins, and L. Hunter Lovins. *Natural Capitalism: Creating the Next Industrial Revolution.* Boston: Little Brown and Company, 1999.

Hinshaw, Mark L. *Design Review.* Planning Advisory Service Report No. 454. Chicago: American Planning Association, 1995.

Hiss, Tony. *The Experience of Place.* New York: Alfred A. Knopf, 1990.

Holusha, John. "Tax Incentive Approved for 'Green' Buildings," *The New York Times,* May 29, 2000.

Hornstein, Jane. "Renewing Urban Renewal," *Planning,* September 2000.

Jackson, Kenneth T. *Crabgrass Frontier: The Suburbanization of the United States.* New York: Oxford University Press, 1985.

Jacobs, Jane. *The Death and Life of Great American Cities.* New York: Vintage Books, 1961.

Katz, Peter. *The New Urbanism: Toward an Architecture of Community.* New York: McGraw-Hill, Inc., 1994.

Kay, Jane Holtz. *Asphalt Nation: How the Automobile Took Over America, and How We Can Take It Back.* New York: Crown Publishers, 1997.

Kinsey, Jon, Mayor of Chattanooga. Remarks at the Second Annual Governor's Conference on Growth, Myrtle Beach, SC, March 12, 2001.

Kunstler, James Howard. *Home From Nowhere: Remaking Our Everyday World for the Twenty-first Century.* New York: Simon and Schuster, 1996.

——. *The Geography of Nowhere: The Rise and Decline of America's Man-Made Landscape.* New York: Simon and Schuster, 1993.

Langdon, Philip. *A Better Place to Live: Reshaping the American Suburb.* Amherst, MA: University of Massachusetts Press, 1994.

Lynch, Kevin. *A Theory of Good City Form.* Cambridge, MA: MIT Press, 1981.

Meck, Stuart, Rodney Cobb, Karen Finucan, Dennis Johnson, and Patricia Salkin. *Planning Communities for the 21st Century.* Chicago: American Planning Association, 1999.

Millard-Ball, Adam. "Putting on Their Parking Caps," *Planning* 68:4, 2002.

Moe, Richard. "The Year in Preservation," *Preservation,* March/April 2001a.

——. President, National Trust for Historic Preservation. Remarks to the National Press Club, May 4, 2001b.

National Association of Home Builders, December 2001. www.nahb.com/hot_topics/regulate.pdf

National Park Service, October 15, 2002. www.cr.nps.gov/nr/about.htm

Natural Resources Conservation Service. *National Resources Inventory* (Revised). Washington, DC: U.S. Department of Agriculture, January 2001.

The New York Times. "Whitman Ends Plan to Shift 900 to Suburb from Trenton," April 28, 2000.

Nishida, Jane, Maryland Secretary of the Department of the Environment. Remarks at the Second Annual Governor's Conference on Growth, Myrtle Beach, SC, March 12, 2001.

Orfield, Myron. *Metropolitics*. Washington, DC: The Bookings Institution and Lincoln Institute for Land Policy, 1997.

Platt, Rutherford H., Rowan A. Roundtree, and Pamela C. Muick, eds. *The Ecological City: Preserving and Restoring Urban Biodiversity*. Amherst, MA: University of Massachusetts Press, 1994.

Preservation: The Magazine of the National Trust for Historic Preservation 52:6, November/December 2000.

Quirsfeld, Kathleen. "West Dundee, Illinois Passes Noise Ordinance," *The Chicago Tribune*, November 17, 1999.

Rusk, David. *Inside Game, Outside Game*. Washington, DC: The Brookings Institution, 1999.

——. *Cities Without Suburbs*. Washington, DC: Woodrow Wilson Center, 1993.

Ryan, Kathleen and Michael Munson. *Outdoor Lighting Manual for Vermont Municipalities*. Essex Junction, VT: Chittenden County Regional Planning Commission, 1996.

Rypkema, Donovan. *Profiting from the Past*. Raleigh, NC: Preservation North Carolina, 1997.

Savoye, Craig. "Vanilla Suburbs Seek an Identity," *The Christian Science Monitor*, December 30, 1999.

Spirn, Anne Whiston. *The Granite Garden: Urban Nature and Human Design*. New York: Basic Books, 1984.

Szold, Terry S. "What Difference Has the ADA Made?" *Planning* 68:4, April 2002.

Szold, Terry. "Look Before You Leap," *Planning*, October 1999.

Urban Land Institute. *The Costs of Alternative Development Patterns: A Review of the Literature*. Washington, DC: Urban Land Institute, 1992.

U.S. Bureau of the Census. *Demographic State of the Nation*. Washington, DC: U.S. Government Printing Office, 1997.

Vermont Forum on Sprawl. *Growing Smarter: Best Site Planning for Residential, Commercial & Industrial Development*. Burlington, VT: VFS, 2001.

White, Bradford J. and Richard J. Roddewig. *Preparing a Historic Preservation Plan*. Planning Advisory Service Report No. 450. Chicago: American Planning Association, 1994.

White, S. Mark. "Neotraditional Development: A Legal Analysis," *Land Use Law and Zoning Digest* 49:8, August 1997.

Whyte, William H. *The Social Life of Small Urban Spaces*. New York: Project for Public Spaces, 2001.

Yaro, Robert D. and Tony Hiss. *A Region at Risk: The Third Regional Plan for the New York-New Jersey-Connecticut Metropolitan Area*. Washington, DC: Island Press, 1996.

CHAPTER 19: PLANNING FOR THE BUILT ENVIRONMENT: GREENFIELD DEVELOPMENT AND SITE DESIGN

Abromowitz, David M. "An Essay on Community Land Trusts: Toward Permanently Affordable Housing," in Geisler and Daneker eds., *Property and Values: Alternatives to Public and Private Ownership*. Washington, DC: Island Press, 2000.

Arendt, Randall. *Rural by Design*. Chicago: American Planning Association, 1994.

Barnett, Jonathan. *The Fractured Metropolis*. New York: HarperCollins, 1995.

Beaumont Constance. *How Superstore Sprawl Can Harm Communities and What Citizens Can Do About It*. Washington, DC: National Trust for Historic Preservation, 1994.

Building Industry Association of Lancaster County, November 1, 2002. www.bialanc.com/bia/policy/growth_pub.cfm

Burby, Raymond J., Arthur C. Nelson, Dennis Parker, and John Handmer. "Urban Containment Policy and Exposure to Natural Hazards: Is There a Connection?" *Journal of Environmental Planning and Management* 44, 2001.

Burchell, Robert. "State of the Cities and Sprawl." Paper presented at the Rocky Mountain Land Use Institute, Ninth Annual Land Use Conference, Denver, CO, March 9, 2000.

California Farm Bureau. News Release. "Farmland Protection Ruling Hailed," February 24, 1998.

Calthorpe, Peter. *The Next American Metropolis: Ecology, Community, and the American Dream*. New York: Simon & Schuster, 1993.

Centers for Disease Control. *Creating a Healthy Environment: The Impact of the Built Environment on Public Health*. Atlanta, GA: CDC, 2001.

Chester County, Pennsylvania. *Landscapes: Managing Change in Chester County 1996-2020*. West Chester, PA: Chester County, 1996.

Corser, Susan Ernst. *Preserving Rural Character Through Cluster Development*. Planners Advisory Service Memo. Chicago: American Planning Association, July 1994.

Craft, Susan. Interview with Susan Craft, Burlington County, New Jersey Office of Land Use Planning, February 27, 2001.

Daniels, Thomas L. "Farm Follows Function," *Planning* 66:1, January 2000.

——. "Where Does Cluster Zoning Fit in Farmland Protection?" *Journal of the American Planning Association* 63:1, 1997.

Daniels, Tom. *When City and Country Collide: Managing Growth in the Metropolitan Fringe*. Washington, DC: Island Press, 1999.

Daniels, Tom and Deborah Bowers. *Holding Our Ground: Protecting America's Farms and Farmland*. Washington, DC: Island Press, 1997.

Davis, Mike. *Ecology of Fear*. New York: Vintage Books, 1999.

Davis, Tony. "Wildcat Subdivisions Fuel Fight Over Sprawl," *High Country News*, April 24, 2000.

Delaware Office of State Planning Coordination. *Managing Growth in 21th Century Delaware: Strategies for State Policies and Spending*. Dover, DE: DOSPC, 1999.

Duany, Andres, Elizabeth Plater-Zyberk, and Jeff Speck. *Suburban Nation: The Rise of Sprawl and the Decline of the American Dream*. New York: North Point Press, 2000.

Easley, V. Gail. *Staying Inside the Lines: Urban Growth Boundaries*. Planners Advisory Service Report No. 440. Chicago: American Planning Association, 1992.

Ehrenhalt, Alan. "The Czar of Gridlock," *Governing*, May 1999.

El Nasser, Haya. "A Comprehensive Look at Sprawl in America," *USA Today*, February 22, 2001.

Etzioni, Amatai. *The Spirit of Community: Rights, Responsibilities, and Communitarian Agenda*. New York: Crown Publishers, 1993.

Ewing, Reid. *Best Development Practices*. Chicago: American Planning Association, 1996.

Farmland Preservation Report. Vol. 5, No. 10. Street, MD: Bowers Publishing, September 1995.

Fisher, Robert, William Ury, and Bruce Patton. *Getting to Yes: Negotiating Agreement Without Giving In*. 2d ed. New York: Penguin Books, 1991.

Freilch, Robert H. *From Sprawl to Smart Growth: Successful Legal, Planning, and Environmental Systems*. Chicago: Section of State and Local Government Law, American Bar Association, 1999.

Garrett, Robert T. and Jennifer Bowles. "Courts Rein in 'Paper Water,'" *The Press-Enterprise* (Riverside, CA), September 25, 2000.

Geisler, Charles and Gail Daneker, eds. *Property and Values: Alternatives to Public and Private Ownership*. Washington, DC: Island Press, 2000.

Greenhouse, Linda. "Justices Weaken Movement Backing Property Rights," *The New York Times*, April 24, 2002.

Healy, Robert G. and John S. Rosenberg. *Land Use and the States*. 2d ed. Baltimore, MD: Johns Hopkins University Press, 1979.

Hirschorn, Joel S. *Quality of Life in the New Economy*. Washington, DC: National Governors Association, 2000.

Howard, Ebeneezer. *Garden Cities of Tomorrow*. Cambridge, MA: MIT Press, 1961.

Hylton, Thomas. *Save Our Land, Save Our Towns*. Harrisburg, PA: Richly Beautiful Books, 1995.

Jefferson County, Kansas. *Draft Comprehensive Plan*, August 2000.

Knaap, Gerrit. "The Urban Growth Boundary in Metropolitan Portland, Oregon: Research, Rhetoric, and Reality." Paper presented at the International Workshop on Urban Growth Management Policies of Korea, Japan, and the United States, Seoul, South Korea, June 23, 2000. Jefferson County, Kansas, *Draft Comprehensive Plan*, August 2000.

Land Trust Alliance, December 20, 2002. www.lta.org/policy/referenda2002.htm

Lang, Robert E. and Karen A. Danielsen. "Monster Homes? Yes!" *Planning* 68:5, May 2002.

Larimer County, Colorado, Larimer County Land Use Code, November 22, 1999.

Libby, James M., Jr. and Darby Bradley. "Vermont Housing and Conservation Board: A Conspiracy of Good Will among Land Trusts and Housing Trusts," in Geisler and Daneker, eds., *Property and Values: Alternatives to Public and Private Ownership*. Washington, DC: Island Press, 2000.

Little, Charles. *Greenways for America*. Baltimore: Johns Hopkins University Press, 1990.

Lucero, Lora and Jeff Soule. "A Win for Lake Tahoe," *Planning* 68:6, June 2002.

Mandelker, Daniel R. Remarks at the American Planning Association Conference, New York, NY, April 18, 2000.

McHarg, Ian. *Design With Nature*. Garden City, NY: Doubleday and Company, 1971.

Meck, Stuart. Remarks at the American Planning Association Conference, New York, NY, April 18, 2000.

Meck, Stuart (ed.). *Growing Smart Legislative Guidebook: Model Statutes for Planning and the Management of Change*. Chicago: American Planning Association, 2002.

Morgan, James. "Golf Sprawl," *Preservation* 53:3, 2001.

National Association of Home Builders, May 12, 2002. www.nahb.com/hot_topics/regulate.pdf

———, August 21, 2001a. www.nahb.com/facts/forecast/sf.htm

———, August 21, 2001b. www.nahb.com/facts/economics/mf.htm

———. Press Release: "Sierra Club Report Ignores Underlying Forces Behind Urban Growth," October 4, 1999a.

———. *Smart Growth: Building Better Places to Live, Work, and Play*. Washington, DC: NAHB, 1999b.

Natural Resources Conservation Service. "National Resources Inventory," Washington, DC: NRCS, January 2001.

Nelessen, Anton. *Visions for a New American Dream*. 2d ed. Chicago: American Planning Association, 1994.

Nelson, Chris. Unpublished manuscript. Department of City Planning, Georgia Institute of Technology, 2000.

New Castle County Council. *New Castle County Comprehensive Development Plan*, Wilmington, DE: New Castle County Council, 1997.

Peirce, Neal. *Citistates: How Urban America Can Prosper in a Competitive World*. Washington, DC: Seven Locks Press, 1993.

The Planning Report, Vol. 12, No. 4, December 1998.

Prairie Crossing, July 30, 2002. www.prairiecrossing.com/principles.htm

Purdum, Todd. "Los Angeles Tests Its Limits to Growth," *The New York Times*, February 13, 2000.

Rusk, David. *Inside Game, Outside Game*. Washington, DC: The Brookings Institution, 1999.

Snyder, Ken and Lori Bird. "Paying the Costs of Sprawl: Using Fair-Share Costing to Control Sprawl," U.S. Department of Energy, June 16, 2001. www.sustainable.doe.gov/articles/sprawl.shtml

Steiner, Frederick R. *The Living Landscape: An Ecological Approach to Landscape Planning*. 2d ed. New York: McGraw-Hill, 2000.

Suskind, Lawrence and Jeffrey Cruikshank. *Breaking the Impasse: Consensual Approaches to Resolving Public Disputes*. New York: Basic Books, 1987.

University of Connecticut Cooperative Extension. *Nonpoint Education for Municipal Officials* project, No. 10. Storrs, CT: University of Connecticut, 2000.

U.S. Bureau of the Census, July 30, 2002. quickfacts.census/gov/qfd

Vermont Forum on Sprawl, August 19, 2001. www.vtsprawl.org

———. "Sprawl and Smart Growth Action Plan," Burlington, VT: VFS, October 1999.

Walters, Jonathan. "Anti-Box Rebellion," *Governing* 13:10, July 2000.

Yaro, Robert D., Randall G. Arendt, Harry L. Dodson, and Elizabeth A. Brabec *Dealing with Change in the Connecticut River Valley: A Design Manual for Conservation and Development*, Amherst, MA: University of Massachusetts Center for Rural Massachusetts, 1988.

CHAPTER 20: POSITIVE TRENDS AND URGENT NEEDS FOR SUSTAINABLE ENVIRONMENTAL PLANNING

Ad Hoc Associates for Governor's Commission on Vermont's Future. Chittenden, VT: Ad Hoc Associates, 1990.

American Planning Association. *Planning Communities for the 21st Century*. Chicago: APA, 1999.

Bingham, Gail. *Resolving Environmental Disputes: A Decade of Experience*. Washington, DC: The Conservation Foundation, 1986.

Bright, Chris. "Anticipating Environmental 'Surprise,'" in Worldwatch Institute, *State of the World 2000*. New York: W.W. Norton, 2000.

Burchell, Robert W. *et al.* (9 co-authors). *The Costs of Sprawl Revisited*. Transit Cooperative Research Program Report 39. Washington, DC: Transportation Research Board, National Research Council, 1998.

Dernbach, John. "Synthesis," in Dernbach, ed., *Stumbling Toward Sustainability*. Washington, DC: Environmental Law Institute, 2002.

Dowie, Mark. *American Environmentalism at the End of the Twentieth Century*. Cambridge, MA: MIT Press, 1995.

Easterbrook, Gregg. *A Moment on the Earth: The Coming Age of Environmental Optimism*. New York: Penguin Books, 1996.

The Economist. "Net Benefits," February 24, 2001.

Farmland Preservation Report. Vol. 10, No. 5. Street, MD: Bowers Publishing, March 2000.

French, Hilary. "Coping with Ecological Globalization," in Worldwatch, *State of the World 2000*. New York: W.W. Norton, 2000.

Glendening, Parris N. "3 Great Challenges: Education, Environment, and Equality," *The Washington Post*, January 21, 1999.

Goodstein, Eban. *The Trade-off Myth: Fact and Fiction About Jobs and the Environment*. Washington, DC: Island Press, 1999.

Greider, William. *One World Ready or Not: The Manic Logic of Global Capitalism*. New York: Touchstone, 1998.

Hahn, Robert W. *Regulatory Reform; What Do the Government's Numbers Tell Us?* Washington, DC: American Enterprise Institute, 1996.

Hart, Betsy. "People are resources, not liabilities." *Times Union* (Albany, NY), October 17, 1999.

Hawken, Paul, Amory Lovins, and L. Hunter Lovins. *Natural Capitalism: Creating the Next Industrial Revolution*. Boston: Little Brown and Company, 1999.

Holmes, Stephen A. "After Standing Up to Be Counted, Americans No. 281,421,906," *The New York Times*, December 29, 2000.

Institute for Southern Studies. *Gold and Green 2000*, February 14, 2001.
www.southernstudies.org/goldgreen2000.htm

International Coral Reef Information Network, May 15, 2002. www.coralreef.org

Johnson, Denny. "Washington," in *Planning Communities for the 21st Century*. Chicago: American Planning Association, 1999.

Johnson, Huey. *Green Plans: Greenprint for Sustainability*. Lincoln, NE: University of Nebraska Press, 1995.

Land Trust Alliance, December 20, 2002.
www.lta.org/policy/referenda2002.htm

Lee, Jean H. "Study Forecasts Population Boom." Associated Press in *Times Union* (Albany, NY), February 28, 2001.

McNeil, J.R. *Something New Under the Sun*. New York: W.W. Norton, 2000.

Orfield, Myron. *Metropolitics*. Washington, DC: The Bookings Institution and Lincoln Institute for Land Policy, 1997.

Orr, David W. *Ecological Literacy: Education and the Transition to a Postmodern World*. Ithaca, NY: State University of New York Press, 1992.

Pioneer Valley Planning Commission, August 2, 2002.
www.pvpc.org/info/docs/Datadigest/Pop.pdf

President's Council on Sustainable Development. *Sustainable America: A New Consensus for the Prosperity, Opportunity, and a Healthy Environment for the Future*. Washington, DC: U.S. Government Printing Office, 1996.

The Trust for Public Land. *Land & People*, Spring 2000.

United Nations Environmental Program. *Geo-3*. New York: United Nations, 2002.

U.S. Bureau of the Census. "Projections of the Total Population of States: 1995 to 2025," June 28, 2002.
www.census.gov/population/projections/state/stjpop.txt

——. Population Quick Facts, October 30, 2001.
www.census.gov

——. *Annual Projections of Total Resident Population, as of July 1, Middle, Lowest, Highest, and Zero International Migration Series, 1999-2100*. Washington, DC: U.S. Government Printing Office, February 14, 2000.

U.S. Environmental Protection Agency. "EPA Supplemental Environmental Projects Policy." EPA 300-F98-006. Washington, DC: USEPA, 2000.
See also, es.epa.gov/oeca/sep

U.S. General Accounting Office. *Community Development: Local Growth Issues—Federal Opportunities and Challenges*, GAO/RCED-00-178. Washington, DC: USGAO, September 2000.

U.S. Office of Management and Budget. Report to Congress on the Costs and Benefits of Federal Regulations. Washington, DC: USOMB, 1997.

Worldwatch Institute. *State of the World 2000*. New York: W.W. Norton & Company.

Index

A

Abandoned Mine Reclamation Fund, 327
Acid rain. *See also* Sulfur dioxide
  case study, 147–148
  cause of, 126, 127
  cost of, 50
  and emissions trading, 137, 138
  impacting forests, 308
Action Strategy
  in built environment planning, 354, 371–372, 393, 422
  in natural areas planning
    coastal zones, 252
    landscape preservation, 203–204
    natural hazards and disasters, 273–274
    wetlands, 238
    wildlife habitats, 225
  overview, 26–27
  in public health planning
    air quality, 144
    solid waste, 162
    toxic substance, 180–181
    water quality, 120
    water supplies, 93
  in working lands planning, 294–295, 316–317, 328
Ad-hoc citizens' groups, 200. *See also* Public
  participation
Administrative law, 46, 48
Aerial photos, 20–21, 23. *See also* Geographic
  Information Systems (GISs)
Aesthetics, in built environment design, 379–380
Aggregates, 323. *See also* Mining
Agricultural districts, 289–290
Agricultural land, 279–304
  case studies, 303–304
  challenges in managing, 281–285, 434
  creating built environment from, 399 (*see also* Built
    environments)
  economic potential of, 296
  federal planning for, 285–288
  local planning for (*see also* Transfer of development
    rights (TDR))
    Action Strategies, 294–295
    CIPs, 300
    development reviews, 302–303
    growth boundaries, 300–301
    inventories, 293–294
    objectives, 294
    right-to-farm laws, 289
    subdivisions, 299–300
    zoning, 295–299
  overview, 279–280

state planning for, 288–290 (*see also* Purchase
  of development rights (PDR))
  trusts in preserving, 292
Ahwahnee Principles, 385
Air pollution. *See under* Pollution
Airports, planning for, 349
Air quality, 125–149
  case studies, 146–149
  challenges in managing, 434
  in development reviews, 146
  federal planning for (*see* Clean Air Act)
  local planning for, 144–146
  in natural resource inventories, 23
  pollution affecting (*see under* Pollution)
  state planning for, 130, 141–144
Alabama, 200, 220, 236
Alarmists, 59
Alaska
  forests in, 305, 309
  landfills in, 152
  landscape protection in, 185, 187, 188
  natural hazards in, 261, 271
  oil production in, 361, 362
  population growth in, 441
  solid waste disposal in, 158
  wildlife habitats in, 214, 219
Alaska National Interest Lands and Conservation Act,
  187
Ambient air quality standards, 128, 129–130. *See also*
  Air quality
American Association of State Highway and
  Transportation Officials, 350
American Farmland Trust (AFT), 285, 409
American Heritage Rivers Initiative, 189–190
American Highway Users Alliance, 336–337
American Planning Association (APA)
  on California water supply, 72
  on ecological footprints, 3
  on environmental justice, 39
  on lot size, 399
  on natural system values, 54
  on state planning legislation, 446
American Rivers, 201, 202
American Rule, 83
American Society of Civil Engineers (ASCE), 1
Americans with Disabilities Act (ADA), 379
American Water Works Association, 84
Amtrak, 347–348
Analysis, of inventories. *See* Inventories
The Andrew W. Mellon Foundation, 201, 202
Animal Unit Monthly (AUM) fee, 220, 288

Anthropocentrics, 58–59
Antiquities Act, 189
Aquifers
    depletion of, 72–73
    in hydrologic cycle, 71
    protection programs for, 91, 94, 286–287
Arizona
    air quality in, 130
    land ownership in, 185
    population growth in, 441
    sprawl in, 401
    water supplies in, 74, 83, 86
    wildlife preservation in, 214
Arkansas, 202, 270
Arrington, G.B., 344
Assimilative capacity, 99–100
Atmosphere, role of, 125
Automobiles. *See* Motor vehicles
Avalanches, 261

B

Bacteria, pollution from, 102–104
Barrier islands, 245, 274–275
Beach Environmental Assessment and Coastal Health
        Act, 248
Benchmarking, 33
Bennett et al. v. M. Spear, 215
Best Available Control Technology (BACT), 135
Best management practices (BMPs), 111, 112, 117, 138
Bicycles, 339, 343, 348, 350. *See also* Transportation
Big-box stores, 413
Biochemical/biological oxygen demand (BOD), 105
BioCycle, 152
Biodiversity, 208–209, 220
Biological pollution, 102–104
Biomass energy, 366
Bioregionalism, 210–212
Biosolids. *See* Sludge
Boats, transportation by, 348
Boca Villas Corporation v. City of Boca Raton, 40
Browner, Carol, 148
Brownfield Assessment Demonstration Pilots program,
        178
Brownfield redevelopment
    elements of, 175–179
    grants for, 386–387, 388
    importance of, 169, 173, 441
Brownfields Economic Development Initiative, 386–387
Building codes, 275, 370
Building Officials and Code Administrators
        International, Inc. (BOCA), 275
Build-out analyses, 408–409
Built environments, 373–397

ADA requirements for, 379
aesthetics in, 379–380
Ahwahnee Principles for, 385
case study, 395–397
challenges in managing, 434
creating livable, 375–378
declining quality of, 1 (*see also* Sprawl)
defined, 11
design of, 378–379, 385 (*see also* Greenfield
        development)
downtowns in, 380–382
energy used by (*see* Energy)
federal planning for, 386–389
inventory of, 23–25, 391 (*see also* Inventories)
and land-value taxation, 382
local planning for, 391–395
neighborhoods in, 385–386
nuisances, noise, and light in, 382–384
overview, 373–375
state planning for, 389–391
transportation systems in (*see* Transportation)
Bush, George W., 141, 188, 307
Bus systems, 343, 344. *See also* Transportation

C

California
    built environment in
        case study, 424–425
        cluster design, 417
        downtown rebuilding, 381
        energy use, 361, 362, 363, 366, 368
        growth boundaries, 40, 407–408
        housing scale, 377
        hydroelectric dams, 363
        impact fees, 418
        limited building permits, 411
        population growth, 441
        public participation, 419, 430
        sprawl, 401, 406
    natural areas in
        coastal zones, 248, 249, 254–256
        conservation easements, 202, 431
        critical concern area, 192
        endangered rivers, 202
        greenways, 196
        land ownership, 185
        land trusts, 197
        national parks, 188
        open space purchase, 193
    natural hazards in
        earthquakes, 261, 262, 271, 272, 275
        high rate of, 258
        volcanoes, 271

wildfires, 268, 269
population growth in, 242
public health in
    air quality in, 132, 133, 140, 433, 445
    landfills in, 152
    ozone damage, 308
    population growth in, 74
    recycling in, 153
    solid waste disposal in, 157, 160
    toxic substances in, 174, 176
    transportation planning in, 131
Sustainability Plan, 28
transportation in
    approaches to, 347
    boats, 348
    bottlenecks, 337
    buses and trolleys, 343–344
    heavy rail, 347
    transit corridors, 432
water in
    price of, 86
    quality of, 248
    supplies of, 60, 72, 74, 81–82, 84
    wetlands, 230, 234
wildlife habitat in
    bioregions, 211, 212
    endangered species, 214, 215
    mitigation bank project, 222
    species conservation, 223
working lands in
    agricultural, 285, 290, 291, 292, 296
    forests, 305, 309, 312, 319–320
    land trusts, 315
    zoning for, 317
*Calvert Cliffs' Coordinating Committee v. Atomic Energy
    Commission*, 43
Capital improvements programs (CIPs)
    in built environment planning, 355, 372, 394–395, 423
    comprehensive plan working with, 13, 16–17
    in natural areas planning, 205, 227, 240, 254, 276
    in public health planning
        air quality, 145–146
        solid wastes, 162–163
        toxic substances, 182
        water quality, 122
        water supplies, 95
    role of, 28, 29, 30
    in working lands planning, 317, 330
Carbon credits, 315
Carbon cycle, 61, 125
Carbon dioxide. *See also* Greenhouse gases
    affecting air quality, 128, 140–141
    from burning trash, 158

landfills emitting, 156
    from wetlands, 230
Carbon monoxide, 61, 127, 130, 134, 139
Carbon sequestration, 315
Carrying capacity, 62
Carson, Rachel, *Silent Spring,* 165, 166
Cautionaries, 59–60
Census of Agriculture, 284–285
The Center for Natural Lands Management, 222
Centers and corridors strategy, 343, 357. *See also*
    Transportation
Certified Forest Products Council, 313
Changes in the Land (Cronon), 47
Chemical pollution, 104–107
Chemical Safety, Site Security and Fuels Regulatory
    Relief Act, 41
Chesapeake Bay Foundation (CBF), 250
Chlorofluorocarbons (CFCs), 128, 140, 166. *See also*
    Ozone
Cities Back from the Edge (Gratz and Mintz), 381–382
A Civil Action (Harr), 168
Clean Air Act, 129–138. *See also* Air quality
    allowing offsets, 136
    car emissions under (*see* Motor vehicles)
    versus Clean Water Act, 107
    control technologies under, 135–136
    cost-benefit analysis of, 56
    enforcement of, 445
    impacting transportation planning, 131–132, 133
    on landfill gas emissions, 156
    on mining industry, 324
    permitting required by, 135
    on private citizens' rights, 47
    quality standards under, 23, 129–131
    role of, 41, 43
    sanctions imposed by, 132–134
    on toxic emissions, 136–137
    tradable credits under, 137–138
    and transportation planning, 341
    violation fine alternative, 439
Clean Water Act, 107–114. *See also* Water quality
    on farmland runoff, 304
    on mining industry, 324, 326
    monitoring and enforcement under, 113–114, 445
    on nonpoint source pollution, 111–112
    nonprofit organizations using, 433
    on pollutant discharge, 109
    on private citizens' rights, 47
    protecting estuaries, 246
    quality ratings, 107, 108, 109
    role of, 41, 43, 107, 108
    state standards under, 114
    TMDL process under, 115

on toxic substances, 172
violation of, 320, 439
on wastewater treatment, 109–111
on wetlands, 38, 221, 230–233
Clean Water Action Plan programs, 116
Clear cutting, 311, 315, 320
Clinton, Bill
creating nature preserve, 245
on landfill locations, 172
on national monuments, 189
on oil pricing, 367
on roadless areas, 187–188, 307
on spotted owl protection, 321
on water protection, 189, 248
wildlife habitats under, 218
The Closing Circle (Commoner), 6, 61
Cluster development
advantages of, 425
disadvantages of, 94
in farmlands, 295
overview, 415–418
wildlife habitat protection in, 226–227
Coal
as energy source, 360, 361, 363–364
mining of, 323, 327 (*see also* Mining)
Coalition Opposed to PCB Ash, 175
Coastal Barrier Resources Act, 245, 247
Coastal Nonpoint Source Pollution Control Programs,
112
Coastal Wetlands Planning, Protection, and Restoration
Act, 235–236
Coastal Zone Management Act (CZMA)
performance of, 247–248
role of, 243–244, 247
state planning under, 236, 272
in wetlands permitting process, 231
Coastal zones, 241–256
case studies, 254–256
challenges in managing, 242–243, 434
Chesapeake Bay protection program, 250
defined, 241
erosion in, 260, 269–270
federal planning for (*see also* Coastal Zone
Management Act (CZMA))
Coastal Barrier Resources Act, 245, 247
Coastal Wetlands Planning, Protection, and
Restoration Act, 235–236
Marine Protection Research and Sanctuaries Act,
41, 219, 231, 243, 244–245
National Estuarine Reserve and National Estuary
Program for, 219, 245–246
Great Lakes Program for, 246–247
local planning for, 251–254, 253, 254

state planning for, 248–249
success of legislation protecting, 247–248
The Code of the Building Officials Conference of America,
370
Cogeneration, 364–365
Colorado
built environment in
brownfield cleanup in, 179
cluster design, 417
downtown rebuilding, 381
sprawl, 401
transportation, 131, 344, 349
natural areas in
endangered rivers, 202
greenways, 196
land ownership, 185
land trusts, 197
open space, 193, 195, 221
ski resorts, 186
wildfires in, 268
wildlife habitat protection in, 225
public health in, 140, 168
working lands in, 292, 325
Common law, 47–48
Community Development Block Grants (CDBGs), 386
Community Reinvestment Act (CRA), 387
Community services, cost of, 409
Commuter rail, 346–348. *See also* Transportation
Commuting. *See* Transportation
Comprehensive Environmental Response
Compensation and Liability Act (CERCLA).
See The Superfund Law
Comprehensive plans
action plans in (*see* Action Strategy; Environmental
action plans)
CIPs in (*see* Capital improvements programs (CIPs))
ecological considerations in, 62–63
role of, 12–14, 27–28
state review of, 44
subdivisions and regulations in, 15–16 (*see also*
Subdivisions)
in wildlife protection, 223 (*see also* Wildlife habitats)
and zoning, 14–15 (*see also* Zoning)
Computers, 174, 361. *See also* Technology
*Concerned Area Citizens for the Environment v. Southview
Farms,* 304
Concurrency policies, 17, 40, 145–146, 437
Confined animal feeding operations (CAFOs), 297,
302–304
Conjunctive Use Doctrine, 83
Connecticut, 68, 133, 172, 290, 350
Conservation easements, 90, 198–200, 202, 431
The Conservation Fund, 196, 200–201

Conservation Reserve Enhancement Program, 286
Conservation Reserve Program (CRP), 286
Constitutional law, 37–40, 48
Consultants, action plans by, 18–19
Contaminant levels, 78–79
Contingent valuation, 54
The Control of Nature (McPhee), 62, 125
Convention on Persistent Organic Pollutants (POPs),
    171
Cornucopians, 59
Corporate Average Fuel Economy (CAFE), 131, 134, 362
Corridors strategy, 343, 357
Cost-benefit analyses. *See also* Economics
    air quality in, 148
    of community services, 409
    in long-range planning, 432
    overview, 54–56
    water quality in, 113
    on wetlands, 230
Council on Environmental Quality (CEQ), 42, 53, 187,
    212
County government, 117–119, 170. *See also under* Water
    supplies
Critical concern areas, 192–193
Critical habitats, 214–215
Current Trends Analyses, 25

D

Daly, Herman, 3
    Toward a Steady-State Economy, 57
Dams. *See also* Rivers
    cost-benefit analysis of, 55
    in flood control, 265, 268
    hydroelectric, 363
    U.S. Bureau of Reclamation building, 75, 77
    in water supply disputes, 68
Data gathering, for action plans, 19, 20–25, 446
The David and Lucille Packard Foundation, 201, 202
Deeds of easement, 290. *See also* Purchase of
    development rights (PDR)
Deer, overpopulation of, 208
Delaware
    agricultural land in, 290
    built environment in, 404, 405
    land trusts in, 197
Density, balancing sprawl with, 378
Design With Nature (McHarg), 243, 406
Development reviews
    in action plan implementation, 372
    in built environment planning, 355, 395, 423, 424
    economic and environmental balance in, 57
    in natural areas planning
        coastal zones, 254

landscape preservation, 205, 206
natural hazards and disasters, 276
wetlands, 240
wildlife habitats, 228
    in public health planning
        air quality, 146
        solid wastes, 163
        toxic substances, 182
        water quality, 122–123
        water supplies, 95, 96
    in working lands planning
        agricultural, 302–303
        forests, 317–318
        mining operations, 330, 331
Developments of regional impact (DRIs), 404–405
Dichlorodiphenyltrichloroethane (DDT), 166, 168, 171,
    175
Dioxins, 165, 171
Disaster Mitigation Act, 262. *See also* Natural hazards
    and disasters
Disney Company, 381
Districts, in built environment design, 378
Dolan v. City of Tigard, 38
The Doris Duke Foundation, 201, 202
Downtowns, designing, 380–382
Drought, 73, 259
Ducks Unlimited, 118, 222
Due diligence, 176

E

Earthquakes, 261–262, 270–271
Earth Summit, 447
Easements. *See also* Land trusts; Purchase
        of development rights (PDR); Transfer
        of development rights (TDR)
    conservation, 90, 198–200, 202, 431
    in forestland preservation, 311, 314
    in wellhead protection programs, 90
    in wildlife habitat preservation, 220
Eco-industrial parks, 152, 160
Ecological footprints, 3, 60
Ecology, 6, 60–63, 209–210
Economics, 48–57. *See also* Cost-benefit analyses
    of agricultural land, 280, 281, 283, 296
    defined, 48
    in development and growth, 56–57
    efficiency in, 49
    environment balancing with, 57
    of pollution cleanup, 53
    subsidies in, 52
    in valuing environmental resources, 49–52, 54–56
Ecosystems, 60–63, 220. *See also* Landscape protection;
        Wildlife habitats

Ecotones, 210
Edge cities, 374
Edge effects, 210
Edges, in built environment design, 379, 413
Electricity, as energy source, 363–365
Emissions standards, 128, 130–131. *See also* Air quality
Empowerment Zone/Enterprise Community program, 387
Endangered species, 241, 320–321, 448–449. *See also* Extinction; Wildlife habitats
Endangered Species Act (ESA)
    mining conflicting with, 326
    role of, 41, 212–215, 217–218
    violation of, 320
    on wetlands development, 231, 236
    on wildlife habitats, 215, 246
Energy, 359–372
    and building codes, 370
    challenges in managing, 335–336, 359–361, 434
    conservation opportunities, 2, 442–443
    federal planning for, 170, 366–367
    Internet impacting use of, 349
    local planning for, 369–372
    pollution from creating, 363
    recycling conserving, 152, 361
    sources of, 361–366 (*see also specific*)
    state planning for, 367–368
    tax credit for conserving, 368, 369
Energy Planning and Community Right-to-Know Act, 170
Enhanced Surface Water Treatment Rule, 79
Environmental action plans, 17–35
    Action Strategy in, 26–27 (*see also* Action Strategy)
    adoption of, 27–28
    case studies, 30, 32–35
    committing people and money to, 18–19
    data gathering and analysis in, 20–25
    implementing, 28–30, 31
    public input in, 19
    recognizing need for, 17–18
    vision, goals, and objectives in, 25–26 (*see also* Goals and objectives)
Environmental Defense, 114, 433
Environmental impact assessments (EIAs)
    for CAFO expansions, 300
    in development reviews, 30, 31
    landfill construction requiring, 162, 181
    in landscape preservation, 205
    for mining operations, 330
    in natural hazard and disaster planning, 275, 276
    sample report, 451–453
    state requirements for, 44, 46
    in wetlands development proposals, 240

    in wildlife habitat protection, 220, 221
Environmental impact statements (EISs), 42–44, 419
Environmentalists, 58–59
Environmental justice, 39, 58
Environmental Needs Assessment Survey, 19, 25
Environmental planning, defined, 11
Environmental planning needs, 435–447
    international, 447–449
    local and regional
        environmental mediation, 438–439
        growth limits, 435–436
        hazard and disaster planning, 440–441
        infrastructure replacement and growth, 439–440
        land use and transportation coordination, 440
        monitoring and enforcement, 440
        planning improvements, 436–437
        property tax reform, 438
    state and federal
        education, data collection, and research, 446
        energy reform, 442–443
        environmental funding, 443–444
        environmental law enforcement, 445
        national environmental vision, 446–447
        national population policy, 441
        program coordination improvements, 445–446
        recycling and reuse, 444
        revitalization of communities, 441–442
        true cost concept, 443
        water cleanup, 444
    summary of, 434, 449–450
Environmental planning trends, 429–435
    crises motivating, 429–430
    green infrastructures, 431
    increasing state role, 433
    local responsibility, 430–431
    long-term views, 431–432
    private organization influences, 433, 435
    transportation modes, 432
Environmental Quality Analyses, 24–25. *See also* National Resources Inventory
Environmental Quality Incentives Program (EQIP), 286
Erie, Lake, 53, 99
Erosion. *See also* Runoff
    of agricultural land, 281, 282, 288
    in coastal zones, 260, 269–270
    from mining operations, 325
Estuaries
    defined, 241
    National Estuarine Reserve and National Estuary Program, 219, 245–246
    pollution of, 242
    wildlife protection in, 219
Ethics, in environmental perception, 57–60

Euclid, Ohio, Village of, v. Ambler Realty Co., 39
Euclidean zoning, 28
Eutrophication, 105, 106
The Everglades (Douglas), 237
Exaction, 51
Extinction, 207, 217. *See also* Endangered species;
    Endangered Species Act (ESA); Wildlife
    habitats

F
Farm Bills, 235, 285–286, 287, 309
Farmland. *See* Agricultural land
Farmland Protection Policy Act, 285, 303
Farmland Protection Program, 285, 443
Federal Aviation Administration (FAA), 349
Federal Emergency Management Agency (FEMA)
    on coastal erosion, 247, 269, 270
    on earthquakes, 262, 270, 271
    on floods, 23, 246, 264, 265–268
    hazard mitigation assistance programs, 262–264
    nuclear power plant approval by, 363
    role of, 262
    on toxic substances, 165, 170
Federal Energy Regulatory Commission (FERC), 77,
    268, 367
Federal Environmental Pesticide Control Act, 41, 169
Federal government planning. *See* Legislation; *specific*
    topic
Federal Highway Administration, 336, 404
Federal Insecticide, Fungicide, and Rodenticide Act
    (FIFRA). *See* Federal Environmental Pesticide
    Control Act
Federal Land Policy Management Act, 189
Federal National Mortgage Association (Fannie Mae),
    351
Federal Register, 42, 214
Federal Transit Administration (FTA), 336
Federal Water Pollution Control Act. *See* Clean Water
    Act
5th Amendment, 37–38, 46
Fires, 258–259, 268–269, 308
Fiscal impact studies, 56
Fisheries, 213, 214, 217, 218, 449. *See also* U.S. Fish and
    Wildlife Service (FWS)
Fixed-area ratio zoning, 296
Floating zones, 329–330
Flood Disaster Protection Act, 41, 246, 265, 266
Floodplains, 23, 264–265
Floods. *See also* National Flood Insurance Program
    (NFIP)
    FEMA on, 23, 246, 264, 265–268
    greenways in mitigation of, 267–268
    National Flood Insurance Reform Act, 41, 265, 269

    planning for, 258, 264–268
    Watershed Protection and Flood Prevention Act, 327
Florida
    agricultural land in, 285
    built environment in
        DRI process, 405
        energy needs, 361, 362
        legislation, 404
        neighborhood design, 386
        parking design, 377
        sprawl, 401
    comprehensive plan review in, 44
    concurrency policy in, 17
    environmental program in, xx
    natural areas in
        critical concern area, 192
        Everglades, 237
        forests, 307
        greenways, 196
        open space, 193, 194, 195
        wildlife habitat, 211, 214, 221
    population growth in, 40, 242, 441
    public health in
        landfills, 152
        natural hazards in, 258, 259, 264, 274–275
        wastewater, 85
        water quality, 248
        water supplies, 68, 72
Food Quality Protection Act, 41
Food Security Act, 41
The Ford Foundation, 201
Forest and Rangeland Renewable Resource Act, 309, 310
Forest Legacy Program
    case study, 318–319
    cause behind, 307
    role of, 311, 314
    spending on, 443, 444
Forestry Incentives Program, 309
Forests, 305–321
    and carbon sequestration, 315
    case studies, 318–321
    certified sustainable, 313
    challenges in managing, 434
    creating built environment from, 399 (*see also* Built
        environments)
    federal planning for, 309–311, 443 (*see also* U.S. Forest
        Service (USFS))
    global loss of, 448
    land trusts in protecting, 314–315
    local planning for, 315–318
    overview, 305–306
    ownership of, 305, 306
    pressures on, 306–308

state planning for, 311–314
types of, 308–309
Forest Stewardship Council, 313
Fossil water, 69
14th Amendment, 39–40, 46
Freeman Foundation, 202
Full Cost Accounting, 155

G

Gaia (Lovelock), 61
Gap Analysis Program (GAP), 216
Garbage. *See* Solid waste
Garden Cities of Tomorrow (Howard), 412
Gasoline storage tanks, 106–107
Gated communities, 376
General Mining Law, 326
Geographic Information Systems (GISs)
in brownfield redevelopment planning, 178
finding nonpoint pollution sources, 119
land trusts using, 197
in layers design technique, 407, 421
mapping water sources, 87
in mining operations, 325, 328
in monitoring and enforcement, 440
natural resource inventories using, 20, 23, 24
in soil surveys, 293–294
Geology, 22
Georgia
air quality in, 132, 133, 445
built environment in, 386, 411
landfills in, 152
natural areas in, 193, 196, 307
regional planning in, 6
transportation planning in, 131, 337
water supply in, 68, 73
wildlife preservation in, 214
Geothermal energy, 366
Global warming. *See also* Greenhouse gases; Ozone
history of, 7
impacting forests, 308
landfills contributing to, 156
timber harvesting affecting, 315
and violent storms, 257, 260
wetlands impacting, 230
Goals and objectives
in built environment planning
energy sources, 370, 371
greenfield development, 421–422
livable communities, 392–393
transportation, 353
in natural areas planning
coastal zones, 251–252
landscape preservation, 203–204

natural hazard and disaster, 273, 274
wetlands, 238, 239
wildlife habitats, 224–225
in planning process, 26
in public health planning
air quality, 144
solid waste, 161
toxic substances, 180, 181
water quality, 120, 121
water supplies, 86–88, 93
in working lands planning, 294, 316, 328, 329
Golden v. Planning Board of the Town of Ramapo, 40
Golf courses, 296, 416
Grasslands Reserve Program (GRP), 220
GrassRoots Recycling Network, 153
Grazing, affecting agricultural land, 287–288
Great Lakes National Program, 246–247
Green accounting, 34, 57
Green Book, 350
Green buildings, 369
Greenfield development, 399–426. *See also* Built
environments
case studies, 424–426
challenges in managing, 400–403, 434
federal planning for, 403–404
local planning for, 420–423, 424
state planning for, 404–406
techniques for guiding (*see also* Cluster
development; Growth boundaries)
build-out analyses, 408–409
community services costs, 409
impact fees, 418
inclusionary housing ordinances, 410–411
layers approach, 406–407
limiting building potential, 411
moratoriums, 411–412
public facilities ordinances, 410, 436–437
public participation, 418–420
PUDs and master planning, 412
septic system ordinances, 91, 94, 410
site design standards, 412–415
sunsetting regulations, 410
urban redevelopment versus, 374, 375, 400–401
(*see also* Sprawl)
Greenhouse effect, 125
Greenhouse gases. *See also* Carbon dioxide; Global
warming; Ozone
global reduction of, 448
Kyoto Protocol on, 141, 315, 448
motor vehicle restrictions reducing, 133
PAYT reducing, 155
recycling reducing, 152–153
Green infrastructure, 2, 63, 205, 431

Greenspaces, 376
Greenways
    corridors meshing with, 210
    defined, 4
    in flood mitigation, 267–268
    role of, 194–196
    urban, 376
Groundwater
    availability of, 70–73
    mapping, 87
    pollution in, 101–102, 154
    recharge rates for, 92
    state laws on, 83
Groundwater Guardians, 118
Growth boundaries
    in agricultural land planning, 300–301
    in greenfield development, 404, 407–408
    in water supply planning, 84
Growth Management Act, 46

H

Habitat Conservation Plans (HCPs), 217–218, 223
Hanly v. Kleindienst, 42
Hardin, Garrett, 51
Harvard University, 365
Hawaii
    coastal zone planning in, 248
    environmental program in, xx, 44
    nature preserve in, 245
    population growth in, 441
    Sierra Club suing, 191
    volcano in, 271
    wildlife habitats in, 211, 212, 214
Hazardous and Solid Waste Amendments, 41
Hazardous chemicals, pollution from, 106–107
Hazardous waste. *See also* Toxic substances
    challenges in managing, 2
    and computer manufacturing, 174
    from nuclear power production, 362–363
    in wellhead protection programs, 90, 91
Hazards. *See* Natural hazards and disasters
Heat islands, 127, 307, 361
Heavy rail, 346–348. *See also* Transportation
High Occupancy Vehicle (HOV) lanes, 337, 351
Highways. *See* Motor vehicles; Roads; Transportation
Historic preservation, 380, 388–389, 393
Hope VI program, 387
Housing. *See also* Built environments
    affordable, 377, 386–387, 410–411
    compact developments versus sprawl, 402–403
    HUD guiding, 95, 386–387
    need for new, 402
Hurricanes. *See* Natural hazards and disasters

Hydroelectric dams, 363
Hydrogen fuel cells, 366
Hydrologic cycle, 61, 69. *See also* Water supplies

I

Idaho
    energy action plan in, 367
    historic preservation in, 389
    landfills in, 172
    land ownership in, 185
    LRMP in, 310
    population growth in, 441
    Teton River dam project in, 77
Illinois
    agricultural land in, 304
    air quality in, 133
    earthquake risk in, 270
    greenfield development in, 424–425
    noise ordinance in, 384
    sprawl in, 401
    water in, 202, 230
Immigration, 441
Impact fees, 418
Impermanence Syndrome, 283
Importing
    affecting forests, 308
    of minerals, 323
    of oil, 336, 360, 361–362
Inclusionary housing ordinances, 410–411
Index of Sustainable Economic Welfare, 57
Indiana, 175, 196, 270, 304
Indicator species, 207
Indoor Radon Abatement Act, 135
Industrial forests, 308–309
Industrial Revolution, 126, 450
Infrastructure. *See also* Built environments
    green, 2, 63, 205, 431
    replacing or planning for new, 439–440
    sprawl impacting, 1
    upgrading, 386–387
    for water supplies, 80, 81
In-holdings, 186
Integrated pest management (IPM), 282
Interagency Ecosystem Management Task Force, 212
Intermodal Surface Transportation Efficiency Act (ISTEA), 340–342, 348, 350, 432
Intermodal transportation, 343, 432. *See also* Transportation
Internal Revenue Service (IRS), 197, 199–200, 387. *See also* Taxes
International Conference of Building Officials (ICBO), 275
International Coral Reef Information Network, 449

Internet, affecting transportation, 349
Interstate highways, 338
Inventories
    analyzing, 24–25
    in built environment planning
        energy sources, 369
        greenfield development, 421
        increasing developed lands, 374–375
        livable communities, 391
        transportation, 352–353
    creating, 20–24
    in layers technique, 406
    in natural areas planning
        coastal zones, 251
        hazards and disasters, 261, 273
        landscape preservation, 203
        wetlands, 238
        wildlife habitats, 224
    in public health planning
        air quality, 144
        solid wastes, 161
        toxic substances, 179–180
        water quality, 119
        water supplies, 92
    in working lands planning, 293–294, 316, 328
Inverse estuaries, 245
Iowa
    agricultural land in, 282, 289
    bus system in, 348
    endangered species in, 220
    water in, 202, 230
Izaak Walton League, 118, 222

J

The John D. and Catherine T. MacArthur Foundation,
    201
Judicial law, 41
Just v. Marinette County, 46

K

Kansas
    greenfield development in, 420–421
    natural hazards in, 259
    water in, 202, 286–287
Kentucky
    agricultural land in, 301
    coal mining in, 323
    earthquake risk in, 270
    growth boundaries in, 407
    solid waste disposal in, 158
    water in, 84, 202
Kyoto Protocol, 141, 315, 448

L

Land and resource management plans (LRMPs), 310
Land and Water Conservation Fund
    overview, 190–191
    spending on, 196, 443, 444
    supporting wildlife refuges, 219
Land and Water Suitability Analyses, 24, 25. *See also*
    National Resources Inventory
Land Conservation, Preservation, and Infrastructure
    Improvement Act, 191
Land development ordinances, 15–16, 205. *See also*
    Subdivisions
Land Evaluation and Site Assessment (LESA) system,
    25, 294, 297–299
Landfills, 154–158. *See also* Hazardous waste; Solid
    waste; Toxic substances
Landmarks, 379
Landscape ecology, 209–210
Landscape protection, 185–206. *See also* Ecosystems;
    Open spaces
    in bioregions, 210–212
    challenges in managing, 185–186, 434
    federal planning for, 187–191, 443–444
    local and regional planning for, 202–206, 431
    in site planning, 413
    state planning for, 191–193
Landslides, 260–261
Land subsidence, 261, 325
Land Trust Alliance, 197
Land trusts. *See also* Easements
    and coastal zone protection, 249
    and farmland preservation, 292
    in forestland protection, 314–315
    history of, xx
    organizations supporting, 201–202
    role of, 197–198
Land use planning. *See also* Environmental action plans
    agricultural, 283 (*see also* Agricultural land)
    locally unwanted, 179, 419, 439
    responsibility for, 2–3, 11–12, 430–431
    for transportation, 335–336, 440 (*see also*
        Transportation)
Land-value taxation, 382
Laws. *See* Legislation
Laws of Ecology, 6
Layers design technique, 406–407, 421
Lead, affecting air quality, 127, 131, 139
Legislation, 37–48. *See also specific*
    administrative, 46
    common law and property rights as, 47–48
    in comprehensive plans, 48
    constitutional, 37–40
    history of, xx

judicial, 46–47
    precedence in, 48
    and quasi-judicial rulings, 47
    state planning and zoning enabling, 44–46
    and statutory law, 40–44
Levees, 265
Lighting, 384
Light rail, 343, 344–346, 432
The Limits to Growth (Meadows *et al.*), 56
Local government planning. *See specific topic*
Locally Unwanted Land Uses (LULUs), 179, 419, 439
Losing Ground (Dowie), 11, 430
Louisiana, 62, 248
Lowest Achievable Emissions Rate (LAER), 135
Lucas v. South Carolina Coastal Commission, 38

M

Maine
    forests in, 307, 309
    hydroelectric dams in, 363
    land trusts in, 197
    water in, 80, 237
Man and Nature (Marsh), 60
Manure management, 287, 304
Marginal benefits/costs, 53
Marine Protection Research and Sanctuaries Act, 219,
    231, 243, 244–245. *See also* Ocean Dumping Act
Market failures, 50
Maryland
    built environment in
        affordable housing, 377
        brownfield redevelopment, 178
        downzoning in, 430
        inclusionary housing, 411
        layers technique, 406–407
        legislation, 404
        neighborhood design, 386
        PUD design, 412
        transportation, 346, 352
    long-range planning in, 432
    natural areas in, 196, 237–238, 248, 250
    public health in
        air quality, 133
        water pollution, 102
        water quality, 248
        water supplies, 68, 117, 118, 124
    Smart Growth legislation in
        Live Near Your Work program, 351, 390, 441–442
        long-term planning, 432
        open space conservation, 404
        overview, 389–391
    working lands in
        agricultural, 289, 290, 291, 302, 433

    forests, 312–314
Massachusetts
    agricultural land in, 290
    built environment in
        build-out scenarios, 409
        cluster design, 416–417
        housing scale, 377
        parking design, 377
    environmental review process in, 44
    natural area protection in
        estuaries, 246
        land trusts, 197
        water quality, 248
        water supplies, 68, 117
        wildlife preservation, 221
    regional planning in, 437
    toxic waste in, 168
Mass transit, 2–3, 339. *See also* Transportation
McHarg, Ian, *Design With Nature*, 243, 406–407
McPhee, John, *The Control of Nature*, 62, 125
Mediation, 438–439
Methane gas, 156, 157, 230, 366
Metropolitan Planning Organizations (MPOs), 131, 141,
    340, 341, 342
Michigan, 117, 237, 289
Migratory Bird Hunting Stamp Act, supporting wildlife
    refuges, 219
Migratory routes, 210. *See also* Wildlife habitats
Mine Safety and Health Administration, 324
Mining, 323–331
    challenges in managing, 324–326, 434
    federal planning for, 41, 114, 324, 326–327
    local planning for, 328–330, 331
    overview, 323–324
    state planning for, 327–328
    waste from, 114, 176
Minnesota
    agricultural land in, 304
    endangered rivers in, 202
    endangered species in, 220
    environmental review process in, 44
    recycling in, 153, 157, 174
    wind energy in, 365
Mississippi, 202, 270
Mississippi River, 62
Missouri
    airport in, 349
    natural hazards in, 261–262, 270
    toxic substances in, 165
    transportation case study, 356
    water in, 202, 230
Mitigation assistance programs, 262–264
Mitigation banks, 222, 232–233, 235

Mixed-use developments, 375–376, 414–415
A Moment on the Earth (Easterbrook), 185
Mono Lake (National Audubon v. Superior Court), 83
Montana, 202, 268, 310, 323
Montreal Protocol, 128
Monuments, protection of, 188. *See also* Landscape
    protection
Moratoriums, 411–412
Motor vehicles. *See also* Transportation
    emissions from, 130–131, 133, 134–135 (*see also* Clean
      Air Act)
    fuel efficiency of, 442
    impacting coastal zones, 242
    mass transit mixed with, 339
    parking for, 377
Muir, John, 58
Multiple Use-Sustained Yield Act, 309–310
Multiple use-sustained yield principle, 187, 189, 288

N

*Named Individual Members of the San Antonio Conservation
    Society v. Texas Highway Department*, 43
National Academy of Sciences, 7, 215, 233, 248
National Ambient Air Quality Standards (NAAQS),
    129–130, 141
National Association of Home Builders (NAHB), 378,
    402
National Audubon Society, 83, 221, 249, 307, 433
National Audubon v. Superior Court, 83
National Drought Mitigation Center, 73
National Earthquake Hazards Reduction Act, 270
National Environmental Policy Act (NEPA)
    continuing sprawl under, 445
    in development proposal review, 30
    inception of, 41
    on mining operations, 326
    preserving biodiversity, 212, 220
    role of, 37, 42–44, 404
    and SEPA, 44–46
    in wetlands development, 231
    wildlife habitats in, 214–215
National Estuarine Research Reserves, 219, 245–246
National Flood Insurance Program (NFIP)
    in coastal protection, 245, 246, 269, 270
    overview, 265, 266–267
National Flood Insurance Reform Act, 41, 265, 269
National Forest Management Act, 309, 310
National Forest System, xx, 309–311
National Geographic Society, 210
National Heritage Area program, 190
National Heritage Inventory, 222
National Historic Preservation Law, 388
National Institute of Standards and Technology, 270

National Interagency Fire Center, 269
National Landscape Conservation System, 189
National Marine Fisheries Service, 213, 214
National Marine Sanctuary Program, 219
National Oceanic and Atmospheric Administration
    (NOAA)
    administering the CZMA, 243, 245, 247
    coastal program spending, 191
    managing estuaries, 219, 246, 247
    on nonpoint source pollution, 112, 244
National Park Service
    coastal zone management by, 242, 247
    role of, 186, 187, 188
    supporting National Heritage Areas, 190
National Pollutant Discharge Elimination System
    (NPDES) permits, 109, 116, 242, 304, 327
National Rails to Trails Conservancy, 348, 350
National Recreation and Park Association, 376
National Recycling Coalition, 174
National Register of Historic Places, 388, 389, 393
National Research Council, 7
National Resources Inventory. *See also* Inventories
    on farmland development, 284
    on forests, 59, 307
    on increase in developed land, 374–375
    on irrigation, 286
    on urban land, 399
    on wetlands, 287
National Science Foundation, 270
National Trails System Act, 190
National Trust for Historic Preservation, 380, 388
National Wild and Scenic Rivers System, 189, 201
National Wilderness Preservation System, 187
National Wildlife Federation (NWF), 214, 222, 433
National Wildlife Refuge System, 218–219, 242
National Wildlife Refuge System Improvement Act, 219
Natural areas, 11. *See also* Coastal zones; Landscape
    protection; Natural hazards and disasters;
    Wetlands; Wildlife habitats
Natural gas, 362
Natural hazards and disasters, 257–276
    air pollution from, 125–126
    challenges in planning for
      avalanches, 261
      coastal erosion, 260
      drought, 259
      earthquakes, 261–262
      floods, 258
      landslides, 260–261
      land subsidence, 261, 325
      violent storms, 259–260
      wildfires, 258–259
    in coastal areas, 252, 253

federal planning for
    coastal erosion, 269–270
    earthquakes, 270–271
    floods, 264–268
    mitigation assistance programs, 262–264
    volcanic eruptions, 271
    wildfires, 268–269
local planning for, 263–264, 272–276
preparation tips, 434, 440–441
state planning for, 262–263, 271–272
trends in, 257–258
Natural resources
    American consumption of, xix
    inventory of (*see* Inventories; National Resources
        Inventory)
    national vision of, 446–447
    placing value on, 54–56
    renewable versus nonrenewable, 49
Natural Resources Conservation Service (NRCS). *See
    also* National Resources Inventory
    conservation programs of, 287
    drought program, 259
    farmland grants from, 285
    farmland ratings, 284
    Forestry Incentives Program, 309
    history of, xx
    Land Evaluation and Site Assessment system, 25
    on loss of natural lands, 1
    on mine drainage, 327
    on soil erosion and runoff, 112
    soil surveys from, 293
    on wetlands, 235, 238, 246
Natural Resources Defense Council (NRDC), 114, 185,
    433
Natural Resources Protection Act, 236
The Nature Conservancy (TNC)
    coastal zone protection by, 249
    role of, 200, 222, 433, 435
    on wildlife habitat, 207, 220
Nebraska, 202
Needs. *See* Environmental planning needs
Negative declaration, 44, 46
Negotiation, of environmental disputes, 420
Neighborhoods
    agricultural land near, 283, 289, 297, 302–303
    mining operations near, 324
    road and street planning for, 351–352
    TND design of, 385–386
Neutral estuaries, 245
Nevada
    landscape protection in, 185, 192
    nuclear waste disposal in, 167
    population growth in, 441

sprawl in, 401
water supplies in, 84
New Hampshire
    Conservation Fund projects in, 201
    forests in, 307, 309, 314–315
    water supplies in, 118–119
    wetlands in, 237
New Information Economy, 68, 174, 349, 431
New Jersey
    agricultural land in, 290, 291
    brownfield cleanup in, 179
    built environment aesthetics in, 380
    critical concern area in, 192
    greenfield development in, 404
    open space planning in, 430
    smart growth program in, 391
    TDR ordinance in, 414
    water in, 84, 117, 202, 236
New Mexico
    buying open space, 195
    conservation easement in, 222
    endangered rivers in, 202
    landfills in, 172
    land ownership in, 185
    population growth in, 441
    sustainable community planning in, 34
New Source Review Rules, 138
New Town movement, 412
New Urbanism, 352, 373, 385–386
New York
    built environment in
        boat transportation, 348
        building size, 394
        downtown redevelopment, 381–382
        green buildings, 369
        historic preservation, 389
        vacant building survey, 391
    concurrency system in, 40
    environmental review process in, 44
    natural areas in
        Conservation Fund projects, 201
        critical concern area, 192–193
        earthquake planning, 271, 275
        endangered rivers, 202
        greenways, 196
        open space, 193
    public health in
        air quality, 133, 147–148
        hazardous waste, 167
        pesticide use, 180
        solid waste disposal, 157, 158
        toxic substances, 172–173, 175
        water pollution, 104

water quality, 248
water supplies, 79, 84, 95–97
working lands in
agricultural, 282, 285, 289, 290
forests, 307, 309
mining, 323
Nitrogen cycle, 62
Nitrogen oxide, 127, 138, 139, 158, 361
Nodes, in built environment design, 378
Noise Control Act, 41
Noise ordinances, 383–384
Nonindustrial forests, 309
Nonpoint sources, 100, 111–112. *See also* Pollution
Nonprofit organizations, 34, 433, 435. *See also under*
Open spaces
Nonrenewable natural resources, 49, 360
North American Wetlands Conservation Act, 235
North Carolina
agricultural land in, 304
brownfield redevelopment in, 178
buying open space, 195
coastal zone planning in, 245, 248
greenways in, 196
historic preservation in, 389
Hurricane Floyd damaging, 257, 268
natural hazards in, 258, 271–272
transportation in, 337, 356–357
water quality in, 248
water supply in, 68
North Dakota, 202, 220, 365
"Not in My Back Yard" people, 418, 430
Nuclear power, 362–363
Nuisance ordinances, 162
Nutrient pollution, 105

O

Objectives. *See* Goals and objectives
Occupational Safety and Health Act, 41
Occupational Safety and Health Administration, 324
Ocean Dumping Act, 41, 114. *See also* Marine Protection
Research and Sanctuaries Act
Odum, Eugene, 37, 209
Office of Surface Mining Reclamation and Enforcement,
326
Offsets, for polluters, 136
Ohio
buying open space, 193
case study, 32–34
coal mining in, 323
downtown rebuilding in, 381
Environmental Action Plan in, 27
environmental planning needs, 17–18
transportation in, 346

water supplies in, 117
wetlands in, 230
Oil Pollution Act, 41, 171
Oil prices, 50, 367. *See also* Petroleum products
Oklahoma, 259, 286–287
Old-growth forests, 305
Open spaces, 193–202. *See also* Landscape protection
private, nonprofit efforts (*see also* Land trusts)
ad-hoc citizens' groups, 200
easement donations, 198–200
national and private foundations, 200–202
overview, 196–197
public efforts, 194–196
Ordinances. *See* Zoning
Oregon
built environment in
dams, 363
design, 373, 377, 386
energy planning, 369
greenways, 196, 376
growth boundaries, 407, 408, 433
legislation, 404
long-range planning, 432
public participation, 419
state planning, 368
coastal zones in, 248–249
comprehensive plan review in, 44
desert in, 211
environmental program in, xx
land ownership in, 185
long-term planning in, 432
regional government in, 437
solid waste disposal in, 157
transportation in, 148–149, 344, 345, 350
volcano in, 271
water supplies in, 84, 117
wildlife protection in
legislation, 221, 226
spotted owl, 306–307, 320–321
working lands in
agricultural, 289, 295
growth boundaries, 300, 301
land trusts, 315
logging management, 312
lot size, 296, 314
LRMP input, 310
zoning for, 317
Organic Act, 309
Overlay zones, 28. *See also* Zoning
Owls, protection of, 306–307, 320–321
The Oxford Foundation, 202
Oxygen cycle, 61

Ozone, 125, 128, 139–140. *See also* Global warming; Greenhouse gases

P

Paper
    Americans' use of, 306
    recycling, 158, 159, 160 (*see also* Recycling)
Parking, design of, 377
Parks, 188, 210. *See also* Greenways; Landscape protection
Particulates, 127–128, 139, 158, 325
Partnership parks, 188
Paths, 378. *See also* Trails
Pay-as-you-throw programs (PAYT), 155
Payments-in-lieu-of-taxes (PILTS), 310
Pedestrians, in transportation planning, 339, 343, 348, 350
Pennsylvania
    air quality in, 133
    built environment in
        brownfield cleanup, 179, 433, 441
        case study, 425–426
        energy use, 366
        growth boundaries, 407, 408, 421
        land-value taxation, 382
        neighborhood design, 386
    natural areas in, 193, 197, 202, 250, 261
    water supplies in, 78, 118
    working lands in
        farmland loss, 285
        growth boundaries, 301
        mining in, 323, 325
        preservation programs, 290, 291, 293–294
        zoning, 296, 413
Pennsylvania Coal v. Mahon, 38
Performance zoning, 28, 29, 394
Permits
    limiting building potential, 411
    for polluters, 136, 142
    for solid waste disposal, 154
    for wetlands development, 230–233, 235
Pesticides, 106, 180. *See also* Toxic substances
Petroleum products
    American consumption of, 336
    as energy source, 360, 361–362, 442–443
    funding land and water conservation, 190
    in nature preserve, 245
    Oil Pollution Act, 41, 171
    and oil prices, 50, 367
    Superfund tax on, 173
    in underground tanks, 106–107, 172
The Pew Charitable Trusts, 201
Phosphorus cycle, 62

Physical pollution, 102
Pigou, A.C., 50
Pinchot, Gifford, xx
Pittman-Robertson Act, 219
Planned-unit developments (PUDs), 412
Planning Enabling Act, 44
Pod-style development, 403, 418
Point sources, 100. *See also* Pollution
A Policy on Geometric Design of Highways and Streets, 350
Policy plans, 13
Pollution
    air (*see also* Air quality; Clean Air Act)
        from landfills, 157
        from mining operations, 324, 325, 361
        progress and challenges in, 138–141
        road building affecting, 337–338
        sources of, 125–127, 363–364, 366
        types of, 127–128
    EPA on treating, 7
    from lighting, 384
    in National Resources Inventory, 21–22
    in natural resource inventories, 23
    from noise, 383–384
    spending on, 53
    sprawl impacting, 1–2
    water (*see also* Clean Water Act; Safe Drinking Water Act (SDWA))
        from agricultural land, 281
        breakdown of, 99–100
        in estuaries, 242
        from manure, 287
        mining causing, 327
        sources of, 100–102, 230, 366
        types of, 102–107
Pollution credits, 137–138, 141
Pollution Prevention Act, 41, 155–156, 170
Polychlorinated biphenyls (PCBs)
    cleanup of, 175
    EPA banning, 168, 169–170
    legislation on, 171
    recycling of, 167
Polyvinyl chloride (PVC), 167
Population
    in coastal zone planning, 242, 243
    distribution of, xix
    and ethical views, 60
    farm-based, 280
    growth of
        challenges from, 434
        energy consumption for, 360
        estimate, xx, 441
        limits on, 435–436, 441, 448
    suburb versus city, 374

U.S. percentage of global, 447
and water supply planning, 73–75, 92
Positive estuaries, 245
Precautionary principle, 7
Preservationists, 58–59
Prevention of Significant Deterioration (PSD), 135
Private inurement, 199
Private sector environmental planning, 27
Proactive environmental planning, 5
Property rights, 47–48
Property taxes. *See* Taxes
Public facility ordinances, 410, 436–437. *See also specific facilities*
Public health. *See* Air quality; Recycling; Solid waste; Toxic substances; Water quality; Water supplies
Public participation, 19, 418–420, 430–431. *See also* Ad-hoc citizens' groups
Public Reporting requirements, 80
Public trust doctrine, 47, 83
Public water systems, 78. *See also* Water quality; Water supplies
Purchase of development rights (PDR), 290–293, 297, 314. *See also* Transfer of development rights (TDR)

Q
Quasi-judicial rulings, 47

R
Radon gas, 135
Ranchland. *See* Agricultural land
Reactive environmental planning, 5
Reasonable Available Control Technology, 135–136
Reclamation, of mine sites, 325–327. *See also* Mining
Recreation. *See also* Landscape protection; Tourism
in coastal zones, 241–242, 247–248
in forests, 310, 311
revenue from, 185
wildlife habitat protection role, 222
Recycling
benefits of, 152–153, 361
goals for, 156, 444
mandatory programs for, 158–160
National Recycling Coalition, 174
of toxic waste, 166–169
Regional planning, 436–437. *See also specific topic*
Regional Transportation Plans (RTPs), 131–132, 133, 144, 340
Reisner, Marc, 68, 77
Renewable natural resources
defined, 49
producing energy, 359–360, 365–366, 442
Resource Conservation and Recovery Act (RCRA). *See also* Solid waste; Toxic substances

inception of, 41
role of, 171–172
standards under, 154–155
violation fine alternative, 439
Resources Recovery Act, 41
Reviews. *See* Development reviews
Revised Universal Soil Loss Equation, 282
Rhode Island, 394
Right-to-farm laws, 289
Ring roads, 337
Risk assessment
in hazard and disaster planning, 263
in toxic waste planning, 168, 176–177, 179
of water quality, 113
River basin planning, 77–78
Rivers, 189–190, 201, 202. *See also* Dams; Water quality; Water supplies
Rivers and Harbors Act, 231
Roadless Area Conservation Rule, 187–188. *See also* Roads
Roads, 187–188, 210, 307, 342. *See also* Transportation
The Robert W. Woodruff Foundation, 201
The Rockefeller Foundation, 201
Rocky Mountain Elk Foundation, 222–223
Rocky Mountain Institute, 359
Roosevelt, Franklin D., 305
Runoff. *See also* Erosion; Water quality
management ordinances, 121–122
pollution from, 2, 100–101, 111, 112
in urban design, 376
Rural Abandoned Mine Program, 327
Rural sprawl, 400

S
Safe Drinking Water Act (SDWA)
affecting mining industry, 327
cost of, 88
inception of, 41
in local water supply planning, 92
risk evaluations under, 113
role of, 78–81
standards set by, 114
and watershed management approach, 75
wellhead protection under, 89
on wetlands, 236, 246
A Sand County Almanac (Leopold), 58
Scarcity principle, 48–49
Schools
chemical exposure at, 180
need for planning by, 436
regional management of, 437
tax funding of, 289, 438
in urban revitalization, 442

Section 8 rent subsidies, 387
Section 404 permits, 246. *See also* Wetlands
Sediment pollution, 102, 103, 122
Selective cutting, 311–312, 315
Septic systems
    ordinances on, 91, 94, 410
    pollution from, 103–104, 105, 230
Shadow prices, 54
Sierra Club, 191, 200, 433
Silent Spring (Carson), 165, 166
Site design, 406–407, 412–415. *See also* Built
        environments; Greenfield development
Ski areas, 186
Sliding scale zoning, 296–297
Sludge, 105, 110, 153–154. *See also* Wastewater treatment
Small Business Liability Relief and Brownfields
        Revitalization Act, 177
Smart growth, xx, 353, 389–391, 411. *See also under*
        Maryland
SmartWood program, 313
Smog, 125, 127, 130, 132, 138. *See also* Air quality
Soil Conservation Service, xx. *See also* Natural Resources
        Conservation Service (NRCS)
Soils, 21–22, 285–286. *See also* Erosion
Solar energy, 365–366
Solid waste, 151–163
    challenges in managing, 2, 151–154, 434
    cost of, 151
    federal planning for (*see* Resource Conservation
        and Recovery Act (RCRA))
    Full Cost Accounting for, 155
    local and regional planning for, 157–163
    mining industry creating, 325
    PAYT program for, 155
    reducing, reusing, and recycling, 155–156 (*see also*
        Recycling)
    state planning for, 156–157
Source Water Assessment and Protection (SWAP)
        programs, 79–80, 89
South Carolina, 68, 195, 249
South Dakota, 202, 220
Southern Building Code Congress International, Inc.
        (SBCCI), 275
The Southern Standard Building Code, 370
Southwest Florida Water Management District, 72
Spotted owls, 306–307, 320–321
Spot zoning, 39
Sprawl. *See also* Built environments; Greenfield
        development
    airports contributing to, 349
    designing to avoid, 378, 441
    disturbing wetlands, 230
    federal management of, 445–446

    impact fees discouraging, 418
    problems caused by, 1–2, 401–402, 406
    regional planning to control, 436–437
    types of, 399–400
    in water supply planning, 84–86
Stafford Disaster Relief and Emergency Assistance Act,
        246, 262
State Environmental Policy Acts (SEPAs), 30, 44–46,
        405–406
State Environmental Quality Review Acts, 192
State government planning. *See specific topic*
State Improvement Plans (SIPs)
    role of, 130, 131, 133, 141–142
    TIP coordinating with, 341
State Pollutant Discharge Elimination System (SPDES),
        109, 111, 116
Storms, planning for, 259–260. *See also* Natural hazards
        and disasters
Stormwater management ordinances, 111, 121–122
Storm Water Pollution Prevention Plan, 111. *See also*
        Runoff
Stream ratings, 70
Street furniture, 382
Streets. *See* Roads; Transportation
Strip Mining Act, 327
Subdivisions
    in built environment, 354, 372, 394, 423
    in natural area planning, coastal areas, 253
    in natural areas planning
        landscape preservation, 205
        natural hazards and disasters, 275–276
        wetlands, 239–240
        wildlife habitats, 226–227
    in planning process, 15–16, 28, 29
    in public health planning
        air quality, 145
        solid wastes, 94–95
        toxic substances, 182
        water quality, 121–122
        water supplies, 94–95
    in working lands planning, 283, 299–300, 317, 330
Subsidence, 261, 325
Subsidies
    farmland, 280, 443
    low-income housing, 387
    mining industry, 326, 443
    politics of, 52
    transportation system, 338, 403
Suburban sprawl, 400
Suburbs, redesign of, 382, 383
Suitum v. Tahoe Regional Planning Agency, 192
Sulfur dioxide, 127, 139, 158, 361. *See also* Acid rain
Sunsetting regulations, 410

Sunshine Laws, 418
Superfund Amendments and Reauthorization Act, 41, 173
The Superfund Law
    on brownfield remediation, 175, 176
    cost-benefit analysis of, 56
    history of, 41, 172–175
    on mine cleanup, 327
    violation fine alternative, 439
Supplemental Environmental Project (SEP), 439
The Surdna Foundation, 201
Surface Mining Control and Reclamation Act, 41, 326–327
Surface Mining Reclamation Act, 114
Surface Transportation Policy Project (STPP), 339
Surface water, 70, 79, 82, 87, 101. *See also* Water supplies
Surface Water Treatment Rule, 79
Surveys, 19, 25, 293–294, 391
Susquehanna River Basin Commission, 78
Sustainable development, 3–4
Sustained yield concept, xx

T

Tahoe-Sierra Preservation Council v. Tahoe Regional Planning Agency, 192, 412
Taxes. *See also* Internal Revenue Service (IRS)
    on agricultural land
        capital gains, 291, 292
        property, 283, 288–289, 290
    on built environment
        energy-related credits, 368, 369
        gasoline, 336, 362, 403, 442
        historic preservation credits, 388–389, 393, 442
        home sales and purchases, 378, 404, 443
        job creation credits, 390, 441–442
        land-value, 382
        school funding, 438
    on forestlands, 310, 314
    on natural areas preservation
        easement donations, 198, 199
        landscape funding, 194, 195
        wildlife protection incentives, 226, 227
    on virgin materials, 444
Taylor Grazing Act, 220
Technology
    in air pollution control, 135–136
    changing farming, 280
    of computers, 174, 361
    increasing energy demands, 360–361
    influencing good science, 7
    reducing transportation needs, 349
Telecommuters, 349
Tennessee

built environment revitalization in, 395–397
    earthquake risk in, 270
    greenways in, 196
    open space legislation in, 404
    ring roads in, 337
    water in, 202, 237
    wildlife preservation in, 214
Tennessee Valley Authority (TVA), 44, 77
Tennessee Valley Authority v. Hill, 44
10th Amendment, 38–39, 46
Texas
    agricultural land in, 285
    energy use in, 361, 363
    natural areas in
        endangered species, 214
        natural hazards, 258, 259
        open space, 195
        wetlands, 237
        wildlife habitats, 211
    population growth in, 242, 441
    public health in
        air quality, 132, 133, 445
        landfills, 152, 172
        water quality, 123–124, 248
        water supplies, 84, 117, 123–124, 286–287
    transportation in
        bicycles and pedestrians, 348, 351, 432
        light rail, 344
        ring roads, 337
        traffic calming, 352
Thermal inversions, 126–127
Thermal pollution, 102
Thoreau, Henry David, 185
Threshold effect, 53
Timber Production Zones (TPZs), 317
Topography, 22
Tornadoes, 259–260. *See also* Natural hazards and disasters
Total Maximum Daily Load (TMDL) process, 115, 116, 433, 445
Tourism, 13, 191, 241–242. *See also* Recreation
Toward a Steady-State Economy (Daly), 57
Toxic substances, 165–182. *See also* Hazardous waste
    affecting air quality, 128, 135, 136–137, 140
    in brownfield remediation, 175–179
    from burning trash, 128
    challenges in managing, 165–166, 434
    disposal of, 166–169
    federal planning for, 169–175
    local planning for, 170, 179–182
    mining industry creating, 176
    state planning for, 178–179
    tax on, 444

Toxic Substances Control Act, 41, 169–170, 175, 439
Traditional neighborhood developments (TNDs), 385–386
Traffic. *See* Motor vehicles; Roads; Transportation
Traffic calming, 352
Traffic impact studies, 350
Trails, 190, 194–196, 348, 350. *See also* Paths
Transfer of development rights (TDR). *See also* Purchase of development rights (PDR)
    in critical concern areas, 192
    preserving historic sites, 389
    role of, 301–302
    in water supply planning, 84
    zoning for, 297
Transit-oriented developments (TODs), 148–149, 343–344, 345
Transportation, 335–357
    and airport planning, 349
    alternative modes of, 339, 348, 350–352
    case studies, 148–149, 355–357
    challenges in managing, 434
    context-sensitivity in planning, 339, 350
    federal planning for, 340–342 (*see also specific legislation*)
    highway construction, 336–338
    impacting air quality, 131–132, 133
    Internet affecting, 349
    interstate systems, 338
    land use patterns, 335–336, 440
    local planning for, 339, 340, 352–355
    mixing motor vehicles and mass transit, 339
    regional planning for, 342, 343–348
    shaping development patterns, 2–3
    trails for, 190, 194–196
Transportation and Community and System Preservation Pilot (TCSP) program, 342
Transportation Efficiency Act, 195
Transportation Equity Act for the 21st Century (TEA-21)
    funding from, 347, 348, 350, 432
    overview, 342
    transit benefits, 351
Transportation Improvement Plans (TIPs), 131–132, 133, 341, 342
Trends. *See* Environmental planning trends
Trout Unlimited, 118, 222
Trust for Public Land (TPL), 200
Trusts. *See* Land trusts
Turbidity, 102

U

Underground storage tanks, 172
The Uniform Building Code, 370
United Nations, 3, 447, 448, 449. *See also* Kyoto Protocol

United Nations Conference on Environment and Development, 447
United States v. 247.37 Acres of Land, 43
Urban redevelopment, versus greenfield development, 374. *See also* Built environments
Urban sprawl, 399–400
U.S. Army Corps of Engineers
    authority of, 238
    in coastal zones, 246
    cost benefit analyses by, 55
    Florida Everglades project by, 237
    mining permits from, 327
    water projects by, 62, 77
    wetlands permits from, 231–233, 236, 237
    writing EIS reports, 43
U.S. Bureau of Land Management (BLM)
    in energy production, 367
    grazing lands owned by, 220, 287–288
    on mine cleanup, 327
    role of, 187, 188–189
    wildfire responsibility of, 268, 269
    wildlife habitat program, 213
U.S. Bureau of Reclamation, 75, 77, 187
U.S. Bureau of the Census, xx, 74, 356, 360
U.S. Conference of Mayors, 169, 441
U.S. Department of Agriculture (USDA)
    on food waste, 153
    LESA system, 294, 297–299
    National Resources Inventory (*see* National Resources Inventory)
    river management by, 189
    setting environmental law, 46
    on soil erosion and runoff, 112, 286
    water project grants from, 95
    on wetlands, 229, 235, 246
U.S. Department of Commerce, 95, 219, 248
U.S. Department of Energy
    nuclear facility monitoring by, 167, 168
    on renewable energy sources, 365
    role of, 367
    setting environmental law, 46
    on U.S. oil imports, 361–362
U.S. Department of Housing and Urban Development (HUD), 95, 386–387
U.S. Department of Labor, 324
U.S. Department of the Interior
    coastal zone responsibility, 248
    funding cuts for, 196
    land management under, 187
    setting environmental law, 46
    Wild and Scenic River system, 189, 201
    wildlife habitat programs, 213
U.S. Department of Transportation, 43, 342

U.S. Environmental Protection Agency (EPA)
on air quality, 23, 126
on biological pollution, 102, 103
on built environment
brownfields, 178, 386–387
energy efficiency, 367
transportation systems, 341, 353
U.S. infrastructure spending, 439
capital improvement grants from, 95
on coastal zones
funding cuts, 196
Great Lakes National Program, 246–247
program coordination, 248
recreation report, 242
water quality, 247
conservation categories, 88–89
cost-benefit analyses by, 56
legislation enforcement by, 445
NEPA exemption, 43
nonprofit organizations influencing, 433
resource information, 22
role of, 46
SEP policy, 439
on solid wastes
accounting for, 155
eco-industrial parks, 152, 160
food-based, 153
grants for disposal of, 160
landfill emissions, 157
paper and wood, 158
on toxic substances (*see also* The Superfund Law)
burning of, 165
Office of Pollution Prevention and Toxics, 170
Rocky Flats investigation, 168
role of, 171–172, 173
tolerance levels, 168
Toxic Release Inventory, 170, 176
underground fuel tanks, 172
water supply bans, 174
U.S. pollution statistics, 99
on water supplies
dilution solution, 7
for drinking, 79, 80–81, 85
quantity of, 67
river basin planning, 78
State Wetlands Grants Program, 236
stormwater runoff, 100–101
wetlands permitting process, 231
on wildlife habitats, 208
U.S. Fish and Wildlife Service (FWS). *See also* Fisheries
coastal zone management by, 242, 246
role of, 187
on wetlands, 23, 235–236, 238

on wildlife habitats
ESA management, 213, 214–215
land requirements, 209
National Wildlife Refuge System, 218–219
U.S. Forest Service (USFS)
on energy production, 367
land ownership by, 186
role of, 187, 310
on subdividing forests, 307–308
wildfire responsibility of, 259, 268, 269
U.S. General Accounting Office (GAO)
on Clean Air Act, 147
on farmland, 279, 284, 285
sprawl research by, 445
on wildfire prevention, 269
U.S. Geological Survey (USGS)
earthquake planning by, 270
Gap Analysis Program, 216
National Landslides Hazards Program, 260–261
topographic maps from, 20, 22
wildlife habitat programs, 213
U.S. Nuclear Regulatory Agency, 363
U.S. Office of Management and Budget (USOMB), 340, 432
U.S. Supreme Court, 48
Utah
coal mining in, 323
earthquake risk in, 272, 275
endangered species in, 220
landfills in, 172
land ownership in, 185
national monuments in, 189
population growth in, 441
recycling in, 153
Utilitarians, 58–59

V
Vegetation, in natural resources inventories, 23
Vehicle miles traveled (VMT), 33, 139, 338, 339, 341
Vermont
built environment in
DRI process, 404–405
energy use, 369
housing, 411
pedestrian mall, 381
planning boards, 13
property taxes, 438
environmental program in, xx
natural areas in, 201, 202, 214, 220
public health in, 60, 160, 433
transportation in, 348, 350
working lands in
agricultural, 290, 292

forests, 307, 308, 309, 315
Virginia
    coastal zone planning in, 250
    landfills in, 152
    mining in, 329
    road system in, 337
    solid waste disposal in, 158
    water supply in, 68
    wildlife preservation in, 214
Vision statements, 25–26
Volatile organic compounds (VOCs), 128, 133–134
Volcanoes, 271

W

The W. Alton Jones Foundation, 201
Washington, D.C.
    air quality in, 133
    coastal zone planning in, 250
    forests in, 307
    transportation in, 337, 339
Washington, State of
    built environment legislation in, 404
    energy use in, 369
    environmental review process in, 44, 46
    green accounting in, 34
    natural areas in
        endangered rivers, 202
        fish farms, 217, 218
        forests, 307, 315
        land ownership, 185
        natural hazards, 261, 270, 271
        open space, 195
    public health in, 130, 157, 158, 248
    transportation in, 348, 351
    wildlife protection in, 306–307, 320–321
Waste disposal. *See* Hazardous waste; Solid waste
Waste Management, 152
Wastewater treatment
    construction and planning, 109–111, 439–440
    reuse in, 85
    wetlands in, 234
Water audits, 86
Water cycle, 61
Water pollution. *See under* Pollution
Water quality, 99–124
    agricultural land impacting, 281, 288
    air pollution impacting, 127, 147
    case studies, 123–124
    challenges in managing, 434, 444
    in coastal zones, 243–244, 246, 247 (*see also* Coastal
        zones)
    energy production harming, 363

federal planning for (*see also* Clean Water Act; Safe
    Drinking Water Act (SDWA))
    American Heritage Rivers Initiative, 189–190
    Land and Water Conservation Fund, 190–191,
        196, 443, 444
    National Wild and Scenic Rivers System, 189, 201
    in forestland, 311
    local planning for, 119–122
    mining impacting, 324–325
    pollution affecting (*see under* Pollution)
    regional and county planning for, 117–119
    in site planning, 413
    state planning for, 114–117
    toxic substances impacting, 174
Watershed Protection and Flood Prevention Act, 327
Watersheds
    county and regional management of, 118–119
    impervious surfaces covering, 72
    overview, 69–70
    protection of, 79, 91, 327
    state management of, 116
Water supplies, 67–97. *See also* Wetlands
    agricultural use of, 286–287
    in bioregions, 211
    case studies, 95–97
    challenges in managing, 67–73, 434
    drought impacting, 73
    federal approach to
        river basin planning, 77–78
        SDWA role in, 78–81
        western water projects, 75–77
    local planning for, 92–95, 96
    mining impacting, 324–325
    in natural resource inventories, 22–23
    need for planning, 73–75
    oceans as source of, 72
    population growth impacting, 2
    regional and county planning for, 83–92
        aquifer and watershed protection, 91, 94
        issues, 84–86
        objectives, 86–88
        recommendations, 88–89
        wellhead protection, 89–91
    in site planning, 413
    state planning for, 81–83
    U.S. spending on, 439–440
    wastewater reuse benefiting, 85
Weatherization, 368
Welfare economics, 50
Wellhead protection
    groups sponsoring, 118–119
    SDWA program requirements for, 79
    in site planning, 413

steps in, 89–91
zoning in, 90, 94
Wells
    oil, 363 (*see also* Petroleum products)
    ordinances governing, 95
    pollution in, 101–102
West Virginia
    coal mining in, 323
    endangered rivers in, 202
    endangered species in, 220
    national parks in, 188
Wetlands, 229–240. *See also* Water quality; Water
        supplies
    challenges in managing, 434
    Everglades restoration project, 237
    on farms and ranches, 287
    federal planning for, 38, 230–233, 235–236
    local planning for, 238–240
    mining operations destroying, 327
    in natural resource inventories, 22, 23
    pressures on, 229–230
    role of, 70, 229
    state management of, 236–238
    types of, 229, 230
    for wastewater treatment, 234
Wetlands Reserve Program, 38, 246, 287, 443, 444
Wild and Scenic River system, 189, 201
Wilderness Act, 41, 187
Wilderness areas, 187–188. *See also* Landscape
        protection
The Wilderness Society, 200, 201, 310
Wildfires, 258–259, 268–269, 308
Wildlands Project, 216
Wildlife, in natural resource inventories, 23
Wildlife Habitat Incentives Program (WHIP), 219–220
Wildlife habitats, 207–228. *See also* Ecosystems
    biodiversity in, 208–209, 210–212
    challenges in managing, 434
    in coastal zones, 246
    estuarine research and marine sanctuaries, 219
    federal government planning for, 218–220, 242 (*see*
        also Endangered Species Act (ESA))
    forest harvesting methods impacting, 311–312, 320
    information sources on, 213
    landscape ecology in, 209–210
    local planning for, 223–228
    mining affecting, 325, 326
    pressures on, 207–208 (*see also* Endangered species)
    principles for protecting, 223–224
    state planning for, 220–223

Willamette Industries, 133–134
The William Penn Foundation, 202
Wind, generating energy, 365
Wisconsin
    air quality in, 133
    historic preservation in, 389
    recycling in, 157
    water in, 102, 202
Woodland protection ordinances, 122
Working landscapes, 11. *See also* Agricultural land;
        Forests; Mining
World Wildlife Fund, 185
Wyoming
    coal mining in, 323
    endangered rivers in, 202
    endangered species in, 220
    energy use in, 363
    land ownership in, 185

Z
Zoning
    in action plan implementation, 28, 29
    in built environment planning
        energy sources, 371
        excess of, 409
        greenfield development, 422–423
        livable communities, 393–394
        transportation, 354
    in natural areas planning
        coastal zones, 252–253
        landscape preservation, 204–205
        natural hazards and disasters, 274–275
        wetlands, 239
        wildlife habitats, 225–226
    in public health planning
        air quality, 144–145
        solid wastes, 162
        toxic substances, 181
        water quality, 120–121
        water supplies, 90, 94
    role of, 14–15
    10th Amendment impacting, 39
    in working land planning
        agricultural lands, 295–299
        forestlands, 317
    in working lands planning, mining operations,
        328–330
Zoning Board of Adjustment, 47
Zoning Enabling Act, 44